CASTLE CLASS CORVETTES

An Account of the Service of the
Ships and of their Ships' Companies

CASTLE CLASS CORVETTES

An Account of the Service of the
Ships and of their Ships' Companies

Compiled by
Norman Goodwin
The Castle Class Corvette (Frigate) Association

Edited by
Steve Bush

Previous Page: *HMCS Petrolia (Musée du Commandement Maritime - Neg No: NF 3848-2)*

First published in the United Kingdom in 2007 by Maritime Books, Lodge Hill, Liskeard, Cornwall, PL14 4EL

CONTENTS

Prologue	vii
Foreword	ix
Acknowledgements	xi
Section 1 - The Ship	1
Section 2 - Service at War and Peace	23
Section 3 - Ships' Histories	
HMS Allington Castle	71
HMS Alnwick Castle	81
HMS Amberley Castle	89
HMS Bamborough Castle	95
HMS Berkeley Castle	103
HMS Caistor Castle	119
HMS Carisbrooke Castle	125
HMS Denbigh Castle	139
HMS Dumbarton Castle	143
HMS Farnham Castle	153
HMS Flint Castle	155
HMS Hadleigh Castle	163
HMS Hedingham Castle	171
HMS Hurst Castle	177
HMS Kenilworth Castle	185
HMS Knaresborough Castle	195
HMS Lancaster Castle	203
HMS Launceston Castle	215
HMS Leeds Castle	225
HMS Morpeth Castle	233
HMS Oakham Castle	241
HMS Oxford Castle	247
HMS Pevensey Castle	255
HMS Portchester Castle	267
HMS Rushen Castle	277
HMS Tintagel Castle	287
HMCS Arnprior	297
HMCS Bowmanville	301
HMCS Copper Cliff	305
HMCS Hespeler	309
HMCS Humberstone	313
HMCS Huntsville	317
HMCS Kincardine	321
HMCS Leaside	325
HMCS Orangeville	329
HMCS Petrolia	337
HMCS St Thomas	341
HMCS Tillsonburg	347
HNoMS Tunsberg Castle	353
Section 4 - Escort Group Reports	359

Appendix 1	Castle Class Production	471
Appendix 2	Commanding Officers	477
Appendix 3	Roll of Honour	480
Appendix 4	Escort Groups Reported to Include Castle Class Corvettes	485
Appendix 5	An Example of Commanding Officer's Standing Orders	487
Appendix 6	HMS Tintagel Castle Boarding Party Standing Orders	494
Appendix 7	Instructions for Forming an Observant Search	497
Appendix 8	Operation Banana	499
Appendix 9	Operation Scabbard	500
Appendix 10	Operation Artichoke	501
Appendix 11	Anti-Gnat Procedures	502
Appendix 12	Exercises at Sea	505
Appendix 13	Douglas Sea and Swell Scale	511
Appendix 14	Beaufort Scale	512
Appendix 15	Problems Arising when Escorting Large Convoys	513
Appendix 16	A Commodore's Complaint	516
Appendix 17	Canteen Messing	518
Appendix 18	Carriage of Bullion	519
Appendix 19	Manoeuvring at Sea	521
Appendix 20	Oiling at Sea	522
Appendix 21	Ships' News Services	523
Appendix 22	U-Boat Surrender Orders	524
Appendix 23	High Tea Barrier	525
Appendix 24	Brittany Barrier	526
Appendix 25	Publication Sponsors	528

PROLOGUE

BOARD MINUTES

Friday, 7th May, 1943.

PRESENT:

THE RIGHT HON. A. V. ALEXANDER, C.H., M.P.
ADMIRAL SIR CHARLES E. KENNEDY-PURVIS, K.C.B.
VICE-ADMIRAL SIR WILLIAM J. WHITWORTH, K.C.B., D.S.O.
VICE-ADMIRAL SIR JOHN H. D. CUNNINGHAM, K.C.B., M.V.O.
VICE-ADMIRAL SIR HENRY R. MOORE, K.C.B., C.V.O., D.S.O.
REAR-ADMIRAL WILFRED R. PATTERSON, C.B., C.V.O.
BARON BRUNTISFIELD, M.C.
CAPTAIN RICHARD A. PILKINGTON, M.C., M.P.
SIR HENRY V. MARKHAM, K.C.B., M.C.
SIR J. SIDNEY BARNES, K.B.E., C.B.
SIR STANLEY V. GOODALL, K.C.B., O.B.E., attended for Minutes 3874 and 3875.
ADMIRAL SIR T. HUGH BINNEY, K.C. B., D.S.O., attended for Minute 3876.

Confirmation of Minutes.
3873. The Minutes of the Meeting of the Board held on 13th April, 1943, which had been circulated, were confirmed, except that in Minute 3869, line 4, it was agreed that for the words "consolidated rate of pay" there should be substituted "existing emoluments."

Lengthened Single Screw Corvettes: Legend and Drawings.
3874. The Board approved the Legend and Drawings of the Lengthened Single Screw Corvettes, the estimated cost, excluding guns and ammunition, being £174,000 per vessel. The Director of Naval Construction explained that the design enabled the number of depth charges carried to be increased if desired. Attention was drawn to the considerable increase in complement over the "Flower" class, viz, 100 compared with 29, and the First Lord asked that the Deputy First Sea Lord would consider in conjunction with the Second Sea Lord whether a reduction in complement to, say 70, could not be made.

FOREWORD

The Castle Class Corvette (Frigate) Association[1] was formed in 1989 with the primary purpose of enabling those who had served in these ships to keep in touch with one another and to maintain the bonds of friendship established during their service.

Inevitably, members sent in photographs and anecdotal stories. These were shared through the Association's newsletter *Ship's Log*.

Many of the photographs had faded and so to preserve the images from further loss they were stored on a computer.

Initially it had been intended that all the material would be catalogued and preserved with a view to eventually depositing the archives in a Naval or Maritime library. However, it soon became apparent that more than sufficient material was being received to form the basis of a book recording the service of the ships' companies and of the ships.

To back up fading memories and to fill in many of the missing details recourse was had to the records of the Public Records Office (PRO), Kew, the libraries of the Royal Naval Museum, Portsmouth and of the Maritime Museum, Greenwich. Later, additional information about the Castle Class Corvettes of the Royal Canadian Navy was obtained from the records of the Directorate of History and Heritage, National Defence Headquarters, Ottawa.

As a result, the Reports Of Proceedings covering almost all the convoys escorted by the Royal Navy ships, and of the patrols carried out by the Castle Class Corvette Support Groups have been incorporated into this account. Unfortunately, it has not been possible to record the voyages of the Canadian Class Corvettes in as much detail or as comprehensively as those of the Royal Navy and Royal Norwegian Navy. The Canadian records are not as accessible as are those at the PRO, Kew.

However, by extracting data from the Pink List, the composition of convoys, escorts and position reports and Ship Movement Orders, it has been possible to record the location of every Castle Class Corvette at seven to ten day intervals from the day the first of the class, **HMS Hadleigh Castle**, sailed after commissioning to slightly beyond the end of World War II in Europe.

None of this work would have been possible without the help of those who provided assistance in searching the records in the U.K namely:- Mr. R.C. Angel, Mr. D. Beckett and Mr. F. Shipp, and in Canada, Mr. R.J. Crothers and Mr. L. Webb. It was our good fortune that Mr. Robert Crothers, in Canadian terms, lived close to Ottawa. It is he who obtained most of the reports of Proceedings on the Canadian Groups that we have recorded here. We are much indebted to Mr. Leonard Webb who has acted throughout as our 'Canadian Correspondent'. Through his contacts on the West Coast he was able to fill many of the gaps in the histories of the post war mercantile conversions of the Castle Class Corvettes that plied the Canadian and Alaska waterways. We are also indebted to Lt Cdr F.R. Pike RCNVR, one time Commanding Officer of **HMCS Orangeville**, who provided us with many details of the ship, her crew and service.

Without the constant interest and encouragement of members of the Association, none of this would have been possible. Their contribution of anecdotes and photographs was an essential contribution. These are acknowledged as they appear in the volume.

---

[1] www.castlecorvette.co.uk

ACKNOWLEDGEMENTS

The production of this account of the service of the Castle Class Corvettes (Frigates) and of their ships' companies would not have been possible without the full and patient support of all the members of the Castle Class Corvette (Frigate) Association.

The original concept for producing such a volume stemmed from the imaginative mind of the late Ron Davies, who at that time was the editor of the Association's news letter the '*Castle Class Ships Log*'. I was invited to join him in this venture after I had submitted some material concerning the convoys that had been escorted by *HMS Tintagel Castle*. Unfortunately, Ron was struck down by cancer in 1998 and I was invited to continue with the work.

An early source of official information was found to be 'The Ship Movement Orders' files. Two sets of these voluminous files are located in the UK. One at the Maritime Museum, Greenwich, and the other at the library of the Royal Navy Museum, Portsmouth. Mr and Mrs Denis Beckett, Mr R.C. Angel and Mr. Frank Shipp, all of the Association, volunteered to help with the extraction of the relevant information from these files. It is very largely due to their work that the basis of the data bank of ship locations and movements was compiled. Subsequently this work was amplified by reference to the files at the Public Record Office; particularly those of the ADM 187/30-50 series, the Pink List, and the ADM 199/1714-1719 series providing information on Convoy and Escort Dispositions at Sea. The help and patience of the staff of the Public Records Office was of considerable value in identifying the sources of relevant information. Of particular importance was the identification of the senior officer's ship of the various escort groups in which the Castle Class Corvettes formed part. This was necessary because the Reports of Proceedings of the escort groups are filed under the names of the senior officers' ships.

With twelve of the corvettes belonging to the Royal Canadian Navy it was essential to form links with Canada. I am particularly indebted to Mr. Leonard Webb of Alberta who became our 'Canadian Correspondent'. He was instrumental in obtaining the initial contact with the Canadian National Defence Directorate of History and Heritage. He also provided some most useful information on the post war mercantile employment of some of the Castles on the West Coast that plied between Vancouver and Alaska. The ships had been owned and converted by the Union Steamship Company.

Subsequently the Canadian work fell into the capable hands of Robert (Bob) Crothers who had served in *HMS Hadleigh Castle* and subsequently as Navigating Officer of *HMCS Humberstone*. Living at Kingston, Ontario, Bob was able to visit the office of the Directorate of History and Heritage. In spite of the restricted access times and difficulties in copying files there, he was instrumental in obtaining a large proportion of the operational records of the Canadian Castles that are reported here. Without Bob's efforts these would indeed have been even further incomplete than they are. I and the Association are most grateful for Bob's contributions.

Mention must also be made of the help and advice received from the Naval Historical Branch of the Ministry of Defence, London. Especially by David Ashby and Malcolm Llewellyn-Jones MBE, MA, psc, both of whom were most helpful in providing solutions to various technical questions that had arisen during the preparation of the book. Thanks are also due to Mr. J.R. Hailey MA, one time Archivist and Research Secretary of the Naval Historical Collectors and Research Association for assistance in checking on information extracted from PRO files.

I am much indebted to Mr. Steve Bush, editor, Maritime Books, for his guidance on the format of the book and for his scrupulous proofing of the text and also to Mr. M.C. Biffen (ex-*Carisbrooke Castle*) and Mr. N.S. Kimberley (ex-*Tintagel Castle*) for their suggestions and proof reading of the draft. However, it must be clearly understood that the whole responsibility for the text is mine; any errors or omissions must be laid at my door. The Castle Class Corvette (Frigate) Association does not necessarily concur with any statements, comments or opinions expressed in the book.

F.N. Goodwin, Archivist and Editor

Section One
THE SHIP

CASTLE CLASS CORVETTES: THE SHIP

HMS Snowflake was a Flower class corvette completed in 1941. Based on a traditional whaler hull, their small size and crowded upperdecks were a hinderance in the emerging submarine war. As the Battle of the Atlantic became more intense a larger more capable vessel was required. (Steve Bush Collection)

Introduction

In its preparations for the Second World War, the Admiralty had assumed that the requirements for the protection of merchant ships and the war supplies that they would carry would be very similar to that of the First World War. Then most of the anti U-boat action occurred in the Western Approaches to the British Isles where an extensive convoy system had proved effective. Convoys made it more difficult for U-boats to find their targets. Whilst the concentration of escorts made it more difficult for the U-boats to attack.

Between the wars the Admiralty had been developing an underwater sound detection system which came to be generally known as the Asdic. This was extensively fitted to HM Ships, especially destroyers as well as to the smaller Flower Class Corvettes. The range at which a submarine could be detected varied considerably depending on the weather, sea tempera-

ture and the skill of the operator. The average value was about 1,300 yards with a maximum of 2,500 yards. In terms of the number of ships that can be protected per escort, large convoys increase the effectiveness of the escort screen. Even so, the short range of the Asdic required large numbers of escorts. Because of the limited resources available, the escorts had to be simple and easy to build; preferably in small yards. The Flower class corvettes fitted these requirements. Eighteen yards were involved in their building in the UK and sixteen in Canada. They were originally developed and designed by the Smith Dock Company of Middlesborough. They were based on an existing design of theirs for a whale catcher.

Although designed for coastal escort work, for want of anything else they were used as ocean escorts. In spite of their deficiencies they and their crews did a remarkable job. They bore the brunt of the Battle of

the Atlantic under extremely arduous conditions. Commenting on their design and habitability, David K. Brown wrote:

"The early, short forecastle Flowers were the worst. They had bunks in the forecastle where the motion was worst and to reach the bridge or engine room meant crossing the open well deck, inevitably getting wet in bad weather. Worse still, the galley was aft and the food had to be brought along the open upper deck to the mess, getting cold, if not spilt on the way. As more equipment was added, over crowding became worse...They were so short (in length) so that pitch and heave motions were severe, which led to a high incidence of sickness and in all probability, of poor decision making, while their standard of habitability was low. Inadequate bilge keels led to heavy rolling and they were too slow to keep up with a surfaced submarine or to return quickly to station."

The fall of France gave the German Navy new bases on the Atlantic seaboard and allowed the battle to spread across the Atlantic. It was realised that more ships would be needed with a longer endurance and with better sea keeping qualities and better weapons.

Based on the ocean experience of the Flower Class, the Smith's Dock Company came up with proposals for two new types of vessels. The single screw corvette, to become the Castle Class and a twin screw corvette, later to be designated as a frigate, that became the River Class. The Board of Admiralty approved the Legend and Design of the new single screw corvette on 7th May 1943. The estimated cost, excluding guns and ammunition, was £174,000 per vessel.

The design called for an overall length of 252 feet, 47 feet longer than the previous Flower class, with a displacement of 1010 tons. The freeboard forward was increased by four feet and by three feet aft as compared to the Flowers. The ship was designed to carry 480 tons of fuel oil and have an endurance at 15 knots of 6,200 miles; 2,200 miles further than the Flower class.

With these dimensions and a beam of 36.5 feet the ships could be built by the smaller shipyards and keep the building capacity fully extended. Much of the superstructure was designed to be pre-fabricated.

Castle Class Specifications

Dimensions (feet)

Length between perpendiculars	225'
Length on waterline	234'
Length overall	252'
Beam amidships	36' 6"
Displacement (tons)	1010
Mean draught, deep condition	13' 2"

Machinery

Engine: 4 cyl triple expansion developing	2,980 IHP
Propeller Shaft	1
Speed in standard condition	17 knots
Speed in deep condition	16.5 knots
Fuel capacity (tons)	480
Endurance at 15 knots , clean bottom	6200 miles
Generators: Port Steam	1 x 60 KW
Starboard Steam	1 x 30 KW
Auxiliary Diesel	1 x 15 KW

Complement

Officers and Men	100-110

Armament

4-inch Mk XVI gun on Mk XXIV mounting; 300 rounds fixed shells

Squid single Mk1	1
Squid projectiles	81
Rocket Flares	64 x Mk II w
Single Oerlikons	2
Twin Oerlikons	2
Depth Charges	15 carried on deck only
Depth Charge Throwers	2 (Mk IV)
Depth Charge Rails	1

Equipment

ASDICs

The Type 144 Asdic complete attack set was the first to be based on war time experience. Two patterns were produced of which the Type 145, with a detachable dome, were fitted to the Flower and Castle class corvettes. The complete equipment included the 'Q' attachment that allowed contact with a submarine to be maintained at close range and the Type 147B which accurately derived the depth of the target. The whole was integrated into a system of automatically firing the Squid bombs and setting the bombs' depth fuses at the moment of firing. Repeaters on the bridge and in the wheelhouse provided information as to the bearing of the target and the course to be steered to intercept it.

An echo sounder Type 761 was also used as an aid in identifying bottomed targets

RADAR

At the time when the Castle class corvettes were being commissioned, this was still known by its British acronym of RDF (Range and Direction Finding). Most of the ships were initially equipped with the Type 272(P) set, although the mast had been designed to take the Type 277, a much more effective and robust piece of equipment. In due course the Type 277 was fitted as the supply position and contingencies of service allowed. The following were fitted with Type 277:-

Amberley Castle; *Copper Cliff*; *Huntsville*; *Bamborough Castle*, *Denbigh Castle*; *Lancaster Castle*, *Bowmanville*; *Dumbarton Castle*; *Launceston Castle*; *Caistor Castle*; *Hedingham Castle*; *Oakham Castle*; *Carisbrooke Castle*; *Hespeler* and *Portchester Castle*.

IFF equipment comprised:-	Interrogator 242
	Responder 255
	RACON 251

HF/DF

All of the Castle class corvettes were fitted with HF/DF. The aerials being placed at the top of the mast. The system could detect very short transmissions and record the bearing on a screen. It was also possible to distinguish between transmissions originating less than 25 miles away or a more distant signal. The receiver was to be found at the rear of the W/T Office

COMMUNICATIONS

Visual communication systems were located on the flag deck immediately aft of and at the same level as the bridge. The equipment included a flag locker containing a complete set of Naval and International flags; two 10-inch search light/signal lamps, one on each side of the flag deck, and Aldis lamps for short range signalling. Inter-ship voice radio was provided by the TBS (Talk Between Ships); a high frequency 'line of sight' system, located in the shelter on the for'ad starboard side of the bridge. A 2,410Kc/s voice radio system was also provided. This was know as the 'TBY'. It was used for communication between escorts and

merchant ships. Usually only the Commodore's and Vice Commodore's ships were equipped with TBY.

The main, Type 150, radio transmitter and four B2 receivers were located in the W/T Office as well as the high frequency radio for inter ship communications.

OTHER EQUIPMENT

Two oar propelled boats were supplied. A standard Naval Whaler (but without sails) mounted on davits on the starboard side and a 16-foot trawler dinghy also on davits on the port side (**Huntsville**, however, reported the possession of a 16-foot motor boat. The other Canadian ships variably reported the 16ft dinghy as a 'skiff'). A recreational 14-foot Naval dinghy was also stowed on the upper deck. Numerous Carley rafts and floatation nets were secured at various places along and upon the superstructure. The anti-Gnat Foxer gear was stowed aft on the uncluttered quarter-deck.

Ninety six vessels were ordered during 1943-44 including twelve for the Royal Canadian Navy. Ten were fitted out for Arctic conditions. With the success of the Allies in the North Atlantic some 52 vessels were cancelled and five were completed as Rescue Ships.

The layout of a Castle class corvette, upperdeck, forward. The 4-inch gun is prominent, as is the Squid A/Sweapon, under canvas, and the rails for the bomb loading carrier. *(CCC(F)A Archives)*

This view of a Castle class quarterdeck, shows the uncluttered stern, where the depth charge throwers and single depth charge rail were situated, a vast improvement over the cluttered decks of the earlier Flower class corvettes.
(CCC(F)A Archives)

SQUID

The vessels were to be built around a completely new and untried weapon, the Squid, and its associated Asdic system. Had these systems failed there was no alternative.

The Asdic Type 144 was the first attempt at an integrated Anti-Submarine (AS) weapon system. This combined with the 'Q' attachment, that allowed contact to be maintained with the submarine at close range, and the Type 147B depth measuring device combined with the Squid was the high-water mark of British anti-submarine technology.

From the concept drawings of the Squid to production took about thirteen months and the Type 147B depth determining Asdic was developed and fitted in the record time, from inception to prototype, of four months. The sea trials of the prototype 147 took place in *HMS Ambuscade* in May 1943. The first opera-

tional set was installed in *HMS Hadleigh Castle* four months later.

The Squid comprised three mortar type barrels on a single gyro controlled mounting. This threw projectiles in a triangular pattern with forty yard sides a distance of nearly 300 yards ahead of the ship. The projectiles contained 200lbs of Minol II explosive and had a rapid sinking speed of 44 feet per second. Automatic fuses were set by the Asdic 147B at the moment of firing so that the projectiles exploded at the depth of the submarine.

The Squid was the only weapon capable of attacking a submarine down to a depth of 900 feet. In 1945 Squid projectiles were fitted with a special shallow depth setting of 20 feet with a view to crippling and combating high speed U-Boats on the surface.

SHIP'S CHARACTERISTICS

The plate below shows off the characteristics of the Castle Class Corvettes. The sheer, flare and tumble home of the hull are considerably increased compared to the Flower Class. The midships section is rectangular and the covered upperdeck is carried right aft to the quarter deck. The whole hull design is strong and sturdy and specifically designed for operations in the North Atlantic. The visual effect is of a well turned out and designed sea boat and to many, especially to those who served on them, the most pleasing and attractive of all the escort classes. The cut away stem is especially attractive. Other points to be noted are the 4-inch gun mounted on a band stand forward of the Squid, thus providing a dry firing platform even in the worst of weathers; the open bridge with wings extended to the full beam of the ship affording a clear view for all purposes and a very wide arc of fire for the single mounted Oerlikons. The Type 272P RDF (Radar)

set is mounted high on the lattice mast with the HF/DF aerials mounted above. The quarterdeck is bounded by solid bulwarks and is comparatively uncluttered with only one depth charge thrower mounted on each side and a single rail over the stern. The hull design provided a very dry ship and it was rare for the bridge personnel to be drenched by spray and adequate shelter was provided for the Squid and Gun crews on watch. There was only one really bad design fault. Under certain conditions of rough weather the quarterdeck would ship green seas thus becoming a hazardous place to work.

The excellent sea keeping qualities of these ships is illustrated by the performance of **HMCS Orangeville** when she encountered hurricane force winds in the general position of 46°N 26°W in February 1945 whilst forming part of the escort for convoy ONS 41. During the afternoon and until shortly after midnight

The ships were designed to operate in the worst of the Atlantic weather. Note the long high freeboard and the flared bow, and the Squid launchers positioned well above the focs'le deck. Crew comfort was also addressed with accomodation as near the centre of the ship as possible to reduce the sensation of movement. (Lt D. Harris)

the wind was blowing from the SW strength 11 with the sea and swell recorded as 77. The convoy was hove to. During the night *Orangeville* realised that she had overtaken part of the convoy and although the wind had moderated to force 9 the sea and swell were 67, *Orangeville* altered course 180° to regain contact with a bunch of straggling ships. Two hours later she again altered course 180° with the sea and swell still recorded as 67 and wind force 9. The ship's deck log does not record that any damage was incurred by these manoeuvres.

In spite of the comparatively large rudder the ships could be difficult to control in heavy weather. Leading Seaman Henry Swain, a quartermaster of long standing, described the difficulties of maintaining a straight course in heavy weather whilst proceeding westwards in *HMS Lancaster Castle* with convoy RA 65. He wrote:

"It took me a while to get the hang of steering in these wild conditions. You couldn't steer the course directly because the ship's head was swinging through 30°. The course was supposed to be 223°. The best that I could do was to make 223° the mean course but the last digit made the mental arithmetic hard. The red numbers of the gyro compass repeater simply flashed in a blur as the waves hit us. I tried desperately to contain the swing between 208 and 238. The Officer of the Watch had evidently been staring at his compass on the bridge unbelievingly. I heard him say down the voice pipe, "Can't you do better than this, quartermaster?" The correct answer to this question, which was not really a question, should have been, "Aye, aye sir" but I didn't give it.

"I was doing my best and I was pretty sure that nobody could steer a better course. I shouted angrily back up the voice pipe "No, I bloody well can't sir." There was silence above. I was not sure who the officer of the watch was. It was hard to recognise voices in the racket of the wind and sea. I knew it was not the First Lieutenant, however, because if it had been, I should have had an immediate response. It would have been on the lines of "Yes, you bloody well can, Henry, and if you can't do it , I'll show you how to drive this sodding ship

myself."

"As the seconds ticked past I imagined being put on a charge for insubordination. I didn't care. As far as I could see, nobody could devise a worse punishment than that which I was already being subjected to - steering a wildly pitching and rolling corvette in the Arctic night in a Force 10 storm.

When the officer of the watch spoke again, he was quite nice. He said "Okay quartermaster, do your best. Try and keep the mean course as near as you can".

"Aye, aye sir," I said, slightly relieved.

"I was working myself to the limits of my strength at the wheel and the officer of the watch was trying to keep the ship in her right position in zero visibility and trying to dodge some of the spray as well. We were both, I reflected, in the same shit."

The rather blunt frontage of the superstructure was blamed by some to produce excessive windage. In one of his Reports of Proceedings for the 30th Escort Group, Commander D.A. Rayner RNVR drew attention to the difficult situation that can arise during stormy weather. He reported that when heading into a Force 9 wind and sea 63, 100 revolutions gave a ships speed made good of a fraction over 1 knot, and in the same wind, but more sheltered waters, when the sea was estimated at 41, 126 revolutions gave a ships speed of 4 knots. In both instances the ships were in waters where Gnats could have been fired from a submerged U-Boat.

It seems probable that it was the steepness of the seas rather than the strength of the wind that was the main factor in causing the slow speeds.

HMCS Orangeville in February 1945, when escorting convoy ONS 41 and in position 46°N 25°30'W encountered winds recorded by the Deck Log as Force 11 and seas 77 (Very heavy seas and heavy swell). Under these conditions speeds of 5 to 6 knots were achieved with engine revolutions varying between 107 and 117 per minute. The next day, after a lull, the wind again increased to Force 10-11 producing a high sea accompanied with a heavy swell (67). Eighty seven to ninety revolutions per minute gave a recorded speed of 3.5 to 4 knots.

Anti-Submarine Weapon Systems

ASDICS

Between the two World Wars the Admiralty continued research on submarine detection. The word 'Asdic' or 'Asdics' was coined; a term sufficiently meaningless not to give away the principle on which the device was based. Following the use of the term in the House of Commons in 1939, the Admiralty said that the word was an acronym of 'Allied Submarine Detection Investigation Committee'. No such committee bearing that name has been found in the Admiralty archives. However, the Admiralty department that initiated the research was known as the 'Anti Submarine Division-ics (*Hackman. W. 'Seek and Strike' HMSO 1984 p.xxv*)

The essential principle of the device is that of transmitting in a 2?° to 5° wide fan shaped underwater sound signal in a selected and controlled direction. If the sound wave should strike a solid object an echo would bounce back to the transmitting device.

In its simplest form, the sound wave is created by feeding an alternating current through an oscillator made up of layers of mild steel and layers of quartz. The current is repeatedly passed at regular short intervals of a few seconds. This causes the plates to vibrate or oscillate. Thus creating a sound wave. When the wave of sound hits an object it bounced back, hitting the oscillator and causing it to vibrate. This homing echo creates a small electric charge and can be recorded, and by time lapse, the distance from the oscillator to the object calculated. The oscillator, with its 'Q' attachment (see later) was housed in a dome shaped protective cover externally, and below the keel of the ship in a forward position

The speed of sound in the water tends to be around 4,900 feet per second. This velocity can be affected by factors such as sea temperature, salinity and depth. Salinity is of importance in the area of the Great Banks, where strongly saline Gulf Stream water mixes with the colder, less saline Labrador current. Temperature variations and gradients in the arctic waters are also an important factor. A rapid decline in temperature with depth, known as the thermocline, results in a decrease of sound speed, and thus a sharp

downward refraction and poor ranges.

The systems installed in the Castle class corvettes were the Type 145, Type 145Q and Type 147B.

Generally the maximum range for detecting an object during WWII was around 2,500 yards. It would take the sound wave 1.5 seconds to travel this distance and should it hit a solid object at extreme range the echo would take 1.5 seconds to return. Thus the transmission intervals were normally 3 seconds. The effective range could be affected by a wide range of local conditions. (Speed of operating ship - optimum about four knots - sea conditions, efficiency of the Asdic set and operator).

The operator had to contend with many factors. Echoes of varying quality may be obtained off a variety of objects, (a submarine, the sea bed, a prominent submerged rock, or a wreck). A variety of other unpredictable and less solid objects, such as a bubbles from fish of all sizes, ships' propellers (H.E. - hydrophone effect) ship wakes, or areas of previous attacks would also produce a response.

A skilful and experienced Asdic operator would be able to classify the echo according to its origin. The difference in pitch between the outgoing pulse and the echo is an important determinant of the contact being a moving object. A receding object giving a lower echo tone and an approaching object a higher one. This is known as the doppler effect. Disturbed water or a shoal of fish produce a 'fizz' of an echo. In coastal waters the tidal stream could induce an illusion of a stationary target moving, whereas in fact it was the investigating ship that was moving with the tide. There would, however be no doppler effect.

The main oscillator, described above, transmitted a horizontal beam of sound with the result that at close range the beam can pass over a submarine and contact be lost. This was largely overcome by the 'Q' oscillator that transmitted its sound wave downward. With the 'Q' attachment contact could be maintained at close ranges and some indication of the depth of the target was possible. The development of the type 147B Asdic provided greater precision in measuring

the depth of the target. The Type 147B oscillator (transducer) produced a fan shaped beam about 3° wide in the vertical plane. It could be depressed from the vertical to 45°. The horizontal range and depth of the submarine were determined by the angle of the tilt of the transducer. The depth could be obtained by the stylus of the recorder travelling across the paper at a speed proportional to the sine of the angle of depression of the Asdic beam. The set was found to be remarkably accurate. Because of the short ranges and steep angles, refraction was relatively unimportant. In the Atlantic the Type 147B was found to be accurate to within 20 feet.

The 'Q' oscillator was attached to the main oscillator which could be trained horizontally through, in effect, 360°, but in practice seldom more than 70° either side of direct ahead. The 147B oscillator (known as the 'Sword') could not be trained. It directed its beam of sound directly ahead and downward.

Each oscillator was connected to a separate recorder, on which a stylus moves across a moving sheet of sensitised paper. One pass across the width of the paper for each transmission 'ping' of the sound wave. This could be heard in the operator's head phones as well as from a repeater on the bridge. A black mark is recorded on the paper when an echo is received. The range is recorded by calibration across the sheet. The direction relative to the ship's head is already chosen and known.

Within the Asdic hut there was also a plotting table, which by combining inputs from the ship's gyro compass and the electric chernokeef log, the ship's course and distance travelled can be recorded. A wide range of scales was available. The Plan Position Indicator (PPI) from the RDF Type 272 or 277 was positioned on the for'ard bulkhead close to the plotting table. Thus the range and bearing of all the other ships engaged in the attack was readily available

During action stations the plot would be manned, usually by the navigating officer, who would plot the movement of the target, the ranges and bearings of the target being passed on by the Asdic team. By this means the target's course and speed was plotted. The Asdic hut at action stations was very crowded. The

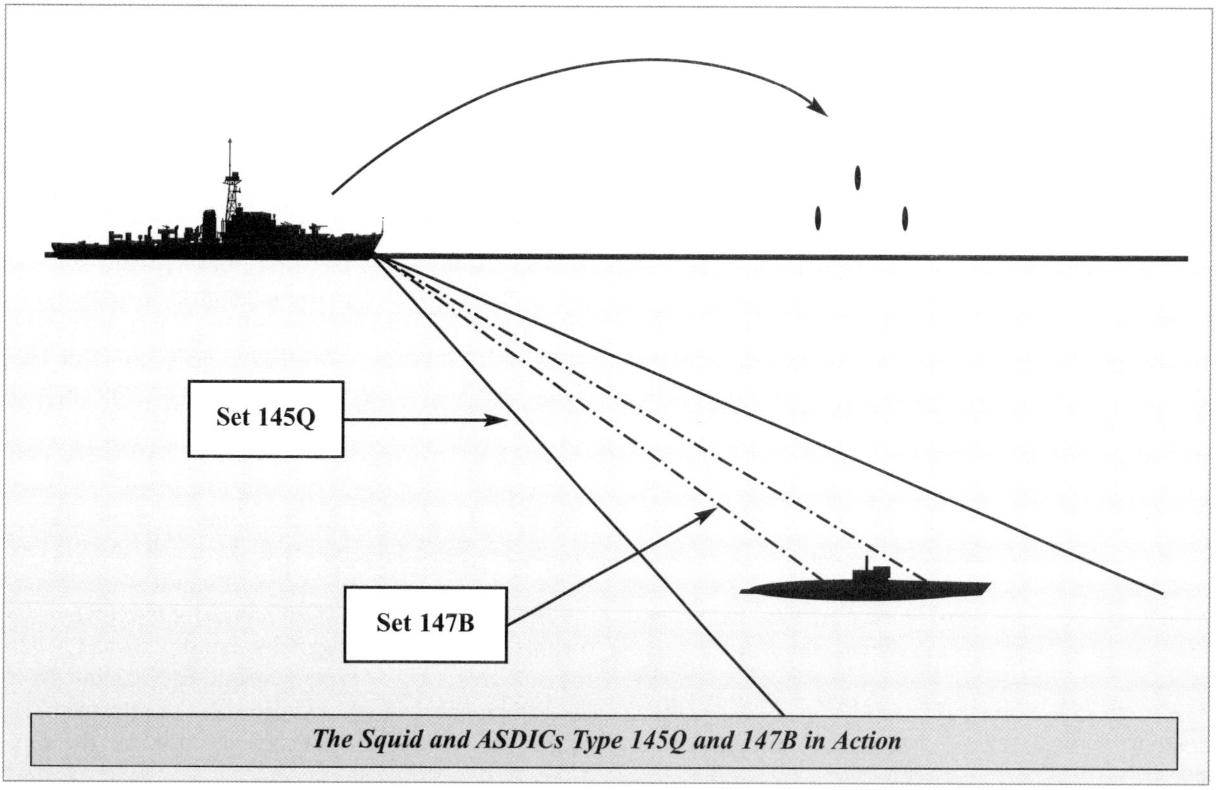

Set 145Q

Set 147B

The Squid and ASDICs Type 145Q and 147B in Action

Asdic Officer and the Plotting Officer stood pressed back to back. Information on range depth and speed of the target was exchanged. The movement of the target, of adjacent ships as well as the convoy was plotted. In the event of the contact being lost valuable information was available as to its likely position and thus the likely direction in which to resume the search, as well as its probable bearing and distance from adjacent hunting vessels.

Once a submarine had been detected, the attacking ship was steamed at the optimum Asdic operating speed, usually at 4 to 5 knots, towards the target. All the information coming from the Asdic operator and the navigation plot. The system was such that an attack could easily be initiated by the Officer of the Watch (OOW). Usually the helmsman was ordered to "Steer by Asdic" by following a repeater indicator located in the wheelhouse (i.e. - in the direction of the target as relayed from the Asdic operator). The Squid was fired automatically as soon as the target came within range and the bombs automatically set to explode at the target's depth.

The Senior Officer of the Escort Group could also listen in on what the Asdic operators were hearing. This was done by the attacking ship placing the microphone of the TBS (Talk Between Ships HF radio) close to the Asdic bridge repeater. In this way the Senior Officer could make his own judgement as to the type of target being investigated or attacked.

In coastal waters the standard navigational echo sounder depth recorder was also used as a submarine detector. The sound signal from this device is directed directly downwards and the echo produces a profile of the sea bed and its depth. It was frequently used to identify a stationary bottomed contact. By steaming over the spot the echo sounder could trace the outline of the contact. Sometimes this could be recognised as that of a U-Boat, or alternatively that of a wreck. It was also possible to measure the length, breadth and height of the object with some degree of confidence.

"The Asdic team consisted of six ratings, one of which was an H.S.D. (Higher Submarine Detector). Sometimes he held a substantive rating though not always. It was his job to see that the A/S sets were always in top condition. He was of course the senior operator. The remaining member of the A/S team was an officer who had been designated and also usually trained as the A/S Officer. It was he who stood behind

the operators during an attack on a U-Boat co-ordinating their reports and liasing with the Commanding Officer and the Navigator.

The Asdic hut was located at the rear of the bridge. All communication between the Asdic hut, the Bridge and RDF Office was by voice pipe. This enabled the Captain or OOW to discuss with the A/S Officer or Asdic operator the characteristics of the echo . The system was designed to enable the Commanding Officer to have as much information as possible about the target, its characteristics and the disposition of neighbouring vessels

"A/S ratings were not allowed to display their SD badge on their uniform. The intention being to deny to the enemy or his agents the knowledge of the presence of an SD rating ashore or as a Prisoner of War.

"A/S ratings were never members of a gun crew; this was to protect their ears. Usually when not on U-Boat action, they would be communication No's. Their nickname on board ship was 'Ping'. This was what the transmissions sounded like. They were also referred to, as being 'Ping happy'. The shore base for these Ping happy creatures was **HMS Osprey**. *Originally at Portland and then at Dunoon. I did my basic training at Campbeltown. The base there was called* **HMS Nimrod**. *It was situated in the old Grammar School. We went to sea each day, marching down to the harbour carrying our food rations. These would be given to the cook on whichever vessel we were sailing on that day. We used a variety of craft ranging from fishing vessels to private yachts that had been requisitioned by the Admiralty. There was also an old French destroyer,* **La Cordelier**. *Each day we practised with our own submarines off Ailsa Craig. We would sit in the mess deck until called to the bridge to take our turn on the A/S set. When the day's training was over the Captain of the ship would order the engine room 'tap the hull'. A stoker would then bang a spanner on the bilges, the submarine captain would hear this and surface and accompany us back to harbour. This demonstrates how well sounds travel under water.*

When on escort duty whenever we got back to harbour our training would continue in an Attack Teacher House (ATH) These were double decker buses fitted out with all the A/S gear and bridge gear that a sea going ship would have. Mock U-Boat attacks were simulated here. There would be a full A/S team and

officers training alongside them. The buses were usually on the jetty and were used during our lay-over *period between voyages".*

OPERATION OF THE ASDIC SETS

An important part of the A/S equipment was the gyro compass repeater which incorporated a cursor. The whole thing looked somewhat like a car's steering wheel. In front of this was a knurled knob that would turn to the left or to the right, and in the middle of this knob was a button. Next to this was a two position switch, one marked 2? degrees and the other 5 degrees. By turning the knurled knob the oscillator was also turned. A common A/S sweep would go 70° either side of each bow. If the sweep was to start on the port side, the operator would turn the knob to the left and hold it there. This would cause the cursor and oscillator to move. When the cursor reached Red 70 it would be released. The cursor and oscillator would then start to move back towards the ship's head automatically in 5° steps, if the two position switch had been set to 5°. Upon reaching the ship's head the oscillator would continue to transmit twice more until it reached Green 10. The operator would then, by means of the knob, move the oscillator down to Green 70 and the whole process would start again. Another standard sweep was one used to detect mines. This was a 40° by 40° sweep and a shorter transmission setting was used.

Each time the oscillator moved it would transmit a pulse of sound in the direction that it was facing. If this sound beam hit anything it would bounce back towards the oscillator as an echo. The original pulse of sound and the returning echo would be heard through the headphones by the operator who would evaluate the difference between the outgoing transmission and the incoming echo. The period from transmission of a pulse to the return of an echo took about three seconds. Thus the complete sweep from one side to the other took about 1? minutes.

If it was a good echo or there was some doubt, the operator would immediately press the button in the middle of the knurled knob. This would cause the oscillator and cursor to step back 5°. The switch would then be set to 2? degree steps and the cursor would start moving back towards the original bearing of the echo in 2?° steps. When the echo was again

reached the position on the left hand side (say) would be noted, the operator would then move the oscillator/cursor manually forward to this position and then allow the oscillator/cursor to step backwards towards the echo bearing. When again meeting the echo the position would be noted thus giving the extent of the target and also whether or not there was any movement. This information as well as other knowledge would be used to determine whether this was a submarine or not. Of course as soon as the first echo was heard the O.O.W. would have been informed through the voice pipe. He might reply that there was one of our ships on that bearing and that we were probably getting an echo from his wake and to disregard that echo and carry on with the sweep.

On cruising watch the two operators would take turn and turn about on the main set and wearing the headphones. In those days these were not light. The task was an onerous one as we were listening to a transmission every three seconds or so. The operator not doing the sweep would man the range recorder attached to the 145 Asdic set. This was a flat bed machine about 12 inches wide and 14 inches long of metallic construction. Sensitised paper was automatically scrolled down and along the top ran a stylus immediately below a range scale calibrated in yards. As the pulse of sound was transmitted, so the stylus moved along the scale and when an echo was obtained it left a brown dot on the paper. The range could be read off the scale. Because the paper was moving down all the time, it gave a visual trace of the echo showing among other things the movement and also the quality of the echo. During an attack the operator would keep a line of light along these dots by means of a wheel which also had on it a steel rod. At the culmination of the attack the range would have diminished, the light and the rod would have been moved following the dot representing the target until it became into Squid range. By this time the rod would make contact with a switch which would automatically fire the Squid. Immediately before this the target would have been so close that the operator would be

hearing 'instant echoes'. That is the transmissions going out were merging with the echoes. This was the time for the operators to ease the headphones from their ears so that they didn't get their eardrums broken when the squid bombs exploded. When the ship had passed over the target the order "*Carry out stern sweep*" was given. The oscillator would be trained directly aft and transmissions would be going out with a limited range of 1,000 yards. On completion of the first stern sweep the 1st Operator would report to the bridge "*First stern sweep carried out Sir*" This was usually a fruitless task because the oscillator would pick echoes from the Squid explosions and also echoes from the ship's wake. In due course the C.O. would turn the ship towards the last known or expected position of the target and the operators would carry out more sweeps until contact was regained.. During the early stages of an attack the operator would 'Switch to Q'. This ensured that, contact was not lost, especially with a U-boat running deep, because of the transmission from the 145 set passing over above the U-Boat.

During an attack the third operator would be manning the 147B set and recorder. This was the 'sword' oscillator which the operator kept in contact with the target by arcing the sword up or down. It recorded the depth of the U-Boat. It worked in conjunction with the range recorder(s) so that when the firing bar made

contact, the depth of the U-Boat was immediately transferred to the Squid depth fuses. This ensured that the Squid bombs exploded at the right depth.

Good operators were valued for their skill in classifying an echo. This was done by considering certain criteria:

How big was it ?	Width of the target. Five degrees at a normal range was suspicious.
Did it sound good?	A sharp hard echo was promising
Was it moving?	If so how fast?
Are there any wrecks in the area?	
Any surface ships about?	
Any hydrophone effect?	i.e. sounds of:- Ships engines, fast , reciprocating? Any mechanical bangs or other noises. Maybe a U- Boat breaking up or blowing tanks. Torpedoes running. Explosions. Torpedoes, depth charges, Squid bombs Shoals of fish, clicking noises made by shoals of shrimps. Whales whistling.

CLOSING UP PROCEDURES

When a new watch took over it was usual for the watch on duty to ask permission to hand over. When this was obtained the new watch would report their names, gyro compass heading, circuits OK, and the on going sweep.   The new watch would also report

"*Chronoscope and stop watch provided sir*". These latter were used if during an attack the range finder broke down. There was a procedure for working out the range and to fire the Squid manually. The chronoscope ands stop watch were required for this.

*Source: This Asdic section was prepared almost wholly by Mr. Derek Wells-Brown ex Lieutenant RNVR and Asdic Officer and R. Hewitt, Asdic Operator, both of **HMS Portchester Castle**.*

Additional material was obtained from:-

Hackman. W.   *Seek and Strike. HMSO 1984*
Gardiner W.J.R. *Anti-Submarine Warfare. Brassey's 1996*
Hague A.   *The Allied Convoy System 1939-1945. Chatham Publishers 2000.*

TACTICAL CONTROL

Reference to the image on page 4 shows the position of the gyro compass and Asdic repeater. Adjacent to this was a loudspeaker which repeated what the Asdic Operator heard in his ear-phones. Thus the Commanding Officer or Officer of the Watch were able to hear the quality of the echo and visualise the direction from which the echo was coming. This information, supplemented by that provided by the Asdic Officer and Plotting Officer, enabled the CO to make a judgement as to the tactical situation and progress of the attack, or hunt, as the case may be. On the basis of the information provided, the CO could decide whether or not an attack should be continued or broken off, sometimes over-ruling the diagnosis of the Asdic team. A good example of this is described by Colin Warwick the Senior Officer of the B2 Escort Group and CO of **Rushen Castle**. The incident occurred during a training exercise off Londonderry.

"At the start of the exercise the A/S Staff Training Officer reported "Commodore torpe-doed on the Starboard side!".
Lt Billany and his Asdic crew working in the lit-tle cabin behind the open bridge had obtained a firm contact and reported "Possible subma-rine".
"Action Stations! Steer by Asdic", I ordered.
***Rushen Castle** was brought head on to the Asdic compass bearing, moving in to make a simulated attack with the Squid. The echo, which had been sharp and clear, now recorded a rather wooly sound.*
"It is a non-sub echo", remarked the staff ASW

officer rather pontifically.
"The convoy has been attacked. The com-modore ship torpedoed on her starboard side. This was a possible submarine contact. We are going to attack without delay," I pointed out.
Lt Billany came out of the A/S cabin. "I think it is a non-sub, Sir," suggesting that I should break off the attack.
"Continue with the attack on this contact, Lt Billany. You picked up a firm, possible subma-rine contact in the area from which the torpedo attack was made. U-Boats can create non-sub effects when they hear that their submarine has been contacted by Asdic."
"It is obviously a non-sub", sniffed the ASW staff expert.
Lt Billany looked at me apologetically and went back to complete the attack. When the Squid was reported as having been fired, I ordered the hand grenade to be thrown overboard. Up came a yellow smoke candle from the subma-rine in response to the explosion. I said nothing and lit a cigarette.
"Who dropped that hand grenade down my con-ning tower, giving me a headache all after-noon?" asked the submarine commander at the post-mortem meeting on the exercise.
"I did, and now you can tell me what you were doing down there making non-sub effects?"
"I was going ahead and astern alternatively on my engines to create a wake of disturbed water around the submarine. It often works quite well".

THE SQUID

In principle the Squid was a long-range depth-charge thrower, automatically operated and controlled. It was a three barrelled mortar, electrically fired and designed to discharge bombs ahead of the attacking ship. The feasibility of doing this from the deck of a small ship arose from the special design of the mount-ing that reduced the size of the recoil forces.

The Squid was the most important A/S weapon to be

developed in WWII and the first in which the Asdics and the weapon were fully integrated. The most important feature was the automatic setting of the depth-pistols by the Type 147B depth determining Asdic set. Unlike the hedgehog projectiles which only exploded on contact, the Squid bombs exploded when they reached their depth setting. The 'big-bang' school of thought in the Royal Navy argued that even

if the bombs missed their target, they would inflict morale damage on the U-Boat's crew. And the explosions certainly proved satisfying to the crew of the attacking ship.

The bombs contained some 200 lbs (91 Kg) of the new Minol II explosive and had a fast sinking speed of 44 ft (13.4m) per second. The Squid was the only wartime weapon capable of attacking submarines down to a depth of 900 feet. At the other end of the scale, a development later in the war enabled the Squid fuses to be set to explode at a shallow setting of 20 feet for the purpose of attacking a semi-submerged U-Boat.

The Squid mounting was gyro stabilised for the roll of the ship and deflection was allowed not only for roll but also for yaw and throw off to allow for the movement of the U-Boat from the time of the firing of the bombs to their explosion. The maximum possible correction for roll was 43° either side of the vertical and 20° for deflection and yaw. A follow-the-pointer gear was provided so that in the event of failure of the power system the cradle could be stabilised and trained by hand. Post war analysis showed that between 1943 and 1945 the Squid was the most effective A/S weapon. A single depth charge attack had roughly a 6 per cent chance of sinking a U-Boat, a Hedgehog pattern roughly 20 per cent, and the Squid pattern roughly 50 per cent.

The Squid A/S weapon comprised a three-barrelled launcher which fired a pattern of depth charges ahead of the ship (note the differing angles of the barrels which produced the spread of bombs). Squid was the first A/S weapon to be fully integrated with Asdic.

(Photograph courtesy of the Imperial War Museum Neg No: A26152)

THE FIRST USE OF THE SQUID IN ACTION

The 15th Escort Group (**HMS Wren** SO) which included **Kenilworth Castle** and **Berkeley Castle** was engaged in an A/S sweep off the north of Ireland on 23 January 1944.

At 1739 **Kenilworth Castle** obtained a contact and **Berkeley Castle** was ordered to join in with her on the hunt. Over the next 16 hours the two ships carried out 13 attacks with Squid (**KC** 6; **BC** 7). This was the first time that the new weapons had been used in Action.

Commenting on the action, Commodore (D),

Londonderry, was of the opinion that the target was not in fact hostile. He concluded that the attacks had been carried out on one or more of the numerous wrecks lying in the area. However, he commented:

"If the target during the hunt had been a submarine, it is considered that the attacks carried out would not only have damaged it severely but would have forced it to reveal its identity."

Discussing the behaviour of the Squid he wrote:

"When it is considered that this is the first action experience of the Squid and that the two ships attacking were inexperienced, the weapon on the whole, behaved extremely well."

Because of the sea conditions (sea rough; swell moderate) the loading of the Squid was difficult largely due to the rolling of the ships. The "drill" as laid down proved adequate. One unsatisfactory point was found to be the wire holding the fuse in position and the smallness of the key. This made the withdrawal of the key difficult and an uncertain business at night and in bad weather.

In both ships, the Type B roll corrector failed. In **Kenilworth Castle** this broke before the 8th attack (of the series) and in **Berkeley Castle** after her 2nd or 3rd attack. In **Kenilworth Castle** the defect was caused by the gyro armature burning out after ten hours running. In **Berkeley Castle** the defect was almost certainly due to a nut shaking loose due to vibration.

During extensive exercises the Type 147 A/S set had achieved remarkable results. These were not repeated during this action. This was attributed to the fact that a bottomed target was being attacked. No clear "cut off" on the bottom edge of the target being discerned.

RADAR

Formerly known as RDF this was a key element in anti submarine warfare. The Castle Class Corvettes were designed to take the Type 277 set but most were initially fitted with the less robust Type 272. The transmitting/receiving aerial was mounted high in the lattice mast and had a 'visual' range to the horizon of 12,800 yards. The aerial was rotated by hand via a 'Bowden' wire drive and the signal displayed on a Plan Position Indicator (PPI) in the Radar room and a repeater close to the plot in the Asdic Hut. In some instances an additional repeater was fitted in the Captain's day cabin. It was one of the early 10cm sets transmitting on 3,000Mhz with a power rating of 5-10 Kw. It was first introduced into the Fleet in 1941.

Several range scales were available for use. Under normal escort or patrol duties the longest range scale would be used, with the shorter scales coming into use once a definite target was being investigated.

The Type 277 was designed primarily for surface and low air warning. Its circular paraboloid aerial, stabilized in elevation, gave a pencil-shaped beam which could be pointed in any direction. On the Castle Class Corvettes it was provided with a 4ft 6in paraboloid aerial. The aerial was continuously rotated. Rotation of the aerial was motor driven and it could be rotated at speeds of up to 16 rpm.

The U-Boats were able to intercept the Radar pulsed transmission and would usually submerge as soon as these were detected. Thus the disappearance after a brief time of a small echo was a good indicator that a U-Boat had been detected. This of course meant that the Radar operators had to be very alert and quick to detect these instances. Early warning of aircraft was also possible, the Type 277 being better at this than the earlier 272 model.

Radar was invaluable for keeping station on the convoy or other escorts as well as an aid in coastal navigation.

THE 4-INCH GUN

The Mk XVI version on the Mk XXIV mounting was provided. The Semi Armour Piercing (SAP) shells that were supplied were of limited value against submarines. The main asset of the 4-inch gun was in providing illuminants. These were in the form of the conventional star shell and a battery of 2 inch rocket flares mounted on each side of the gun shield.

THE "SHARK" ANTI-SUBMARINE PROJECTILE

This was a projectile developed for use in 4-inch guns for attacking U-Boats on the surface. It was known during development by the code name "Shark" and that name stuck. It was a cumbersome weapon some 41 inches long (104cm). The "Shark" was intended to hit the water just short of the U-Boat and strike the boat underwater when the water tamping would make its detonation more effective.

The purposes underlying the development was that to be effective, the semi armour piercing (SAP) shell, had to hit a vertical surface; on a U-Boat this was a very small area. Even if this was hit the SAP shell was likely to glance off the pressure hull.

If these shells hit the conning-tower, they often travelled on before bursting and, even if they burst, were unlikely to prevent the boat diving. An H.E. shell will detonate if it hits the target anywhere but only under exceptional circumstances would the fragments from a 4-inch shell hole the pressure hull.

The "Shark" was heavy and unwieldy but its AP head enabled it to pierce tanks or superstructure before bursting. It was immune from ricochet, at all angles greater than 3?° which meant that, if fired from a gun mounted not less than 15ft above the waterline, it would not ricochet at any angle of gun elevation. Its fuse gave sufficient delay to permit penetration and its charge, 25lbs of Torpex, could cause a large hole in the pressure hull.

On hitting the water the "Shark" continues to move substantially along the same trajectory but loses its velocity rapidly. It follows that the "Shark" was essentially a short range weapon, because the greater the range the steeper the trajectory inclined downwards and the projectile would miss under the U-Boat unless it fell very close to her.

Owing to the unhandiness of the projectile the rate of fire was particularly slow if there was any degree of motion of the ship. Starting with the gun loaded, it would be a smart crew that fired three rounds in a minute.

The muzzle velocity was only 500ft a second, which meant that the "forecast" to be applied by the gunlayer when there is motion on the ship would need to be five times that required by an ordinary shell. This would be so difficult to assess that it was advised to restrict firing to the end of the roll towards - there could be insufficient depression to be able to fire on the roll away - when no forecast would be required. However, the main constraint on the rate of fire was the unhandiness of the projectile and the small number of rounds carried.

Firing would always be in Quarter Firing, range being set on a special "Shark" scale on the Range dial. For further details see CB 04050/44(1) monthly Anti-Submarine report January 1944.

OERLIKONS

Anti aircraft defence was provided wholly by these weapons. Two twin powered mountings were placed abaft the funnel and two single mountings near the wings of the bridge. Ample ready use ammunition was provided in lockers nearby.

RADIO

The W/T Office was the kingpin for all other than visual external communications.

All W/T messages were in Morse and taken down by hand. These were invariably in a numerical code. Numbers were the easiest to read. One dot followed by 4 dashes was numeral 'one'. Two was two dots followed by three dashes and so on until numeral five which consisted of 5 dots. Six was one dash followed by 4 dots and progressed through 9 (4 dashes and one dot) to zero which was 5 dashes.

At the signal school dots and dashes were taught as de's and dah's. This gave every letter its distinctive sound. A good example of this is the letter Q which being Dah Dah De Dah would sound like 'Here comes the Queen'. Even complete words could sound like a tune. It was not until about mid 1945 that telegraphists began to be taught touch typing. There is no record of type-writers being issued to Castle Class Corvette's wireless offices during war time. Coders sat in the Wireless Office so as to minimise the time spent in coding and decoding messages.

VISUAL SIGNALLING

Not all the Flower Class corvettes had been equipped with TBS, so communication with them had to be by either by light or flags. Generally the distance between escorts was too great for the use of flags. The most usual method being the use of the 10 inch signal lamps. Aldis lamps were only suitable for compara-tively short ranges. The Aldis was rarely used on the Russian Convoy operations. The cold necessitated the wearing of mittens and one cannot operate the Aldis 'trigger' when wearing these. The cold also interfered with the use of signal flags. The signal halyards tend-ed to freeze up.

HF/DF (HIGH FREQUENCY DIRECTION FINDING)

Early in 1944 Frank Rees was one of a new bunch of specialist telegraphists, trained in the use of the HF/DF equipment. He was in the advance party for the commissioning of the **Pevensey Castle** and remained with the ship for the whole of her first commission. He wrote:

"I had just completed my training and passed out as a Tel(S), a new grade to man the anti-submarine equipment - HF/DF. The Huff Duff (as it became known) was initially viewed with some scepticism by the Captains as it was yet to prove itself which it soon did on the first convoy and thereafter.

"Whilst on watch we sat in our small cabin with headphones firmly on surrounded by the H.F receivers with the large Goniometre in the centre. Our job was to search the ether within a spectrum and pick up any U-Boat transmissions. These were usually very brief coded messages and when preceded by what we called "B-Bar" (sent twice) we knew that there could be trouble ahead as it was a convoy sighting report. This being picked up by the German Naval land base would be rebroadcast to all U-Boats who would then form their packs and home in on the convoy. As soon as we heard the U-Boat transmit we had to be very quick to get a bearing by swinging the Gonio and decreasing its swing until we had a peak signal. We then flicked a switch to 'Sense', to confirm its true bearing and not its reciprocal. Sometimes, If one was lucky, we would hear the peculiar whine of the U-Boat drying out its aerials before transmitting. This provided extra time for getting a bearing. The equip-ment enabled a skillful operator to determine if the transmission had occurred close to, within 25 miles, or at a distance. All the other escorts similarly equipped would also have heard the transmission and passed the bearing to the Senior Officer. All being well the combination of the bearings would give a plotted position for the U-Boat. Subsequent action would depend on the tactical situation."

LORAN

The Canadian Castle Class Corvettes were required to complete a Fighting Equipment Report. Parts of these have survived and it can be shown that LORAN Type DAS-1 was carried by *Hespeller*, *Huntsville*, *Orangeville* and *Tillsonberg*.

This equipment was also carried by *Tintagel Castle* and may well have been carried by other RN Castle Class Corvettes.

SMOKE FLOATS

All the Canadian Castle Class Corvettes reported carrying smoke floats, usually 6, Mk III. These were also reported in the Reports of Proceedings as having been used/carried by the RN ships. It is assumed that the complement would have been the same.

WAVEMETER

The Canadian corvette *Orangeville* reported carrying one WAVEMETER Type G-73.

A pencil sketch by Henry Swain showing the accommodation in No.6 Mess, *HMS Lancaster Castle*.

RECREATIONAL AND OTHER EQUIPMENT

Both **Hespeler** and **Huntsville** report having two washing machines. **Hespeler**'s was donated by Hespeler City. **Huntsville** was also fortunate in having a Bell & Howell Projector complete with screen and speaker. She also had one complete drum kit, an alto saxophone and one trumpet.

Leeds Castle had, reportedly, somehow managed to manoeuvre a piano down to one of the mess decks .

MESSDECK ACCOMMODATION

Conditions on the messdecks were very crowded. There was little room for stowing personal gear and only the benches for relaxation for those off watch. Once hammocks had been slung there was even greater restriction on movement.

Describing conditions during heavy weather, J.C. Montier, a signalman on the **Allington Castle**, wrote:

"Cooking was No Go in these conditions and the crew lived on hard biscuits, jam and cheese until the weather improved."

A heavily rolling ship also contributed to the general discomfort. Coming off the middle watch, he wrote:

"When I arrived in the mess the ship rolled heavily to port just as one of the telegraphists was turning out of his hammock to go on watch. The roll of the ship helped him on his way straight across the table and on to the other side of the mess. Before he could grab hold of some-thing, the ship rolled back and he came sliding across the deck the other way. At the same moment a large tin of flour came adrift and spilt onto the deck spreading flour all over the place. By the time that he was able to stand up again, he looked quite pale and ill covered from head to foot with flour. The vigour of his language belied his ghostlike appearance".

An additional problem, especially when in arctic waters was condensation. Outward bound, once past the Faroes, it was not long before the bulkheads, deck head, pipes and air ducts were covered with a thickening layer of frozen condensation. This stayed in place until things began to warm up again when homeward bound. As it got warmer the ice thawed and we then became saturated by water dripping down from overhead. If you happened to have your hammock slung, then you were more than likely to have wet blankets. There was infact few facilities for drying out either clothing or bedding.

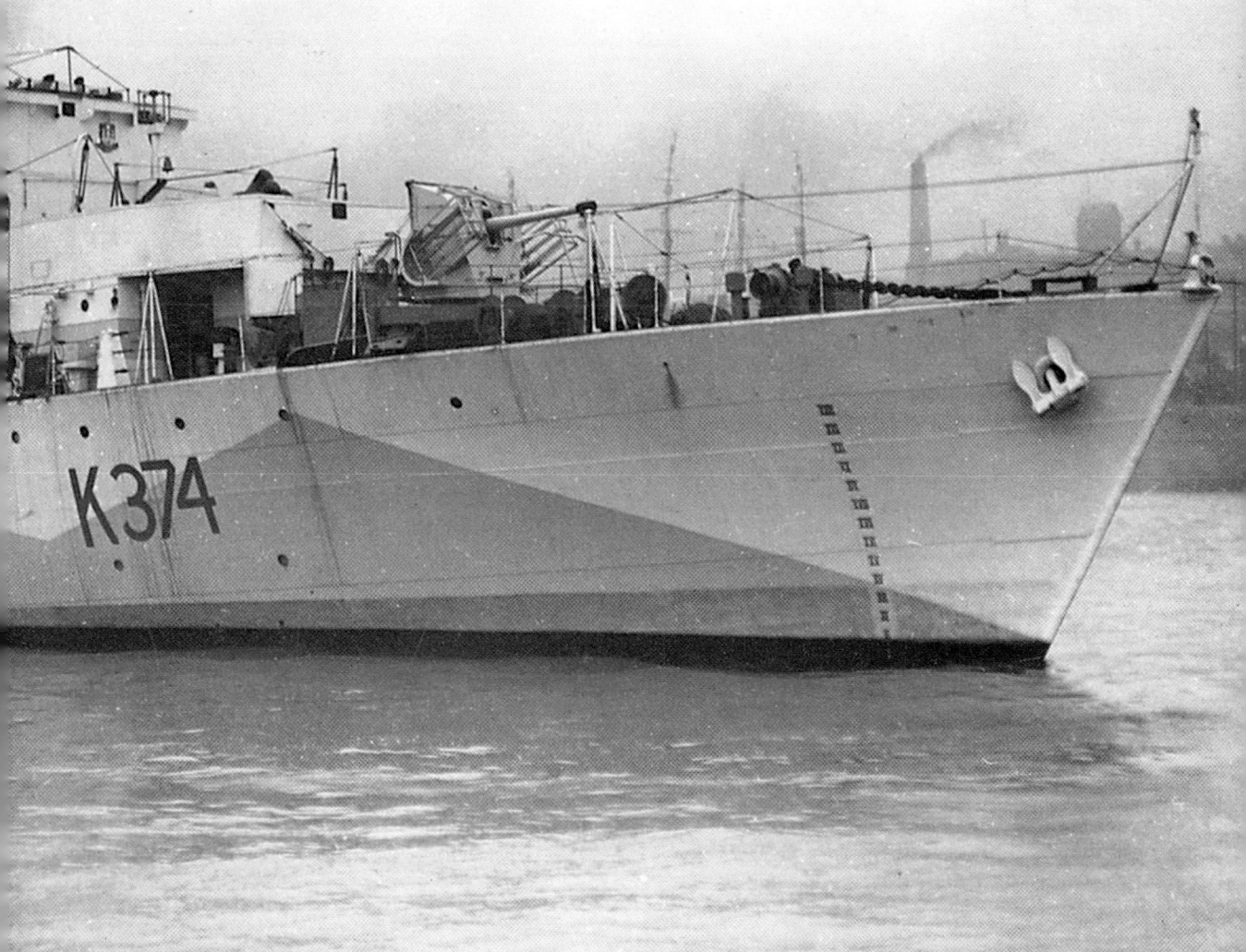

Section Two
SERVICE AT WAR AND PEACE

K374

SERVICE AT WAR AND PEACE

HMS Launceston Castle off Rathlin Island - in typical Atlantic weather. (R.W. Burke)

THE PROTECTION OF CONVOYS

The ships were designed primarily to protect merchant ships from attacks by U-boats, and to provide a certain amount of protection from close range air attack. In particular the ships were designed with the expectation that their main sphere of operation would be in the North Atlantic. In this they were particularly successful. During the period 11 December 1943 to 6 June 1945 the Castle class corvettes escorted 237 ocean convoys comprising just over 12,000 ships for a loss of less than 10 merchant ships by enemy action. During that time they were associated with the destruction of seven U-boats for the loss of three corvettes. As the ships were commissioned they were placed under the command of the Commander-in-Chief Western Approaches (CinC W.A.) and allocated to Escort Groups.

ESCORT GROUPS

Convoy escorts were organised into Escort Groups. Each Group comprising some six ships. The Senior Officer of the Group was usually accommodated in a Frigate - larger and faster than the corvettes that formed the bulk of each Group. At the time when the Castle class corvettes began to come into service the Flower class corvettes formed the main body of the Escort Groups escorting convoys. At this time specialised Support Groups were being formed. These comprised of Groups of Frigates

which moved from convoy to convoy in response to the tactical situation and concentration of U-boats. They provided additional anti-submarine detection and fire power to individual convoys as they passed through areas of heightened danger.

The one Royal Norwegian Navy Castle class corvette and the Royal Navy Castle class corvettes were distributed between the B1 to B7 Escort Groups, B21, B22 and B23 Escort Groups. Castle class corvettes were also included in the 7th and 8th Escort Groups for Russian Convoy duties. Two Escort Groups, the 30th and 31st, were formed wholly from Castle class corvettes. These two Groups were allocated patrol and convoy support roles in the western and northern coastal waters of the United Kingdom.

The Royal Canadian Navy Castle Class Corvettes were distributed between the C1 to C8 Escort Groups. These groups never included more than 2 Castle class corvettes. The Canadian Escort Groups were wholly occupied in escorting trans-Atlantic convoys, whereas the British Groups were also involved in escorting convoys between the UK and Gibraltar.

The Castle class corvettes were primarily concerned with the protection of the 'Trade Convoys'. That is, ships engaged in 'normal' commercial traffic and plying between North America and the UK; between the UK and Gibraltar and the convoys to northern Russia.

These series of convoys were identified by the following codes:-

HX	Halifax to UK, and also New York City to UK
ON	Outward North; Liverpool etc. to North America
ONS	Outward North Slow. Liverpool etc. to North America
KMF	UK to Mediterranean, Fast
KMS	UK to Mediterranean, Slow
OS	Outward, Southbound. Liverpool etc. to Freetown

The KMS and OS convoys were frequently combined as far south as Gibraltar.

MKF	Mediterranean to UK Fast
MKS	Mediterranean to UK Slow
SL	Freetown to UK
SLF	Freetown to UK Fast
SLS	Freetown to UK Slow.

The MK and SL series were frequently combined from Gibraltar to UK.

JW	UK to North Russia. These replaced the PQ series.
RA	North Russia to UK. These replaced the QP series.

The 30th and 31st Escort Groups were often required to support 'local' convoys. The most frequent of these were:-

BB	Clyde to Bristol
MH	Milford Haven to Holyhead
EN	Methil to Oban via Loch Ewe.

UC/CU New York to UK tanker series; and reverse direction. These were 14 -14.5 knot convoys not necessarily confined to tankers. The close escorts were normally American but supported by RN escorts when passing through UK waters.

A complete list of Convoy Codes may be found in Arnold Hague's *The Allied Convoy System 1939-45'* which formed the basis of the above list.

The B2 and B3 Escort Groups plied between the U.K. and Gibraltar escorting the OS/KMS series of convoys. These were frequently used as 'shakedown' voyages for corvettes on completion of their training at the Tobermory School for corvettes. Fourteen of the Royal Navy Castle Class Corvettes served at one time or another in these two Escort Groups.

COMMAND STRUCTURE

The convoy itself would be under the command of the Convoy Commodore, who with his staff, was accommodated in one of the merchant ships forming the convoy. Frequently the Commodore was a retired Flag Officer or a senior Merchant Navy Captain.

A great deal of understanding and tolerance was required between the Commodore and the Senior Officer of the Escort (SOE). The Commodore was in command of the convoy, but the SOE was responsible for its protection and safe passage. As the SOE was invariably junior in rank to the Commodore, it was laid down that the Commodore had no right to interfere with the handling of the escort. The SOE could, in the light of the tactical situation, give a mandatory instruction to the Commodore. The SOE, at the specific request of the Commodore, would provide any assistance required in controlling the convoy or detail another escort to do so. The system worked very well. The only difference to this situation arose with the convoys to and from northern Russia. The passage of these convoys was a major Naval operation under the command of a Flag Officer sailing with the convoy escort. The SOEs of the Escort Groups involved in these operations came under the command of the Flag Officer in command of the operation.

Elsewhere in the North Atlantic the whole body, convoy and escort, was controlled by the CinC WA. from his headquarters in Liverpool. The general organisation operated under Western Approaches General Orders (WAGOs) and Western Approaches Convoy Instructions (WACIs). Westbound convoys were controlled up to the point known as the Change of Operation Control Line (CHOP line) where command was transferred to the Eastern coast of America. East bound convoys came under the command of CinC WA when crossing the same line.

It should not be thought that WAGOs and WACIs rigidly controlled or strictly directed the actions of SOEs. They retained the right to take any action they deemed appropriate. This was emphasised in a minute made by a senior staff officer and is worth quoting in full.

The convoy was escorted by only three escorts. The Senior Officer Escort suggested that under these circumstances the distance between columns should be reduced. He suggested :-

"that where the ocean escort is small the distance between columns should be reduced to four cables and even to three in good weather. This would result in practice of getting the columns five to four cables apart, because in practice the tendency is always to increase the distance between columns."

A staff officer commenting on this wrote:-

"Columns are placed 5 cables apart to preclude too solid a target for the U/B when attacking. This applies however many or few the escort is".

D.C
So(c).

To this the senior staff officer wrote:-

"It does not necessarily apply if I am SOE! There is I feel, a tendency in Derby House to consider that what always has been must always continue to be. It is doubtless correct to lay down that distance apart of columns should normally be 5 cables. But no shore authority, however many stripes on his arm, can take away the Divine Right of the S.O.E., who alone is responsible for the tactical safety of the convoy at sea, to modify the application of instructions in the light of existing facts.
2)."ACI" are instructions (not orders), for guidance. "Instructions to Commanders" are presumably the same.
3). The realistic point which B21 makes, is that if the distance apart of 5 cables is ordered, the convoy will - in real life - suffer from middle-aged-spread, and open to six cables. Therefore, he says, in order to achieve compliance with instructions, why

not tell them to take station at four cables? Which he is perfectly entitled to do, subject to Commodore's concurrence.

4). To say that, because ships are told to be at 5 cables, therefore they will be at 5 cables, is to live in a fool's paradise.

5). For the better protection of some convoys by the escorts available, I have frequently - in agreement with the Commodore - closed columns to four cables, and did not think it necessary to put it in my ROP. If I get a chance, and the need arises, I shall do so again.

6). I do not know Lt Cdr Warwick, but I suggest it would be useful to encourage him in a little ebullient independence. We don't want him to feel that he is hamstrung by orders. Propose;-

"WRT Para A of Section 4 of Minute I, There is no objection to the Senior Officer, Escorts, in agreement with the Commodore, taking any reasonable steps he may devise to ensure compliance by the convoy with the instructions given to them; nor to his amending such instructions in the light of the tactical situation prevailing."

7). Sorry to be so long, but I think that an important point of principle is at stake".

SOO

(A) I do not think it is necessary to give B21 quite so much encouragement as SOO suggests

Propose to Admiralty.
Copy to F.O.G.M.A, Captain D Liverpool.
Forward for the information of their Lordships

2. With reference to Section 4 paragraph (A) of the report it is not considered that any amendment to the existing instructions is called for. (X) It is always at the discretion of the Senior Officer Escort in conjunction with the Commodore of the Convoy to make such adjustments should the tactical situation demand.

SOT

"I fully appreciate SOO's feelings and agree with what he thinks. However I agree with SOT at (A) and propose to approve (X)

THE SECRETARY OF THE ADMIRALTY

Forwarded for the information of Their Lordships

2). With reference to Section 4 paragraph (A) of the report it is not considered that any amendment to the existing instructions is called for. It is always at the discretion of the Senior Officer of Escort in conjunction with the Commodore of the Convoy to make such adjustment should the tactical situation demand."

Admiralty instructions to convoys and merchant ships generally (or specifically) were given in British Admiralty Mercantile Signals (BAMS). These were transmitted at specific times on a daily basis using a code held by all merchant ships. In an emergency, orders could be passed via the SOE for the attention of the Commodore who would receive them in plain language after decoding by the escort.

A dual command situation also existed between the Senior Officer of the Support Group and the close escort. Generally, whilst in support of the convoy, the Senior Officer of the Support Group disposed the ships under his command as requested by the SOE. This too required a similar degree of understanding and tolerance as was required between the Convoy Commodore and the SOE. Only two incidents of discord were noted concerning convoys that were escorted by Castle class corvettes.

In April 1945 **Knaresborough Castle**, at this time allocated to the Liverpool Pool, was, with four other corvettes escorting KMS99/OS125. Instructions in force at the time required Foxers to be streamed at a minimum speed of 12 knots. With a convoy speed of 7? knots this required the escorts to undertake "a violent zig zag (70° -70° constant wheel) in order for the ships to remain in station". **Knaresborough Castle** considered that because of the interference from Foxers of adjacent ships it was not possible to carry out an effective A/S sweep

when zig zagging together and disposed his ships, including the 8th Escort Group who were in support, in alternative screening positions which in his view enabled the escorts to zig zag independently at 12 knots and still provide good A/S cover ahead and on the flanks. The SOE 8th Escort Group disagreed, made known his views to **Knaresborough Castle**, conformed to the latter's requirements, but at the same time conveyed his concerns to CinC WA. After a two hour delay CinC WA ordered the S.O. 8th Escort Group, being the Senior Officer present, to assume command of all escorts present while in company with **Knaresborough Castle**.

The other incident of discord occurred when the B1 Escort Group were to take over the ocean escort duties of an HX convoy from a local Canadian Escort Group at the usual western change over point (usually in the vicinity of 44°N 55°W to the south of St John's, Newfoundland). However, because of U-boat dispositions the frigates of the B1 Group were ordered to leave St John's N.F. early and proceed at best speed to rendezvous early with the convoy. On meeting the convoy the SOE B1 signalled his instructions for the disposition of the escorts. However, the SO of the Canadian Group asserted that he was in command of the escorts until the convoy arrived at the normal handing over point. Several acrimonious signals were exchanged, with the situation not improved by the prevailing very poor visibility. Finally the SO B1 being the Senior Officer present, asserted his authority and took command of all the escorts.

These incidents were the exception. The Reports of Proceedings (ROPs) by SOEs are full of examples of genuine respect and co-operation between Commodores and SOEs. A typical example being when in March 1945 two convoys were on collision courses in thick fog. Commander J.V. Brock R.C.N.V.R. SO of C6 (the Group included RCN **Tillsonburg**) reporting on the voyage of convoy ON 293 wrote:-

" Thursday 29th March, during thick weather whilst the convoy was still being formed at 11.00 the Bristol Channel section did not join us in one unit because the Milford Haven section were fog bound and some sailed late."

"12.45 - during thick weather , visibility 4 to 5 cables and while the convoy was still in an unformed state, Radar indicated the approach of MRF/41 on a collision course with a relative speed of 23 knots. Disaster was narrowly averted by the prompt action as both convoys executed without incident emergency turns to port. This reflects great credit on all Merchant Vessels in both convoys, in that the turns were executed in both cases approximately 90 seconds after receipt of the order from Escort Commanders."

"In view of the fact that the Support Groups and three close Escort Groups were jockeying for positions, forming and reforming on their respective convoys with the unavoidable congestion of R/T traffic, it is noteworthy to record how recent intensive training in R/T discipline made possible complete control of the situation by both Escort Commanders." "This hair raising occurrence took place in position 51° 53'N 06° 24' W (Approx.). It is thought that the inward bound convoy was to the south of its route and it is known that the outward bound convoy was too far North, but in poor visibility and the lack of the most modern navigation equipment made it difficult to determine relative positions. However without resorting to Bargee language SOE EG 24 and I relieved the tension by exchanging recriminations, all of which were promptly forgotten on learning that we had successfully passed clear of one another , and the whole question amicably settled by a further exchange of compliments and congratulations."

CONVOY AND ESCORT MANAGEMENT

An insight into the management of convoys and escorts is provided by the following signals and memo:-

On 2 September 1944 the Admiralty issued the following message:-

"It is appreciated that a considerable U-boat threat must be expected in the UK inshore waters, such as the Northern, North Western and South Western approaches. In fact, one ship was torpedoed 20 miles North of Malin Head on 30th, and another in the same area on 1st.

The formation of additional support groups is urgently required, and to effect this the following steps are approved.

Reduce the nominal strength of all existing British support groups to five.

Withdraw fast escorts from the Trans-Atlantic B groups, when the new cycle reduces present large size of convoys. The resulting nominal strength of six corvettes per group to be accepted.

Reduce the escort of KMS/MKS convoys to three ships. This has been approved in AM 242303 August.

*The escort of KMF/MKF convoys is **not** repetition **not** to be reduced below the present figure*

A separate signal is being made to NSHQ (National Security HQ) 021605B/Sep/44

The following related signals and memo were found amongst Canadian papers:

From NSHQ to Admiralty

AM 221140 Concur

(2) It is assumed effective strength of C groups as in NSHQ's 082217 para 2 (c) is acceptable even with increased size of convoys.

(3) In (arranging) convoy cycles request you bear in mind that 8 knot ships loading timber in Gulf of St. Lawrence will require not less than 3 weeks from the time of arrival Sydney inbound to leaving Sydney outbound if conditions allow independent sailing in that area.

242058Z

221140-Re abolishing SC/ONS convoys

From CinC CNA to NSHQ,® FONF, Admiralty C in C WA etc

The following is the intended allocation of Canadian Mid Ocean Groups.

C-1 **Chebougue, Arnprior, Giffard, Chammly, Orangeville, Halifax, Frontenac**

C-2 **Longueuil, Kincardine, Asbestos, Kamloops, Morden, Chilliwack, Fennel**

C-3 **Kokanee, St Thomas, Forest Hill, Trillium, Bittersweet, La Mal, Baie, Eyebright.**

C-4 **Wentworth, Petrolia, Waitby, North Bay, Atholl, Mapanee.**

C-5 **Runnymede, Hespeler, Huntsville, Long Branch, New Westminster, Dauphin.**

C-6 **Eastview, St. Lambert, Cobourg, Peterborough, Tillsonburg, Brandon.**

C-7 **Lanark, Hawkesbury, Copper Cliff, Collingwood, Fredericton, Owen Sound.**

C-8 **Stonetown, Leaside, Edmunston, Etaskiwin, Humberstone, Amherst.**

2. In the event of unforeseen delays it may be necessary to make minor changes to these groups.

3. It will be noted that the paper strength of certain groups is seven (repetition) seven ships. This is due to the necessity of having to refit 2 ships in each of these groups at approximately the same time.

From FONF To C in C CAN

It is assumed that B groups will be withdrawn Admiralty 221140 your ??? consider 5C groups can maintain existing HX and ON schedules without difficulty on basis standard route C and following times on passage Oversay to WESTOMP HX Fast 9 days, medium 10 slow 11 ON Fast 10 days medium 11 slow 12 which should be bettered as weather improves.

Strongly recommend that HX convoys be sailed 2 days later and ON convoys 1 day earlier than in present schedule this to increase layovers mid-ocean groups at St. John's by 3 days for consideration of both maintenance and recuperation vide my 161225 Jan. I do not consider the resultant layover in UK of 7 to 9 days would be incompatible with a satisfactory training programme while boiler cleaning and improved maintenance of groups could be undertaken here.

It is noted that a rotation of groups throughthe fast medium and slow convoys will be accomplished in this schedule.
(251915)

221140 - Changes in convoy cycles to provide additional A/S force.

141906 - Request Admiralty remarks on 221140

181225 Jan - Adverse weather forces reduced turn round in St. John's.

From C in C CAN to NSHQ ® FONF

Admiralty's 221140 and FONF's 251915. Concur with FONF that 5 C groups could handle entire mid-ocean escort requirements

(2) Our calculations, on the basis of the present cycle which Admiralty proposes to retain, indicate that layovers in Londonderry will be 10, 8, 10, days in rotation and in Newfoundland 7, 3, 7, days. FONF's proposed changes in cycle while adding 3 days to Newfoundland layover would reduce Londonderry layover to 7, 5, 7 days, which I do not consider would be acceptable to C in C. WA, though if B groups are eliminated and complete period is available for training without leave complications, might be prevailed upon to accept it.

(3) If this cannot be arranged, suggest that Admiralty be requested at least to sail ON convoys 2 days earlier, the resultant layovers being Londonderry 8, 6, 8 days, Newfoundland 9, 5, 9 days. This proposal would also assist in keeping HX and ON convoys clear of each other in the North Channel.

(4) The above figures are based on the following estimates for winter passage on standard route C between New York and Liverpool HX convoys 16, 18, and 21 days. ON convoys 17, 20 and 23 days.

Monthly Operations Memo 8/12/44

C Groups: General

The Mid-Ocean Escort Force (MOEF) is based on St. John's. NF, and is employed between that base and Londonderry, Northern Ireland. The MOEF is now comprised of eight C Groups, C1 to C8, and three British Groups, B1 - B3

The Western Escort Force (WEF) is based on Halifax, NS and is employed escorting ocean convoys between Westomp and New York. The WEF is now comprised of eight W Groups. W1 - W8.

W8 was formed on 22nd November. Previously seven groups had handled the

CASTLE CLASS CORVETTES DISPOSITIONS 20th to 30th NOVEMBER 1944

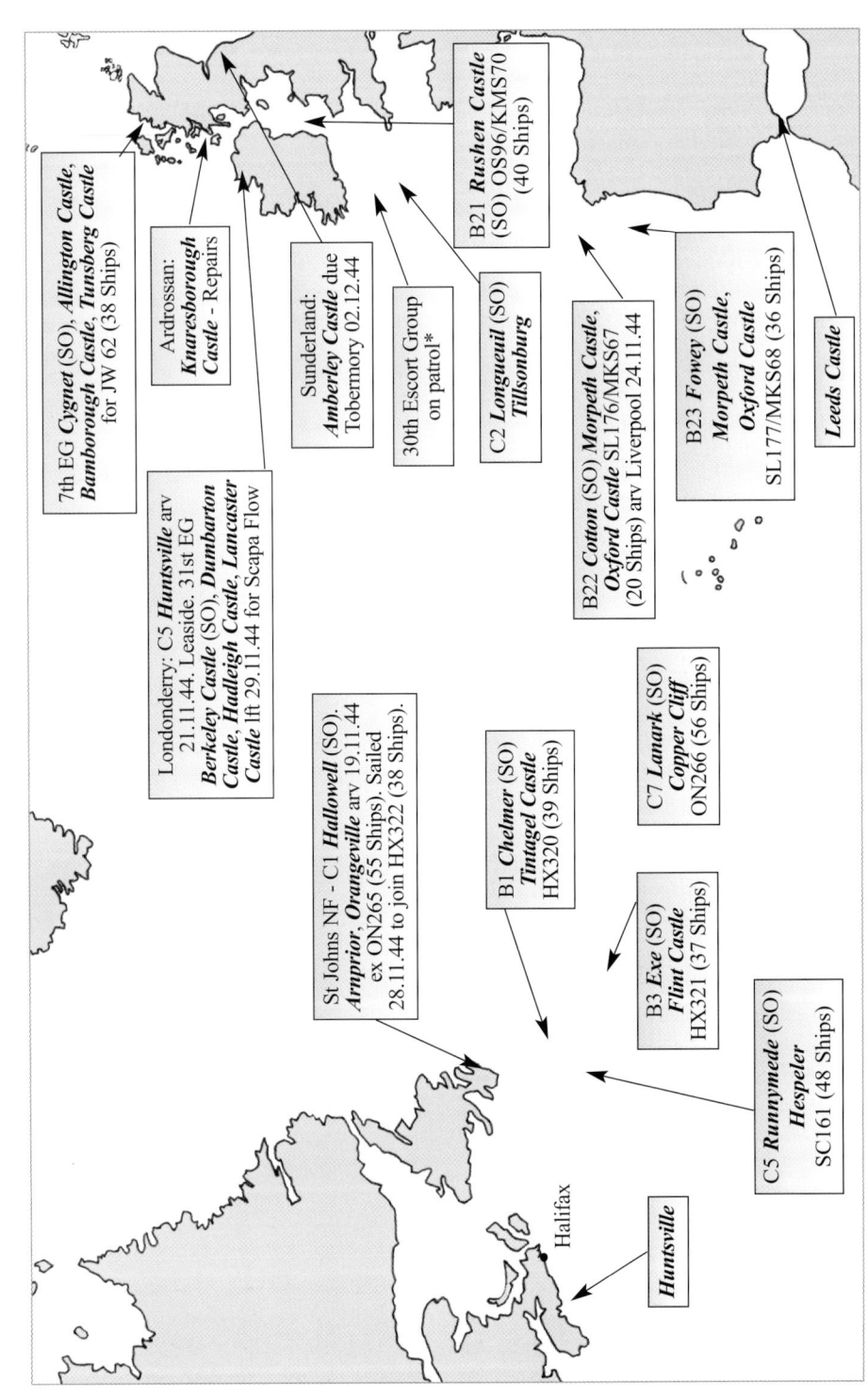

7th EG *Cygnet* (SO), *Allington Castle*, *Bamborough Castle*, *Tunsberg Castle* for JW 62 (38 Ships)

Ardrossan: *Knaresborough Castle* - Repairs

Sunderland: *Amberley Castle* due Tobermory 02.12.44

30th Escort Group on patrol*

C2 *Longueuil* (SO) *Tillsonburg*

B21 *Rushen Castle* (SO) OS96/KMS70 (40 Ships)

B22 *Cotton* (SO) *Morpeth Castle*, *Oxford Castle* SL176/MKS67 (20 Ships) arv Liverpool 24.11.44

B23 *Fowey* (SO) *Morpeth Castle*, *Oxford Castle* SL177/MKS68 (36 Ships)

Leeds Castle

Londonderry: C5 *Huntsville* arv 21.11.44. Leaside. 31st EG *Berkeley Castle* (SO), *Dumbarton Castle*, *Hadleigh Castle*, *Lancaster Castle* lft 29.11.44 for Scapa Flow

St Johns NF - C1 *Hallowell* (SO). *Arnprior*, *Orangeville* arv 19.11.44 ex ON265 (55 Ships). Sailed 28.11.44 to join HX322 (38 Ships).

B1 *Chelmer* (SO) *Tintagel Castle* HX320 (39 Ships)

C7 *Lanark* (SO) *Copper Cliff* ON266 (56 Ships)

B3 *Exe* (SO) *Flint Castle* HX321 (37 Ships)

C5 *Runnymede* (SO) *Hespeler* SC161 (48 Ships)

Halifax

Huntsville

* Note:
30th Escort Group comprised *Pevensey Castle* (SO), *Kenilworth Castle*, *Launceston Castle* and *Portchester Castle*.

ocean convoy cycle between Westomp and New York, but the delay in sailing and in winter passage of ON convoys made the formation of an additional group necessary.

Six Frigate Support Groups are now operating, EG.6, EG.9, EG.16, EG.25, EG.26, EG.27.
EG.6, EG.9, EG.25, EG.26, are at present operated by C in C WA

EG.16, and EG.27 are operated by C in C. C.N.A.

*Destroyer support group EG.11 has been virtually disbanded. Out of a nominal strength of nine ships, seven are under refit or repair and one is working up. The only operational ship left, **HMCS Assiniboine**, is attached to EG.14, in the Western Approaches Command.*

There can be little doubt that the convoy ocean escorts were amongst the hardest worked ships of the fleet. This is not surprising considering that the Navy's primary task has always been considered to be the protection of the country's trade and shipping

The chart opposite illustrates the disposition of 35 Castle Class corvettes over a ten day period late in 1944. The only Castle class corvettes not included are:

Alnwick Castle	Arrived Tobermory 05.12.44 for working up.
Oakham Castle	At Tobermory, working up 20.12.44
Carisbrooke Castle	Under repair at Avonmouth since 27.10.44
Denbigh Castle	Not completed until 20.12.44
Farnham Castle	Not yet completed
Hedingham Castle	Not yet completed
Hurst Castle	Sunk 09.09.44

Of the remaining 35 ships, two were under repair, and all the others were either at sea, or as in the case of 7th Escort Group, the C1 Escort Group and the 31st Escort Group, where their ships were in port for a short layover between convoys or patrol duties.

A typical example of the amount of sea time that these ships did, is that of *Tintagel Castle*. From 7th May 1944 to 8th May 1945 she spent 214 days at sea on convoy escort duty. That is just under 60 per cent of the available days. The layover period between convoys was in the region of seven days. During that period, time had to be found for routine maintenance, training ashore as well as training at sea. Two to three days leave would also be given to half the ship's company. There was very little idle time.

ANTI-SUBMARINE TACTICS

This Sub Section is not intended to be a definitive treatise on this subject. It is presented so as to provide a basis for understanding the actions described later. The information provided relates to tactics employed by Castle Class Corvettes and has been derived from various ROPs involving this class of escort; from discussions and correspondence with Commanding Officers and Asdic Officers and from personal recollections of the compiler.

OFFENSIVE TACTICS

A convoy of merchant ships is both an offensive and defensive device. The concentration of U-boat targets draws U-boats to the convoy whilst at the same time brings the U-boat into close proximity of the defending escorts .

Ocean convoys were formed by disposing short columns of ships (rarely more than six ships) on a broad front. This enables the ships to collectively pass through a danger zone more rapidly than if they were strung out in fewer long columns.

A typical convoy screen diagram is presented below. The convoy of 60 ships was disposed in ten columns each of six ships. Each ship was allocated a pendant number corresponding to her position in the convoy. The leading ships bearing pendants 01 to 11 and the rear ships, pendants 16 to 106. The Commodore's ship would be positioned in the lead of one of the central columns. The ship at the rear of the fourth column, pendant number 46 was a rescue Ship fitted with HF/DF. The escort comprised three frigates (Fr) located in positions A, X, and I;

Five Flower Class Corvettes (Fl) were stationed in positions L and B; N and half way between positions F and G on the starboard flank of the convoy. The only Castle Class Corvette (CC) in the Group was stationed in position D. The diagram is derived from the actual dispositions of the escorts of the B1 Escort Group escorting an HX convoy. The positions shown are the day stations. At night the escorts were probably drawn in to their respective inner stations.

The only effective weapon the corvettes had

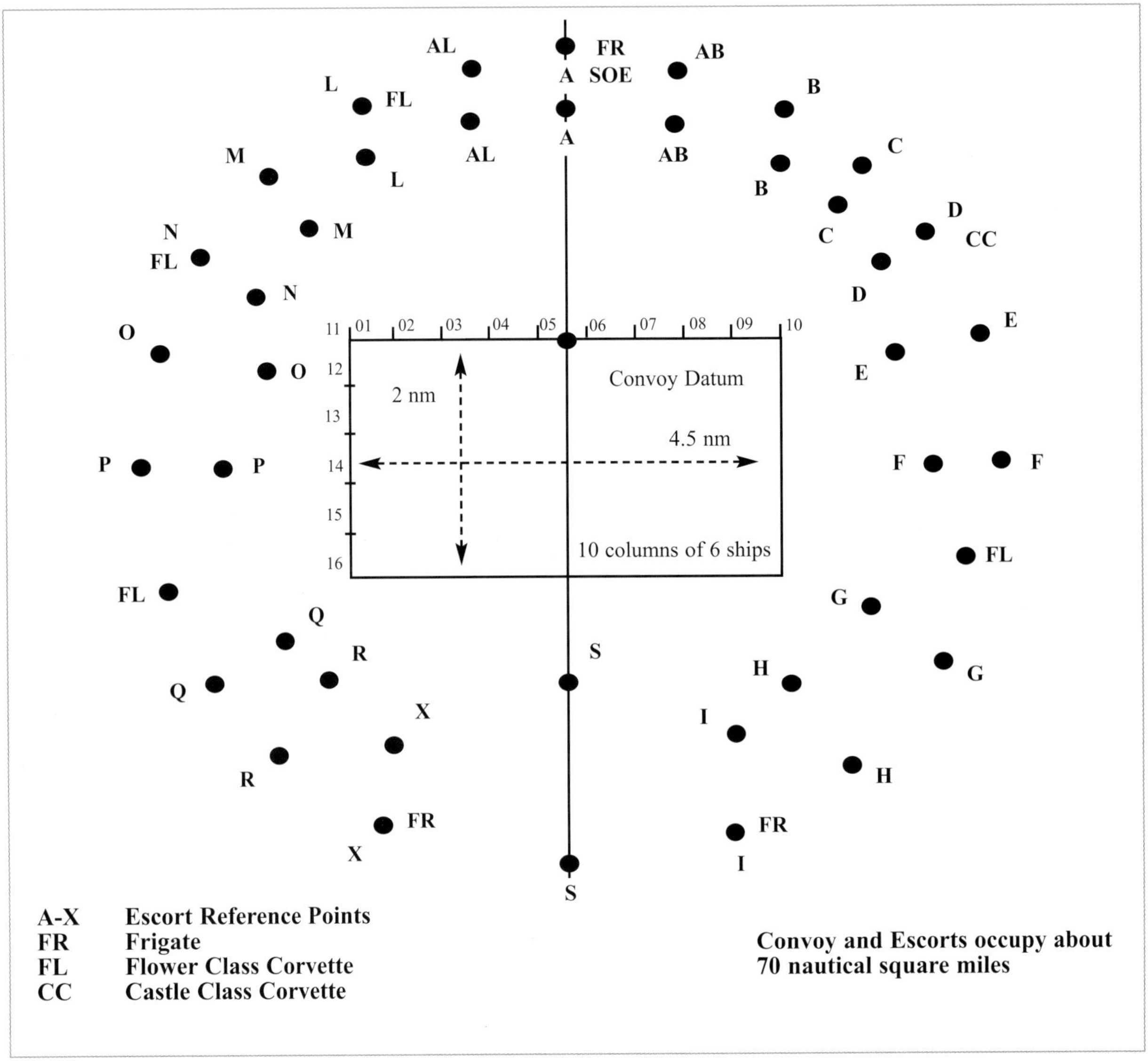

A-X	Escort Reference Points
FR	Frigate
FL	Flower Class Corvette
CC	Castle Class Corvette

Convoy and Escorts occupy about 70 nautical square miles

CONVOY ESCORT DIAGRAM

against a surfaced U-boat was the Squid and Depth Charge thrower with the bombs and depth charge set at 20 or 25 feet. This required a very close encounter with the U-boat with ramming as an alternative. The 4-inch gun's semi armour piercing shells were virtually ineffective against the curved surface of the U-boats hull. However, the firing of star shell or the launching of the 2-inch illuminating rockets were usually sufficient to cause a U-boat to dive. A submerged U-boat under the threat of attack by escorts had little opportunity to threaten the convoyed ships. Thus the aggressive tactic of a Castle Class Corvette was to turn to attack a surfaced U-boat as soon as it was detected by Radar, or sight, so as to be able to contact it by Asdic and attack with the ship's main armament, the Squid. Commanding Officers expected their Officers of the Watch, to initiate an attack immediately, and on his arrival on the bridge to find that the ship was already 'steering by Asdic'.

Commanding Officers were always anxious to obtain proof that their attack had been successful and tended to linger over the contact for as long as possible and repeatedly attack it. The SOE on the other hand had other priorities and would be anxious not to reduce his escort strength around the convoy. A U-boat deeply submerged astern of the convoy was no longer an immediate threat. The SOE would be inclined to recall his escort(s) to station as soon as possible.

The priorities were shifted towards a more aggressive attitude by a signal issued by C in C W.A on the 14th December 1943. This directed resources to the destruction of U-boats even at the expense of temporarily reducing the strength of the ocean escort.. It should be noted that the signal was issued before the true effectiveness of the Squid had been demonstrated (*See signal page 34*).

The importance of keeping the U-boat submerged was given prominence in a memorandum, part of which read:-

"It cannot be emphasised too often that a prolonged hunt to exhaustion of a U-boat which has disclosed its position is the fundamental requirement and the thing most feared by any submarine. In inshore operations spare escorts should search offshore and upwind. Whenever possible the operation should continue with day and night air support for a minimum period of 48 hours. By day any type of aircraft can be used to keep the U-boat down since even if it is not equipped with offensive weapons it can report the position of the U-boat and home surface craft to the new datum position. By night A.S.V. aircraft of any type will be of great value or even non-ASV aircraft searching across the moon will be effective."

(Source ADM 199/2061)

With two ships engaged in attacking a U-boat, both would endeavour to keep in Asdic contact with the target. A critical period being immediately after an attack when the sea was disturbed by the explosions. Depending on the situation, one of the ships might patrol around the last known position of the U-boat with the objective of intercepting it should it attempt to creep away. This manoeuvre by the escort being known as 'Observant'. With a Support Group in position, more ships would be available to carry out an Observant and thus considerably improve the chances of intercepting the U-boat

A diagram of a tactical hunt for a U-boat, including an 'Observant' is provided on page 35. The designation FL1 is obscure. The convoy was HX 342. The incident occurred in the proximity of 'Westomp', the line where the ocean escorts took over from the local Canadian escorts. It will be observed that the convoy took avoiding action to the north of the reported position of the U-boat. The first emergency turn was executed in 1? minutes from the time that the SOE (C6) had informed the Commodore.

Instructions for forming an 'Observant' are detailed in Appendix Seven.

If the tactical situation allowed, escorts would remain in contact with a submerged U-boat for up to 72 hours. After this time it was assumed that its crew had exhausted their oxygen supply and had succumbed.

There was, however, always the prospect of boarding and capturing a disabled U-boat should the opportunity arise. The problems involved in

HUSH MOST SECRET
CYPHER MESSAGE

From: C in C W.A.

BATTLE OF THE ATLANTIC RECENT CHANGES IN ENEMY TACTICS

Following review is promulgated for the guidance of Senior Officers Escort Groups.

2. Experience during the last few weeks has shown that U-.boats are now rarely found on the surface by day, This implies a very marked change of tactics which calls for a corresponding change in our counter-meas ures

3. By remaining submerged by day the enemy reduces the risk of detection and counter-attack but at the same time denies himself the following important advantages of his previous policy

 (a) Surface reconnaissance and immediate receipt of sighting reports by consorts.
 (b) Subsequent shadowing and homing of consorts.
 (c) The ability to trail a convoy and carry out a series of attacks extending over a number of days.
 (d) The mobility which enables the more distant U-boats to intercept a reported convoy.

4. Such tactics have already greatly promoted the safe and timely arrival of the convoys, but they must inevitably give us fewer opportunities to destroy the enemy. It is my intention now to take full advantage of the enemy's weakened offensive by neglecting no opportunity to destroy him whenever contact is made.

5. To this end orders may be expected under certain circumstances for Support Groups, and even a proportion of the Close Escort, in the aftermath of a battle to leave the convoy and return to the battle area for mopping up.

6. I desire that Commanding Officers should henceforward use more care and deliberation in the execution of their attacks on U-boats which are not an immediate threat to the convoy. It has become increasingly clear that the old methods of depth charge attack which, provide such ample warning of their approach, are not effective against a deep and highly maneuverable U-boat.

7. In the Hedgehog and in the Squid are combined the two attributes of precision and surprise which ensure its effectiveness in a deliberate attack, For a U-boat which is too deep for the Hedgehog, the 'Creeping attack', which has the same attributes, has recently proved on three occasions its deadly day accuracy.

8. It is my view that, when Escorts are hunting in pairs, the delivery of the standard depth charge attacks on a deep submarine are no longer justified except for the purpose driving it deeper for a Creeping Attack .

T.O.O, 142141A December 1943
C..S.O.(M).
Source:- PRO ADM 217/358

this were regularly exercised during home port lay-overs. These could involve some tricky seamanship when going alongside a semi submerged U-boat. For example when the crew of *U- 877* abandoned ship they were all rescued without loss of life even though three whalers were capsized in the process having been washed onto the U-boat's hull by the swell. An example of 'Boarding Party' standing orders is given in Appendix Six.

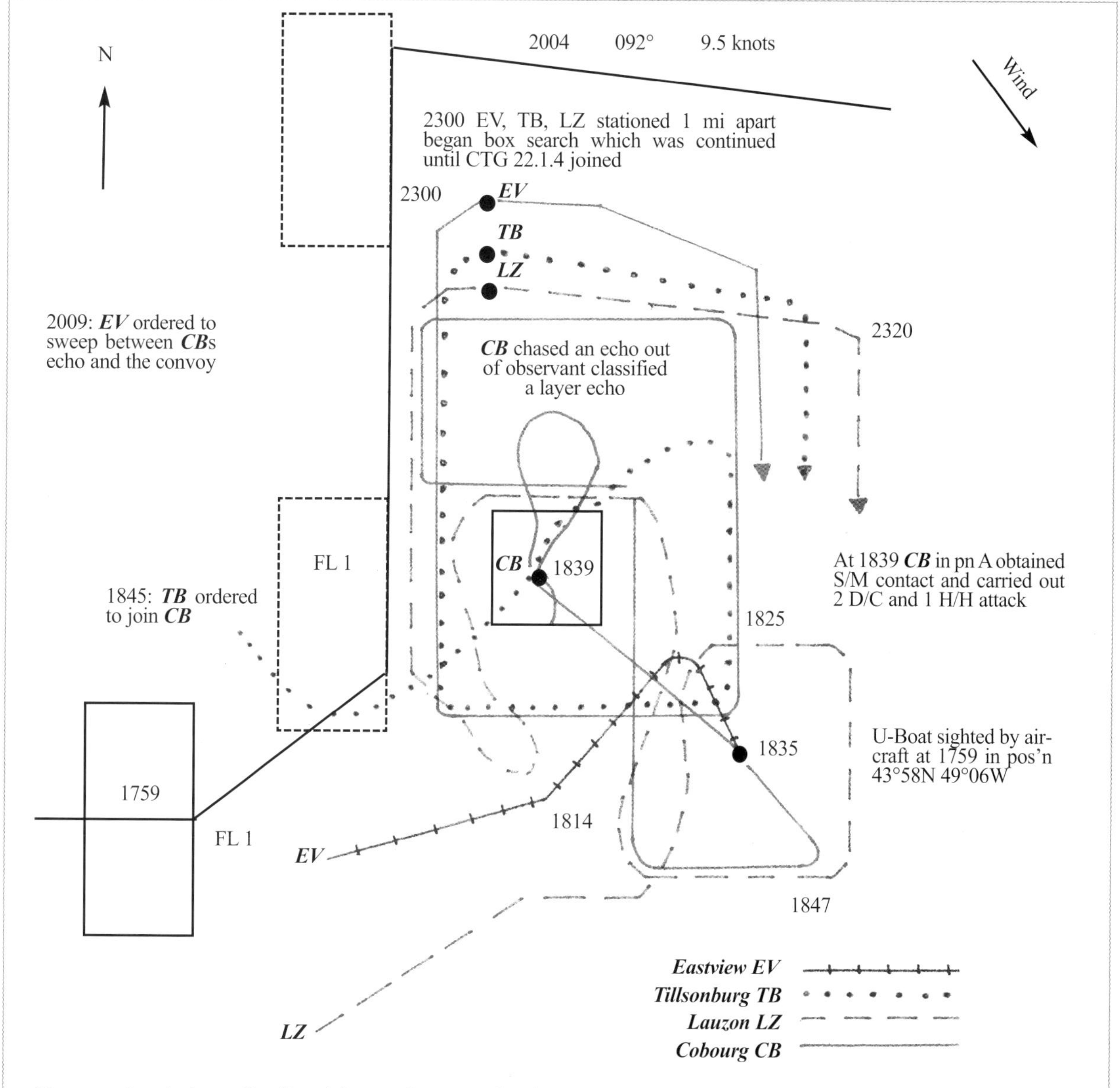

N

2004   092°   9.5 knots

Wind

2300 EV, TB, LZ stationed 1 mi apart began box search which was continued until CTG 22.1.4 joined

2300   *EV*

TB

LZ

2009: *EV* ordered to sweep between *CB*s echo and the convoy

2320

CB chased an echo out of observant classified a layer echo

FL 1

CB   1839

1845: *TB* ordered to join *CB*

1825

At 1839 *CB* in pn A obtained S/M contact and carried out 2 D/C and 1 H/H attack

U-Boat sighted by air-craft at 1759 in pos'n 43°58N 49°06W

1835

1759

FL 1

EV

1814

1847

LZ

Eastview EV	—+—+—+—+—
Tillsonburg TB	· · · · · · ·
Lauzon LZ	— — — — —
Cobourg CB	————————

Not to confuse the issue, Box Search has not been completed in this reduced scale copy of the original plot, and for a similar reason most of the times have been omitted. It is therefore to be merely looked upon as a sketch of the movements of four ships hunting a U-Boat

TACTICAL PLOT OF HUNT FOR A U-BOAT SIGHTED BY SHORE BASED AIRCRAFT IN POSITION 43°58N 49°06W ON 09.03.45

ANTI-SUBMARINE DEFENSIVE TACTICS

The only defensive Anti Submarine (A/S) tactics considered are those against torpedoes. Normal straight running torpedoes would usually be detected by the Asdic operator, who on hearing the hydrophone effect of the torpedo's propeller would immediately report its bearing. If the relative bearing was before 70° the normal procedure would be to turn towards, and turning away if it was abaft that bearing.

ANTI-GNAT PRECAUTIONS

The major threat to escorts was the German Naval Acoustic Torpedo (the Gnat). This was a 21-inch electric driven acoustic homing torpedo. Its speed was in the region of 24 knots with a range of 6,000 yards and an overrun at decreasing speed. It could not travel for more than 15 minutes and its homing range was of the order of 300 yards from an escort vessel doing revolutions for 15 knots. The Gnat was designed to home onto the noise of ships' propellers. It could not home onto Asdic transmissions. It could be set to run either straight, or in circles after running a pre-set distance. It could also be angled at up to 90°. The torpedoes could be fired singly from bow or stern tubes on the surface or when submerged at a depth not greater than about 70 ft.

There were three means of defence; to steam at speeds greater than 24 knots, or at 7 knots or less. At this slower speed the cavitation noise from the ship's propellers was not sufficient to attract the Gnat. The third method was to tow a noise maker as an expendable decoy.

Tests had shown that in ships with reciprocating engines or electric drive, a sudden reduction in shaft revolutions caused temporary but pronounced increase in cavitation noise because of the braking effect of the propellers. The absence of cavitation noise during speed reduction could be achieved by the smooth and gradual reduction of shaft revolutions; ideally so that the propellers neither drove or braked the ship.

This resulted in orders being issued for the phased reduction of revolutions over periods of 15 seconds, with the engine room being made responsible for reducing shaft revolutions in accordance with a complex Table (*See ADM 207/231*). Ships developed their own system for carrying out these instructions. Frequently, after leaving harbour, the order would be passed down to the engine room "Gnat revolutions for slow speed". From this time on whenever the telegraph was put to SLOW the engine room automatically reduced shaft speeds in accordance with the scale laid down. Prior to entering harbour the order "Normal revolutions for slow speed" would be passed to the engine room. Should normal revolutions for slow speed be required at sea the revolution telegraph would be rung down to 50 revolutions.

FOXERS

The towed noise generator, generally known as 'Foxers' or 'Uni-Foxers', consisted, in essence, of parallel iron bars towed by a bridal. The shape of the Foxer frame was similar to that of a metal clothes hangar. The Foxer consisted of two round chilled metal bars about 2-inches in diameter and 18-24 inches long. They were held close together at both ends in a steel frame from each of which was the 'hanger' to which the towing wire was attached.

On each towing wire was a device similar to that used by minesweepers to spread their cutting devices. Thus when both Foxers were streamed by hand from the stern, one went out to the port quarter and one to the starboard quarter.

When towed the chilled steel bars on each Foxer vibrated against each other emitting a high pitched

'chatter' or 'natter' attracting the acoustic torpedo which proceeded to run from port to starboard and vice versa until it blew up. The two Foxers could be streamed by hand or from a hand reel. Later models consisted of only one 'chattering' unit and

were known as 'Unifoxers'. The minimum towing speed for effective protection, and in coastal waters to keep the Foxers above defensive minefields, was 10 knots.

STEP ASIDE

An additional anti-Gnat procedure, known as 'Step Aside', was developed for use by ships that did not have Foxers streamed. If a U-boat was detected or suspected to be present at a range exceeding 4,000 yards, maximum speed would be maintained whilst approaching the U-boat, but a position directly ahead or astern of the U-boat being avoided. Illuminants and gunfire would be used to induce the U-boat to dive.

To clear the ship of the danger zone area from a Gnat, an alteration of course was to be made to bring the U-boat 60° on the bow as soon as it dives if the range was under 5,000 yards or in any event when the range was down to 4,000 yards from the last known position of the U-boat.

If the U-boat was initially on one bow, preference was given to altering course so as to place it on the other bow. After proceeding for about 2,000 yards the ship would be turned parallel to the estimated bearing of the U-boat at the time of starting avoiding action, and then steam for a further 2,000 yards before beginning the hunt at 7 knots; reduction to this speed being achieved during this latter run. The procedure is illustrated overleaf.

Operational experience brought to light various practical problems in carrying out anti-Gnat precautions.

The most significant perhaps was the disparity of engine revolutions required to maintain patrol speed arising from differences in the cleanliness of the ships' bottoms.

Commander Rayner RNVR SO 30th EG reported that the normal patrolling speed of the Group was 11 knots. To achieve this:-

Caistor Castle	Clean bottom - required 126 revolutions
Launceston Castle	4 months old - required 128 revolutions
Pevensey Castle	6 months old - required 130 revolutions
Kenilworth Castle	10 months old - required 140 revolutions
Portchester Castle	12 months old - required 145 revolutions

He concluded that in those ships where the revolutions were higher to provide an equal speed of ships, the greater percentage reduction in revolutions to achieve anti-gnat speed was offset by the quicker reduction in speed of the hull due to its dirty state, so that the cavitation from the breaking effect of the propellers was not likely to be any greater in the ships with dirty bottoms than those ships with clean bottoms. He therefore intended to rely on straight reduction of shaft speed to 90 revolutions as the Group's anti gnat precautions.

The anti-Gnat policy of 30th EG when operating as a Support Force in coastal waters, was for all ships to stream Unifoxers from dawn to dusk. This was to allow ships to close U-boats without the delay necessitated by the Step Aside procedure. In fog and at night (except bright moon light nights) the Group swept at anti-Gnat speed.

Immediately a U-boat disclosed its presence by sighting, H.E, torpedo track or an unexplained explosion and the like, all ships were to drop one depth charge set to 100 feet (unless unifoxers were streamed) and alter course by at least 20°. When clear of coastal waters (i.e. outside the 100m fathom line) the 'Step Aside' procedure was to be followed by ships which do not have unifoxers streamed. Full details are given in Appendix Eleven.

By the time that the attacking ship reaches the U-Boat sighting position it would have travelled 2,500 yds at 3.5 kts. Under good conditions this would be within Asdic range.

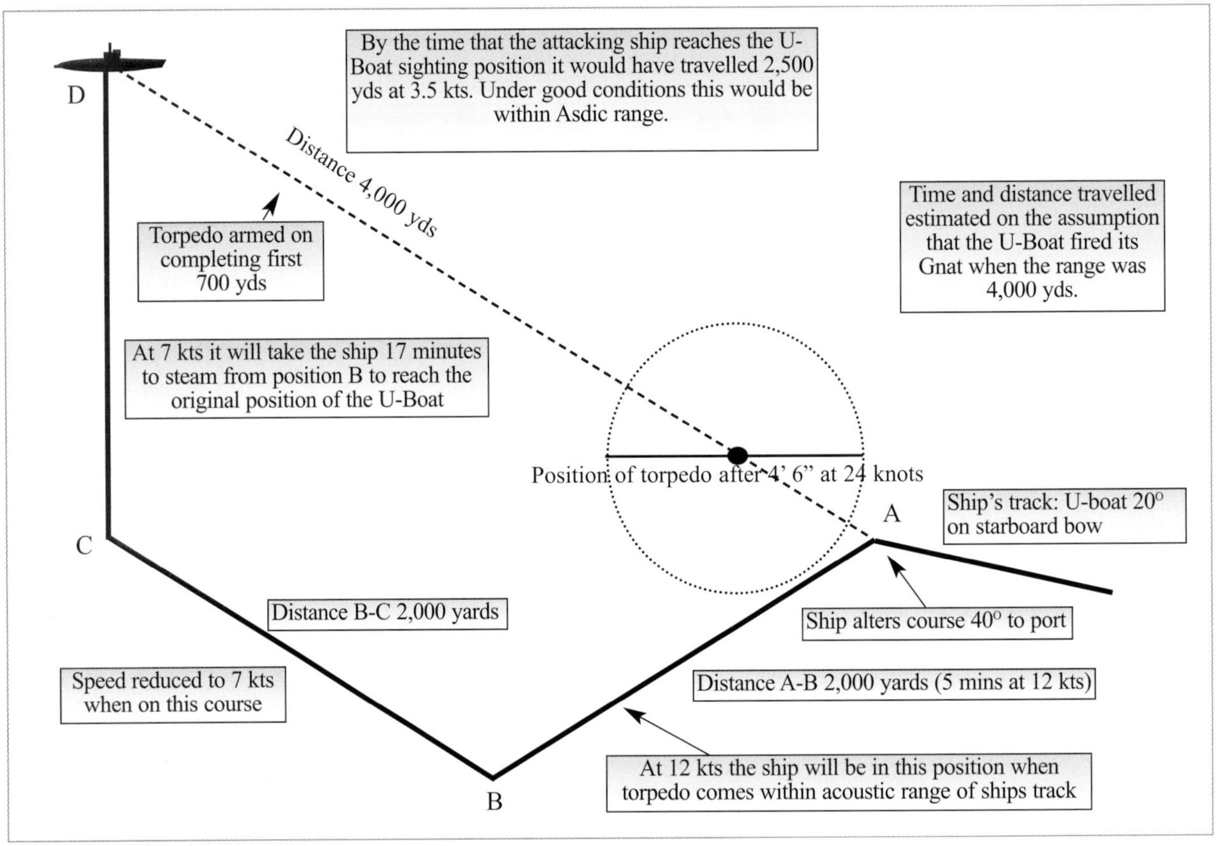

D

Distance 4,000 yds

Torpedo armed on completing first 700 yds

Time and distance travelled estimated on the assumption that the U-Boat fired its Gnat when the range was 4,000 yds.

At 7 kts it will take the ship 17 minutes to steam from position B to reach the original position of the U-Boat

Position of torpedo after 4' 6" at 24 knots

A

Ship's track: U-boat 20° on starboard bow

C

Distance B-C 2,000 yards

Ship alters course 40° to port

Speed reduced to 7 kts when on this course

Distance A-B 2,000 yards (5 mins at 12 kts)

At 12 kts the ship will be in this position when torpedo comes within acoustic range of ships track

B

THE 'STEP ASIDE' PROCEDURE

ANTI-AIRCRAFT TACTICS - EGs ON THE UK-GIBRALTAR CONVOYS

By the time that the Castle Class Corvettes became operational Merchant Aircraft Carriers (MAC ships) were usually sailed with the Gibraltar convoys.

The underlying appreciation of the tactical situation was that although these convoys were unlikely to be attacked by torpedo bombers the threat from attacks with glider bombs was real. Defensive measures were designed to thwart these.

Not infrequently one or more MAC ships would transfer from a south to north bound convoy (or vice-versa) as the convoys approached a section of their route vulnerable to air attack. Defensive measures centred on providing adequate screening of the MAC ships whilst flying aircraft off or on and in disposing the escorts to provide the maxi-

mum practical close range defensive gunfire on the probable sector of attack. It was not unusual for the escorts and the convoyed ships to practice making smoke and laying a smoke screen in anticipation of an attack. This would not be done until it was known that the convoy had been detected. Pages 39 and 41 provide an example of the actual disposition of the escorts during a period when attacks were expected. The decision to operate the carriers in a 'Bull Ring' close to the convoy, rather than as a separate carrier squadron some ten miles from the convoy with its own escorts was based on the following considerations:-

If the enemy pressed home their attack with a series of sorties the carrier squadron might become the focus for the first attacks. In view of the lack of

gunpower in the carriers and escorts this would be most unfortunate.

With the carriers astern of the convoy they would receive better gunnery protection. They would have the armament and physical obstruction of up to sixty ships to support them. This, notwithstanding that all the guns would be of a close range nature.

The carriers were not such obvious targets to select being part of a force of up to sixty ships instead of being a small unit on their own.

The A/S protection given in the 'Bull Ring' astern of the convoy was probably much better than any that could be given by six escorts to two or three carriers which would frequently be making large alterations of course.

These precautions combined with the Luftwaffe's failure to press home attacks resulted in no losses from aircraft after October 1944 from the SL/MKS convoys. Only three ships were lost to aircraft in 1944 and one in 1945 in the OS/KMS series of convoys.

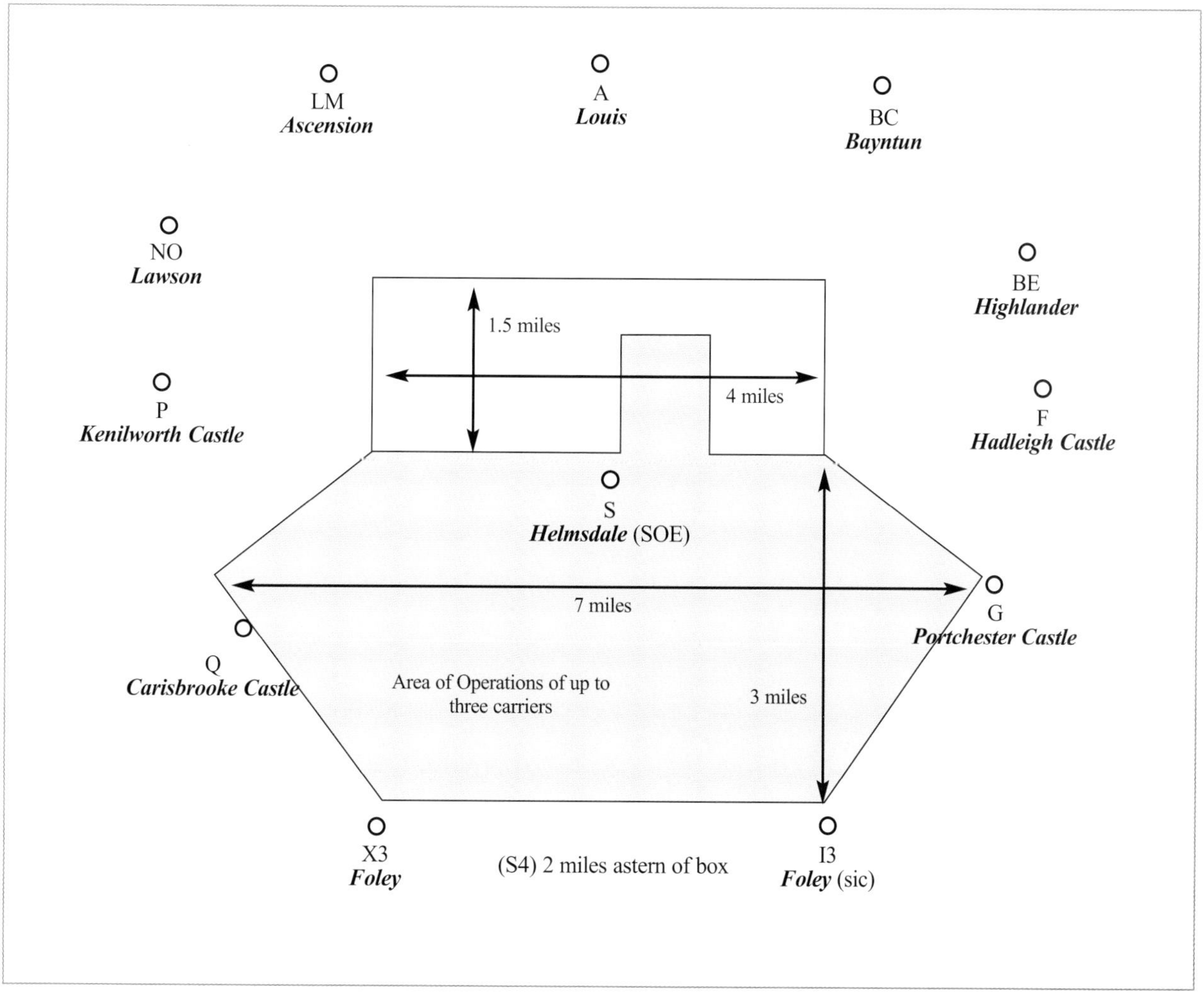

○
LM
Ascension

○
A
Louis

○
BC
Bayntun

○
NO
Lawson

○
BE
Highlander

1.5 miles

4 miles

○
P
Kenilworth Castle

○
F
Hadleigh Castle

○
S
Helmsdale (SOE)

7 miles

○
G
Portchester Castle

○
Q
Carisbrooke Castle

Area of Operations of up to three carriers

3 miles

○
X3
Foley

(S4) 2 miles astern of box

○
I3
Foley (sic)

ANTI-AIRCRAFT ESCORT DISPOSITIONS - EXPECTED GLIDER BOMB ATTACK

ANTI-AIRCRAFT TACTICS - RUSSIAN CONVOYS

Castle Class Corvettes were involved with escorting the Russian Convoys from September 1944 with the sailing of JW 60 to the conclusion of the voyage of RA 66 in May 1945. During this series of convoys enemy air activity, apart from aerial shadowing of the convoys, comprised attacks by torpedo bombers.

These attacks generally came from a westerly direction early in the day or from a easterly direction in the evening. This allowed the enemy aircraft to approach with the convoy silhouetted against the lightest horizon. Furthermore, since for much of the voyage, the convoys were steaming in a Northerly or Southerly direction, attacks from the preferred direction provided the greatest number of visual targets.

To counter this the convoy would, whenever possible, be manoeuvred by a series of emergency turns to present either the rear or the van of the convoy to the attacking aircraft.

The normal night escort dispositions were such that the escorts formed two concentric circles around the convoy. This formation was also found to provide good protection to the convoy from the escorts anti-aircraft weapons, even though most of these were of the short range variety. Since attacks at dawn and dusk were also favoured by the enemy, this escort disposition involved the minimum amount of station changing.

Further valuable air defence was provided by the fighters of the escorting carriers which also attempted and often succeeded in shooting down the shadowing aircraft. However, none of these tactics would have been so successful had it not been for the effectiveness of the Type 277 radar in detecting the approach of attacking formations. The Castle Class Corvettes equipped with this type of radar played a valuable part in this. The carrier **Campania**, that frequently formed part of the escort, had a blind spot astern with her 277 and this was covered by **Denbigh Castle** and later by **Alnwick Castle** after the former had been sunk. When carrying out these duties the ships were provided with a Flight Direction Officer from **Campania**.

None of this would have been possible without good communications. TBS and TBY being the essential media between escorts and between the FAO i/c and the convoy. Further more good communications between the escorts allowed those on the screen to give quick warning of the approach of torpedoes and this enabled the convoy to be manoeuvred to comb their tracks. It is satisfactory to note that the 7th Escort Group were especially commended for the Group's excellent communication skills.

The success of these anti-aircraft tactics, combined with the failure of the enemy to vigorously press home his attacks, is demonstrated by the fact that only one ship, the **Hendy Bacon**, was sunk by aircraft attack in this series of convoys.

CONVOY DUTIES AND SPECIAL OCCASIONS

Although the primary duty of the close escort and the escorts of the support groups was to protect the convoy from the violence of the enemy, escorts inevitably became involved in the convoys' administration. Particularly those of the close escort.

When a convoy was being assembled it was common practice for the ships to be sailed from several ports. This invariably occurred with outward bound Atlantic convoys from the UK. As the different sections of the convoy joined the main body it often fell upon individual escorts to guide and chivvy the ships into their proper stations. This became particularly arduous when a convoy was forming up under stress of fog or high winds. On these occasions the skill and responsiveness of the radar operators of the escorts played a vital role in identifying straying vessels. A similar situation would also arise in the aftermath of severe weather that had caused the convoy to become dispersed. Escorts would be despatched to retrieve errant ships and

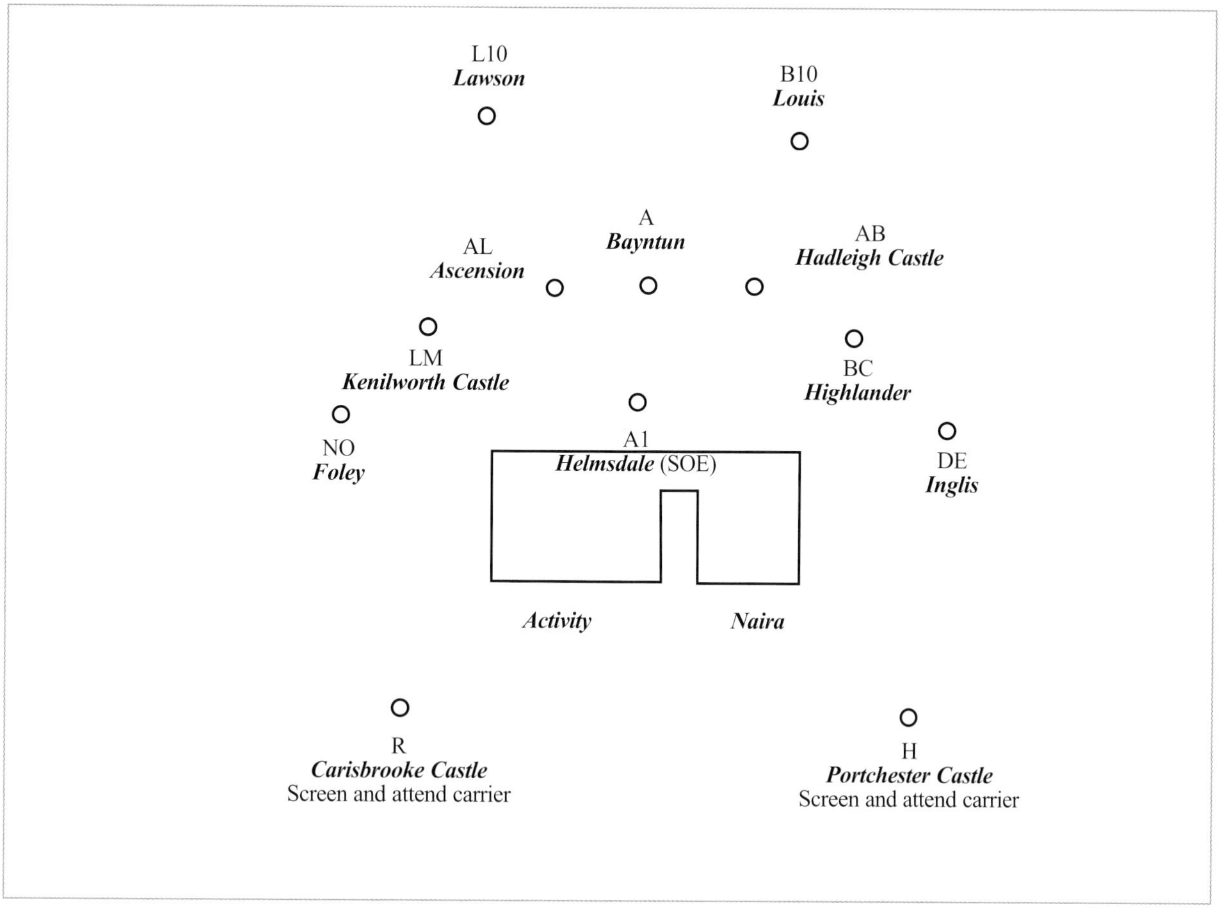

L10
Lawson
O

B10
Louis
O

A
Bayntun

AL
Ascension
O   O

AB
Hadleigh Castle
O

O
LM
Kenilworth Castle

O
BC
Highlander

O
NO
Foley

O

A1
Helmsdale (SOE)

O
DE
Inglis

Activity   *Naira*

O
R
Carisbrooke Castle
Screen and attend carrier

O
H
Portchester Castle
Screen and attend carrier

ANTI-AIRCRAFT ESCORT DISPOSITIONS - DAY STATIONS

bring them back to the fold. It was not surprising that terms associated with driving sheep entered the Naval vocabulary.

Transferring personnel and stores at sea from one ship to another was usually done by boat. This would arise when medication or technical stores were required and sometime specialist personnel as well to repair defective equipment. In the Castle class corvettes the whaler was used for this manoeuvre. This was not motorised nor provided with a mast or sails. It was propelled by oars, making transfers a potentially painfully slow business.

To alleviate this , some escort groups, including the B1, B3 and B21 Escort Groups developed the procedure illustrated overleaf. It should be noted that the whaler towing pendant was carried right forward thus maximising the potential lateral move-ment of the boat. Following this drill transfers could be made very rapidly and the whalers' crews rarely had to do more than stabilise the boat with the flat of their oars. *Rushen Castle* using this method to transfer her medical officer to one of the ships in her convoy, recorded a time from slipping to recovering the whaler of 14 minutes. The merchant ship lost little less than 3 cables distance in her column. Transfers between escorts are thought to have been quicker than this.

Severe weather frequently tested the seamanship and endurance of the escorts in providing assistance to ships in distress. The event surrounding convoy OS92/KMS66 between the 18th and 23rd of November 1944 provide an outstanding if somewhat extreme example of this.

The convoy, escorted by *HM Ships Fowey* (SO),

Allington Castle and *Knaresborough Castle*, comprised 35 ships, 3 Submarines (*Thresher, Sea Scout, & Trident*) and 9 Tank Landing Craft (TLC). The latter were in tow by 5 merchant ships.

The first hint of trouble occurred on the 16th when the Milford Haven section was joining. *LCT 488* one of the two LCTs being towed by *SS Samfoyle* reported hull defects, but "able to continue voyage, providing weather conditions did not deteriorate".

The next day when the convoy was to the North West of Lands End and halfway across the Celtic Sea to the S E of Ireland, the weather did indeed worsen. By the 18th the wind was from the West Force 8 raising a sea and swell estimated at 67 (High Seas and Heavy Swell). *LCT 488* still in tow was suffering heavy weather damage. Around 1100 that morning the Commodore ordered all the towing ships to heave to. The S.O ordered *Allington Castle* and *Knaresborough Castle* to render what assistance they could and at the same time signalled the Admiralty (repeated CinC WA) requesting that additional escorts be sent. During the afternoon further signals were received reporting LCTs in various stages of distress. *Allington Castle*, whilst making preparations to assist *Knaresborough Castle*, who was standing by *LCT 488*, had a working party on the quarter-deck securing depth charges and preparing a grass line for use in rescue work. A large sea broke aft over both quarters and four hands were swept overboard. Two managed to hold onto the bight of the grass line and were quickly recovered. The other two were swept straight overboard followed quickly by a life buoy and flare, landing within 20 yards of them. Although the ship was quickly turned only one of the men was recovered.

Finding that *Knaresborough Castle* did not require assistance, *Allington Castle* altered course to go to the assistance of *LCT 491*. An hour later *Allington Castle* observed two dim red lights one over the other. On closing and illumination "..this was shown to be a raft definitely not under command"..containing survivors of *LCT 480* which was in sight, listing heavily with the foredeck half submerged. The survivors, three officers and sixteen ratings, the full crew of LCT 480 were recovered from the raft in which they had spent two hours.

The wreck of the LCT was sunk by gunfire.

In the meantime *Knaresborough Castle* who was standing by *LCT 488* which was running before the sea, managed to take off most of the crew, who had taken to the LCT's Carley Rafts. Unfortunately some of the crew had scrambled back on board the LCT, which was now without any life saving equipment. Because of the darkness and sea conditions further attempts to rescue the crew failed. The remaining crew managed to get the LCT under way and appeared to be managing well. However at 0500 on the 19th the LCT capsized and sank. Without life saving equipment the remaining crew became scattered in the water and all efforts to lay alongside were fruitless.

At this point Lt. W.A.E. Sheppard RCNVR volunteered to take away the seaboat. Unfortunately it capsized in the attempt, but all the crew were saved. Subsequently a search for survivors from the LCT was continued until after 1330. One officer was picked up.

After sinking the LCT by gunfire *Allington Castle* proceeded to home onto the Tug that was by now standing by *LCT 7014*. Shortly after midnight she was informed by the Tug that the LCT had sunk and the crew recovered. *Allington Castle* then proceeded towards *SS Badjistan* that was standing by *LCT 491*. *Allington Castle* lay alongside the LCT whilst *SS Badjistan* steamed up wind and laid an oil slick. *Allington Castle* placed herself on the weather side of the LCT with the LCT's Oerlikon platform abreast the ship's port forward scrambling net.

The ship and craft were rolling heavily but only touching on the roll All the ships company of *LCT 491* three officers and sixteen ratings were brought on board in a little over an hour since the start of the operation. One rating who had to be manhandled aboard suffered a smashed pelvis and the ship received a small hole in the hull. On clearing the wreck it was sunk by gunfire and Squid. This rescue operation was carried out in the dark from 0330 to 0540 during which time the wind and seas were slowly moderating to NW 7, sea and swell 57.

Whilst proceeding to rejoin the convoy *Allington Castle* was ordered to investigate the condition of three ships of the convoy reported to be in difficulties. Pendant (PT) 34 was found hove to astern of

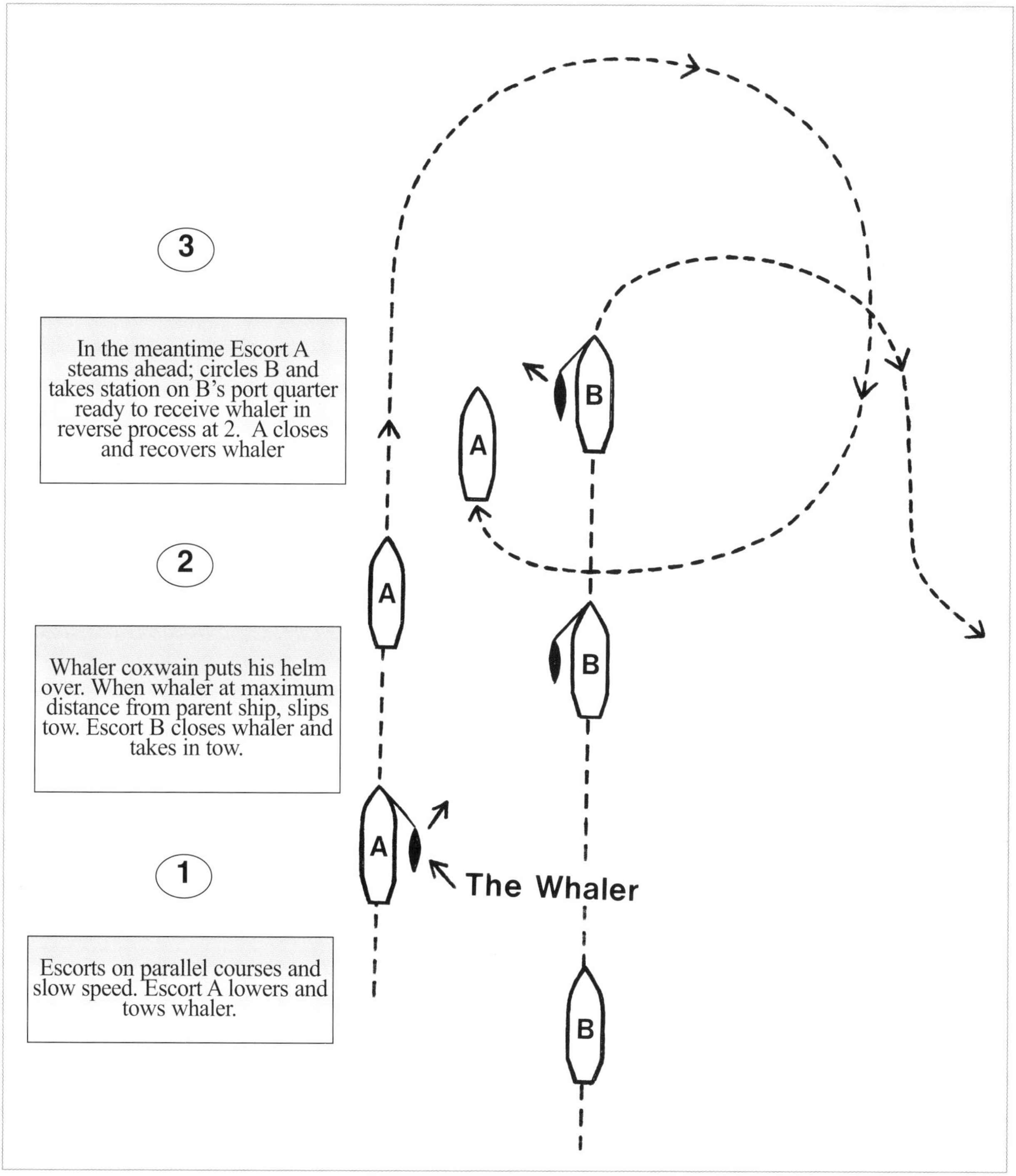

3

In the meantime Escort A
steams ahead; circles B and
takes station on B's port quarter
ready to receive whaler in
reverse process at 2. A closes
and recovers whaler

2

Whaler coxwain puts his helm
over. When whaler at maximum
distance from parent ship, slips
tow. Escort B closes whaler and
takes in tow.

1

Escorts on parallel courses and
slow speed. Escort A lowers and
tows whaler.

A

B

A

B

A   The Whaler

B

TRANSFERS BY WHALER

the convoy with shifted cargo and one lifeboat washed away. PT 32 was steering by hand but reported that no assistance was required and PT 64 contacted at 1150 on the 20th also reported as not needing any help.

At 1600 on the 20th *Allington Castle* had to heave to so as to secure depth charges that had broken adrift. Then in response to orders, proceeded towards *SS Laganto* to render assistance. W/T contact was made at 1900/20th and *Allington Castle* homed onto her. Rockets fired by *SS Laganto* were seen forty minutes later and the ship was sighted steaming down wind at 8 knots. She was not in great distress. The starboard side of her bridge had been stove in and her compass damaged or carried away. The starboard bulwarks on the fore deck were stove in and all lifeboats either damaged or washed away. Some of her deck cargo had shifted and one man had been lost overboard.

Allington Castle laid oil ahead of her until daylight. She was also in W/T contact with **HMS Drury** who was to take over 'stand by' duty from *Allington Castle*. By 1400/21st *SS Laganto* had secured her deck cargo and was able to heave to; *Allington Castle* spreading oil to windward of her. At 1710/21st *Drury* was sighted and relieved *Allington Castle* who set course to rejoin the convoy at the best possible speed. On the way back to the convoy she gathered in 13 stragglers and with them rejoined the convoy at 1750/22nd; that is 4 days 8 hours since she had been ordered to render assistance to *LCT 488*. *Knaresborough Castle* had also rejoined the convoy at about the same time, having stood by and escorted the submarine *Trident*. The latter had suffered from one screw being fouled by wire and had been proceeding at only 8 knots *(This episode is described in more detail in Section Three).*

A different sort of incident occurred in the Western end of the English Channel on the 28th January 1945. The 30th Escort Group was supporting convoy TBC 50 when it was noticed that one of the ships, **MV Cromarty** had hauled out of line on fire.

Pevensey Castle (S.O.) closed her at full speed. On approaching the ship it was found that two boat loads of the crew had abandoned ship. In the meantime the ship's officers and remainder of the crew were plying hoses through scuttles and ventilators of the amidships accommodation that was well on fire.

Pevensey Castle lay alongside the weather side of the ship and put aboard three fire fighting parties, whilst *Launceston Castle* carried out Observant. The fire parties were able to enter the blazing accommodation using smoke helmets and spray nozzles.

Cromarty's main fire pump was out of action. *Pevensey Castle* coupled up *Cromarty*'s fire pumps as well as using her own 70 ton portable pump. Additional hoses were provide by *Launceston Castle*.

After 1? hours the fire was extinguished and the fire parties, with most of their fire fighting gear, returned on board. A light touch was provided by *Cromarty*'s two boat loads of men, clean, dry and complete with cat, dog and suitcases boarding their ship across *Pevensey Castle* as her fire parties, wet and grimed returned to her.

Whilst alongside, the two ships were pounding together in the moderate sea, *Pevensey Castle's* fenders were chewed up. Perhaps this partially accounts for the fact that she only suffered slight structural damage.

Significant contacts with the Enemy

ARTILLERY FIRE

A unique episode occurred on 6th January 1945 when **Caistor Castle** accompanied by **Kenilworth Castle** and **Launceston Castle** were on patrol in the vicinity of the Channel Islands. The Group approached a little too temptingly close to Alderney and came under fire from the German batteries on the Island. The Group retired north at high speed after three salvoes fell within 200 yards of **Kenilworth Castle**'s stern. More significant occasions are outlined in chronological order below

THE SINKING OF U-744

On the 5th March 1944 the C2 Escort Group whilst escorting Convoy HX 280 obtained a HF/DF bearing indicating the close proximity of a U-boat. Two minutes later **HMCS St Catherines** obtained a contact. The plot indicated that the U-boat was heading for the convoy. Numerous attacks were made with depth charges and hedgehog.

After three and a half hours **Kenilworth Castle** joined the hunt at 1330, but before she could attack she had to recover her Foxers so that she could operate at slow speed.

Kenilworth Castle's first attack was considered unsuccessful. The U-boat had altered course, and **St Catherines** who had been directing ship, lost contact.

An hour later **Kenilworth Castle** attacked again but failed to obtain a depth with 147B; this was followed by a creep attack by **HMCS Fennel** directed by **St Catherines**.

Between 1800 and 1922 **Kenilworth Castle** made three attempts to attack but broke off during the first two. On the first occasion the U-boat made a large alteration in course, and in the second attempt she lost contact. On the third attack she again failed to obtain a depth with 147B. After this **Kenilworth Castle** reported a failure in the Asdic training gear and therefore took no further active part in the action. She was detached at 0730 the next morning as she had been unable to repair her Asdics.

The C2 Group continued to attack and keep contact with the U-boat which finally surfaced at 1532 on the 6th March; the crew abandoning ship. Attempts to board were thwarted by the sea conditions. Three seaboats being capsized in the attempt. All the boarding parties were recovered and 2 officers and 25 ratings of the U-boat were rescued. The U-boat was finally sunk by torpedo. The action lasted 30 hours. The U-boat was subjected to five hedgehog attacks, three Squid attacks and some 10 depth charge attacks using 244 depth charges.

The ships credited with the sinking of **U-744** were **HMS Icarus**, **HMCS St Catherines**, **HMCS Chilliwack**, **HMS Kenilworth Castle**, **HMCS Chaudine** and **HMCS Gatineau**.

HURST CASTLE TORPEDOED

HMS Hurst Castle in company with **Oxford Castle** were sailed from Londonderry in the evening of 30th August 1944 with orders to join the Senior Officer Force 33 on patrol off the north west of Ireland. In the afternoon of the 31st **Hurst Castle** was placed under the orders of **Pevensey Castle** and proceeded to patrol between 56°16'N and Tory Island. **Pevensey Castle**, **Launceston Castle** and **Ambuscade** being in company. At 0800, 1st September, the ships were manoeuvring so as to sweep in a line abreast through the sighting point of a U-boat that had been reported by a Liberator. At 0820 **Hurst Castle** was 15° astern of station and had increased speed to 14 knots to regain bearing.

Foxers were not streamed "because the Senior Officer's intentions could only be surmised" (*Commanding Officer's Report*).

The ship was struck by a torpedo at 0825 and sank in about 6 minutes. The torpedo struck on the port side aft. The after engine room bulkhead collapsed and almost immediately so did the forward engine room bulkhead.. The ship took a list to port and slowly settled by the stern. 102 survivors were picked up by **HMS Ambuscade**.

U-484 SUNK BY HM SHIPS PORTCHESTER CASTLE AND HELMSDALE

On the 9th September 1944 the 30th Escort Group, as part of Force 33, was screening in support of Convoy ONF 305 to the west of Northern Ireland in position 55°46'N, 11°41'W. **Portchester Castle** had only joined the Group the day before. The Group were steaming in line abreast ahead of the convoy with **Portchester Castle** being the port wing ship of the screen. At approximately 0740 she obtained a contact at 2,100 yards, and having reduced speed to 7 knots, attacked with Squid. Although the depth of the U-boat was over estimated, the attack was accurate. The U-boat was forced to the surface at a range of 200 yards from the ship in the centre of the disturbed water from the explosion. **U-484** was attacked with 4-inch and

Oerlikon. The former having difficulty in depressing far enough in the close range. As the U-boat came level, depth charges were fired from the No 2 starboard thrower. The U-boat appeared to roll over and sink.

Helmsdale then made contact and acted as directing ship. At 0909 **Portchester Castle** attacked with Squid again. This attack was well conducted and was followed by a slight under water explosion. This in turn, five minutes later, was followed by a heavy underwater explosion together with wreckage rising to the surface. This attack was considered to have destroyed the U-boat. This was the first occasion when a U-boat was sunk entirely by the action of a Castle class corvette.

THE DESTRUCTION OF U-1200

On the 11th November 1944 the 30th Escort Group was on patrol in the Celtic Sea. The Group were disposed in line abreast on a course of 224°, zig zagging at 12 knots. **Launceston Castle** being the starboard wing ship, then **Pevensey Castle**, **Kenilworth Castle** and **Portchester Castle** the port wing ship.

At 0058 on the 11th **Portchester Castle** reported a radar contact bearing 183° range 23,000 yards. At first this was thought to be a ship echo, and later when she lost contact, as possibly that of an aircraft. **Pevensey Castle** investigating this bearing obtained a small echo at the extreme range of 25,000 yards. The plot gave the target's course and speed of 250°, 4 knots. The contact was held continuously until 0116. Assuming that, if it was a U-boat, it would continue on this course and speed, the Group reformed on a course of 187° to intercept.

When the Group passed through the diving position, **Launceston Castle** , the starboard wing ship,

reported a contact. This was at first classified as non -sub. She regained contact at 0235, reporting a firm contact with a course and speed of 250° 2? knots. She attacked at 0240 with Squid. Thus started a series of attacks that were to continue at intervals for three days, culminating in a mass attack by the 4th Escort Group which had arrived on the scene at 1015. This attack by four ships was carried out at 1316 on the 11th with four ships in line abreast on a course of 270°. **Pevensey Castle** was stationed 360° 1,500 yards from the contact to give the order "Fire". This spectacular attack produced a very large air bubble 300 feet long in the position of the contact.

At 1355 **Pevensey Castle** carried out a further Squid attack. After this, further attacks were considered to be a waste of ammunition. The echo had become duller and lost its bell like note. During the three days of the action, the score of attacks was :-

Launceston Castle	10 with Squid, and one depth charge attack.
Portchester Castle	5 with Squid, and one depth charge attack
Pevensey Castle	2 with Squid
Kenilworth Castle	1 with Squid
Drury	1 Hedgehog attack
4th Escort Group	1 massed depth charge attack.

The echo sounder traces provided by *Portchester Castle* were well preserved and indicated a target length of 243 feet and a possible conning tower structure 10 feet high.

Launceston Castle did the greatest number of attacks and was also responsible for most of the fine contact keeping of the Group. Post war investigations indicated that *U-1200* was the subject of these attacks.

BAMBOROUGH CASTLE SINKS U-387

Towards the conclusion of the voyage of JW 62 enemy signal activity and HF/DF reports indicated that U-boats were active in the approaches to Kola Inlet. Even so, all the convoyed ships were to arrive safely at their destinations.

The departure of RA 62 was therefore preceded by A/S sweeps along the intended route of the convoy. The 7th Escort Group, *Cygnet* (SO) with *Lapwing*, *Allington Castle* and *Bamborough Castle* sailed from Vaenga on the 9th December 1944 with orders to sweep an area south of 69° 59'N between longitudes 33° and 35° East.

At 1800 *Cygnet* obtained a small disappearing radar contact at 21,800 yards, but no Asdic contact.

An hour and a half later *Bamborough Castle* also obtained a radar contact. This was at 4,000 yards and disappeared after six minutes. This precipitated an A/S hunt by *Cygnet*, *Lapwing*, *Allington Castle* and *Bamborough Castle*.

Ten minutes after losing radar contact *Bamborough Castle* gained Asdic contact at 1,400 yards. This was classified as 'submarine' and attacked with Squid. Type 147B gave a depth of 360 feet and the bombs were set to explode at 380 feet. Loud whistle effect was heard immediately after the bombs exploded.

Although contact was lost immediately after the

attack, it was regained two minutes later. *Cygnet* also obtained contact on the same target and acted as directing ship. *Bamborough Castle* attacked again. After closing the range for a third attack contact was lost at 650 yards and not regained for 23 minutes.

At 1729 the contact was regained at 2,100 yards. *Bamborough Castle* made a run over with Type 147B and echo sounder in order to confirm the contact. This was confirmed by 147B, but no result was obtained by the echo sounder. The Squid was fired at 1735 after which contact was lost.

In the location of the third attack a patch of oil appeared in the centre of which were several pieces of apparently freshly broken wood. The oil slick continued to spread downwind. The hunt was abandoned at 2035 because the position of the attack was some distance away from the convoy's route.

The U-boat Assessment Committee assessed the attack as "U-boat probably destroyed". Subsequently, *Bamborough Castle* was credited with having sunk *U-387*.

An important feature of this action is the manner in which *Bamborough Castle* was able to so readily regain contact in these waters where Asdic conditions were notoriously bad.

TUNSBERG CASTLE MINED

Tunsberg Castle sailed from Loch Ewe as part of the close escort for the Russian Convoy JW.62, arriving at the Kola Inlet on 7th December 1944. This was in conjunction with the decision to deploy

Norwegian naval vessels to Finmark, the result of the Russian liberation of the Eastern part of Finmark.

A task force comprising *Tunsberg Castle*, the

corvette *Eglantine* and four Isles Class auxiliary minesweepers, *Jelöy*, *Karmöy*, *Oksöy* and *Tromöy* was sailed from Kola Inlet on 11th December 1944. *Tunsberg Castle* had embarked 1 officer and 10 soldiers of the Norwegian Army. The force was bound for Batsfjörd with supplies for the civilian population there.

On approaching the Fjord on 12th December 1944, two of the minesweepers with oropesa sweeping gear escorted the corvettes. Some blinking lights were observed close to the Makkur lighthouse and *Tunsberg Castle* was ordered to investigate. The minesweepers hauled their gear and *Eglantine* turned out to sea in the cleared channel. When within 1,500 metres of the Makkur Lighthouse the *Tunsberg Castle* was hit beneath the stern. Twenty to twenty five metres of the stern were blown off and five of the crew located at the stern were killed.. Two others were wounded. Both the engine and the boilers were put out of action. The wreck drifted back into the swept channel. *Eglantine* was able to come alongside and remove all the remainder of the crew as well as the soldiers without further loss. The ship sank two hours and forty minutes after the explosion.

It was considered that the *Tunsberg Castle* had hit one of the mines laid by the German destroyer *Z-33* on 31st October 1944.

Source: Royal Norwegian Naval Museum and Rear Admiral Ole F Berg who was a Midshipman on the *Tunsberg Castle* *at the time: both personal communications.*

ST THOMAS SINKS U-877

The C3 Escort Group (**HMCS Kakanee** SO) joined convoy HX 527 (47 ships) in position 44° 02'N, 49°44'W at 1810 on 24th December 1944. On 26th December HF/DF bearings indicated the presence of a U-boat a considerable distance from the convoy.

The next morning (27th) *Edmunton* obtained a doubtful Asdic contact at 0755 which she investigated and then lost. At 0815 *St Thomas* picked up and attacked a doubtful A/S contact. Contact was lost after the attack and then regained and a second attack was made at 0917. At 0930 *St Thomas* reported that the contact was more promising, having made firm contact both with Q and 147B. The latter giving a depth of 450 feet. *Sea Cliff* was detached to assist. Contact was not regained and at 1030 after an unsuccessful search, course was about to be set to rejoin the convoy. At this point a U-boat surfaced two and a half miles away. It sank shortly afterwards and the complete crew of fifty four were picked up by the two corvettes.

Survivors reported that the first attack caused no damage to the U-boat. The second attack was accurate and caused severe leaks all over the hull. The U-boat sank steeply stern first to the unprecedented depth of 350 metres (1,150 feet). At this depth the pressure hull could be heard bending. By going full speed ahead and blowing all tanks (heard by *St Thomas* as 'whistle effect') the U-boat rose to 160 metres (525 feet). It was not possible to maintain this depth. The Engineer Officer reported that the only chance of survival was to blow tanks and surface. These events account for the time (67 minutes) between the second attack and the final surfacing and sinking of the U-boat. The U-boat sank in approximately 46°25'N 36°38'W.

DENBIGH CASTLE TORPEDOED, BEACHED AND DECLARED A TOTAL LOSS

The Russian convoy JW 64 sailed from the Clyde on 3rd February 1945. The outstanding feature of this and the return convoy RA 64 was the persistent bad weather, attacks by torpedo bombers in spite of the bad weather and the close approach of the U-boats to the entrance of Kola Inlet.

The convoy was almost certainly detected by the enemy during the forenoon of 6th February when it was in the vicinity of 64°N. It was shadowed by enemy aircraft at intervals by day and by night until the day before it reached Kola Inlet.

On the morning of 7th February the convoy

screen was ordered to remain at their night stations. This provided two concentric circles of escorts around the convoy and had proved a very effective anti aircraft tactic.

At 0745 that morning the convoy was attacked by a number of Ju-88 torpedo aircraft. One of these was quickly shot down by *Denbigh Castle* (Lt Cdr G. Butcher DSC RNVR). A very creditable performance considering that this was her first operation since commissioning.

Air attacks culminated on 10th February. Several attacks developed. Seven enemy aircraft were shot down and no ships were damaged.

Late, during the night of 12th February, *Denbigh Castle* was in station 2? miles on the port quarter of the convoy. The convoy was forming into two columns in preparation for entering harbour. The leading ships being in the vicinity of Toros Island within the Kola Inlet.

Shortly after midnight *Denbigh Castle* altered course to 180° to open her station on the convoy and also to drop back as the convoy speed appeared to have been reduced and probably because the leading ships had stopped to pick up pilots.

Four minutes later, when in position estimated as 69°20.5'N 33°37.5'E, at 0008, an explosion took place in the fore part of the vessel. It was originally thought that the ship had struck a mine. Later considerations concluded that she had been torpedoed by *U-992*.

Although the ship was severely damaged and down by the head, it was apparent that she was not in immediate danger of sinking. *Bluebell* (Lt. G.H. Walker RN) came alongside at 0045 and the medical officer from *Serapis* was embarked from her whaler. All casualties and all hands that could be spared from their duties on board were transferred to *Bluebell*. Preparations for towing were immediately put in hand.

Bluebell started towing from aft at 0217 at 3 knots. At 0300 the Russian tug *Krasner* came alongside on the port side and her 100 ton motor pump was transferred to *Denbigh Castle*. This pump was able, for a time, to check the rise of water which was about 4-5 feet deep in the centre of the wardroom flat.

At 0515, with the ship very deep by the head, all ratings still on board were embarked on the tug. The Tug's Captain decided to beach the ship in Bolshaya Volokovaya Bay so as to prevent her from sinking in the fairway. At 0615 the tug received the tow from *Bluebell*. At 0730 the *Denbigh Castle* grounded in the bay by the bow. The tug slipped the tow and pushed the stern round. At 0900 the ship began to list to port and the officers remaining on board abandoned ship by the whaler. The ship capsized to port at 0910 and was observed to move bodily into deeper water.

Subsequent diving operations were carried out with a view to destroying secret equipment and recover secret documents. Diving operations continued, with little success, over three days. The extreme cold, and the rapid freezing of helmet air valves and loss of circulation in the divers' hands, rendering work in enclosed spaces impracticable. However in spite of all these difficulties the Type 277 radar office was wrecked by an explosive charge.

Casualties comprised 11 killed (one of whom died of his wounds) and six wounded.

Tragically, *Bluebell*, that was so instrumental in taking off survivors and taking the wreck in tow, was, on the homeward bound voyage, torpedoed and blew up. There was only one survivor.

ALNWICK CASTLE AND LARK SINK U-425

On the night of 16/17th February 1945 ships of the 7th and 8th Escort Groups were carrying out an A/S search in the approaches to Kola Inlet prior to the sailing of RA 64. The ships were disposed in line abreast with *Alnwick Castle* and *Lark* adjacent ships on the northern end of the line. *Lark* obtained a contact 0016/17th and *Alnwick Castle* was ordered to assist. *Lark* not being fitted with A.T.W. or Type 147B directed *Alnwick Castle* onto the target. The latter reported a firm contact at 0043 and attacked with Squid at 0059 but quickly lost contact after the explosion of the bombs. At this point she started to carry out 'Observant', when *Lark* reported having gained contact and then almost immedi-

ately reported "Submarine in Sight". Both ships engaged with 4-inch and close range weapons, a pattern of Squid set shallow and Port D.C. thrower.

At 0123 the U-boat was seen to sink stern first and the crew abandon ship. *Alnwick Castle* lowered her whaler and succeeded in picking up one survivor. It was concluded that the extreme coldness of the water accounted for the loss of most of the remainder of the crew. The sole survivor thought that he was one of the last to leave the submarine.

TINTAGEL CASTLE AND VANQUISHER SINK U-878

On 10th April 1945, three days out from the UK, the *Tintagel Castle* was 13 miles astern of Convoy ON295 being escorted by the B1 Escort Group. She had been investigating some doubtful contacts and was on her way back to rejoin the convoy when, at 2147, *Vanquisher* on the outer screen reported sighting a schnorkel and periscope. *Tintagel Castle* was ordered to join her which she did at 2252. *Vanquisher* who had been carrying out Observant regained contact and acted as directing ship. *Tintagel Castle* gained contact at 2321 and started a slow and deliberate attack. At 800 yards range 147B gave a depth of 700 feet and at 600 yards range the depth was observed to be stabilised at 600 feet. The Squid was fired at 2327 and three minutes after the bombs exploded a muffled explosion was heard followed half a minute later by a second much louder explosion that shook the ship.

Contact was regained and a second attack with the target at 300 feet was carried out at 2338. Two small underwater explosions were heard nine minutes after this attack. The contact slowly faded. An attack was initiated an hour later but abandoned because of the poor quality of the contact. A search was then organised by *Vanquisher* and at 0225 *Tintagel Castle* was ordered to rejoin the convoy. The target was subsequently identified as *U-878*.

TRAINING

None of the above would have been possible unless the crews had been trained to a high degree of proficiency and welded together as a coherent ship's company. The latter was largely dependent on the Commanding Officer and his First Lieutenant.

Training started even before the ships were commissioned. Ships' Officers were generally appointed whilst the ship was still in the builder's yard and several weeks before the expected completion date.

Officers would be despatched to training courses appropriate to the duties that they would be expected to perform. The Commanding Officer and perhaps also his Navigating Officer would attend the Tactical School at Liverpool; the Gunnery Officer to Portsmouth for gunnery training and where he would meet up with and train with the 4-inch Gun crew elect. The same would apply to the Asdic Officer. In many instances the specialist rates, Asdics, Telegraphy, Visual Signals, HF/DF, and engine room ratings would come straight from their specialist training schools. The Officer to be in charge of the Squid would also train with the operating crew. Although in the case of the early ships to be commissioned there was not a great deal of difference in the knowledge of the specialists and the trainees - the weapon was so new.

THE SCHOOL FOR CORVETTES

This was established at Tobermory under the command of Vice-Admiral Sir Gilbert. O. Stephenson. He had come to Tobermory from serving as a Convoy Commodore. He was responsible for the initial training of all newly built or re-commissioned escort vessels. He, together with his

staff, put the ships through every conceivable evolution and exercise that they were likely to encounter. Often it seemed simultaneously. A major theme of the training was to make all hands "Think". His name became widely known, respected and admired.

Describing his own recollections of Tobermory, Peter De Beavoir Carey Hart, one time Sub lieutenant and AS CO of the newly commissioned **Dumbarton Castle** wrote.

"*He (the Commodore) would arrive on board*

ship like a charge of dynamite - "Number One, the Captain is dead, there is a fire in the engine room and a mine under your bows - DO SOMETHING- If he thought any officer was inefficient, from the COs downwards, they would be replaced and sent aboard Western Isles for several months of extensive training."

It is difficult to underestimate the contribution that "Monky" Stephenson made towards the winning of the Battle of the Atlantic.

SUBSEQUENT TRAINING

Training did not cease after passing out from Tobermory. It was a continuous business. Senior Officers of Escort Groups were required to regularly carry out training exercises at sea whenever conditions allowed. These would include gunnery exercises, practice in the Step Aside procedure, visual signalling, and rarely would an opportunity be missed for practice in homing in aircraft . Examples of the sort of exercises carried out at sea are given in Appendix Twelve.

Training continued during lay-over periods, mainly at Liverpool and at Londonderry. Much use was made of the 'Asdic Bus' with its plot on the upper deck and the Asdic operators on the lower deck. This provided training in A/S tactics as well as for Asdic operators.

Time was usually found for a training session at sea with a 'tame' submarine. Similarly boarding techniques were exercised, providing an opportunity for some vigorous, but friendly, horse play between the submariners and the boarding party.

Considerable emphasis was placed on signalling procedures. This became increasingly important with the widespread use of TBS radio inter-ship communications.

The home port training programmes were aimed in particular in overcoming problems that had become highlighted in the Senior Officers' Report of Proceedings. Training could be carried out in individual ships to solve problems particular to the ship.

CONVOY RESCUE SHIPS - THE CASTLES THAT NEVER WERE

As the requirement for A/S corvettes increased it was originally envisioned that the Castle class would be ordered in large numbers - indeed 96 ships were ordered for both RN and RCN service.

By the middle of 1943 the Battle of the Atlantic was beginning to swing in favour of the Allies - to such an extent, that by December 1943, much of the Castle class programme was cancelled (see Appendix One).

The need for A/S vessels may have gone, but there was still an Admiralty requirement for Convoy Rescue ships - those vessels which sailed in convoy to provide rescue and medical services to those sailors whose vessels had been lost during the voyage.

The role had traditionally been fulfilled by requisitioned merchant tonnage, but, by the end of 1943, merchant shipping was at a premium, and with one eye on the build up of troops and equipment for the invasion of Europe and another on the massive sealift requirement for D-Day itself, the Ministry of War Transport was loathe to release any more merchant shipping for the role.

The Admiralty reluctantly decided to convert five of the incomplete Castle class hulls into Convoy Rescue ships. Reluctantly because although the ships would have the endurance and speed required for the task, the large slab sided hull and flared bows made recovery of casualties by boat quite a hazardous operation. Added to these concerns were the warship origins of the hulls - heavily compartmentalised internally and not ideal for the accommodation of large numbers of survivors. However, in their favour, they were already under construction and were under naval control.

Following conversion the five ships were mercantile manned and operated and the ships carried naval boats, Carley Floats and rafts along the length of the upperdeck.

Armament comprised a 12-pdr gun aft and five 20mm AA guns.

Once in service the ships were to undertake a series of trial voyages, in order to prove the concept of the design, before being deployed on the Atlantic runs. These proving voyages were usually conducted on the UK-Gibraltar route and would involve up to three passages, the ships usually leaving the southbound convoy part way through the trip to take passage back to the UK with the northbound convoy.

Empire Comfort (ex-***York Castle***)   Builder: Ferguson Brothers Limited

Sailed from the builders on 6 February 1945 and completed her UK-Gibraltar transits with little need for her services. She completed her westbound transit of the North Atlantic only days before the German surrender. Laid up in the Gareloch on her return to the UK, she eventually served as an Accommodation ship for the 3rd Submarine Flotilla in Holy Loch, before being deployed as an Army Ferry in the Channel and Mediterranean. As with the other five vessels she spent periods of her time in the Eastern Mediterranean transporting illegal imigrants. She was sold in July 1955 for breaking up in Belgium.

Empire Lifeguard (ex-***Maiden Castle***)   Builder: Fleming and Ferguson, Paisley

During trials she sailed to Liverpool where she was inspected by Admiral Sir Max Horten, CinC Western Approaches. Damage to one of her boilers during the return passage delayed her entry into service until March 1945 - as a result she only completed two proving trips to the South, before being deployed to the North Atlantic. Laid up at Rosneath at the end of the war, she was returned to service in October 1945 to ferry UK troops from Murmansk, with a similar voyage to Kiel. During immigrant transporting operations in the Eastern Mediterranean in 1947 she was holed by underwater explosions caused by limpet mines which had been attached to the hull in Cyprus; She listed and sank in Haifa Harbour soon after dis-

embarking Jewish immigrants brought from detention camps in Cyprus. She was refloated on 8th August and dry-docked at Port Said on 22nd August. She too was broken up in Belgium in 1955.

Empire Peacemaker (ex-*Scarborough Castle*)   Builder: Fleming and Ferguson, Paisley

Sailed from Paisley on 18 January 1945, embarking on her first Southbound voyage in early February. The ship completed just one North Atlantic run before returning to Rosneath for a short lay-up. There followed a trooping run to Archangelsk to repatriate UK troops. After a period of operation as an army transport the ship was sold in 1955 to be scrapped at Antwerp.

Empire Rest (ex-*Rayleigh Castle*)   Builder: Ferguson Brothers Limited

The first of the conversions to complete, the ship sailed on 26 October 1944. Following her proving trips to the south, she managed to complete two Atlantic runs, during the first of which she encountered hurricane force winds! She completed a repatriation trip from Kiel to Devonport and a brief period of service as an Army transport before being laid up in the River Fal. She arrived at Briton Ferry for breaking up in June 1952.

Empire Shelter (ex-*Barnard Castle*)   Builder: George Brown & Company, Greenock

Completing in March 1945, the ship had only completed two proving voyages before the German surrender. Like her sister, *Empire Comfort* she served as an Accommodation ship on Holy Loch before a brief period as an Army transport in the Mediterranean. After a lay up in the River Fal she arrived at Antwerp for scrapping in July 1955.

*A 1949 view of **Empire Peacemaker** in the Mediterranean. Note the large number of liferafts, floats and boats dispersed around the upperdeck. By this time the 12-pdr, sited on the quarterdeck had been removed.*

(Portsmouth Royal Naval Museum)

POST WAR SERVICE

After the German surrender the Western Approaches Command was quickly run down and the ships dispersed to other commands. The Royal Canadian Navy Castle class corvettes returned to Canada either to the North West Atlantic Command or to the Pacific Coast Command.

To support the repatriation of American soldiers by air a number of Castle class corvettes were allocated to Air/Sea Rescue duties with the ships placed on static patrol along the expected routes of the aircraft. The ships operated from the UK, Gibraltar, Freetown and Dakar. Fourteen Castle class corvettes were allocated for these duties from the end of May 1945 to the end of the year. Castle class corvettes not mentioned in the Table below would have been allocated to the Reserve Fleet.

ALLOCATION OF CASTLE CLASS CORVETTES:
POST GERMAN SURRENDER

Period	Command	Ships	Notes
End May 45 - end Jul 45	Western Approaches Air Sea Rescue Duties	*Amberley Castle* *Berkeley Castle* *Carisbrooke Castle* *Dumbarton Castle* *Leeds Castle* *Rushen Castle*	All ships on station by the end of July *Rushen Castle* under repair. Completed June 45
	FOGMA Air Sea Rescue Duties	*Caistor Castle* *Hadleigh Castle* *Knaresborough Castle* *Lancaster Castle*	*Caistor Castle* left Christiansands end of Jun 45. All ships on station, based at Gibraltar by the end of June 45.
	FOCWAF Air Sea Rescue Duties	*Kenilworth Castle* *Launceston Castle* *Pevensey Castle* *Portchester Castle*	All ships on station based at Freetown by the end of July '45
	CinC Rosyth Misc Duties	*Flint Castle* *Oakham Castle* *Oxford Castle* *Tintagel Castle*	Left St Johns NF 4.6.45. At Narvik 23.7.45 Escorting POW ship Tromso to France. Arrived Rosyth 29.7.45

Period	Command	Ships	Notes
	Reserve Fleet	*Allington Castle* *Alnwick Castle* *Bamborough Castle* *Farnham Castle*	
	RCN North Atlantic Command	*Hespeler* *Huntsville*	At Digby Refit at Halifax. Completed 31.7.45. At Halifax
		Orangeville *St Thomas* *Bowmanville*	At Halifax Arrive Halifax 27.7.45 St Johns NF. Refit completed 8.9.45
		Petrolia *Tillsonburg* *Arnprior* *Kincardine*	At Digby
	Pacific Coast Command	*Leaside* *Copper Cliff* *Humberstone*	All at Esquimalt by 18.7.45
July 45 - 7 Sept 45	A/S Training Flotilla	*Flint Castle* *Oakham Castle* *Oxford Castle*	Arv Campbeltown 8 Sept Arv Campbeltown 24 Aug At Leith. Repairs complete 14.9.45
	Air Sea Rescue Duties Stations 16 & 17	*Amberley Castle* *Berkeley Castle* *Dumbarton Castle* *Leeds Castle* *Tintagel Castle*	At Chatham 20.10.45
7 Sep 45 -18 Oct 45	CinC Plymouth Air Sea Rescue Duties Station 18	*Carisbrooke Castle* *Rushen Castle*	
	FOGMA Air Sea Rescue Duties	*Caistor Castle* *Hadleigh Castle* *Knaresborough Castle* *Lancaster Castle*	

Period	Command	Ships	Notes
	FOCWAF Air Sea Rescue Duties Freetown and Dakar	*Kenilworth Castle* *Launceston Castle* *Pevensey Castle* *Portchester Castle*	
	RCN	*Arnprior* *Huntsville* *Orangeville*	At Halifax, tentatively for disposal
	North Atlantic Command	*Bowmanville* *Petrolia*	Training Duties At Charlottetown. Repairs complete 1 Oct.
	Pacific Coast Command	*Tillsonburg* *Kincardine* *Leaside* *Copper Cliff* *Hespeler* *Huntsville* *St Thomas*	
19 Oct 45 - 30 Dec 45	CinC Rosyth A/S Training Flotilla Campbeltown	*Flint Castle* *Oakham Castle* *Oxford Castle*	
	Air Sea Rescue Stations 16 & 17	*Amberley Castle* *Berkeley Castle* *Dumbarton Castle* *Leeds Castle*	
	CinC Plymouth Air Sea Rescue Station 18	*Tintagel Castle* *Carisbrooke Castle* *Rushen Castle*	At Chatham under Nore Command from 30.10.45
	FOGMA Air Sea Rescue Duties	*Caistor Castle* *Knaresborough Castle* *Lancaster Castle* *Portchester Castle* *Hadleigh Castle*	Preparing for service and Allocated to FOG Ex Reserve, *Kenilworth Castle* - refit Plymouth completed 19.1.46. *Launceston Castle* - ready 8.12.45. *Tintagel Castle* at Chatham completes 6.12.45

Period	Command	Ships	Notes
	FOCWAF Freetown & Dakar	None	The four corvettes left Freetown between 1-6 Oct.
	Home Fleet Fishery Protection Flotilla	*Allington Castle* *Bamborough Castle*	Both allocated from Reserve
	RCN Pacific Coast Comand	None	All Castle class that had been listed under this command were not listed after the end of November.
	North Atlantic Command	*Arnprior* *Bowmanville* *Huntsville* *Kincardine* *Petrolia* *Tillsonburg*	All listed for disposal

The primary duty of those on Air/sea Rescue duties being to act as radio beacons and rescue ships for the fleet of aeroplanes ferrying American soldiers back to their home country. Four ships continued as Weather Ships. One of these ships was withdrawn from service after about thirty years and three continued this arduous Mid Atlantic duty of sending out regular detailed weather reports for thirty five years. They would be at sea for 3-4 weeks. Much of the time stopped and drifting with boilers banked during the day. Come nightfall the engine would be started and the ship move back to the centre of its tiny Weather Station square. Whilst hard on the fabric of the ships it was even harder on the crews. There are few situations that are more uncomfortable than being at sea in a stopped ship. Apart from the discomfort of the rolling ship there was the unremitting tedium of really not having very much to do.

As the need for Air/Sea Rescue ships declined, the ships were returned to the UK and allocated to other duties or placed into the Reserve Fleet. The Air/Sea Rescue period proved the capability of the Castle class corvettes to sustain prolonged static patrols in the North Atlantic, and thus their suitability as 'Weather Ships'. Four Castle class corvettes were used for this purpose.

TRAINING SHIPS

From 1945 to 1956 twelve Castle Class Corvettes, re-designated as Frigates after the formation of NATO in 1948, were involved in training.

In May 1945 the Anti Submarine (A/S) Flotilla was established at Campbeltown. It comprised three Flower Class Corvettes. By November 1945 the strength had risen to nine ships which included the *Tintagel Castle* and the *Oxford Castle*.

The A/S Flotilla was moved to Portland in January 1946 and was joined there by *Leeds Castle*. During the year the Flotilla was re-designated the Third Escort Flotilla. At that time it was composed of a wide range of ships; destroyers, frigates, corvettes, a minelayer, a tug and a maintenance ship. The Castle class dominated the Flotilla.

By the autumn of 1956 the Flotilla had been subjected to further name changes; 2nd Training Flotilla in February 1949 and 2nd Training Squadron in January 1952.

The Castle Class Corvettes/Frigates were primarily employed as Anti-Submarine training ships. They generally operated in pairs, accompanied by a submarine. They sailed each day with trainee Asdic operators, searching for and making runs over the submarine. On occasion this would be varied by 4-inch gun and AA armament firing exercises.

The *Carisbrooke Castle* and the *Launceston Castle* had a different training role. They operated as Air Training Target Ships. The ships operated alternatively from Londonderry and Plymouth, and occasionally together.

They generally operated on a 'day run' basis. To sea first thing. Steam up and down to be located by aircraft and back into harbour during the dog watches. The ship operating out from Plymouth usually exercised with aircraft from RNAS Culdrose. The training included operating with Dragonfly helicopters exercising the recovery of ditched airmen from the sea using the 'Sproule' net. The Sproule net was like a large anglers net. Dangled from the helicopter it in effect scooped a ditched man from the sea. The helicopters had no winches and this required great skill from the helicopter pilot and thus a lot of training. The system was capable of recovering either unconscious or dead bodies.

The main function of the Air Training Target Ships in these exercises was to receive the recovered personnel who were 'dropped' onto the quarterdeck.

Sometime trainee QR3s from Devonport Gunnery School would be taken to sea to train on the 4-inch

HMS Carisbrooke Castle exercising Air Sea Rescue (ASR) techniques with a Dragonfly helicopter.
(*L.J. Boulden*)

A Dragonfly helicopter, with a casualty in the Sproule Net, approaches *HMS Carisbrooke Castle*'s quarterdeck. *(L.J. Boulden)*

gun. *Carisbrooke Castle*'s gun by this time was not very accurate - it had developed so much backlash in laying and training.

When operating out of Londonderry the ships' roles were more varied. They exercised with aircraft from RNAS Eglinton and submarines from Holy Loch. The ship had a triple role, guiding the aircraft in submarine hunting using their Sonar Buoys and the ship's Asdic and RADAR; being

hunted and attacked by the same submarines and simulated attacks on the submarines with squid and depth charges. The days work invariably ended with the task of recovering the Sonar buoys used in the exercises.

The periods over which the various ships contributed to this training effort were:

CASTLE CLASS CORVETTES/FRIGATES AS TRAINING SHIPS						
DESIGNATION OF FLOTILLA OR SQUADRON						
Ship	Campbeltown A/S Training Flotilla May 45 - Nov 45	Basic A/S Training Flotilla (Rosyth) Nov 45 -	Basic A/S Training Flotilla (Portland) Feb 46 -	3rd Escort Flotilla Aug 46- Feb 49	2nd Training Flotilla Feb 49 - Jan 52	2nd Training Squadron Jan 52 - 1959
Caistor Castle						Feb 53- 1955 (1)
Carisbrooke Castle						1952- 1956 (2)
Flint Castle			Jun 46 - Aug 46 (3)	1946 - 1949	1949 - 1952	1952 - 23/03/56
Hedingham Castle				1946 - 1949	1949 - 1952	1952 - 1956 (4)

Ship	Campbeltown A/S Training Flotilla May 45 - Nov 45	Basic A/S Training Flotilla (Rosyth) Nov 45 -	Basic A/S Training Flotilla (Portland) Feb 46 -	3rd Escort Flotilla Aug 46- Feb 49	2nd Training Flotilla Feb 49 - Jan 52	2nd Training Squadron Jan 52 - 1959
Kenilworth Castle				1946 - 1948		
Knaresborough Castle						09/1952 - 1954 (1)
Launceston Castle						10/1951 - 1956 (1) (6)
Leeds Castle			Jan/Feb 46 - Aug 46	1946 - 1948	1949 - 1952	1952 - 20/11/56 (1)
Oakham Castle			1946 - 1951 (5)	1946 - 1948	1948 - 1950	
Oxford Castle	? - Nov 45	Nov 45 - Feb 46				
Portchester Castle					May 51 - Jan 52	1952 - 1956
Tintagel Castle			27/01/46 Aug 46	1946 - 1949	1949 - 1952	1952 - June 56 (1)

(1)   1953 participated at the Coronation Review.

(2)   Operated as an Air Target Training Ship; mostly out of Londonderry.

(3)   The Naval Historical Branch (1980) records *Flint Castle* as having joined the Rosyth Escort Force in June 1946 and moving to Campbeltown in September 1946.

(4)   In June 1955 she provided a naval contingent for the unveiling of the Normandy War Memorial at Bayeux.

(5)   According to 'Paticulars of War Vessels', October 1946, the ship's Squid was replaced by Hedgehog 24.

(6)   Operated as an Air Target Training Ship, mostly out of Plymouth.

WEATHER SHIPS

The post war increase in transatlantic air traffic caused the International Civil Aviation Organisation to sponsor an international agreement in 1946 which set up the Ocean Weather Ship Service.

Thirteen weather stations were established; two to be manned by the UK. Originally four Flower class corvettes were selected for this service. Between 1958 and 1961 these were replaced by Castle class frigates.

Amberley Castle (1961)	re-named *Weather Adviser*	Disposed of 12/1981
Pevensey Castle (1960)	re-named *Weather Monitor*	Disposed of 01/1982
Oakham Castle (1958)	re-named *Weather Reporter*	Disposed of 09/1977
Rushen Castle (1961)	re-named *Weather Surveyor*	Disposed of 09/1977

Lloyds have a continuous record of these ships. All ships of this class were required to have the shelter and weather decks specially examined each year.

In 1975 the World Meteorological Organisation obtained an agreement for the joint financing of the North Atlantic Ocean Stations (NAOs). Under this agreement, ratified in December 1976, the stations were reduced to four with the UK manning one of them (Lima 57°00'N 20°00'W).

In 1971/72 *Weather Adviser* underwent a major refit and was subsequently re-named *Admiral Fritzroy*. In 1977 *Weather Monitor* was given a similar major refit. On completion she was re-named *Admiral Beaufort*. The two ships completed their careers as Weather Ships in December 1981 and January 1982 respectively.

Weather Reporter and *Weather Surveyor* were withdrawn from service in 1977 and sold by the Ministry of Defence, *Weather Reporter* for scrap, whilst *Weather Surveyor* started a new career as a salvage ship.

During their heyday Weather Ships manned six Ocean Stations: Charlie, Alpha, India, Juliet, Kilo and Mike.

• Charlie was on the Western side of the Atlantic and manned by the USA.

• Alpha was at 62°N 33°W and was manned by the UK, France, Netherlands and Norway in rotation.

• India was at 59°N 19°W and was manned by the UK and the Netherlands in rotation.

• Juliet was at 52°30'N 20°W and was manned by the UK, France and the Netherlands in rotation.

• Kilo was at 47°N 15°W and was manned by the UK France and The Netherlands in rotation.

• Mike was in the Norwegian Sea and was manned by Norway and The Netherlands in rotation.

The stations were a 200 km square divided into 20 km squares with the centre spot located in the above positions.

The four British Ocean Weather Ships (OWSs) were painted with a dark grey hull and orange superstructure. The 4-inch gun was replaced by a large winch (for depth sounding purposes). The Squid and the Bofors mounted on the amidships sponsons, port and starboard had been retained and cocooned. The ships were based at Greenock. They normally berthed in the James Watt Dock. They flew the Blue Ensign modified with the OWS crest.

The OWSs were required to collect weather information and to provide a navigation beacon and direction services for aircraft crossing the Atlantic. Operating expenses were high; a large amount of the funding coming from the International Civil Aviation Organisation.

The time on station was 28 days with a 2 - 3 day transit time to and from India and Juliet and 4-5 days to and from Alpha and Kilo. The pattern of duties was such that two ships did I, I, J, A for two years and the other pair did I, J, A, K for two years before they swapped patterns.

The Meteorological staff numbered seven and were attached to the ship for a twelve month period which could be extended if so wished. The compliment was an 'Officer in Charge', two Supervisors and four Scientific Assistants. The ship's crew amounted to 40-45 men and were a mixture of Merchant Navy and ex-RN personnel. The radio and RADAR staff were usually ex-RN. The Masters and 1st Officers were mostly static with a low turnover. The 2nd and 3rd Officers usually turned over quite quickly. A similar pattern was repeated on the engineers' side. The regime of voyages enabled the 2nd and 3rd Officers time to study for their 'tickets' or to fill in between berths in the Merchant Navy. The low pay compared with the Merchant Navy standards was accepted as the forfeit for knowing when the ship sailed or docked for up to two years ahead. There were usually eight trips a year each of around one month's duration

with about 14 days leave between each trip.

A voyage started and ended when the ship was abeam the Cloch Lighthouse at Gourock. Met observations started and ended when the ship was abeam of Ailsa Craig at the mouth of the Clyde.

On passage 3 hourly surface observations where carried out by the Met staff; recording cloud amounts and type, surface wind speed and direction, sea level pressure, air temperature, visibility, sea state (i.e. the wind & waves) height and period, and swell conditions, direction, height, period. These were coded up and transmitted to the Meteorological Headquarters at Bracknell. The upper air programme was started once the ship was west of 10°W. This consisted of soundings (temperature, pressure, humidity, wind speed and direction) at 0001 and 1200 GMT, and just wind finding soundings at 0600 and 1800 GMT.

When over the continental shelf bathythermograph soundings were carried out at 6 hourly intervals using the 'Rocket' which went down to 450 feet. This device was known as the 'Rocket' as it looked like a missile. In addition one shallow sounding was done in the pit off Rathlin Island off the north coast of Ulster. These soundings were

Weather Reporter at James Watt Dock, Greenock. (©Mik Cass)

done whilst the ship was underway and required a fair bit of skill in driving the winch. On reaching the edge of the 'grid' mail was transferred to the home going ship. The aircraft radio navigation beacon was switched on. The centre of the square would be approached at 3 knots. Normally the ship steamed a short distance upwind of the centre, stopped engines and hove to port side to the wind. The main entrance into the ship from the upper deck was on the starboard side.

For the Met staff the 'on station' routine changed to hourly observations, of the full upper air sounding programme, but the 450 foot bathy soundings stopped and twice daily 900 foot soundings were done instead. In addition wind speed and direction was calculated at each upper air sounding at 1000ft levels from the surface to 45,000 feet.

Whilst the rest of the ship worked the normal 4 on 8 off, the Met staff followed a version of the 'shore' routine. There was always one member of staff (Scientific Assistant) on duty for the hourly observations. The full soundings at 0001 and 1200 GMT required another 3 on duty (1 Supervisor and 2 Scientific Assistants). The wind only soundings at 0600 and 1800 only required one extra person, a Supervisor, who carried out the sounding with the help of the observing Scientific Assistant.

For the radio staff the 'on station' routine changed from one to two being on duty. One handled the Met traffic and any other administrative traffic, whilst the second looked after the aircraft side. This entailed ensuring the navigation beacon was transmitting the correct call sign for the grid square that the ship was wallowing in and passing details by VHF to any aircraft requesting information.

This information was the ships position, wind speed and direction at the flight level the aircraft was at, and a radar fix - distance and bearing from the ship.

The radar staff tracked all upper air soundings and provided the range and bearing to the Met staff. They also provided the radar fixes to the aircraft. In between times they maintained and repaired the Met, radio and radar equipment.

Once an aircraft started to call the ship, the DF equipment picked up the transmission and a blip appeared on the radar screen. On the **Weather Reporter** it was a matter of pride to the radar staff

to supply the radio room with the aircraft's bearing and range before the pilot had finished asking for what he wanted. This was in the days before GPS and satellite navigation.

The majority of the conversations between ship and aircraft were formal - "Ocean Station India/Juliet/Alpha or Kilo, this is (aircraft call sign), request ship's position, radar fix and wind at flight level (whatever height the aircraft was flying at)". There were the odd occasions when the pilots were quite chatty, realising that we were stuck 1,000's of feet below them for about a month. If you were really lucky the pilot let one of the stewardesses make the call. One BOAC (British Overseas Airline Corporation) - pre British Airways - pilot on the Heathrow to Bermuda run was quite chatty and always had a few words if it wasn't busy and until he went out of range. One BOAC pilot made the mistake of asking what conditions were like, where upon one rather dry radio operator advised him "not too bad really, slightly damp underfoot though". There was a deathly hush after that!!

Likewise one of the Pan American pilots on the Heathrow to New York run was 'human'. The call sign for the Pan-Am flights was 'Clipper' followed by the flight number. It was noticeable that Flight 001, regardless of the pilot, was always announced as "This is THE Clipper."

The odd time Qantas called, it was always "This is Qantas, the world's airline, flight number etc". Alitalia, the Italian state airline, always called up approaching the ship and when past the ship requesting a radar fix on each occasion. It didn't matter who the pilot was, they wanted two fixes. The radar operator was always ready for them the second time around and always had the information ready before the pilot had got past "Ocean Station".

The Weather Ships had one other function, air sea rescue. Whilst on Kilo, the **Weather Reporter** was called upon to act in this capacity.

Three light aircraft were flying together on a delivery trip from the States to Europe. They encountered electrical storms and one lost contact with the other two. He also got zapped by lightning and lost the majority of his instrumentation. It was night, cloudy, and he didn't know where he was or which direction he was flying. Luckily a USAF aircraft on transit from Spain to the States picked up

Weather Adviser at Station India circa 1966/67.   (©Mik Cass)

his distress calls. The USAF air sea rescue control centre at Lajes in the Azores scrambled a Hercules to rendezvous with the aircraft.

Having ascertained how much fuel he had on board and the distance to the nearest land - Spain, he was advised that he wasn't going to make it and that he should ditch alongside **Weather Reporter** on Kilo. In due he course he ditched alongside, we picked him up, and a day or so later transferred him to a Royal Mail Ship for passage to the UK.

The Castles were very good sea boats. The top end of a Gale Force 8 and the bottom of a Severe Gale Force 9 being the worst times. Under those conditions the wave length was not quite long enough and the ship would ride three before digging the bow in on the fourth. Having dug her nose in, the stern then came out in sympathy and dug in as the bow lifted clear and shipped one over the gunwhales straight into the balloon shed. It is possible to go from a standing start to atop the hydrogen cylinders and grabbing hold of the fire sprinklers at about 8 feet above deck level in one swift movement!! All the Met staff very quickly developed a sixth sense when a wave was going to thump inboard and they didn't get caught out that often. Once the wind got well into a Force 9 and above, the wavelength was such that the ship remained dry. She might roll severely but at least it was a dry one! It did make life interesting when launching the 0001 or 1200 upper air sounding, wondering if the equipment would clear the next wave crest before the balloon started to lift clear of the ship.

Source: Mik Cass

LIFE ON OCEAN WEATHER SHIPS 1966-1969
Mik Cass, one time Meteorological Officer, recalls his time on Ocean Weather ships;

Messing followed the normal RN routine. Wardroom for the officers, PO's Mess for the Met, radio and radar staff and the Seamen's Mess for the rest. Those residing in the Wardroom were allowed spirits and beer to drink, the rest had a choice of Export Guinness, McEwans or Tennents Lager - canned not bottled. However, this was rationed to two cans per day. It was all down to the vagaries of the Customs legislation as the ships, although leaving UK territorial waters, never docked anywhere else before returning to UK waters. The troops weren't considered responsible to be allowed spirits etc. However, you had the daft situation of being allowed spirits if you were promoted to the Wardroom for a trip, before returning below decks again the next trip and not being considered responsible!

As it was in the days before satcoms, communication with the UK was by old fashioned Morse key. No radio teleprinters, faxes, telephones etc, in those days. The radio receivers used were RCA 88's which were very good sets, eagerly snapped up by amateurs when put up for sale on the open market. The main ships radar was a Model 277 with a circular dish, with a Marconi set as the navigating radar. The 277 was used for the upper air soundings and for providing aircraft with range and bearing from the ship.

One could always tell when the **Queen Elizabeth** was at sea criss-crossing the Atlantic as she had a very deep Morse transmission when on 500Hz - commonly known as '5 ton' - due to the length of the aerials. Even I, as a humble Metman, could recognise it.

Ship's position was calculated in two ways - the original manner as in the days of yore, the sextant, or else using an old US Coast Guard 1944 Loran set. No Loran A, B C etc. this was the original, just plain Loran, housed in a 'black box'. To obtain your position it entailed counting the number of 'gates' at different settings and then transferring them to the chart. One didn't interrupt whoever was on watch at the time when they were working out the position and they lost count of the number of 'gates' they had counted. Your ancestry was called into question in no uncertain terms as it meant starting from scratch again.

Light aircraft were reasonably frequent 'visitors' on their delivery flights to the UK or Europe. Without exception there was always something not working - VHF but no HF or vice versa, no heating, no DF and so it went on. I remember one occasion when we were on Juliet when we were requested by Shanwick Oceanic Control to keep the ships navigation beacon on continuously and to keep a continuous radar watch on from a certain time. An aircraft being ferried to Europe via the UK had taken off from Gander and lost his radio compass before he had even reached the US Coast Guard cutter manning Ocean Station Charlie. They had 'brought' him over the top of them using their radar; set the radar beam in the direction of Juliet and guided the pilot as far as they could along the beam till out of range. We did likewise when he reached our part of the ocean, setting the beam in the direction of Shannon Airport in Ireland and guiding him along that until he passed out of range. In the meantime Shannon did the same when he got in range of them. He was lucky, he made it, crossing the Atlantic courtesy of three radars!

It was quite common not to see any ships apart from the ship you relieved and the ship relieving you until reaching the Clyde again. So any ship passing was a great event. I can remember the odd merchant ship, a Canadian anti-submarine frigate who got a trifle upset when we tried to raise him by radio as he wished to be incognito, a Russian 'RFA' waiting for a cruiser, three Russian destroyers, a Russian survey ship who was monitoring waves generated by depressions, and **HMS Hecate** an RN survey vessel.

The Russian survey ship was a converted deep sea trawler which stayed around us for 3-4 days. We exchanged cinema films, but I think they were the outright winners as they lent us god knows how many reels of the Russian Revolution, dramatised version, and needless to say all in Russian. They got the latest blockbuster and of course Bugs Bunny.

The greatest number of ships occurred one summer as part of an international oceanographic survey when we were on Juliet. There were survey ships up the yingyang all carrying out an intense programme of bathy soundings. We had embarked a RN party of Survey Recorders to carry out the soundings as we

wouldn't have been able to cope with doing that and the normal routine which still had to be adhered to. It was the only time that I saw a ship anchor in mid-Atlantic. The ship in question was an American survey vessel which had an enormous winch immediately in front of the bridge, the housing for which was the size of a house. We learnt that they broke the anchor cable on the foc'sle and then connected the winch cable to it before letting the anchor go - and they still had plenty of cable to spare. The UK Hydrographic Office had issued a 'Notice to Mariners' advising ships to stay clear of the area. Instead we never saw so many ships that trip as anyone crossing the Atlantic in either direction had to come for a look. The best was a Swedish merchantman with a deck cargo of timber stacked to a great height, a slight list to port, chugging eastwards at about 8-10 knots right through the middle of the assembled ships, trailing a plume of black smoke and not a soul in sight!

Occasionally we saw the odd maritime reconnaissance aircraft - a US Navy P-3 Orion or a RAF Shackleton. On one trip whilst on India we were visited by a Buccaneer from Lossiemouth which buzzed us a couple times before standing it on its tail and heading back home. It's quite good standing on the bridge wing with eyelevel about 40-45 feet above the water and looking down into the cockpit of a Shackleton as it thundered past! The only other time a Shackleton was seen was if the ship was at sea over Christmas when they dropped mail, goodies, newspapers and even the Christmas tree a few days before the big day.

For the Met staff there wasn't a lot of spare time during a trip because of the extensive programme to be carried out. If you weren't on watch, then you were sleeping or getting ready to go on watch! But there was still time for the Mess competitions - darts, whist, crib, bridge and of course Uckers!! There was a

Admiral Fitzroy (ex-Weather Monitor, ex-Pevensey Castle) - clearly recognisable from her hull lines as a Castle class corvette.
(Ben Warlow Collection)

library on board, and even time to study. Whist was played most of the time regardless if it was as part of the Mess competition or not. Games usually started around the mid-morning 'smoko' and lasted well into the evening. Players changed as the watches changed. Film shows were run twice a week in each mess. And there was always the BBC World Service.

Although you knew what date it was, you lost track of what day it was. The only reason you knew it was Sunday was because of the tot of neaters issued in the forenoon and that it was always roast chicken for Sunday lunch! Very occasionally the Cook threw everybody by serving roast chicken mid-week, and then you were totally confused.

I've seen the North Atlantic in all its moods, from flat calm to standing in the wheelhouse and looking up to the crest of the waves. I've sailed through two 'official' hurricanes, the first of which was a trifle draughty to say the least! For the second one we were on India and the ship on Juliet took a hammering whilst we just managed a Gale Force 8! We felt a bit embarrassed when both ships received a 'well done' signal for maintaining the programme from the Director General of the Met Office. However, that was more than made up by the numerous occasions when we had to contend with the infamous 'deep Atlantic depression' of the BBC Shipping Forecast and no slaps on the back, except of cold water!

All that venture before the mast know seamen are great practical jokers. Halfway through my first trip as we wrapped up from the midday upper air sounding, the duty Supervisor asked me to go down to the engine room and ask for the 'long wait'. He had forgotten that I had already spent seven months at sea, a big mistake. I remained po-faced and duly presented myself to the Second Engineer for the 'long wait.' The conversation went along the lines of "I've been sent down for the long wait, so and so has forgotten that this isn't my first trip to sea and as you have been saying come down for a guided tour, here I am". For the next 45 minutes or so I had a great time clambering around first of all the boiler room, which only took a couple of minutes, and then learning the intricacies of the innermost workings of the triple expansion steam reciprocating engine in the engine room itself. After about 45 minutes the Supervisor came to the engine room entrance and yelled down and asked if everything was OK. Very po-faced again the reply was that it wasn't 'as some sod had nicked the 'wait' and we couldn't find it". Twenty or so minutes later, on completion of my guided tour, I returned to the upper levels, feeling quite pleased with myself.

Section Three
SHIPS' HISTORIES

SHIPS' HISTORIES

Tabulated data on ships' voyages is derived from the Pink List, the listing of Ship and Convoy Dispositions and from the Ship Movement Orders. The former are included in the Public Record Office (PRO), Greenwich, ADM187/30-49 series and the ADM199/1719 series of files (the latter cover the period from 08/01/44 to 31/01/45 and provide information of the sea locations of the Escort Groups). The Ship Movement Orders belong to a different series of files to be found in the Royal Navy Museum Library, Portsmouth and also in the library of the Maritime Museum, Greenwich. As may be expected the three series of records were not necessarily consistent one with the other. Where there has been a conflict the entries consistent with the Senior Officer Escort Group Reports of Proceedings have been used. These however could not always be traced if the name of the Senior Officer's ship was not known.

A fourth useful source of information was provided by the detailed listing of convoys in Arnold Hague's book *The Allied Convoy System 1939-1945*. By comparing the dates of sailing and arrival of individual convoys with those of individual ships it was frequently possible to match escorts with convoys. Where there is doubt as to the accuracy of any entry in the ship history tabulations, this is placed in parentheses. Both time, distance and cost placed restrictions on the resources that could be expended on researching the PRO files. As a result there are gaps in the accounts of the ships voyages. This applies particularly to the voyages of the Canadian Navy Castle Class Corvettes. Only a few records of these are available at the PRO and the files of the Directorate of History and Heritage, National Defence Headquarters, Ottawa, are difficult to access and copy.

The Ship Movement Orders provide details of the date when a ship left a port. Sometimes supplementary information was provided in the form of a brief summary of a signal indicating the state of readiness or intended sailing of the ship in question. These extracts are frequently the source of the remarks given under the 'Notes' heading in the Ship History tabulations.

Common abbreviations used were:-

AM	Admiralty (sometimes only A was used)
C.in C. W.A.	Commanding Officer in Chief Western Approaches.
F.O.I.C	Flag Officer in Command
F.O.G.M.A	Flag Officer Gibraltar and Mediterranean Approaches.
N.O.I.C	Naval Officer in Command
ETA	Estimated Time of Arrival
ETD	Estimated Time of departure

The Time of Origin (TOO) of a signal usually took the form of 101619/9 indicating that the signal was originated at 1619 on the tenth of September

HMS ALLINGTON CASTLE

Battle Honours
Atlantic 1944-45   Arctic 1944-45

*HMS Allington Castle taken from a Swordfish from **Campania** during a 1944 Convoy run to Gibraltar.*

(Lt D. Harris)

HMS *Allington Castle* was originally allocated to the B3 Escort Group and continued with that Group escorting convoys to and from Gibraltar/UK until the end of August 1944 when she was transferred to the 7th Escort Group for Russian Convoy duties. She made five round trips to and from Kola Inlet with that Group. She had a brief interlude with the B23 Escort Group between mid October and early November 1944. On the conclusion of the voyage with RA 65 *Allington Castle* was reduced to Reserve on 24/05/45 at Sheerness. In November 1945 she was allocated to the Fishery Protection Flotilla and based at Fleetwood. Her area of patrol stretched from the South Western Approaches to the UK northwards to Iceland. She reverted to reserve in 1947 and was scrapped in 1958/59.

Details of her wartime voyages are given below, but a description of her voyages with the 7th Escort Group are given under the heading of that Group

Allington Castle formed part of the escort for 12 convoys of which eight were in the JW/RA series, and four in the OSKMS/SLMKS series. She escorted a total of 403 merchant ships of which only five were lost, four from the Russian Convoys.

HISTORY

09.12.42	Ordered.
22.07.43	Laid down. **Builder:** Hull and Engine - Fleming & Ferguson (Paisley).
29.02.44	Launched.
19.06.44	Completed.

WARTIME VOYAGES

Date	ESG	Senior Officer	Convoy	No of Ships	Arrive/ Sail	Location	Notes
26.06.44	EG B3	*Towy*			Arv	Paisley	
30.06.44	EG B3	*Towy*			Arv	Tobermory	
16.07.44	EG B3	*Towy*			Sail	Tobermory	
17.07.44	EG B3	*Towy*			Arv	Larne	
17.07.44	EG B3	*Towy*			Sail	Larne	
23.07.44	EG B3	*Towy*			Arv	Clyde	
01.08.44					Arv	Londonderry	
02.08.44	EG B3	*Tintagel Castle*	OS 85/ KMS 59	34	Sail	Londonderry	
03.08.44	EG B3	*Tintagel Castle*	OS 85/ KMS 59	34		5528N 1107W	
13.08.44	EG B3	*Tintagel Castle*	OS 85/	34	Arv	Gibraltar	
19.08.44	EG B3	*Tintagel Castle*	SL 167/ MKS 58	36	Sail	Gibraltar	
19.08.44	EG B3	*Tintagel Castle*	SL 167/ MKS 58	36		3540N 0643W	260139/8 - *AC* has slight fire damage
27.08.44	EG B3	*Tintagel Castle*	SL 167/ MKS 58	33		5009N 0652W	
30.08.44	EG B3	*Tintagel Castle*	SL 167/ MKS 58	33	Arv	Clyde	
07.09.44	7th EG	*Cygnet*			Arv	Clyde	
13.09.44	7th EG	*Cygnet*			Arv	Aultbea	For JW 60
15.09.44	7th EG	*Cygnet*	JW 60	31	Sail	Aultbea	Joined 7th Escort Group on Russian Convoy duty arriving Kola Inlet 24.09.44 (SMO)
18.09.44	7th EG	*Cygnet*	JW 60	31		6738N 0201W	
22.09.44	7th EG	*Cygnet*	JW 60	31		7256N 3315E	
24.09.44	7th EG	*Cygnet*	JW 60	31	Arv	Kola Inlet	
28.09.44	7th EG	*Cygnet*	RA 60	32	Sail	Kola Inlet	
01.10.44	7th EG	*Cygnet*	RA 60	32		7155N 0403E	
04.10.44	7th EG	*Cygnet*	RA 60	32		N of Minches	
05.10.44	7th EG	*Cygnet*			Arv	Clyde	
13.10.44	EG B23	*Fowey*	OS92/ KMS66	34	Sail	Clyde	Convoy OS 92/KMS 66 B 23 Escort group. Convoy included LCTs. On 18.10.44 *AC* involved in heavy weather rescuing person

Date	ESG	Senior Officer	Convoy	No of Ships	Arrive/ Sail	Location	Notes
							nel from L.C.Ts. On 20th standing by **SS Lagarto**. **AC** lost one man over board.
15.10.44	EG B23	*Fowey*				At Clyde	
18.10.44	EG B23	*Fowey*	OS 92/ KMS 66	38		5025N 10007W	
23.10.44	EG B23	*Fowey*	OS 92/ KMS 66	34		4110N 1202W	
26.10.44	EG B23	*Fowey*	OS92/	36	Arv	Gibraltar	
30.10.44	EG B23	*Fowey*	SL174/ MKS65	44	Sail	Gibraltar	
08.11.44	EG B23	*Fowey*	SL 174/ MKS65	44	Arv	Clyde	
27.11.44	7th EG	**Cygnet**				At Clyde	
28.11.44	7th EG	**Cygnet**	JW 62	38	Arv	Aultbea	
29.11.44	7th EG	**Cygnet**	JW 62	38	Sail	Aultbea	
05.12.44	7th EG	**Cygnet**	JW 62	31		7240N 3120E	
10.12.44	7th EG	**Cygnet**	RA 62	29	Sail	Kola Inlet	
12.12.44	7th EG	**Cygnet**	RA 62	30		7148N 1832E	
20.12.44	7th EG	**Cygnet**			Arv	Clyde	
28.12.44	7th EG	**Cygnet**	JW 63	38	Sail	Clyde	
01.01.45	7th EG	**Cygnet**	JW 63	37		At Sea	
01.01.45	7th EG	**Cygnet**	JW 63	37		6301N 0310W	
06.01.45	7th EG	**Cygnet**	JW 63	37		7235N 3210E	
08.01.45	7th EG	**Cygnet**	JW 63	38	Arv	Kola Inlet	
11.01.45	7th EG	**Cygnet**	RA 63	31	Sail	Kola Inlet	
15.01.45	7th EG	**Cygnet**	RA 63	29		6745N 0450E	
18.01.45	7th EG	**Cygnet**	RA 63	30		6220N 0510W	
20.01.45	7th EG	**Cygnet**	RA 63	30	Arv	Faroes	
24.01.45	7th EG	**Cygnet**	RA 63	30	Sail	Faroes	
27.01.45	7th EG	**Cygnet**	RA 63	30	Arv	Clyde	
09.02.45					Sail	Clyde	Escorting **Ranagar**: Foi/c Glasgow 291181A. **AC** is being taken in hand today 29.1 by Messrs D&W Henderson
11.02.45	7th EG	**Cygnet**			Arv	Barrow	
13.02.45	7th EG	**Cygnet**			Arv	Clyde	
14.02.45	7th EG	**Cygnet**			Arv	Rothesay	
11.03.45	7th EG	**Cygnet**	JW 65	26	Sail	Clyde	

Date	ESG	Senior Officer	Convoy	No of Ships	Arrive/ Sail	Location	Notes
20.03.45	7th EG	*Cygnet*	JW 65	26	Arv	Kola Inlet	
23.03.45	7th EG	*Cygnet*	RA 65	26	Sail	Kola Inlet	
01.04.45	7th EG	*Cygnet*	RA 65	26	Arv	Clyde	
19.04.45	7th EG	*Cygnet*			Sail	Scapa Flow-	
20.04.45	7th EG	*Cygnet*			Arv	Clyde	
26.04.45	7th EG	*Cygnet*			Arv	Milford Haven	
02.05.45	7th EG	*Cygnet*			Sail	Milford Haven	
10.05.45	7th EG	*Cygnet*			Arv	Clyde	
15.05.45	7th EG	*Cygnet*			Arv	Clyde-	
24.05.45	SAR				Arv	Sheerness	1801/1946 FOCRF *AC* has been accepted into Reserve Fleet Cat A 25.6
22.06.45					Reserve	Sheerness	
09.11.45						Dover	AM 092101/11 *AC* is allocated to Fishery Protection Flotilla & is to be brought forward and manned as soon as practicable
20.01.46					Arv	Portland	202354z/1 CinC Nore 161606/1 *AC* sail a 18.1 to Dover
24.01.46					Arv	Swansea	242100/1 *AC* 182215/1 Intend to proceed 19/1 to Swansea
28.01.46					Arv	Pembroke Dock	281925/1 SOFP *Stork* 241121Z/1 Intend *AC* to arrive Chatham 1 March
02.02.46					Arv	Fleetwood	021019/2 *AC* 270950/1 Intend proceeding to Milford Haven 28/1 enter 28/1
13.02.46							Capt. Supt Pembroke Dock 13/0635Z *AC* should arrive 27.2 at Pembroke Dock. SOFP. 170941/2 Intend *AC* to arrive Belfast returning Fleetwood 22.2 arv Pembroke Dock 27.2

Date	ESG	Senior Officer	Convoy	No of Ships	Arrive/ Sail	Location	Notes
15.02.46					Arv	Fleetwood	161042/2 *AC* 300945Z/1. Intend proceeding 30/1 to patrol Outer Fastnet Fishing ground thence Fleetwood ETA 3/2
18.02.46							*AC* 181330/2 Proceeding on Patrol ETA Belfast now 21.2
20.02.46					Arv	Belfast	201147/2 010952/2 ETA Fleetwood 1000/2.2
22.02.46							*AC* ETA Pike Lighthouse 1130/20.2
25.02.46							*AC* 22 1111/2 Intend proceeding 2100/23.2 to Fleetwood ETA 1600 24.2
25.02.46							*AC* 25 0921/25 Intend proceeding 0600/26.2 to Milford Haven ETA 0900 27.2
27.02.46					Arv	Pembroke Dock	270943Z/2 *AC* 091800/2 Intend patrol N Irish Sea area ETA Fleetwood 1000/15.2

1947 - 1958	Reserve Fleet at Harwich and West Hartlepool.
08.49	Completed refit at Tyne.
1958	Sold to T. Young.
20.12.58	Arrived Sunderland for scrapping.

Between convoys RA 60 and JW 62 *Allington Castle* was attached to the B23 Escort Group, escorting convoy OS92/KMS 66. The convoy, to Gibraltar, encountered severe weather in the Western Approaches. *Allington Castle* was heavily involved in rescuing crews of LCTs that were being towed by Merchant Ships in the convoy. Her Commanding Officer's account of the episode follows.

HMS ALLINGTON CASTLE
SO B23
26TH OCTOBER 1944

Sir,

1. I have the honour to submit the following report of proceedings during the time that *HMS Allington Castle* was absent from the close screen of convoy OS 92/KMS 66.

2. On being ordered to proceed to the assistance of *HMS Knaresborough Castle*, standing by *LCT 488*, course and speed were altered at 1050/18 to close her. At 1230, having been led astray, by chasing radar wave echoes, W/T homing bearings put her on the port beam and she was closed and sighted at 13004/18 distant six miles.

3. Having worked up to windward of *Knaresborough Castle* at 11 knots course was altered to run with wind and sea, wind, West, Force 8, sea and swell West 67 and speed was increased to 13 knots at 1330A. Hands were working on the quarterdeck at this time securing depth charges and preparing a grass line for use in rescue work.

4. At 1346A, position estimated as 50°33'N 09°22'W (approx) a large sea came on board aft over each quar-

HMS Allington Castle on Fishery Protection duties, Fleetwood 1946.   *(CCC(F)A Archives)*

ter and four hands were washed overboard. Two of them managed to hold on to a bight of the grass line with which they were working and were immediately recovered - O/Seaman Barnes D. C/JX 549647 and AB Heady R. W. C/JX 406489 were swept straight overboard. A life-buoy with flare quickly followed them, landing within 20 yards and the ship was turned about.

5.   The ship was stopped close to the men at 1350A but was making more leeway, than had been allowed for and although she was within line-throwing distance of them soon drifted away. A Carley float was dropped to within 30 yards of them. Both men were swimming, Heady had removed all his clothing except a singlet and also his lifebelt. Barnes was still wearing all his clothing including a heavy sheepskin coat.

6.   While turning into wind it was noticed that Barnes' face was down and he appeared to be drowning. At 1403A the ship was again close but to windward this time of the men and Barnes' body came alongside, the top of his head breaking surface. Although he could be seen from the bridge he was not so easily visible from the main deck and the rescue parties were unable to get hold of him before his body drifted astern, not to be sighted again.

7.   Heady, however, was recovered at 1406A and appeared none the worse for the experience. After searching for Barnes' body without success course and speed were resumed to overtake *Knaresborough Castle*. Convoy ON 260 sighted ahead, and on confirming from *Knaresborough Castle* that she did not require assistance, course was altered at 1430A to proceed to the assistance of *LCT 491*. The purport of your 181424A was passed to *HMS Manners* at 1530 and to *HMS Highland* at 1540A.

8.   Three Merchant vessels were sighted at about 1850A and on being asked their pendants the *SS City of Lyons*, after enquiring as to whether it was an escort vessel signalling, made SOS by V/S and a red Very Light was sighted near to her. Course was altered to close and speed increased. *City of Lyons* reported that LCT astern of her had abandoned ship. At 1922A a white buoy and light in the water near to the *City of Lyons* was closed but nothing was attached to it. Two dim red lights one over the other were sighted at 1935A and on closing and illuminating this was shown to be a raft definitely "Not under command" containing survivors. The LC. was sighted close to, listing heavily, foredeck half submerged. Three Officers and 16 ratings, full crew of *LCT 480* were picked up from the raft, in which they had spent two hours.

9.   Having sunk *LCT 480* by gun fire at 2040A course and speed altered to home on Tug standing by *LCT 7014*. *LCT 480* sunk in approx. Lat 50°20'N Long 09°31'W. At 2130A sighted convoy ON 260 ahead once more and hove to on closing them to inform *HMS Manners* by V/S that LCT had been sunk ahead of convoy and that all survivors had been picked up. Inquired from *HMS Highlander* as to position of Tug and *LCT 7014*. On learning that they were ten miles astern of convoy continued to home onto them until informed by signal from Tug at 0015A that *LCT 7014* had sunk then altered course to proceed to assistance of *SS Badjestan* who was standing by LCT in distress, speed 11 to 14 knots as weather permitted and commenced homing *HMS Tobago* by W/T. The loom of a white light was sighted on the port beam at 0215A and course was altered to close at 15 knots.

10. W/T communication with *SS Badjestan* confirmed that she was ship ahead and that LCT was still afloat. *LCT 491* was sighted and closed at 0310A and an endeavour was made to tow a Carley float on a grass line into position so that LCT would drop alongside it. This proved too difficult to accomplish in the dark and it was considered that the sea which was running, the LCT may lose men overboard in attempting to lay hold of a line or float. Wind NW 7 Sea and Swell 5.7.

11. It was decided to lay alongside the LCT and at 0330A ship was stopped close to craft to recover Carley float

and observe relative drift of ship and LCT. **SS Badjestan** steamed up to windward to lay oil slick. When she was in position and the float recovered at 0417A proceeded to go alongside weather side of LCT. The ship dropped alongside from close to windward spreading oil fuel from quarter and lay alongside the starboard quarter of the LCT, the craft's Oerlikon platform abreast the ships port forward scrambling net, the stern just forward of the ships compass platform.

12. Ship and craft were rolling heavily but only touching on the roll. No damage would have been suffered by **Allington Castle** had not one rating in the LCT refused to jump or lay hold of the scrambling net. He made no effort whatsoever to save himself and appeared stupefied. The ship was brought close alongside so that the flare of the bow overhung the craft and as the ship rolled heavily towards the craft, the rescue party on the forecastle lay hold of him and picked him off. He was found to smell strongly of alcohol and a bottle containing white rum was found on his person. Both the ship and the rating were slightly damaged by this manoeuvre. The ship receiving a hole about one foot square in the shell above the main deck, the frame damaged in the way of the hole and two punctured dents. The rating was badly crushed and it is suspected that his pelvis is fractured.

13. All the ships company of **LCT 491** three Officers and 16 ratings were on board by 0440A and on clearing the wreck it was sunk in approximate position Lat 50°12'N Long 09°11'W by gunfire and Squid at 0540A/19. Course was set to re-join convoy at best possible speed. A section of ON 260 was sighted at dawn and three stragglers from that convoy well to the southward were directed to re-join. The position course and speed of OS 92/KMS 66 were passed to **PT 23** at 1010A and at 1325A the convoy was sighted and position 'Sugar' taken up.

14. In close company with the convoy until 0958/20 at which time proceed to stand by **PT 34** hove to astern of convoy with shifted cargo and one lifeboat gone, **PT 32** with steering gear broken down and steering by hand reported that no assistance was required and an closing **PT 64** at 1150/20 he also required no assistance. It was found very difficult to steer convoy course or reciprocal without damage. Wind NW force 7 sea and swell 57.

15. At 1600A/20 hove to securing Depth Charges which had broken adrift, orders were received by signal to proceed to the assistance of **PT 18**. Course was altered to home on to **PT 43** by W/T at best possible speed when all was secured at 1655A/20. V/S contact was made with **PT 42** at 1820A/20 and it was confirmed that **PT 18** had passed close to steaming at 8 knots down wind. W/T contact was established with **PT 18** at about 1900A/20 and homed on to her. Rockets, which she had been instructed to fire, were sighted at about 1940A/20 and the ship herself was sighted at about 20001/20.

16. The **SS Lagarto** was not in great distress but the starboard side of her bridge was stove in, her compasses damaged or carried away, the starboard bulwark on fore deck stove in, all lifeboats damaged or carried away; a launch carried on deck cargo on the fore dock had shifted and she had lost one man overboard. Oil was laid ahead of her until daylight and she maintained the same course reducing speed to four knots at 0937/21 by stopping one engine. W/T contact had been made with **HMS Drury** at about 0130A/21 and had commenced homing her at about 0200A/21.

17. **SS Lagarto** reported that his deck cargo was secured and that he could heave to at 1353A/21 and at 1400 she hove to, oil being spread to windward for her. **HMS Drury** was sighted at 1710A/21 and the **SS Lagarto** turned over to her. Course was then set to re-join convoy at best possible speed.

18. At 0915A/22 stragglers were met with and formed up into four columns. Thirteen ships were gathered in, one straggler well astern, and we were formed up by 1100A/22. **HMS Knaresborough Castle** and **HMS Trident** were sighted astern at 1200A/22. The stragglers section re-joined at about 17350A/22 and **Allington**

Castle re-joined the screen and closed *HMS Fowey* to transfer Medical Officer to attend injured survivor.

I am, Sir, your obedient Servant,

(Sgd) P. A. READ.
Lieut. Cdr. RNR

In ADM 199/317 it is minuted that approval had been given for a Letter of Praise be sent to the Master of *SS Badjestan.* The Senior Officer of the Group concluded his report with the following observation:-

General Remarks.

Escort Group B23 consisting of only three ships, *HM Ships Fowey*, *Allington Castle* and *Knaresborough Castle*, recently formed, and operating together for the first time. Events during the voyage very definitely proved that three ships are inadequate when escorting a convoy of the dimensions of KMS 66/OS 92, which consisted of no less than 35 merchant ships, 3 HM Submarines and 9 Tank Landing Craft in tow. Although the likelihood of submarine attack is much smaller than formerly, risk of such attacks must still be deemed to exist, and it was impossible to afford anything remotely resembling an anti-submarine screen with this small number of escorts. Furthermore the fact of other emergencies arising such as heavy weather, scattered convoy, casualties and heavy weather damage, ships requiring urgent assistance and medical assistance, must not be overlooked. All the above occurred during the voyage and it was most obvious that the Group was all too pitifully small to cope with the situation. Had there been more escorts present, much needless loss of life from the LCT's could have been prevented. It is therefore strongly urged that in future no Escort Group consist of less than five ships, and that more than one ship in the Group should carry a Medical Officer.

(Sgd.) G.E. NEWEY
Lieutenant Commander R.N.R,
Senior Officer B 23 Escort Group

The passage of RA 63 was characterised by severe gales almost from the day that it left Kola Inlet on 11 January 1945. The storms culminated, reaching Force 12 with wind speeds recorded as high as 80 knots. The convoy and escorts became widely scattered, with the convoy running southward before the wind, whilst many of the escorts, excluding *Allington Castle* hove to. On 15 January *Allington Castle* reported the loss of one man overboard. D. Beckett, who was an AB on *Allington Castle* at the time, wrote:

> *"The White watch was piped to assemble on the quarterdeck to secure Foxer displacers that had come adrift. I arrived on the quarterdeck and, with the rest of the duty watch and under the directions from a leading seaman, we started to secure the displacers.*
> *While we were doing this I noticed that the bos'n and the cox'n were on the quarterdeck, hands behind their backs, riding the ship's movement. Suddenly there was an urgent yell from the leading hand "Hang on". I grabbed some part of the displacer and looked along the starboard side of the ship and saw a huge wall of water about to hit us. The ship rolled heavily. When we returned to an even keel there was a shout of "Man Overboard!" from the cox'n. He and the bos'n had together been thrown over to the port side. The cox'n had managed to grab hold of something but the bos'n had gone over*

the side. On hearing the shout from the cox'n I looked astern and there was a little red light going up on top of a wave as we went down into the trough. Then the red light went down as we went up. This was repeated once more and then the light vanished and the bos'n was gone. The rest of the voyage was completed in a state of utter disbelief at the loss of PO Lawrence."

As the weather improved all ships were directed to the Faeroe Islands. Unfortunately they arrived there in a severe blizzard, with visibility reduced to one cable. Only eighteen ships were able to anchor in Nalso Fjord. One ship, **SS Fort Highfield**, elected to stay at sea all night. The following morning she reported that she had been in collision (it was suspected that she had in fact probably grounded). However, she was still underway and **Allington Castle** was sent to her assistance and guided her to an anchorage to the eastward of Thorshaven.

Attention was then diverted to **SS Longwood** who, anchored 6 miles from the Burin Light, reported that she could not start her main engines. Repairs would take four days. It was appreciated that should the wind blow hard from the east, the ship was in danger of dragging onto a lea shore.

Attempts to tow her to a safe anchorage failed and she re-anchored not far from her original anchorage. Fears for the crews safety rose because of the weather conditions and the threat from U-boats so it was decided to remove them. Two trawlers failed to go alongside, one of them having to return to harbour with a damaged rudder. During the night **Allington Castle** made repeated attempts to go alongside but was prevented from doing so by the sea conditions. Recalling the incident J. C. Montier, who was a signalman at the time wrote:

"My job was to train the 10-inch signal lamp down the side of the tanker. I was sitting on the gunwale with one of the hands hanging onto my legs as I directed the lamp. We were rolling quite bit and if we had come into contact, I am sure that the damage would have been extensive and my own position was somewhat precarious. It was also very cold."

The next day in calmer weather **SS Longwood**'s crew left their ship by their own boats. They were picked up and carried to safety.

Allington Castle and **Alnwick Castle** were detailed to protect and remain in support of the **Longwood** pending the arrival of a rescue tug and then to escort her to the UK. This was done without further incident.

HMS ALNWICK CASTLE

Battle Honours
Atlantic 1945   Arctic 1945

HMS Alnwick Castle seen just days after completion in November 1944.   (MoD/Crown Copyright)

Having taken longer to build than most ships of her class, she joined the 8th Escort Group on 23 December 1944. The Group was on loan from the Western Approaches Command to the Home Fleet for North Russian escort duties. *Alnwick Castle* formed part of the escort for the JW/RA 63, 64, 65 and 66 series of convoys. A total of 236 ships were escorted of which four were sunk by enemy action. On 17 February 1945 she shared with *HMS Lark* in the sinking of *U-425* at the entrance to the Kola Inlet. Several days later she was largely instrumental in detecting and driving off a torpedo bombing attack on convoy RA 64.

Alnwick Castle remained in reserve from late May

HISTORY

19.01.43	Ordered.
12.06.43	Laid down. **Builder:** Hull - G Brown (Greenock); Engine - J. Kincaid (Greenock).
23.05.44	Launched.
11.11.44	Completed.

WARTIME VOYAGES

Date	ESG	Senior Officer	Convoy	No of Ships	Arrive/ Sail	Location	Notes
05.12.44	Unall				Arv	Tobermory	
15.12.44	8th EG	*Lark*				Tobermory	
23.12.44	8th EG	*Lark*			Sail	Tobermory	
24.12.44	8th EG	*Lark*			Arv	Greenock	
29.12.44	8th EG	*Lark*	JW 63	38	Arv	Aultbea	
30.12.44	8th EG	*Lark*	JW 63	38	Sail	Aultbea	
01.01.45	8th EG	*Lark*	JW 63	37		6301N 0310W	
01.01.45	8th EG	*Lark*	JW 63	37		At Sea	
06.01.45	8th EG	*Lark*	JW 63	37		7235N 3210E	
08.01.45	8th EG	*Lark*	JW 63	38	Arv	Kola Inlet	
11.01.45	8th EG	*Lark*	RA 63	31	Sail	Kola Inlet	There is some uncertainty to which EG she had been attached for this return voyage
15.01.45	7th EG	*Cygnet*	RA 63	29		6745N 0450E	
18.01.45	8th EG	*Lark*	RA 63	29	Arv	Faroes	
18.01.45	8th EG	*Lark*	RA 63	30		6220N 0510W	
24.01.45	8th EG	*Lark*	RA 63	30	Sail	Faroes	
27.01.45	8th EG	*Lark*	RA 63	30	Arv	Clyde	
04.02.45	7th EG	*Cygnet*	JW 64	29	Sail	Scapa	
13.02.45	7th EG	*Cygnet*	JW 64	29	Arv	Kola Inlet	16/17th Feb 7th & 8th Escort Groups carried out A/S sweeps in approaches to Kola Inlet prior to the sailing of RA 64. *AC* sank *U-425* & picked up the sole survivor.
17.02.45	7th EG	*Cygnet*	RA 64	33	Sail	Kola Inlet	
01.03.45	7th EG	*Cygnet*	RA 64	31	Arv	Clyde	
11.03.45	7th EG	*Cygnet*	JW 65	26	Sail	Clyde	
20.03.45	7th EG	*Cygnet*	JW 65	26	Arv	Kola Inlet	
23.03.45	7th EG	*Cygnet*	RA 65	26	Sail	Kola Inlet	
01.04.45	7th EG	*Cygnet*	RA 65	26	Arv	Clyde	
16.04.45	7th EG	*Cygnet*	JW 66	27	Sail	Clyde	
27.04.45	7th EG	*Cygnet*	JW 66	27	Arv	Kola Inlet	
29.04.45	7th EG	*Cygnet*	RA 66	26	Sail	Kola Inlet	
24.05.45	SAR				Arv	Sheerness	AM 171753B *AC* has been ordered to reduce to category C forthwith
24.05.45					Arv	Sheerness	FO RF.271641/6 *AC* has been accepted into Reserve Fleet Cat B 25.6

December 1958   Sold to J.J. King and arrived Gateshead for scrapping.

HMS Alnwick Castle laid up at Harwich as part of the Reserve Fleet from 1953. *HMS Dumbarton Castle* can be seen astern.
(*Ben Warlow Collection*)

ACTION WITH U-425

AN EXTRACT FROM THE REPORT BY THE SENIOR OFFICER, 7th ESCORT GROUP HMS CYGNET

3RD MARCH 1945

SECTION II: ENCOUNTER WITH THE ENEMY (ALL TIME ZONE 1).

3.   Sinking of German U-Boat by *HM Ships Lark* and *Alnwick Castle*.

On the night of 16/17 February, ships of the 7th and 8th Escort Groups were employed in carrying out an A/S search in the approaches to Kola Inlet prior to the sailing of RA 64.

Ships were disposed in line abreast in the order *Lapwing*, *Bamborough Castle*, *Cygnet* (SO), *Alnwick Castle* and *Lark* from left to right 2,000 yards apart, course 280 degrees, speed 10 knots, carrying out zigzag No.45. Visibility was good, wind WSW force 3, no swell. Escorts had unifoxers streamed, and apart from their slight interference, Asdic conditions were good.

At 0016 *Lark* reported on TSB that she was investigating an Asdic contact on her starboard side, and since it was classified as 'firm' at 1,200 yards *Alnwick Castle* was ordered to join her, and the remainder of the Group turned 180 degrees. *Lark* passed ranges and bearings to *Alnwick Castle* until the latter reported firm contact at 0043. *Lark* not being fitted with ATW or Type 147, wisely ordered her consort to attack with squid and a pattern was fired at 0059.

Meanwhile *Cygnet*, *Lapwing* and *Bamborough Castle* were forming up to carry out operation Observant, sides North and South, but using 3 mile legs so as to minimize interference by unifoxers to the attacking ships.

At 0101 *Lark* reported her Asdic set out of action, so *Bamborough Castle* was ordered to join *Alnwick Castle*. This was cancelled at 0109 when *Lark* reported her Asdics fit for action again. three minutes later *Alnwick Castle* reported lost contact, and commenced Observant on a datum course of 240 degrees, round the calcium flare dropped on her Squid pattern. *Lark* reported she had regained contact at a range of 800 yards at 0017, followed almost immediately by the report "Submarine in sight bearing 110 degrees". Starshell were first sighted, and then a lively encounter witnessed when both *Lark* and *Alnwick Castle* engaged the U-boat with 4-inch guns, close range weapons, a pattern of Squid set shallow, and Port D/C thrower. During the action the U-boat was observed to fire a red and green coloured cartridge.

From: The Commanding Officer,
HMS Alnwick Castle.

Date: 19th February, 1945.
Ref: No. AC 145.

To: The Senior Officer, 7th Escort Group

REPORT OF PROCEEDINGS (All times GMT)

On the night of 16 February, 1945, whilst on sweep off Kola Inlet, ships in company *Cygnet* (EG 7 SO), *Lark*, *Lapwing*, *Bamborough Castle*. Course of sweep 280°. *Alnwick Castle* being one mile on *Lark*'s Port Beam, Unifoxers streamed. At 2315 *Lark* gained contact and *Alnwick Castle* was ordered by Senior Officer to join her. *Alnwick Castle* turned towards, and reduced to 8 knots and gained contact at 2340, ran over, confirmed contact was submarine and, at 2359, attacked with Squid; depth of submarine by 147, 40 feet. Contact was lost in run out. *Alnwick Castle* turned and steered course as advised by plot, no contacts gained, and about to commence Observant round last known position of submarine, when, at 0017 on 17 February 1945, radar reported small echo bearing 001° at 1100 yards. *HM Ship* increased to full speed to close, illuminated the target with rocket projectors, and engaged with close range weapons and 4-inch gun. Hits on the conning tower obtained by bridge Oerlikon, but no hits by 4-inch observed. A pattern of Squid set to 20 feet was fired by eye, but fell short by about 50 yards. *Lark* crossed ahead firing at submarine; cease fire ordered. When within 100 yards of submarine searchlight was switched on and depth charge from port thrower fired which fell about 10 to 15 yards short, but in line. Conning tower was observed to be very badly damaged and crew abandoning, and many were in the water shouting. Submarine was observed to sink, stern first, at 0036, bows coming out of the water.

   Alnwick Castle closed position to pick up survivors, boat being lowered, but only one survivor was found, it is considered that extreme cold overcame the remainder before they were reached.

   HM Ship then rejoined group to continue sweep. On passing over area at daylight, the Senior Officer reported seeing oil and one corpse in rubber dinghy.

Sgd   H. A. Stonehouse
Lieutenant Commander RNR
Source : ADM 199/759 page 121

Recalling the voyages to Russia, Frank Fiddler who was a quartermaster on *Alnwick Castle* wrote:-

During the great gale experienced on the homeward passage with RA 64, the ship's steering failed and we feared that we would be driven on to the Norwegian coast. However, the fault was repaired in time and we did not have to steer by hand from the tiller flat.

Comforts
The Women's Guild of South Africa supplied us a good supply of socks, gloves and balaclavas all of which they had knitted. Letters of good wishes were often found in these comforts.
`Those of us who had to go on watch on the upper deck frequently shared coats. The one going off watch handing his coat over to his 'oppo' coming on watch - such was the comradeship on the Alnwick Castle.

Hammocks and Rum
One could not sling a hammock at sea, but made do sleeping on the deck or mess lockers or anywhere where you could jam yourself against a bulkhead or table. In our mess we did have a couple of men who could not face sleeping down below in the messdeck once we left harbour. They would find a cubby hole for the whole trip. They had both seen action in the Mediterranean and Atlantic. One reported sick whilst on leave and was sent to a mental home to recover from his ordeal and then discharged.

Beards
On each trip a sweep was run; 6d a time in the hat. The winner was the one who had grown the best

set and scooped the kitty. On the first trip, the Captain won it with a wonderful ginger set. He never shaved it off. My 'oppo' and I used to rub Vaseline hair tonic on our chins, hoping to make the beard grow.

Washing
The bathroom was closed at sea to save water, but opened for an hour one evening a week. We got over this by acquiring a bucket. One did one's dhobying, wash down and then got someone to tip the bucket over you for a shower, all with the one bucket full. Then dry off with a wrung out flannel then a towel.

Sinking the U-425
My action station was Quartermaster with the Coxswain. It was 16 February 1945. First watch, and just as we went into the middle watch I mentioned to the Coxswain "The 17th now, my birthday, 19 years old." Two years had gone by so quickly since I joined the Andrew.

*We had Asdic contact - "Steer by Asdic." - "Fire Squid." We heard Asdic report 'Lost contact' then Radar reported 'Target on the surface'. The next order from the bridge was 'Double Full Ahead!' Coxswain said "We will most likely ram it." Then the next order was 'hard a starboard' We had fired the Squid again while **U-425** was on the surface but not a hit this time. We opened the steel doors in the wheelhouse and on looking out there was the **U-425** on the surface, a star shell was fired and the search light and Aldis lamp played on her. The crew on the U-Boat were lined up very orderly on their upper deck and an officer had a white flare burning. The crew had their hands up in surrender. We were so close it was as if we and them were making a film. Our Oerlikon guns were firing to keep them away from their guns and the U-Boat crew were kicking the tracer shells off the casing. They seemed to be welding themselves to the deck.*

I was told to leave the wheel and give a hand on the deck. I now had a ring-side view. The U-Boat was now sinking so they jumped into the water. A killick gave an order for another man and myself to release the scramble net aft. After doing this the German survivors were drifting past us shouting. In the meantime Lt McInnes took away the sea boat to pick up survivors. The sea boat returned with one. The survivor, Herbert Lochner, was carried down to the sick bay where our SBA, Lawrence Robinson, cut off his clothing and after massaging the body he came to life.

My job after doing a spell at the wheel was to walk the prisoner on the upper deck for fresh air.

*Much later Herbert Lochner placed a 'Where are you?' advert in the Navy News seeking contact with ex-crew members of the **Alnwick Castle**. After much thought I responded, but my letter arrived just after he died from a heart attack. However, a correspondence developed with his wife and his son and I was invited to met them at Meissen. Out of this I was made an honorary member of the German U-Boat Club Dresden and have since attended some of their reunions.*

HMS Lark
*On the same day that we sunk the **U-425**, our consort **Lark** was torpedoed. We went alongside and took off the survivors who could step from their ship to ours. They stayed with us until we got back to base. Within days the food on the **Alnwick Castle** began to run out owing to the large number of men onboard for the greater part of the three weeks it took to reach the Clyde and the delays caused by the appalling weather. It was hard tack all the way with very occasionally a tin of meat being opened. Thankfully the Rum lasted out!*

Gongs

Back at base our Captain Lt Cdr Stonehouse cleared lower deck to read out who had been awarded medals. The ones that I can recall were:-

Coxswain	M.i.D.
L/S W. Maxwell	D.S.M.
A/B McKriel	D.S.M.
L.T.O. Harvey	M.i.D.
Lt: McInnes	DSC
Lt. Cmdr Stonehouse	Bar to DSC

L/S Maxwell was the senior Asdic operator and AB McKrill's action station was in the magazine. We were told that these awards were picked out of a hat and everyone agreed that they went to the right people.

I once had to take a message down below to the magazine during an action. Sitting there on a ammo box was McKrill reading a cowboy paperback book. Personally I could not get back to the wheel house quick enough.

On 29 April, with RA 66, we sailed out of Kola Inlet when we had a near miss with a torpedo. We were told on the mess deck that some of the lookouts actually saw it approaching us. It missed by a few yards. Shortly before **HMS Goodale** had been torpedoed. She was close to us. However, **Honeysuckle** got there first. She was commended for the manner in which she went alongside for survivors. We went in near, but there was nothing we could do. I remember the sea was ablaze when we turned away. A sight one will always remember.

Undertaker

One trip we made we were tied up to the jetty when an SBA came aboard and asked to see the Officer of the Day. Being the QM I was on the brow. I asked him what it was for and he replied that they wanted a couple of volunteers for preparing the dead boys up at the hospital for burial. The next day two men did go with him and on their return to the ship the Captain gave them a bottle of gin to share. A reward well deserved.

The next morning on the jetty were the rows of bodies in canvas. An old Russian woman dressed in black heavy clothes, and scarfed head, placed a green bunch of leaves on one of the boys. I found this so sad to see.

They were carried across our ship to two ships tied alongside of us, to be taken out of the Kola Inlet to be buried at sea.

HMS AMBERLEY CASTLE

Battle Honours
Atlantic 1945

HMS Amberley Castle on 15 March 1945. *(Ben Warlow Collection)*

Although laid down in mid 1943 *Amberley Castle* was not completed until late November 1944. After working up at Tobermory she was allocated to the Liverpool Escort Pool (LEP) and engaged in escorting convoys to and from Gibraltar. Overall, she escorted 11 convoys comprising 235 ships. On the conclusion of the war in Europe she was allocated for Air/Sea Rescue services operating under the Rosyth Command for Stations 16 and 17 and later transferred to Weather Reporting duties. In 1960 she is recorded under the name of *Weather Adviser* and was transferred to the Air Ministry in 1971 and to the Director General Meteorological Services in 1972. She underwent major repairs in 1972 and was renamed *Admiral Fitzroy*. She was sold and broken up in 1983 after 39 years of service.

HISTORY

02.03.44	Ordered.
31.05.43	Laid down. **Builder**: Hull - Austin (Sunderland); Engine - G. Clark (Sunderland).
27.11.43	Launched.
24.11.44	Completed.

WARTIME VOYAGES

Date	ESG	Senior Officer	Convoy	No of Ships	Arrive/ Sail	Location	Notes
9.11.44					Arv	Tyne	
19.11.44					Sail	Sunderland	
29.11.44					Sail	Tyne	
30.11.44					Arv	Methil	
30.11.44					Sail	Methil	
02.12.44	Unall.				Arv	Tobermory	
15.12.44	LEP					Tobermory	
22.12.44					Arv	Londonderry	
24.12.44	LEP				Sail	Londonderry	
01.01.45	LEP					Londonderry	
02.01.45	LEP				Sail	Londonderry	
08.01.45		*Fowey*	MKS 74	13		N of Lundy	
11.01.45	LEP		OS104/ KMS78	19	Sail	Liverpool	
13.01.45	LEP		OS104/ KMS78	24	Sail	Milford Haven	
19.01.45	LEP		OS104/ KMS78	24	Arv	Gibraltar	
25.01.45	LEP		HKS79G	22	Sail	Gibraltar	
02.02.45	LEP		HKS 79G	22	Arv	Liverpool	

Quarterdeck Crew (CCC(F)A Archives)

Forecastle Crew
(CCC(F)A Archives)

Date	ESG	Senior Officer	Convoy	No of Ships	Arrive/ Sail	Location	Notes
14.02.45	LEP					Liverpool	
17.02.45	LEP		OS112/ KMS86	22	Sail	Liverpool	
25.02.45	LEP		OS112/ KMS86	22	Arv	Gibraltar	
01.03.45	LEP		MKS86G	28	Sail	Gibraltar	CinC W.A. 1911159Z OS/KMS85 1500Z 5024'N 0802'W (?) MKS 86G seems more likely
09.03.45	LEP		MKS86G	28	Arv	Liverpool	Probably with MKS 86G (28 ships)
18.03.45	LEP	*Knaresborough Castle*	OS 117/ KMS 91	5	Sail	Liverpool	
24.03.45	LEP		MKS117/ KMS 91	25	Arv	Liverpool	Apparently detached from OS117/KMS 91 early in the voyage

*Quarterdeck PT
(CCC(F)A Archives)*

Date	ESG	Senior Officer	Convoy	No of Ships	Arrive/ Sail	Location	Notes
28.03.45	LEP		OS119/ KMS93	16	Sail	Liverpool	
06.04.45	LEP		OS119/ KMS93	16	Arv	Gibraltar	
10.04.45	LEP		MKS94G	20	Sail	Gibraltar	
18.04.45	LEP		MKS94G	20	Arv	Liverpool	
27.04.45	LEP	*Knaresborough Castle*	OS125/	23	Sail	Liverpool	30.04.45 with *Knaresborough Castle* supported convoy MKS 97 03/05/45 both ships escorted the detached Clyde Section. (SMO).
04.05.45	LEP		MKS97G	28	Arv	Liverpool	
06.05.45	LEP	*Knaresborough Castle*	OS 127/ KMS 101	15	Sail	Liverpool	S.O. & Convoy probably as indicated.
09.05.45	LEP	*Knaresborough Castle*	OS 127/ KMS 101	15	Arv	Falmouth	S.O. & Convoy probably as indicated.
11.05.45	LEP	*Knaresborough Castle*	OS 127/ KMS 101	15	Sail	Falmouth	S.O. & Convoy probably as indicated. Convoy dispersed 13.05.45.
20.05.45	LEP	*Knaresborough Castle*	MKS102G	21	Sail	Gibraltar	
28.05.45	SAR	*Knaresborough Castle*	MKS102G	21	Arv	Liverpool	

Date	ESG	Senior Officer	Convoy	No of Ships	Arrive/ Sail	Location	Notes
20.06.45					Arv	Londonderry	
22.06.45					Sail	Londonderry	
05.07.45					Arv	Clyde	
18.07.45					Sail	Clyde	
08.09.45					Arv	Clyde	
21.09.45					Sail	Clyde	AC 070615A/9 Relieved by *Berkeley Castle* ETA Sept 8th M.C. Greenock 151505/9 AC returns from A/SR duties approx 12/10
23.09.45					Arv	Station 17	*Dumbarton Castle* 240047/9 Relieved by *AC* on ASR Station 17 at 00300/24th AC 090830/10 Relieved by *Berkeley Castle* at 9th October.
11.10.45					Arv	Greenock	
23.10.45					Sail	Greenock	*AC* 10065Z/11 Relieved by *Berkeley Castle* ASR 16 at 0600Z/10th
11.11.45					Arv	Clyde	
24.11.45					Sail	Clyde	FO I/c Greenock. Intend to sail *AC* to ASR 17 24/11.

Bridge
(CCC(F)A Archives)

Date	ESG	Senior Officer	Convoy	No of Ships	Arrive/ Sail	Location	Notes
13.12.45					Arv	Clyde	*AC* ETA ASR 17 0700/26.11 *AC* relieved by **Berkeley Castle** in ASR 17 at 0830 ETE Greenock 2200Z/13.12.
16.01.46					Arv	Greenock	FO I/c Greenock261035/12 intend to sail *AC* to ASR 16 arv 0300/27.12 *AC* 272121Z/12 ETA ASR 16 2359/28.12
04.02.46					Sail	Greenock	041039Z/2 Intend sailing AC to Portsmouth4/2 *AC* 06010/2. Amended ETA 1530/6.2
06.02.46					Arv	Portsmouth	Record ends.

1947-52	Reserve at Portsmouth.
1953-1957	Reserve at Penarth.
September 1960	Mercantile: **Weather Adviser** Air Ministry.
1971/72	Major repairs at Manchester Dry Dock and renamed **Admiral Fitzroy**.
May 1983	Sold and broken up.

HMS BAMBOROUGH CASTLE

Battle Honours
Atlantic 1944   Arctic 1944-45

HMS Bamborough Castle in 1944.   (MoD/Crown Copyright)

After working up at Tobermory at the end of June 1944 *Bamborough Castle* was allocated to the B5 Escort Group for the remainder of the arctic convoy closed season. The group was engaged in escorting convoys to and from Gibraltar. She escorted three of these amounting to 95 merchant ships.

On 7 September 1944 *Bamborough Castle* was allocated to the 7th Escort Group on arctic convoy duties. She remained with that group for the remainder of the war in Europe. She escorted 12 convoys to and from the Kola Inlet; more than any other Castle class corvette. These convoys comprised a total of 358 merchant ships of which only 8 were lost to enemy action. On 9 December 1944 she sank *U-387*

outside Kola Inlet just prior to the sailing of convoy RA 62. On 20 February 1945 whilst on the outer screen of RA 64 she distinguished herself when engaging a formation of Ju-88 torpedo bombers. With Oerlikon fire she obtained a 'probable' hit on the formation leader. The vigour of the defensive fire of the escorts on the outer screen was sufficient to deter the enemy from pressing home his attacks.

On the conclusion of the voyage with RA 66 *Bamborough Castle* was reduced to reserve. In January 1946 she was re-commissioned and allocated to the Fishery Protection Flotilla for duty in the English Channel area. She was replaced in reserve in 1947 and scrapped in 1959.

HISTORY

19.12.42	Ordered.
01.07.43	Laid down. **Builder**: Hull & Engine - Lewis (Aberdeen).
11.01.44	Launched.
30.05.44	Completed.

WARTIME VOYAGES

Date	ESG	Senior Officer	Convoy	No of Ships	Arrive/Sail	Location	Notes
17.06.44					Sail	Aberdeen	SMO
19.06.44	EG B5	*Exe*			Arv	Tobermory	
24.06.44	EG B5	*Exe*				At Tobermory	
30.06.44	EG B5				Sail	Tobermory	
08.07.44					Sail	Tobermory	This departure is not consistent with the 'Pink List' record Fo i/c Greenock 091238B/7 Proceed on completion of calibration to arrive Larne for Cambelltown. (SMO)-SMO
09.07.44					Arv	Clyde	This movement is not consistent with the 'Pink List' record.-SMO
16.07.44	EG B5	*Exe*			Arv	Clyde	
24.07.44					Sail	Clyde	CinC W.A. 211826B/7 When ready 24/7 BC is to be sailed to Campbeltown and is to remain there until 7th August when she is to be sailed to Greenock to join her Group. SMO
24.07.44	EG B5	*Exe*			Arv	Campbeltown	
09.08.44	EG B5	*Hadleigh Castle*			Arv	Larne	
11.08.44	EG B5	*Hadleigh Castle*	OS86/ KMS60	23	Sail	Londonderry	
23.08.44	EG B5	*Hadleigh Castle*	OS86/ KMS60	24	Arv	Gibraltar	
30.08.44	EG B5	*Hadleigh Castle*	SL168/ MKS 59	35	Sail	Gibraltar	
01.09.44	EG B5	*Hadleigh Castle*	SL 168/ MKS 59	35		3925N1030W	
06.09.44	EG B2	*Cotton*	OS 88/	37		5029N0901W	Arrived Clyde 07.09.44 for 7th E.G.
07.09.44	7th EG				Arv	Clyde	
14.09.44	7th EG	*Cygnet*			Arv	Aultbea	For JW 60
15.09.44	7th EG	*Cygnet*	JW 60	31	Sail	Aultbea	Joined 7th Escort Group on Russian Convoy duty arriving Kola Inlet 24.09.44 (SMO)
18.09.44	7th EG	*Cygnet*	JW 60	31		6738N0201W	
22.09.44	7th EG	*Cygnet*	JW 60	31		7256N3315E	
24.09.44	7th EG	*Cygnet*	JW 60	31	Arv	Kola Inlet	
28.09.44	7th EG	*Cygnet*	RA 60	32	Sail	Kola Inlet	

Date	ESG	Senior Officer	Convoy	No of Ships	Arrive/ Sail	Location	Notes
01.10.44	7th EG	*Cygnet*	RA 60	32		7155N 0403E	
04.10.44	7th EG	*Cygnet*	RA 60	32		N of Minches	
05.10.44	7th EG				Arv	Clyde	
13.10.44	7th EG	*Cygnet*			Sail	Clyde	
15.10.44	7th EG	*Cygnet*				At Clyde	
05.11.44	7th EG	*Cygnet*			Arv	Clyde	
17.11.44	7th EG	*Cygnet*				Clyde	Repairs completes 22 Nov SMO
27.11.44	7th EG	*Cygnet*			Sail	Clyde	SMO
28.11.44	7th EG	*Cygnet*	JW 62	38	Arv	Aultbea	
29.11.44	7th EG	*Cygnet*	JW 62	38	Sail	Aultbea	
05.12.44	7th EG	*Cygnet*	JW 62	31		7240N 3120E	
10.12.44	7th EG	*Cygnet*	RA 62	29	Sail	Kola Inlet	
12.12.44	7th EG	*Cygnet*	RA 62	30		7148N 1832E	
01.01.45	7th EG	*Cygnet*	JW 63	37		6301N 0310W	
01.01.45	7th EG	*Cygnet*	JW 63	37		6301N 0310W	
01.01.45	7th EG	*Cygnet*	JW 63	37		At Sea	
06.01.45	7th EG	*Cygnet*	JW 63	37		7235N 3210E	
08.01.45	7th EG	*Cygnet*	JW 63	38	Arv	Kola Inlet	
11.01.45	7th EG	*Cygnet*	RA 63	31	Sail	Kola Inlet	
15.01.45	7th EG	*Cygnet*	RA 63	29		6745N 0450E	
18.01.45	7th EG	*Cygnet*	RA 63	30		6220N 0510W	
20.01.45	7th EG	*Cygnet*	RA 63	30	Sail	Faroes	
23.01.45	7th EG	*Cygnet*	RA 63	30	Arv	Clyde	
02.02.45	7th EG	*Cygnet*	JW 64	29		Clyde	
17.02.45	7th EG	*Cygnet*	RA 64	33	Sail	Kola Inlet	
01.03.45	7th EG	*Cygnet*	RA 64	31	Arv	Clyde	
11.03.45	7th EG	*Cygnet*	JW 65	26	Sail	Clyde	
20.03.45	7th EG	*Cygnet*	JW 65	26	Arv	Kola Inlet	
01.04.45	7th EG	*Cygnet*	RA 65	26	Arv	Clyde	
16.04.45	7th EG	*Cygnet*	JW 66	27	Sail	Clyde	
27.04.45	7th EG	*Cygnet*	JW 66	27	Arv	Kola Inlet	
29.04.45	7th EG	*Cygnet*	RA 66	26	Sail	Kola Inlet	
08.05.45	7th EG	*Cygnet*	RA 66	26	Arv	Clyde	AM 171753B/5 **BC** has been ordered to reduce to reserve category 'C' forth with. F.O.C.R.F. 271641/6 BC accepted into Cat B reserve fleet 25.6 SMO -
24.05.45	SAR				Arv	Sheerness	
09.12.45							S.O.F.P. 091035/12 **BC** allocated to Channel Area I(?) P.D: taking up duties 1.1.46 (SMO)-SMO

Date	ESG	Senior Officer	Convoy	No of Ships	Arrive/ Sail	Location	Notes
02.01.46					Sail	Sheerness	AM 092101/11 **BC** at present in 'B' is allocated to Fishery Protection Flotilla & is to be brought forward & manned as soon as practicable (SMO)-SMO.
03.01.46							CinC Nore 311746Z/12 Intend sailing **BC** 2/1 ETA Portsmouth 0800/3.1 (SMO)-SMO
07.01.46							CinC Plymouth 071514Z/1 Intend sailing **BC** 8/1 to Portland ETA 1400. **BC** 190917/1 Intend to proceed on patrol 22.1 visiting St Ives and Scillies returning Plymouth 27.1 Intend leave Plymouth 30.1 ETA Spithead 1.2 (SMO)-SMO
08.01.46					Sail	Portsmouth	arrived and departed same day.-SMO
18.01.46					Arv	Plymouth	SMO
02.02.46					Arv	Portsmouth	End of record.-SMO

SMO: Ship Movement Order

1946	Recommissioned and joined the Fishery Protection Flotilla. Based at Plymouth.
1947-48	Reserve at Devonport.
15.09.49	Completed refit at London.
1950-51	Reserve at Devonport.
1952-58	Reserve at Penarth.
1959	Sold to E Rees, arrived Llanelli 22.05.59 for scrapping.

HMS Bamborough Castle in July 1946.   *(Portsmouth Royal Naval Museum)*

RA 62: Sinking of U-387 by HMS Bamborough Castle

On 9 December 1944 the 7th Escort Group sailed from Kola Inlet ahead of the convoy with instructions to carry out A/S searches south of 69°59'N and between longitudes 33° and 35° East.   During this operation *Bamborough Castle* obtained a disappearing RADAR contact. The report of the subsequent action follows:-

Précis of Attack by Bamborough Castle
(Source: A.U.D. 2028/44)

Date: 09/12/44   Time: 1621
Position: 69°41'N 33°12'E,
Weather Condition: Wind SS. Force 3; Sea 12: Visibility: 1.5 miles.
Depth of Water: 75 fathoms.
Duty: Supporting Convoy RA 62.

Narrative:
HF/DF indicated that U-Boats were waiting in the approaches to Kola Inlet for Convoy RA 62, and the 7th EG was instructed to search for them.
   Ships were sweeping in line abreast on course 345° at 11 knots, when *Bamborough Castle*, the port wing ship obtained a Radar contact on her port bow, bearing 292° at 5,700 yards. A Radar contact previously gained by *Cygnet* had been classified as "Doubtful", but *Bamborough Castle* held hers for six minutes, when it faded at 3,500 yards. Speed was reduced to 6 knots and an anti -gnat charge was dropped. (Foxers were not function-

ing correctly, and had been recovered).

At 1638, ten minutes after losing radar contact, *Bamborough Castle* gained Asdic contact bearing 233° at 1,400 yards. This was classified as "submarine" and a Squid attack was commenced at 700 yards. Type 147B gave a depth of 360 feet, and the pattern was fired at 1648 set to 380 feet. The U-Boat appeared to take evasive action, but remained stern-on at 3 knots. Immediately after the bombs exploded loud whistle effect was heard on the bearing.

Contact was lost on the run out at 1,206 yards due to interference from Foxers of ships in company, but regained two minutes later at 1,100 yards. At 1659 *Cygnet* confirmed the contact, and took over duties of directing ship while *Bamborough Castle* delivered a further Squid attack at 1705, depth setting 420 feet.

On closing the range for a third attack contact was lost at 650 yards, and not regained for 23 minutes. However, at 1729 by sweeping the arc suggested by the plot, contact was regained at 2,100 yards. In order to confirm the contact *Bamborough Castle* made a run over with Type 147B and echo sounder. The contact was confirmed by Type 147B and the plot, but no result was obtained by echo sounder. Squid was fired at 1757, after which contact was lost.

In the position of the third attack a patch of oil was discovered, at least 1,000 yards in diameter, in the centre of which several pieces of wood were seen. These appeared freshly broken. It was not possible to recover any wreckage as Foxers were streamed. The oil patch ended in a long streak to windward, and though the source appeared to be 2,000 yards from the centre of the oil patch at 1930 and appeared from the plot to be half a mile further to windward at 2020, no Asdic contact could be gained. At 2035 the hunt was abandoned since the position of the attack was some distance to the Convoy's route and the object of the search was to sweep the Kola approaches.

Decision of U-Boat Assessment Committee:

There is little doubt that the contact was a U-Boat. Three Squid attacks were carried out in all of which contact was obtained on Type 147B. The first and second attacks were very accurate for range, but the Bearing recorder traces are not analysable.

In view of the oil and wooden wreckage seen on conclusion of the action, it is considered probable that the U-boat was destroyed and the hunt accordingly assessed "U-Boat probably sunk."

Subsequently the *Bamborough Castle* was accredited with having sunk *U-387*.

Prior to the sailing of RA 64 in February 1945, *Bamborough Castle* was used as the base ship from which divers worked in their attempt to recover Confidential and Secret documents from the wreck of *Denbigh Castle* which had been torpedoed at the entrance of the Kola Inlet when ships of the convoy JW 64 were entering harbour. *Denbigh Castle*'s Type 277 office was destroyed by explosives.

On 7 February 1945, *Lark* which was part of the screen sweeping ahead of the convoy emerging from Kola Inlet was torpedoed, losing her stern. *Lapwing* and *Bamborough Castle* swept around *Lark* but were unable to obtain any firm contacts. About an hour later Pendant No.34 *Thomas Scott* was torpedoed within sight of *Lark*. *HM Ships Onslaught, Bluebell, Alnwick Castle* and *Bamborough Castle* searched the area but without success. The 7th Escort Group remained in the vicinity for the next seven hours before the Russian escorts had been persuaded to take over *Lark*. Before leaving to rejoin the convoy they took off all surplus Officers and men. They rejoined the convoy at 0503 18 February. With her extra passengers, food supplies became critically short towards the end of the homeward passage.

On 20 February the Group were involved in reforming the convoy that had become widely dispersed by gales. Starting at 1000 the convoy was attacked by torpedo bombers. *Onslow, Zealous* and *Nairana*'s fighters each shot down an aircraft - confirmed; *Bamborough Castle* and **Nairana**'s fighter each got a 'probable'. *Bamborough Castle*'s report on this action follows:

HMS BAMBOROUGH CASTLE's REPORT

HMS Bamborough Castle
27th February 1945

Sir,

1.   I have the honour to submit the following report on action between His Majesty's Ship **Bamborough Castle**, escorting convoy RA 64, and enemy torpedo bombers which attacked at 1006A on 20 February, 1945 in position 72°58'N 17°46'E.

2.   HM Ship was distant 10 miles, on bearing 250° from the centre of the convoy, stationed 360° distant 4,000 yards from **Allington Castle**, (Senior Officer of Group IV of the extended screen) carrying out an independent zigzag on convoy course of 270°.

3.   The weather at the time was; wind SW Force 4, sea and swell 34, visibility variable from 2 to 3 miles with drizzle.

4.   At 1000A when on course 300°, enemy aircraft were sighted, bearing 180° distant three miles on course of approximately 360°. These aircraft were identified as nine Ju-88 torpedo bombers, in a 'V' formation of three groups of three. Oerlikon fire was opened on the leader when he came within range. Two planes quickly released their torpedoes and all turned away. The leader was seen to be hit several times with Oerlikon fire and was on fire when last seen. This plane disappeared in the mist on a bearing of 150° steering about 180°. This plane was not considered sufficiently damaged to justify claiming a probable.

5.   On seeing the torpedoes dropped course was altered to comb the tracks. Two underwater explosions were heard about ten minutes later. It was thought that these were torpedoes exploding at the end of their run. No W/T report of these torpedoes being fired was made as they were seen to be running clear of all ships and W/T traffic was already heavy.

6.   Several more enemy aircraft were sighted between 1010A and 1045A but none came within gun range or attempted to attack. They all appeared to be trying to thread their way between groups of the outer screen and sheered off as soon as they sighted an escort. All the planes which were sighted were Ju-88 torpedo bombers.

Sgd Magnus Work
Lieutenant Commander RNR
Commanding Officer

HMS BERKELEY CASTLE

Battle Honours
Atlantic 1944

HMS Berkeley Castle, 3 December 1943.   (MoD/Crown Copyright)

After working up at Tobermory, the ship's first operational voyage was with the 15th Escort Group, leaving Londonderry on 20 January 1944 to provide support for convoy SL145/MKS 36. This was followed by a round trip to St John's, Newfoundland (NF). Outward bound she had *Carisbrooke Castle* in company who broke down in mid-Atlantic. She was towed to Argentia by *Berkeley Castle*. No official report of this incident was found. However, descriptions of this episode provided by members of the ship's company of *Carisbrooke Castle* are provided under that ship's heading.

On 1 March 1944 *Berkeley Castle* joined the 40th Escort Group engaged in escorting convoys to and from Gibraltar. She continued with that task, but with the B5 Escort Group, from 23 May to 10 September 1944. Other ships forming the Group were *Hadleigh Castle*, *Carisbrooke Castle*, *Dumbarton Castle* and *Lancaster Castle*. The 31st Escort Group was formed on that day with *Berkeley Castle* as the Senior Officer and the other Castle Class Corvettes from the B5 Escort Group.

The 31st Escort Group was destined to operate as a patrol and support group operating in the UK coastal waters - chiefly within the 100 fathom line. The Group operated in the Western Approaches, Western English Channel, and in the Scapa Flow/ Faeroes area until the end of the war in Europe.

From July 1945 to mid 1946 *Berkeley Castle* was on air/sea rescue operations, operating out of Greenock under the Rosyth Command, occupying stations 16 or 17. In mid 1946 she was placed in reserve at Harwich.

On 1 February 1953 she was under refit in No 2 Dry Dock at Sheerness. That night a severe gale induced an unusually large tidal surge up the Thames estuary. The water flooded over the gates of the three dry docks. *Berkeley Castle* was lifted off her blocks and capsized.

Subsequent inspection of the ship led to the conclusion that she was beyond economic repair. She was towed to Chatham, laid up and eventually scrapped in September 1955.

HISTORY

02.02.43	Ordered.
23.04.43	Laid down. **Builder**: Hull & Engine - Barclay Curle (Whiteinch).
19.08.43	Launched.
18.11.43	Completed.

WARTIME VOYAGES

Date	ESG	Senior Officer	Convoy	No of Ships	Arrive/ Sail	Location	Notes
07.12.43	EG B7				Arv	Tobermory	For working up
26.12.43	Unall				Sail	Tobermory	
27.12.43	Unall				Arv	Londonderry	
16.01.44	Unall				Sail	Londonderry	
20.01.44	EG 15	*Wren*	HX274	38		5457N 1201W	ADM 199/315 places **Berkeley Castle** on 21st January with SL145/ MKS 36 in 15 EG (S.O. *Wren*)
23.01.44	Unall				Sail	Londonderry	
02.02.44	Unall				Sail	Londonderry	To overtake ON222. *Carisbrooke Castle* 071800Z/2. Am proceeding direct to St Johns NF towed by *BC*.
04.02.44						5332N 1310W	
06.02.44						5245N 3245W	To St Johns, 13 knots
08.02.44						4945N 4640W	To St Johns, 8 knots
09.02.44	40th EG				Arv		St Johns
10.02.44	Unall				Arv	Argentia	
10.02.44						4618N 5225W	*Berkerley* towing *Carisbrooke* 8.5 knots
11.02.44	Unall		HX 278	60	Sail	Argentia	
12.02.44			HX 278	60		4550N 5105W	Overtake HX 278, 13 knots
17.02.44	EG B2	*Mourne*	HX 278	60		5130N 2101W	
19.02.44	40th EG		HX 278	60	Arv	Clyde	
01.03.44	40th EG	*Exe*			Sail	Clyde	For exercises

Date	ESG	Senior Officer	Convoy	No of Ships	Arrive/ Sail	Location	Notes
04.03.44	40th EG	*Exe*			Sail	Londonderry	Arrived and departed same day to join OS70/KMS44
07.03.44	40th EG	*Exe*	OS 70/ KMS 44	46		5330N 1540W	
17.03.44	40th EG	*Exe*	OS 70/ KMS 44		Arv	Gibraltar	
22.03.44	40th EG	*Exe*	SL 152/ MKS 43	26	Sail	Gibraltar	
24.03.44	40th EG	*Exe*	SL 152/ MKS 43	26		3601N 1030W	Hague lists 75 ships
02.04.44	40th EG	*Exe*	SL 152/ MKS 43	87		5448N 1020W	Hague lists 75 ships
03.04.44	40th EG				Arv	Clyde	
04.04.44					Arv	Clyde	F.O.I.C. Glasgow BC can be docked by D & W Henderson's Dry Dock Govan approx 9 April
07.04.44	EG B5	*Exe*				At Clyde	
13.04.44	EG B5	*Exe*			Sail	Londonderry	Having arrived at Londonderry the day before (SMO)

Portside profile of **HMS Berkeley Castle** *3 December 1943.*   (MoD/Crown Copyright)

Date	ESG	Senior Officer	Convoy	No of Ships	Arrive/ Sail	Location	Notes
14.04.44	EG B5	*Exe*	OS 74/ KMS 48	29		5552N 0952W	
14.04.44	EG B5	*Exe*	OS 74/ KMS 48	29	Sail	Clyde	
22.04.44	EG B5	*Exe*	OS 74/ KMS 48	29		3712N1333W	
24.04.44	EG B5	*Exe*	OS 74/ KMS 48	29	Arv	Gibraltar	
01.05.44	EG B5	*Exe*	SL 156/ MKS 47	65	Sail	Gibraltar	
06.05.44	EG B5	*Exe*	SL 156/ MKS 47	65		4116N1829W	Hague gives 46 ships
12.05.44	EG B5	*Exe*	SL 156/ MKS 47		Arv	Clyde	
20.05.44	EG B5	*Exe*			Sail	Clyde	
21.05.44	EG B5	*Exe*			Arv	Londonderry	
23.05.44	EG B5	*Exe*	OS78/ KMS52	25	Sail	Londonderry	
24.05.44	EG B5	*Exe*	OS 78/ KMS52	25		5550N 1010W	
06.06.44	EG B5	*Exe*	OS78/ KMS52	25	Arv	Gibraltar	
09.06.44	EG B5	*Exe*	MKS 51	14	Sail	Gibraltar	
10.06.44	EG B5	*Exe*	SL160/ MKS 51	44		3540N 0705W	
13.06.44	EG B5	*Exe*	SL 160/ MKS 51	50		3710N 1640W	44 ships according to Hague
20.06.44	EG B5	*Exe*	SL160/ MKS 51		Arv	Clyde	
29.06.44	EG B5	*Exe*			Sail	Clyde	
02.07.44	EG B5	*Exe*	OS82/ KMS56	26	Sail	Londonderry	Having arrived at Londonderry the day before.
06.07.44	EG B5	*Exe*	OS 82/ KMS56	29		4818N 1935W	
13.07.44	EG B5	*Exe*	OS82/ KMS56	29	Arv	Gibraltar	
19.07.44	EG B5	*Exe*	SL164/ MKS55	33	Sail	Gibraltar	
21.07.44	EG B5	*Exe*	MKS 55	19		3435N 1020W	
21.07.44	EG B5	*Exe*	SL 164/ MKS 55	35		3525N 1248W	
29.07.44	EG B5	*Exe*	SL 164/ MKS 55	33		5140N1520W	

Date	ESG	Senior Officer	Convoy	No of Ships	Arrive/ Sail	Location	Notes
31.07.44	EG B5	*Exe*	SL 164/ MKS 55	33	Arv	Clyde	
09.08.44	EG B5	*Hadleigh Castle*			Arv	Larne	
11.08.44	EG B5	*Hadleigh Castle*	OS86/ KMS60	23	Sail	Londonderry	
12.08.44	EG B5	*Hadleigh Castle*	OS86/ KMS60	25		5550N 0855W	
23.08.44	EG B5	*Hadleigh Castle*	OS86/ KMS60	24	Arv	Gibraltar	
30.08.44	EG B5	*Hadleigh Castle*	SL168/ MKS 59	35	Sail	Gibraltar	
01.09.44	EG B5	*Hadleigh Castle*	SL168/ MKS 59	35		3925N 1030W	
08.09.44	EG B2	*Cotton*	OS 88/ KMS 62	32		4530N 1128W	Arrived Clyde 10.09.44 for 31st E.G
10.09.44	31st EG	*Berkeley Castle*			Arv	Clyde	Having left Londonderry on 05.09; date of arrival there not known.
22.09.44	31st EG	*Berkeley Castle*			Arv	At Larne	
23.09.44	31st EG	*Berkeley Castle*			Sail	Londonderry	Having arrived there the same day. (SMO)
09.10.44	31st EG	*Berkeley Castle*			Arv	Clyde	
16.10.44	31st EG	*Berkeley Castle*				Clyde	Boiler cleaning to 18th.
20.10.44	31st EG	*Berkeley Castle*				At Clyde	
23.10.44	31st EG	*Berkeley Castle*				At Larne	
23.10.44	31st EG	*Berkeley Castle*			Sail	Londonderry	
10.11.44	31st EG	*Berkeley Castle*				At sea	
16.11.44	31st EG	*Berkeley Castle*			Arv	Clyde	
29.11.44	31st EG	*Berkeley Castle*			Sail	Londonderry	
02.12.44	31st EG	*Berkeley Castle*			Sail	Scapa Flow	Having arrived there the same day. (SMO)
13.12.44	31st EG	*Berkeley Castle*			Arv	Clyde	
21.12.44	31st EG	*Berkeley Castle*			Sail	Clyde	
23.12.44	31st EG	*Berkeley Castle*			Sail	Lamlash	Having arrived there on 21.12.44. (SMO)
03.01.45	31st EG	*Berkeley Castle*			Sail	Londonderry	
18.01.45	31st EG	*Berkeley Castle*			Arv	Clyde	
22.01.45	31st EG	*Berkeley Castle*				Clyde	Repairs complete 26 Jan
29.01.45	31st EG	*Berkeley Castle*				At Lochalsh	
02.02.45	31st EG	*Berkeley Castle*			Sail	Belfast	Having arrived there the day before. (SMO)
10.02.45	31st EG	*Berkeley Castle*			Arv	Belfast	
10.02.45	31st EG	*Berkeley Castle*			Arv	Clyde	
12.02.45	31st EG	*Berkeley Castle*			Sail	Clyde	

Date	ESG	Senior Officer	Convoy	No of Ships	Arrive/ Sail	Location	Notes
27.02.45	31st EG	*Berkeley Castle*			Arv	Clyde	
10.03.45	31st EG	*Berkeley Castle*			Sail	Clyde	
23.03.45	31st EG	*Berkeley Castle*			Arv	Clyde	
25.03.45	31st EG	*Berkeley Castle*			Sail	Clyde	
14.04.45	31st EG	*Berkeley Castle*			Sail	Clyde	
19.04.45	31st EG	*Berkeley Castle*			Sail	Belfast	
30.04.45	31st EG	*Berkeley Castle*			Arv	Milford Haven	
02.05.45	31st EG	*Berkeley Castle*			Sail	Milford Haven	
13.05.45	31st EG	*Berkeley Castle*			Sail	Lochalsh	To escort surrendered U-Boats to Lough Foyle
29.05.45	31st EG	*Berkeley Castle*			Sail	Clyde	
21.06.45	W.A.				Arv	Clyde	
21.07.45					Arv	Clyde	
02.08.45					Sail	Clyde	*BC* 220910/8. Relieved by *Leeds Castle* in ASR Station 17 at 0800A 22 August.
23.08.45					Arv	Clyde	
05.09.45					Sail	Clyde	*BC* 051901/9 ETA Samop (?) 6.0500A Sept 7th to ASR Position 17 *Amberley Castle* relieved by *BC* in A.S.R. 17 9th Oct.

HMS Berkeley Castle Ship's Company, whilst steaming through the convoy on V.E. Day. (CCC(F)A Archives)

Date	ESG	Senior Officer	Convoy	No of Ships	Arrive/ Sail	Location	Notes
23.09.45					Arv	Greenock	
07.10.45					Sail	Greenock	
27.11.45					Arv	Greenock	ETA A.S.R. Position 16 0630Z.10th Nov. ***Amberley Castle*** 100654Z.11 relieved by ***BC*** in A.S.R. station 16 at 0600z.10
11.01.46							F.O.I.C. Greenock 1111613.1; Intend to sail ***BC*** to A.S.R. 16 12.1
07.02.46							F.O.I.C. Greenock 071603/2 Intend sailing ***BC*** to Harwich ETA 12/2

June 1946	In Reserve Harwich.
February 1953	Capsized in Dry Dock at Sheerness. Declared an un-economic loss and towed to Chatham.
26.09.55	Sold to T.W. Ward.
24.02.56	Arrived Grays for scrapping.

GREAT DAMAGE AT DOCKYARD WORST PEACE-TIME CATASTROPHE YET..

Report by the *Sheerness Times* 7 February1953

Civil Secretary's story

The full story of flood damage in Sheerness Dockyard, which has been estimated at 1? million pounds, was given by Mr. J. E. Melville (civil secretary to the Captain-in-Charge) in an Interview with the *Sheerness Times* and *Guardian*.

"We had been warned that it would be an abnormally full tide," Mr. Meville said, "and two hours before high water, we realised that the warning was more than justified, but we still hoped that it would not bring flooding. However, at high tide a terrific swell of water came over the wall. The wall wasn't damaged - the water simply surged over.

"The tide was ten feet above normal, four feet higher than the 22 foot flood wall and if you add to this the tremendous pressure of the gale, you can realise the force of the river water that surged in.

SUBMARINE AND FRIGATE

"The wave went over the top of the dock gates and into the dry docks. The submarine **Sirdar,** in No.1 dock was sunk and the frigate **Berkeley Castle**, in No.2 dock, rode high on the waters, and eventually turned over and capsized, with part of her bows resting on the side of the dock.

"The yard was completely flooded, with bulks of timber, barrels, oil drums and all sorts of debris being carried along in the wake of the water. Dockyard officers, who had been called out at midnight, could only

HMS Berkeley Castle capsized in Sheerness dry dock, February 1953.   *(CCC(F)A Archives)*

watch the havoc - probably the worst catastrophe in Dockyard history. At one moment, as onlookers scattered before the tidal waves, the Captain-in-Charge (Capt. V.N. Surtees DSO) had to climb a ladder and take refuge for some time on a rooftop. He suffered slight injury to his leg.

"We could do nothing until daylight - a Dockyard is such a dangerous place in a situation like this, as it has so many obstacles and deep places", Mr. Melville pointed out.

"One of our most difficult tasks has been to restore electric engines and power to the yard. All generating stations were flooded, and many electrical engines have had to be rewound.

The submarine was regarded as a "good possibility for salvage", and work began on her on Tuesday. It was thought possible that she could be stripped of machinery and the hull refloated. At the time of her sinking, the inlets were open and hull plates removed during an extensive refit.

The frigate *Berkeley Castle* described by Mr. Melville "as a much more difficult matter", has been the subject of consultation by naval architects and salvage experts. It is thought that she will be broken up. Dockyard quarters and offices were flooded to a depth of several feet, but so well did the 2,000 clearance workers do their job that, by Tuesday afternoon few traces of tide marks or debris remained. In Mr. Meville's office, for instance, where on Sunday morning sea water three feet deep engulfed the furniture only a trace of rust on the fireplace remained, the whole having been swept and garnished with true naval thoroughness.

"The workmen turned in and did a good job: but our main worry at the moment is lack of electrical power," Mr. Melville repeated. "Meanwhile, we are helping the town by running transport to Chatham, and bringing back supplies of fresh water, food, milk, mails, newspapers and all other essentials. Vessels are loading and unloading all day long-except for a small number of military craft, only naval transport is in use. Fresh water is the chief need, of course, and every endeavour is being made to supply this.'

Mr. Melville's admirable broadcast report of the Dockyard situation heard in the B.B.C. news on Sunday evening, was almost impromptu. After his exhausting night and day of continuous work, he had only five minutes' notice before giving this brief but lively account to B.B.C. commentator Douglas Willis; their two way conversation being recorded at Chatham naval headquarters.

A more complete account was compiled by Mr. Malcolm Maclean:

During the night of 1 February 1953, a violent storm struck the Thames area. Despite warnings of an abnormally high tide of ten feet above normal level, there was little that could be done to protect the low-lying area of Sheerness, where a number of Royal Navy Reserve Fleet vessels were either laid up or in refit at the Naval Dockyard. As high tide approached, the storm blew up a huge tidal wave which washed over the 22-foot wall of the dockyard's Great Basin. The inrush of water flooded over the gates of all three dry-docks. In No.2 Dock the Castle class frigate *HMS Berkeley Castle* was in refit. The 1,000-ton ship was lifted off of her blocks and capsized soon after. Her keel coming to rest on the dock steps above the broad altar with her bows protruding over the end of the dock. Her mast barely missed a dockside crane as the ship came to rest on her port side. In the neighbouring, No.1 dock the submarine *HMS Sirdar*, with much of her hull plating removed, was also lifted off of her blocks and became totally submerged. The only man aboard the frigate at the time managed to escape by jumping from the ship onto a Carley float, which was washed away, depositing the shaken watchman near the dockyard's Main Gate. Several other vessels, including the water tanker *Freshwater*, the salvage vessel *Uplifter* and a number of R.N.V.R. minesweepers were also damaged.

There was little that could be done that evening until the flooding, had subsided. The following morning revealed extensive damage, including the submergence of all generating stations under several feet of water, and debris deposited in huge quantities around the area. Over 2000 employees spent the next few days working feverishly to restore electrical power supplies and clear up the mess. The cost of the damage to the dockyard was estimated at around £1.5m and was regarded at the time as the worst catastrophe

HMS Berkeley Castle capsised to port in the dry dock. *(CCC(F)A Archives)*

in the Dockyard's history.

Following inspection of **Berkeley Castle** by the Naval Constructor and salvage experts her stem was burned off. The dock was then flooded leaving the ship floating on her side. Attempts were made to pull her upright, but this was unsuccessful as she rolled over onto the opposite beam, sending dockyard workers scattering for their lives. The ship was then ballasted and rivet holes plugged. In the middle of February the vessel re-docked. As the vessel's collision bulkhead had failed a temporary bow of steel tubing and fairing plates was fitted. Further inspections of the hull resulted in the conclusion that the ship was beyond economical repair and she was later towed to Chatham, where she was laid up. The ship was sold and was scrapped at Grays on 26 September 1955. **HMS Sirdar** was returned to service following repairs and served until the 1960s.

Arthur Brough (AB ST), served in **Berkeley Castle** during the whole of the ship's first commission as well as standing by her for two months prior to commissioning. Describing his time aboard he wrote:-

"I was drafted from Chatham to Glasgow alone and arrived there broke after being taught how to play Pontoon on the train. By sheer chance I met two other matelots. We teamed up and eventually got "civvie digs" in Arthurlie St, Govan.
Standing by the ship was like a day job. I travelled from Govan by tram, then under the Clyde by the underground. On by tram again to Merkland Street for Barclay Curle's Yard at Whiteinch. At first there were just eight of us, including the coxswain. Lt Darrar, Commanding Officer, joined us later. We were there early, supposedly, to get familiar with the ship. One man for each Department. I was only 17 when I joined up. I hadn't a clue! Lt Hedges, after working up trials, gave me a fatherly talk, in his cabin, explaining I was in complete charge of the Department. Just do my best and he would give me an AB to help with the depth charges. He tried hard to obtain an experienced LTO. Luckily, the night we sailed to rendezvous with our first convoy, Boland LTO, joined

us at the eleventh hour. Just as well. We'd only been at sea a matter hours, it seemed, when all the electrical equipment went dead. Boland was experienced. So he and I dodged about running an emergency supply from the diesel engine - which the stokers, after a struggle, had managed to get going - to the many essential junction boxes throughout the ship. We were both seasick at the time. So we'd do a spell below, with the miner type lamps strapped to our heads, then nip up to be ill. That's how it went for the best part of the night. There were a few red faces when we docked. It was found that the builders had not sufficiently protected the main switchboard in the engine room. Condensation had dripped on to the buzz bars and shorted them.

In the early stages I, with many more, suffered from seasickness. We would curl up near the warmth of the engine room or on the messdeck lockers.

THE TOW

Berkeley Castle and **Carisbrooke Castle** *were despatched to reinforce an escort group. When we were a day or so out from Derry,* **Carisbrooke** *broke down. We fully expected a recall. To our dismay, we were ordered to proceed to St John's, Newfoundland, with* **Carisbrooke Castle** *in tow. When we approached the Newfoundland coast we were met by a Flower Class corvette with orders to escort us in. Because of the threat of ice we were diverted from St. John's to the American base at Argentia in the south of Newfoundland. We arrived there in a blinding snowstorm. We requested a tug for* **Carisbrooke**. *The Yanks told us it was too hazardous to send one out. We must cruise around until the weather abated. Our Skipper disagreed and proceeded to take us alongside with* **Carisbrooke** *still in tow. We only lost a scrape of paint on the port bow.*

I volunteered, with a small party, to go ashore for supplies. The snow was about three feet deep. We went to a US warehouse that made our "starved" eyes pop. It was filled with every kind of food and goodies. We sauntered too near a tub of boiled sweets. The Yank diverted us! We loaded the trucks and headed back. Later we were issued with mammoth tins of fruit. Paid for by us through Canteen Messing. Although I was duty watch, LTO Boland fixed it so I could go ashore later. Free buses ran around the base. Just signal and they stopped. After visiting shops for nylons etc, we finished up in a dance hall where cigarettes, coffee and soup were free. There were dance hostesses, but they seemed to prefer their own kind. Yanks!

"My first action station was firing the rockets on the sides of the 4-inch gun. Through earphones I took direct orders from the bridge. The loaders, when they thought that the gun was about to be fired, would bend down behind the gun sheltering their ears and eyes. One night, orders to fire the gun were suddenly cancelled and the gun was swung around and I was given the order to fire the rockets. The PO, in charge, grabbed me to stop me firing. The loaders were, unknowingly, now crouched behind the rockets. Later I was transferred to the Squid. At action stations I would switch it on and run a series of tests before it was fired. I was given an official warning to divulge nothing about the Squid. Top secret.

"In Gibraltar we cooks of the mess that day, forget to put a watchkeeper's dinner up to keep warm. The Killick (the one above, I used to go ashore with him) took us to task. I laughed. He said get your caps. The other two got a warning. Being the senior one I got punishment, so that afternoon I was painting the ship instead of going ashore. I was taken ill next day. The miserable Sick Berth Tiffy wouldn't let me soil his sickberth. He used to sleep in it. Also, he said that if I wanted to go ashore to hospital they'd probably keep me in Gibraltar until the war ended and I was due leave next time home. Between hammock and lockers I tossed and turned for a week. I heard every bang of the depth charges dropped at the harbour entrance, to stop U-boats entering during the night. The day we left the fever left me as suddenly as it had arrived.

"Still in Gibraltar Striper May gained a reputation as the only Naval Patrol (May was in charge)

to crawl back through the dockyard on all fours, drunk out of their heads. After one run ashore May got us to push a concrete mixer through the dockyard as he contemplated getting it up the mast! Lt. Hedges came up behind and told him not to bother.

"I went ashore on a Naval Patrol with May in Greenock. It was a case of off gaiters etc, then into the nearest boozer till closing time. Often in Greenock one of us would dodge over to the dockyard canteen and fill a tea fanny with beer. One night Roy Pritchard was caught and made to empty all the beautiful beer over the side. A bit like losing blood - those days."

"One night in the River Foyle it took us nearly all night to tie up to a buoy it was so rough. Paddy, a lad from Belfast, managed to jump it eventually. Then lower deck was cleared and we coaled ship for the galley. Talking of coal, it was a strange sight when we first went to Gibraltar to see women humping bags of coal off a ship."

"Brooks (King of the Heads) was a bit of an entertainer. Balancing brooms etc. on his chin. We used to do dockyard sentry duty in Gourock. Very lonely during the night. We were told not to load the gun. I always had one up the spout. I wouldn't have hesitated to use it. Brooks returned to the messdeck after a spell of such sentry duty with his rifle and starting messing about with it. A killick took him to task. He assured him it wasn't loaded and pulled the trigger to prove it. The bullet went through a locker narrowly missing a man seated there. He wasn't put in the rattle but his ears were red for a day or two.

"We thought we had finished with the sea when the German war ended. Some hope. We were redeployed as a mid-Atlantic weathership. About a month out and a week in. It was worse than convoys. We'd stop engines and drift. Then start them in a gale or to regain our station again.

"When we needed a doctor during the war we didn't have one. When the war ended we got one - in case (I suppose), we picked up Yanks that were being flown home across the Atlantic.

"We also got a cinema and when in harbour other ship's crews would join us. I'd play it very loud and we'd dance to the music sometimes. One of the films I vividly remember was, 'To Have and Have Not' starring Humphrey Bogart and Lauren Bacall in her debut."

Tom Tribe served aboard **Berkeley Castle** as a signalman from commissioning until the end of November 1945. He wrote :-

*"We arrived at the Barclay Curle & Co. Ltd. yard at Whiteinch, Glasgow probably in September 1943, workmen all over the place. After shaking down and sea trials, a ceremony handing over the ship took place. We were based at Greenock and Londonderry, and on occasion when sailing up to Londonderry and passing Moville a lady living in a small white house would run up a Union Flag as we passed by. When leaving Greenock we oiled at the tanker which was laying moored off. On one occasion, moored not far away in one line were **SS Queen Mary**, **SS Queen Elizabeth** and **SS Mauritania**, two, three and four funnelled liners.*

*"We did our running up trials at Tobermory on the Isle of Mull. Admiral "Monkey" Stevens would arrive without notice at any time of the day or night, and raise HELL. One day we landed by ship's boat on an Island covered with sheep as a landing exercise. The only thing I recall was that all our chocolate rations vanished! One evening a raiding party from **Carisbrooke Castle** borrowed (?) our forward riding light. On the way back possibly with **Carisbrooke**, we carried out an attack on a possible U-boat. Together with **Watchman**, **Wanderer**, **Strule** and **Carisbrooke Castle** we set off for the Bay of Biscay. Off Ireland, **Berkeley Castle** and **Carisbrooke Castle** were diverted to St. Johns, Newfoundland. After a short distance **Carisbrooke's** 'Big End' broke down. We took her in tow and proceeded across the Atlantic. It was possibly that day that Winston Churchill gave his speech proclaiming that 'The Battle of the Atlantic has been won'. Reports of U-boats were received continually, we understood that three large packs were grouping ready for an attack on the*

next convoy. One night a large blip appeared on the Radar and we were instructed to challenge. 'Was it a large German Armed Cruiser?' No, we survived. It was the **SS Queen Mary***!*

In 1991, at a Castle Class Corvette reunion, it was reported that in the German naval records in Jersey are reports from a U-boat in mid-Atlantic that a Castle Class boat was seen towing another but that no action was taken due to lack of torpedoes.

Unable to use St. John's due to reports of ice we made for the American base at Argentia, some miles west along the coast. On arrival we were told to anchor off as the weather was too bad for a tug to take **Carisbrooke** *in tow. This didn't seem to deter the Skipper who managed to go alongside complete with* **Carisbrooke** *still in tow!*

Having asked for green vegetables we were surprised to see a veritable convoy of supplies heading for us.

Leaving **Carisbrooke** *for repairs we left early the next morning after clearing some three or four feet of snow off the bridge, and hauling the mooring lines in by hand as the capstan was frozen solid. We rendezvoused with a very heavily escorted convoy. We were told that all the merchant ships in the convoy were carrying high octane spirit! Escorts outnumbered merchant ships by at least two to one. Arriving off the north of Ireland we passed an outward convoy of empty merchant ships escorted by a Canadian flotilla of Flower Class Corvettes. Just over the horizon they were attacked by a pack of U-Boats and we understood sustained heavy losses. All our escorts were almost out of fuel and were unable to help; at this point most of the escorts left.*

We belonged to Escort Group 40 together with **Carisbrooke***,* **Dumbarton***,* **Hadleigh** *and* **Kenilworth Castle** *and escorted convoys to Gibraltar, usually a long trip half way out into the Atlantic to avoid the Bay of Biscay, away from possible air attacks. On occasions Walker with his flotilla came along at dusk and left early next morning.*

(he) Usually came and went at change of watch. On one occasion, shortly after they had left us and sweeping away from the convoy they sank two U-Boats. Some of the Group together with two fleet' sweepers escorted **HMS Iron Duke** *(built in 1921) to Gibraltar arriving there on 5 June, the eve of D-Day.*

"We appeared to steam closer to the shore than previously, on hearing the news the following morning, we thought "another decoy".

Our Captain, Lieut. Darrer lived in Liverpool and one of our seaman brought back from leave a cutting from the Liverpool Echo reporting how many miles the **Berkeley** *had sailed etc. Shortly after Lieut. Darrer left after being taken ill with an ulcer, his replacement was Lieut. Farmer. Either before or after this, Cdr. Duck DSO RNR, together with his staff, came on board as SO EG 31. It had been reported that he was to have gone to the* **Carisbrooke***, but transferred to the* **Berkeley***. Why? It was suggested because of the 'Duck' painted on her funnel, or perhaps had she broken down once again? The following day as duty Signalman, I handed a signal to the Commander and asked "if it was in order to congratulate him?" He just replied 'thank you'. Shortly afterwards he appeared on deck with four rings on his jacket!*

"After one escort trip we called at Moville to 'oil ship' as SO. We went up river to Londonderry. As duty Signalman I went ashore for urgent orders. Quite a swell on, going alongside, thought I would jump the one foot or so drop. I must have thought too long, it was more like six feet, not so good in sea boots! After hobbling up to Naval HQ and immediately arriving back on board we put to sea. I was in sick bay with a bad foot, which is still with me today. Reports were that every boat that could float joined in to attack suspect U-Boats refuelling on the west coast of Ireland. I don't know if we were in charge of the operation. If Captain Duck was with us, we probably were. I only know that a lot of high explosive sounds worse when below deck. I was told it was thought a number of U-Boats had a fright!

"Shortly after the D-Day landings, **Berkeley Castle** *together with a flotilla of Castle boats were*

ordered to attack old wrecks in the English Channel. It was reported that U-Boats were laying alongside them. Our job was to bomb these wrecks. We blew very many extremely large conger eels to the surface and some of the smaller ones, still over six feet in length, we ate. Refuelled and ammunitioned at Falmouth. On this mission we attacked a moving object, ending up with a huge mound of mackerel. A French fishing boat was invited to help themselves to the catch. We never found out what was in the bottles taken on board in exchange for the fish.

Orders for Berkeley together with another Castle boat, I believe the Carisbrooke and two trawlers were to escort an ocean going tug towing a dry dock from the Bristol Channel to Gibraltar. Its eventual journey (destination) being Suez.

Three times we got near the Bay of Biscay, each time the tow parted and twice the dry dock ended up nearer to the Bristol Channel. On the third occasion we had orders to sink her. Unable to sink by gunfire a PO and our very able seaman, Alan Stanley, placed charges on her.

"At the end of one of our convoy duties we, together with another Castle picked up an American convoy of landing craft and escorted it to Swansea. Signalling Mumbles signal station for a long time, giving details of ships, it was not until we reached Greenock and received post, that I realised I had been signalling to a Wren that I had met at Coalhouse Fort on the Thames at East Tilbury. We refuelled at Milford Haven. Is it correct or only a buzz, that some of the crew collected a piano from the NAAFI and got (it) as far as the dockyard gate?

"Next day leaving harbour we felt our way very nervously up the Irish Sea through a minefield. Patrolled the minefields above Scapa, luckily our very able bodied seaman, Alan Stanley, who could sink a mine with oerlikon fire was on board. We were to meet again in 1990, 91 and 92. This happened before 20 November 1944, my 21st birthday, when I left the ship. I was to meet many of the crew again at Chatham whilst being demobbed in June 1946."

'Postie' and Potatoes
Alan Stanley ex Berkeley Castle

Alan Stanley wrote:

"During my service aboard Berkeley Castle I managed to land myself the job of 'Postie'. A dream job, although I never let on to the others what a skive it was. I earned countless 'sippers' for little favours performed ashore for their shopping needs. The job required two visits to the Fleet Mail Office, forenoon and afternoon, then a stroll round the shopping centre for items requested by members of all ranks. There would also be time for a stop at the local before my tot and earned 'sippers' and lunch. The afternoon collection was preceeded by attendance at the cinema or football match; there was always something going on. I was never in any duty watch, so after clearing the mail box at 1800 for the wardroom to censor, I went ashore. I usually went to the 'Church Services Club' for a social evening playing cards and chatting to the ladies of all ages."

"There was a particular lady that I was acquainted with who told me that there was a serious shortage of potatoes. She and her family were going to miss their usual roast potatoes for Sunday lunch. This was just a couple of days before we were due to sail with another convoy. I then decided to repay her and her family for all the kindness shown by smuggling a few pounds of potatoes on my last trip ashore before sailing."

"Before collecting the censored mail from the wardroom I visited the vegetable locker and put about 3lbs into the mail bag. I then stuffed the post, about 20 letters, on top of the 'rabbits' and proceeded to the gangway. There stood Lieutenant Usher, like the Rock of Gibraltar saying 'Let's go ashore together, I've never seen a mail office.' He and I had stood many middle and morning watches on the bridge discussing every subject under the sun.

Unfortunately he followed me down the gangway, so with the mail bag over my shoulder he could not fail to see that there was more than post in the bag. "What on earth have you in the pack?" he enquired, "I censored the mail post last night , and there was only about 20 letters." I had visions of all sorts of calamities falling on me. "Potatoes Sir." I replied meekly. He repeated quietly "Potatoes." And for several minutes never uttered a word. Seizing the chance I explained my reasons. I like to think that I had made a deep impression on him. But no. He replied with a lecture that could have stripped the paint off the ship's side. The fact that a few pounds of fresh vegetables did go bad before there was a chance to eat them, did not weigh much in my favour. However, by the time that we had reached the Mail Office he had calmed down and told me to deliver the 'King Edwards', then to return to the ship. The incident was never referred to again, but I noticed that on several future occasions he gave me a knowing look at the mail bag."

HMS CAISTOR CASTLE

Battle Honours
North Sea 1945

*A 25 January 1945 view of **HMS Caistor Castle**.* (Ben Warlow Collection)

On completion of working up at Tobermory *Caistor Castle* joined the 30th Escort Group, sailing with them for the first time on 21st November 1944. She remained with that group on patrol and convoy support duties until the end of the war in Europe.

From time to time *Caistor Castle* was the Senior Officer of the 2nd division of the group and from 31.12.44 to 07.01.45 she carried out the duties of the Senior Officer of the group whilst *Pevensey Castle* was retained in harbour with engine defects.

On 11 May 1945 whilst on patrol with the group *Caistor Castle* intercepted *U-956* on the surface and flying the designated black flag of surrender.

After the group had been despatched to Loch Erribol, *Caistor Castle* was loaned to the 21st Escort Group to assist in the escort of ten U-boats to Loch Alsh.

Caistor Castle sailed with the 30th Escort Group on 24 May 1945 from Scapa Flow to Bergen, arriving there on 26th May. She was left behind when the group sailed from Bergen to the UK escorting surrendered U-Boats and proceeded to Christiansands. From there, leaving on the 10 June 1945, she escorted three Type XXI U-boats to the UK.

From 14 June 1945 to the end of January 1946 *Caistor Castle* was engaged in Air/Sea Rescue (ASR) duties. Firstly based at Gibraltar under the command of Flag Officer Gibraltar and Mediterranean Approaches (FOGMA) and secondly, from mid November 1945 under N.O.I.C. Freetown.

At the end of January 1946 *Caistor Castle* was sailed to the UK for reduction into reserve. However, enroute she stood by an L.C.I in distress and escorted it to Bermuda. From there she sailed to the UK via New York.

HISTORY

19.12.42	Ordered.
26.08.43	Laid down. **Builder:** Hull and Engine Lewis (Aberdeen).
22.05.44	Launched.
29.09.44	Completed.

WARTIME VOYAGES

Date	ESG	Senior Officer	Convoy	No of Ships	Arrive/ Sail	Location	Notes
30.09.44							AM 3011200A/9 When ready for sea C should be sailed for Tobermory to work up on conclusion of which she is to join Western Approaches Command
18.10.44					Sail	Aberdeen	To Scapa Flow
20.10.44	30th EG	*Pevensey Castle*					At Tobermory
20.10.44	30th EG	*Pevensey Castle*			Arv	Clyde	
30.10.44	30th EG	*Pevensey Castle*			Arv	Tobermory	
06.11.44	30th EG	*Pevensey Castle*				At Tobermory	
10.11.44	30th EG	*Pevensey Castle*				At Tobermory	
19.11.44	30th EG	*Pevensey Castle*			Arv	Londonderry	
21.11.44	30th EG	*Pevensey Castle*			Sail	Londonderry	Patrol in area 52N 11W. Group attacked suspected U-boat on 26th Nov & held contact for 73 hrs. Then supported passage of HX 321 & relieved 2nd EG on 5th Dec. Group returned to Londonderry
28.11.44	30th EG	*Pevensey Castle*				5110N0945W	On Patrol
02.12.44	30th EG	*Pevensey Castle*			Sail	Larne	
09.12.44	30th EG	*Pevensey Castle*			Arv	Londonderry	
18.12.44	30th EG	*Pevensey Castle*			Sail	Belfast	Having arrived there the same day (SMO)
21.12.44	30th EG	*Pevensey Castle*			Sail	Milford Haven	
28.12.44	30th EG	*Pevensey Castle*			Sail	Portsmouth	For a short lay-over
31.12.44	30th EG	*Caistor Castle*			Sail	Portsmouth	Patrol area north of Cherbourg
08.01.45	30th EG	*Pevensey Castle*				S of Needles	On Patrol: *Pevensey Castle* resumed command of the 30th EG
15.01.45	30th EG	*Pevensey Castle*			Arv	Londonderry	

Date	ESG	Senior Officer	Convoy	No of Ships	Arrive/ Sail	Location	Notes
15.01.45	31st EG	*Berkeley Castle*				Off Holyhead	On Patrol This is not substantiated by the S.O. 31st E.G's R.O.P. (S.M.O.)
29.01.45	30th (B)	*Caistor Castle*				Off Hartland Point-On patrol	
06.02.45	30th EG	*Pevensey Castle*			Sail	Plymouth	
19.02.45	30th EG	*Pevensey Castle*				Londonderry	Boiler cleaning ready 22.02.45
24.02.45	30th EG	*Pevensey Castle*			Sail	Londonderry	
27.03.45	30th EG	*Pevensey Castle*			Arv	Lochalsh	
30.03.45	30th EG	*Pevensey Castle*			Sail	Londonderry	
02.04.45	30th EG	*Pevensey Castle*			Arv	Scapa Flow	
11.04.45	30th EG	*Pevensey Castle*			Arv	Scapa Flow	
13.04.45	30th EG	*Pevensey Castle*			Sail	Scapa Flow	
04.05.45	30th EG	*Portchester Castle*			Sail	Londonderry	
07.05.45	30th EG	*Pevensey Castle*			Sail	Londonderry	
17.05.45	30th EG	*Pevensey Castle*			Arv	Londonderry	
20.05.45	30th EG	*Pevensey Castle*			Arv	Loch Eribol	
25.05.45	30th EG	*Pevensey Castle*			Arv	Scapa Flow	
27.05.45	30th EG	*Pevensey Castle*			Arv	Bergen	
02.06.45	30th EG	*Pevensey Castle*			Sail	Bergen	
10.06.45	F.O.G.M.A				Sail	Christiansand	
14.06.45	F.O.G.M.A				Arv	Londonderry	
09.07.45					Arv	Gibraltar	On ASR Duty
14.07.45					Sail	Gibraltar	
06.08.45					Arv	Gibraltar	T 19.8. F.O.GM. 0110226/8 *Knaresborough Castle* proceeding to relieve *CC* ETA ASR Station 4/9
07.09.45					Arv	Gibraltar	
24.09.45					Sail	Gibraltar	to A.S.R. position 20 *CC* 080701/10 Have been relieved by *St Austell Bay* at A.S.R. Station 20. *CC* relieved *Portchester Castle* in position 19
10.11.45					Arv	Gibraltar	
17.11.45					Sail	Gibraltar	*CC* 071832/11 Have been relieved on ASR Station 19 by *St Brides Bay*.
23.11.45					Arv	Freetown	F.O.G.M.A. *CC* ETD 1400/17 for Freetown. F.O.G.M.A. *CC* ETA Freetown p.m. for A.D.R. duties as ordered by

Date	ESG	Senior Officer	Convoy	No of Ships	Arrive/ Sail	Location	Notes
							Capt.; (?) Freetown 260946/1 Intend sailing *CC* 27.11 to A.D.R. 22
13.12.45					Arv	Freetown	
19.12.45							N.O.I/c Freetown 1900901/12 Intend sailing *CC* to A.S.R. No 22
06/01.46					Arv	Freetown	***Knaresborough Castle*** have been relieved on A.S.R. M by *CC* . *CC* 110844/12 have been relieved by *Fal* Station 22 0805/11 ETA Freetown 13/12.
28.01.47							Capt. I/c W.A.F. 280934/1 intend sailing *CC* from Freetown 28/1.
29.01.47							F.O.G.M.A. 291628/1 *CC* is to proceed direct to Las Palmas ETA 2/2.
29.01.47							AM 291611/1 F.O.G.M.A. is requested to sail *CC* to UK as soon as practicable to reduce to Cat "B" on arrival.
31.01.47							G.O.G.M.A. 311952A/1 Arrival of *CC* delayed expected to R/V/ with L.C.I. 1100/3.1 *CC* 722/2 Proceeding to assistance of ship in distress in position 2120'N 2330'W.
27.02.47							Com. I/c Bermuda 271400Z/2 Intend to sail *CC* (escorting L.C.I.(L) 1400/1.3 to New York then *CC* to Plymouth. end of record

1947 to 1948	Reserve at Devonport.
1949	Refit at Cardiff.
1951	Refit at Sheerness.
Feb 1953 to 1955	2nd Training Squadron, Portland.
1953	Represented Home Command, Portsmouth at the Coronation Review.
1955 - 1956	Reserve at Devonport.

1956	Sold to Arnott Young.
March 1956	Arrived Dalmuir for scrapping.

Summaries of the patrols with the 30th Escort Group are provided under that group's heading.

*A post war picture of **HMS Caistor Castle** displaying an 'F' pendant number following reclassification to a frigate.* (*World Ship Society*)

HMS CARISBROOKE CASTLE

Battle Honours
Atlantic 1944

HMS Carisbrooke Castle in November 1943.   (MoD/Crown Copyright)

HMS *Carisbrooke Castle*, in terms of human life would have been described as one destined to suffer ill health all her life. Trouble started soon after she was commissioned. She had left Dundee on 17 November 1943 and was proceeding northwards but had to put into Aberdeen on the 29th to correct engine room defects. On completion of repairs she then went to Tobermory for working up. There she remained until Christmas Eve, arriving at Londonderry on the 27th with a recurrence of engine defects.

Carisbrooke Castle was not immediately allocated to any specific Escort Group, serving as a spare ship. She briefly supported the 15th Escort Group in January which was escorting convoy HX 274. However, later in the month engine room problems re-occurred.

On 2 February 1944 she left Londonderry in com-

pany with *Berkeley Castle*, apparently with orders to proceed to St. John's, Newfoundland, and to overtake and provide additional support to ON 222.

On 13 February 1944 the two ships were reported as being in position 52°45'N; 32°45'W steaming at 13 knots towards St. John's. Sometime during the following day *Carisbrooke Castle* suffered a major breakdown of a main engine crankshaft bearing and was unable to proceed under her own power.

She was taken in tow by *Berkeley Castle* under difficult conditions. Anecdotal tales tell of the tow line parting at least once. As the weather improved the towing speed increased to 8 knots and after a three day tow the two ships arrived off Argentia.

The authorities told *Berkeley Castle* that the two ships should anchor outside the harbour because conditions were too severe for their tug. *Berkeley Castle* discounted the bad weather and brought the two ships

into harbour and alongside without the tug's assistance.

Carisbrooke Castle remained at Argentia for six days and then proceeded to St. John's where she joined the 40th Escort Group (*HMS Exe* SO), leaving with them on convoy escort duty. The Group arrived at the Clyde on 28 February 1944.

For the next month *Carisbrooke Castle* remained with the 40th Escort Group on convoy support and patrol duties.

Early in April 1944 *Carisbrooke Castle* joined the re-organised B5 Escort Group under Commander N. W. Duck. RNR in *Berkeley Castle*. Other ships forming the Group were - *Hadleigh Castle*, *Dumbarton Castle* and *Lancaster Castle*.

In October 1944 the Group was re-designated as the 31st Escort Group and placed on A/S patrol and convoy support duties in the western and northern coastal waters of the UK. This continued until mid-May 1945 when the Group was disbanded after VE Day.

Prior to the formation of the 31st Escort Group *Carisbrooke Castle* had escorted 13 convoys comprising a total of 500 ships; all without loss due to enemy action.

At the end of the war in Europe *Carisbrooke Castle* was allocated to Air/Sea Rescue duties based at Devonport. In April 1946 she was loaned to the Fishery Protection Flotilla for service off the West coast of Scotland. In the late autumn of that year she was placed in reserve. She was brought back into service in 1952 and based at Devonport, where she worked as an Air Target Training Ship. In January 1957 she replaced the badly damaged destroyer *Orwell* as the leader of the Plymouth Local Squadron. This continued until the *Orwell*'s repairs were completed and *Carisbrooke Castle* was laid up on 10 May 1957.

HISTORY

02.02.43	Ordered.
12.03.43	Laid down. **Builder**: Hull - Caledon (Dundee); Engine - G Clark (Sunderland).
31.07.43	Launched.
17.11.43	Completed.

WARTIME VOYAGES

Date	ESG	Senior Officer	Convoy	No of Ships	Arrive/ Sail	Location	Notes
12.11.43	Unall				Arv	Leith	
15.11.43	Unall				Arv	Dundee	
30.11.43	Unall				Arv	Aberdeen	Having left Dundee on the same day. N I/c Dundee 291937/11 *CC* Developed engine trouble proceeding to Aberdeen. FO I/c Aberdeen 041158/12 Defects in *CC* will be completed 2/12. (SMO)
08.12.43	EG B7				Arv	Tobermory	
24.12.43	Unall				Sail	Tobermory	
27.12.43	Unall				Arv	Londonderry	Engine room defects (SMO)
16.01.44	Unall				Sail	Londonderry	
20.01.44	EG 15		HX 274	38		5457N 1201W	
23.01.44	Unall				Sail	Londonderry	
02.02.44	Unall				Sail	Londonderry	Engine room defects (SMO).
04.02.44-						5332N 1310W	To St John's
06.02.44						5245N 3245W	To St John's, 13 knots
08.02.44						4945N 4640W	To St John's, 8 knots
09.02.44	40th EG				Arv	St John's	
10.02.44						4618N 5225W	*Carisbrooke Castle* being towed by *Berkeley Castle* 8.5 knots
10.02.44					Arv	Argentia	
16.02.44	40th EG				Sail	Argentia	
18.02.44	EG C3		HX 279	54		4301N 4725W	Hague lists 59 ships
19.02.44	40th EG				Sail	St John's	
27.02.44	3rd EG		Not given			5435N 1055W	To Clyde Convoy scattered
28.02.44	40th EG*Exe*				Arv	Clyde	
06.03.44	40th EG*Exe*				Sail	Clyde	HX 279 (SMO).
14.03.44	40th EG*Exe*				Arv	Londonderry	
16.03.44	40th EG*Exe*				Sail	Londonderry	
28.03.44	40th EG*Exe*				Sail	Aultbea	Having arrived on the same day.
01.04.44	40th EG*Exe*				Arv	Clyde	
07.04.44	EG B5	*Exe*			Arv	Clyde	
10.04.44	EG B5	*Exe*			Arv	Greenock	
13.04.44	EG B5	*Exe*			Sail	Londonderry	
14.04.44	EG B5	*Exe*	OS 74/ KMS 48	29		5552N 0952W	
22.04.44	EG B5	*Exe*	OS 74/ KMS 48	29		3712N 1333W	

Date	ESG	Senior Officer	Convoy	No of Ships	Arrive/ Sail	Location	Notes
24.04.44	EG B5	*Exe*			Arv	Gibraltar	
01.05.44	EG B5	*Exe*			Sail	Gibraltar	
06.05.44	EG B5	*Exe*	SL 156/ MKS 47	65		4116N 1829W	Hague gives 46 ships
12.05.44	EG B5	*Exe*	SL 156/ MKS 47	65	Arv	Clyde	
13.05.44	EG B4	*Helmsdale*	OS 76/ KMS 50	35	Arv	Gibraltar	
20.05.44	EG B5	*Exe*			Sail	Clyde	
22.05.44	EG B5	*Exe*			Arv	Londonderry	
23.05.44	EG B5	*Exe*	OS78/ KMS52	23	Sai	Londonderry	
29.05.44	EG B4	*Helmsdale*	SL 158/ MKS 49	51		4730N 2150W	Convoy size increased with the joining of the SL section on 21 May. *CC* Joined convoy on 28 May. Detached to southbound convoy 29th
06.06.44	EG B5	*Exe*	OS78/ KMS52	23	Arv	Gibraltar	
09.06.44	EG B5	*Exe*	MKS 51	14	Sail	Gibraltar	
10.06.44	EG B5	*Exe*	SL160/ MKS 51	44		3540N 0705W	
13.06.44	EG B5	*Exe*	SL 160/ MKS 51	50		3710N 1640W	44 ships according to Hague
20.06.44	EG B5	*Exe*	SL160 MKS 51	50	Arv	Clyde	
29.06.44	EG B5	*Exe*			Sail	Clyde	
02.07.44	EG B5	*Exe*	OS82/ KMS56	26	Sail	Londonderry	Having arrived at Londonderry the day before
06.07.44	EG B5	*Exe*	OS 82 KMS56	29		4818N 1935W	
13.07.44	EG B5	*Exe*	OS82/ KMS56	29	Arv	Gibraltar	
21.07.44	EG B5	*Exe*	MKS 55	19		3435N 1020W	
21.07.44	EG B5	*Exe*	SL 164/ MKS 55	35		3525N 1248W	
31.07.44	EG B5	*Exe*	SL 164/ MKS 55	33	Arv	Clyde	
09.08.44	EG B5	*Hadleigh Castle*			Arv	Larne	Having left Clyde the day before.
11.08.44	EG B5	*Hadleigh Castle*			Arv	Londonderry	
12.08.44	EG B5	*Hadleigh Castle*	OS86/ KMS60	23	Sail	Londonderry	
12.08.44	EG B5	*Hadleigh Castle*	OS 86/ KMS60	25		5550N 0855W	
22.08.44	EG B5	*Hadleigh Castle*	OS86/ KMS60	24		3548N 0840W	

Date	ESG	Senior Officer	Convoy	No of Ships	Arrive/ Sail	Location	Notes
23.08.44	EG B5	*Hadleigh Castle*	OS86/ KMS60	24	Arv	Gibraltar	
30.08.44	EG B5	*Hadleigh Castle*	SL 168/ MKS 59	35	Sail	Gibraltar	
01.09.44	EG B5	*Hadleigh Castle*	SL 168/ MKS 59	35		3925N 1030W	
06.09.44	EG B2	*Cotton*	OS 88/ KMS 62	37		5029N 0901W	
08.09.44	EG B2	*Cotton*	OS 88/ KMS 62	32		4530N 1128W	Arrived Clyde 10.09.44 for 31st E.G
10.09.44	31st EG	*Berkeley Castle*			Arv	Clyde	
21.09.44	31st EG	*Berkeley Castle*			Arv	Londonderry	
23.09.44	31st EG	*Berkeley Castle*			Sail	Londonderry	
09.10.44	31st EG	*Berkeley Castle*			Arv	Clyde	
11.10.44	31st EG	*Berkeley Castle*				Clyde	Clyde for lay over
16.10.44	31st EG	*Berkeley Castle*				Clyde	To 18th
20.10.44	31st EG	*Berkeley Castle*				At Avonmouth	Refit & Repairs
23.10.44	31st EG	*Berkeley Castle*				At Avonmouth	Refit
27.10.44	31st EG	*Berkeley Castle*				At Avonmouth	Refit Repairs
03.11.44	31st EG	*Berkeley Castle*				Avonmouth	Refit completes 19 Dec
01.12.44	31st EG	*Berkeley Castle*				Avonmouth	Refit comp 19 Dec
21.12.44	31st EG	*Berkeley Castle*				At Avonmouth	
24.12.44	31st EG	*Berkeley Castle*			Sail	Avonmouth	
04.01.45	31st EG	*Berkeley Castle*			Sail	Clyde	
22.01.45	31st EG	*Berkeley Castle*				Clyde	
29.01.45	31st EG	*Berkeley Castle*				At Lochalsh	
02.02.45	31st EG	*Berkeley Castle*			Sail	Belfast	May have visited Great Yarmouth and Harwich before arriving at Belfast.(SMO)
10.02.45	31st EG	*Berkeley Castle*			Arv	Belfast	
10.02.45	31st EG	*Berkeley Castle*			Arv	Clyde	
12.02.45	31st EG	*Berkeley Castle*			Sail	Clyde	
27.02.45	31st EG	*Berkeley Castle*			Arv	Clyde	
10.03.45	31st EG	*Berkeley Castle*			Sail	Clyde	
23.03.45	31st EG	*Berkeley Castle*			Arv	Clyde	
25.03.45	31st EG	*Berkeley Castle*			Sail	Clyde	
14.04.45	31st EG	*Berkeley Castle*			Sail	Clyde	
19.04.45	31st EG	*Berkeley Castle*			Sail	Belfast	
30.04.45	31st EG	*Berkeley Castle*			Sail	Milford Haven	
13.05.45	31st EG	*Berkeley Castle*			Arv	Clyde	
29.05.45	31st EG	*Berkeley Castle*			Sail	Clyde	
18.06.45					Arv	Clyde	
18.06.45	WA				Arv	Clyde	
28.06.45					Sail	Clyde	
29.06.45					Arv	Londonderry	And left same day.
19.07.45					Arv	Plymouth	For ASR Duties
02.08.45					Sail	Plymouth	
08.08.45					Arv	Plymouth	

Date	ESG	Senior Officer	Convoy	No of Ships	Arrive/ Sail	Location	Notes
17.09.45					Sail	Plymouth	CinC Plymouth 231117/9 *CC* is to be relieved by *Knaresborough*.
27.09.45					Arv	Plymouth	
22.10.45					Arv	A.D.R.18	
15.11.45					Arv	Plymouth	
27.11.45					Sail	Plymouth	ETA ASR 18 0400Z/29/11.
16.12.45					Arv	Plymouth	
29.12.45					Sail	Plymouth	CinC Plymouth 25/1149/12. Sail about 1600 29/12 to relieve *Rushen Castle* on ASR 2.
21.01.46					Arv	Plymouth	*CC* 191730/1 Relieved on ADR 10. ETA 1800 21/1.
17.02.46					Sail	Plymouth	CinC Plymouth 161255/2 Sail to relieve *Rushen Castle* on ASR 19. End of record

HMS Carisbrooke Castle Ship's Company 4 September 1945.   *(CCC(F)A Archives)*

A post war photograph of
HMS Carisbrooke Castle
looking a little negleted.
(MoD/Crown Copyright)

Apr 1946	Loaned to the Fishery Protection Flotilla, Rosyth, for service off the West Coast of Scotland.
Late Autumn 1946	Relieved by the Fleet Minesweeper *Welcome*; paid off and laid up in reserve.
1947-49	Devonport Reserve.
1949-50	Refit.
Sep 1951	Refit at Falmouth then reserve at Devonport.
May 1952 - 56	2nd Training Squadron; 30 May to 5 June 1953 at Ramsey, Isle of Man, participated 2 June in the official coronation celebrations including ceremonial parade and provided a much appreciated 30 minute firework display in the evening. She also represented the Home Command, Plymouth, at the Coronation Fleet Review.
Dec 1956	Reduced to reserve.
Jan to Apr 1957	Brought back into service as leader of the Plymouth Squadron to replace *Orwell*.
10 May 1957	Placed in reserve and laid up at Devonport.
1958	Sold to Shipbreaking Industries.
14 Jun 1958	Arrived Faslane for scrapping.

THE ATLANTIC TOW

Unfortunately, no definitive official report on this incident has been found. The various ship location, Ship Disposition Reports and the Ship Movement Orders do throw some light on the affair.

The two ships, *Carisbrooke Castle* and *Berkeley Castle* had been ordered to proceed together towards St Johns, N.F, possibly with a view to supplementing the escort strength of convoy ON 222. On 6 February they were reported as being in position 52°45'N 32°45'W steaming at 13 knots. On 8 February they are reported at 49°54'N, 46°40'W at 8 knots. This may coincide with John Leggett's account. He recalls that they experienced severe weather, resulting in the radar aerial coming adrift and the decision to send 'volunteers' aloft to secure it with rope. This was done when conditions had calmed down a little. Soon after this the weather further moderated and there was a dramatic drop in temperature. In thickening fog the ship's engine stopped. John, who was also Captain of the 4-inch gun, was engaged in regularly moving the gun so as to prevent it from freezing up. Meanwhile, all the rest of the watch were lining the rails on the lookout for icebergs. The conditions for the hands were not helped by the shortage of cold weather clothing - "...we had to turn our duffel coats over to each other when changing watch". The two ships made contact, still in fog. A tow was connected which eventually parted but was re-connected. The tow continued for about three days with the ships reaching up to 8 knots. They were directed to Argentia in worsening weather. When they arrived there they were told to anchor outside the harbour because conditions were too severe for a tug to operate. However, the Commanding Officer of *Berkeley Castle*, ignoring this advice, successfully brought both ships into harbour and alongside.

The Ship Movement Orders for *Carisbrooke Castle* record several incidents of engine defects starting from very soon after she was commissioned. On one of these occasions she went into Cardiff docks for repair. This was over the Christmas-New Year period 1943/44. John Leggett recalls the very cold weather and no power on board. In desperation to get warm they tried "...to get into pubs and working men's clubs just for a drink or anything for a warm. They wouldn't let us in. We finished up in a Sally Club about the size of a double toilet getting tea. After that, on the way back to the ship, we found a pub open. They were selling Blue Elephant Beer, at today's price of 35/-; needless to say we couldn't have more than one."

Mr. H.C. Reed who was a signalman on the *Carisbrooke Castle* commenting on their subsequent departure from Argentia wrote:-

> "..We had to have an ice-breaker to assist us out. There was loads of snow and ice and it really was cold. As usual we all closed up for leaving harbour. I was not expecting to take over the watch when we were under way, so I had come up with just my duffle coat on instead of waterproofs. As we went out to sea it really roughed up. I got chatting with a 10-inch lamp to the signal station on the headland. That kept me busy. The seas were coming over the top. The spray was lashing onto my back, freezing as it made contact. The surplus ran down my short duffle dripping into my sea boots. The seaman's watch was closed up on deck every half hour to clear the ice from the guns and squid.
> After about an hour I was shouting for a relief. I had no direct contact with the messdeck and remember pleading with the wheelhouse to get a message down below. It was the coldest I had been in my life, and quite honestly I was nearly in tears when my oppo appeared to take over the last half hour of the watch."

Normally the only people who stood a whole watch in the open at sea were the signalmen and Officers on watch. Lookouts changed every hour or half hour depending on conditions. The 4-inch gun and Squid crews could find shelter.

HMS Carisbrooke Castle photographed from *HMS Berkeley Castle* during the Atlantic Tow in 1944. The Ship's Company are busy recovering the parted tow line prior to recommencing the tow. *(CCC(F)A Archives)*

Carisbrooke Castle 1952 - 1954
Recollections of M.C. Biffen AB, RP3, Navigator's Yeoman and Motor Boat Coxswain W.J. Laidler, AB GL3 and Quartermaster's Mate.

The first of the crew since 1947 joined the ship at Flag Staff Steps, Devonport August/September 1952. Lieut. Commander T. G. Ridgeway, the Commanding Officer, had transferred along with some of his crew from the destroyer **HMS Ulysees**. Working up trials in Plymouth Sound soon demonstrated the considerable handling differences between a twin screwed destroyer and a single screwed corvette, now designated a Frigate. This was especially apparent when coming alongside or manoeuvring up to a mooring buoy.

On completion of working up, the ship joined the 2nd Training Squadron based at Portland. However **Carisbrooke Castle**'s main operational base was Londonderry.

From there the ship worked with Gannets from RNAS Eglinton and with submarines from the Holy Loch. The ship had a triple role; guiding the Gannets in sub hunting using their sonar buoys and her own Asdics and radar; being hunted and attacked by the same submarine; attacking the submarine with Squid and depth charges. These also involved the recovery of the sonar buoys that had been used during the exercises.

When the ship was based at Londonderry many families benefited from the trips ashore to the Free State,

*A March Past by **HMS Carisbrooke Castle** contingent at Ramsay on 2nd June 1953 for the Coronation of HM Queen Elizabeth II.*
(CCC(F)A Archives)

resulting in parcels of butter, bacon, nylons and toys being sent home to ration impoverished Britain.

Christmas and the 1952/53 New Year period was spent at Rosyth, where the numerous defects that had come to light were put right.

The usual routine at Londonderry was interrupted by preparations for and the visit to Ramsey, Isle of Man 31 May to 5 June for the Coronation celebrations.

Bad weather prevented the ship remaining alongside the Ramsey Pier. The ship anchored in the bay. Guests invited aboard found the motor boat trip across the bay to the ship more than many stomachs could withstand.

The boats' crews worked hard conveying guests as well as the coronation guard comprising 20 blue jackets, one Commissioned Gunner and the Navigating Officer who paraded through Ramsey with fixed bayonets.

The following day the town council repaid the crew by laying on coaches for a tour of the TT course with a boot load of refreshments half way up Snae Fell.

Later in the month **Carisbrooke Castle** repaired to Spithead to participate in the Fleet Review. The ship then returned to Londonderry. Once again she was lavished with more paint, but this time on the port side only. This being the only side that the Queen would see on her visit to Londonderry. It was hoped that she would be able to distinguish the **Carisbrooke Castle** from the fishing fleet which had apparently obtained paint similar to that used by the RN.

In October the ship participated in NATO exercises with the Dutch and French Navies. Disappointingly there were no opportunities for runs ashore in foreign ports.

In December 1953 the ship went into dry dock at Devonport. On completion, and whilst alongside the wall, a young executive Midshipman, on his first ship since leaving Dartmouth, was OOW during an exercise attack by Royal Marine Commandos. He made the mistake of trying to draw a side arm on a frogman attempting to board ship. The Midshipman began to realise the true facts of life when a lifebelt landed alongside him in the cold waters of the Tamar.

In 1954 the ship moved to Falmouth where she worked with **RNAS Culdrose**. During this time ". . .we went to the rescue of a merchant ship abandoned and on fire off the south Wales coast. We moored alongside and put aboard an anchor party and a fire party. The ship's condition was under control by the time that the salvage tugs came to tow her away.

Commenting on the work of the training squadron, Commander B.H. Wainwright OBE RN wrote:-

"Lt Cdr Brian Wainwright took over command from Lt Cdr Tom Lancaster on 16 August 1955 and until paying off on 18 December 1956 (the ship being unexpectedly recommissioned shortly after to replace the damaged **Orwell** *for Captain (D) Plymouth).*

With **Launceston Castle** *(Lt Cdr Mike Godden and later Lt Cdr Kay),* **Carisbrooke Castle** *was one of the two ATTS (Air Training Target Ships) in the Plymouth Local Division operating alternately from Plymouth and Londonderry, and on very rare occasions exercising together.*

Out of Plymouth the ship was generally day running - to sea first thing, out past the Eddystone, to steam up and down in mid-Channel to be located by aircraft from Culdrose, and back to harbour in the dog watches. Occasionally classes of makee-learn QR3's from Devonport Gunnery School would be taken to sea to have the experience of firing the 4-inch gun - it was said to sort out those who couldn't stand the noise! The gun was not terribly accurate; it had developed so much backlash in laying and training. On one occasion we took territorial soldiers to sea, led by a RAMC major. We did have visits to other ports and I remember St Ives where we were well received, but bad weather made boatwork difficult and there were fears of the anchor dragging. We also paid a visit to Nantes in France. I recollect that we took up overnight anchorage once off Penzance where there were mixed emotions among the locals who mistook us for a fishery protection ship. At dawn the fishing boats making for home drew alongside and chucked over quantities of fish. The first and only time I have had conger eel for breakfast, but what a time Jack had dodging these beasts with their snapping jaws on the quar-

terdeck before they were battered to death.

It was off Plymouth one time that, while doing about 15 knots, the CERA rang up for the engine to be stopped because the MP bottom end was running hot. So there we laid motionless for a worrying length of time while his team look down the bearing and applied new whitemetal. There was a sequel months later when a former wartime Commanding Officer - RNR - asked to visit with his family. After lunch with me he asked to be allowed to visit the engine-room. Afterwards a much-embittered Chief told me that his visitor had been responsible, while the ship lay dead in the water in mid-Atlantic, for sending seamen to help the stokers to true up the crankshaft with bastard files, hence our problems with running the MP bottom end bearing. Was this the origin of the tale in one of Nicholas Montserrat's novels?

"A more dramatic incident involved our taking to sea 20 Wren reservists, for what was supposed to be a day run. Approaching the breakwater around 1600 the W/T Office intercepted a Mayday for an aircraft ditched off the Lizard. Without a thought I put the wheel over and ordered full ahead down Channel while reporting my intentions. With the evening came the problem of feeding and bedding down the girls. They were fed on the messdecks and retired to cabins surrendered by the officers - several in the cuddy - watched over and stoutly defended by their Chief Wren. Around midnight we were in the search area enlisting the help of a merchant ship and a RNLI lifeboat but finding no wreckage or survivors. By then there was another worry. One of the Wrens, suffering it emerged from some chronic illness, was in a coma as she lay in the First Lieutenant's bunk while the SBA was helpless to find a remedy. But the search took priority until after a couple of hours we were closed by two destroyers sent at full speed from Devonport with orders for us to return to port forthwith. So we steered for home and at daybreak called the signal station for medical assistance. An irate Surgeon Captain, aroused from his bed, came out in a launch to meet us in the Sound, saying he had never heard of such a thing as a sick woman all night aboard a warship, and what did I think I was up to! The casualty was landed in the boat and on our arrival alongside we found that the CinC had been besieged by the Press who were on to the sensation of women being at sea overnight. Hence the despatch of the destroyers to relieve us. Some time later the girls visited the ship with chocolates etc. for the ship's company.

"At Londonderry our task was in support of training for Gannet crews from Eglinton and RAF Shackletons from Aldergrove. We usually sailed from Derry on Sunday night or Monday morning and returned on Friday night. Mid-week, if not required for night operations, we usually anchored inside the mouth of the Foyle. Fuelling was at Lisahally. Anti-submarine training for the air observers involved up to six UX9s a day, telling our submarine to dive, directing the joining aircraft, and when we obtained contact dropping grenades to surface the submarine before recovering all the sonabuoys. When rolling about in a heavy sea this required good seamanship on the quarterdeck. Then we opened the range and started all over again . Occasionally we were the target Shackletons on photo-reece and, at night, practising with their Leigh lights. They would also drop torpedoes which had to be recovered as well as the sonobuoys. We had some visits, notably to Liverpool and Belfast, as well as to the distillery and creamery on Islay - the latter run by an ex-MTB coxswain.

"One evening, having got the 'secure' from Eglinton and heading for the Foyle, an aircraft was reported lost and we went off to search. Using a guess at the position and taking into account a strong breeze we found Lieut. Moseley RN in his dinghy twenty miles downwind and crossing the Atlantic in the dark very fast. He was a very grateful officer!

Romance at Christmas 1955.

Young John Boulden on leave from *Carisbrooke Castle* pops the question and is accepted. They went to see their local vicar to set the arrangements in motion. "Ah!" he said, you must have the bans called at your home parish. "But that's not so easy when, like me, you are serving on *Carisbrooke Castle*."

"O.K. see what you can do." So No.1 was consulted who in turn looked it up in Q.RE.& A.I. There were two choices. To publish the bans or to call them. Knowing his shipmates, it was realised the first choice would require a glass fronted notice board, to stop graffiti. Since this did not exist, the only course open was to call the bans.

So, to do this, divisions were called on three successive Sundays. This did not go down well with the ship's company and John's popularity went into a decline.

Another problem was the No.l, not being a Cornishman, found John's fiance's Cornish name something of a tongue twister. After the first attempt of calling out 'VELLENOWETH' he asked "How did |I do?" "Well not too bad Sir. You are pretty close, and at least you have another two goes at it to get it perfect."

All went well and the couple were spliced on Easter leave in 1956. He had a wonderful wedding present from the ship's company. But, it was Sippers, gulpers and wedding cake all round before he was in their good books.

An Essay from a young orphan girl in France following a children's party onboard

Great was our joy last Tuesday when at dinner we were told that in the afternoon we would be taken to visit an English ship anchored in the Bassin D'Arcachon.

On arrival at the landing place we saw two big warships. The F379 (*Carisbrooke Castle*) and the F397 (*Launceston Castle*) anchored together.

A motor boat manned by pirates with painted faces was at our disposal. The pirates were disguised sailors. They frightened us at first, but we were quickly reassured by the big smiles that lit up their faces, we got into the boat and went to F379.

At our destination, a sailor helped us to climb on to the deck. There it was impossible to understand anyone, fortunately gestures and a few words caught in passing helped us to understand that, for the visit there would be a sailor as guide to eight children. The one given to my group was very friendly. He tried by gestures to make himself understood (which was very funny) and succeeded every time. With much patience, and a smile on his face, he showed us the guns and made them move, the seasaw - how happy he was to see how quickly each one of us wanted to try it. There was certainly everything for our happiness on board this ship and the time passed by and the tour continued. The Galley, which was very warm; the Captain's cabin- in those two, was something amusing, a voice pipe which we were allowed to try, someone spoke and people up above replied.

On the deck in front, right at the end, we saw a red and gold crown which we admired very much. Truly we were allowed everything that day, even as far as the telephone on board, which were put at our service.

Next was the cinema, where sweets were distributed causing a battle, but order and silence were soon restored. We had a film of '*Charlie*' in English but very funny all the same. This was not all - we had surprise after surprise. Soon we were taken to a big room where long tables were covered with many plates of cakes, each one of us had our place. After Grace we started to enjoy English delicacies. The paper hats! One for each of us and quickly they were place on our heads. Nearly all the crew were there and each one

pressing us to fill our plates and cups which to our great astonishment were made of cardboard. Cakes and fruits followed each other very quickly to our 'Poor Stomach'. We got up from our abundant refreshment, very heavy with English food inspite of that we sang two French songs under the fatherly smiles of those who were now our friends. A pair of earrings were given to each of us as a souvenir then we got into the boat again which took us away from the dream which this visit had been to us.

Brother English! This little French girl wishes, in retelling that day, to inframe the friendship which lies between us and which ought to be amongst all peoples of the world. But you are leaving and going back to the business which you like so much. Perhaps will you remember again those little girls whom you amused so much and parted from there cares. They cannot say to much for you as if you were big brothers who are leaving never to return.

Anne Marie
Of the Aorius St. Vincent de Paul
Le mulleau Arcachon.

(Note: The spelling and text is as of the original)

*Children's party on board **HMS Carisbrooke Castle** at Arcachon on 30 July 1955, with PO J. Boulden.* *(J. Boulden)*

HMS DENBIGH CASTLE

Battle Honours
Arctic 1945

HMS Denbigh Castle in 1945.

(Steve Bush Collection)

HISTORY

19.12.42	Ordered.
30.09.43	Laid down: **Builder**: Hull and Engine - Lewis (Aberdeen).
05.08.44	Launched.
30.12.44	Completed.
09.01.45	Left Aberdeen and arrived Scapa Flow.
10.01.45	Left Scapa Flow.
12.01.45	Arrived Tobermory.
29.01.45	Arrived Scapa Flow.
04.02.45	Left Scapa Flow with 7th Escort Group to escort Russian Convoy JW 64.
13.02.45	Torpedoed at the entrance to Kola Inlet by *U-992*. Towed into Bolshaya Volkovaya Bay where she capsized and was written off as a total constructive loss.

After completion, the ship under the command of Temp Lt Cdr Graham Butcher DSC RNVR proceeded to Tobermory via Scapa Flow, arriving at Tobermory on 12 January 1945. She was allocated to the 7th Escort Group (*Cygnet* SO) and joined the Group at Scapa Flow on 29 January after completing working up training at Tobermory.

On 4 February 1945 she left with the Group to form the close escort for convoy JW 64. (Operation Hotbed; VA 10th Cruiser Squadron in *Campania*). The outstanding feature of the passage of JW 64 was the persistent bad weather, attacks by torpedo bombers and the close proximity of U-Boats to the Kola Inlet.

Denbigh Castle, which was fitted with Type 277 radar liased with *Campania* in detecting approaching aircraft. Because of the position of *Campania*'s aerial she had a blind spot 25° either side of the stern. *Denbigh Castle* was instructed to pay particular attention to stern bearings with her Type 277 and she was included in the air reporting organisation and later on placed in the inner screen.

The convoy was shadowed by enemy aircraft by day and night from 6 February. The first attack by torpedo bombers was at 0745 on 7 February and *Denbigh Castle* quickly shot down one of them. A fine piece of work for a ship on her first operation. She was on the outer screen at that time.

The next main attack occurred during the forenoon of 10 February. Some 20-25 Ju-88's participated in the attacks which caused no casualties. Of those attacking 7 were assessed as shot down, 4 probables and 8 damaged.

As the convoy approached the Kola Inlet, air patrols had been unable to detect any U-Boats and in the evening of the 12th these patrols were discontinued because of bad visibility.

The convoy was formed into two columns and proceeded into the Kola Inlet under conditions of variable visibility - almost nil during snow showers and up to two miles between showers.

Denbigh Castle was stationed 2,500 yards on the port quarter of the convoy. Because of broken chattering bars her unifoxer had been recovered and not streamed again because of the slow speed of the convoy.

The radar scan was very complicated, displaying nearly all the ships of the convoy and escorts as well as the high land. At 2345 on the 12th a radar echo was reported astern at 2,500 yards. This was thought to be one of the Russian patrol craft.

Just after midnight (0014, 13 February 1945) an explosion took place in the fore part of the ship. From the bridge it appeared that as a result the bow was either missing or submerged up to the 4-inch gun platform. At the time it was thought that the ship had struck a mine.

With the First Lieutenant, J.F. Watt RNVR, Damage Control Officer in charge, damage control, rescue and first aid parties were rapidly at the scene of the damage. It was soon apparent that the ship was in no immediate danger of sinking. The main damage was in the forward upper messdecks and in the lower messdecks to a lesser extent. The wounded were removed from the upper messdeck. Once the evacuation of all living persons had been completed the water tight door was closed and flooding boundaries established on the upper deck at No 23 Bulkhead, and on lower decks at No 41 Bulkhead. The Water Tight door dividing the two lower messdecks was reported as having been blown off by the explosion.

Between 0030 and 0045 the lights of *Serapis* and *Bluebell* were observed. *Bluebell* came alongside the starboard quarter and the medical officer from *Serapis* was transferred by whaler. Casualties were transferred to *Bluebell* and as many hands as could be spared were also transferred.

Preparations were immediately put in hand to be taken in tow by *Bluebell* which was specially fitted for towing. *Denbigh Castle*'s pendant of 20 fathoms of 3 inch wire was shackled to *Bluebell's* pendant of 20 fathoms of 15-inch manila. This operation took about 30 minutes. *Bluebell* started towing at 0205, two hours after the explosion.

Denbigh Castle had to be turned nearly 180° before the ships steadied on a course of 230°. Speed was gradually worked up to about 2 knots. *Serapis* stood by and screened the two ships for the whole time that *Bluebell* had *Denbigh Castle* in tow.

At 0330 a Russian tug arrived to assist but "the curse of Babel" lasted an hour. At 0430 the tug went alongside and transferred a 100 ton salvage pump to assist in controlling the inrush of water. By this time the depth

of water in the wardroom flat was 4ft 6 inches. The flooding boundary having been extended to No 48 Bulkhead on all decks.

At 0501 *Denbigh Castle* was very deep by the head and all hands were transferred to the tug, the officers only remaining on board.

The Captain of the tug, fearing that *Denbigh Castle* would founder in the fairway, cast off and proceeded alongside *Bluebell* and took the tow from her at 0615. By this time the water had filled the wardroom flat and the ship was very high by the stern, the water level on the upper deck now reaching the after end of the bridge house (No.50 frame).

At 0730 the ship grounded in Bolshaya Volkovaya Bay. The bow touched first, and the tug, slipping the tow, pushed the stern round. At this time the tide was two hours after high water springs. The ship began to list to port with the ebbing tide and at 0905 the officers abandoned ship by the whaler. At 0910 the ship capsized to port and moved bodily into deeper water.

Subsequent examination showed that the damage extended 27 feet along the upper deck and 9 feet along the keel. The entire structure of the bow was bent downwards. Very limited structural damage occurred abaft No.23 Bulkhead on the upper deck. Articles from the forward Naval Store were found on the bridge. The 4-inch gun was thrown onto the port extremity of the Squid platform pointing in the reverse direction. Three wire reels from the centre of the forecastle had been thrown, two to the port side of the bridge deck and one to the port extremity of the forecastle deck abaft the galley.

The subsequent Board of Inquiry considered that *Denbigh Castle* had been torpedoed. There had been nothing to show that the torpedo was a Gnat. It was thought that this could possibly have been a 'Curly' fired at the convoy. The reasons for believing that the ships had been torpedoed were:-

HMS Denbigh Castle capsized in the Kola Inlet, Russia.   *(CCC(F)A Archives)*

(a)   It is most improbable that a single moored mine would be encountered, and if there had been any number of these, they would certainly have been disclosed by Russian sweepers on the following days.

(b)   A drifting mine in this position would necessarily have debauched from the Kola Inlet. Observing that the tidal stream sets permanently N.E. It is known that no mines have been laid that could have drifted into such a position.

(c)   The depth of water was too great for the operation of a ground mine.

It is known that U-Boats were in the area and remained there some days. It is considered most unlikely that U-Boats would frequent an area mined by themselves."

Attempts were made to destroy or recover secret documents and equipment remaining on board after the ship capsized. Demolition and diving parties went to the ship on *Dumbarton Castle*, however, it was found that she could not anchor in the bay because of the depth of water and lack of room to swing.

The severe cold was a great handicap. The helmet valves quickly froze and the loss of circulation in the divers' hands rendered work in enclosed spaces impractical. The air temperature was 11°F and ice had to be broken before divers could descend. Upon removing the divers' suits to restore circulation, they froze up in such a manner as to render further diving impracticable without returning on board to thaw them out.

In spite of these extreme conditions the Radar Office was wrecked with a 25lb demolition charge, but attempts to demolish the driving mechanism of the Squid had to be abandoned. The very keen and able diving team was from *Bellona* under the example and direction of Lt (E) K Morgan RN, who made the first descent, remaining below for forty minutes.

HMS DUMBARTON CASTLE

Battle Honours
Atlantic 1944-45

HMS Dumbarton Castle in 1944.   *(MoD/Crown Copyright)*

Two days after completion the *Dumbarton Castle* (Lt Cdr P.F. Broadhead RNR) sailed for Tobermory on 27 February 1944 for working up at Tobermory. She was initially allocated to the 40th Escort Group (*Exe* SO) but in fact joined the B5 Escort Group which had been taken over by *Exe* on 7 April 1944. The ship's movements between arriving on the Clyde on 17 March 1944 after working up and joining the B5 Escort Group are not recorded. It is probable that she was used as a 'spare' escort during this period.

Dumbarton Castle continued with the B5 Escort Group and its successor, the 31st Escort Group, until the latter was disbanded soon after VE Day in May 1945.

With the B5 Escort Group *Dumbarton Castle* escorted eight convoys comprising 296 ships without loss to enemy action

The record of her service with these Groups is given later under the heading of B5 and 31st Escort Groups.

She remained in commission with a reduced compliment for Air Sea Rescue duties and subsequently underwent a refit early in 1946 and was then reduced to reserve.

HISTORY

02.02.43	Ordered.
06.05.43	Laid down: **Builder:** Hull - Caledon (Dundee); Engine - H. Hargreaves.
28.09.43	Launched.
25.02.45	Completed.

WARTIME VOYAGES

Date	ESG	Senior Officer	Convoy	No of Ships	Arrive/ Sail	Location	Notes
27.02.44	40th	*Exe*			Sail	Dundee	
01.03.44	40th	*Exe*			Arv	Tobermory	
17.03.44	40th				Arv	Clyde	
30.03.44	40th				Arv	Greenock	
07.04.44	EG B5	*Exe*			Arv	Clyde	
13.04.44	EG B5	*Exe*			Sail	Londonderry	
14.04.44	EG B5	*Exe*	OS 74/ KMS 48	29		5552N 0952W	
22.04.44	EG B5	*Exe*	OS 74/ KMS 48	29		3712N 1333W	
24.04.44	EG B5	*Exe*			Arv	Gibraltar	
01.05.44	EG B5	*Exe*			Sail	Gibraltar	
06.05.44	EG B5	*Exe*	SL 156/ MKS 47	46		4116N 1829W	
13.05.44	EG B4	*Helmsdale*			Arv	Clyde	
23.05.44	EG B5	*Exe*	OS78/ KMS52	23	Sail	Londonderry	
24.05.44	EG B5	*Exe*	OS 78/ KMS52	23		5550N 1010W	
06.06.44	EG B5	*Exe*	OS78/	23	Arv	Gibraltar	
09.06.44	EG B5	*Exe*	MKS 51	14	Sail	Gibraltar	
10.06.44	EG B5	*Exe*	SL160/ MKS 51	44		3540N 0705W	
13.06.44	EG B5	*Exe*	SL 160/ MKS 51	44		3710N 1640W	44 ships according to Hague
20.06.44	EG B5	*Exe*	SL160/ MKS 51	44	Arv	Clyde	
29.06.44	EG B5	*Exe*			Sail	Clyde	
02.07.44-	EG B5	*Exe*			Sail	Londonderry	
06.07.44-	EG B5	*Exe*	OS 82/ KMS 56	26		4818N 1935W	
13.07.44	EG B5	*Exe*	OS82 KMS 56	26	Arv	Gibraltar	
19.07.44	EG B5	*Exe*-	SL164/ MKS55	33	Sail	Gibraltar	
21.07.44	EG B5	*Exe*	MKS 55	19		3435N 1020W	
21.07.44	EG B5	*Exe*	SL 164/ MKS 55	33		3525N 1248W	
29.07.44	EG B5	*Exe*	SL 164/ MKS 55	33		5140N1520W	
09.08.44	EG B5	*Hadleigh Castle*			Arv	Larne	
12.08.44	EG B5	*Hadleigh Castle*	OS86/ KMS60	23	Sail	Londonderry	

Date	ESG	Senior Officer	Convoy	No of Ships	Arrive/ Sail	Location	Notes
12.08.44	EG B5	*Hadleigh Castle*	OS 86/ KMS60	23		5550N 0855W	
22.08.44	EG B5	*Hadleigh Castle*	OS86 KMS60	23		3548N 0840W	
23.08.44	EG B5	*Hadleigh Castle*	OS86/ KMS60	23	Arv	Gibraltar	
30.08.44	EG B5	*Hadleigh Castle*	SL168/ MKS 59	35	Sail	Gibraltar	
01.09.44	EG B5	*Hadleigh Castle*	SL 168/ MKS 59	35		3925N 1030W	
06.09.44	EG B2	*Cotton*	OS 88/ KMS 62	37		5029N 0901W	
08.09.44	EG B2	*Cotton*	OS 88 KMS 62	37		4530N 1128W	Arrived Clyde 10.09.44 for 31 EG
10.09.44	31 EG	*Berkeley Castle*			Arv	Clyde	
22.09.44	31 EG	*Berkeley Castle*			Arv	At Larne	
23.09.44	31 EG	*Berkeley Castle*			Sail	Londonderry	
27.09.44	31 EG	*Berkeley Castle*				5430N 1412W	Force 33. On Patrol
01.10.44	31 EG	*Berkeley Castle*				NW of Donegal Bay	On patrol in support of ONS 33
09.10.44	31 EG	*Berkeley Castle*			Arv	Clyde	
11.10.44	31 EG	*Berkeley Castle*				Clyde	Clyde for lay over
16.10.44	31 EG	*Berkeley Castle*				Clyde	Boiler Cleaning til 18th
20.10.44	31 EG	*Berkeley Castle*				At Clyde	
23.10.44	31 EG	*Berkeley Castle*				At Larne	
30.10.44	31 EG	*Berkeley Castle*				4910N 0538W	On A/S sweep
10.11.44	31 EG	*Berkeley Castle*				At Sea	
17.11.44	31 EG	*Berkeley Castle*				Clyde	Repairs complete 22 Nov
29.11.44	31 EG	*Berkeley Castle*			Sail	Londonderry	
02.12.44	31 EG	*Berkeley Castle*			Sail	Scapa Flow	
05.12.44	31 EG	*Berkeley Castle*				6020N 0459W	On Patrol
13.12.44	31 EG	*Berkeley Castle*			Arv	Clyde	
21.12.44	31 EG	*Berkeley Castle*			Sail	Clyde	
23.12.44	31 EG	*Berkeley Castle*			Sail	Lamlash	
03.01.45	31 EG	*Berkeley Castle*			Sail	Londonderry	
08.01.45	31 EG	*Berkeley Castle*				WA	On Patrol
18.01.45	31 EG	*Berkeley Castle*			Arv	Clyde	
29.01.45	31 EG	*Berkeley Castle*				At Lochalsh	
02.02.45	31 EG	*Berkeley Castle*			Sail	Belfast	
10.02.45	31 EG	*Berkeley Castle*			Arv	Belfast	
10.02.45	31 EG	*Berkeley Castle*			Arv	Clyde	
12.02.45	31 EG	*Berkeley Castle*			Sail	Clyde	
10.03.45	31 EG	*Berkeley Castle*			Sail	Clyde	

Date	ESG	Senior Officer	Convoy	No of Ships	Arrive/ Sail	Location	Notes
23.03.45	31 EG	*Berkeley Castle*			Arv	Clyde	
25.03.45	31 EG	*Berkeley Castle*			Sail	Clyde	
14.04.45	31 EG	*Berkeley Castle*			Sail	Clyde	
19.04.45	31 EG	*Berkeley Castle*			Sail	Belfast	
02.05.45	31 EG	*Berkeley Castle*			Sail	Milford Haven	
13.05.45	31 EG	*Berkeley Castle*			Sail	Lochalsh	
29.05.45	31 EG	*Berkeley Castle*			Sail	Clyde	
22.06.45	W.A				Arv	Clyde	
25.09.45					Arv	Greenock	No record between 22.06.45 & 25.09.45.
07.10.45					Sail	Greenock	To ASR 16 ETA 9/10.
26.10.45					Arv	Clyde	
08.11.45					Sail	Clyde	081649/11 from ASR Station 16 *Cosby* 101235Z/11. Relieved by *DC* at 1200Z/11. Operation Archer.
27.11.45					Arv	Greenock	*DC* 26/0528Z/11 Relieved by *Amberley Castle* at ASR 17 ETA Greenock 27.11.45.
10.12.45					Sail	Greenock	
30.12.45					Arv	Greenock	
08.01.46					Sail	Greenock	FOIC Greenock 071115/1. Intend sailing *DC* Jan 8 to Birkenhead. ETA Jan 9.
09.01.46					Arv	Liverpool	

January - March 1946	Refitting at Liverpool.
04.46 - 48	Reserve at Portsmouth.
15.07.49	Completed refit at Grimsby.
1950-1952	Reserve at Harwich.
1953-1959	Reserve at West Hartlepool.
16.11.60	Sold to B.I.S.
03.61	Arrived Gateshead for scrapping by J.J. King & Co.

Sub/Lt Peter De Beavoir Carey Hart served during the first year of **Dumbarton Castle**'s first commission. His account of that time provides an insight into the working of these corvettes and the duties of a junior officer serving on them.

Dumbarton Castle
Dec 1943 to Dec 1944
Sub/Lt Peter De Beavoir Carey Hart

My new ship, one of the first Castle class corvettes, had been built by Caledons and was lying alongside the quay at Dundee. Spencer Shelley, a Lieutenant RNVR and Old Cheltonian who had served in Flower'class corvettes, and I were the first to arrive and to report to our Commanding Officer, Lt Cdr Broadhead RNR who had been at one time a master in the B.I. Line but had subsequently become a very successful barrister specialising in maritime law. Immediately prior to joining **Dumbarton Castle** he had brought a northern trawler with a mutinous crew back to the U.K from the Med: - he told me that during that voyage, he had always slept with a loaded pistol under his pillow; possibly because of this experience he was a very firm disciplinarian.

Shelley and I found our CO in a Nissen hut, on the quay, which was our temporary office until the arrival of the ships company. After we had reported to Broadhead, he strode up and down - he was rather short and slightly tubby and reminded me of Captain Bligh as portrayed in the picture entitled "Mutiny on the Bounty". He gave Shelley the choice of either taking over the duties of gunnery officer, navigator or ASCO, and although Shelley decided that he would prefer to be 'Guns' he was told that he was to be navigator whilst I became the 'pinger'. We were both sent on appropriate weekly courses, my destination being **Osprey** at Dunoon and **Nimrod** at Campbeltown. At the latter we 'played' with a submarine in which my cousin David Carey was serving as a sub-lieutenant and who later was to lose his life in X craft.

After our return from our respective courses, the commissioning party, which included Lt Roskill RNVR (First Lieut.), Lt Jones (Gunnery Officer) and Sub/Lt Colvin arrived. Following several days of sea-trials, we sailed for Tobermory, the Western Approaches working-up base in Mull. Before leaving Dundee, Broadhead had written to the Admiral Contract Built Ships, proposing that a change in the pitch of the propeller could give the ship an extra 1.5 knots, an extra 10% in speed. Some weeks later a rather curt letter arrived, suggesting that Broadhead would do better to mind his own business. He was rather incensed but had the last laugh since the pitch was later changed and he was proved to be right.

Commodore Western Isles, with his HQ aboard **Western Isles**, was Admiral Sir Gilbert Stephenson, better known as Monkey Stephenson, a man for whom I had the most tremendous admiration and someone I got to know after the War when I was commanding a Sea Cadet Corps unit. The War had brought him from retirement and, as an old man, he was a beach-master at Dunkirk and a commodore of convoys. Everybody was terrified of him and dreaded his visits to their ships. He would arrive on board a ship like a charge of dynamite - "Number One, the captain is dead, there is a fire in the engine-room and a mine under your bows - DO SOMETHING". Twice, whilst I was ashore in charge of a squad of seamen undergoing field-training, he came running towards me with "Do something, make them think, MAKE THEM THINK". If he thought that any officer was inefficient, from COs downwards, they would be replaced and sent aboard **Western Isles** for several months of extensive re-training. I made two visits, in different ships, and felt certain that I would be imprisoned in **Western Isles** but I need not have worried as, after the War, when I was sailing with Broadhead, he told me that 'Monkey' had been pleased with me. He used to send his aides, during the dark hours, to steal ships logs from sleeping QMs. On a previous visit to Tobermory, Shelley had climbed the **Western Isles** cable during the middle watch, entered Monkey's cabin and told him that he had captured his ship. Monkey was thrilled and kept the ship's company at action stations whilst he and Shelley enjoyed several whiskies.

On leaving Tobermory, after three weeks of hell, we sailed to Greenock where we joined an escort group

- B5. Our senior officer was in *Exe*, a River class frigate, and the rest of the group comprised *Antigua*, an all-welded American built frigate, and three other Castles: - *Hadleigh*, *Berkeley* and *Carisbrooke*. After one or two anti-submarine patrols, we found ourselves escorting convoys to and from Gibraltar. In order to avoid the German aircraft, we used to sail to 30° West before steaming either due South or due North. At that time the escort carriers were arriving from the States (*Campania*, *Nairana*, *Emperor* etc, all of which, as soon as they arrived in the UK from the States, went into dockyard hands so that their bunks and canteens could be removed), and, in our customary escort position of 'S for sugar' we were frequently acting as escort to one of these carriers when she was turning into the wind so that her aircraft could take-off and land. Landing was not so easy and we witnessed frequent crashes. Sometimes we escorted the tankers which sailed from one convoy to another in order to re-fuel the escort vessels. These convoys were of the 8 knot variety, a speed which was often reduced due to bad weather and 'stragglers'.

As ASCO, my action station was, of course, in the Asdic compartment which was situated aft of the bridge and where I had a team of four, a Leading Hand and three ABs, operating the bearing, range and depth recorders. We were one of the first ships to be fitted with the Squid ahead throwing weapon and the Sword depth-recording oscillator. The dome for the main Asdic oscillator could not be housed internally, as in later vessels. It had to be raised and lowered using a small davit situated on the upper-deck. An operation which could be extremely tricky and I am unlikely to forget Broadhead's wrath on the occasion when we missed the tide on our maiden voyage because I took so long at my first attempt to put the dome in place. My entering harbour station was always on the bridge with Broadhead who could handle this single-screw vessel like a motor-car and never ever got ruffled, chatting to me during the most tricky pieces of ship-handling - "Hart, Are you going to see that Wren of yours this evening? Starboard five. Are you going to take her out to dinner? Slow ahead. Taking her to the Bay Hotel no doubt. Midships. I say, that is a jolly pretty MT driver on the quay! Stop engines. If she has some signals for us let us invite her on board for a coffee. Slow astern. I like her hair-do. Stop engines". We were based in Greenock and the round-trip to 'Gib' and back usually took five weeks, followed by a week alongside either at Gourock Pier or Great Harbour whilst boiler-cleaning was in progress. From time-to-time we carried the odd passenger and on one occasion, when we were oiling at Moville after exercising with *Isle of Sark* (formerly one of the mail-boats running between Southampton and the Channel Islands) in the Irish Sea, we received a signal to say that there was an outbreak of smallpox in Gibraltar and that no one would be allowed ashore there unless they had been very recently vaccinated. Fortunately a Polish Air Force doctor was taking passage with us and he vaccinated the entire ships company with a sewing needle sterilised in the flame of a candle. On another occasion we brought an RAF commodore back from 'Gib' to Greenock. Whilst customs officials were boarding us from their launch on our port side, all the commodore's duty free rabbits were being loaded into an RAF launch lying on our starboard quarter!

'Stragglers' were a great problem as they would slow-down a convoy. We often had to 'chase' them which made their captains, frequently bowler-hatted, most indignant as they swore at us through their megaphones whilst we steamed alongside, telling them to catch-up the convoy. Yet, when the order was given as we were nearing the Scottish coast, for ships of the convoy to carry-on independently, it was often the one-time stragglers', with black smoke pouring out of their funnels, which made the best speed. We once spent a night drifting astern of the convoy with a major engine-room defect and it certainly filled one with a sense of being very much alone although I do not recall that anyone was frightened as was depicted in the film 'Cruel Sea' when *Compass Rose* was in a similar situation. I certainly did not lose a wink of sleep nor do I remember anybody being so nervous that they remained on the upper deck rather than going below to sleep.

After escorting our final convoy to the 'Med' we entered 'Gib' on the morning of D-Day. A few day's later we sailed to escort the first UK bound convoy to take the inshore route and whilst we were in the Bay of Biscay we received signals advising us that there were thirty-five U-boats in our vicinity and it was with a sigh of relief that we sighted the Scilly Isles but, because of the U-boat activity, we were ordered to

return, as an additional escort, with the South-bound convoy. Another sigh of relief was cut-short when we received orders to turn round and strengthen the group (Senior Officer in *Wellington*) escorting the North-bound convoy.

After our return to the UK, we were detached from Western Approaches and spent a month chasing submarines in the Channel. I practically lived in the A/S compartment since we were constantly attacking contacts. The shallow water of the Channel made it very difficult to differentiate between a submarine and wreck. We overcame this problem by steaming over contacts whilst running our echo-sounder and were able to pick-out the shape of the wrecks. During this period we spent two days in Devonport, refuelling and amunitioning. We had dropped all our depth-charges and fired all our Squid bombs. Our spell in Devonport convinced us that Greenock administration was far superior to that in Devonport but, to be fair to the latter they probably just did not understand corvettes. We were kept constantly on the move and would be dispatched at full speed, for example, to the Scillies where there had been a submarine sighting and, before we had a chance to check whether our attacks had been successful, there would be another signal dispatching us to a sighting off the coast of Alderney, followed by another and another. We were sometimes ordered to escort Channel convoys, and this we found difficult as they were made-up of a long single line of ships whereas we were accustomed to convoys with nine or ten columns of vessels.

Finally, rather to our relief, we returned to Western Approaches where our group became a support group and was involved in more varied work than convoy escorting and we would be sent to expected trouble-spots. Occasional sweeps in 'The Rose Garden', stretching from the North coast of Scotland to the Shetlands, as it covered the route used by German submarines leaving or entering the Atlantic (Broadhead, the following year when in command of *Loch Shin* sank three U-boats in this area). The strengthening of escorts of important convoys, one in particular was the largest convoy which had ever left the UK. Instead of the normal escort of six or seven escort vessels there were seven escort groups; this convoy covered a vast area and *Dumbarton Castle* was stationed on the starboard side of the convoy, further North than any other vessel as we steamed though the North Channel between Northern Ireland and Islay. I had the Middle watch and we were being forced closer and closer to the coast, until I could see white breakers when I had to go hard-a-port, waking half the ships company. On another occasion in 'The Rose Garden' and, again, a middle when we were carrying-out an A/S sweep in line abreast and were slightly astern of station, as the engine-room were not giving me the revs I had ordered. *Exe* ordered an easy item turn for quite a small change of course, considerably less than that recommended and, then, in the darkness, I saw, approaching us rapidly, the trellis mast of one of our sister-ships. I leaped to the voice pipe to yell, again, hard-a-port. We were so close that I was even able to look down on the other vessel's quarterdeck. A quavering voice came up on the RT, 'Did I miss you by very much?" I had a midshipman RN as second OOW (C-in-C Western Approaches laid-down that at night there had to be two OOWs) who remarked, "According to the rule of the road, Sir, we should have turned to starboard."

I explained to him that if I had we would both have found ourselves in the 'drink'. He was seventeen and I was twenty, the signalman was seventeen and the two look-outs eighteen. Broadhead would have roasted me and the Chief ERA (we carried no Engineer Officer) but Broadhead had left the ship a week earlier and when I awoke his successor, to tell him how near we had been to disaster, he just grunted and went back to sleep. At that time, we were carrying two midshipmen, very unusual for a corvette, but I suspect it was because, thanks to Broadhead, *Dumbarton Castle* had earned a tremendous reputation for efficiency and discipline.

During a patrol in the North Atlantic we were detached to escort a dry-dock and its tug situated a hundred miles off the West coast of Iceland. I had seen some very severe weather in Northern waters but I think that the conditions which we encountered on this particular trip were worse than any I had ever experienced, driving rain reducing visibility to practically nil. We finally located the tug and her tow, making little or no headway as one of the towing-wires had parted, at the same time very seriously injuring a member of the tug's crew. This resulted in the tug asking us for medical assistance, just as I arrived on the

bridge for a 'shufti'. Quite the wrong moment because I was promptly detailed to take away the seaboat's crew to the tug with our SBA (a young farm labourer whose medical knowledge was even less than mine. We carried no doctor). As the sea-boat's crew was being piped away, I felt extremely nervous. I had had no experience in handling a boat under such extreme conditions of weather. I felt certain that the chances of survival would be very slim indeed with little chance of even lowering the whaler into the water without disastrous results. I could picture her being smashed like match wood against the ship's side. Relief came just as we were about to board the whaler. The tug signalled that their injured seaman had died. I am sure that our SBA, had we ever reached the tug, would have been of little help to the dying man.

During one of our anti-submarine patrols, several hundred miles to the West of Ireland, one of our sister-ships made Asdic contact with a U-boat at a distance which was too great for us to pick-up the echo at our normal automatic transmitting range of 2,500 yards, so, which we were not supposed to do, I went over to hand transmissions and found the contact at a range of almost 4,000 yards. It was an excellent contact which we were able to hold until we fired a pattern of Squid bombs. This resulted in some underwater explosions and, a little later in the light of our searchlight, we saw a patch of oil. We picked-up a half-eaten orange on which was printed 'Sunkist' - a name which we thought might well be German, as did C-in-C WA who sent us a signal congratulating us and ordering us to continue sweeping in that area until further notice. At about 0400 hours he sent us another signal instructing us to discontinue the search as 'Sunkist' was the brand-name of an orange grown in California. It had probably been dumped with the 'gash' from a passing hospital-ship. We were however credited with a probable kill. As we know, U-boats frequently released oil in order to fool the escorts.

We had our lighter moments in harbour and I recall, whilst lying alongside the destroyer *Ambuscade* at Gourock Pier, receiving an RSVP from her captain to attend a conference covering the mark 5 pea-shooter. In the wardroom we divided into two sides, armed with these mark 5 weapons, and, when the lights went-out, we shot our peas across the wardroom at one another, using matches as star-shells. Frequent cease-fires were celebrated with large glasses of neat gin, a drink which I have never touched since!

On several occasions we passed the Monsters in mid-Atlantic - they were the very large fast ships which travelled independently, carrying troops from USA, as they were considered to be fast enough to avoid any attacks from U-boats; - amongst them *Queen Mary* and *Queen Elizabeth*, both of them rolling almost to their boat-decks so I can only suppose that their ant-roll stabilisers were not being used. One day, lying-off the Tail of the Bank, in the Clyde, I saw both the Queens plus the *Aquitania*, *Mauritania* and *New Amsterdam*.

We never drank at sea but several of our commanding officers imbibed large quantities of alcohol when in harbour. Not surprising really, as they were under constant strain and never dared, for example, to get undressed and have a bath, although our spells at sea varied between fourteen and twenty-eight days!

Broadhead was the sort of man that one either liked and respected greatly, as Shelley and I did, or loathed because he was a perfectionist and a severe disciplinarian. If one wanted to learn, then he was very happy to teach one and after dinner in harbour, I learned so much from him as ships were represented by match-sticks on the table-cloth.

Broadhead was appointed to command a Loch class frigate, still under construction, and before leaving *Dumbarton Castle* , asked the Admiralty if I might be appointed to the same ship, to this they agreed and I only made one more trip after his departure before leaving the ship myself. Life in a corvette in Western Approaches suited me admirably and I had the greatest affection for *Dumbarton Castle*, of which I have so many happy memories and where I was a member of the nicest wardroom of which I have ever been a member".

Stoker George Charlton joined *Dumbarton Castle* in October 1944 when he was 17 years old. As the youngest member of the crew he was delegated to do Captain's Rounds on Christmas Day wearing the CO's hat.

He recalls standing in the engine room flat with the stoker P.O. during a force ten gale "so as to be near

the upper deck should she go over and waiting for the boiler room stokers to come tumbling out of the funnel." Also of being on watch in No 2 Boiler room whilst closed up at action stations and "definitely not feeling so Jolly Jack Tar when the Squid was fired and the spanners jumping out of the bulkhead racks and looking up to see the small blue line painted well up on the bulkhead with the letters DWL."

He remembers a run ashore at Londonderry, "when having walked through a village, complete with dirt road, chickens and kids to the railway line. When the train came along you just held up your hand to stop it and climbed aboard. We obtained our tickets on the train. They were printed 'To Londonderry and Back'. Back to where was anybody's guess."

"Air Sea rescue duty was a dull time. One boiler was shut down and the other banked up and used to start engines to bring us back on station every 24 hours.

As we sat on station for about three weeks boredom soon set in. Various things were done to keep us busy. On one station near the Azores it was all hands off watch, over the side, to paint ship. The weather was balmy. Sporting events were organised; Tug of War, Boxing matches and so on. We also made mats - ornaments and models. One of the officers was working in the small workshop using a bench mounted drill. He slipped and fell forward catching his face on the revolving drill. A really nasty wound. We only carried a Sick Bay Tiffy. The nearest ship with a doctor on board was **HMS Ottawa**. We transferred him to her by boat.

One killick stoker scrounged a number of empty cigarette tins and made a model destroyer about four feet long. He made a really good job of it and painted it Pusser grey. Going on leave through the Dockyard gates at Greenock it was greatly admired by the Dockyard Police. What they did not know was that before he soldered the deck and superstructure to the hull, he had packed it with tickler's tobacco and NAAFI cigarettes.

We had a three month refit and then went to Pompey to pay off. We realised that we could not go ashore without lanyards and they were in very short supply. The gentlemen of the seaman's branch collected tot after tot by making up lanyards from Coston Gun Line."

HMS FARNHAM CASTLE

Battle Honours
Arctic 1945

*An undated image of **HMS Farnham Castle**.*   *(MoD/Crown Copyright)*

After completion on the 31 January 1945 *Farnham Castle* arrived at Tobermory on the 9th February 1945 for working up. Subsequently she joined the 7th Escort Group at Scapa Flow to form part of the escort for the Russian convoy JW 65. An account of this voyage and her subsequent voyages with the 7th Escort Group is detailed later in the following Section under the heading "7th Escort Group".

HISTORY

19.12.42	Ordered.
25.06.43	Laid down. **Builder**: Hull - Crown (Sunderland); Engine - C. Clark (Sunderland).
25.04.44	Launched.
31.01.45	Completed.

WARTIME VOYAGES

Date	ESG	Senior Officer	Convoy	No of Ships	Arrive/ Sail	Location	Notes
01.01.45	Unall					Sunderland	
05.01.45	Unall					Sunderland	
12.01.45	Unal						
15.01.45	8 EG					Sunderland	
27.01.45	8 EG				Arv	Tyne	
09.02.45	8 EG				Arv	Tobermory	
01.03.45	8 EG	*Lapwing*			Sail	Tobermory	
02.03.45	8 EG				Arv	Scapa Flow	
13.03.45	7 EG	*Cygnet*	JW 65	26	Sail	Scapa Flow	
20.03.45	7 EG	*Cygnet*	JW 65	26	Arv	Kola Inlet	
01.04.45	7 EG	*Cygnet*	RA 65	26	Arv	Clyde	Boiler cleaning; complete 9 April.
16.04.45	7 EG	*Cygnet*	JW 66		Sail	Clyde	
27.04.45	7 EG	*Cygnet*	JW 66	27	Arv		Kola Inlet
29.04.45	7 EG	*Cygnet*	RA 66	26	Sail		Kola Inlet -
08.05.45	7 EG	*Cygnet*	RA 66	26	Arv		Clyde
24.05.45	SAR				Arv		Sheerness-FOCRF 271641/6 FC has been accepted into Reserve Fleet. Record ends.

HMS FLINT CASTLE

Battle Honours
Atlantic 1944-45

HMS Flint Castle *seen post war.*   *(Portsmouth Royal Naval Museum)*

HMS Flint Castle, after completion arrived at Tobermory on the 12th January 1944 for working up. Whilst there she grounded and after being refloated was sent to Belfast for repair. She joined the 39th Escort Group in mid-March and did one Atlantic convoy operation with that Group. She was then re-allocated to the Liverpool based B2 Escort Group engaged on escorting convoys to and from Gibraltar. In September 1944 she was allocated to the B3 Escort Group engaged on trans-Atlantic work and remained with that Group until the end of the war in Europe. Voyages with these Groups are described later in the following Section under B2 (B21) and B3 Escort Groups. After the European war **Flint Castle** served in various training roles until 1956. Her period of unbroken service of ten years was only exceeded by that of the **Leeds Castle**.

During her wartime service **Flint Castle** escorted some 714 ships in 17 convoys. All these voyages were uneventful in that no ships were lost from any cause. The actual number of ships escorted should be treated with caution because there was not always agreement between the sources as to the actual number of ships in all the convoys.

HISTORY

19.01.43	Ordered.
20.04.43	Laid Down: **Builder:** Hull - Robb (Leith); Engine - G Plenty (Newbry).
01.09.43	Launched.
31.12.43	Completed.

WARTIME VOYAGES

Date	ESG	Senior Officer	Convoy	No of Ships	Arrive/ Sail	Location	Notes
09.01.44	Unall				Arv	Leith	CinC WA 281129/9 *FC* is allocated to Londonderry
10.01.44					Sail	Leith	
12.01.44	Unall				Arv	Tobermory	
17.01.44					Sail	Tobermory	
18.01.44					Arv	Tobermory	F.O i/c Greenock 181204/1 *FC* has been re-floated.
19.01.44	B1				Arv	Belfast	Repairs
09.02.44	39 EG					Belfast	
21.02.44	39 EG				Arv	Stornoway	
21.02.44	39 EG				Sail	Stornoway	
25.02.44					Arv	Oban	With tow
25.02.44					Sail	Oban	
26.02.44	39 EG				Arv	Stornoway	
15.03.44	39 EG				Arv	Londonderry	Having left Stornoway the day before. (SMO)
15.03.44	39 EG				Arv	Londonderry	Boiler cleaning
26.03.44	39 EG				Arv	Londonderry	
26.03.44	39 EG				Sail	Londonderry	
10.04.44	B2	*Hesperus*			Arv	Londonderry	
15.04.44					Arv	Clyde	
15.04.44					Sail	Clyde	
17.04.44	B2	*Hesperus*			Sail	Clyde	
21.04.44	B2	*Hesperus*			Arv	Londonderry	
24.04.44	B2	*Hesperus*			Sail	Londonderry	
25.04.44	B2	*Hesperus*	OS 75/ KMS 49	23		5556N 1010W	
27.04.44	B2	*Hesperus*	OS 75/ KMS 49	23		5224N 1558W	
01.05.44	B2	*Hesperus*	OS 75/ KMS 49	23		4021N 1935W	
06.05.44	B2	*Hesperus*	OS 75/ KMS 49	23	Arv	Gibraltar	
12.05.44	B2	*Hesperus*	MKS48	32	Sail	Gibraltar	
14.05.44	B2	*Hesperus*	SL 157/ MKS 48			3840N 1630W	To overtake the convoy
15.05.44	B2	*Hesperus*	SL 157/ MKS 48	49		4125N 1830W	
22.05.44	B2	*Hesperus*	SL157/ MKS 48	49	Arv	Liverpool	
30.05.44	B2	*Hesperus*			Arv	Larne	Having left Liverpool the same day. Developed condenseritis after dropping 'scaring' DCs (SMO)

Date	ESG	Senior Officer	Convoy	No of Ships	Arrive/ Sail	Location	Notes
03.06.44	B2	*Hesperus*			Sail	Londonderry	
05.06.44	B2	*Hesperus*	OS 79/ KMS 53	27		?420N 1245W	
14.06.44	B2	*Hesperus*	OS 79/ KMS 53	27	Arv	Gibraltar	
20.06.44	B2	*Hesperus-*	MKS 52	19	Sail	Gibraltar	Carrying 30 boxes of bullion: N Pickford 1999; Hague records 17 ships
21.06.44	B2	*Hesperus*	MKS 52	19		3525N 0830W	
23.06.44	B2	*Hesperus*	SL 161/ MKS 52	45		3620N 1535W	Hague records 41 ships
30.06.44	B2	*Hesperus*	SL 161/ MKS 52	44		5430N 1101W	
01.07.44	B2	*Hesperus*			Arv	Liverpool	
02.07.44	B2	*Hesperus*	SL 161/ MKS 52	44	Arv	Londonderry	
09.07.44	B2	*Hesperus*			Sail	Liverpool	
13.07.44	B2	*Hesperus*	OS 83/ KMS 57	29	Sail	Londonderry	
14.07.44	B2	*Hesperus*	OS 83/ KMS 57	32		5557N 0945W	Hague gives 29 ships
22.07.44	B2	*Hesperus*	OS 83/ KMS 57	31		3810N 1750W	
25.07.44	B2	*Hesperus*	OS 83/	31	Arv	Gibraltar	
29.07.44	B2				Sail	Algiers	Having left Gibraltar the same day. (SMO)
30.07.44	B2	*Hesperus*	SL 165/ KMS 57	39	Sail	Gibraltar	Carrying 30 boxes of bullion: N Pickford 1999; Hague gives 35 ships
05.08.44	B2	*Hesperus*	SL 165/ MKS 56	39		4615N 1824W	
07.08.44	B2	*Hesperus*	SL165/ MKS 56	32		5152N 1540W	
08.08.44	B2	*Hesperus*	SL 165/ MKS 56	37		5522N 0830W	
09.08.44	B2	*Hesperus*			Arv	Liverpool	
22.08.44	B2	*Hesperus*			Arv	Belfast	Having left Liverpool on 27.08.44. (SMO)
24.08.44	B2	*Hesperus-*	OS 87/ MKS 56	34	Sail	Belfast	
01.09.44	B2	*Hesperus*	OS 87/ KMS 61	36		3850N 1156W	
04.09.44	B21	*Hesperus*	OS 87/ KMS 61	36	Arv	Gibraltar	
09.09.44	B21	*Hesperus*	MKS 50	23	Sail	Gibraltar	

Date	ESG	Senior Officer	Convoy	No of Ships	Arrive/ Sail	Location	Notes
10.09.44	B21	*Hesperus*	MKS 50	23		3554N 0840W	
16.09.44	B21	*Hesperus*	SL 169/ MKS 60	20		Hartland Point	
18.09.44	B21	*Hesperus*			Sail	Clyde	Having arrived Clyde the same day. (SMO)
18.09.44	B3				Arv	Liverpool	Note change in Escort Group designation
25.09.44	B3					At Liverpool	Boiler Cleaning
28.09.44	B3	*Exe*	ONF 256	67	Sail	Belfast	Having arrived the day before.(SMO)
29.09.44	B3	*Exe*	ONF 256	67		5201N 0620W	
07.10.44	B3	*Exe*	ONF 256	76		4806N 4752W	
08.10.44	B3	*Exe*	ONF 256	76	Arv	St John's	
14.10.44	B3	*Exe*	HX 313	43	Sail	St John's	
23.10.44	B3	*Exe*	HX 313	32		5103N 1012W	Hague gives 43 ships
25.10.44	B3	*Exe*	HX 313	32	Arv	Liverpool	
30.10.44	B3	*Exe*				Liverpool	Boiler cleaning
03.11.44	B3	*Exe*				At Liverpool	
04.11.44	B3	*Exe*	ON 264	67	Sail	Liverpool	ON 264 (SMO)
18.11.44	B3	*Exe*	ON 264	67	Arv	St John's	
25.11.44	B3	*Exe*	HX 321	36	Sail	St John's	
28.11.44	B3	*Exe*	HX 321	37		4315N 4312W	
06.12.44	B3	*Exe*	HX 321	36	Arv	Liverpool	
11.12.44	B3	*Exe*	ON 272	45	Sail	Liverpool	
12.12.44	B3	*Exe*	ON 272	45	Arv	Campbeltown	
12.12.44	B3	*Exe*	ON 272	45	Sail	Campbeltown	
13.12.44	B3	*Exe*	ON 272	45	Arv	Belfast	
14.12.44	B3	*Exe*	ON 272	45	Sail	Belfast	
16.12.44	B3	*Exe*	ON 272	45	Sail	Milford Haven	To rejoin ON 272. (SMO)
27.12.44	B3	*Exe*	ON 272	45	Arv	St John's	
02.01.45	B3	*Exe*	HX 329	36	Sail	St John's	
13.01.45	B3	*Exe*	HX 329	36	Arv	Liverpool	A 172129.1 *FC* can be taken in hand for refit Hill Dry Dock Co: Cardiff 23 Jan. (SMO)
21.01.45					Arv	Cardiff	
26.01.45	B3	*Exe*				Cardiff	Refit
02.02.45	B3	*Exe*				Cardiff	Repairs complete 10 March
20.03.45	B3	*Exe*			Sail	Cardiff	FO I/c Cardiff 161556B *FC* completion March 19th postponed.
28.03.45	B3	*Exe*			Arv	Milford Haven	
29.03.45	B3	*Exe*			Sail	Milford Haven	
30.03.45	B3	*Exe*			Arv	Milford Haven	
04.04.45	B3	*Exe*			Arv	Plymouth	
04.04.45	B3	*Exe*			Arv	Falmouth	

Date	ESG	Senior Officer	Convoy	No of Ships	Arrive/ Sail	Location	Notes
05.04.45	B3	*Exe*			Sail	Plymouth	
05.04.45	B3	*Exe*			Sail	Plymouth	
09.04.45	B3	*Exe*	ONS 47	17	Arv	Liverpool	
12.04.45	B3	*Exe*	ONS 47	17	Sail	Belfast	Having left Liverpool on 10th and arrived Belfast 11th (SMO)
13.04.45	B3	*Exe*	ONS 47	17	Sail	Londonderry	
28.04.45	B3	*Exe*	ONS 47	17	Arv	St John's	
03.05.45	B3	*Exe*	(HX 353)	64	Sail	St John's	
16.05.45	B3	*Exe*	(HX 353)	64	Arv	Liverpool	
21.05.45	B3	*Exe*	(ON 304)	70	Sail	Liverpool	Convoy dispersed NYC ships arrived 05.06.45: Hague.
06.06.45	B3				Sail	St John's	
26.06.45	Rosyth Command				Arv	Rosyth	

HMS Flint Castle Ship's Company 1944.

(CCC(F)A Archives)

Date	ESG	Senior Officer	Convoy	No of Ships	Arrive/ Sail	Location	Notes
29.06.45					Sail	Rosyth	
30.06.45					Arv	Sheerness	
05.07.45					Sail	Sheerness	
06.07.45					Sail	Rotterdam	To Tilbury
07.07.45					Arv	Nore (Southend)	
07.07.45					Sail	Southend	
09.07.45					Arv	Rosyth	
12.07.45					Sail	Rosyth	
13.07.45					Arv	Christiansand	
16.07.45					Sail	Christiansand	
17.07.45					Arv	Trondheim	
18.07.45					Sail	Trondheim	
19.07.45					Arv	Narvik	
24.07.45					Sail	Narvik	
28.07.45					Sail	Christiansand	
30.07.45					Arv	Bremerhaven	
18.08.45					Sail	Christiansand	
20.08.45					Arv	Rosyth	
23.08.45					Sail	Rosyth	
25.08.45					Arv	Rosyth	
03.09.45					Sail	Rosyth	For Cambeltown NO I/c Cambeltown 221315/1 intend sailing FC 23.1. to Portland.
05.09.45					Arv	Campbeltown	
23.01.46					Sail	Campbeltown	
25.01.46					Arv	Portland	Record ends

June 1946	Joined the Rosyth Escort Force, which was employed as a training organisation, moving to Campbeltown and becoming the Basic A/S Training Flotilla in September, when the Escort Force was disbanded.
January 1947	The Flotilla moved to Portland, where it became the Portland Flotilla, the 3rd Escort Flotilla in March 1947, the 2nd Training Flotilla in January 1949 and finally the 2nd Training Squadron in January 1952.
1953	Represented Home Command, Portsmouth, at the Coronation Fleet Review.
March 1956	Placed in reserve at Devonport after 13 years continuous service.
1956	Sold Ship Breaking Industries.
10.07.58	Arrived Faslane for scrapping.

Ship's Dog

Amongst the corvette community both at Londonderry, Liverpool and Portland, *Flint Castle* was well known for her longest serving member of the ship's company. This was Judy CSW 1 (Canine Sea Woman 1st Class). She was recruited in a pub late in December 1943 by five members of Red Watch. During the evening one of the civvy regulars came in carrying a puppy. He, lacking the cost of a drink, offered the pup for 2/6d. The five members of the Red Watch each contributed 6d and triumphantly carried the pup back to the ship.

Judy quickly endeared herself to all hands and the CO and No.1 quietly adopted the Nelson touch towards her.

Judy was quickly trained to attend to her personal business at the gash shoot at the stern on the quarterdeck. Although she learned to go up the ladders from the messdeck, coming down again was another matter. Her normal means of decent was to wait at the top of ladder and descend down on the shoulder of the first man to go down. Judy was also encouraged to bark a warning at the approach of anyone in square rig.

Under the normal process of drafting Judy had, in the course of time, several minders. These she usually chose herself. The minder was responsible for her well being. These duties including ensuring that Judy did not go ashore when the ship was under sailing orders.

All was well until Friday 13th April 1945. Orders were received to put to sea at 2000 hours. Judy's minder was told that Judy was under stoppage of shore leave. Judy could not be found. All hands not on watch were ordered ashore to find her, but to no avail. The ship sailed without her. It so happened that one of the ship's company, Able Seaman Smith was ashore at the Londonderry Naval Hospital. A signal was sent to him repeated to Commodore (D). The following day Smith told the R.C Chaplain of the problem. He said that shortly after midnight he had been given a shake by the duty SBA with a signal from the ship. This read "Don't die. You are under orders to bring Judy back on board." The Chaplain informed the police, the Royal Naval Patrol, Coast Guards, Boy Scouts and other bodies in a attempt to organise a city wide

HMS Flint Castle endures the type of weather frequently encountered on convoy escort work.
(CCC(F)A Archives)

search. The Londonderry police brought several dogs to Smith's bedside for his inspection.

A week later Judy was recognised waiting patiently at Pier 19 for her ship's return. She was promptly arrested and the RC Chaplain informed. From the pulpit of his church he explained the Able Seaman's predicament. A Mr and Mrs Barrett volunteered to look after Judy until Smith came out of hospital. On his discharge from hospital Smith was given 7 days leave. With his ship still at sea he had no option but to take Judy with him. The ship went to Cardiff for a refit and Smith and Judy rejoined her there to the great relief and joy of all hands.

When *Flint Castle* joined the Portland Flotilla Judy soon became a favourite at the various pubs frequented by her shipmates. She also became enamoured with another dog 'Skipper'. Through the generosity of the publicans and the matelots the two dogs frequently got drunk together.

As Judy got older, she would avoid going to sea with the ship on her daily training trips, during bad weather. She soon developed the knack of knowing exactly where the ship was going to berth and was always waiting at the right spot.

Captain C.N. MacEacharn C.B.E. RN. who was *Flint Castle*'s Navigating Officer from 1954-56 wrote:

"I can well remember Judy having gone ashore with the postman to collect the mail, would return to the jetty, but if she remained there one could guarantee that the weather would be bad after we had sailed. As the weather was one of my main concerns with regard to the operations, I began to rely more on Judy than on the Met Office. She was always waiting on the jetty when we berthed and seemed to know our ETA with uncanny accuracy.

"She was trained to bark at Officers but this did not prevent her from fraternising with Officers wives. When I was on duty over the weekend my wife and small child would get the bus from Rodwell, and on arrival at Portland would be met at the Dockyard gate by the gunner's mate and Judy - having just come out of the Portland Road pub - and escorted to the gangway.

"She became ill at a time when we were carrying a medical officer and I recall the coxswain carrying her into the wardroom in a blanket and putting her in front of the fire whilst the doctor did what he could to help her. Unfortunately he could not save her.

"It was approximately 1000 hours that the First Lieutenant broadcast to the ship's company the news that Judy had died, that she would be buried at sea in an hour's time and that anyone wished to witness the committal they would be welcome. I went down from the bridge at 1100 hours to find most of the ship's company present to bid their last farewells. It was a very moving ceremony, carried out with almost as much feeling as that experienced when we buried friends at sea".

HMS HADLEIGH CASTLE

Battle Honours
Atlantic 1943-44

HMS Hadleigh Castle in September 1943.   *(MoD/Crown Copyright)*

HMS *Hadleigh Castle* was the first of the class. She was laid down and completed in six months. After successful trials she worked up at Tobermory and then visited the USA via St. John's Newfoundland and Halifax. She demonstrated the effectiveness of the Squid and associated Asdic equipment during January 1944.

En route to the USA she formed part of the escort for the convoy ON 215 with the C4 Escort Group (*Hotspur* SO). On the return voyage to the UK from St. John's she joined the B5 Escort Group (*Havelock* SO) escorting convoy HX 277. The convoy arrived at Liverpool on 13 February 1944. *Hadleigh Castle* assumed the mantle of SO B5 Escort Group and escorted convoy ON 225 (60 ships), arriving at Argentia, Newfoundland, on 3 March 1944. When in the vicinity of the Great Banks her consort, *HMS Lavander*, encountered a radar Decoy spar buoy.

Deep explosions were heard and it was assumed that these were caused by torpedoes fired in the vicinity.

The Group returned to the UK escorting convoy HX 282 (96 ships). Subsequently the Group was enlarged to include *Dumbarton Castle* , *Carisbrooke Castle* , and *Berkeley Castle* with *Exe* taking over as Group SO from *Hadleigh Castle*, which remained with the Group. The Group was employed in escorting convoys between the UK and Gibraltar. On two occasions *Hadleigh Castle* carried 20 boxes of bullion from Gibraltar.

In September 1944 the Group was reorganized and designated the 31st Escort Group. The new Group operated as a patrolling and Support Group in the UK western and northern coastal waters. The voyages and services of the B5 and 31st Escort Groups are described later in more detail under the heading B5 and 31st Escort Groups.

HISTORY

19.12.42	Ordered.
04.04.43	Laid down. **Builder**: Hull and Engine - Smiths Dock (Middlesborough).
21.06.43	Launched.
18.09.43	Completed.

WARTIME VOYAGES

Date	ESG	Senior Officer	Convoy	No of Ships	Arrive/ Sail	Location	Notes
22.09.43					Sail	Tees	From builder, Smith's Dock Co: Middlesborough. AM 182001B/7. When ready for sea *HC* to be sailed Clyde First of Class Trials. On completion, on to Tobermory for working up, thence to West Apps command.
25.09.43	Unall					Clyde	Trials
17.10.43	Unall					At Clyde	
01.11.43	Unall				Sail	Clyde	
02.11.43	Unall				Arv	Tobermory	
17.11.43	Unall				Arv	Clyde	Other reports state that *HC* left Tobermory 23rd Nov & arrived Clyde 24th Nov. (SMO)
23.11.43	Unall				Sail	Tobermory	
24.11.43	Unal				Arv	Clyde	
24.11.43	Unall				Arv	Clyde	
09.12.43	EG C4	*Hotspur*	ON 215	58	Sail	Clyde	
11.12.43	EG C4	*Hotspur*	ON 215	63		5510N 1145W	With ON 215 from 09.12.43. Hague list 58 ships
22.12.43	EG C4	*Hotspur*			Arv	St John's	
27.12.43	Unall				Sail	St John's	
29.12.43	Unall				Arv	Halifax	
13.01.44					Sail	Halifax	CinC NA 292040/Dec *HC* to be taken in hand until Jan 6. BAD Washington 032242/Jan *HC* will complete pro gramme at New London 20/Jan Intend she will

Date	ESG	Senior Officer	Convoy	No of Ships	Arrive/ Sail	Location	Notes
							visit New York for two days.
14.01.44	Unall					At Sea	
15.01.44	Unall				Arv	New York	
24.01.44	Unall					At Sea.	Left New York 27.01.44
27.01.44	Unall				Sail	New York	
31.01.44					Arv	Argentia	
31.01.44					Sail	Argentia	
01.02.44					Arv	St John's	
01.02.44	EG B5	*Havelock*	HX 277	69	Sail	St John's	
03.02.44	EG B5	*Havelock*	HX 277	71		4452N 4848W	
05.02.44	EG B5	*Havelock*	HX 277	71		4359N 3901W	
12.02.44	EG B5	*Havelock*	HX 277	69	Arv	Greenock	
13.02.44	EG B5	*Hadleigh Castle*			Arv	Liverpool	
21.02.44	EG B5	*Hadleigh Castle*			Sail	Londonderry	
21.02.44	EG B5	*Hadleigh Castle*			Arv	Belfast	Left Liverpool 20.02/44 (SMO)
22.02.44	EG B5	*Hadleigh Castle*			Arv	Londonderry	
22.02.44	EG B5	*Hadleigh Castle*	ON 225	59	Sail	Belfast	
23.02.44	EG B5	*Hadleigh Castle*	ON 225	59	Sail	Londonderry	

*Starboard bow view of **HMS Hadleigh Castle**.*   *(MoD/Crown Copyright)*

Date	ESG	Senior Officer	Convoy	No of Ships	Arrive/ Sail	Location	Notes
23.02.44	EG B5	*Hadleigh Castle* ON 225			Sail	Londonderry	
23.02.44	EG B5	*Hadleigh Castle* ON 225		61		N Channel	
24.02.44	EG B5	*Hadleigh Castle* ON 225		60		5615N 1225W	
03.03.44	EG B5	*Hadleigh Castle* ON 225		60	Arv	Argentia	
10.03.44	EG B5	*Hadleigh Castle* HX 282		96	Sail	Argentia	
21.03.44	EG B5	*Hadleigh Castle* HX 282		96	Arv	Liverpool	
07.04.44	EG B5	*Exe*			Arv	Liverpool	
08.04.44	EG B5	*Exe*			Arv	Clyde	
13.04.44	EG B5	*Exe*			Sail	Londonderry	
14.04.44	EG B5	*Exe*	OS 74/ KMS 48	29		5552N 0952W	
22.04.44	EG B5	*Exe*	OS 74/ KMS 48	29		3712N 1333W	
24.04.44	EG B5	*Exe*			Arv	Gibraltar	
01.05.44	EG B5	*Exe*			Sail	Gibraltar	

HMS Hadleigh Castle in cold weather - notice the iced up 4-inch gun in the background.   *(CCC(F)A Archives)*

Date	ESG	Senior Officer	Convoy	No of Ships	Arrive/ Sail	Location	Notes
06.05.44	EG B5	*Exe-*	SL 156/ MKS 47	65		4116N 1829W	Hague gives 46 ships
12.05.44	EG B5	*Exe*	SL 156/ MKS 47	46	Arv	Clyde	
22.05.44	EG B5	*Exe*			Sail	Clyde	
23.05.44	EG B5	*Exe*	OS78/ KMS52		Sail	Londonderry	
24.05.44	EG B5	*Exe*	OS78/ KMS52	25		5550N 1010W	
29.05.44	EG B4	*Helmsdale*	SL 158/ MKS49	51		4730N 2150W	Convoy size increased with the joining of the SL section on 21 May. *HC* Joined convoy on 28 May. Detached to southbound convoy 29th
06.06.44	EG B5	*Exe*	OS78/ KMS52		Arv	Gibraltar	
09.06.44	EG B5	*Exe*	MKS51	14	Sail	Gibraltar	
10.06.44	EG B5	*Exe*	SL160/ MKS51	44		3540N 0705W	
13.06.44	EG B5	*Exe*	SL160/ MKS51	50		3710N 1640W	44 ships according to Hague
21.06.44	EG B5	*Exe*	SL160/ MKS51		Arv	Clyde	
29.06.44	EG B5	*Exe*			Sail	Clyde	
02.07.44	EG B5	*Exe*	OS82/ KMS56	26	Sail	Londonderry	
06.07.44	EG B5	*Exe*	OS 82/ KMS56	29		4818N 1935W	
13.07.44	EG B5	*Exe*	OS82/ KMS56	29	Arv	Gibraltar	
19.07.44	EG B5	*Exe*	SL164/ MKS55	33	Sail	Gibraltar	
21.07.44	EG B5	*Exe*	MKS 55	19		3435N 1020W	
21.07.44	EG B5	*Exe*	SL 164/ MKS55	35		3525N 1248W	
29.07.44	EG B5	*Exe*	SL 164/ MKS 55	33		5140N1520W	
31.07.44	EG B5	*Exe*	SL 164/ MKS 55	33	Arv	Clyde	
09.08.44	EG B5	*Hadleigh Castle*			Arv	Larne	
12.08.44	EG B5	*Hadleigh Castle*	OS86/ KMS60	23	Sail	Londonderry	

Date	ESG	Senior Officer	Convoy	No of Ships	Arrive/ Sail	Location	Notes
23.08.44	EG B5	*Hadleigh Castle*	OS86/ KMS60	24	Arv	Gibraltar	
30.08.44	EG B5	*Hadleigh Castle*	SL168/ MKS59	35	Sail	Gibraltar	Carrying 20 boxes of bullion (N.Pickford 1999)
01.09.44	EG B5	*Hadleigh Castle*	SL 168/ MKS59	35		3925N 1030W	
09.09.44	31 EG	*Berkeley Castle*			Arv	Clyde	
22.09.44	31 EG	*Berkeley Castle*			Arv	At Larne	
23.09.44	31 EG	*Berkeley Castle*			Sail	Londonderry	
27.09.44	31 EG	*Berkeley Castle*				5430N 1412W	Force 33. On Patrol
01.10.44	31 EG	*Berkeley Castle*				NW of Donegal Bay	On Patrol in support of ONS33
09.10.44	31 EG	*Berkeley Castle*			Arv	Clyde	
11.10.44	31 EG	*Berkeley Castle*				Clyde	Clyde for lay over
16.10.44	31 EG	*Berkeley Castle*				Clyde	To 18th
20.10.44	31 EG	*Berkeley Castle*				At Clyde	
23.10.44	31 EG	*Berkeley Castle*			Sail	Londonderry	
23.10.44	31 EG	*Pevensey Castle*				At Larne	
30.10.44	31 EG	*Berkeley Castle*				4910N 0538W	On A/S sweep
10.11.44	31 EG	*Berkeley Castle*				At Sea	
16.11.44	31 EG	*Berkeley Castle*			Arv	Clyde	
29.11.44	31 EG	*Berkeley Castle*			Sail	Londonderry	
02.12.44	31 EG	*Berkeley Castle*			Sail	Scapa Flow	Having arrived Scapa same day
05.12.44	31 EG	*Berkeley Castle*				6020N 0459W	On Patrol
11.12.44	31 EG	*Berkeley Castle*			Arv	Lerwick	
12.12.44	31 EG	*Berkeley Castle*			Arv	Clyde	
21.12.44	31 EG	*Berkeley Castle*			Sail	Clyde	
23.12.44	31 EG	*Berkeley Castle*			Sail	Lamlash	Having arrived there 21.12.44 (SMO)
02.01.45	31 EG	*Berkeley Castle*			Arv	Avonmouth	
03.01.45	31 EG	*Berkeley Castle*			Sail	Londonderry	FOIC Cardiff 050945.1 *HC* taken in hand 04.01.45 by Messrs Dhas Hill Bristol to complete 24.02.45
08.01.45	31 EG	*Berkeley Castle*				WA	On Patrol
22.01.45	31 EG	*Berkeley Castle*				Bristol	For Repairs
29.01.45	31 EG	*Berkeley Castle*				Bristol	
02.02.45	31 EG	*Berkeley Castle*				Bristol	Repairs completed 24 Feb
27.02.45	31 EG	*Berkeley Castle*			Arv	Bristol	

Date	ESG	Senior Officer	Convoy	No of Ships	Arrive/ Sail	Location	Notes
08.03.45	31 EG	*Berkeley Castle*			Arv	Cardiff	NO I/c Avonmouth 071110A/3 *HC* fouled a buoy in Portished Dock when proceeding and has returned to wharf.
11.03.45	31 EG	*Berkeley Castle*			Sail	Belfast	
23.03.45	31 EG	*Berkeley Castle*			Arv	Clyde	
25.03.45	31 EG	*Berkeley Castle*			Sail	Clyde	
14.04.45	31 EG	*Berkeley Castle*			Sail	Clyde	
19.04.45	31 EG	*Berkeley Castle*			Sail	Belfast	
24.04.45	31 EG	*Berkeley Castle*			Sail	Holyhead	
30.04.45	31 EG	*Berkeley Castle*			Arv	Milford Haven	
02.05.45	31 EG	*Berkeley Castle*			Sail	Milford Haven	
13.05.45	31 EG	*Berkeley Castle*			Sail	Lochalsh	
14.05.45	31 EG	*Berkeley Castle*			Arv	Clyde	
29.05.45	31 EG	*Berkeley Castle*			Sail	Clyde	
04.06.45					Sail	Clyde	
22.06.45					Sail	Clyde	
22.06.45					Arv	Liverpool	
23.06.45	FOGMA				Sail	Liverpool	

HMS Hadleigh Castle *in January 1945.*

(Portsmouth Royal Naval Museum)

Date	ESG	Senior Officer	Convoy	No of Ships	Arrive/ Sail	Location	Notes
28.06.45					Arv	Gibraltar	
29.06.45					Sail	Gibraltar	
19.07.45					Arv	Gibraltar	
31.07.45					Sail	Gibraltar	
03.09.45					Sail	Gibraltar	To relieve *Lancaster Castle*. *LC*'s 041920A/9 Relieved by *HC* FOGMA 120949/9 *HC* is being relieved in Pos 20 by *St Brides Bay* AM 211354.1 *HC* is to reduce to reserve Cat B on arrival in UK. FOGMA 251222A ETD 26.1. ETA Portsmouth 31.1.
31.10.46					Arv	Portsmouth	

August 1946 -49	Reserve at Portsmouth.
1949-50	Refit at Birkenhead.
1951-52	Reserve at Harwich.
1958	Sold to C.W. Dorkin.
01/59	Arrived Gateshead for scrapping.

HMS Hadleigh Castle at Gateshead in 1959 awaiting scrapping.   (Ben Warlow Collection)

HMS HEDINGHAM CASTLE

HMS Hedingham Castle seen on completion in May 1945.　　　　　　　　*(MoD/Crown Copyright)*

HMS Hedingham Castle was originally ordered under the name of *Gorey Castle* and renamed in 1943. Although allocated to the Western Approaches Command on completion of working up, she took no active part in Naval operations prior to V.E Day and was reduced to reserve in August 1945.

HISTORY

09.12.42　Ordered as *Gorey Castle* K529.
02.11.43　Laid down. Builder: Hull - Crown (Sunderland); Engine - G Clark (Sunderland).
30.10.44　Launched.
12.05.45　Completed as *Hedingham Castle*.

HMS Hedingham Castle in May 1946.
(Portsmouth Royal Naval Museum)

WARTIME VOYAGES

Date	ESG	Senior Officer	Convoy	No of Ships	Arrive/ Sail	Location	Notes
26.05.45					Sail	Blyth	NO I/c Blyth 131150/5 to Admty Anticipate *HC* will be available to sail 21/5
28.05.45					Arv	Tobermory	Work up
18.06.45					Sail	Tobermory	
19.06.45					Arv	Clyde	
29.06.45					Sail	Clyde	
29.06.45					Arv	Belfast	
17.07.45					Sail	Belfast	
18.07.45					Arv	Douglas (IOM)	
19.07.45					Sail	Douglas (IOM)	
20.07.45					Arv	Clyde	
06.08.45					Sail	Clyde	
09.08.45					Arv	Plymouth	
10.08.45					Sail	Plymouth	
11.08.45					Arv	Plymouth	
14.08.45					Sail	Plymouth	
15.08.45					Arv	Sheerness	
23.08.45					Sail	Southend	
24.08.45					Arv	Plymouth	
25.08.45					Sail	Plymouth	

Date	ESG	Senior Officer	Convoy	No of Ships	Arrive/ Sail	Location	Notes
27.08.45					Arv	Clyde	
06.09.45					Arv	Fairlie (Clyde)	
06.09.45					Sail	Clyde	
02.10.45					Sail	Fairlie (Clyde)	
03.10.45					Arv	Plymouth	
06.11.45					Sail	Plymouth	
08.11.45					Arv	Greenock	
24.11.45					Sail	Greenock	131135/12 FOIC Greenock Intend to sail *HC* to ASR 16 24/11: 251621/11 ETA ASR 16 0800/26/11
13.12.45					Arv	Greenock	HC 260718Z Relieved by *Berkeley Castle* on ASR 16 0800/26/11.
17.01.46					Arv	Clyde	
06.02.46					Arv	Portland	End of record.

August 1945	At Chatham in reserve.
October 1945	Recommissioned for Air/Sea Rescue duties, Rosyth Command.
1946	3rd Escort Flotilla, Portland.
January 1949	2nd Training Flotilla, Portland.
1952-1956	2nd Training Squadron, Portland.
1953	Represented Home Command, Portsmouth, at the Coronation Fleet Review.
June 1955	Provided a naval contingent for the unveiling of the Normandy War Memorial at Bayeux.
1956-57	Reserve at Plymouth.
21.10.57	Sold to BIS for breaking up.
04.58	Arrived Grangemouth for scrapping.

The ship seen a year later in June 1947 . (Portsmouth Royal Naval Museum)

Visit to Castle Hedingham

Hedingham Castle visited Harwich in June 1947 from Portland. The purpose of the visit was to make contact with the people of Castle Hedingham who had adopted the ship. There was an exchange of visits between the villagers and the ship's company. This included a successful party held on board *Hedingham Castle*, when the ship was visited by 70 children from the village.

   In response to the hospitality shown to the ship's company the Commanding Officer wrote to the editor of the *Halstead Gazette* in the following terms:-

HMS Hedingham Castle

Sir,
May I express, in your columns, the appreciation of myself and my ship's company for all that was done to make our visit to Castle Hedingham so enjoyable and so successful. It was a very real pleasure for us to meet the people of Castle Hedingham In their lovely village, and to be able to show some of them our ship, in which they have shown so much interest, and to which they have been so kind. In conclusion I would like to offer a special vote of thanks to the Vicar the Rev. W.H.H. Cossens and Mrs Cossens, for their untiring efforts. We all hope that we shall be able to meet the people of the village again and I have no doubt but that at some future weekend or leave period, some of us will be found in the village sampling the many kind and generous offers of hospitality.

yours faithfully

Robert A. Purves
Lieutenant Commander Royal Navy
Commanding Officer

Hedingham Castle recollections

P.J. Carroll served in **Hedingham Castle** over two periods. The first time was in 1948 and again in 1952. He recalled that on the first commission, "Except for refits at Pompey we never went anywhere, once to Cowes as guardboat at Cowes Week."

   During his second spell it seems that they had a more active time. On one occasion, in thick fog, orders were received from Captain (D) to anchor at Weymouth. "However our chap decided he would ping the opening in the breakwater. He hit it and everyone was laid aft jumping up and down with the engines at full astern to get us off. The C.O. left very shortly after that."

   "On another occasion on a Friday afternoon as we entered harbour, I was already dressed for a long weekend. The pipe went '*All leave is cancelled, the ship is returning to sea*'. We spent the weekend steaming up and down between Dover and the French coast; some VIP was flying across the channel and we were there in case of any incident. Nothing happened of course. I was on watch in the engine room. We were at slow ahead and had been there most of the night. Approaching Portland suddenly everything changed. Up went the revs and we started to circle. The tiffy said "nip up quick and have a look'. There to my amazement was this huge four masted sailing ship. It was either the **Pamir** or **Passat**.

   The OOW was filming the ship with a cine camera. No one believed me on the mess deck. They said it was probably the **Mary Celeste**. But we saw it later on during a film show."

   "In July 1953 we were told that we were swapping crews with the **Launceston Castle**, she being a Devonport ship with a Pompey crew and us being the opposite."

   "We were told we would be running out of Londonderry working with the local Fleet Air Arm Station.

The Captain told us he would try and give us all a long weekend on route. The West country men left us in Portland. Our next stop was at Liverpool for the northern lads. We were told when we went alongside we would connect up for steam and lights. We could not get the connection and stayed flashed up all the time."

"We were independent command and if our service was not required the skipper would take us off somewhere. Scotland normally, but once we went to Antwerp."

HMS HURST CASTLE

Battle Honours
Atlantic 1944

*An undated image of **HMS Hurst Castle**.*   *(MoD/Crown Copyright)*

HMS Hurst Castle completed working up at Tobermory on 3 July 1944 and joined the B3 Escort Group. She sailed with that Group on 2 August escorting Convoy OS 85/KMS 59 to Gibraltar. On completion of the return voyage with Convoy SL 167/MKS 58 on 30 August 1944, *Hurst Castle* was ordered to join Force 33. She was torpedoed off Tory Island on 1 September 1944 and sank in six minutes with the loss of 17 lives.

HISTORY

02/02/1943	Ordered.
06/08/1943	Laid down: **Builder**: Hull - Caledon (Dundee); Engine - Thornycroft (Woolston).
23/02/1944	Launched.
09/06/1944	Completed.
01/09/1944	Torpedoed and sunk in six minutes by *U-482* off Tory Island.

REPORT ON THE LOSS OF *HMS HURST CASTLE*

Enclosure No.1a to Commodore (D), Western Approaches' Letter No. DW. 042.OP dated 19th September, 1944 (ADM 199/958)

HMS Hurst Castle was sailed from Londonderry at 2015B August 30th 1944 in company with *HMS Oxford Castle*, with orders to join Senior Officer, Force 33.

I proceeded to the westward of Inistrahull Island with the intention of joining Force 33 until ordered to patrol the area enclosed by Inistrahull Island, Oversay Light, Mull or Oa and Innishowen Head. During the night various ships were met but they were not identified by name. Orders were received at about 0600/31 to rendezvous with Force 33. A rendezvous position was later given as 072BB41 at 1330. *HMS Oxford Castle* was detached at about 1030/31 to join *HMS Kenilworth Castle* patrolling inside Tory Island. Junction was made at 1420/31 with *HM Ships Helmsdale, Foley, Pevensey Castle, Launceston Castle* and *Ambuscade*, and *HMS Hurst Castle* was put under the orders of *HMS Pevensey Castle* and proceeded to patrol North and South in company with *HM Ships Pevensey Castle, Launceston Castle* and *Ambuscade* between 56°16'N and Tory Island.

The ships turned North at 1607/31, North again at about 0303/1 September and South again at 0620/1, zigzag No. 20 being carried out, speed 12 knots. At 0700/1 course was altered by blue turn from 180° to 160° speed 15 knots. At 0750 orders were received to close distance to two miles for day sweeping. At 0750 course was altered to 135°, and 090° at 0810, ships being ordered to form a line of bearing 000° S/O in the order *Launceston Castle*, from *Pevensey Castle, Hurst Castle, Ambuscade*. A signal was intercepted at 0605 from *HMS Helmsdale* to *HMS Oxford Castle* repeating a sighting report by Liberator W26 and it was appreciated that the Senior Officer's turn at 0810 was with the intention of sweeping through the sighting position.

At 0810/1 September the order to spread on a line of bearing North and South was received, the ship at the time being about 070° two miles from *Pevensey Castle*. *Hurst Castle* turned through 180° to starboard to take up station 000° two miles from *Pevensey Castle*. Course was then 080° and the ship about 15° astern of station speed being increased to 13 knots and then to 14 knots to regain bearing. *HMS Launceston Castle* was at that time (0820) about five miles astern and *HMS Ambuscade* bearing about 030° five to six miles. *HM Ships Kenilworth Castle* and *Oxford Castle* were in sight to the eastward about ten miles distant and had been ordered by *HMS Pevensey Castle* to join her.

At 0824 *HMS Hurst Castle* was on a course of 080° speed 14 knots, ship at cruising stations, HSD closed up as the Senior Officer's intentions could only be surmised. Gland space watertight hatch was open with duty Stokers carrying out routines in the gland space. All other red openings were shut with the possible exception of the tiller flat hatch. Weather at the time being - wind Southwest force 3, sea and swell 23, visibility extreme.

HMS Hurst Castle was struck by torpedo at 0825 when in position 55°35' N 8° 11' W, while on course 080° at 14 knots, sinking in about 6 minutes. The torpedo struck port side aft probably in No. 14 oil fuel tank, flooding the tiller flat, after peak tank, Engineer's store and workshop, main naval store and provision room, instantly. The after engine room bulkhead collapsed within a minute. Other damage observed was a buckling of the forecastle deck on the port side abreast the bridge, and the upper deck forward collapsed. The ship took a list to port and settled slowly by the stern. By the time the smoke had cleared it was obvious that the ship was sinking and I gave the order to abandon ship.

The dinghy was lowered on the weather side but filled with a breaking sea. Six Carley floats were launched (three above establishment), but the whaler could not be turned out against the list (whaler not fitted with gripping spar). There was little difficulty in getting away from the ship and there was no fire except for live coals thrown from the galley range and no further explosions. All superstructure remained intact but it is believed that one or two ratings were entangled in the funnel guys. With very few exceptions inflatable lifebelts were being worn, and Officers were evenly distributed among the rafts and nets to organise rescue attempts.

The Ship sank stern first, bows rising vertically out of the water and hung for some minutes with about 40

feet of bow above water; probably the stern on the bottom.

HMS Ambuscade, brilliantly handled, was very soon on the spot and commenced picking up survivors. 102 survivors including all Officers, were picked up and were shown every kindness by the ship's company of *HMS Ambuscade*, outstanding among whom was Stoker Petty Officer Jordan who repeatedly dived into the oil to rescue exhausted men.

H G Chesterman
Lieutenant, RNR

HMS Hurst Castle *seen from the starboard quarter.*   *(MoD/Crown Copyright)*

HMS Hurst Castle provisioning a convoyed RN submarine (above) and conducting an oiling at sea (below). (CCC(F)A Archives)

From: **Commanding Officer,**
              HMS Pevensey Castle,
              C/o G.P.O. London.

Date: **3rd September , 1944**
To: **Senior Officer Force 33.33,**
Copy To: **Commodore (D) W.A.**
              (Relevant Signals and Track Chart with Original only)

REPORT OF PROCEEDINGS LEADING UP TO LOSS OF HMS HURST CASTLE at 0825

(All times "B")
1st September, 1944

Course 270 speed 12 knots, **HM ships Ambuscade**, **Launceston Castle** and **Hurst Castle** in company, ships spread on a line bearing 000° - 180°, distance apart 2 miles, carrying out zig-zag No. 20.

At 1800 in position 284 Tory Island, 12 miles, ships turned by E.1, turn to 000° -180° and a Gamma patrol commenced between the limits of the area on course 000° and 180°. At 2145 distance apart of ships was increased to 4 miles. **HMS Ambuscade** requested permission to return to Moville at 0700/1st for fuel.

1st September: At 0615/1st a signal was intercepted between one ship of Force 33 passing on an aircraft ASV contact in position 55°28'N 08°32'W. My division was then approaching the northern limit of the patrol and ships were immediately turned towards this position and speed increased to 15 knots,

A search with 242 Radar Set giving responses showing Stud 5 and homing signals indicated that the aircraft was more to the eastward than the original position given and this was confirmed by C in C WA's 0160610B giving the position as 55°28'N 08°05'W. At 0725 course was altered to 135° and the Senior Officer informed that I was closing this position giving an ETA 0830.

A signal TOO 0714 was intercepted from **HMS Oxford Castle** giving his position as 106°.BB. 43 miles and stating he was in the vicinity of aircraft marker. This position was taken to be the most accurate datum point.

At 0810 course was altered to 090° and speed reduced to 12 knots with the intention of forming the ships up in station and commencing sweep from the westward. In view of latest U-boat tactics I felt that the U-boat would have bottomed on being detected.

HMS Launceston Castle was well astern of station having been on the outside of all turns. **HMS Hurst Castle** and **Ambuscade** were ahead. **HMS Ambuscade** was ordered to remain until prudent limit of endurance and she stated that she would remain until 0900. Ships were ordered to form on a line of bearing 000° - 180°, **HMS Hurst Castle** Port 2, **HMS Ambuscade** Port 4, **HMS Launceston Castle** Starboard 2.

HMS Hurst Castle turned back to lose bearing, and had just turned again into station when a loud explosion was heard and a flash, followed by smoke which was seen to rise from her starboard quarter. Time 0825, position 111°.BB. 36 miles.

HM Ships Oxford Castle and **Kenilworth Castle** had been sighted at 0820 and were proceeding towards, distance about 6 miles.

All ships were immediately ordered to carry out operation "Observant" and ordered to out "Foxers".

I swept through the wreck area and investigated a contact which classified as echoes from the wreck.

Communication was established with aircraft W/17, who was ordered to Patrol around wreck at 4,000 yards distance.

HMS Ambuscade was then ordered to pick up survivors and return to Moville for fuel, first marking the position of the wreck with a dan buoy.

At 0940 Senior Officer, Force 33 had arrived and took over direction of the of the operation.
(*Note*) In streaming displacer paravanes at 70 R.P.M. (safe speed for Castle class) Port paravane sank below crushing depth or hit bottom and was flattened, subsequently towing on surface.

(Sgd) . . . .
COMMANDING OFFICER
LIEUTENANT COMMANDER, R.N.R.**

A SURVIVORS TALE

Fred Kemp the P.O. Tel of the ***Hurst Castle*** had stood by the ship whilst she was being built. He was somewhat horrified to find that when all his 'staff' joined ship, none of them had been to sea before and that they had all come straight from the training school at Skegness. Their first convoy was quite a strain. Fred felt that he had to be in the W/T Office, full time. He complained to the C.O. All he could say was "Sorry - its the drafting Officers fault - Carry on."
Eventually they settled down and got over having to have a bucket alongside them when on watch.
Fred recalls that when re-fuelling at Belfast, the Cox'n was distributing the mail. He called out to a young seaman, not more than a boy, "Here you are lad - a parcel from your Mum." "Its not from my Mum, I aint got no Mum. Its from my Gran."
On the following morning whilst on patrol, Fred had managed to get a few hours sleep on a camp bed under the bench in the W/T Office. Waking up and going to have a wash, he stopped to look through the signals in the 'In Tray' and found one - addressed to the ship from Admiralty "The following has been received from an aircraft. Have sighted conning tower of a U-Boat in position ....." The signal had been received about an hour previously. He asked if they had reported it to the bridge "...and they looked blank." Fred continued, "I just threw down the towel and flew up to the bridge where naturally the Captain was sitting on his High Chair. I handed him the signal, which he read and then hit the roof, screaming. "What the hell is the matter with your bloody sparkers?" All I could say was to remind him of my earlier conversation and misgivings. And he calmed down and said "OK P.O. Tel, I see what you mean, but when you get back there tell them to Buck Their Bloody Ideas up." Which is what I did as they sat quietly getting on with their morning watch. I added "You'd better get your life jackets blown up - you may need them sooner than you think." And with that I stowed my savings in an oiled silk tobacco pouch in the CB Chest and went below."
"I had just got to the bathroom when we were hit. One hell of an explosion and complete darkness except for as few emergency lights. I ran back to the W/T office and told the lads to get their life jackets blown up and to BEAT IT. I did not think that she would last long and I also knew that none of them could swim. I went looking for my oiled silk tobacco pouch but I couldn't find the bloody key to the CB chest.
Then I did what I should have done and got the emergency transmitter working. By the time I had got the emergency signal off, I had difficulty in getting out of the office and on to the upper deck as the ship was not far from sliding straight under.
As I slowly slid across the deck towards the guard rails I saw someone hanging onto one of the funnel guy ropes. It was the young boy seaman. He had his life jacket on, blown up. I grabbed hold of him but he wouldn't budge - "I can't swim." I pointed to his life jacket but it was no good. Then a stoker PO and a "Tiffy" clambered out of the engine room and crawled over and took off his own life jacket and put it on the lad (I had not got mine - I couldn't find it) and tried to get him to let go and follow us, but we just couldn't budge him.

At that time the ship was on her beam ends and we slid down to the port side guard rails. There were no boats or Carley Rafts. I'm sure that we were the last two to leave the ship and just jumped. As I surfaced I looked up and the mainmast with the HF/DF aerial on the top was coming down fast towards me, so I turned and did the fastest 50 yards fully clothed I've ever done, only to realise I was in the oil fuel which was running up my nose and it went into my eyes. Then I just turned and swam on my back. It seemed a very long time before I was picked up by the Ambuscade. In the meantime I had got very tired. I began to sink. I can honestly say that when you get to that stage drowning is the easy way out. I felt that as though I was sitting in a big easy chair at home and I could see the lovely roaring fire and said to myself "Oh well drowning isn't so bad after all" - "Then there must have been some brain cells still working as I remembered - I'd got married on the day before we sailed for Gib and if I could get out of this I'd get 7 days survivors leave, and I struck out to get back to the surface."

"After I had been hauled aboard and recovered a little I went down to the messdeck to see if I could find any of my lads. But not very confident as all my lad were non swimmers. I could not believe my eyes. Every one of them was there and when I asked them how they had managed it - "Well POTS someone lowered the whaler and we just stepped into it"

CASUALTIES SUFFERED BY HMS HURST CASTLE WERE:-

ARBUCKLE, Leading Seaman, GEORGE; Age 23
ASH, Able Seaman, WILLIAM ERNEST; Age 19
BENNETT, Ordinary Seaman, DONALD LIONEL; Age 16
BYNER, Stoker 1st Class, ALBERT LEONARD; Age 33
DARBY, Stoker 2nd Class, ALFRED; Age 21
DUFFY, Engine Room Artificer 4th Class, MICHAEL; Age 21
EARL, Stoker 1st Class, SIDNEY ALBERT; Age 20
ELLIS, Able Seaman, SAMUEL JOSEPH; Age 21
KELLY, Leading Cook(S), JAMES HANN; Age 28
LINKLATER, Canteen Manager, WILLIAM WRIGHT; Age 36
LUCAS, Able Seaman, MAURICE EDWARD; Age 21
NAYLOR, Chief Stoker, ROBERT MADDOCKS; Mentioned in Despatches Age 34
ROFF, Ordinary Seaman, LEONARD; Age 19
SAVIDGE, Ordinary Seaman, STANLEY ERNEST; Age 18
TURNER, Leading Stoker, SIDNEY GEORGE; Age 30
WARES, Ordinary Seaman, JOHN HENRY; Age 19
WRIGHT, Ordinary Seaman, WILLIAM; Age 19

HMS KENILWORTH CASTLE

Battle Honours
Atlantic 1944   North Sea 1945

HMS Kenilworth Castle, fresh from the builders in November 1943.   *(MoD/Crown Copyright)*

HMS *Kenilworth Castle* completed working up at Tobermory on 20 December 1943. The records of her movements during January 1944 are confused. She was variously reported as operating with the B3 Escort Group, the 39th Escort Group and the 6th Escort Group. In February 1944 she joined the B7 Escort Group; at first on mid-ocean escort duty in the Atlantic and then, from April 1944 until the end of August, escorting convoys to and from Gibraltar. In September the Group was reformed as the 30th Escort Group. This was allocated to patrol and convoy support duties in the UK coastal waters.

Kenilworth Castle was involved with the sinking of two U-boats - *U-744* on 6 March 1944 and *U-1200* on 11 November 1944.

Upon the conclusion of the war in Europe *Kenilworth Castle* was allocated for Air/Sea Rescue duties, subsequently in 1946 joining the Training Squadron at Portland. She was reduced to reserve in 1948 and scrapped in 1959.

HISTORY

19.12.43   Ordered.
07.05.43   Laid down: **Builder**: Hull and Engine - Smiths Dock (Middlesborough).
17.08.43   Launched.
22.11.43   Completed.

WARTIME VOYAGES

Date	ESG	Senior Officer	Convoy	No of Ships	Arrive/ Sail	Location	Notes
30.11.43	Unall				Arv	Tobermory	
20.12.43	EG B7				Sail	Tobermory	
21.12.43	EG B7				Arv	Londonderry	
15.01.44	EG B7				Sail	Londonderry	
17.01.44	EG B3	*Burza*	OS 65/ KMS39	53		5350N 1209W	
21.01.44	39 EG	*Rochester*	SL145/	36		5335N 1202W	ADM 199/315 places *KC* working with 6th EG escorting this convoy 22 Janaury 1944
23.01.44	EG B7				Sail	Londonderry	

*A Commissioning photograph of **HMS Kenilworth Castle**'s ship's company, September 1943.*

(CCC(F)A Archives)

Date	ESG	Senior Officer	Convoy	No of Ships	Arrive/ Sail	Location	Notes
25.01.44	EG B7				Arv	Londonderry	CinC WA 252256/Jan Com Leggasaich is to be accommodated in *KC*. Ship sails 26th
08.02.44	EG B7	*Chelmer*			Sail	Londonderry	
09.02.44	EG B7				Sail	Londonderry	
09.02.44	EG B7	*Chelmer*	ON 223	54		5545N 1057W	
18.02.44	EG B7	*Chelmer*	ON 223	55		4355N 5015W	
19.02.44	EG B7	*Chelmer*			Arv	Argentia	
24.02.44	EG B7				Sail	Argentia	
07.03.44	EG B7	*Chelmer*	HX 280	64		5355N 1450W	To join B7? 13.5 knots
08.03.44	EG B7	*Chelmer*			Arv	Londonderry	
16.03.44	EG B7	*Chelmer-*	ON 228	73	Sail	Londonderry	
17.03.44	EG B7	*Chelmer*	ON 228	73		5525N 1101W	SO may have been *Vidette*: Hague lists 70 ships
27.03.44	EG B7	*Vidette*			Arv	Argentia	
31.03.44	EG B7	*Vidette*			Sail	Argentia	
02.04.44	EG B7	*Vidette*	SC 156	59		4515N 4925W	Hague lists 40 ships
08.04.44	EG B7	*Vidette-*	SC 156	54		4820N 2730W	
13.04.44	EG B7	*Vidette*			Arv	Londonderry	
24.04.44	EG B4	*Helmsdale*			Sail	Londonderry	
28.04.44	EG B4	*Helmsdale*			Arv	Londonderry	
03.05.44	EG B4	*Helmsdale*	OS 76/ KMS50	35	Sail	Londonderry	
05.05.44	EG B4	*Helmsdale*	OS 76/ KMS50	35		5415N 1245W	Gale force head winds encountered (ADM 217/364)
15.05.44	EG B4	*Helmsdale*	OS 76/ KMS50	35	Arv	Gibraltar	
20.05.44	EG B4	*Helmsdale*	SL 158/ MKS 49	31	Sail	Gibraltar	
21.05.44	EG B4	*Helmsdale*	MKS 49	29		3530N 0625W	
29.05.44	EG B4	*Helmsdale*	SL 158/ MKS 49	51		4730N 2150W	Convoy size increased with the joining of the SL section on 21 May
01.06.44	EG B4	*Helmsdale*	SL158/ MKS49	47		5255N 1518W	
03.06.44	EG B4	*Helmsdale*	SL158/ MKS49	47	Arv	Londonderry	
12.06.44	EG B4	*Helmsdale*	OS80/ KMS54	29	Sail	Londonderry	
13.06.44	EG B4	*Helmsdale*	OS80/ KMS54	29		5540N 0758W	

Date	ESG	Senior Officer	Convoy	No of Ships	Arrive/ Sail	Location	Notes
24.06.44	EG B4	*Helmsdale*	OS80/ KMS54	29	Arv	Gibraltar	
29.06.44	EG B4	*Helmsdale*	SL162/ MKS53	36	Sail	Gibraltar	
30.06.44	EG B4	*Helmsdale*	SL162/ MKS53	36		3535N 0659W	
11.07.44	EG B4	*Helmsdale*	SL162/ MKS53	36	Arv	Londonderry	Convoy subjected to unsuccesful air attack on 3rd; believed glider bombs used.
22.07.44	EG B4	*Helmsdale*	OS84/ KMS58	24	Sail	Londonderry	
26.07.44	EG B4	*Helmsdale*	OS84/ KMS58	27		4901N 1935W	Hague gives 24 ships
02.08.44	EG B4	*Helmsdale*	OS84/ KMS58	35	Arv	Gibraltar	
08.08.44	EG B4	*Helmsdale*	SL166/ MKS57	16	Sail	Gibraltar	
09.08.44	EG B4	*Helmsdale*	SL166/ MKS57	16		3541N 0652W	
19.08.44	EG B4	*Helmsdale*	SL 166/ MKS57	31	Arv	Londonderry	
25.08.44	EG B4	*Helmsdale*				Londonderry	Boiler clean
29.08.44	30 EG	*Pevensey Castle*			Sail	Londonderry	
14.09.44	30 EG	*Pevensey Castle*	ONF 252		Sail	Londonderry	Operating under Force 33
23.09.44	30 EG	*Pevensey Castle*			Arv	Londonderry	On completion of Group training 30 EG is to be sailed to top up fuel at Morville thence to join force for operation CW (SMO)
29.09.44	30 EG	*Pevensey Castle*			Sail	Londonderry	
03.10.44	30 EG	*Pevensey Castle*			Arv	Larne	
05.10.44	30 EG	*Pevensey Castle*			Sail	Londonderry	
11.10.44	30 EG	*Pevensey Castle*				NW App	On patrol
15.10.44	30 EG	*Pevensey Castle*				At Sea	
18.10.44	30 EG	*Pevensey Castle*			Arv	Londonderry	
21.10.44	30 EG	*Pevensey Castle*			Sail	Londonderry	
28.10.44	30 EG	*Pevensey Castle*			Arv	Londonderry	
06.11.44	30 EG	*Pevensey Castle*				Londonderry	
09.11.44	30 EG	*Pevensey Castle*			Sail	Londonderry	To patrol NW Approaches.

Date	ESG	Senior Officer	Convoy	No of Ships	Arrive/ Sail	Location	Notes
19.11.44	30 EG	*Pevensey Castle*			Arv	Londonderry	11 Nov: Group attacked U-boat and hold contact for three days
21.11.44	30 EG	*Pevensey Castle*			Sail	Londonderry	Patrol in area 52N 11W. Group attacked suspected U-boat on 26 Nov & held contact for 73 hrs. Then supported passage of HX321 & relieved 2 EG on 5 Dec. Group returned to Londonderry
28.11.44	30 EG	*Pevensey Castle*				5110N 0945W	On patrol
03.12.44	30 EG	*Pevensey Castle*			Sail	Milford Haven	
06.12.44	30 EG	*Pevensey Castle*			Arv	Londonderry	
18.12.44	30 EG	*Pevensey Castle*			Sail	Belfast	
28.12.44	30 EG	*Pevensey Castle*			Sail	Portsmouth	For a short lay-over
31.12.44	30 EG	*Caistor Castle*			Sail	Portsmouth	Patrol area north of Cherbourg
08.01.45	30 EG	*Pevensey Castle*				S of Needles	On patrol
13.01.45	30 EG	*Pevensey Castle*			Arv	Londonderry	
15.01.45	30 EG	*Pevensey Castle*				Off Holyhead	On patrol
29.01.45	30 (B)	*Caistor Castle*				Off Hartland	On patrol
06.02.45	30 EG	*Pevensey Castle*			Sail	Plymouth	
13.02.45					Arv	Londonderry	
19.02.45	30 EG	*Pevensey Castle*				Londonderry	Boiler cleaning. Ready 22.02.45
24.02.45	30 EG	*Pevensey Castle*			Sail	Londonderry	
27.03.45	30 EG	*Pevensey Castle*			Arv	Lochalsh	
31.03.45	30 EG	*Pevensey Castle*			Sail	Scapa Flow	
02.04.45	30 EG	*Pevensey Castle*			Arv	Scapa Flow	
11.04.45	30 EG	*Pevensey Castle*			Arv	Scapa Flow	
13.04.45	30 EG	*Pevensey Castle*				Scapa Flow	
14.04.45	30 EG	*Pevensey Castle*				Clyde	
19.04.45					Arv	Scapa Flow	
20.04.45	30 EG	*Pevensey Castle*			Sail	Scapa Flow	
04.05.45	30 EG	*Portchester Castle*			Sail	Londonderry	
07.05.45	30 EG	*Pevensey Castle*			Sail	Londonderry	
17.05.45	30 EG	*Pevensey Castle*			Arv	Londonderry	
19.05.45					Sail	Londonderry	
20.05.45	30 EG	*Pevensey Castle*			Arv	Loch Eriboll	
24.05.45		*Pevensey Castle*			Sail	Loch Eriboll	
25.05.45					Sail	Scapa Flow	
27.05.45	30 EG	*Pevensey Castle*			Arv	Bergen	
31.05.45	30 EG	*Pevensey Castle*			Arv	Scapa Flow	

Date	ESG	Senior Officer	Convoy	No of Ships	Arrive/ Sail	Location	Notes
02.06.45	30 EG	*Pevensey Castle*			Arv	Londonderry	
28.06.45					Sail	Londonderry	
08.07.45					Arv	Cape Vincent	
09.08.45					Sail	Freetown	*KC* 160900/4 Have taken over ASR Station 32 relieving *Portchester Castle*
06.10.45					Sail	Freetown	
08.10.45					Sail	Dakar	
08.10.45					Arv	Dakar	
11.10.45					Arv	Las Palmas	
16.10.45					Sail	Las Palmas	Escorting *Sustler* and Tow
25.10.45					Arv	Falmouth	
25.10.45					Sail	Falmouth	
26.10.45					Arv	Portsmouth	
28.10.45					Sail	Portsmouth	
29.10.45					Arv	Plymouth	AM 102257/11 *KC* is re-allocated to FOGMA for Air Sea Rescue Duties. Record ends.

1946		Portland Training Squadron.
1948		Reserve.
1949-51		Reserve at Devonport.
1952-58		Reserve at Penarth.
1959		Sold to E. Rees.
20.06.59		Arrived Llanelli for scrapping.

THE SINKING OF U-744

In March 1944 **Kenilworth Castle** as part of the B7 Escort Group was reported to be escorting the homeward bound convoy HX280. The B7 Reports of Proceedings for this convoy were not found in the ADM 217 series of files at the Public Records Office, Kew. This is unfortunate because on 5 March 1944, the C2 Escort Group, also escorting this convoy, was in action with **U-744**. C2's report merely records that **Kenilworth Castle** joined in the hunt at 1304 and was ordered to recover Foxers so as to be able to operate at slow speed.

The action had started at 1000 on 5 March when the C2 Escort Group obtained D/F bearings indicating the close proximity of a U-boat. Two minutes later **HMCS Gatineau** obtained a contact. The contact was promptly attacked heralding the start of an action lasting 30 hours culminating in the eventual scuttling of **U-744**.

At 1447 **Kenilworth Castle** had recovered her Foxers and the C2 Group held their contact whilst **Kenilworth Castle** attacked with Squid. This attack fell short of the target. **Kenilworth Castle** regained contact and attacked with Squid at 1538 but failed to make a contact with her Type 147B. Between 1808 and 1933 she made three attempts to attack but broke off during the first two. On one occasion the U-boat made a large alteration of course and on the second attempt **Kenilworth Castle** lost contact. She failed to make contact with her 147B during the third attack. After this **Kenilworth Castle** reported that her Asdic training gear had broken down. She was then stationed close astern of **HMCS St Catherine** (whose radar was faulty) to assist in detection should the U-boat surface.

During the night sporadic attacks were made so as to keep the U-boat down. **Kenilworth Castle** was detached at 0730 on 6 March. She had not been able to repair her Asdic and her radar was no longer required.

The C2 Group continued with the action. Shortly after noon the U-boat was on a steady course. Contact was firm and the weather settled. It was assumed that the U-boat would not attempt to surface until about 2100.

It was decided to postpone any further attacks until about 1600 and from then on to attack at regular intervals with a view to discouraging offensive action when the U-boat surfaced.

At 1532 the U-boat surfaced and was immediately attacked with gunfire. Ships ceased fire when the U-boat's crew were seen to be abandoning ship.

What followed was a practical demonstration of the difficulties involved in successfully boarding a U-boat at sea. **Chilliwac**'s boarding party was the first to arrive. The U-boat was boarded and numerous books collected. By this time there was quite a bit of sea running. The books had been transferred to the whaler when it capsized on the U-boat's saddle tank. All the books and gear were lost and several of the boarding party thrown into the sea. At this point **St. Catherine**'s boarding party had arrived from the other side. They misjudged the distance from the U-boat; a wave carried the whaler onto the casing and that too capsized.

Seeing two boarding parties going to the U-boat, **Fennel** had launched her skiff to pick up survivors. It was swamped and capsized alongside her.

At this point, **Chaudiere** arrived and seeing both whalers capsize, very smartly lowered her motor boat. This spent the next 30 minutes rescuing boarding parties and U-boat survivors. It had just completed this when its engine broke down.

The U-boat was finally sunk by a torpedo from **Icarus**.

During the 30 hour period of the hunt, **U-744** was subjected to five Hedgehog attacks, three Squid attacks and some ten depth charge attacks using 244 depth charges. This was the first time that a Castle Class Corvette was involved in the sinking of a U-boat. The ships credited with the sinking of **U-744** were **HM Ships Icarus** and **Kenilworth Castle** , **HMC Ships St Catherines**, **Fennel**, **Chilliwack**, **Chaudiere**, and **Gatineau**.

Before the formation of the 30th Escort Group **Kenilworth Castle** escorted ten convoys comprising 480 ships of which two were lost due to enemy action.

SINKING OF U-1200

On 10 November 1944 the 30th Escort Group on patrol in position 50°24'N 05°42'W was steaming in line abreast when *Pevensey Castle* obtained a radar contact at a range of 23,000 yards. This faded but *Portchester Castle* obtained a radar contact at 25,000 yards and held it for 18 minutes until it too slowly faded. It was assumed that this was a U-boat and that it would continue on its same course of 250° at 4 knots. The Group then altered course to intercept. *Launceston Castle* obtained an Asdic contact at 0130 on 11 November, one hour and 32 minutes after the initial radar contact.

Launceston Castle subsequently carried out two further attacks. After the third attack she reported that the target had bottomed.

The Group then held this contact continuously for three days. During that time the contact was subjected to 17 Squid attacks, two depth charge attacks (*Launceston Castle* and *Portchester Castle* one each) one Hedgehog attack (*HMS Drury*, 4th Escort Group) and a massed depth charge attack by the 4th Escort Group. *Launceston Castle* carried out most of the Squid attacks. *Kenilworth Castle* made one attack.

Subsequently the Group was credited with the destruction of *U-1200*.

HMS Kenilworth Castle *stands by the yacht* ***Vanity V.***   *(Illustrated London News 25th January 1947, p124)*

KENILWORTH CASTLE STANDS BY THE YACHT VANITY V

The accompanying photograph is that of a painting by the marine Artist Major Tom Linsey. It depicts the 12-metre yacht *Vanity V* running before a strong gale 15 miles south of Portland, whilst **Kenilworth Castle** stands by to render assistanc. *Vanity V* was the last 12-metre to be built before the war by W. Fife for Mr. J.R. Payne. He had sold the yacht to Sir Hartley Shawcross. It was while she was being delivered for her new owner to Falmouth that *Vanity V* ran into the gale, the artist being a member of the crew at the time.

Vanity V was sighted by **Kenilworth Castle** at a range of 12 miles when the yacht was hard-driven by the gale and decided to stand by her. It was then blowing Force 9, and after an exchange of signals under very difficult conditions, *Vanity V* declined the offer of a tow, but accepted the escort of **Kenilworth Castle** into harbour. (*Source: Illustrated London News January 25th 1947, p124*)

HMS KNARESBOROUGH CASTLE

Battle Honours
Atlantic 1944-45

HMS Knaresborough Castle in May 1944.   *(MoD/Crown Copyright)*

After completing working up at Tobermory *Knaresborough Castle* was allocated to the B3 Escort Group (*HMS Towy* SO) engaged in escorting convoys between the UK and Gibraltar.

Following the reorganisation of Escort Groups in August/September 1944, *Knaresborough Castle* became the Senior Officer of the B23 Escort Group, similarly engaged on the UK - Gibraltar run. The composition of the Group varied from time to time, but usually include two Castle class corvettes.

Following a refit at Ardrossan from November - December 1944 she returned to Tobermory for working up and was allocated to the Liverpool Escort Pool (LEP) where she resumed escorting convoys to and from Gibraltar. She escorted 16 convoys comprising 490 merchant ships, none of which were lost due to enemy action.

On the conclusion of the war in Europe *Knaresborough Castle* was allocated to Air Sea Rescue (ASR) duties based at Gibraltar from June to October 1945 and then to Freetown until January 1946 from where she returned to the UK and reduced to reserve.

Following a refit from September - October 1952 she was brought out of reserve for employment as an air training target ship under the Plymouth Command. She was replaced in reserve in July 1954 at Devonport.

Knaresborough Castle claimed to have the longest cap tally in the Fleet.

HISTORY

19.01.43   Ordered.
22.04.43   Laid down. **Builder**: Hull - Blyth Dry Dock; Engine - Whites Marine Engineering (Hebburn).
28.09.43   Launched.
05.04.44   Completed.

WARTIME VOYAGES

Date	ESG	Senior Officer	Convoy	No of Ships	Arrive/ Sail	Location	Notes
10.04.44	EG B3	*Towy*			Arv	Greenock	
14.04.44	EG B3	*Towy*			Arv	Tobermory	
05.05.44	EG B3	*Towy*			Sail	Tobermory	
08.05.44	EG B3	*Towy*			Arv	Clyde	Boiler clean.
14.05.44	EG B3	*Towy*	OS 77/ KMS51	31	Sail	Londonderry	
21.05.44	EG B3	*Towy*	OS 77/ KMS51	33		3808N 1857W	
25.05.44	EG B3	*Towy*	OS 77/ KMS51		Arv	Gibraltar	
30.05.44	EG B3	*Towy*	SL 159/ MKS 50	33	Sail	Gibraltar	
31.05.44	EG B3	*Towy*	SL 159/ MKS 50	33		3550N0630W	
01.06.44	EG B3	*Towy*	SL 159/ MKS 50	33		3530N 1025W	
11.06.44	EG B3	*Towy*			Arv	Clyde	
12.06.44	EG B3	*Towy*			Arv	Londonderry	
23.06.44	EG B3	*Towy*	OS 81/ KMS 55	33	Sail	Londonderry	Detached to escort oiler *Scottish American* to the convoy; rejoined 27.06.44
26.06.44	EG B3	*Towy*	OS 81/ MKS 55	33		Not Given	
04.07.44	EG B3	*Towy*	OS 81/ MKS 55	33	Arv	Gibraltar	
10.07.44	EG B3	*Towy*	SL 163/ MKS 54	42	Sail	Gibraltar	
11.07.44	EG B3	*Towy*	SL 163/ MKS 54	42		3535N 0730W	
21.07.44	EG B3	*Towy*	SL 163/ MKS 54	42	Arv	Clyde	
02.08.44	EG B3	*Tintagel Castle*	OS 85/ KMS59	34	Sail	Londonderry	
03.08.44	EG B3	*Tintagel Castle*	OS 85/ KMS59	34		5528N 1107W	
13.08.44	EG B3	*Tintagel Castle*	OS 85/ KMS59	34	Arv	Gibraltar	
19.08.44	EG B3	*Tintagel Castle*	SL167/ MKS58	36	Sail	Gibraltar	
19.08.44	EG B3	*Tintagel Castle*	SL 167/ MKS58	36		3540N0643W	Hague gives 29 ships

Date	ESG	Senior Officer	Convoy	No of Ships	Arrive/ Sail	Location	Notes
27.08.44	EG B3	*Tintagel Castle*	SL 167/ MKS58	33		5009N0652W	Hague gives 29 ships
30.08.44	EG B3	*Tintagel Castle*	SL 167/ MKS58	33	Arv	Clyde	
10.09.44	B23	*Knaresborough Castle*			Arv	Belfast	
11.09.44	B23	*Knaresborough Castle*			Arv	Clyde	
12.09.44	B23	*Knaresborough Castle*	OS 89/ KMS63	33	Sail	Clyde	
15.09.44	B23	*Knaresborough Castle*	OS 89/ KMS63	33	Sail	Belfast	
19.09.44	B23	*Knaresborough Castle*	OS 89/ KMS63	34		4506N 1144W	
23.09.44	B23	*Knaresborough Castle*	OS 89/ KMS63	33	Arv	Gibraltar	
29.09.44	B23	*Knaresborough Castle*	SL 171/ MKS62	17	Sail	Gibraltar	
30.09.44	B23	*Knaresborough Castle*	SL 171/ MKS62	17		3601N0901W	
07.10.44	B23	*Knaresborough Castle*	SL 171/ MKS62	17		5013N 0521W	
09.10.44	B23	*Knaresborough Castle*	SL 171/ MKS62	17	Arv	Clyde	
13.10.44	B23	*Fowey*	OS 92/ KMS66	34	Sail	Clyde	
18.10.44	B23	*Fowey*	OS 92/ KMS66	34		5025N 10007W	
30.10.44	B23	*Fowey*	SL174/ MKS65	44	Sail	Gibraltar	
18.12.44	LEP					Ardrossan	Repairs completed 21 Dec
05.02.45	LEP						
18.02.45	LEP				Arv	Tobermory	
28.02.45	Sail					Tobermory	
01.03.45	LEP				Arv	Clyde	
04.03.45	LEP				Sail	Barry	
09.03.45	LEP				Arv	Liverpool	
18.03.45	LEP	*Knaresborough Castle*	OS 117/ KMS91	25	Sail	Liverpool	
27.03.45	LEP	*Knaresborough Castle*	OS 117/ KMS 91	25	Arv	Gibraltar	Ex OS 117/KMS 91 *HMS Woodruff* took over the convoy on 26.03.45

HMS Knaresborough Castle

Date	ESG	Senior Officer	Convoy	No of Ships	Arrive/ Sail	Location	Notes
31.03.45	LEP	*Knaresborough Castle*	MKS 92	41	Sail	Gibraltar	
08.04.45	LEP	*Fowey*	MKS 92	41	Arv	Liverpool	*Fowey* assumed command of the escorts on 05.03.45
11.04.45	LEP				Sail	Liverpool	
14.04.45	LEP				Arv	Liverpool	
24.04.45	LEP				Arv	Campbeltown	Having left Liverpool the same day. (SMO)
26.04.45	LEP	*Knaresborough Castle*	OS 125/ KMS 99	23	Sail	Campbeltown	Convoy dispersed 01.05.45
30.04.45		*Sweetbriar*	MKS 97	28		4722N1023W	Joined in support
04.05.45	LEP				Arv	Liverpool	
05.05.45		*Sweetbriar*	MKS 97	28		Skerries	Detached with Mersey Section 270°/7 miles
07.05.45	LEP	*Knaresborough Castle*	OS 127/ KMS 101	15	Sail	Liverpool	Departure date suggests that the convoy may have been OS 127/KMS 101
15.05.45	LEP	*Knaresborough Castle*	OS 127/ KMS 101	15	Arv	Gibraltar	Convoy escorted was probably OS 127/KMS 101
20.05.45	LEP	*Knaresborough Castle*		21	Sail	Gibraltar	The date of departure suggests that she escorted MKS102G to Liverpool
27.05.45	LEP	*Knaresborough Castle*		21	Arv	Liverpool	Possibly having escorted MKS from Gibraltar
02.06.45					Sail	Liverpool	
23.06.45	FOGMA				Sail	Liverpool	
28.06.45	FOGMA				Arv	Gibraltar	
30.06.45	FOGMA				Sail	Gibraltar	
19.07.45	FOGMA				Arv	Gibraltar	
31.07.45	FOGMA				Sail	Gibraltar	
04.08.45	FOGMA				Arv	Gibraltar	
05.08.45	FOGMA				Sail	Gibraltar	
22.08.45	FOGMA				Arv	Gibraltar	To relieve *Caistor Castle* on ASR Station *Caistor Castle* 04009Z/9 Have been relieved by *KC* on ASR 19.
02.09.45	FOGMA				Sail	Gibraltar	
16.09.45	FOGMA				Arv	Gibraltar	FOGMA 101619/9 *KC* is being relieved by *St Brides* in ASR 19.

Date	ESG	Senior Officer	Convoy	No of Ships	Arrive/ Sail	Location	Notes
01.10.45	FOGMA				Sail	Gibraltar	
14.10.45	FOGMA				Arv	Gibraltar	
30.10.45	FOGMA				Sail	Gibraltar	To ASR 21.
10.11.45	FOCWAF				Arv	Freetown	
12.11.45	FOCWAF				Sail	Freetown	*KC* will be relieved on ASR 22 by *Caistor Castle* on 27.11.
02.12.45	FOCWAF				Arv	Freetown	
08.12.45	FOCWAF				Sail	Freetown	NO I/c Freetown 071207/12 intend to sail *KC* 0700/8/12 to ASR 21 to relieve *Lancaster Castle* 10.12 to 21.12.
17.12.45	FOCWAF				Arv	Freetown	
11.01.46	FOGMA				Arv	Gibraltar	FOTA 271208a.12 *KC* to be sailed Gibraltar immediately on arrival of *Pevensey Castle*.
27.01.46					Arv	Harwich	AM 211354.1 *KC* is to reduce to Reserve on arrival in UK at Harwich. *KC* 2520035Z.1 ETA Harwich 27/1. Record ends.

1946-48	Reserve at Harwich.
27.08.49	Completed refit at Grimsby and returned to Harwich for reserve.
1953	Represented Home Command, Plymouth, at the Coronation Fleet Review.
09/52-54	2nd Training Squadron at Portland.
15.02/54	Completed refit at Devonport.
1955-56	Reserve.
1956	Sold to Smith & Houston.
16.03.56	Arrived Port Glasgow for scrapping.

On October 1944 **Knaresborough Castle** and **Allington Castle** were heavily involved in standing by and rescuing the crews of several LCTs that were being towed by merchant ships in convoy KMS66/OS92.

On the third day out from the UK the weather rapidly deteriorated and on the following day several of the LCTs became in serious trouble. Both Castles were fully occupied in the rescue operation over a four day period. The report of the incident by the Commanding Officer of **Knaresborough Castle** Lt Cdr J.F. Marchant RNR follows.

The complete report from the Senior Officer B23 Escort Group for that voyage, **HMS Fowey** is given under the heading B23 Escort Group, which also provides details of the other voyages of **Knaresborough Castle** with the B23 EG.

B23 ESCORT GROUP - CONVOY OS92/KMS 66
14th - 26th OCTOBER 1944
KNARESBOROUGH CASTLE

25.10.44

REPORT ON THE LOSS OF HM LCT 488

I have the honour to report on the loss of **HM LCT 488**. Extracts from Signal Log and Deck Log of **HMS Knaresborough Castle** and a copy of the report of S/Lt K.W. Steele RNVR (Surviving Officer) are attached.

After my conversation with S/Lt K.W. Steele, RNVR, I consider that **LCT 488** should have returned to Milford Haven on October 16th 1944, as at this early stage she was not in a fit state for sea passage.

After **HM LCT 488** had slipped tow and altered course to run before the sea she appeared to be quite comfortable and it was my considered opinion that to try and make port was less hazardous than to take off the crew. Later in the day the LCT was getting less seaworthy and an attempt was made to take off the crew at 1730. This was successful and recovered all the crew that remained on Carley Floats and in the water.

Unfortunately, several members of the crew who had taken to the rafts clambered back on board the LCT whilst rafts were still alongside. In my opinion if all the crew had left LCT at this stage they would have been safely picked up. LCT was now left without any life saving gear and owing to the darkness, further attempts to render assistance to the remainder of crew were unsuccessful.

The crew remaining on board were able to get LCT under way again and appeared to be getting along well.

I informed them of the importance of keeping going until daylight, unfortunately at 0500 on 19 October it became necessary to abandon ship. Immediately afterwards LCT capsized and sank.

In the absence of any life-saving apparatus, crew became scattered in water and all efforts to lay alongside were fruitless.

At this stage Lt. W.A.E. Sheppard RCNVR came to me and volunteered to take away seaboat, although the seaboat was lost, and their rescue attempt a failure, I consider Lt. W.A.E. Sheppard's action highly commendable.

After recovering the seaboat's crew I continued the search for LCT survivors, picking up one officer. The search was carried out until 1324 and then left to rejoin convoy.

One seaboat, 4 Carley Floats and 2 Floatnets were lost by us in rescue attempts.

(sgd) J.F. Marchant
Lieutenant Commander, RNR
Commanding Officer.

REPORT ON THE LOSS OF HM LCT 488
K.W. STEELE SUB LIEUTENANT RNVR
SURVIVING OFFICER

The first defects were reported on Monday morning 16th of October, 1944 to the **SS Samfoyle** who passed the signal on to SO B23. An armed trawler came alongside and asked if we were OK. Commanding Officer replied, "Yes, as long as weather does not get any worse".

These defects were:-

(1)   Barrels in space between door and water tight doors adrift.
(2)   Welding had gone in several places in the combing.
(3)   Welding gone in after end of gun deck that overlaps quarterdeck, the ammunition in locker was removed from this part to ease the strain on the after gun deck.
(4)   Galley Funnel had been smashed owing to the springing of the gun deck.

During Monday and Tuesday we were suffering very heavy pounding and sea did not get any calmer. The Commanding Officer at this time was of the opinion that we should be turned to Milford Haven for shelter as the ship was getting so shaken due to the pounding.

At 0335 on Wednesday, 18th October, whilst in tow, we took a wave green that washed back to the Bridge. This wave tore away the after part of the hold cover and smashed the spreaders, the spreaders parted at the welding on the combing. F'ward of that they were very badly buckled.

The water getting through to the tank space broke the canvas adrift, the securing gear for the caravan had been examined by me during the Tuesday forenoon and by S/Lt Bell during the last dog watch. The only explanation for this was that the welding of the eyebolts must have been torn adrift. The pumps were started to get the water out, but more was being shipped and the pumps were only just holding their own. The caravan broke several more things adrift. Attempts were made to secure the caravan but owing to the amount of water in the tank space this was impossible.

During this time the weather did not get any better and we were shipping water.

We had been pumping out all this by F'ward pump and Suction pump but, the F'ward pump gave out after a very short while and at 1020 the suction pump stopped working, we could not account for this unless bedding and clothing from caravan had been drawn into suction and so blocking it.

The Commanding Officer then decided that we could not last very much longer and **Knaresborough Castle** was standing by to take us off, we slipped the tow.

After receiving signal from **Knaresborough Castle** to try to follow her, we tried to get ship round on course of about 060 degrees. After great difficulty managed to steer this course.

We found that we did not take nearly as much water running before the weather, which now had reached about Force 7. A pump was rigged from the fire main, also to the Mono Pump - this pump would not work.

We could not repair damage done to Hold Cover owing to the spreaders having gone. The pump was then rigged from the fire main but it broke down owing to a fractured pipe and more efforts were made with the hand pump but to no avail. Buckets were used in a human chain but this was hopeless. The line from the fresh water tank to the Galley had gone by this time - (Fractured). All the barrels forward had gone and all the tank cover given in.

At 1724 Commanding Officer, decided to abandon ship. **Knaresborough Castle** said she would take off crew. Carley Floats were got ready and crew ordered to jump. They did, but seven came inboard as they got panicky trying to get Carley Floats round to stern and aft of the screws, although engines were stopped, thus causing the Officers to remain onboard.

All that stayed on the Carley Floats were saved. **Knaresborough Castle** made two more attempts to pass lines

but each time they parted and it was decided that remaining people on board should try to keep LCT afloat till morning, we got under way again as far less water was shipped than when 'Hove To'. LCT was very sluggish even though she did not appear to be so from *Knaresborough Castle*, there must have been five feet of water in the tank apace.

We steered a suitable course and then received a signal that we must steer South, this was done but shipped more water than when steering ESE. After a time course was altered to ESE but by this time we were very full of water and we reduced speed so that we should go down to the backs of waves more than riding along in the surf which came over the combing and stopped (slopped?) into the tank space.

At 0431 the situation became impossible as we took water every time we came down on the back of a wave. Commanding Officer 'Hove To'. Red Very lights were fired as arranged by signal.

LCT was foundering and could not hold out any longer.

A line was passed over from *Knaresborough Castle* which broke and as LCT was listing heavily to starboard it was decided that we must leave her. We jumped and as I swam clear away from LCT she capsized and sank. I thought that there were two people on the deck but could not tell who they were, as even at this stage the crew were panicky and loath to make the jump. *Knaresborough Castle* did everything possible to save crew but weather was far too heavy. I was eventually picked up at 0805 after being in the water 3 hours.

(sgd.) K. W. STEELE
Sub. Lieutenant RNVR
Source PRO: ADM 217/48

HMS LANCASTER CASTLE

Battle Honours
Atlantic 1944

An undated image of **HMS Lancaster Castle**.   (MoD/Crown Copyright)

After completing her working up at Tobermory, *Lancaster Castle* joined the 31st Escort Group (Commander N.W. Duck RNR in *Berkeley Castle*) in October 1944. The group was employed in A/S patrols and convoy support work in the Western Approaches. She was loaned to the 7th Escort Group to form part of the close escort for convoys JW/RA 65 to and from Russia during March 1945. On conclusion of the war in Europe, she, together with her consorts, was allocated for Air Sea Rescue duties operating out of Gibraltar and Freetown.

HISTORY

19.12.42   Ordered.
10.09.43   Laid down. **Builder**: Hull and engine - Fleming & Ferguson (Paisley).
14.04.44   Launched.
15.09.44   Completed.

WARTIME VOYAGES

Date	ESG	Senior Officer	Convoy	No of Ships	Arrive/ Sail	Location	Notes
29.09.44	Unall				Arv	Tobermory	
02.10.44	31 EG	*Berkeley Castle*				At Tobermory	
06.10.44	31 EG	*Berkeley Castle*				At Tobermory	
10.10.44	31 EG	*Berkeley Castle*				At Tobermory	
11.10.44	31 EG	*Berkeley Castle*				Clyde	*LC* working up
15.10.44	31 EG	*Berkeley Castle*				At Tobermory	
16.10.44	31 EG	*Berkeley Castle*				Tobermory	To 18th
17.10.44					Sail	Tobermory	
18.10.44					Arv	Clyde	FOIC Glasgow 1953Z/10 *LC* can be docked Govan by Barclay Curle, Govan Approx Oct 27
20.10.44	31 EG	*Berkeley Castle*				At Clyde	
27.10.44	31 EG	*Berkeley Castle*				At Clyde	Repairs. CinC WA 30227/10 When ready on 1/11 FOIC Greenock is requested to sail *LC* to Plymouth to join 31 EG operating under CinC Plymouth.
30.10.44	31 EG	*Berkeley Castle*				At Clyde	The two reports on this Group for this date are from different Admiralty sources
30.10.44	31 EG	*Berkeley Castle*				4910N 0538W	On A/S sweep
01.11.44	31 EG	*Berkeley Castle*			Sail	Clyde	
16.11.44	31 EG	*Berkeley Castle*			Arv	Clyde	
29.11.44	31 EG	*Berkeley Castle*			Sail	Londonderry	
02.12.44	31 EG	*Berkeley Castle*			Sail	Scapa Flow	
05.12.44	7 EG					6020N04459W	On patrol
13.12.44	31 EG	*Berkeley Castle*			Arv	Clyde	
23.12.44	31 EG	*Berkeley Castle*			Sail	Lamlash	
03.01.45	31 EG	*Berkeley Castle*			Sail	Londonderry	
08.01.45	31 EG	*Berkeley Castle*				WA	On patrol
18.01.45	31 EG	*Berkeley Castle*			Arv	Clyde	
22.01.45	31 EG	*Berkeley Castle*				Clyde	Repairs complete 27 Jan
29.01.45	31 EG	*Berkeley Castle*				At Lochalsh	
02.02.45	31 EG	*Berkeley Castle*			Sail	Belfast	
10.02.45	31 EG	*Berkeley Castle*			Arv	Clyde	
10.02.45	31 EG	*Berkeley Castle*			Arv	Belfast	
12.02.45	31 EG	*Berkeley Castle*			Sail	Clyde	
27.02.45	31 EG	*Berkeley Castle*			Arv	Clyde	

Date	ESG	Senior Officer	Convoy	No of Ships	Arrive/ Sail	Location	Notes
11.03.45	7 EG	*Cygnet*	JW 65	26	Sail	Clyde	
20.03.45	7 EG	*Cygnet*	JW 65	26	Arv	Kola Inlet	
23.03.45	7 EG	*Cygnet*	RA 65	26	Sail	Kola Inlet	
01.04.45	31 EG	*Berkeley Castle*			Arv	Clyde	
14.04.45	31 EG	*Berkeley Castle*			Sail	Clyde	
19.04.45	31 EG	*Berkeley Castle*			Sail	Belfast	
30.04.45	31 EG	*Berkeley Castle*			Arv	Milford Haven	
02.05.45	31 EG	*Berkeley Castle*			Sail	Milford Haven	
13.05.45	31 EG	*Berkeley Castle*			Sail	Lochalsh	
29.05.45	31 EG	*Berkeley Castle*			Sail	Clyde	
29.05.45	FOGMA				Sail	Clyde	
05.07.45					Arv	Londonderry	
05.07.45					Sail	Londonderry	
06.09.45					Arv	Gibraltar	
22.09.45					Sail	Gibraltar	
05.10.45					Arv	Gibraltar	FOGMA 020949B/29 intend to sail *Hadleigh Castle* 2000B/29 to relieve *LC* who then returns to Gibraltar.
20.10.45					Sail	Gibraltar	
03.11.45					Arv	Gibraltar	

HMS Lancaster Castle escorting surrendered U-Boats.   *(CCC(F)A Archives)*

Date	ESG	Senior Officer	Convoy	No of Ships	Arrive/ Sail	Location	Notes
12.11.45					Sail	Gibraltar	
18.11.45					Arv	Freetown	
21.11.45					Sail	Freetown	NO I/c Freetown. Intend sail *LC* to ASR Station 21 21/11 to relieve *Fal* Patrols 23.11-8.12.
12.12.45					Arv	Freetown	
21.01.46					Arv	Freetown	
15.02.46					Sail	Gibraltar	AM 2916/11 *LC* to reduce to Cat B on arrival UK. FOGMA 141209A/2(*LC*) sail 15/2 to Portsmouth ETA 19/2. Record ends.

1946-60	Reserve at Portsmouth, Harwich and West Hartlepool.
1949	Completed refit at Cardiff.
1957	Offered to Norway but deal not completed.
1960	Sold to J.J. King.
06.09.60	Arrived Gateshead for scrapping.

HMS Lancaster Castle ship's company in Freetown, 1944.   *(CCC(F)A Archives)*

Henry Swain was a Quartermaster for most of the time that he served on ***Lancaster Castle***. His experiences on the ship were recorded in his book *Return to Murmansk*. Recalling the working up period at Tobermory he wrote:-

> *"The First Lieutenant had one good quality that appealed to very young men who made up most of the crew. He had a reputation for recklessness.*
>
> *I had been an unwitting agent for creating this reputation. The event had occurred when the ship had been based in Tobermory harbour in September 1944 for working up training after commissioning. The Flag Officer, Commodore Stephenson, through whose hands all new Western Approaches ships passed ran a fairly tough outfit. Day-long anti-submarine exercises off the west coast of Mull were followed by simulated emergencies in harbour - the ship is on fire, the anchor is dragging, the Skipper is dead. The Commodore's training staff speeded up the solution to these problems by tossing thunder flashes. It was a hard two weeks but the Commodore was much hard-*

er on the Skipper and the officers than the crew. The crew began to resent this and tried quite hard to help them. In a new ship where people hardly knew each other, there was gradually born a sense of solidarity and a loyalty to the officers. I didn't appreciate it then but this was precisely what the Commodore intended.

"It was rumoured that when a corvette was at moorings at night with officers and men enjoying a brief and exhausted sleep the Commodore with his gang of gunners mates wearing gaiters would creep out in a whaler with muffled oars and unshackle the ship's mooring chain. Next day her skipper would be put on a charge for failing to guard his ship. On our first night in Tobermory I came on duty for the first watch - 2000 to midnight.

"As sentry, I was wearing a regulation watch coat and webbing equipment. The Smith & Wesson revolver on its white lanyard was more of a badge of office than a weapon. I had just taken over when the First Lieutenant appeared on the main deck in the fading light.

"Here you are, Quartermaster," he said. "Take these."

"He handed me five .38 cartridges. I must have looked rather surprised. I said politely,

"Thank you, sir," and put them gingerly into my pocket.

"Not there," he said, "in the bloody gun".

"I was puzzled but took the revolver out of its holster and slowly loaded it.

"Now," he said, "if any boat approaches the ship I want you to fire at it."

"I couldn't see how there could be any Germans in Tobermory so I said, "Supposing it's the train

HMS Lancaster Castle Chiefs and POs.

(CCC(F)A Archives)

ing people from ashore, sir?"

"That's precisely who it will be," he said, "and they'll be trying to unshackle the cable. It's your job to stop them."

"Shouldn't I give them a hail first, sir? I might shoot the Commodore."

The First Lieutenant looked exasperated. I didn't know what orders the Skipper had given him but it must have been on the lines of, " ... and by the way, No. 1, make sure those dozy quartermasters are on their toes."

He said patiently, "I want you to kill him. As far as you are concerned he's the enemy and by the way take off the safety catch, you'll have to shoot fast."

He could see I was getting the message. He grinned and said "Pass those orders on to your relief at midnight."

He left me staring uneasily into the growing darkness. The revolver was back in its holster but my hand was on the butt. Nothing happened in the night.

THREE MEN IN A BOAT

A true story by Anthony Baynon, ex-Able Seaman, HMS Lancaster Castle

*It happened in 1944 at Tobermory. Having passed her sea trials **Lancaster Castle** had just arrived at the Isle of Mull for the obligatory working up fortnight.*

We lay at anchor in Tobermory Bay. One of those rare moments of relief from the endless round of evolutions at sea; tracking the 'clockwork mouse', firing our guns, putting out imaginary fires, being taken in tow, launching the whaler etc.

Together with a shipmate, AB Alan Culham, I was busy on the fo'c'sle greasing and cleaning the four-inch gun. Suddenly Alan had a brilliant idea.

"Time for a smoke", he said, "Nobody's looking."

We slunk round in front of the gun-shield, crouched down and lit up.

A moment later, the Buffer appeared in our midst.

"Aha!" he cried, "Baynon and Culham, I see, Smokin' during workin' hours. Loafin', as usual, and," he looked down and his tone hardened, "droppin' ash on my fo'c'sle."

Our mumbled apologies at the enormity of our transgression were brushed aside. "To me on the quarterdeck at 1400 sharp." He ordered, "I've got the very job for the pair of you, you'll see."

He strode off, calling over his shoulder, "In your oldest-working clothes, mind." Punctually and appropriately clad, we reported. "Down there, pronto!" The Buffer pointed over the side. Alan and I peered over the guard-rail. Tied up alongside and bobbing on a choppy sea was a tiny dinghy. In the stern-sheets, a wizened, aged Petty Officer sat hunched, puffing at a pipe. The rest of the dinghy appeared occupied by a huge pile of something, covered with a tarpaulin.

We clambered down and just managed to squeeze ourselves in around the mysterious heap.

The P.O. was a man of few words, and those extremely gruff. A series of grunts indicated that we were to row him out to the middle of Tobermory Bay. Alan and I rowed in silence, the P.O. ignoring us as he drew noisily on his pipe. I noticed, without at that moment realising its significance, the Torpedo Gunner's Mate badge on the sleeve of his grimy jacket.

At last we stopped. With a sudden movement, the P.O. lent forward and jerked aside the tarpaulin to reveal a huge pile of parcels, each one wrapped in brown grease-proof paper.

"TNT!" he proudly announced. "Demolition charges!" He jabbed at them with the stem of his pipe. I wondered what there was to demolish in the middle of Tobermory Bay.

"Making a film," he explained briefly. He pronounced the word in two syllables - fill-um.

"There's film folk on the hill over there, watching us through telescopes." He stabbed his pipe in the general direction of a distant headland, *"Seem they needs a gigantic whirlpool thing, fit to swallow up a boat. Sort of special effect, like. They wants the Navy to do the trick so we're going to show em a thing or two!"*

He paused to knock out the glowing embers of his pipe on the gunwale, then reloaded with a generous charge of evil black tobacco. He fished out a large brass lighter and spun the flint-wheel to produce blow-lamp-sized flame. A paroxysm of furious sucking and puffing followed, and the tobacco became an incandescent mass. I dodged a shower of sparks and blazing fragments, borne on the stiff westerly breeze.

"Now," went on the PO, selecting one of the parcels, *"When I shouts 'give way together' you pulls on them oars like buggery, understand?"* We nodded enthusiastically.

Feeling, perhaps, that some reassurance was in order, the PO added *"Course, today's only a practice.* He dunked the fuse in the bowl of his pipe, tossed the fizzing package over his shoulder and shouted. Alan and I pulled exactly as requested. A loud bang, a storm of water and drenching spray rose twenty feet in the air, the dinghy lurched.

The PO sounded disappointed. *"Not nearly enough."* He picked up two parcels, dunked both fuses and tossed. We pulled. Louder bang, a tempest of water, the dinghy was briefly airborne.

"Now to ginger it up a bit." Observed the PO, seizing three parcels.

A little dinghy was rather too frail to share with a deranged torpedoman, I reflected, but at least it was too small to carry depth-charges.

By now a demon possessed our PO. Three charges, then four, five, more, in rapid succession, tossed to right, to left, astern. Again and again. The sea boiled up, erupted around us. The dinghy performed evolutions previously undreamed of, even in Tobermory. Alan and I pulled and pulled. Had there been a Blue Riband of Tobermory Bay, we would have won it - no contest!

An hour later, there were no parcels left. Alan and I slumped over our oars soaking wet and gasping for breath. Then, with aching arms, we baled out the water-logged dinghy.

Slowly we rowed back to **Lancaster Castle**. The PO didn't speak again. He sucked at his pipe and gazed into the distance, no doubt inwardly brooding on the inadequacies of Admiralty explosives .

Alan and I tied up alongside. Painfully we clambered on board, abandoning the dinghy and its silent occupant. Presumably a motor-boat would appear and tow them both back to wherever they came from.

The Buffer was busy on deck, repairing a mooring rope. He looked around and acknowledged our return with a slight nod. I swear that his lips moved briefly in the faintest outline of a triumphant smile. He turned back to his work. Not a word was said on either side. Alan and I went below.

Being a quartermaster at the helm can be a routine job; reactions can be almost automatic. Sometimes things go wrong. Henry Swain wrote:

*"It began as a perfectly ordinary day. The forenoon watch was nearly over and I was steering 040 degrees through the St. George's Channel. **Lancaster Castle** was the fourth corvette steaming in line ahead. The sea was calm under a cloudless blue sky and although it was 15 November it was warm enough to have the starboard side door of the wheelhouse open. Glancing through it I could see the distant green coast of Pembroke. I had been quartermaster since the ship commissioned in September 1944 and lining up the lubber line with the compass course on the gyro repeater was now an automatic skill. At 1200 hours the order came down the voice pipe from the bridge,*

"Starboard twenty." "Starboard twenty," I repeated and smartly turned the wheel to port. Filling the view through the wheelhouse door there was suddenly the sight of three ships heading in line towards the distant coast. We were steaming away from them at an angle of 90 degrees. Time stood still. Then came a shocked realisation that I had got it wrong. I was twenty one and the bottom fell out or my world. Clipped orders came down the voice pipe, "Midships, starboard twenty, revolutions 180." For a moment, nothing. and then the officer of the watch said. "The Captain is very angry. Report to the bridge at the end of the watch". His voice sounded frighteningly normal. When the afternoon quartermaster relieved me I put on my cap and reluctantly climbed the ladder to the compass platform. I stood woodenly in front of the Captain. There was a long silence as he looked at me. The visor of his cap shadowed his face from the sunshine. Any second the sky was going to fall: I had a vision of the skipper meeting his opposite numbers in their favourite hotel in Glasgow. I had made him look a proper idiot. After a bit he seemed to make up his mind, "You're no longer quartermaster". he said. Then he turned to the officer of the watch, "Arrange for his relief." His voice was quite mild. I think he had decided that if any punishment was needed I was quite capable of handing it out myself. In the seamen's mess deck I was greeted with hilarious remarks and grins. I hated it, but there was no malice - we all made mistakes. For the next few weeks I stood my watches as lookout and gun's crew. These jobs were easier than steering but all the time I was saying to myself, "You're a failure, you can't even steer a bloody ship". In the new year I found myself back on the wheel; nobody explained why. Probably my various reliefs had made similar or worse balls-ups. In the event I steered the ship for what seemed like forever. At the time I made no excuses for my spectacular mistake but quite recently it has occurred to me that there was a mitigating factor - you couldn't see ahead from the steering position. In the Castle Class ships the anti-submarine Squid mortar was mounted in front of the wheel-house. My former ship had been a new fleet destroyer and there had been perfect forward vision for the man at the wheel. It is inconceivable that a quartermaster, seeing three ships ahead altering course to starboard in succession, would have put the wheel the wrong way. The thought comforts me a little but, even today, I can sometimes relive the awful moment when our ship went in the wrong direction and I saw three corvettes steaming away from us in line ahead across a blue and sunlit sea.

When **Lancaster Castle** was loaned to the 7th Escort Group, Henry Swain had been reinstated as Quartermaster.

Although the extremes of weather experienced during the passage of RA 64 were not repeated with the JW/RA 65 convoys, winds of Force 10 and the accompanying heavy turbulent seas were encountered. Steering through seas such as these presented several difficulties as explained by Henry Swain.

"I steered through the midnight to 0400 middle watch on 26th March. I was glad it was dark and I couldn't see the waves. Since the strength of the wind and the size of the seas very much affected my standard of living, I had taken every opportunity to read about them when I had the chance to look at the books in the chart room. I guessed the wind was now blowing Force 10 on the Beaufort Scale, 44 to 55 knots velocity-storm. The definition for Force 10 was 'very high waves with long overhanging crests. The rolling foam in great patches is thrown in dense white streaks along the direction of the wind. On the whole the waves take on a white appearance. The tumbling of the sea becomes heavy and shock like. Height of waves 24-40ft'. This described what I had seen. It took me a while to get the hang of steering in these wild conditions. You couldn't steer the course directly because the ship's head was swinging through 30°. The course was supposed to be 223° degrees True. The best I could do was to make 223 the mean course but the last digit made the mental arithmetic hard. The red numbers on the gyro compass repeater simply flashed in a blur as the waves hit us. I tried desperately to contain the swing between 208 and 238. The Officer of the

Watch had evidently been staring at his compass on the bridge unbelievingly. I heard him say down the voice pipe, "Can't you do better than this, quartmaster?" The correct answer to this question, which was not really a question, should have been, "Aye, aye, sir," but I didn't give it. I was doing my best and I was pretty sure that nobody could steer a better course. I shouted angrily back up the voice pipe "No, I bloody well can't, sir." There was silence above. I was not sure who the OOW was. It was hard to recognise voices in the racket of the wind and sea. I knew it was not the First Lieutenant, however, because if it had been, I should have had an immediate response. It would have been on the lines of, "Yes, you bloody well can, Henry, and if you can't do it, I'll show you how to drive this sodding ship myself". As the seconds ticked past, I imagined being put on a charge for insubordination. I didn't care. As far as I could see, nobody could devise a worse punishment than that which I was already being subjected to - steering a wildly pitching and rolling corvette in the arctic night in a Force 10. When the OOW spoke again, he was quite nice. He said, "Okay, quartermaster, do your best. Try and keep the mean course as best you can".
"Aye, Aye, Sir" I said, slightly relieved.
I was working myself to the limits of my strength at the wheel and the OOW was trying to keep the ship in her right position in zero visibility and trying to dodge some of the spray as well. We were both, I reflected, in the same shit".

Storm conditions caused considerable discomfort on the mess decks. Henry Swain again.

"The seamen's messdeck had by this time become squalid even by our standards. We were endlessly wiping up things and putting things away, establishing some semblance of order. The ship would hit a specially big wave - we called them millstones - and everything again would be dislodged and spilt and men not holding on would go flying. Seamen coming from the bridge and the upper deck dripped pools of water and snow. The mess smelt of sweat, oilskins and toast. The glare of the bare electric light bulbs shone on the dirty brown cortiscene covered deck and the white tired faces. Eating was the worst thing. First you had to clear the mess table of discarded oilskins and arctic clothing, then you rolled down the oil-cloth on the deal table. George Seeley's hammock knocked against my back as I tried to cut bread and all the cups slid together like skaters from side to side of the table. At one point, one of the tables, regarded as a fixed item in our world, itself became unseated from its base, tipping tea onto the men sitting on the inboard benches. The problem of actually eating diminished into insignificance when compared with the chaos of dirty dishes, greasy washing up water and refuse which eating entailed. Every object not actually bolted down or held in your hand was potentially a dangerous missile". The crowded conditions on the messdeck are illustrated by pencil sketch on page 18.

By contrast life when on Air/Sea Rescue Duty following on from the end the war in Europe was much easier. Tony Baynon wrote:-

"Any sailor who claimed to have crossed the Equator a few hundred times in rather less than a year might well be accused of seeking a fraudulent mention in the Guinness Book of Records. From another matelot he would expect a cynical "Oh Yeah?, well just swing the lamp some Jack!".
And yet there may well have been a few hundred sailors who could in all modesty and truth , say "But that's exactly what we did, all in the line of duty".
Shortly after VE Day we were despatched to Freetown as part of a little flotilla of Castle class involved in a novel air-sea rescue mission.
Faced with the challenge of repatriating and demobilising a large part of its huge armies in Europe and in the Middle East, the US Government responded with typical American inventiveness.

Time expired GIs were packed into Flying Fortresses and transport planes in a vast airlift following one of several pre-ordained routes westwards across the Atlantic. The southern-most of these headed south to West Africa, then turned west to follow exactly the line of the Equator.

At intervals along this route, corvettes were to be stationed, transmitting a radio beacon to guide the pilots and to be on hand should an aircraft and its human cargo be unlucky enough to ditch in the ocean.

For us, it was a leisurely, stress free existence. Each morning on station, we positioned ourselves a few miles south of the Equator, stopped engines and, wafted by a tropical breeze, drifted northwards over the line until evening. Engines we re-started, the ship turned around and we dawdled sedately back to our starting point, ready to repeat the process the next day and each succeeding day.

Our first ever crossing the Line was observed with traditional rituals. Wiggy Bennet, the genial Chief Stoker, with wooden trident and profuse cotton-wool beard, became a suitable portly and rumbustious Neptune, inflicting us "first timers" into the unprintable mysteries of his realm. Thereafter, twice daily passage between the north and south hemispheres passed unmarked and unremarked - all in a days (and nights) work.

There was the peace time luxury of four watches. Off-watch we tittivated the ship and painted her in the latest Admiralty pastel shade (Boudoirs blue? - Hawaiian haze ? - I forget what) with the most expert brush-stokes being applied to the starboard side, this being the profile, when in harbour, presented to the Senior Naval Officer there.

*Back in Freetown for a few days boiler cleaning after each month on station, the **Lancaster Castle** moored well out in the river, beyond mosquito range; malaria was still a potent hazard. Ashore, we wore long-sleeved shirts with white duck trousers tucked into regulation brown suede ankle-boots. Each morning we dutifully swallowed an obligatory mecaprine tablet, washed down with a*

*A water colour image of **HMS Lancaster Castle** in dry dock at Gibraltar by H. Swain.*

copious draught of pure lime juice - more welcome in the African heat than any daily rum tot. The vivid yellow of the mecaprine soon transferred itself to our skins. Combined with a deepening sun-tan it quickly transformed the most unlikely amongst us into mahogany-hued precursors of Baywatch beach boys. Alas! Mecaprine proved more durable then the African sun; soon after our return to the UK the next year, our tans quickly faded and erstwhile 'beach-boys' were reduced to terminal jaundiced patients for an episode of 'Casualty' to the great consternation of family and friends.

Hammocks were slung on the upper deck where we slept, stripped to the buff, shielded by tropical awnings from the nightly storms that thundered and drenched overhead.

For a while, an inter ship shark fishing contest yielded a generous haul of these huge creatures hoisted on to the quarter deck to lash about and snap in fury until dispatched by a rifle bullet through the head. Finally the Captain ordered an end to what he rightly saw as a pointless and barbaric pastime. No argument therefore with the pipe "Hands are not, repeat not, to bathe over the side!". Instead a lorry from Kissy Naval Barracks would sometimes transport libertymen down the coast to Lumlet Beach - now, I understand, a sophisticated tourist resort, but in 1945 an iso-lated paradise of opal sea and palm-fringed glistening sand.

We sunbathed, read, dozed and wrangled over politics.

A hand-picked cast of officers and men rehearsed and broadcast over the ship's tannoy a radio pro-duction of Bernard Shaw's Pygmalion received by the whole ship's company to critical acclaim.

Our numbers were slightly increased, and our chores much diminished, by recruiting three cheer-ful young Sierra Leonies, each confusingly named Sam, who lived on board at sea and in harbour. They enlivened the dog-watches with African songs and dances, and the mornings by taking ener-getic charge of all our dhobying. Never have matelots' white tropical uniforms glistened so daz-zlingly nor been so crisply starched and ironed. We would have been instantly conscripted lock stock and barrel, onto the Royal Yacht, had she had the good fortune to call in at Freetown

We calculated wildly optimistic demob dates. We talked of home and fantasised about unmention-able things we'd do when we got there. And of course, being matelots, we grumbled incessantly - the food, endless dehydrated potatoes, tinned vegetables, bread invariably riddled with baked wee-vils. Besides, where were all those planes we'd come so far to guide and rescue. From time to time, a solitary aircraft would pass overhead, calling us up by radio with words of thanks for our lone-ly vigil. The word was - probably truthfully - that by the time the poor old Andrew had got its air/sea rescue act together the Yanks were nearly all back at home; what we were getting were the "last knockings".

Occasionally, a Flying Fortress would swoop in, mast head high, open its bomb doors and drop a large bundle of girlie magazines. Being rather less than aerodynamic, these of course splashed down in the ocean to sink before our lascivious eyes. But one plane, surely a pathfinder, scored a direct hit with its thanksgiving offering on our deck, its erotic contents further fuelling our fan-tasies".

Freetown and air/sea rescue - a slightly surreal experience, sharply at odds with the harshness of our previous time in the North Atlantic.

*Later, in 1946, **Lancaster Castle** steamed into Portsmouth, her paying-off pennnant streaming in a stiff breeze astern in a stiff, chilly breeze, and took her final moorings at the back of the harbour near the mud-flats.*

Demob loomed, leave, reunion with families, jobs to be found, training courses to be looked for, easy promises made "to keep in touch".

HMS LAUNCESTON CASTLE

Battle Honours
Atlantic 1944

HMS Launceston Castle *31 October 1944.*   *(Ben Warlow Collection)*

HMS Launceston Castle was completed in June 1944 and allocated to the B4 Escort Group which was re-formed as the 30th Escort Group with whom she remained until the end of the war in Europe. On 11 November 1944 she along with other ships of the 30th Escort Group sank *U-1200* in the North Atlantic south of Cape Clear.

On the conclusion of the war in Europe she escorted a group of U-Boasts from Bergen to Scapa Flow.

She was transferred to Air/Sea Rescue duties operating out of Freetown. She left Freetown for Plymouth in October 1945 and entered the reserve fleet.

After a refit *Launceston Castle* operated as an Air Target Training Ship from 1951 to 1956, attached to Captain (D) Plymouth but operating mainly out of Londonderry. After a year in the reserve fleet again she was sold for breaking up in 1959.

HISTORY

19.01.43   Ordered.
27.05.43   Laid down. **Builder**: Hull - Blyth Dry Dock Co; Engine - Whites Marine Engineering (Hebburn).
27.11.43   Launched.
20.06.44   Completed.

WARTIME VOYAGES

Date	ESG	Senior Officer	Convoy	No of Ships	Arrive/ Sail	Location	Notes
02.11.43	Unall				Arv	Tobermory	Trials completed today
26.06.44	EG B4	*Helmsdale*			Arv	Blyth	
29.06.44	EG B4	*Helmsdale*			Arv	Tobermory	
11.07.44	EG B4	*Helmsdale*			Sail	Tobermory	
19.07.44	EG B4	*Helmsdale*			Arv	Londonderry	
23.07.44	EG B4	*Helmsdale*			Sail	Londonderry	
26.07.44	EG B4	*Helmsdale*	OS 84/ KMS 58	27		4901N 1935W	Hague gives 24 ships
02.08.44	EG B4	*Helmsdale*	OS 84/ KMS 58		Arv	Gibraltar	
08.08.44	EG B4	*Helmsdale*	SL 166/ MKS 57	16	Sail	Gibraltar	
09.08.44	EG B4	*Helmsdale*	SL 166/ MKS 57	16		3541N 0652W	
19.08.44	EG B4	*Helmsdale*	SL 166/ MKS 57	31	Arv	Londonderry	
25.08.44	EG B4	*Helmsdale*				Londonderry	Boiler clean
29.08.44	30 EG	*Pevensey Castle*			Sail	Londonderry	
14.09.44	30 EG	*Pevensey Castle*	ONF 252	81	Sail	Londonderry	Operating under Force 33
23.09.44	30 EG	*Pevensey Castle*			Arv	Londonderry	
03.10.44	30 EG	*Pevensey Castle*			Arv	Larne	
05.10.44	30 EG	*Pevensey Castle*			Sail	Londonderry	
11.10.44	30 EG	*Pevensey Castle*				NW Apps	On patrol
15.10.44	30 EG	*Pevensey Castle*				At Sea	
18.10.44	30 EG	*Pevensey Castle*			Arv	Londonderry	
27.10.44	30 EG	*Pevensey Castle*				Londonderry	
30.10.44	30 EG	*Pevensey Castle*				Londonderry	
03.11.44	30 EG	*Pevensey Castle*				Londonderry	
06.11.44	30 EG	*Pevensey Castle*				Londonderry	
09.11.44	30 EG	*Pevensey Castle*			Sail	Londonderry	To patrol NW Approaches.
19.11.44	30 EG	*Pevensey Castle*			Arv	Londonderry	11th Nov: Group attack U-boat and hold contact for three days. *LC* was the first to gain asdic contact & held contact for 73 hrs. Then supported passage of HX 321 & relieved 2nd EG on 5th Dec. Group returned to Londonderry

Date	ESG	Senior Officer	Convoy	No of Ships	Arrive/ Sail	Location	Notes
21.11.44	30 EG	*Pevensey Castle*			Sail	Londonderry	Patrol in area 52N 11W. Group attacked suspected U-boat on 26th Nov
28.11.44	30 EG	*Pevensey Castle*				5110N 0945W	On patrol
06.12.44	30 EG	*Pevensey Castle*			Arv	Londonderry	
18.12.44	30 EG	*Pevensey Castle*			Sail	Belfast	
25.12.44	30 EG	*Pevensey Castle*				Portsmouth	
31.12.44	30 EG	*Caistor Castle*			Sail	Portsmouth	Patrol area north of Cherbourg
08.01.45	30 EG	*Pevensey Castle*				S of Needles	On patrol
13.01.45	30 EG	*Pevensey Castle*			Arv	Londonderry	
13.01.45					Arv	Londonderry	
16.01.45					Sail	Plymouth	
29.01.45	30 (A)	*Pevensey Castle*				Mounts Bay	On patrol
09.02.45	30 EG	*Pevensey Castle*				Plymouth	
12.02.45	30 EG	*Pevensey Castle*				At Sea	
19.02.45	30 EG	*Pevensey Castle*				Londonderry	Boiler cleaning ready 22.02.45
24.02.45	30 EG	*Pevensey Castle*			Sail	Londonderry	
26.03.45	30 EG	*Pevensey Castle*			Sail	Londonderry	
30.03.45	30 EG	*Pevensey Castle*			Sail	Londonderry	
03.04.45	30 EG	*Pevensey Castle*			Arv	Scapa Flow	
12.04.45	30 EG	*Pevensey Castle*			Arv	Scapa Flow	
14.04.45	30 EG	*Pevensey Castle*			Sail	Clyde	
20.04.45	30 EG	*Pevensey Castle*			Sail	Scapa Flow	
05.05.45	30 EG	*Pevensey Castle*			Sail	Londonderry	
07.05.45	30 EG	*Pevensey Castle*			Sail	Londonderry	
17.05.45	30 EG	*Pevensey Castle*			Arv	Londonderry	
20.05.45	30 EG	*Pevensey Castle*			Arv	Loch Eriboll	
25.05.45	30 EG	*Pevensey Castle*			Arv	Scapa Flow	
27.05.45	30 EG	*Pevensey Castle*			Arv	Bergen	
31.05.45	30 EG	*Pevensey Castle*			Arv	Scapa Flow	
02.06.45	30 EG	*Pevensey Castle*			Arv	Londonderry	
23.06.45	FOCWAF				Sail	Londonderry	
09.07.45					Sail	Freetown	
13.08.45					Arv	Dakar	
22.08.45					Sail	Dakar	
16.09.45					Arv	Freetown	On relief by *Pevensey Castle*
03.10.45					Sail	Freetown	
11.10.45					Sail	Gibraltar	
14.10.45					Arv	Plymouth	
27.12.45					Sail	Plymouth	
10.01.46					Arv	Plymouth	
16.01.46					Sail	Plymouth	

Date	ESG	Senior Officer	Convoy	No of Ships	Arrive/ Sail	Location	Notes
06.02.46					Arv	Plymouth	From 14.10.45 records indicate that *LC* was on ASR duties operating out of Plymouth.

1946-1947	Reserve Fleet at Devonport.
1949	Refit at Bristol.
1951-56	2nd Training Squadron after a refit at Falmouth operating as Air Target Training Ship. mainly out of Londonderry.
1953	Represented Home Command, Portsmouth, at the Coronation Fleet Review.
11.56	Reserve Fleet at Devonport.
1959	Sold to A.J. White.
03.08.59	Arrived St Davids-on-Forth for scrapping.

DESTRUCTION OF U-1200, 11TH NOVEMBER 1944

U-1200 was sunk by the 30th Escort Group in position 50°24'N 05°42'W. *Launceston Castle* played a major part in this action.

As recorded by HQ Staff, *Launceston Castle* did the greatest number of attacks, and was also responsible for most of the fine contact keeping of the Group, whose combined effort extended over a prolonged period.

The Group was in continuous Asdic contact with the U-Boat for a total of 70 hours of which *Launceston Castle* was in contact for 44 hours 25 minutes. As a result she was given the main credit for the success of this operation. Her Narrative of the Attack is given below in full:-

HMS Launceston Castle
Narrative of Attack on U-boat -11th November 1944

Situation	EG 30 carrying out A/S Patrol in line abreast, course 224° speed 12 knots, zig-zag Group 3 - 30°. *Launceston Castle* starboard wing ships, *Pevensey Castle*, *Kenilworth Castle*, *Portchester Castle* - distance apart 1.5 miles.
Radar contact by *Pevensey Castle*	At 0026/11 course was altered to 187° to close radar contact obtained by *Pevensey Castle* at a range of 25,000 yards; and which disappeared shortly afterwards. This was classified as possible submarine - amplitude of echo 2X.
A/S Contact by *Launceston Castle*	At 0130.11 *Launceston Castle*'s A/S operator reported contact at Green 15 (230°), range 2,100 yards: with H.E of fast reciprocating engines. Although the speed of approach given as 30 knots was too high for the contact to be classified as submarine, course was altered towards and speed reduced to safe anti-gnat, the contact being reported to S.O. E.G. 30. Contact was lost at 750 yards: but regained at 1,000 astern when a second run in was made with a Squid attack - emergency settings of 100 ft: being
First Attack	used. This attack was at 0158.11. Action Stations had been sounded just before but the Action team could not close up before the attack was made. It was subsequently found that the Range Recorder Operator had failed to switch from cruising to attacking speed and this accounted for the high rate of approach first observed. The firing time was also affected by this
Cause of inaccuracy movement	and the first attack must therefore be considered inaccurate. Slight high Doppler and slight movement left indicated that the target was moving westward.
Second attack 147B in contact	At 0143.11 the Plot was started and the second attack carried out at 0159.11 with 147B in contact - 400 ft: Depth of water by E/S was 420 ft: In this attack Doppler was slight low and Plot gave course and speed of target as 270° - 2 knots. Ship's course and speed was 254° - 6 knots.

Third Attack	Contact was regained at 400 yards astern with moderate to high Doppler and a third attack was carried out at 0214.11 - 147B giving a depth of 400 ft: and the Plot still showing a slight westerly movement. Ship's course and speed was 098° - 6 knots. Range recorder trace during run in was poor and subsequent analysis suggests that U-boat bottomed at this time. After this attack 147B traces, although showing an additional echo close to the bottom, were generally poor and for all subsequent attacks a depth setting of 420 ft: was used.
Range recorder gave trouble	The Range recorder stylus gave considerable trouble from 0230 onwards owing to failure of Magnetic Clutch. A new assembly was shipped at 0408 and, although this helped, occasional trouble was still experienced.
Fourth Attack Dan Buoy laid	At 0256.11 the fourth attack was carried out with Squid - course 097° speed 4 knots. Firm contact with 'Q' was obtained and the target appeared to be stationary. After this attack a lighted Dan Buoy was laid 800 yards bearing 016° from the contact at 0312.11.
Fifth Attack	At 0335.11 the fifth attack was carried out with Squid, firing on the 'Q' trace. Course 190°, speed 4 knots - target stationary.
Sixth Attack	At 0428.11 the sixth attack was made with Squid, firing on the 'Q' trace. Course 147°, speed 6 knots - target stationary.
Seventh Attack	At 0603.11 the seventh Squid attack was carried out, firing on the main trace. Course 073° speed 5 knots - target stationary.
Eight Attack	At 0707.11 the eight squid attack was carried out, firing on the 'Q' trace. Course 263° speed 5 knots - target stationary.
Ninth attack with D/Cs	At 0825.11 the ninth attack was made with depth charges - a pattern of three only being dropped from the rails set at H, 500 ft: One of these, the first, fired prematurely at between 50 and 100 ft: The cause of this has not been established . Course was 307° speed 14 knots. The target appeared to be stationary and firing was on the 'Q' trace.
Tenth Attack	At 0951.11 the tenth attack was carried out with Squid, firing on the 'Q' trace. Course 147° speed 5 knots - no target movement.
Eleventh & last attack	At 1104.11 the eleventh and last attack was carried out with squid, firing on the main trace. Course 270° speed 4 knots, target stationary. On this attack the 147B gave a depth of 200 ft: but it is considered that this was due to disturbance from Drury's hedgehog attack. Contact was lost until 1134.11 when it was regained in its original position.

Oil observed	After the third attack, when running in with the E/S, a strong smell of oil, rather similar to tar, was noticed; but owing to the darkness nothing could be seen. At daylight a considerable area was found to be covered with oil. By mid-day this oil patch was about a mile in diameter; during the afternoon the oil drifted off the Southward leaving a long slick starting about 300 yds: from the contact - attempts were made to obtain a sample but were not altogether successful owing to its thin quality. A sample was collected on a piece of flannel and this was passed over to the Senior Officer EG 30.
oil samples	
Observant Radar out of action	At 1715.11 orders were received to leave the *Portchester Castle* in contact and carry out Observant with the remainder of the Group. Shortly afterwards Radar became unserviceable and at 1930.11 ship resumed the duties of holding contact - *Portchester Castle* proceeding to carry out Observant. Contact was held throughout the night without difficulty and at daybreak oil was seen to be rising still. At 0800.12 *Kenilworth Castle* took over the contact - *Launceston Castle* resuming Observant.
holding contact	
E/S runs	*Launceston Castle* resumed duties of contact keeper from 1700.12 until 0830.13 - during this time twelve runs were made over the target with E/S but only slight traces of an object on the bottom were noticeable.
Oil traces	*Launceston Castle* took over contact again 1630.13 when traces of oil were observed to be still coming to the surface.
Contact left	At 0015.14 the Group was ordered to leave the contact which had been held continuously for 70? hours.
A/S conditions	A/S conditions were very good for the first 24 hours, the only Non-subs: owing obviously caused by other ships' wakes and disturbances due to attacks. Conditions deteriorated after the first day, but remained fair until time of leaving the contact.
E/S	Many runs were made over the target with E/S (Type 761) but only two good traces were obtained. These unfortunately faded before they could be preserved, but an approximate sketch is shown hereunder. Height of target 15 to 20 ft: and length about 150ft: Subsequent E/S traces showed nothing but a slight irregularity on the bottom.
Mistake made	The only error made was the failure of the Range Recorder Operator to switch from Cruising to Attacking during the first attack thus rendering it inaccurate and giving a false impression of relative speed of the target.
reasons for abandoning hunt	The target was held continuously for 70? hours on the bottom and the reason for abandoning the hunt was the order of C in C W.A.
Evidence of damage	The main evidence of damage to the U-boat , apart from its failure to surface, was the strong smell of oil after the third attack, probably released by

	the second attack. This oil was sighted at daybreak and was still evident after 62 hours.
Value of S.T.U.	The S.T.U. (Short Transmission Unit) was found of great value through-out the attack in distinguishing the contact from the wakes and distur-bances caused by other ships' attacks. On the second night it was found much simpler to hold the contact by using S.T.U., and also this rested the Operators ears. On subsequent nights it was not found to be of such value.
Value of 'Q'	The 'Q' attachment was found extremely valuable throughout and it is considered that, if possible, arrangements should be made for the bridge loud Speaker to be switched to 'Q'.

November 17th 1944   signed: R. M. Roberts

Lieutenant R.N.R.
Commanding Officer

*A post war shot of **HMS Launceston Castle** leaving Portsmouth, with the Isle of Wight in the background.*
(Steve Bush Collection)

LAUNCESTON CASTLE'S FIRST VOYAGE WAS TO GIBRALTAR AND BACK.

For the majority of the newly assembled crew this was their first voyage and first time of 'going foreign'. Ray Hewitt who joined the ship as O.D A.S/D straight from the training school *HMS Nimrod*, Campbeltown. Recalls his impressions:-

Launceston Castle *was on her way on her one and only slow convoy to Gibraltar. We were all excited. We were mostly a young ships company having never been out of the UK in our lives, and here we were on our way to sunshine and foreign climes. I don't remember much about the outward voyage, but I do remember my first view of the Rock. It was at night and wonder of wonders, it was all lit up! Being so close to neutral Spain it wasn't thought necessary to impose a blackout on the Rock. You can imagine what a shock it was to us, having suffered about three years of total blackout at home. Well, we enjoyed Gib: to the full. The good weather, the bars, the Spanish dancing girls with their Mantillas, castanets, etc. And the very Englishness of Gibraltar, its red pillar boxes, even the policemen looked like they did at home, and yet there was a difference, it seemed an altogether different way of life.*

I think that convoy changed us a ships company, we were different, we had got some sea time in and we had been 'foreign'. To prove it most of us now sported Mediterranean blue collars. Due to a great deal of work with the scrubbing brush I might add. The ship had changed too. It was not only an A/S escort ship, it was a cargo ship because every nook and cranny on board contained one or two hands of green bananas. During our war years we had had to live without fresh fruit of any kind, so it was no surprise that with such an abundance available at Gibraltar we all took advantage of it and stocked up in order to give our loved ones a treat. Sadly it was it was all to be in vain. Every day on the voyage home saw bundles of black over ripe bananas being ditched over the side. Not many survived to Londonderry.

On another occasion when on patrol off the southern coast of Ireland, they picked up a strong contact. It was a very strong echo and we proceeded to classify it. It soon became obvious that it was a non-sub. It was much too large and various other things bore this out. All the information was passed to the Captain and the A/S Officer. We continued to hold this echo and then the Captain told us that we were in contact with a known wreck. It was the **Lusitania**. *We continued to ping on it, went over it, at the same time running the echo sounder. This painted a picture on the sensitized paper of the ship lying on the sea bed.*

MEMORIES OF THE LAUNCESTON CASTLE AND BISCAY
By Harry Clarke ex-Coder

The Captain was a stocky, swarthy Lt. Cdr. RNR, thought to have been involved in gun running up the Yangtse at one time.

Returning to Devonport from Finisterre after 28 days on station he just seemed to point the ship in the right direction and make full revs regardless of the weather. One middle watch he came into the Wireless Office bringing half the Bay with him on his way from the bridge and from roughly a horizontal position uttered the immortal words; "It must be force 11 up there." From a position hanging vertically from an Admiralty transmitter the size of a wardrobe I wondered what force he thought it was down here. No one showed it much but I suspect I wasn't the only one with doubts about whether we would make it home. I wonder if he is still with us? He must have been about 40 then and as I was about 20 he would be 90 now! A born survivor I would think. If I met him now I would give him a bit of my mind, but then, he did get us home every trip. Do they still make them like that? I hope so.

But things weren't always like that, although sometimes it seemed so. During little over 12 months

I saw the sea from 'dead calm, glassy' to 'hurricane, white out' more or less. One day we even had a slight swell with sun, 'Hands to Bathe'. It was a memorable experience swimming in water a mile deep, seeing your ship for the first time from outboard at sea in a swell. The feeling was exquisite, but at the time I thought about those who had watched their ship sinking from such a position, perhaps surrounded by burning oil, injured or dying. I thought to myself, "You lucky Sod."

HMS LEEDS CASTLE

Battle Honours
Atlantic 1945

*An aerial view of **HMS Leeds Castle**.*   (MoD/Crown Copyright)

After working up at Tobermory **Leeds Castle** joined the B3 Escort Group escorting convoys to and from Gibraltar and in September 1944 was allocated to the B23 Escort Group on the same duty. In December of that year she was allocated to the Liverpool Escort Pool (LEP) and continued with the same duties. Between 18 January and 7 April 1945 she underwent a refit at Cardiff. She undertook one more voyage escorting a convoy to and from Gibraltar before the end of the war in Europe.

She escorted 16 convoys totalling some 510 ships. These voyages were generally without incident and no ships were lost from enemy action. On 6 August 1944 whilst escorting OS85/KMS59 her HF/DF sense aerial fell down the funnel, but was retrieved from its hiding place amongst the tubes of No1 boiler and successfully replaced.

In mid-June 1945, like several others of her sister-ships, she was assigned to Air Sea Rescue duties oper-ating out of the Clyde. On 10 October 1945 she grounded on Pladda Island, Arrran and had to be beached. Her magazines were completely flooded and machinery spaces partly flooded. She was refloat-ed and towed to Ardrossan where she was fully repaired, completing on 27 December 1945. In January 1946 she was allocated to training duties, joining the Basic A/S Training Flotilla, Portsmouth Command. This unit was successively re-named the Portland Flotilla and the 3rd Escort Flotilla during the year. In January 1949 this became the 2nd Training Flotilla, being finally re-named the 2nd Training Squadron in 1952. She continued to serve at Portland until relieved by the Type 14 Frigate **HMS Grafton**. She paid off at Chatham on 20 November 1956 and was laid up until June 1958. Her length of continuous service, interspersed only by refits and periods under repair, extending from February 1944 until November 1958, was unequalled by any of her sister-ships.

HISTORY DETAILS

23.01.43	Ordered.
22.04.43	Laid down. **Builder**: Hull - Pickersgill (Sunderland); Engine - C Clark (Sunderland).
12.10.43	Launched.
15.02.44	Completed.

WARTIME VOYAGES

Date	ESG	Senior Officer	Convoy	No of Ships	Arrive/ Sail	Location	Notes
11.01.44	LEP				Sail	Liverpool	
23.02.44					Arv	Tyne	
23.02.44	EG B3	*Towy*			Sail	Sunderland	
09.03.44					Sail	Tyne	*LC* delayed by minor collision damage.
09.03.44	EG B3	*Towy*			Sail	Tyne	
11.03.44					Arv	Tobermory	
11.03.44	EG B3	*Towy*			Arv	Tobermory	
25.03.44	EG B3				Sail	Tobermory	
25.03.44	EG B3				Sail	Tobermory	Taken in hand 28/3 Clyde for fitting Foxer Gear, completes 03/04.
26.03.44	EG B3				Arv	Clyde	
04.04.44	EG B3	*Towy*			Sail	Londonderry	
07.04.44	EG B3	*Towy*	OS 73/ KMS 47	45		5215N 1601W	
15.04.44	EG B3	*Towy*	OS 73/ KMS 47	48		3559N 1122W	
17.04.44	EG B3	*Towy*	OS 73/ KMS 47	45		5215N 1601W	
17.04.44	EG B3	*Towy*	OS 73/ KMS 47		Arv	Gibraltar	
22.04.44	EG B3	*Towy*	MKS 46	49		5580N 0605W	
01.05.44	EG B3	*Towy*	SL 155/ MKS 46	49		5325N 1247W	
03.05.44	EG B3	*Towy*	SL 155/ MKS 46	49	Arv	Clyde	
14.05.44	EG B3	*Towy*	OS 77/ KMS 51	31	Sail	Londonderry	
15.05.44	EG B3	*Towy*	OS 77/ KMS 51	33		5557N 0935W	*LC* not included after 17 May; no indication of where she went
16.05.44	EG B3	*Towy*			Sail	Londonderry	

Date	ESG	Senior Officer	Convoy	No of Ships	Arrive/ Sail	Location	Notes
18.05.44	EG B3	*Towy*				4546N 1732W	To overtake OS 77
21.05.44	EG B3	*Towy*	OS 77/ KMS 51	33		3808N 1857W	
25.05.44	EG B3	*Towy*	OS 77/ KMS 51		Arv	Gibraltar	
30.05.44	EG B3	*Towy*	SL 159/ MKS 50	33	Sail	Gibraltar	
31.05.44	EG B3	*Towy*	SL 159/ MKS 50	35		3550N 0630W	
31.05.44	EG B3	*Towy*	SL 159/ MKS 50	35		3550N 0630W	
01.06.44	EG B3	*Towy*	SL 159/ MKS 50	43		3530N 1025W	
10.06.44	EG B3	*Towy*			Arv	Clyde	
23.06.44	EG B3	*Towy*	OS 81/ KMS 55		Sail	Londonderry	
23.06.44	EG B3	*Towy*	OS 81/ KMS 55		Arv	Londonderry	
26.06.44	EG B3	*Towy*	OS 81/ KMS 55	34		Not Given	
04.07.44	EG B3	*Towy*	OS81/ KMS 55	33	Arv	Gibraltar	
10.07.44	EG B3	*Towy*	SL 163/ MKS 54	42	Sail	Gibraltar	
11.07.44	EG B3	*Towy*	SL 163/ MKS 54	42		3535N 0730W	
21.07.44	EG B3	*Towy*	SL 163/ MKS 54	42	Arv	Clyde	
02.08.44	EG B3	*Tintagel Castle*	OS 85/ KMS 59	34	Sail	Londonderry	
03.08.44	EG B3	*Tintagel Castle*	OS 85/ KMS 59	34		5528N 1107W	
13.08.44	EG B3	*Tintagel Castle*	OS 85/ KMS 59	34	Arv	Gibraltar	
19.08.44	EG B3	*Tintagel Castle*	SL 167 MKS 58	36		3540N 0643W	
19.08.44	EG B3	*Tintagel Castle*	SL 167/ MKS 58	36	Sail	Gibraltar	Hague gives 29 ships
27.08.44					Sail	Londonderry	
27.08.44	EG B3	*Tintagel Castle*	SL 167/ MKS 58	33		5009N 0652W	Hague gives 29 ships
30.08.44	EG B3	*Tintagel Castle*	SL 167/ MKS 58	33	Arv	Clyde	
02.09.44					Arv	Clyde	

Date	ESG	Senior Officer	Convoy	No of Ships	Arrive/ Sail	Location	Notes
10.09.44					Sail	Clyde	
10.09.44	B23	*Knaresborough Castle*			Arv	Belfast	
12.09.44	B23	*Knaresborough Castle*	OS 89/ KMS 63	33	Sail	Clyde	
15.09.44	B23	*Knaresborough Castle*	OS 89/ KMS 63	33	Sail	Belfast	
19.09.44	B23	*Knaresborough Castle*	OS 89/ KMS 63	34		4506N 1144W	
23.09.44	B23	*Knaresborough Castle*	OS 89/ KMS 63	33	Arv	Gibraltar	
23.09.44	B23	*Knaresborough Castle*	OS 89/ KMS 63	33	Arv	Gibraltar	
29.09.44	B23	*Knaresborough Castle*	SL 171/ MKS 62	17	Sail	Gibraltar	
30.09.44	B23	*Knaresborough Castle*	SL 171/ MKS 62	17		3601N 0901W	
07.10.44	B23	*Knaresborough Castle*	SL 171/ MKS 62	17		5013N 0521W	
09.10.44	B23	*Knaresborough Castle*	SL 171/ MKS 62	17	Arv	Clyde	
23.10.44	B23					At Clyde	
27.10.44	B23					At Clyde	
03.11.44	B23					At Clyde	
10.11.44	B23					At Campbeltown	
12.11.44	B23	*Fowey*	OS 95/ KMS 69	31	Sail	Clyde	
23.11.44	B23	*Fowey*	OS 95/ KMS 69	31	Arv	Gibraltar	
25.11.44	B23	*Fowey*	SL 177/ MKS 68	35	Sail	Gibraltar	Having arrived the day before (SMO)
28.11.44	B23	*Fowey*	SL 177/ MKS 68	36		4012N 1030W	
12.12.44	7th EG	*Cygnet*			Sail	Clyde	
13.12.44	LEP		OS 98/ KMS 72	36	Sail	Clyde	
20.12.44	LEP		OS 98/ KMS 72	36	Arv	Gibraltar	
26.12.44	LEP		MKS73G	26	Sail	Gibraltar	
03.01.45	LEP		MKS73G	26	Arv	Liverpool	
11.01.45	LEP		OS 104/ KMS 78	16	Sail	Liverpool	
15.01.45	?	*Leeds Castle*	OS 104/ KMS 78	24		4732N 0850W	16 ships according to Hague. Convoy dispersed 15.01.45

Date	ESG	Senior Officer	Convoy	No of Ships	Arrive/ Sail	Location	Notes
21.01.45	LEP				Arv	Liverpool	A 182301.1 *LC* can be taken in hand 26.01 Penarth Dry Dock Co: FOIC Cardiff Intend to sail *LC* on completion of satisfactory trials to Liverpool 06/04.
07.04.45	LEP				Sail	Milford Haven	
12.04.45	LEP				Arv	Milford Haven	
16.04.45					Arv	Clyde	
16.04.45					Sail	Clyde	
16.04.45					Arv	Belfast	
17.04.45					Sail	Belfast	
18.04.45	LEP				Arv	Liverpool	
22.04.45	LEP				Sail	Liverpool	
28.04.45	LEP				Arv	Liverpool	
07.05.45	LEP	*Knaresborough Castle*	OS 127/ KMS101		Sail	Liverpool	
15.05.45	LEP	*Knaresborough Castle*	OS 127/ KMS101		Arv	Gibraltar	
20.05.45	LEP	*Knaresborough Castle*	MKS 102G	21	Sail	Gibraltar	
27.05.45	LEP	*Knaresborough Castle*	MKS 102G		Arv	Liverpool	
04.06.45					Arv	Sheerness	
14.06.45	W.A.				Sail	Liverpool	
05.07.45					Arv	Clyde	
18.07.45					Sail	Clyde	
05.08.45					Arv	Clyde	
20.08.45					Sail	Clyde	*Berkeley Castle* 2209 10/8 Relieved by *LC* in ASR Station 17. *LC* relieved by *Dumbarton*
10.10.45					Arv	Lamlash	*LC* 100954/10 Have grounded off Pladda. Am making water. Intend to beach.
12.10.45					Sail	Lamlash	
04.01.46					Arv	Greenock	FOIC Glasgow 181034.10 *LC* is to dock at Ardrossan 29.10. FOIC Greenock 281035.1 Intend sailing *LC* 29/1 to Portland ETA 31/1

Date	ESG	Senior Officer	Convoy	No of Ships	Arrive/ Sail	Location	Notes
30.01.46					Arv	Portland	Record ends

1946 - 1956	Training Squadron at Portland.
13.01.50	Completed refit at Chatham. The departure from Chatham was marred by grounding in thick fog in the estuary. The ship was left high and dry by the ebbing tide and exposed for all to see when the fog cleared. Ammunition and stores were unloaded into lighters brought alongside and the ship re-floated on the rising tide. All hands being engaged in off-loading and reloading the stores and ammunition.
1953	Represented Home Command, Portsmouth, at the Coronation Fleet Review.
11.56	Reserve at Chatham.
1958	Sold to T.W. Ward.
06.06.58	Arrived Grays for scrapping.

STUCK IN THE MUD - LEEDS CASTLE

Leeds Castle sailed from Portland to her home port of Chatham for a refit. We spent several weeks in dry dock cleaning and painting the hull, cleaning boilers and getting the engine overhauled. On completion we stored and ammunitioned ship. Early the next day on a foggy morning we slipped and eased out of the basin into the Thames Estuary at Sheerness for our return to Portland. Thirty minutes later on an ebb tide we stuck fast on a mud bank. A race began to off-load all the ammunition and stores into flat bottomed barges that had been hurriedly brought alongside. Around midday at low water we sat 'high and dry' and to make matters worse the fog had cleared and the sun shone brightly on our predicament.

At full tide we did in fact float off, the ship being somewhat lighter. Then came the job of reloading the stores, victuals and ammunition. All hands turned to and after an exhausting time we resumed our voyage back to Portland.

(Ted Wild, one time Postie and Coxswain of the motorboat)

STUCK IN THE MUD

Into the treacherous current
Of the Medway stream
Slipped the **Leeds Castle**
With full ahead steam
The engineers' runner was happy and gay
For he knew he was sailing Portland way
The Engine Room Branch were in fine fettle
The Boiler Room stoker had put on the kettle
ERA Goldsworthy Chief of the Watch
Put weight to the throttle and revved up a notch

But alas and alack came fog unforeseen
Visibility nil abaft the beam
The Navigating officer was busy that morning
For of the fog he had no warning

Then sluggishly the engines slowed
The condenser gauge no vacuum showed
The engine room telegraph clanged astern
But the HPs and LPs the shaft would not turn

ERA Goldsworthy went straight to the trouble
We're up to the poop with mud and rubble
The upper deck was all panic and confusion
Half the crew were in ablution.
But Jimmy the One soon brought out his whip,
And gave the order "de-ammunition ship."
The seaman dug in, I will give them this,
Helped by the Engineer boys free gratis.

So this ended the unhappy trip
Of the gallant **Leeds Castle**
His majesty's ship.
For the very next morning with very little joy
The crew were anchored to No 3 Buoy.

                                        Anon

HMS MORPETH CASTLE

Battle Honours
Atlantic 1944-45

HMS Morpeth Castle, 17 July 1944.   *(MoD/Crown Copyright)*

On completing working up at Tobermory, *Morpeth Castle* joined the B2 Escort Group which was operating on escorting convoys to and from Gibraltar. Her first voyage being with Convoy OS 88/KMS 62 of 37 ships early in September 1944. The Group was renamed the B22 Escort Group on arrival at Gibraltar and retained that designation until the end of December 1944 when the designation reverted to the B2 Escort Group. Up until then the Senior Officer of the Group was carried by **HMS Cotton**. When the renamed or reformed Group started escorting the HX/ON convoys across the Atlantic the ship dispositions lists omitted the name of the Senior Officer's ship. The voyages of this Group were derived from the 'Pink Lists' with the result that the convoys escorted have had to be estimated by reference to the sailing and arrival dates of the convoys. Furthermore the PRO series of ADM/217 files cover-

ing the relevant period do not contain any reference to the B2 Escort Group or to *Cotton* that may have continued to be have been the Senior Officer of the Group. The tabulation below provides an estimate of the designations of the convoys and number of ships that were escorted by **Morpeth Castle**. The total number of ships that she escorted is estimated as being 753 made up from 16 convoys. Eight of these were convoys to and from Gibraltar, and eight comprised the HX/ON series across the Atlantic. On completion of convoy escort duties *Morpeth Castle* was allocated to Flag Officer Submarines for use as a Submarine Escort with the 3rd Submarine Flotilla. In the course of these duties she visited numerous ports in the UK and Europe. *Morpeth Castle* was reduced to reserve in July 1946. She remained with the Reserve Fleet until August 1960, when she was sold for scrap.

HISTORY

23.01.43   Ordered.
23.06.43   Laid down: **Builder**;:Hull - Pickersgill (Sunderland) Engine - C Clark (Sunderland).
26.11.43   Launched.
13.07.43   Completed.

WARTIME VOYAGES

Date	ESG	Senior Officer	Convoy	No of Ships	Arrive/ Sail	Location	Notes
26.06.44	EG B4	*Helmsdale*			Arv	Sunderland	
29.06.44	EG B4	*Helmsdale*			Sail	Sunderland	
15.07.44	EG B4	*Helmsdale*			Sail	Sunderland	
15.07.44	EG B4	*Helmsdale*			Arv	Tyne	
21.07.44					Sail	Tyne	
23.07.44	EG B4	*Helmsdale*			Arv	Tobermory	
05.08.44	EG B4	*Helmsdale*			Sail	Tobermory	
08.08.44					Arv	Aultbea	
09.08.44					Arv	Stornoway	*Mentor* 091725/9 *MC* has developed leaks intend to sail her to Londonderry August.
09.08.44					Sail	Aultbea	
10.08.44					Arv	Londonderry	A 131324/8 *MC* can be taken at Tobermory for further 9 days work up.
19.08.44	EG B4	*Helmsdale*			Arv	Tobermory	
27.08.44					Sail	Tobermory	
29.08.44	EG B4	*Helmsdale*			Sail	Londonderry	
03.09.44	EG B2	*Cotton*			Sail	Londonderry	
06.09.44	EG B2	*Cotton*	OS 88/ KMS 62	37		5029N 0901W	
08.09.44	EG B2	*Cotton*	OS 88/ KMS 62	32		4530N 1128W	
10.09.44	EG B2	*Cotton*	OS 88/ KMS 62	31		3750N 1108W	
12.09.44	EG B2	*Cotton*	KMS 62	20		Nr Gibraltar	
18.09.44	B22	*Cotton*	SL 170/ MKS 61	43	Sail	Gibraltar	Carrying 20 boxes of bullion: N. Pickford 1999
20.09.44	B22	*Cotton*	SL 170/	43		3812N 1010W	
26.09.44	B22	*Cotton*			Arv	Liverpool	
04.10.44	B22	*Cotton*			Arv	Belfast	Having left Londonderry the day before. (SMO)

Date	ESG	Senior Officer	Convoy	No of Ships	Arrive/ Sail	Location	Notes
04.10.44	B22	*Cotton*			Sail	Belfast	
07.10.44	B22	*Cotton*	OS 91/ KMS 65	29		4743N 1123W	
11.10.44	B22	*Cotton*	KMS 65	25		3545N 0615W	
11.10.44	B22	*Cotton*	KMS 65	25	Arv	Gibraltar	
19.10.44	B22	*Cotton*	SL 173/ MKS64	39	Sail	Gibraltar	
23.10.44	B22	*Cotton*	SL 173/ MKS64	39		4445N 0945W	
29.10.44	B22	*Cotton*	SL 173/ MKS64	39	Arv	Liverpool	
03.11.44	B22	*Cotton*	OS 94/ KMS68	34	Sail	Liverpool	
13.11.44	B22	*Cotton*	OS94/ KMS68	34	Arv	Gibraltar	
17.11.44	B22	*Cotton*	SL 176/ MKS 67	28	Sail	Gibraltar	
24.11.44	B22	*Cotton*	SL 176/ MKS 67		Arv	Liverpool	
03.12.44	B22	*Cotton*	OS 97/ KMS71	29	Sail	Belfast	

HMS Morpeth Castle *post war in Holy Loch.*　　　　　　　　　*(CCC(F)A Archives)*

Date	ESG	Senior Officer	Convoy	No of Ships	Arrive/ Sail	Location	Notes
10.12.44	EG B2		OS 97/ KMS71	29	Arv	Gibraltar	
16.12.44	EG B2		MKS71G	24	Sail	Gibraltar	
24.12.44	EG B2		MKS71G	24	Arv	Liverpool	
08.01.45	EG B2		ON 271	69	Sail	Liverpool	
18.01.45	EG B2		ON 271	69	Arv	St John's	
27.01.45			HX 334	74	Sail	St John's	
06.02.45	EG B2		HX 334	74	Arv	Liverpool	
14.02.45	EG B2				Sail	Liverpool	
17.02.45	EG B2		ON 285	70	Sail	Clyde	
28.02.45	EG B2		ON 285	70	Arv	St John's	

HMS Morpeth Castle in drydock at Hamburg.
(CCC(F)A Archives)

Date	ESG	Senior Officer	Convoy	No of Ships	Arrive/ Sail	Location	Notes
11.03.45	EG B2		HX 342	71	Sail	St John's	
22.03.45	EG B2		HX 342	71	Arv	Liverpool	
26.03.45	EG B2					Liverpool	Repairs complete 31 March
02.04.45	EG B2		ONS 46	24	Sail	Clyde	
18.04.45	EG B2		ONS 46	24	Arv	St John's	
21.04.45	EG B2		HX 351	57	Sail	St John's	
05.05.45	EG B2		HX 351	57	Arv	Liverpool	
10.05.45	EG B2	*Morpeth Castle*	ON 302	75	Sail	Liverpool	
24.05.45	EG B2	*Morpeth Castle*	ON 302	75	Arv	St John's	Convoy dispersed 27.05.44
29.05.45	EG B2	*Morpeth Castle*	HX 358	56	Sail	St John's	
07.06.45	EG B2	*Morpeth Castle*	HX 358	56	Arv	Liverpool	The last HX convoy
08.06.45					Arv	Rosyth	Attached to FO Submarines for escort duty with 3rd Submarine Flotilla
15.06.45					Sail	Liverpool	
16.06.45					Arv	Clyde	
25.06.45					Sail	Clyde	
26.06.45					Arv	Barrow	
27.06.45					Sail	Barrow	
28.06.45					Arv	Greenock	
04.07.45					Arv	Londonderry	
04.07.45					Sail	Greenock	
06.07.45					Sail	Londonderry	
06.07.45					Arv	Clyde	
06.08.45					Sail	Clyde	
10.08.45					Sail	Rosyth	
12.08.45					Arv	Loch Ryan	
13.08.45					Sail	Loch Ryan	
13.08.45					Arv	Londonderry	
15.08.45					Arv	Holy Loch	
15.08.45					Arv	Loch Ryan	
15.08.45					Sail	Londonderry	
15.08.45					Sail	Loch Ryan	
25.08.45					Sail	Holy Loch	
29.08.45					Arv	Kiel	
01.09.45					Sail	Kiel	
06.09.45					Arv	Greenock	
24.09.45					Arv	Londonderry	
25.09.45					Sail	Londonderry	
25.09.45					Arv	Holy Loch	
26.09.45					Sail	Holy Loch	
27.09.45					Arv	Clyde	

Date	ESG	Senior Officer	Convoy	No of Ships	Arrive/ Sail	Location	Notes
11.10.45					Sail	Clyde	
15.10.45					Arv	Hamburg	
20.10.45					Sail	Hamburg	To Brunsbuttel for O/R Kiel
29.10.45					Sail	Cuxhaven	
04.11.45					Arv	Barrow	FOSM 17/11012 SM is requested to sail **MC** escorting JOP to Hamburg 25.11.
14.12.45					Arv	Cuxhaven	NSCO Inverness 271625/11 **MC** will R/V with German JOP 0900/28.11
16.12.45					Arv	Sheerness	NO I/c Keil 181446.12 **MC** leaves Kiel 0800 14.12 ETA WG 17.12
21.12.45					Arv	Barrow	ETA 18.12 to Barrow postponed 24 hrs; CinC Nore postponed further 24 hrs.
22.12.45					Arv	Clyde	

U-Boats at Lisahally, N. Ireland, August 1945. (CCC(F)A Archives)

*U-Boats at Lisahally, N. Ireland, August 1945 as seen from **HMS Morpeth Castle**.*

(CCC(F)A Archives)

Date	ESG	Senior Officer	Convoy	No of Ships	Arrive/ Sail	Location	Notes
09.02.46					Arv	Clyde	*MC* ETA Clyde 22/12
06.06.46							SMS 06 1637Z Intend sailing *MC* to Inchmarnock South 7.2
03.07.46							SM 3 071550Z/2 Intend sailing *MC* 9/2 to R/V with ***Unsparing*** off Lough Foyle.
02.10.46							SM 3 10 1442/2 Intend sailing *MC* 11/12 to Firth of Forth & Blyth

1946-49	Reserve at Devonport and then Penarth.
1960	Sold to E. Rees.
09.08.60	Arrived Llanelli for srapping.

HMS OAKHAM CASTLE

Battle Honours
Atlantic 1945

HMS Oakham Castle.   *(MoD/Crown Copyright)*

H*MS Oakham Castle* completed working up at Tobermory on 10 January 1945, where she had the misfortune to suffer a minor grounding. She was allocated to the Liverpool Escort Pool (LEP). She made three complete voyages to and from Gibraltar, but she was also employed in supporting other convoys as they passed through the then dangerous waters of the Western Approaches.

Comparisons with her sailing and departure dates with those of convoys sailing to and from Gibraltar suggest that she was involved in escorting 5 convoys comprising 134 ships between February and May 1945. On 22 May 1945 her departure from Liverpool coincided with that of convoy OS130/KMS 104 (25 ships). This convoy dispersed two days later. *Oakham Castle* must have then continued on her way to Gibraltar since she is reported as having left Gibraltar on 30 May, when in company with *HMS Columbine*, she escorted the submarine *HMS Spirit* to Portsmouth.

On her return to the UK *Oakham Castle* sailed to Stavangar followed by a visit to Bergen to collect two merchantmen carrying German POWs. She escorted the two ships to Brunbutten via the Kiel Canal. From there she went to Rosyth.

Oakham Castle was then employed in anti submarine training duties, firstly at Campbeltown and later at Portland. It must have been during this time that, according to 'The Particulars of War Vessels' for October 1946, that whereas, other Castle Class Corvettes retained their Squid 81 Ahead Throwing Weapons, the *Oakham Castle* had her's removed and replaced by Hedgehog 241.

The ship went through a series of periods in dockyard hands for various modifications, repairs and refits from early 1946 to June 1950 when she was reduced to reserve. In July 1957 she was transferred to the Air Ministry and converted for weather ship duties and in May 1958 renamed as *Weather Reporter*. She continued in this role until sold for scrap in September 1977, some 33 years after her first commissioning.

HISTORY

19.12.42   Ordered
30.11.43   Laid down. **Builder**: Hull - Inglis (Pointhouse); Engine - Harland and Wolff (Govan) & Robey (Lincoln)
20.07.44   Launched
10.12.44   Completed

WARTIME VOYAGES

Date	ESG	Senior Officer	Convoy	No of Ships	Arrive/ Sail	Location	Notes
11.12.44	Unall					Clyde	
20.12.44	Unall				Arv	Tobermory	
01.01.45	LEP					Tobermory	
10.01.45	LEP				Sail	Tobermory	
11.01.45	LEP				Arv	Liverpool	
22.01.45	LEP				Sail	Liverpool	
26.01.45	LEP				Arv	Belfast	
27.01.45	LEP				Sail	Clyde	Escorting OS 107/KMS 81 (8 ships) for 3 days
02.02.45	LEP				Arv	Liverpool	
04.02.45	LEP		OS 110/ KMS 84	21	Sail	Liverpool	
16.02.45	LEP		OS 110/ KMS 84	21	Arv	Gibraltar	
19.02.45	LEP		MKS84G	26	Sail	Gibraltar	
27.02.45	LEP		MKS84G	26	Arv	Liverpool	
04.03.45	LEP				Arv	Liverpool	
08.03.45	LEP				Sail	Liverpool	
10.03.45	LEP				Arv	Milford Haven	
13.03.45	LEP				Arv	Liverpool	
14.03.45	LEP				Sail	Liverpool	
15.03.45	LEP				Sail	Clyde	
15.03.45					Arv	Belfast	
16.03.45	LEP				Arv	Liverpool	
16.03.45	LEP				Sail	Belfast	
17.03.45	LEP				Sail	Liverpool	
18.03.45	LEP				Arv	Liverpool	
18.03.45	LEP				Arv	Milford Haven	
18.03.45	LEP				Sail	Milford Haven	
23.03.45	LEP		OS 118/ KMS 93	29	Sail	Liverpool	
31.03.45	LEP		OS 118/ KMS 93	29	Arv	Gibraltar	
05.04.45	LEP		MKS93G	33	Sail	Liverpool	

Date	ESG	Senior Officer	Convoy	No of Ships	Arrive/ Sail	Location	Notes
13.04.45	LEP		MKS93G	33	Arv	Liverpool	
27.04.45	LEP				Arv	Liverpool	
01.05.45	LEP				Sail	Liverpool	
03.05.45	LEP				Arv	Liverpool	
07.05.45	LEP				Sail	Liverpool	
13.05.45	LEP				Arv	Liverpool	
15.05.45	LEP				Arv	Liverpool	
22.05.45	LEP		OS 130/ KMS 104	25	Sail	Liverpool	Convoy dispersed 24 May 1945
30.05.45	LEP				Sail	Gibraltar	Having arrived the day before (SMO) in company with *HMS Columbine* and *HM Submarine Spirit*
03.06.45	LEP				Sail	Portsmouth	
05.06.45	LEP				Arv	Liverpool	
16.06.45					Arv	Rosyth	
19.06.45					Sail	Rosyth	
27.07.45					Arv	Stavangar	
28.07.45					Sail	Stavangar	
29.07.45					Arv	Bergen	
03.08.45					Arv	Kiel	
07.08.45					Arv	Hamburg	
07.08.45					Sail	Hamburg	
07.08.45					Sail	Kiel	
09.08.45					Arv	Christiansand	
11.08.45					Sail	Christiansand	
12.08.45					Arv	Rosyth	
24.08.45					Arv	Campbeltown	
25.01.46					Arv	Portland	

1946-1951	Training duties, Portland.
1951 - 1957	In Reserve, Category B at Plymouth.
1957	Mercantile; converted for weather reporting duties. The conversion carried out by James Lamont & Co, Port Glasgow was completed on 3rd April 1958.She was re-named *Weather Reporter* on 16th May 1958. She continued to serve as a weather ship until September 1977.
09.77	Sold to Tees Marine.
1977	Arrived Middlesborough for scrapping.

*An undated image of **HMS Oakham Castle** wearing a dark grey colour scheme.*   (*Steve Bush Collection*)

OAKHAM CASTLE - EARLY DAYS AT PORTLAND
E.W. Stanton - Signalman.

A few incidents that have stuck in my memory:-

*1. **Oakham Castle** was moored alongside **Kenilworth Castle** in Portland harbour (1946) when a seaman put his leg in the bight of a wire rope on the bits. The ships drifted apart and the rope tightened on his leg. Then his luck was in. Wind and weather pushed the ships together and he was able to pull his leg out intact.*

2. Signalman Riley was about to throw a mills bomb over the side to signal to a submarine below, when his hand caught on the oerlikon gun stanchion and the grenade fell down his watch coat sleeve. He slung it out and it rolled underneath the platform by the 10-inch signal projector. At first he thought to pick it up and then thought otherwise and ran away from it. The resulting explosion blew up the little platform, penetrated the flag locker and tattered some of the flags and chipped the paint on the ready-use locker. The door to the companion way was pitted - but no one was hurt, thank goodness.

*3. **Oakham Castle** was acting as part of the screen for the battleship **HMS King George V** out of Portland in 1945 or 1946 and three submarines were taking part in the exercise to attack the battleship. We were off the flagship's port bow and I was on watch on the flag deck. I hoisted a pendant upside down, much to the annoyance of the yeoman and the CO. Shortly afterwards I reported sighting a periscope off the port beam and we were credited with that one. Then I looked astern into our wake and spotted another periscope. We were also credited with that submarine and so I was 'let off the hook' for my mistake at the beginning of the exercise.*

4. Two members of the mess blacked up and made a commando-style raid on a warehouse and brought back a crate of marmalade and one of crayfish. We were fed up with both of the commodities before

they were consumed.

5. A signalman's nightmare: This started when the ingelfield clip on the top of the flag which I was about to hoist broke and the halyard shot up to the yard leaving the flag and a mass of rope at my feet. I climbed the mast to the platform from which the yard stretched out towards the dockside and then realized that the foot rope fitted on a modern ship is useless for working ones way across the yard. I had to lie down on the 4-in wide girder and pull myself out to the end. Then I had to release one hand grip and pull the halyard out. There was no one on the upper deck to catch the rope as it was 'Stand -Easy' time. I was immensely relieved when the boatswain's mate came on deck and was able to help me. Having secured the halyard below I was then had to wriggle backwards to the platform before I could stand upright. That is something I am very glad that I never had to repeat.

PASSENGERS

*Most of the passengers we took on board for our 'day runs' were trainees from **HMS Osprey** who were to qualify for a torpedo and anti-submarine substantive rate. However, one day as we were preparing to take the ship to sea , we were alerted that we were to take on board a group of army personnel; Officers who had recently completed their exams at Sandhurst Military Academy. A day at sea was to be an award following their passing out parade. I was detailed to be their minder for the day and began to explain what would be happening during the A/S exercises, and what the ship would be doing. Unfortunately, all but one of them turned green and became seasick before we had even cleared the breakwater. The remaining succumbed as soon as the breakwater was cleared.*
It took a considerable time and great effort to get the unfortunates down to the forward mess deck, where they lounged the day away. We had to assist them to disembark on the ship's return to harbour that evening. I wondered what sort of obligatory essays they would write on their days experience.

HYPNOTISM

*R. Gillman on the **Oakham Castle** in 1949 recalls that one of his messmates was a hypnotist. One day his friend decided to demonstrate his skills in the seamen's messdeck. After briefing everyone on what he expected to achieve he chose one member of the mess, who he thought would make a good subject. He went through his routine and gave his first command, "When I snap my fingers you will wake up and do so and so". The subject did not obey, he had not really been hypnotised, but several others including R.G did so.*
As a result R.G. became his friend Eric's subject. They gave regular performances just for the fun of it. Word got round to the Wardroom and they were invited to perform there. The Ship's Officers and their ladies were suitably impressed and they were rewarded with plenty of food and not a little liquid refreshments.
The performance was repeated on other ships in Portland and the pair became well known. Unfortunately one day things got a bit out of hand and they could easily have been landed in trouble. The 1st Lieutenant advised them to stop the shows and in fact banned them from doing any more.

OAKHAM CASTLE'S CRASHING DEPARTURE
By Mik Cass

*In 1977, between 24th October and 24th November, **Oakham Castle** was moored in the Cattewater at*

Plymouth for a few days before proceeding under her own steam to Lowestoft to be broken up. At that time Mik was stationed at the Meteorological office on RAF Mount Batten and had a good view of her from there. Subsequently a Captain Silas Oats who had been given the task of taking the ship to Lowestoft called in at the office for a weather forecast. He told of the ship's interesting demise. She was longer than the dock which was going to be used to break her up in. So he had to steam at full ahead into the dock with the hope that when she rammed the head of the dock it would 'shorten' her. It worked!

*This account could not be confirmed. An authority on Teeside shipping confirmed that the dock was indeed small, but could accommodate **Oakham Castle** there being a 3ft clearance, but there may have been a problem with the depth.*

HMS OXFORD CASTLE

Battle Honours
Atlantic 1944-45

HMS Oxford Castle seen in March 1944.   (MoD/Crown Copyright)

After completing working up *Oxford Castle* was allocated to the B2 Escort Group (SO *HMS Hesperus*) engaged in escorting Gibraltar convoys. Work she continued to do until the end of the war in Europe.

On 26 June 1944 she was ordered to join the destroyer *HMS Bulldog* hunting a submarine northwest of Bloody Foreland. However, she arrived on the scene after *Bulldog* had successfully concluded the action with the destruction of *U-719*.

On 31 August 1944 *Oxford Castle* participated in the hunt for a U-boat that had sunk the US tanker *Jacksonville* between Aran Island and Invrahull, but without success.

In September 1944 she was allocated to the B22 Escort Group (SO *HMS Cotton*) and in December 1944 to the Liverpool Escort Pool (LEP).

Oxford Castle was transferred to the Anti-Submarine Training Flotilla under the Rosyth Command and operated out of Campbeltown. A year later she was laid up at the Penarth Docks near Cardiff where she remained until September 1960 when she left Penarth for Briton Ferry to be broken up. In the meantime she had been placed on the disposal list for sale as an Ocean Weather Ship. She was also offered to the Finnish Navy as a prospective flagship.

HISTORY

23.01.43   Ordered.
21.06.43   Laid down. **Builder**: Hull & Engine - Harland & Wolff (Belfast).
11.12.43   Launched.
23.02.44   Commissioned.
10.03.44   Completed.

WARTIME VOYAGES

Date	ESG	Senior Officer	Convoy	No of Ships	Arrive/ Sail	Location	Notes
14.03.44	EG B2	*Hesperus*			Arv	Tobermory	
30.03.44	EG B2	*Hesperus*			Arv	Liverpool	Having left Tobermory the day before. (SMO)
21.04.44	EG B2	*Hesperus*			Arv	Londonderry	
25.04.44	EG B2	*Hesperus*	OS 75/ KMS 49	23	Sail	Londonderry	
27.04.44	EG B2	*Hesperus*	OS 75/ KMS 49	23		5224N 1558W	
01.05.44	EG B2	*Hesperus*	OS 75/ KMS 49	23		4021N 1935W	
06.05.44	EG B2	*Hesperus*	OS 75/ KMS 49	23	Arv	Gibraltar	
10.05.44	EG B2	*Hesperus*	MKS 48	26	Sail	Gibraltar	
12.05.44	EG B2	*Hesperus*	MKS 48	32		3530N 1020W	26 ships according to Hague
15.05.44	EG B2	*Hesperus*	SL 157/ MKS 48	49		4125N 1830W	
22.05.44	EG B2	*Hesperus*	SL157/ MKS 48	49	Arv	Liverpool	
26.05.44	EG B2	*Hesperus*			Sail	Liverpool	
02.06.44	EG B2	*Hesperus*			Arv	Liverpool	
03.06.44	EG B2	*Hesperus*				At Liverpool	
12.06.44	EG B2	*Hesperus*			Sail	Londonderry	In operation 'CW' with *Bulldog* (SO) supported by B4 EG. 12/13 June Convoy OS80/KMS54. (SMO)
25.06.44	EG B2				Sail	Londonderry	
01.07.44	EG B2	*Hesperus*			Arv	Londonderry	
13.07.44	EG B2	*Hesperus*	OS 83/ KMS 57	29	Sail	Londonderry	
14.07.44	EG B2	*Hesperus*	OS 83/ KMS 57	32		5557N 0945W	Hague gives 29 ships
22.07.44	EG B2	*Hesperus*	OS 83/ KMS 57	31		3810N 1750W	
25.07.44	EG B2	*Hesperus*	OS 83/ KMS 57	31	Arv	Gibraltar	
29.07.44	EG B2	*Hesperus*	MKS 56	18	Sail	Algiers	
30.07.44	EG B2	*Hesperus*	SL 165/	39	Sail	Gibraltar	Hague gives 35 ships
05.08.44	EG B2	*Hesperus*	SL 165/ MKS 56	39		4615N 1824W	

Date	ESG	Senior Officer	Convoy	No of Ships	Arrive/ Sail	Location	Notes
07.08.44	EG B2	*Hesperus*	SL 165/ MKS 56	32		5152N 1540W	
08.08.44	EG B2	*Hesperus*	SL 165/ MKS 56	37		5522N 0830W	
10.08.44	EG B2	*Hesperus*	SL 165/ MKS 56	37	Arv	Liverpool	
21.08.44	EG B2	*Hesperus*			Sail	Liverpool	
22.08.44	EG B2	*Hesperus*			Arv	Belfast	
22.08.44	EG B2	*Hesperus*			Arv	Londonderry	
22.08.44	EG B2	*Hesperus*			Sail	Londonderry	
22.08.44	EG B2	*Hesperus*			Arv	Belfast	
24.08.44					Sail	Belfast	
26.08.44	EG B2	*Hesperus*			Arv	Londonderry	
30.08.44	Force 33				Sail	Londonderry	To join Force 33 *Hurst Castle* in company
02.09.44					Sail	Loch Ewe	
04.09.44	EG B2	*Cotton*	OS 88/ KMS 62	37	Sail	Belfast	
06.09.44	EG B2	*Cotton*	OS 88/ KMS 62	37		5029N 0901W	
08.09.44	EG B2	*Cotton*	OS 88/ KMS 62	32		4530N 1128W	
10.09.44	EG B2	*Cotton*	OS 88/ KMS 62	31		3750N 1108W	
12.09.44	EG B2	*Cotton*	KMS 62	20		Nr Gibraltar	
18.09.44	B22	*Cotton*	SL 170/ MKS61	43	Sail	Gibraltar	Carrying 20 boxes of bullion: N Pickford 1999
20.09.44	B22	*Cotton*	SL 170/ MKS61	43		3812N 1010W	
26.09.44	B22	*Cotton*	SL 170/ MKS61	43	Arv	Liverpool	
03.10.44	B22	*Cotton*			Sail	Liverpool	
04.10.44					Arv	Campbeltown	
07.10.44	B22	*Cotton*	KMS 65	25	Sail	Milford Haven	
11.10.44	B22	*Cotton*	KMS 65	25	Arv	Gibraltar	
19.10.44	B22	*Cotton*	SL 173/ MKS 64	39	Sail	Gibraltar	
23.10.44	B22	*Cotton*	SL 173/ MKS 64	39		4445N 0945W	
27.10.44	B22	*Cotton*	SL 173/ MKS 64	39	Arv	Liverpool	
07.11.44	B22	*Cotton*	OS 94/ KMS 68	35		4852N 1130W	Convoy sailed from Liverpool 03.11.44 and dispersed 12.11.44
10.11.44	B22	*Cotton*				At Campbeltown	

Date	ESG	Senior Officer	Convoy	No of Ships	Arrive/ Sail	Location	Notes
13.11.44	B22	*Cotton*			Arv	Gibraltar	Ex OS94/KMS 68
17.11.44	B22	*Cotton*	SL 176/ MKS 67	28	Sail	Gibraltar	
24.11.44	B22	*Cotton*	SL 176/ MKS 67	28	Arv	Liverpool	Having been detached to support SC 161(49ships)
03.12.44	B22	*Cotton*	OS 97/ KMS 71	29	Sail	Belfast	Having arrived from Liverpool the day before. (SMO).
06.12.44	LEP				Arv	Liverpool	
15.12.44	LEP					Liverpool	Repairs.
18.12.44	LEP					Liverpool	Repairs
11.01.45	LEP				Arv	Liverpool	
12.01.45	LEP				Sail	Liverpool	
15.01.45	?	*Leeds Castle*	OS 104/ KMS 78	24		4732N 0850W	
22.01.45	LEP				Arv	Liverpool	
27.01.45	LEP		OS 107/ KMS 81	21	Sail	Liverpool	
05.02.45	LEP		OS 107/ KMS 81	21	Arv	Gibraltar	
09.02.45	LEP		MKS 82	17	Sail	Gibraltar	
17.02.45	LEP		MKS 82	17	Arv	Liverpool	
26.02.45	LEP				Sail	Liverpool	CinC WA 271909/2 OS113/KMS87 0600Z/28
04.03.45	LEP				Arv	Liverpool	
08.03.45	LEP		OS 115/ KMS 89	24	Sail	Liverpool	
10.03.45	LEP		OS 115/ KMS 89	24	Sail	Londonderry	
16.03.45	LEP		OS 115/ KMS 89	24	Arv	Gibraltar	
23.03.45	LEP		MKS 90	18	Sail	Gibraltar	
29.03.45	LEP		MKS 90	18	Arv	Liverpool	
07.04.45	LEP				Sail	Liverpool	
16.04.45	LEP				Sail	Clyde	
18.04.45	LEP				Arv	Liverpool	
26.04.45	LEP				Sail	Belfast	
27.04.45	LEP		*Knaresborough Castle* OS 125/ KMS 99	23	Sail	Liverpool	SO 8th EG assumed command of all escorts 30.04.45. Convoy dispersed 01.05.45
03.05.45	LEP		OS 125/ KMS 99	23	Arv	Gibraltar	Convoy dispersed 01.05.45

Date	ESG	Senior Officer	Convoy	No of Ships	Arrive/ Sail	Location	Notes
10.05.45	LEP		MKS 100	23	Sail	Gibraltar	21 ships according to the ROP
17.05.45	LEP		MKS 100	21	Arv	Liverpool	
27.05.45	LEP		OS 131/ KMS 105	13	Sail	Liverpool	Convoy dispersed 30.05.45
04.06.45	LEP		OS 131/ KMS 105	13	Arv	Gibraltar	
10.06.45					Arv	Liverpool	
18.06.45					Sail	Liverpool	
20.06.45					Sail	Rosyth	
20.06.45					Arv	Rosyth	
07.11.45					Arv	Greenock	1946: FO I/c Glasgow 041116/2 *OC* is to proceed down river to Tail of Bank 5/2.
13.02.46					Arv	Portland	132359/2 CinC Plymouth *OC* can be accepted for reduction.
20.02.46							Capt. I/c Portland 181248/2 Intend sailing *OC* to Plymouth ETA 20/2
20.02.46					Arv	Plymouth	200739Z/2 FO I/c Glasgow 090956/2 *OC* sails 9/2. FO I/c Greenock 091705/2 Intend to sail 0700.10/2 to Portland ETA 1500 13/2.

1946-1949	In reserve at Devonport.
February 1950	Completed refit at Russels, Liverpool.
1951-56	Reserve at Devonport and then Penarth (1952).
November 1956	Placed on disposal list to sale to a European country or as an Ocean Weather Ship.
March 1957	Offered to the Finnish Navy for use as a flagship.
March 1960	Sold to T.W. Ward.
September 1960	Arrived Briton Ferry for scrapping.

During her active service *Oxford Castle* escorted 20 convoys comprising 580 ships. These voyages were mostly without incident. Exceptions did, however, occur.

HMS COTTON B22
OS 91/KMS 65
4th - 11th OCTOBER 1944

The convoy started to form up on 4th October . The Clyde portion included two submarines. *Oxford Castle* was detailed to bring on the Belfast joiner. *Morpeth Castle* joined the Group and Convoy at K2 buoy having made good repairs to her Asdic and TBS at Bangor Bay.

On 5th October at 2010 occurred what was described as a short action. In position 51°38'N 07°58'W three echoes were picked up on the SG Radar 227° 14,000 yards. Both *Morpeth Castle* and *Oxford Castle* reported no IFF on the bearing. The ship went to Action Stations and the echoes were closed. At 2035, when the leading ship bore 201° 5,200 yards, the challenge was made twice through on the white open box light. As there was no reply this procedure was repeated at 2027. There still being no reply a bouquet of three star shell was fired and 'A' arcs opened.

The star shells illuminated three ships. One ship then identified herself as *Coldstream*, and at 2031 reported "have *Northern Spray* and two tugs in company".

The action had therefore to be abandoned. These ships were not in the situation report received on board for 2000/5th October. This incident provoked several responses in minutes by HQ staff. Firstly the Officer who drafted the Situation Reports defended his not putting the ships in the broadcast Situation Report (they were in the 'land' sit reports) because he was unaware that the ships were 60 miles astern of their estimated position.

It was then suggested that Capt D should be asked to instruct *Cotton* in the proper use, as opposed to abuse of the challenge. You challenge only a suspected enemy. If a reply is not received at once, or the wrong reply is received, then you blow the suspect out of the water.

A suspected friend should merely be asked for his pendants.

Explanations from *Coldstream* were that his IFF was working (One Staff Officer thought that the range of 14,000 yards might be too long for the system to work properly). He also suggested that in view of the shore lights beyond the bearing of *Cotton*, that the dim lamp used by *Cotton* was not recognised as another ship. These explanations were apparently accepted.

On 6 October *Oxford Castle* developed a hot Plumber Block and was detached to Milford Haven. It transpired that the trouble arose with the plumber block because the vessel mixed special mineral oil obtained from Gibraltar with that supplied from the home base. The plumber block is of the enclosed Michell pad type and the mixing of the oils proved detrimental to the bearing. *Oxford Castle* rejoined on 9 October in position 09°32'N 10°42'W. But she was in trouble again on the night of 10th/11th with condenseritis and went into Gibraltar as soon as possible in the morning.

In spite of vigorous maintenance efforts during lay-over periods, breakdowns still occured at sea. On 30 January 1945 the piston of *Oxford Castle's* Distiller Feed Pump broke at the crosshead. Temporary repairs were made and the pump brought into use again. The reserve feed tanks for boiler feed were filled to capacity and strict economies imposed on the use of fresh water. The patched up piston broke again on 4 February and was repaired with a stronger joint. The repaired piston was still in use two weeks later.

Medical facilities on most merchant ships and escorts were very basic. It was a fortunate convoy when a doctor was carried on one of the ships. Whilst escorting convoy OS 115/KMS 89 in March 1945 medical assistance was sought on three occasions. On the 10 March 1945 *Oxford Castle* received permission from the SO to obtain the services of the medical officer of the rescue ship *SS Lifeguard*. The medical officer was transferred by the ship's whaler and he successfully removed a piece of steel from a rating's eye. Shortly after this all the escorts, except *Oxford Castle* and the rescue ship, detached. The next day the Master of *SS Mary Kingsley* urgently required drugs to control a heart problem. These were not carried by *Oxford Castle* but were

eventually obtained from **SS Antilochus** and transferred by Coston gun line. The following day the medical officer of **SS Antilochus** was transferred by whaler to **SS Mary Kingsley** to attend the latter's Captain who was seriously ill. A similar service was provided by **Oxford Castle** on 13 May when, once again using her whaler, a doctor was transferred to and from another merchant vessel and back again the next day.

In spite of the disastrous occasion when several LCTs were lost in heavy weather when being towed by merchant ships in convoy KMS 66/OS 92 in the previous October, the practice continued.

On her last convoy to Gibraltar there were four LCTs being towed by two merchant ships. The convoy was dispersed on 30 May 1945 with the exception of the two ships towing LCTs. **Oxford Castle** escorted them into the Mediterranean. One of the ships continued, proceeding independently with her two LCTs. The other entered Gibraltar Bay and slipped her tows. **Oxford Castle** closed her and recovered the two towing pendants for transfer to the two LCTs and escorted them into harbour.

HMS PEVENSEY CASTLE

Battle Honours
Atlantic 1944

*A pristine looking **HMS Pevensey Castle**.* (*MoD/Crown Copyright*)

On completion of working up ***Pevensey Castle*** was allocated to the 4th Escort Group (SO ***Helmsdale***) engaged on convoy escort to and from Gibraltar. Her first voyage with the Group was on 3 June 1944 with convoy OS 80/KMS 54, Londonderry to Gibraltar. At that time the Group included ***Kenilworth Castle***, ***Portchester Castle*** and ***Pevensey Castle***, later to be augmented by ***Launceston Castle*** and ***Morpeth Castle***. On 13 September 1944 these Castle Class Corvettes were formed into the 30th Escort Group with ***Pevensey Castle*** as Senior Officer. On 11 November 1944 the Group sank ***U-1200*** in the North Atlantic, south of Cape Clear. For the remainder of the war the 30th Escort Group was employed in anti submarine patrols in the Western Approaches and in the North Sea. At the end of May 1945 the Group escorted thirteen U-Boats that had surrendered at Bergen, from Norway to Scapa Flow and Lisahally.

HISTORY

23.01.43 Ordered.
21.06.43 Laid down. **Builder**: Hull & Engine - Harland and Wolff (Belfast).
11.01.44 Launched.
10.06.44 Completed.

WARTIME VOYAGES

Date	ESG	Senior Officer	Convoy	No of Ships	Arrive/ Sail	Location	Notes
21.04.44	EG B4	*Helmsdale*			Arv	Belfast	
24.04.44	EG B4	*Helmsdale*			Sail	Belfast	
28.04.44	EG B4	*Helmsdale*			Sail	Belfast	
01.05.44	EG B4	*Helmsdale*			Arv	Belfast	
08.05.44	EG B4	*Helmsdale*			Sail	Belfast	
22.05.44	EG B4	*Helmsdale*			Arv	Belfast	
02.06.44	EG B4	*Helmsdale*			Sail	Belfast	
03.06.44	EG B4	*Helmsdale*			Sail	Belfast	
12.06.44					Sail	Belfast	For Tobermory, arrive 13.06.44. Allocated to B4 Escort Group
13.06.44	EG B4	*Helmsdale*			Arv	Tobermory	
29.06.44	EG B4	*Helmsdale*			Arv	Londonderry	Having left Tobermory the same day. (SMO).
02.07.44	EG B4	*Helmsdale*			Sail	Londonderry	
04.07.44							R/V *Vindex*
15.07.44	EG B4	*Helmsdale*			Arv	Londonderry	
22.07.44	EG B4	*Helmsdale*	OS 84/ KMS 58	24	Sail	Londonderry	
26.07.44	EG B4	*Helmsdale*	OS 84/ KMS 58	27		4901N 1935W	Hague gives 24 ships
02.08.44	EG B4	*Helmsdale*	OS 84/ KMS 58		Arv	Gibraltar	
08.08.44	EG B4	*Helmsdale*	SL 166/ MKS 57	16	Sail	Gibraltar	
09.08.44	EG B4	*Helmsdale*	SL 166/ MKS 57	16		3541N 0652W	
19.08.44	EG B4	*Helmsdale*	SL 166/ MKS 57	31	Arv	Londonderry	CinC WA 041208/10 On completion of group training 30th EG is to be sailed to top up with fuel at Moville thence to join Force 33 opera tion CW, 7/09 carrying out sweeps in Area C with *Inman* & *Braithwaite*, and B4 EG.
25.08.44	EG B4	*Helmsdale*				At Londonderry	Boiler clean
29.08.44	30 EG	*Pevensey Castle*			Sail	Londonderry	The Group was formed out of the B4 EG on 13 September 1944.

Date	ESG	Senior Officer	Convoy	No of Ships	Arrive/ Sail	Location	Notes
14.09.44	30 EG	*Pevensey Castle* ONF 252			Sail	Londonderry	Operating under Force 33
23.09.44	30 EG	*Pevensey Castle*			Arv	Londonderry	
29.09.44	30 EG	*Pevensey Castle*			Sail	Londonderry	
03.10.44	30 EG	*Pevensey Castle*			Arv	Larne	
05.10.44					Sail	Larne	
05.10.44	30 EG	*Pevensey Castle*			Sail	Londonderry	
11.10.44	30 EG	*Pevensey Castle*				NW Apps	On patrol
15.10.44	30 EG	*Pevensey Castle*				At Sea	
18.10.44	30 EG	*Pevensey Castle*			Arv	Londonderry	
22.10.44	30 EG	*Pevensey Castle*			Sail	Londonderry	Patrol NW Approaches.
28.10.44	30 EG	*Pevensey Castle*			Arv	Londonderry	Problems occurred on this patrol in co-operat ing with air patrols
03.11.44	30 EG	*Pevensey Castle*				At Londonderry	Boiler clean.
06.11.44	30 EG	*Pevensey Castle*				Londonderry	
09.11.44	30 EG	*Pevensey Castle*			Sail	Londonderry	Patrol NW Approaches.
19.11.44	30 EG	*Pevensey Castle*			Arv	Londonderry	11th Nov: Group attack U-boat and hold contact for three days Resumed patrol in heavy weather & Group attacked another suspected U-boat & held contact for 65.5 hours, being relieved by 4 EG.
21.11.44	30 EG	*Pevensey Castle*			Sail	Londonderry	Patrol in area 52N 11W. Group attacked suspect ed U-boat on 26 Nov & held contact for 73 hrs. Then supported passage of HX 321 & relieved by 2 EG on 5 Dec. Group returned Londonderry.
28.11.44	30 EG	*Pevensey Castle*				5110N 0945W	On patrol
06.12.44	30 EG	*Pevensey Castle*			Arv	Londonderry	
15.12.44	30 EG	*Pevensey Castle*			Arv	Campbeltown	Group arrived for exer cises, but these seriously interrupted by gales until moderated on 17th. Proceeded to sea p.m. & exercised with subma rine before proceeding to Belfast Lough.

Date	ESG	Senior Officer	Convoy	No of Ships	Arrive/ Sail	Location	Notes
18.12.44	30 EG	*Pevensey Castle*					30 EG to patrol in the South West Approaches. On 20th Dec Group under the command of CinC Plymouth & patrol area moved to the entrance of English Channel, and later to areas North of Cherbourg Peninsular.
18.12.44	30 EG	*Pevensey Castle*			Sail	Belfast	30 EG sailed for exercises in Campbeltown area.
29.12.44	30 EG	*Pevensey Castle*			Arv	Portsmouth	
31.12.44	30 EG	*Pevensey Castle*			Sail	Portsmouth-	But returned to harbour shortly after sailing with engine defects. *Caistor Castle* assumed SO duties. On patrol in central Channel and supported various convoys passing through, and later patrolling N of Cherbourg.
08.01.45	30 EG	*Pevensey Castle*				S of Needles	On patrol. *Pevensey Castle* resumed command of the 30 EG
10.01.45	30 EG	*Pevensey Castle*			Arv	Portland	As well as the remainder of the Group
11.01.45	30 EG	*Pevensey Castle*			Sail	Portland	Arrived having been relieved by 17th EG. On passage to Portland to Londonderry took *Kenilworth Castle* in tow (engine room defects) for 5 hours before defect rectified.
13.01.45	30 EG	*Pevensey Castle*			Arv	Londonderry	
15.01.45	30 EG	*Pevensey Castle*				Off Holyhead	On Patrol
22.01.45	30 EG	*Pevensey Castle*			Sail	Londonderry	On patrol in central Irish Sea. Later under CinC Plymouth's command to the Western English Channel and in support of various convoys. On

Date	ESG	Senior Officer	Convoy	No of Ships	Arrive/ Sail	Location	Notes
							28 January *PC* successfully extinguished a fire aboard *MV Cromarty*.
29.01.45	30 EG	*Pevensey Castle*				Mounts Bay	On patrol
05.02.45	30 EG	*Pevensey Castle*			Arv	Plymouth	
08.02.45	30 EG	*Pevensey Castle*			Sail	Plymouth	
09.02.45	30 EG	*Pevensey Castle*				Plymouth	
13.02.45	30 EG	*Pevensey Castle*			Arv	Londonderry	Boiler cleaning at Londonderry late February. Patrol western approaches to North Channel and in support of convoys. Various non-sub contacts encountered and attacked.
19.02.45	30 EG	*Pevensey Castle*				Londonderry	Boiler cleaning ready 22.02.45
19.02.45	30 EG	*Pevensey Castle*			Arv	Portsmouth	And proceeded to & arrived at Londonderry the same day.
24.02.45	30 EG	*Pevensey Castle*			Sail	Londonderry	
28.02.45	30 EG	*Pevensey Castle*			Sail	Londonderry	
07.03.45	30 EG	*Pevensey Castle*			Arv	Londonderry	
09.03.45	30 EG	*Pevensey Castle*			Sail	Londonderry	
12.03.45	30 EG	*Pevensey Castle*			Arv	Londonderry	
26.03.45	30 EG	*Pevensey Castle*			Sail	Londonderry	Departures and arrivals between 07.03 and 26.03 not confirmed by Pink List.
27.03.45	30 EG	*Pevensey Castle*			Arv	Lochalsh	
30.03.45	30 EG	*Pevensey Castle*			Sail	Lochalsh-	On passage to Scapa Flow.
03.04.45	30 EG	*Pevensey Castle*			Arv	Scapa Flow	
06.04.45	30 EG	*Pevensey Castle*			Sail	Scapa Flow	Patrol off Moray Firth and also Cape Wrath areas.
12.04.45	30 EG	*Pevensey Castle*			Arv	Scapa Flow	
14.04.45	30 EG	*Pevensey Castle*			Sail	Clyde	
20.04.45	30 EG	*Pevensey Castle*			Sail	Scapa Flow	To patrol off Cape Wrath before proceeding to Londonderry.
24.04.45	30 EG	*Pevensey Castle*			Arv	Londonderry	

Date	ESG	Senior Officer	Convoy	No of Ships	Arrive/ Sail	Location	Notes
04.05.45-30 EG		*Pevensey Castle*			Sail	Londonderry	Left for patrol, but aborted owing to engine defect. SO EG trans ferred to *Portchester Castle*. Group patrolled Irish Sea as Force 36.
05.05.45	30 EG	*Pevensey Castle*			Sail	Londonderry	*PC* rejoined EG at 1000/6 but returned to Moville to embark stores. Group then proceeded to become Force 33 in support of RA 66 until 8th. Boarded surrendered *U-956* on 11th, subsequently patrolling the 'Blue Route'.
07.05.45	30 EG	*Pevensey Castle*			Sail	Londonderry	
17.05.45	30 EG	*Pevensey Castle*			Arv	Londonderry	
19.05.45	30 EG	*Pevensey Castle*			Sail	Londonderry	
20.05.45	30 EG	*Pevensey Castle*			Arv	Loch Eriboll	
24.05.45	30 EG	*Pevensey Castle*			Sail	Loch Eriboll	Escorted U-boats to Loch Alsh on 21st returning to Loch Eriboll the same day. Proceeded to Scapa Flow on 24th.
26.05.45	30 EG	*Pevensey Castle*			Arv	Bergen	Having arrived and left Scapa on the 25th (SMO). Ship open to the public on 27th some 300 children fed. 28th official return of Bergen to rightful owners. Ship escorted 13 U-boats to UK. (SMO).
31.05.45	30 EG	*Pevensey Castle*			Arv	Scapa Flow	
02.06.45	30 EG	*Pevensey Castle*			Arv	Londonderry	Having left Scapa Flow on 1st June & escorted U-boats to Lisahally.
28.06.45					Sail	Londonderry	
08.07.45					Arv	Bathurst Cape St Vincent	
19.07.45					Sail	Freetown	
08.08.45					Sail	Freetown	

Date	ESG	Senior Officer	Convoy	No of Ships	Arrive/ Sail	Location	Notes
25.08.45							*PC* 251630/8 Relieved by ***Portchester Castle*** proceeding to Dakar.
25.09.45							From *PC* 251200Z/9 ASR Station closed down am returning to Freetown.
03.10.45					Sail	Freetown	
10.10.45					Arv	Gibraltar	
12.10.45					Sail	Gibraltar	
18.10.45					Arv	Portsmouth	AM 102257/11 *PC* is re-allocated to F.O.G.M.A. for Air Sea Rescue duty.
08.12.45					Sail	Portsmouth	
20.12.45					Arv	Gibraltar	
26.12.45					Sail	Gibraltar	
02.01.46					Arv	Freetown	

HMS Pevensey Castle, *as seen from* ***HMS Lancaster Castle***. *Note OOW and duty signalman on the bridge - fully exposed to the weather.* (*CCC(F)A Archives*)

Date	ESG	Senior Officer	Convoy	No of Ships	Arrive/ Sail	Location	Notes
16.01.46					Sail	Freetown	
03.02.46					Arv	Freetown	AM 291611.1 FOGMA is requested sail PC to UK to reduce to Category B. Capt. I/c W Africa 300955.1 You are to return to Freetown leaving ASR Station 31.1.

02.46 - 54		Reserve at Portsmouth, Chatham & West Hartlepool.	
12.08.49		Completed refit at Hull.	
1954-55		Dehumidified & preserved at Dowsons, South Shields.	
1960		Acquired by Air Ministry and converted at Blyth for weather reporting duties and re-named *Weather Monitor*, later 78-79 re-named *Admiral Beaufort*.	
1982		Scrapped.	

Soon after the formation of the 30th Escort Group *Pevensey Castle* had an interesting encounter with a wreck.

On 6th October 1944 the 30th Escort Group was patrolling north-west of Ireland. At 1120 a Swordfish aircraft reported by V/S that an oil slick was coming to the surface approximately 10 miles west of Oversay. The Group closed the position with all dispatch. It had been anticipated that the oil slick would turn out to be no more than strong tidal eddies that are frequent in that area. However, on arrival it was found that oil was actually coming to the surface. A firm Asdic contact was made by *Pevensey Castle*. This was attacked by *Portchester Castle* with squid with the bombs set to explode ten fathoms clear of the bottom. It was common practice in the Group that the first ship to attack a contact dropped a calcium flare as she passed through the disturbed water from the Squid Bombs. This gave the other ships a reference point. By night from its small flame and by day from its white smoke. According to Derek Wells-Brown, who was the *Portchester Castle*'s Asdic Officer, this was done on this occasion. *Pevensey Castle* being some two cables astern and approaching to make her attack. As *Pevensey Castle* approached, the sea caught fire. "Fortunately the bows of the ship were clear of the flames, which rose to a great height with a column of black smoke going up a few thousand feet, otherwise the upper deck personnel must have been fried like so many kippers. The fierceness of the blaze was our salvation, because the air drawn into the gap in the wall of flame made by the bows and forepart of the ship was sufficient to give us cool air to breathe.

"In the first shock of surprise I think we, in *Pevensey Castle*, thought that it was our own oil tanks on fire but, as we realised that it could not be and that we were drawing clear, full ahead was rung on the telegraphs and we left the area with no damage except to the First Lieutenant's paintwork.

" In the photograph taken by *Kenilworth Castle* the smoke plume (measured by using the length of the

ship as the scale) is a fraction under 4,000ft high and 400 yards wide at sea level. The most memorable aspects were the cool wind blowing over our bows and the great noise of the flames."

Sources: i).   *30th Escort Group; Report of proceedings 5th October 1944 to 18th October 1944.*

           ii).   *Monthly Anti Submarine Reports Vol 5 1944.*

           iii).   *Derek Wells-Brown personal communication.*

<u>Comment</u>:

The only reference to the prevailing weather conditions in the Monthly Anti Submarine Report (MASR) was that the forenoon of the 5th October was "one of the only really fine days that we have had this autumn." The first discrepancy is the date. The ROP is quite definite that the fire occurred on the 6th October. The rising vertical column of smoke in the photograph indicates that the wind was very light. The fact that the Group had anticipated that the 'slick' would turn out to be 'tidal eddies' also suggests that the weather was good, with a light wind and calm sea.

Pevensey Castle would have been travelling between 4 and 7 knots. Thus unless there was a stern wind of greater velocity, a cigarette thrown overboard would have been swept aft. With the Squid about to be fired the only personnel on the upper deck, forward of the quarter deck, would have been the 4-inch Gun crew and the Squid Crew. A cigarette thrown by any of them would not be likely to ignite gas ahead of their position.

The account in the MASR speculates that ignition may "have been spontaneous combustion of gasses suddenly released, or it may have been a spark from the galley funnel, or a piece of burning soot from the main funnel shaken out by the Squid explosions and gently drifting down wind, or it may have been the unseen rating who was smoking at action stations."

Neither of the official reports states which ship fired the pattern of Squid. If Derek's memory is false and that it was *Pevensey Castle* that attacked the wrecked tanker, then the calcium flare could not have started the fire because the flare would not have been dropped overboard until the stern of the ship passed through the disturbed water from the Squid bombs. If Derek is right then the mostly likely ignition agent would be the calcium flare.

Failing the calcium flare, the key unknown is the relative direction of the wind. If *Pevensey Castle* fired the Squid pattern, then the wind must have been from astern of her. If *Portchester Castle* fired the squid, then the wind must have been from ahead, since there seems to be little doubt that *Pevensey Castle* was astern of *Portchester Castle*.

In either case, the cigarette as the agent, seems less likely than a spark or burning soot from a funnel. [The target was the after part of the 10,500 ton tanker *Jacksonville* which was sunk on 30th August, 1944. A similar incident occurred off Eddystone on 9th January, 1940, as a result of attacks by *HMS Scarborough*.]

The Report of Proceedings for the period 22nd January to 5th February 1945(ADM 217/573) described another fiery occasion. Commenting on this incident Commodore 'D' Londonderry wrote:

*"It is considered that the handling of **Pevensey Castle** on the windward side of **MV Cromarty** showed good seamanship on the part of Commander Hewitt. The fire parties, under the able leadership of Lieutenant Campbell RNVR, Executive Officer of **Pevensey Castle**, worked with courage and determination and their action is highly commendable."*

The entry in the Report of Proceedings for the 28th January 1945 was:-

28th January 1945. Convoy BTC51 was supported from 0345A until 0840A when it left division's area. Division went to support T.B.C.50, when it entered the area, it was straggling badly, distance between leading and rear ships being about 8 miles, and efforts were being made to hasten up the stragglers when at 1400A, it was seen one of the ship's, *MV Cromarty*, belonging to Messrs. B & W Sutherland, had hauled out of line with smoke pouring from her. *Pevensey Castle* closed her at full speed, but by the time we got there 2 boat loads of her crew had prematurely abandoned ship, and were some distance away. *Pevensey Castle* went alongside her weather side at 1420 and put three fire parties on board while *Launceston Castle* carried out 'observant'. *Cromarty*'s officers and crew were playing with the fire through the scuttles and ventilators, They would not go into the amidships accommodation which was all ablaze, *Pevensey Castle*'s fire parties led by Temp. Lieutenant J. Campbell MBE, RNVR, ably assisted by ERA V.T. Garnett, ERA W.G. Akers, PO R. Jennings, Sto. PO L. Marsham, R. Thompson, AB W. R. Adair, F. W. Stacey, F. W. Shreeve, and others, fought their way into the accommodation using smoke helmets and spray nozzles and tackled the fire which was raging in all cabins, storerooms, pantry and saloon. Ready use accommodation lockers on the boat deck were heated due to the fire below them and the gunners party, led by Sub Lieutenant J. R. Robjant RNVR, dumped some ammunition from the endangered lockers over the side and transferred all the remainder of the Oerlikon ammunition including the magazines from the guns to *Pevensey Castle* together with C.B.'s etc. It was then reported by *Cromarty*'s officers that the engine room was ablaze and my signal requesting a fire boat was made. Subsequently this report was found to be exaggerated, there was only a small fire down the engine room, and this was tackled successfully by *Cromarty*'s engine room staff,

The fire was eventually got under control amidships and finally extinguished at 1600 when fire parties

HMS Pevensey Castle *laid up in 1955.*   *(Ben Warlow Collection)*

and most of their fire fighting gear were returned to **Pevensey Castle**. As the two ship's were pounding in the moderate sea running and as all fenders had by this time been chewed up, I did not want to return the stores removed from **Cromarty**, but cast off at 1606 and joined **Launceston Castle** carrying out operation 'Observant' while **Cromarty** recovered her boats which been towed back by the 2 M.L's that had come out from Penzance to stand by.

A light touch was provided by **Cromarty**'s two boat loads of men, clean and compete with cat, dog, and suitcases boarding their ship across **Pevensey Castle** as our assisting fire parties, wet and dirty, left her.

Slight structural damage was caused to **Pevensey Castle** as she lay alongside and, two scuttles were stove in and sundry fire gear was lost and damaged, a list of which is shown in the Appendix, but it is considered this was well expended, as without help the fire would probably have gutted the ship, as when we arrived we were told her main fire pump was out of action. **Pevensey Castle** obtained additional hoses from **Launceston Castle** and was able to supply them all by using the 70 ton portable pump, both fire and bilge pumps and the after 20 ton pump. In addition **Pevensey Castle** coupled up to **Cromarty**'s five main pumps, and supplied water for use by ship's hoses. The use of the portable damage control lamps assisted greatly in the fire fighting and it was also found that the jet spray (FIREX) nozzles were superior to the Oilfyre nozzles for clearing away the smoke which was most dense. Pattern 230 smoke helmet were also invaluable. One of **Cromarty**'s junior engineer officer was reported missing and a first aid party under Temp. Surg. Lieutenant. G. C. Foster-Smith. RNVR stood by to render artificial respiration, but the man was not found, and it was assumed he had got away in one of the lifeboats. Subsequently it was reported to me that **Cromarty** flew her ensign at half mast, so it is possible he may have been found later, dead.

Cromarty got under way at 1640 and at 1705 **Ilfracombe** arrived to escort her. Division gave support until eastern end of patrol area, when three travelers arrived from Penzance and patrol was resumed.

Appendix No III.

Gear expended and lost while fire fighting in **SS Cromarty** and damage caused by ships lying alongside in sea way (No rate book on board).

DAMAGED.

8 Hoses, canvas unlined, 40 ft lengths fitted with No 3 size instantaneous couplings.
1 Hose Compoflex suction, 8 ft lost(sic) for 70 ton portable pump.
4 Spreaders on Port forward scrambling nets.
3 Sixty fathom lengths manila 6-inch.*
1 Six inch single sheaf block.
1 Wooden scotchman for dome in haul wire.
Bulwarks on Port side of Quarterdeck slightly damaged and one stiffening bracket buckled.
1 hinged scupper plate, Port side of Quarterdeck.
Ship's side plating stove in at scuttles to ERA's mess and Crews heads. Scuttle frames forced away from plating and glass smashed.
Wind baffles on Port side bridge slightly damaged.
Several small dents in ships side.

LOST.

9 Coir fenders.
5 heaving lines.

Four 40 foot lengths unlined Canvas hose fitted No3 instantaneous couplings.
* Three 20 foot lengths unlined canvas hose, fitted No3 instantaneous couplings
* 1 instantaneous coupling .
* 3 Branch pipes for 2? inch instantaneous couplings fitted with ? inch nozzle. Pattern 1557.
* 1 Branch pipe with ? inch nozzle.
* 7 jet spray nozzles fitted with 2? inch instantaneous- couplings.

NOTE. Items marked * were dropped in fire fighting. Application has been made to NOIC Falmouth in signal TOO 291700 for their return.

In June 1945 *Pevensey Castle* was allocated for Air/Sea Rescue duties in the South Atlantic and returned to Portsmouth six months later. Where she was placed in Reserve. In April 1960 she was sold to the Air Ministry, converted for weather reporting duties and renamed **Weather Monitor** and later (1979), **Admiral Beaufort.** She continued to be recorded by Lloyds Register under that name until 1983 when she was broken up.

HMS PORTCHESTER CASTLE

Battle Honours
Atlantic 1944

HMS Portchester Castle on 3 November 1943.   *(MoD/Crown Copyright)*

Portchester Castle was one of the earliest of the Castle Class corvettes to be commissioned. She completed working up by the end of December 1943 and was allocated to the B1 Escort Group. However the 'Ship Disposition Reports' place her in January 1944 with the 15th Escort Group. In fact it is not at all clear what the ship was doing during January 1944. In February 1944 she was allocated to the B7 Escort Group (**HMS Chelmer** S.O.) and sailed with them on the 8th February with convoy ON 223 (54 ships). She remained with that Group on trans - Atlantic convoy duty until April 1944 when she was allocated to the B4 Escort Group escorting convoys to and from Gibraltar. Early in September 1944 the 30th

Escort Group was formed out of the B4 Escort Group. The 30th Escort Group was one of two single class Escort Groups comprising Castle Class Corvettes and employed on anti submarine patrols and convoy support duties in the Western Approaches, Western English Channel and the North Sea.

Two days after joining the 30th Escort Group *Portchester Castle* sank *U-484* near Tory Island. This was the first occasion when a U-boat had been sunk entirely by an attack with a ship mounting a single three barrelled Squid unit. Two months later she and other members of the Group sank U-1200 off Cape Clear, Ireland.

HISTORY

06.02.43	Ordered.
17.03.43	Laid down. **Builder**: Hull & Engine - Swan Hunter and Wigham Richardson (Wallsend).
21.06.43	Launched.
08.11.43	Completed. This 8 month building time being one of the fastest for her class.

WARTIME VOYAGES

Date	ESG	Senior Officer	Convoy	No of Ships	Arrive/ Sail	Location	Notes
10.11.43	Unall				Arv	Tyne	
16.11.43	Unall				Arv	Clyde	
22.11.43	EG B1				Arv	Tobermory	
11.12.43	EG B1				Arv	Londonderry	
18.12.43	EG B1				Arv	Clyde	
25.12.43	EG B1				Arv	Londonderry	
12.01.44	EG B1				Sail	Londonderry	
18.01.44	EG B1				Sail	Londonderry	
20.01.44	EG 15	*Saladin*	HX 274	38		5457N 1201W	ADM 199/315 places *Portchester Castle* on 21 Janaury with SL145/MKS 36 in 15 EG (S.O. *Wren*)
22.01.44					Arv	Londonderry	
23.01.44	EG B1				Sail	Londonderry	
25.01.44	EG B1				Arv	Londonderry	
04.02.44						To St Johns 5332N 1310W	
07.02.44	EG B1	*Chelmer*			Arv	Londonderry	
08.02.44	EG B7	*Chelmer*			Sail	Londonderry	Allocated to B7 Escort Group.(SMO)
09.02.44	EG B7	*Chelmer*	ON 223	54		5545N 1057W	
18.02.44	EG B7	*Chelmer-*	ON 223	55		4355N 5015W	
19.02.44	EG B7	*Chelmer*			Arv	Argentia	
24.02.44	EG B7				Sail	Argentia	
07.03.44	EG B7	*Chelmer*	HX 280	64		5505N 1345W	
09.03.44	EG B7	*Chelmer-*			Arv	Londonderry	
16.03.44	EG B7	*Chelmer*	ON 228	73	Sail	Londonderry	
17.03.44	EG B7	*Chelmer*	ON 228	73		5525N 1101W	SO may have been *Vidette*: Hague lists 70 ships
27.03.44	EG B7	*Vidette*			Arv	Argentia	
31.03.44	EG B7	*Vidette*			Sail	Argentia	
02.04.44	EG B7	*Vidette*	SC 156	59		4515N 4925W	Hague lists 40 ships
08.04.44	EG B7	*Vidette*	SC 156	54		4820N 2730W	Hague lists 40 ships
12.04.44-	EG B7	*Vidette*			Arv	Londonderry	
24.04.44	EG B4	*Helmsdale*			Sail	Londonderry	
27.04.44	EG B4	*Helmsdale*			Sail	Clyde	
01.05.44	EG B4	*Helmsdale*			Sail	Greenock	
03.05.44	EG B4	*Helmsdale*	OS 76/ KMS 50	35	Sail	Londonderry	Convoy narrowly averted collision with a small USA convoy GK2 in thick fog. (SMO)

Date	ESG	Senior Officer	Convoy	No of Ships	Arrive/ Sail	Location	Notes
05.05.44	EG B4	*Helmsdale*	OS 76/ KMS 50	35		5415N 1245W	Gale force head winds encountered (217/364)
15.05.44	EG B4	*Helmsdale*	OS 76/ KMS 50	35	Arv	Gibraltar	
20.05.44	EG B4	*Helmsdale*	SL 158/ MKS 49	31	Sail	Gibraltar	
21.05.44	EG B4	*Helmsdale*	MKS 49	29		3530N 0632W	
29.05.44	EG B4	*Helmsdale*	SL 158/ MKS 49	51		4730N 2150W	
01.06.44	EG B4	*Helmsdale*	SL 158/ MKS 49	47		5255N 1518W	
03.06.44	EG B4	*Helmsdale*	SL 158/ MKS 49	47	Arv	Londonderry	
12.06.44	EG B4	*Helmsdale*	OS 80/ KMS 54	29	Sail	Londonderry	
13.06.44	EG B4	*Helmsdale*	OS 80/ KMS 54	29		5540N 0758W	
24.06.44	EG B4	*Helmsdale*	OS 80/ KMS 54	29	Arv	Gibraltar	
29.06.44	EG B4	*Helmsdale*	SL 162/ MKS 53	36	Sail	Gibraltar	Night attack by moonlight possibly using Glider Bombs - no casualties, Convoy protected by smoke screen.
30.06.44	EG B4	*Helmsdale*	SL 162/ MKS 53	36		3535N 0659W	
11.07.44	EG B4	*Helmsdale*	SL 162/ MKS 53	36	Arv	Londonderry	Convoy subjected to unsuccessful air attack 3rd July. Believed glider bombs used.
22.07.44	EG B4	*Helmsdale*	OS 84/ KMS 58	24	Sail	Londonderry	
26.07.44	EG B4	*Helmsdale*	OS 84/ KMS 58	27		4901N 1935W	Hague gives 24 ships
02.08.44	EG B4	*Helmsdale*	OS 84 KMS 58	35	Arv	Gibraltar	
08.08.44	EG B4	*Helmsdale*	SL 166/ MKS 57	16	Sail	Gibraltar	
09.08.44	EG B4	*Helmsdale*	SL 166/ MKS 57	16		3541N 0652W	
18.08.44					Arv	Londonderry	For boiler cleaning
25.08.44	EG B4	*Helmsdale*				At Londonderry	Boiler clean
29.08.44	EG B4	*Helmsdale*			Sail	Londonderry	

Date	ESG	Senior Officer	Convoy	No of Ships	Arrive/ Sail	Location	Notes
03.09.44	30 EG	*Pevensey Castle*			Sail	Londonderry	In support of HXF 305 then ONF352 (B2 EG). Attacked and sank U-boat 9th Sept:
14.09.44	30 EG	*Pevensey Castle*	ONF 252		Sail	Londonderry	Operating under Force 33
23.09.44	30 EG	*Pevensey Castle*			Arv	Londonderry	
03.10.44	30 EG	*Pevensey Castle*			Arv	Larne	Left Londonderry the same day CinC WA 041208.10. On completion of Group training EG is to be sailed to top up with fuel at Moville thence to join Force 33 for operation CW.
05.10.44	30 EG	*Pevensey Castle*			Sail	Londonderry	
11.10.44	30 EG	*Pevensey Castle*				NW Approaches	On patrol
15.10.44	30 EG	*Pevensey Castle*				At Sea	
18.10.44	30 EG	*Pevensey Castle*			Arv	Londonderry	
21.10.44	30 EG	*Pevensey Castle*			Sail	Londonderry	Patrol NW Approaches
28.10.44	30 EG	*Pevensey Castle*			Arv	Londonderry	
06.11.44	30 EG	*Pevensey Castle*				Londonderry	
09.11.44	30 EG	*Pevensey Castle*			Sail	Londonderry	To patrol NW Approaches.
19.11.44	30 EG	*Pevensey Castle*			Arv	Londonderry	11th Nov: Group attack U-boat and hold contact for three days Group attacked suspected U-boat on 26 Nov & held contact for 73 hrs. Then supported passage of HX 321 & relieved 2nd EG on 5th Dec. Group returned to Londonderry
21.11.44	30 EG	*Pevensey Castle*			Sail	Londonderry	Patrol in area 52N 11W.
28.11.44	30 EG	*Pevensey Castle*				5110N 0945W	On Patrol
06.12.44	30 EG	*Pevensey Castle*			Arv	Londonderry	
15.12.44	30 EG	*Pevensey Castle*			Arv	Campbeltown	Group arrived for exercises, these interrupted by gales until 17th. Group proceeded to sea in afternoon & exercised with

Date	ESG	Senior Officer	Convoy	No of Ships	Arrive/ Sail	Location	Notes
							submarine before proceeding to Belfast Lough.
17.12.44	30 EG	*Pevensey Castle*			Sail	Campbeltown	
18.12.44	30 EG	*Pevensey Castle*			Sail	Belfast	30 EG to patrol in the South West Approaches. On 20th Dec Group came under the command of CinC Plymouth & patrol area moved to the entrance of English Channel, and later to areas North of Cherbourg Peninsular
18.12.44	30 EG	*Pevensey Castle*			Arv	Belfast	
27.12.44	30 EG	*Pevensey Castle*			Arv	Cardiff	F.O.I.C. Cardiff. 0111210.1 *PC* taken in hand C.H. Bailry Hills 01 1045 CD 20th Feb revised CP March 26th. Refit at Cardiff. Fitted with Type 277 Radar during this refit.
29.12.44	30 EG	*Pevensey Castle*					Cardiff-AM 151249.12 to CinC WA *PC* can be T.I.H. for refit 27.12 at Cardiff.
08.01.45	30 EG	*Pevensey Castle*					S of Needles-On Patrol Ship returned to Londonderry 6th Dec & apparently joined Group at Campbeltown
15.01.45	31 EG	*Berkeley Castle*				Off Holyhead	On Patrol
02.02.45					Sail	Londonderry	
03.03.45	30 EG	*Pevensey Castle*				Cardiff	Refit complete 19 March
24.03.45	30 EG	*Pevensey Castle*			Arv	Loch Alsh	Arrival date assumed.
24.03.45	30 EG	*Pevensey Castle*			Sail	Cardiff	
30.03.45	30 EG	*Pevensey Castle*			Sail	Loch Alsh	
03.04.45	30 EG	*Pevensey Castle*				On passage	To Londonderry
07.04.45	30 EG	*Pevensey Castle*			Arv	Londonderry	
08.04.45	30 EG	*Pevensey Castle*			Arv	Scapa Flow	Ship rejoined 30 EG.
10.04.45	30 EG	*Pevensey Castle*			Sail	Scapa Flow	
12.04.45	30 EG	*Pevensey Castle*			Arv	Scapa Flow	

Date	ESG	Senior Officer	Convoy	No of Ships	Arrive/ Sail	Location	Notes
14.04.45	30 EG	*Pevensey Castle*			Sail	Clyde	Sailed with 1st Division of 30 EG (*Pevensey Castle*, *Launceston Castle*, *Portchester Castle*)
18.04.45	30 EG	*Pevensey Castle*			Arv	Scapa Flow	
20.04.45	30 EG	*Pevensey Castle*			Sail	Scapa Flow	To patrol off Cape Wrath before proceeding to Londonderry.
20.04.45	30 EG	*Pevensey Castle*			Sail	Scapa Flow	
24.04.45	30 EG	*Pevensey Castle*			Arv	Londonderry	
04.05.45	30 EG	*Portchester Castle*			Sail	Londonderry	SO of EG transferred to *Portchester Castle*
06.05.45	30 EG	*Pevensey Castle*			Arv	Londonderry	
07.05.45	30 EG	*Pevensey Castle*			Sail	Londonderry	
07.05.45	30 EG	*Pevensey Castle*			Sail	Londonderry	Group proceeded to become Force 33 in support of RA 66 until 8th. Boarded the surrendered U-boat *U- 956* on 11th, subsequently patrolling the 'Blue Route'
17.05.45	30 EG	*Pevensey Castle*			Arv	Londonderry	
17.05.45	30 EG	*Pevensey Castle*			Arv	Londonderry	
23.05.45	30 EG	*Pevensey Castle*			Sail	Londonderry	Escorted U-boats to Loch Alsh on 21st returning to Loch Eriboll the same day. Proceeded to Scapa Flow on 24th.
23.05.45	30 EG	*Pevensey Castle*			Sail	Londonderry	
25.05.45	30 EG	*Pevensey Castle*			Arv	Scapa Flow	
25.05.45	30 EG	*Pevensey Castle*			Sail	Scapa Flow	
27.05.45	30 EG	*Pevensey Castle*			Arv	Bergen	
31.05.45	30 EG	*Pevensey Castle*			Arv	Scapa Flow	Ships open to the public on 27th. Group represented at ceremony of returning Bergen to its rightful owners. Group escorted 13 U-boats to the UK leaving Bergen 30.05.45.
01.06.45	30 EG	*Pevensey Castle*			Sail	Scapa Flow	
02.06.45	30 EG	*Pevensey Castle*			Arv	Londonderry	
23.06.45	F.O.C.W.A.F				Sail	Londonderry	

Date	ESG	Senior Officer	Convoy	No of Ships	Arrive/ Sail	Location	Notes
06.07.45					Arv	Freetown	Assumed date of arrival.
09.07.45					Sail	Freetown	
13.08.45					Arv	Dakar	
21.08.45					Sail	Dakar	*PC* 250630/8 Have arrived to relieve *Pevensey Castle* from ASR 22
18.09.45					Arv	Freetown	
01.10.45					Sail	Freetown	
08.10.45					Arv	Gibraltar	
22.10.45					Sail	Gibraltar	
05.11.45					Arv	Gibraltar	F.O.G.M.A. 181249A.11 Intend to sail *PC* at 1900A. to relieve *St Brides Bay* on AS To patrol off Cape Wrath before proceeding to Londonderry. ASR Station 19
04.12.45					Arv	Gibraltar	F.O..G.M.A. *PC* to be relieved by *Start Bay* ETA Gibraltar 24.12.
11.12.45					Sail	Gibraltar	
19.12.45					Arv	Gibraltar	
27.12.45					Sail	Gibraltar	To relieve *Start Bay* on ASR 20.
07.01.46					Arv	Gibraltar	
16.01.46					Sail	Gibraltar	F.O.G.M. 161219A OC ETD 1800.16.1 to Chatham ETA 21.1. CinC Nore 191523.1 *PC* to proceed direct to Harwich
21.01.46					Arv	Harwich	AM 21 1354.1 *PC* is to reduce to Cat B Reserve at Harwich.
31.08.48		Refit on the Tyne.					
April 1951		Taken in hand for service.					
15.05.51		Recommissioned and allocated to 2nd Training Squadron, Portland for Anti submarine warfare and general seamanship training.					
June 1956		Relieved by new Type 14 Frigate, *HMS Keppel* and laid up.					
1958		Sold to West of Scotland Shipbreaking, Broke adrift from tug *Brigadier* night 15-16 May.					
17.05.58		Arrived Troon for scrapping.					

HMS Portchester Castle in June 1952.　　　　　　　　　(*Portsmouth Royal Naval Museum*)

THE SINKING OF U-484

On 9 September 1944 **Portchester Castle** was part of Force 33 screening convoy ONF 305. Other escorts included **HM Ships Helmsdale** (SO B4 EG), **Inman**, **Braithwaite**, **Pevensey Castle**, **Portchester Castle** and **Launceston Castle**. SO B4 being in charge of these ships supporting the convoy, whilst S.O. B2 was in command of the convoy's close escort. Contact was made with a U-Boat and **Portchester Castle** attacked at 0753Z. **U-484** surfaced immediately after this attack, dead in the centre of the water disturbed by the Squid bomb's explosions. Fire was opened immediately with the 4-inch and Oerlikons, but the range was too short for the 4-inch which could not be depressed enough. As the U-Boat came level depth charges were launched from the starboard thrower. The U-Boat then appeared to roll over and sink with no apparent forward movement. A second attack was made thirty minutes later but this was believed to have been on a non-sub. **Portchester Castle** attacked a third time. This was thought to have to have been well conducted and most accurate and was considered to have destroyed the U-Boat.

Commenting on this action the U-boat Assessment Committee wrote:

> *"The contact attacked at 0824 (**Portchester Castle**'s third attack) is considered "non-sub". When **Helmsdale** regained the contact lost by **Portchester Castle**, the decision to refrain from attacking and to direct the Squid fitted ship is considered entirely correct and showed good team-work. **Portchester Castle**'s subsequent Squid attack was well conducted and most accurate and is considered to have destroyed the U-boat. After this, an additional slight under-water explosion, followed five minutes later by a heavy under-water explosion, together with wreckage later observed on the surface, is considered as sufficient evidence of destruction; the hunt is accordingly assessed U-boat known sunk."*

This was the first time that a U-Boat had been destroyed solely by a Castle class corvette.

SINKING OF U-1200

Portchester Castle was involved in a supporting role in this action which is described in some detail under the heading *Launceston Castle* .

Summaries of the Reports of Proceedings for B4 and 30 Escort Groups are provided later in this volume.

Portchester Castle underwent a lengthy refit from 1st January to 1st May 1945 and saw no further action. She was allocated to the West Africa Command in mid June 1945 for Air Sea Rescue duties and served there until 1st October 1945, when she left for Gibraltar to take up similar duties. She proceeded to Harwich early in 1946 where she was laid up in reserve.

When at Freetown, in 1945, *Portchester Castle* was involved with the sinking of the liner *Edinburgh Castle* which had been used as a base ship there. To avoid the cost of towing the ship back to the UK she was taken 60 miles out to sea and sunk by gunfire and depth charges. Ships involved in this task were the armed trawler *Cape Warwick*, *Portchester Castle* and *Lancaster Castle*.

In April 1951 *Portchester Castle* was prepared for service and re-commissioned on the 15 May 1951. She was allocated to the 2nd Training Squadron. Whilst at Portland she was chosen to portray the fictional frigate *HMS Saltash Castle* in the film *The Cruel Sea*. The ships pennant number, F 362, continued to be used during the film. The filming was done at Portland and in the Channel. At one time several of the ship's company were sent over the side, covered in grease, to represent shipwrecked survivors.

The ship's bell now hangs in Cobham Hall, the Scout Hut in White Lane, Portchester.

HMS RUSHEN CASTLE

Battle Honours
Atlantic 1944-45

HMS Rushen Castle on 17 February 1944.   (MoD/Crown Copyright)

After completing working up at Tobermory *Rushen Castle* was allocated to B2 Escort Group engaged on escorting the Gibraltar convoys. In September 1944 B2 EG was disbanded and *Rushen Castle* became the Senior Officer of the newly constituted B21 Escort Group. This group too was disbanded in late December 1945 and *Rushen Castle* was allocated to the Liverpool Escort Pool. She continued in the role of Senior Officer of the much reduced escort size of the convoys between the UK and Gibraltar until the end of the war in Europe. She was then allocated to the Plymouth Command for Air Sea Rescue duties.

From October 1945 to January 1946 she was under repair at Devonport, prior to being reduced to reserve Category B. In February 1948 it was proposed to transfer her with other Castle Class ships to the Royal New Zealand Navy. However, they opted for the larger Loch Class frigates. *Rushen Castle* was accordingly reduced to Category B2 reserve at Devonport.

In September 1956 the ship was offered to the Air Ministry for conversion to a weather ship and finally sold for this purpose on 23 September 1960. She was converted at Blyth and started operating as a weather ship in November 1961 under the name *Weather Surveyor*. The *Weather Surveyor* continued in service as a weather ship until the middle of 1970. In July 1977 she was sold for use as a salvage ship at Portsmouth From 1980 to 1983 she was registered under the ownership of Pounds Marine Shipping Co: In 1983 her entry was stamped "Delete Class" with the remark "Broken up 1982".

HISTORY

06.02.43	Ordered.
08.04.43	Laid down: **Builder**: Hull & Engine - Swan Hunter and Wigham Richardson (Wallsend).
16.07.43	Launched.
24.02.44	Completed.

WARTIME VOYAGES

Date	ESG	Senior Officer	Convoy	No of Ships	Arrive/ Sail	Location	Notes
27.02.44	EG B2	*Hesperus*			Sail	Tyne	
29.02.44	EG B2	*Hesperus*			Arv	Tobermory	Having left Tyne the same day.
16.03.44					Sail	Tobermory	Allocated to B2 Escort Group
17.03.44	EG B2	*Hesperus*			Arv	Liverpool	
24.03.44	EG B2	*Hesperus*			Arv	Liverpool	
27.03.44	EG B2	*Hesperus*			Sail	Liverpool	
28.03.44	EG B2	*Hesperus*			Arv	Clyde-	
28.03.44	EG B2	*Hesperus*			Sail	Clyde	
29.03.44	EG B2	*Hesperus*			Arv	Londonderry	
30.03.44	EG B2	*Hesperus*			Arv	Falmouth	
30.03.44	EG B2	*Hesperus*			Sail	Londonderry	
30.03.44	EG B2	*Hesperus*			Sail	Clyde	
01.04.44					Sail	Falmouth	
03.04.44	EG B2	*Hesperus*			Arv	Liverpool	
10.04.44	EG B2	*Hesperus*			Sail	Liverpool	
21.04.44	EG B2	*Hesperus*			Arv	Londonderry	
24.04.44	EG B2	*Hesperus*	OS75/ KMS 49	23	Sail	Londonderry	
25.04.44	EG B2	*Hesperus*	OS 75/ KMS 49	23		5556N 1010W	
27.04.44	EG B2	*Hesperus*	OS 75/ KMS 49	23		5224N 1558W	
01.05.44	EG B2	*Hesperus*	OS 75/ KMS 49	23		4021N 1935W	
06.05.44	EG B2	*Hesperus*	OS 75/ KMS 49	23	Arv	Gibraltar	
10.05.44	EG B2	*Hesperus*	MKS 48	26	Sail	Gibraltar	
12.05.44	EG B2	*Hesperus*	MKS 48	32		3530N 1020W	26 ships according to Hague
15.05.44	EG B2	*Hesperus*	SL 157/ MKS 48	49		4125N 1830W	
21.05.44	EG B2	*Hesperus*	SL157/ MKS 48	49	Arv	Liverpool	

Date	ESG	Senior Officer	Convoy	No of Ships	Arrive/ Sail	Location	Notes
31.05.44	EG B2	*Hesperus*			Arv	Londonderry	
03.06.44	EG B2	*Hesperus*			Sail	Londonderry	
14.06.44	EG B2	*Hesperus*	OS 79/ KMS 53	27	Arv	Gibraltar	
20.06.44	EG B2	*Hesperus*	MKS 52	19	Sail	Gibraltar	Carrying 40 boxes of bullion: N Pickford 1999. Hague records 17 ships
21.06.44	EG B2	*Hesperus*	MKS 52	19		3525N 0830W	
23.06.44	EG B2	*Hesperus*	SL 161/ MKS 52	45		3620N 1535W	Hague records 41 ships
30.06.44	EG B2	*Hesperus*	SL 161/ MKS 52	44		5430N 1101W	
02.07.44	EG B2	*Hesperus*	SL 161/ MKS 52	44	Arv	Londonderry	
13.07.44	EG B2	*Hesperus*	OS 83/ KMS 57	29	Sail	Liverpool	
13.07.44	EG B2	*Hesperus*	OS 83/ KMS 57	29	Sail	Liverpool	
14.07.44	EG B2	*Hesperus-*	OS 83/ KMS 57	32		5557N 0945W	Hague gives 29 ships
22.07.44	EG B2	*Hesperus*	OS 83/ KMS 57	31		3810N 1750W	
25.07.44	EG B2	*Hesperus*	OS 83/ KMS 57	31	Arv	Gibraltar	
29.07.44	EG B2	*Hesperus*	MKS 56	18	Sail	Algiers	
30.07.44	EG B2	*Hesperus*	SL 165/ MKS 56	39	Sail	Gibraltar	Carrying 15 boxes of bullion: N Pickford 1999; Hague gives 35 ships
05.08.44	EG B2	*Hesperus*	SL 165/ MKS 56	39		4615N 1824W	
07.08.44	EG B2	*Hesperus*	SL165/ MKS 56	32		5152N 1540W	
08.08.44	EG B2	*Hesperus*	SL 165/ MKS 56	37		5522N 0830W	
09.08.44	EG B2	*Hesperus*			Arv	Liverpool	
18.08.44					Sail	Liverpool	
22.08.44	EG B2	*Hesperus*			Arv	Belfast	
24.08.44	EG B2	*Hesperus*	OS 87/ KMS 61	34	Sail	Belfast	
01.09.44	EG B2	*Hesperus*	OS 87/ KMS 61	36		3850N 1156W	
04.09.44	EG B21	*Hesperus*	OS 87/ KMS 61	36	Arv	Gibraltar	

Date	ESG	Senior Officer	Convoy	No of Ships	Arrive/ Sail	Location	Notes
09.09.44	EG B21	*Hesperus*	MKS 50	23	Sail	Gibraltar	
10.09.44	EG B21	*Hesperus*	MKS 50	23		3554N 0840W	
16.09.44	EG B21	*Hesperus*	SL 169/ MKS 60	20		Hartland Point	
17.09.44	EG B21	*Hesperus*			Arv	Liverpool	
26.09.44	EG B21	*Rushen Castle*	OS 90/ KMS 64	30	Sail	Milford Haven	
29.09.44		*Rushen Castle*	OS 90/ KMS 64	33		4230N 1201W	
02.10.44	EG B21	*Rushen Castle*	OS 90/ KMS 64	30	Arv	Gibraltar	
08.10.44	EG B21	*Rushen Castle*	SL 172/ MKS 63	23	Sail	Gibraltar	
11.10.44	EG B21	*Rushen Castle*	SL 172/ MKS 63	24		3(?) 4N 1030W	
16.10.44	EG B21	*Rushen Castle*	SL 172/ MKS 63	23	Arv	Liverpool	
22.10.44	EG B21	*Rushen Castle*			Arv	Campbeltown	
24.10.44	EG B21	*Rushen Castle*	OS 93/ KMS 67	30	Sail	Belfast	
27.10.44	EG B21	*Rushen Castle*			Arv	Liverpool	
30.10.44	EG B21	*Rushen Castle*	OS 93/ KMS 67	30		3950N 1201W	
02.11.44	EG B21	*Rushen Castle*	OS 93/ KMS 67	30	Arv	Gibraltar	
07.11.44	EG B21	*Rushen Castle*	(SL 175/ MKS 66)	38	Sail	Gibraltar	
15.11.44	EG B21	*Rushen Castle*	(SL 175/ MKS 66)	38	Arv	Liverpool	
20.11.44	EG B21	*Rushen Castle*				Liverpool-	Boiler clean ready 22 Nov
23.11.44	EG B21	*Rushen Castle*	OS96/ KMS70	40	Sail	Liverpool	
30.11.44	EG B21	*Rushen Castle*	OS 96/ KMS70	40	Arv	Gibraltar	
05.12.44	EG B21	*Rushen Castle*	SL 178/ MKS 69	39	Sail	Gibraltar	Bad weather reduced convoy speed at times to 3.5 - 4.0 knots.
15.12.44	B 21	*Rushen Castle*	SL 178/ MKS 69	61	Arv	Liverpool	
22.12.44					Sail	Liverpool	
23.12.44	LEP				Sail	Belfast	

Date	ESG	Senior Officer	Convoy	No of Ships	Arrive/ Sail	Location	Notes
23.12.44					Arv	Belfast	Capt: D Liverpool. *RC* has leaking keel request she may be T.I.H. at Belfast
24.12.44					Sail	Belfast	
30.12.44					Arv	Liverpool	
31.12.44					Arv	Belfast	
31.12.44	LEP				Arv	Belfast	
31.12.44					Sail	Liverpool	
02.01.45	LEP				Sail	Belfast	
03.01.45					Sail	Belfast	
08.01.45		*Rushen Castle*	KMS 76	16		3946N 1154W	
11.01.45	LEP	*Rushen Castle*	KMS 76	16	Arv	Gibraltar	

*A single depth charge dropped by **HMS Rushen Castle**. This was frequently done as a 'scaring' charge to encourage the U-Boat to remain submerged. The cannister above the depth charge rail is a smoke float. The Foxer displacers can be seen to the right of the watching sailors. (CCC(F)A Archives)*

Date	ESG	Senior Officer	Convoy	No of Ships	Arrive/ Sail	Location	Notes
15.01.45	LEP	*Rushen Castle*	MKS 77	32	Sail	Gibraltar	
23.01.45	LEP	*Rushen Castle*	MKS 77	32	Arv	Clyde	
01.02.45	LEP				Sail	Liverpool	
07.02.45	LEP				Arv	Liverpool	
11.02.45	LEP	*Rushen Castle*	KMS 84	21	Sail	Liverpool	
19.02.45	LEP	*Rushen Castle*	KMS 84	21	Arv	Gibraltar	
24.02.45	LEP	*Rushen Castle*	MKS 85	23	Sail	Gibraltar	
03.03.45	LEP	*Rushen Castle*	MKS 85	23	Arv	Liverpool	
13.03.45	LEP				Sail	Liverpool	
19.03.45	LEP				Arv	Liverpool	
23.03.45					Sail	Liverpool	
29.03.45					Arv	Liverpool	
29.03.45	LEP				Arv	Liverpool	
02.04.45	LEP	*Rushen Castle*	OS 120/ KMS 94	21	Sail	Liverpool	
10.04.45	LEP	*Rushen Castle*	OS 120/ KMS 94		Arv	Gibraltar	
15.04.45	LEP	*Rushen Castle*	MKS 95	22	Sail	Gibraltar	
23.04.45		*Rushen Castle*	MKS 95	22	Arv	Liverpool	
02.05.45	LEP	*Rushen Castle*	OS 126/ KMS 100		Sail	Liverpool	
02.05.45	LEP				Arv	Liverpool	
08.05.45	LEP	*Rushen Castle*	MKS 98	15	Arv	Liverpool	Transferred to MKS 98 5th May escorted by *Lavander*. *RC* assumed duty of S.O. EG 31 also in support. Convoy then had 11 escorts
11.05.45					Sail	Liverpool	
12.05.45	LEP				Arv	Cardiff	
17.05.45	LEP				Arv	Liverpool	
22.05.45	LEP				Sail	Liverpool	
27.05.45	LEP				Arv	Liverpool	
25.06.45	W.A					Liverpool	Repairs complete 29 June
10.07.45					Sail	Liverpool	
11.07.45					Arv	Plymouth	
06.08.45					Arv	Plymouth	
19.08.45					Sail	Plymouth	
07.10.45					Sail	Plymouth	
19.10.45					Arv	Plymouth	
20.10.45					Arv	Plymouth	
31.01.46					Sail	Plymouth	

13.07..46	Reserve at Devonport category B.
24.09.47	Taken in hand for docking; completing 02.10.47.
28.07.48	Reduced to reserve Category B2.
23.09.60	Sold to Air ministry for conversion to a weather ship and left Cardiff under tow the same day for Blyth.
Nov 1961	Conversion completed and re-named *Weather Surveyor*.
Jul 1977	Sold for use as a salvage vessel at Portsmouth.
1982	Scrapped.

ODD ODES FROM RUSHEN CASTLE

The following 'Odes' were provided by Colin Warwick one time Senior Officer of the B2 Escort Group and Commanding Officer of the **Rushen Castle**. In explanation he wrote:

"As to S.R.E this would refer to the internal communication system for which there was a microphone on the bridge. Lt Alan Weeks RNR was the navigator and fond of using it.
In regard to A.S.C.O. this I feel fairly stood for Lt. Billany RNVR as the A/S Control Officer. The poet would have been in signals or navigation".

Odd Ode Number One   ***The Sea***

In my Crystal ball appears to be
A little ship upon the sea,
With mountainous waves she has to 'wrassle'
Ah hah, it is the **Rushen Castle**.

Oh what hell tis to be sick
On this uproarious Atlantic,
When one could be quite pleasantly chokker
Midst the dust and dirt of Gladstone Docker

But those memories live on,
"Canada One, and Huskisson".
And a stoker P.O. in the depths of gloom
Thinking of ivy and her blue room.

Dont despair, alas alack,
Those happy days will soon be back,
And in the meantime everyone
Be prepared to bash the Hun.
Pull up your socks with one big heave,
If we're bloody lucky we may get leave.

Odd Ode Number Two

Clarabelle

Here is the story of Clarabelle Cat
Who thought she had the world off pat.
She went ashore on the rock of Gibraltar,
Met a handsome tom by the name of Walter.

'Walters' eyes began to glint,
She comes from a Castle, prefixed Flint.
He did his worst and left her blushin'
So she quit the Flint and came to Rushen.

She stepped aboard -Oh what, a thrill,
First person she saw, Petty Officer Gill,
Somewhat distracted with oil and water,
Looked at her and thought he oughter
Put her in Reggie Parsons Locker,
A devilish plan: the rotten shocker.

But Clarabelle, she wa'nt waitin'
She went to the locker of Tubby Layton,
Who took it as an awful shock
And thrust the cat on Young Enoch.

The Withington Wonder stood in surprise
With gaping mouth and popping eyes.
And when at last she started to fidget
Enoch called 'Radar - Forebridge'.

The Officer of the Watch, the Navigator,
Until then an amused spectator,
Surveyed Flint's Clarabelle. So fair,
Grabbed S.P.E. - Said 'D'Ye hear There'.
What I want to know is are you single?
If you are then the midwife shall be Dingle.

But Dingle gave an awful look
And said I've mislaid my Pay Book.
I really cannot tend this lady.
I suggest Ordinary Seaman Kennedy!

But Kennedy was not so sweet
His thoughts were all for Sauchiehall Street.
And so it went on 'Hey, not too roughly'
Until it lapsed on Steward Tuffley.

Who took one look and cried "Hong, Hong"
And soon she reached the Ships Cook, Strong
Remembering our last poor little doggie,
Said "My dear, you'll make a wonderful oggie!"

Oh Clarabelle, don't be much longer,
Or you'll find that Strong is very much stronger.
The A.S.C.O has bet a plumber,
As to the date of birth ,and the number.
So come on cat, and do not stint,
This is the Rushen, not the Flint.
You may rest assured, they will be fed,
So don't have the bastards on my bed.

Odd Ode Number Three   ***The Hopeful Plumbers***

Oh hopefull plumbers, I agree,
This is the best ships Company
Of any escort in B Two,
And here I say "Just thanks to you."

But as for rum, it is a sin,
The crystal ball only drinks gin.
So if you want to rot your socks on,
Make applications through the Cox'on

Odd Odc Numbcr Four   ***The Canteen Manager***

In future, Joe, I'll smile and say,
Good morning to you, its such a fine day.
You've a worthy stock of all good things,
You probably sell these non-sub pings.

The service is fine without a doubt,
And much as I hate to put you out
Please don't let sailing the Canteen catch
Without a Masters Safety Match.
Cos cigarettes without ignition
Might just as well be in the Cats condition!

Odd Ode Number Five

Oiling at Sea

I think of all the evolutions
Oil at sea has most confusions
With buoyant hose and steadying lines
And many other devilish signs.
I do admire the gallant buffer,

At slinging the hook he is no duffer.
Rivalled only by one for his audacity;
You know who I mean; young man Cassidy!

Killick Miller and his boys,
Heaving in; lifes full of joys.
2.4.6. ; no one abide;
Party ended on its backside!
Leapt to its feet with, sheepish grins.
Much too late; we'd seen their sins.

Then there was the Gunners Mate,
A soul no one could emulate.
Stead close to the barrel when taking, up slackers;
Ropes end slipped; hit G.I .in the 'worst spot possible!'

And so we've done it once again.
Water, sweat, oil fuel and pain
There's room for improvement; It must be found,
Cos we're bound to do it homeward bound.

HMS TINTAGEL CASTLE

Battle Honours
Atlantic 1944-45

HMS Tintagel Castle in 1944.   *(MoD/Crown Copyright)*

Tintagel Castle was ordered as part of the second batch of Castle Class Corvettes. She was laid down at the Ailsa Ship Building Company's yard at Troon at the end of April 1943. She took a year to build.

On completion of working up she was allocated to the B3 Escort Group escorting convoys to and from Gibraltar. She was transferred to the B1 Escort Group in September 1944 and remained with that group on mid ocean trans-Atlantic escort duty for the remainder of the war in Europe. Whilst with both groups she, at times, carried the Senior Officer when the Senior Officer's ship was not available.

On 10 April 1945 she, together with the escort Destroyer *Vanquisher* sank *U-878* to the south of Ireland.

HISTORY

23.01.43	Ordered.
29.04.43	Laid down: **Builder**: Hull & Engine - Ailsa (Troon).
13.12.43	Launched.
07.04.44	Completed.

WARTIME VOYAGES

Date	ESG	Senior Officer	Convoy	No of Ships	Arrive/ Sail	Location	Notes
21.04.44	EG B4	*Helmsdale*			Arv	Tobermory	
28.04.44	EG B4	*Helmsdale*			Sail	Tobermory	
05.05.44	EG B3	*Towy*			Sail	Tobermory	
07.05.44	EG B3	*Towy*			Arv	Greenock	
15.05.44	EG B3	*Towy*	OS 77/ KMS 51	33		5557N 0935W	
21.05.44	EG B3	*Towy*	OS 77/ KMS 51	33		3808N 1857W	
25.05.44	EG B3	*Towy*	OS 77/ KMS 51		Arv	Gibraltar	
27.05.44		*Leith*	OS 77/ KMS 51	22		2715N 1420W	
30.05.44	EG B3	*Towy*	SL 159/ MKS 50	33	Sail	Gibraltar	
31.05.44	EG B3	*Towy*	SL 159/ MKS 50	35		3550N0630W	
01.06.44	EG B3	*Towy*	SL 159/ MKS 50	43		3530N 1025W	
10.06.44	EG B3	*Towy*			Arv	Clyde	
16.06.44	EG B3	*Towy*				At Clyde	Repairs
19.06.44					Sail	Clyde	
23.06.44	EG B3	*Towy*	OS 81/ KMS 55		Sail	Londonderry	Detached to escort oiler *Scottish American* to the convoy; rejoined 27.06.44
26.06.44	EG B3	*Towy*	OS 81/ MKS 55	34		Not Given	
04.07.44	EG B3	*Towy*	OS 81/ MKS 55	33	Arv	Gibraltar	
10.07.44	EG B3	*Towy*	SL 163/ MKS 54	42	Sail	Gibraltar	
11.07.44	EG B3	*Towy*	SL 163/ MKS 54	42		3535N 0730W	
21.07.44	EG B3	*Towy*	SL 163/ MKS 54	42	Arv	Clyde	
02.08.44	EG B3*	*Tintagel Castle*	OS 85/ KMS 59	34	Sail	Londonderry	Having left Clyde and arrived Londonderry the day before. (SMO)
03.08.44	EG B3	*Tintagel Castle*	OS 85/ KMS 59	34		5528N 1107W	
13.08.44	EG B3	*Tintagel Castle*	OS 85/ KMS 59	34	Arv	Gibraltar	
19.08.44	EG B3	*Tintagel Castle*	SL 167/ MKS58	36	Sail	Gibraltar	

Date	ESG	Senior Officer	Convoy	No of Ships	Arrive/ Sail	Location	Notes
27.08.44	EG B3	*Tintagel Castle*	SL 167/ MKS58	33		5009N 0652W	Hague gives 29 ships
30.08.44	EG B3	*Tintagel Castle*	SL 167/ MKS58	33	Arv	Clyde	
07.09.44	EG B1	*Chelmer*			Arv	Londonderry	
12.09.44	EG B1	*Chelmer*			Arv	Larne	
16.09.44	EG B1	*Inman*	SC 158		Sail	Londonderry	
18.09.44	EG B1	*Inman*	ONS 254	84		5540N 1010W	It is probable that the Escort Group was B1 & the SO *Chelmer*
21.09.44	EG B1	*Inman*	ONS 254	83		5132N1602W	Note: change of Group's name in mid-ocean
24.09.44	EG B1	*Chelmer*	ONS 254	83		4650N 2935W	
29.09.44	EG B1	*Chelmer*	ONS 254	83	Arv	St John's	
29.09.44	EG B1	*Chelmer*	ONS 254	83		4601N 5040W	
30.09.44	EG B1	*Chelmer*	ONS 254		Arv	St John's	Different file sources give slightly different arrival dates
06.10.44	EG B1	*Chelmer*	SC 158		Sail	St John's	
07.10.44	EG B1	*Poppy*	SC 158	7		4630N 5059W	St John's Section; left St John's same day
11.10.44	EG B1	*Lotus*	SC 158	75		4710N 3550W	
18.10.44	EG B1	*Chelmer*	SC 158		Arv	Londonderry	
19.10.44	EG B1	*Chelmer*	SC 158		Arv	Londonderry	Uneventful passage
23.10.44	EG B1					At Londonderry	Boiler cleaning.
27.10.44	EG B1					At Londonderry	
29.10.44	EG B1	*Chelmer*	ONS 35		Sail	Londonderry	
29.10.44	EG B1	*Chelmer*	ONS 35		Sail	Larne	
07.11.44	EG B1	*Chelmer*	ONS 35	52		4401N 3709W	
13.11.44	EG B1	*Chelmer*	ONS 35	51	Arv	St John's	
17.11.44	EG B1	*Chelmer*	HX 320		Sail	St John's	*Tintagel Castle* recovers periscope like wooden spar by whaler
30.11.44	EG B1	*Chelmer*	HX 320		Arv	Londonderry	
09.12.44	EG B1				Sail	Belfast	
09.12.44	EG B1	*Tintagel Castle*	ON 271	69		5430N 0540W	Heavy weather encountered 17th & convoy had frontage of 25 miles
12.12.44	EG B1	*Tintagel Castle*	ON 271	70		4902N 1230W	
22.12.44	EG B1	*Tintagel Castle*	ON 271	70	Arv	St John's	
28.12.44	EG B1	*Tintagel Castle*	HX 328	56	Sail	St John's	

Date	ESG	Senior Officer	Convoy	No of Ships	Arrive/ Sail	Location	Notes
01.01.45	EG B1	*Tintagel Castle*	HX 328	55		4710N 3736W	
08.01.45	EG B1	*Tintagel Castle*	HX 328			Carnearvon Bay	*Tintagel Castle* arriving Londonderry the same day
18.01.45	EG B1	*Tintagel Castle*	ON 279	47	Sail	Londonderry	Junction of the various sections of the convoy effected under hazardous conditions in heavy weather
22.01.45	EG B1	*Tintagel Castle*	ON 279	47		4733N 1601W	
29.01.45	EG B1	*Tintagel Castle*	ON 279	46		4425N 4632W	Arriving St John's the same day (SMO)
30.01.45	EG B1	*Tintagel Castle*			Arv	St John's	
06.02.45	EG B1	*Tintagel Castle*	HX 336	48	Sail	St John's	No enemy encountered. Just as well, 6 escorts suffered various breakdowns
16.02.45	EG B1	*Tintagel Castle*	HX 336	48	Arv	Londonderry	Supported by EG 23, EG 19 & EG 31 during NW passage through Irish Sea
25.02.45	EG B1	*Chelmer*	ON 287	93	Sail	Londonderry	Considerable congestion in St Georges Channel because of combination of ON, OS, & KMS convoys.
27.02.45	EG B1	*Chelmer*	ON 287	93	Sail	Milford Haven	*Tintagel Castle* escorting the Milford Haven section in persistent fog
05.03.45	EG B1	*Chelmer*	ON 287	93		At Sea	
09.03.45	EG B1	*Chelmer*	ON 287	93	Arv	St John's	Convoy handed over to W5 on 8th in severe weather
15.03.45	EG B1	*Chelmer*			Sail	St John's	Group evacuated St John's due to threat of ice and proceeded to Argentia
16.03.45	EG B1	*Chelmer*			Arv	Argentia	
18.03.45	EG B1	*Chelmer*	HX 344	71	Sail	Argentia	RV effected with HX 344 in fog.
29.03.45	EG B1	*Chelmer*	HX 344	71	Arv	Londonderry	English Channel section detached in thick fog on 27th March
02.04.45	EG B1					Londonderry	*TC* Ready 6 Apr
08.04.45	EG B1	*Chelmer*	ON 295	96	Sail	Cardiff	Group had sailed the day before, *Tintagel Castle* & *Poppy* having been detached for local escort duties

Date	ESG	Senior Officer	Convoy	No of Ships	Arrive/ Sail	Location	Notes
20.04.45	EG B1	*Chelmer*	ON 295	96	Arv	St John's	*Tintagel Castle* & *Vanquisher* sank *U-878* 10th April
27.04.45	EG B1	*Chelmer*	HX 353		Sail	St John's	The passage was undertaken almost entirely in fog
08.05.45	EG B1	*Chelmer*	HX 352		Arv	Londonderry	
17.05.45	EG B1	*Chelmer*	ON 303	74	Sail	Londonderry	Ships of the EG sailed at various times on May 16th & 17th; *Tintagel Castle* to Clyde
30.05.45	EG B1	*Chelmer*	ON 303	74	Arv	St John's	Convoy encountered icebergs in thick fog on 27th May; Emergency turn resulted in 19 ships damaged by collisions.
04.06.45					Sail	St John's	The B1 EG was disbanded whilst at St John's & *Tintagel Castle* ordered to UK independently
23.06.45					Sail	Londonderry	
25.06.45					Arv	Rosyth	
27.07.45					Sail	Rosyth	
28.07.45					Sail	Humber	
28.07.45					Arv	Humber	
28.07.45					Arv	Humber	
29.07.45					Arv	Rosyth	Having left Humber the day before
19.08.45					Sail	Granton	
21.08.45					Arv	Oslo	
25.08.45					Sail	Oslo	
03.09.45					Sail	Christiansands	
07.09.45					Arv	Sheerness	
26.01.46					Sail	Sheerness	
27.01.46					Arv	Portland	Record ends.

27.01.46 - 06.56	A/S Training duties; Portland Flotilla and the numerous name changes of that unit.
1953	Represented Home Command, Portsmouth at Coronation Fleet Review.
June 1956	Reduction to reserve at Devonport.
August 1956	Paid off and laid up.
1958	Sold to West of Scotland Shipbreaking.
June 1958	For scrapping.

On her final passage from St John's N.F. to the UK and when a few days out from the UK, a U-Boat was encountered flying the black flag of surrender and was escorted towards Londonderry. The U-Boat was ordered to take up a position on the port bow and warned that any deviation from this would result in dire consequences.

An undated picture of **HMS Tintagel Castle**, *probably taken post-war.*   *(Steve Bush Collection)*

During June and July 1945 **Tintagel Castle** spent much of her time at anchor some 50 miles east of Aberdeen and at the western end of the swept channel across the North Sea acting as a radio beacon guiding shipping down the swept channel.

Tintagel Castle's voyage to Norway was in connection with escorting a group of passenger liners conveying the King of Norway's entourage back home. The King and immediate family having already proceeded ahead.

The ship spent several delightful days in Oslo. The ship rang with the sound of children invited aboard by the crew and the NAAFI Canteen was soon denuded of chocolates and other goodies generously given by the lower deck. The Officers had little part in this. F.N. Goodwin's recollection is that it was considered by the crew that the children were not allowed on board. "At that time whenever I ventured below decks there always seemed to be a scuffle of children rapidly disappearing from view, which one pretended not to notice."

From Oslo she steamed through the Norwegian fjords to Tromso to rendezvous with a an old freighter bringing back French POWs from Russia. The ship had no suitable charts and was escorted to Boulounge.

The **Tintagel Castle** escorted 19 convoys comprising 1,076 ships. No ships were lost due to enemy action.

No record of the ship's first voyage with a convoy could be found, thus these highlights of her voyages start with the homeward passage following that first convoy. However, at the conclusion of her first voyage with a convoy it was apparent, as demonstrated by the following account by Lieut. R.V. Dykes DSC RNVR (who at that time was not yet the Executive Officer), there was still lessons to be learnt.

HE MARCHED THEM UP TO THE TOP OF THE HILL AND MARCHED THEM DOWN AGAIN...

Oh what a beautiful morning! Yes indeed it was a beautiful morning in Gib harbour. A clear blue sky with bright sunshine, a slight breeze which did not effect the calm of the harbour water. Silence only broken by the

noise of a motor boat crossing the harbour. Warm and comfortable was the day. Hopefully the beginning of what was to be a perfect day perhaps an afternoon swimming, who knows. 'Twas a Saturday morning, so of course Captains Rounds. A spanking new ship, clean as whistle. All hands clear lower deck - mess decks perfect for Captain's inspection. Mess cutlery neatly laid out on the mess tables, plus all the other gear of kettles, fannies etc. Oiler alongside so there was that acceptable smell of fuel oil about the ship as we oiled.

Captain walks for'ard accompanied by the coxswain's pipe together with Divisional Officers. First stop - lower forward stokers mess deck - starboard side - Captain takes his first few steps down the ladder - stops - seen to bend over to look into the mess and then quietly returns to the deck with his index finger to his lips - hush. Beckons No.1 to do likewise which he does and then returns looking rather shaken and very very angry..

Next I took a look. My, oh my, what do we see? Nothing but a stoker quietly sitting on the hatch cover to a fuel tank intently reading a book whilst all around him was an expanding creeping sea of fuel oil quitely gurgling up through a breathing pipe. I am not sure how he was able to get to dry deck without getting his feet "wet".

No afternoon swim for the stokers mess to be sure because it was their task to clean the entire mess deck and clean it they did.

I am not sure if I displayed some form of amusement at seeing that stoker on his little island, but next morning No.1 detailed me to take the entire stokers mess and march them up to the top of the Rock - and march them down again. It was a hot and exhausting event that Sunday morning and coming down was no better.

Should that stoker be a member of the Association, I think he owes his mates a pint, including ME.

Dick Dykes
Tintagel Castle

CONVOY HX 320 (32 SHIPS) NF TO UK 17TH - 30TH NOVEMBER 1944.

The *Abrial Gibbon* (No 83) created a diversion by reporting sighting a periscope. Three officers including the Master and the watch on deck had seen the periscope. Although B1 seemed to doubt the authenticity of this report an emergency ship-shore was broadcast. In due course ***Tintagel Castle*** recovered an old weighted wooden spar. This was done from the whaler in difficult seas.

Away sea boats Crew

The day was overcast with a strong wind and broken disturbed seas. A merchant ship had reported sighting a periscope and TC was sent to investigate. Sure enough there over on the starboard side was a spar bobbing up and down. The Skipper ordered the sea boat away. Lt. Dykes, the sea boat Officer, viewed the affair with much doubt and apprehension. It was difficult to launch the whaler under those conditions and in the high seas, rowing in unison would not be easy.

During the launching process, the ***Tintagel Castle*** had been turned to give the whaler a lee. This put the spar on the port side, but in the limited visibility this was not noticed by the whaler which gamely set out to starboard away from the ***Tintagel Castle***. By the time this was realised the spar was well astern and to get to it under oars in that sea way would be a long and exhausting effort. The Skipper approached the whaler with the intention of passing a tow line and towing the whaler to the spar. We turned a full circle and closed the whaler. Let Dykes continue in his own words:-

> *"A Seaman crouched astride the forecastle bullring to hand us a line - 'To hand' indeed was very much a feasibility. Being approached bow on, presented us with a towering raking bow one moment and the next, so low in the water that we could have stepped from the whaler onto the forecastle."*

Meanwhile, to F. N.Goodwin, from his position on the compass platform it seemed almost impossible that we could avoid running the whaler down and he started to rehearse in his mind what we would have to do to rescue the whaler crew from the sea. Dykes continued:-

> *"The process of going from high to low presented us in the whaler with the possibility of the rakish bow presenting itself to the side of the whaler as it was a saw- the consequences of which I could plainly see- either being sawn in half down to the keelson or gradually being turned over port side first. With a large degree of strength and certainly urgency, we endeavoured to maintain a small distance of a foot or so from the plunging bow, by pushing ourselves away until we secured the tow line."*
>
> *"Inspite of the numerous expletives and other seaman like words of the whaler crew, by now very wet and chokker, the tow was passed to us and secured to the tabernacle. The tow began. I cannot recall whether we were towed astern of the* **Tintagel Castle** *in her wake or alongside starboard side a matter of an oars length from the ship's side. Although the* **Tintagel Castle** *could not have gone any slower without loosing steerage way, we, in the whaler, felt we were proceeding at a very fast rate. Certainly too good for comfort and with a degree of danger because of the large seas and strong wind."*

Once close to the object the whaler slipped the tow and painfully pulled the remaining short distance by oars. With difficulty the 12 foot 4" x 3" plank was hauled aboard. One end had a metal collar with a swan neck secured to the wood, hence the reason why the plank stood on end in the water, looking, from a distance, like a periscope.

It was a difficult pullback to the ship and even more difficult to secure the falls in that type of seaway. In Dykes' words:-

> *"We eventually came alongside and engaged the falls fore and aft.* **Tintagel Castle** *proceeded to get under way slowly and our troubles began once more. Unfortunately* **Tintagel Castle** *did not roll in the same direction as the swell.* **Tintagel Castle** *would roll to starboard, the sea would roll towards the ship.*

HMS Tintagel Castle's sea boat searching for a 'spar'.   (CCC(F)A Archives)

Gunnery practice. Note the complete absence of anti-flash gear and ear muffs.   (*F.N. Goodwin*)

The whaler would find itself on the crest of the sea, the falls and disengaging gear snatched with a loud bang as if it was all being pulled from the keel of the boat. As the roll to port continued we were inclined to be pulled from the sea and swung towards the ship's side. Then the ship would right itself and start to roll back to starboard and dump us in the sea."

"The slacking and snatching of the falls in those moments presented the bowman with a difficulty which nearly cost him his fingers- but we made it. The Ship's Company 'cleared lower deck' to hoist us clear of the water. The whaler was secured on the davits and the crew returned to their messes. The Boat's crew were given an additional tot of rum……."

CONVOY ON 271; 9th - 22nd DECEMBER 1944 (70 SHIPS).

Rendezvous effected with the Clyde and Belfast sections on 9th December. The Milford Haven section joined on the 10th and the English Channel section on the 11th. Heavy weather encountered. On the 17th the convoy was spread out over a frontage of 25 miles and a depth of 35 miles. On the 20th, with a southerly gale wind force 8 veering slowly and increasing in strength one vessel with only 2? days fuel remaining was detached to St John's NF escorted by *Poppy*.

LIEUTENANT R.F. DYKES, WRITING IN THE ASSOCIATION'S NEWSLETTER, RECALLS CHRISTMAS DAY 1944

"The Commanding Officer informed me that he would not be onboard for Christmas dinner because he had been invited for lunch at the Governor's House. Would I instruct the QM to inform the Captain when the Governor's car arrived for him.

Time lapsed to the Governor's car arriving on the jetty. The Governor's Naval Attaché (Commander RCN) gets out, immediately it seems he becomes confused when the sentry on the brow presents arms and the RCN Commander returns the salute but cannot quite fathom why the sentry on the brow was a Surgeon Captain RN. Robert, with due ceremony, left the ship.

In the late afternoon when Robert returns on board, says that the Governor's Christmas lunch was just a sandwich buffet, so was there any Christmas lunch left? Steward rustles up some re-warmed spuds, carrots and sprouts. A Leading Hand, much encouraged by his numerous tipples at lunch, insists that it is his privilege to serve Christmas Lunch to his Captain.

Captain sits at the end of the wardroom long table which on this occasion does not have a cloth covering its polished surface. Leading Hand accepts two silver platters from Steward with the vegetables whilst the Steward places cold turkey in front of Captain. Leading hand with a platter in the palm of each hand presents the image of an Egyptian about to do his national dance (whatever that may be) starts at the end of the table near the wardroom hatch, and finding it difficult to stand upright, places his left elbow on the polished table and slides up the table towards the Captain on his elbow with both platters balanced in the palm of his hands. Reaches Captain, waits in this awkward position whilst the Captain helps himself to vegetables. The Leading Hand then disappears into pantry. Captain did not enjoy his meal.

Captain not amused - gives rocket to Dick on the quiet for such behaviour - Dick pleads the customs of the Service especially on Christmas Day. Teaches Robert not to forsake Wardroom hospitality in future."

Note - 'The Surgeon Captain RN' on sentry duty - often seen in ships company group photographs which you may recall it was my responsibility to develop on board because of security. Whenever he appeared in the photographs identification was difficult until one day I found the mystery man to be none other than the sick bay tiffie dressed in a clever copy of an officer's jacket complete with painted yellow braid sleeves and of course branch colour (red) between the yellow stripes. His spell on sentry duty on Christmas Day was his boldest venture in uniform onto the upper deck- he did not expect to be confronted by a Commander RCN - However, the Commander RCN overcoming his surprise, saluted the present arms and realised the situation.

HMCS ARNPRIOR

Battle Honours
Atlantic 1944-45

HMCS Arnprior.   (*Ken MacPherson via Vanwell Publications*)

She was laid down as **HMS Rising Castle** (K398) and was renamed and handed over to the Canadian Navy as **HMCS Arnprior** (K494) in June 1944.

After working up at Tobermory she was allocated to the C1 Escort Group.

Arnprior continued with the C1 Escort Group on mid ocean escort duties until the end of the war in Europe. She escorted 14 convoys totalling 992 ships non of which were lost to enemy action. At times she acted as the Senior officer of the escort group.

Early in June 1945 she started a major refit at St Johns, NF. From September that year she was based at Halifax. She was sold to the Uruguayan Navy later in 1946 and renamed **Montevideo**.

HISTORY

23.01.43	Ordered as **Rising Castle** (K398).
21.06.43	Laid down: **Builder**: (Hull & Engine) Harland and Wolff (Belfast).
08.02.04	Launched.
26.06.44	Commissioned as **HMCS Arnprior** (K494).

WARTIME VOYAGES

Date	ESG	Senior Officer	Convoy	No of Ships	Arrive/ Sail	Location	Notes
30.06.44					Sail	Belfast	
01.07.44					Arv	Tobermory	
10.07.44	EG C1	*New Glasgow*			Sail	Tobermory	
21.07.44	EG C1				Arv	Londonderry	
31.07.44	EG C1	*New Glasgow*			Arv	Campbeltown	
12.08.44	EG C1	*New Glasgow*			Arv	Londonderry	
17.08.44	EG C1	*New Glasgow*			Arv	Londonderry	
19.08.44	EG C1	*New Glasgow*	ONM 249	153	Sail	Londonderry	
24.08.44	EG C1	*New Glasgow*	ONM 249	153		5417N3448W	ADM 217/520. *Orangeville* is included in the escort of ONM 249
27.08.44	EG C1	*New Glasgow*	ONM 249	154	Arv	St John's	
05.09.44	EG C1	*New Glasgow*	HXS 306	121	Sail	St John's	
07.09.44	EG C1	*New Glasgow*	HXS 306	120		4513N4745W	
17.09.44	EG C1	*New Glasgow*	HXS 306	121	Arv	Londonderry	
22.09.44	EG C1				Arv	Londonderry	
27.09.44	EG C1				Arv	Larne	
30.09.44	EG C1	*Cheboque*	ONS 33	51	Sail	Londonderry	
10.10.44	EG C1	*Cheboque*	ONS 33	51	Arv	St John's	
19.10.44	EG C1	*Arnprior*	HX 314	63	Sail	St John's	
29.10.44	EG C1	*Arnprior*			Arv	Londonderry	
09.11.44	EG C1	*Arnprior*	ON 265	55	Sail	Londonderry	
19.11.44	EG C1	*Arnprior*	ON 265	55	Arv	St John's	
28.11.44	EG C1	*Hallowell*	HX 322	38	Sail	St John's	
05.12.44	EG C1	*Hallowell*	HX 322	3		5045N2208W	
09.12.44	EG C1	*Hallowell*	HX 322	39	Arv	Londonderry	
18.12.44					Arv	Londonderry	
19.12.44	EG C1	*Hallowell*			Sail	Belfast	
26.12.44	EG C1	*Hallowell*	ON 272	62		4420N3415W	Hague gives 45 ships
29.12.44	EG C1	*Hallowell*	ON 272	62	Arv	St John's	Hague gives 45 ships
07.01.45	EG C1	*Hallowell*	HX 330	46	Sail	St John's	
15.01.45	EG C1	*Hallowell*	HX 330	46		5020N1210W	
18.01.45	EG C1	*Arnprior*	HX 330	46	Arv	Londonderry	
30.01.45	EG C1	*Arnprior*	ON 282	55	Sail	Londonderry	

Date	ESG	Senior Officer	Convoy	No of Ships	Arrive/ Sail	Location	Notes
17.02.45	EG C1	*Arnprior*	ON 282	55	Arv	St John's	
22.02.45	EG C1	*Arnprior*	HX 339	79	Sail	St John's	
04.03.45	EG C1	*Arnprior*	HX 339	79	Arv	Londonderry	
09.03.45	EG C1	*Arnprior*			At	Londonderry	Repairs complete 11 March
11.03.45	EG C1	*Arnprior*	ON 289	78	Sail	Londonderry	
28.03.45	EG C1	*Arnprior*	ON 289	78	Arv	St John's	
03.04.45	EG C1	*Arnprior*	HX 347	62	Sail	St John's	
15.04.45	EG C1	*Arnprior*	HX 347	62	Arv	Londonderry	
21.04.45	EG C1	*Arnprior*	ON 298	70	Sail	Liverpool	
03.05.45	EG C1	*Arnprior*			Arv	Halifax	
11.05.45	EG C1				Sail	Halifax	
28.05.45					Arv	Clyde	
29.05.45			ON 305	79	Sail	Clyde	
04.06.45	EG C1				Arv	St John's	
26.06.45	EG C1				Arv	Londonderry	
21.08.45					Sail	St John's	FO I/c N.F. 201320/8 'A' refit completed 20/08 (SMO)

09.46	Based at Halifax.
1946	Sold to the Uruguayan Navy and renamed *Montevideo* and operated as a training ship until 1975 when she was scrapped.

Arnprior's first convoy, 19-27 August 1944, ONM 249 of 153 ships, was the largest ON convoy to be sailed across the Atlantic. Nearly six months later she was escorting convoy ONS 41 of 35 ships, her smallest convoy. It was during this voyage that *Arnprior* experienced the severest weather of all her voyages. It started well enough with winds of force 3 to 4 for the first few days. During the early hours of 3 February strong head winds slowed the convoy down and flying from the MAC ship was cancelled. After a brief lull, heavy rain squalls and force 7 winds, followed by fog, reduced visibility to less than two miles. The wind slowly veered north westerly. During the night the wind was gusting to Force 9 and rain squalls reduced visibility to three cables. By 1600 on the 4th the convoy was hove to facing storm force winds with sea and swell rising to 7/7. It was not long before the convoy became widely scattered. The peak of the storm occurred during the evening of 7 February with the convoy nominally hove to on a course of 255°. Ships were becoming widely scattered. By noon on 8 February the wind eased and stragglers began to rejoin the convoy. However, the respite was short lived. During the night of the 8th/9th the gale recovered in strength producing winds of force 10 to 11 and these persisted until midday on the 9th when for a short while the winds reduced to force 7 rising again to force 9. Conditions slowly improved but it was not until after midday on 11 February that all 35 ships were present in a coherent convoy. That is eight days after 3 February following the first hint of trouble to come on.

HMCS BOWMANVILLE

Battle Honours
Atlantic 1944-45

HMCS Bowmanville *in October 1944.* (MoD/Crown Copyright)

Originally laid down as **Nunnery Castle** K 446 and transferred to the Royal Canadian Navy in 1943 and re-named **Bowmanville** K 493. After working up at Tobermory she was allocated to the C4 Escort Group in October 1944. With her consort **Petrolia** she continued with that Group until the end of the war in Europe escorting Mid Ocean Atlantic convoys. She formed part of the escort to ten convoys comprising a total of 620 merchant ships without sustaining any losses due to enemy action.

HISTORY

23.01.43	Ordered as **Nunnery Castle** K 446.
12.08.43	Laid down: **Builder**: Hull - Pickersgill (Sunderland); Engine - G. Clark (Sunderland).
26.01.44	Launched.
08.10.44	Completed.

WARTIME VOYAGES

Date	ESG	Senior Officer	Convoy	No of Ships	Arrive/ Sail	Location	Notes
03.10.44		*Bowmanville*			Sail		
03.10.44		*Bowmanville*			Arv	Tyne	
12.10.44		*Bowmanville*			Sail	Tyne	
14.10.44	EG C4	*Bowmanville*			Arv	Tobermory	
27.10.44	EG C4	*Bowmanville*				At Tobermory	
30.10.44	EG C4	*Bowmanville*				At Tobermory	
10.11.44	EG C4	*Bowmanville*				Corpatch	Repairs complete 11/11
11.11.44	EG C4	*Bowmanville*			Arv	Londonderry	
22.11.44	EG C4	*Bowmanville*			Sail	Londonderry	
24.11.44	EG C4	*Bowmanville*				At Larne	
24.11.44	EG C4	*Bowmanville*			Arv	Belfast	
24.11.44	EG C4	*Bowmanville*	ON 268	60	Sail	Belfast	
28.11.44	EG C4	*Bowmanville*	ON 268	60		4728N1620W	
05.12.44	EG C4	*Bowmanville*	ON 268	60	Arv	St John's	
10.12.44	EG C4	*Bowmanville*	HX 325	57	Sail	St John's	48 ships according to Hague
19.12.44	EG C4	*Bowmanville*	HX 325	57		4850N 3117W	

*A starboard side view of **HMCS Bowmanville** showing the slab-sided appearance of the hull. Despite this, these ships have a well proportioned appearance.* (Ken MacPherson via Vanwell Publications)

Date	ESG	Senior Officer	Convoy	No of Ships	Arrive/ Sail	Location	Notes
24.12.44	EG C4	*Bowmanville*	HX 325	57	Arv	Londonderry	
03.01.45	EG C4	*Bowmanville*			Sail	Belfast	
04.01.45	EG C4	*Bowmanville*			Arv	Londonderry	
08.01.45	EG C4	*Bowmanville*			Sail	Londonderry	
08.01.45	EG C4	*Bowmanville*			Sail	Belfast	
08.01.45	EG C4	*Bowmanville*			Arv	Belfast	
09.01.45	EG C4	*Bowmanville*	ON 276	69	Sail	Londonderry	
15.01.45	EG C4	*Bowmanville*	ON 276	69		4810N 4510W	14 knots to Halifax
17.01.45	EG C4	*Bowmanville*	ON 276	69	Arv	Halifax	
21.01.45	EG C4	*Bowmanville*	HX 333	53	Sail	Halifax	
29.01.45	EG C4	*Bowmanville*	HX 333	53		4959N 2222W	
02.02.45	EG C4	*Bowmanville*	HX 333	53	Arv	Londonderry	
12.02.45	EG C4	*Bowmanville*	ON 284	66	Sail	Milford Haven	
24.02.45	EG C4	*Bowmanville*	ON 284	66	Arv	St John's	
04.03.45	EG C4	*Bowmanville*	HX 341	71	Sail	St John's	
16.03.45	EG C4	*Bowmanville*	HX 341	72	Arv	Londonderry	
22.03.45	EG C4	*Bowmanville*	ON 292	68	Sail	Londonderry	
07.04.45		*Bowmanville*	ON 292		Arv	St John's	
12.04.45	EG C4	*Bowmanville*	HX 349	56	Sail	St John's	
24.04.45	EG C4	*Bowmanville*	HX 349	56	Arv	Londonderry	
02.05.45	EG C4	*Bowmanville*			Sail	Londonderry	
03.05.45	EG C4	*Bowmanville*	ONS 49	56	Sail	Moville	
16.05.45	EG C4	*Bowmanville*	ONS 49	56	Arv	St John's	
23.05.45	EG C4	*Bowmanville*	HX 357	83	Sail	St John's	
02.06.45	EG C4	*Bowmanville*	HX 357	83	Arv	Londonderry	
09.06.45		*Bowmanville*			Sail	Londonderry	
09.06.45		*Bowmanville*			Arv	Clyde	
10.06.45		*Bowmanville*			Sail	Clyde	
16.06.45		*Bowmanville*			Arv	St John's	
30.07.45						At Halifax	

03 - 16.09.45	Reported to be at Digby for training duties.
23.09.45	Placed on disposal list.
30.09.45	Reported to be at Halifax until 15 February 1946 when she was paid off.
1947	Sold mercantile; Chinese flag and re-named *Ta Shun*, then later *Yan Pei.*
1949	Acquired by the Chinese Communist Government, re-armed and renamed *Kuang Chou.* Sold at a later date.

HMCS COPPER CLIFF

Battle Honours
Atlantic 1944-45   North Sea 1944

HMCS Copper Cliff.   (*Ken MacPherson via Vanwell Publications*)

She was originally allocated to the C6 escort group, but on completion of working up at Tobermory she was assigned to the C7 Escort Group then being assembled at Londonderry. She was the only Castle Class Corvette and the only Squid equipped ship in the group. She remained with that group until the end of May 1945. During that time the group was employed exclusively on mid ocean escort duties. The group escorted 12 convoys totalling 680 ships; loosing only two to enemy action.

After returning to Canada in June 1945 she was sold and became the Chinese flag merchant ship *Ta Lung*, and later re-named *Wan Lee*. She was taken over by the Chinese Communist Navy and sold in 1949.

HISTORY

23.01.43	Ordered as **HMS Hever Castle** K 521.
29.06.43	Laid down. **Builder**: Hull - Blythe Shipbuilding; Engine - Whites Marine Engineering (Hebburn).
24.02.44	Launched.
15.08.44	Completed and handed over to the Canadian Navy and renamed **HMCS Copper Cliff** K521.

WARTIME VOYAGES

Date	ESG	Senior Officer	Convoy	No of Ships	Arrive/ Sail	Location	Notes
29.08.44					Arv	Methil	
29.08.44	EG C6				Arv	Tobermory	CinC NA 0817192/8 request *Tillsonburg* or *CC* be sailed to Canada on completion of working up in order to join Group (SMO)
30.08.44					Sail	Methil	
31.08.44	EG C6				Arv	Tobermory	
15.09.44	EG C6					At Tobermory	
19.09.44					Sail	Tobermory	For Londonderry
20.09.44	EG C6				Arv	Clyde	
20.09.44	EG C6				Sail	Tobermory	
24.09.44					Sail	Clyde	
26.09.44					Sail	Lamlash	
28.09.44					Sail	Greenock	
29.09.44	EG C6				Arv	Londonderry	
02.10.44	EG C7					At Londonderry	
06.10.44	EG C7					At Londonderry	
07.10.44	EG C7				Sail	Belfast	
07.10.44	EG C7		ONS 258	55	Sail	Londonderry	
11.10.44	EG C7		ONS 258	55		4952N 2019W	
18.10.44	EG C7		ON 258	54		4625N 4450W	
19.10.44	EG C7		ON 258	54	Arv	St John's	
25.10.44	EG C7		HX 315	43	Sail	St John's	
30.10.44	EG C7		HX 315	43		4845N 2822W	
04.11.44	EG C7		HX 315	43	Arv	Londonderry	
14.11.44	EG C7		ON 266	56	Sail	Londonderry	
16.11.44			ON 266	56	Sail	Liverpool	
21.11.44	EG C7		ON 266	56		4337N 2844W	
27.11.44	EG C7		ON 266	56	Arv	St John's	
06.12.44	EG C7		SC 162	61	Sail	St John's	
12.12.44	EG C7		SC 162	61		5255N 2555W	
16.12.44	EG C7		SC 162	61	Arv	Clyde	
16.12.44	EG C7				Sail	Clyde	
17.12.44	EG C7				Arv	Londonderry	
22.12.44	EG C7					Londonderry	
29.12.44	EG C7		ONS 39	37	Sail	Londonderry	
01.01.45	EG C7		ONS 39	37		5152N 1645W	
08.01.45	EG C7		ONS 39	37		4310N 4248W	
10.01.45	EG C7		ONS 39	37	Arv	St John's	
17.01.45	EG C7		HX 322	49	Sail	St John's	

Date	ESG	Senior Officer	Convoy	No of Ships	Arrive/ Sail	Location	Notes
22.01.45	EG C7		HX 322	49		4730N 3359W	
28.01.45	EG C7		HX 322	49	Arv	Londonderry	
07.02.45					Sail	Milford Haven	
08.02.45	EG C7		(ON 283)	58	Sail	Liverpool	
22.02.45	EG C7		(ON 283)	58	Arv	St John's	
28.02.45	EG C7		(HX 340)	53	Sail	St John's	
11.03.45	EG C7		(HX 340)	53	Arv	Londonderry	
18.03.45	EG C7		(ON 291)	71	Sail	Londonderry	
28.03.45	EG C7		ON 291	71		St John's	Not compatible with entry 31.03.45
31.03.45	EG C7		(ON 291)	71	Arv	St John's	
07.04.45	EG C7		(HX 348)	80	Sail	St John's	
21.04.45	EG C7		(HX 348)		Arv	Londonderry	Two ships sunk 18.04.45 by *U-1107*
28.04.45	EG C7		(ON 299)	71	Sail	Londonderry	From D.W.A. 261520/5 *C* will complete April 27th Orkneys regret *C* has been in collision with Orkney no serious damage 26100/4
08.05.45	EG C7		(ON 299)	71	Arv	St John's	
17.05.45	EG C7		(HX 356)	47	Sail	St John's	
27.05.45	EG C7		(HX 356)	47	Arv	Londonderry	
31.05.45	EG C7				Sail	Londonderry	
01.06.45					Sail	Clyde	
07.06.45					Arv	St John's	
16.06.45					Sail	St John's	
18.06.45					Arv	Halifax	
03.07.45					Sail	Balbas	
18.07.45						Esquimalt	For Disposal

18.07.45	At Esquimalt; Pacific Coast Command: for disposal.
30.11.46	All the Castle Class Corvettes that had been listed for disposal by the 'Pink List' as being at Esquimalt for disposal were not listed after this date.
1946	Mercantile *Ta Lung*.
1947	Mercantile *Wan Lee*.
?	Taken over by the Chinese Communist Navy.
1949	Sold.

HMCS HESPELER

Battle Honours
Atlantic 1944-45

HMCS Hespeler.   *(Ken MacPherson via Vanwell Publications)*

After working up **HMCS Hespeler** was allocated to the C5 Escort Group joining the Group on 18 April 1944. She remained with that Group until the end of the war in Europe.

Hespeler escorted 20 convoys comprising 1,543 ships. These included the largest HX Convoy, HX 300 of 166 ships. She was in mercantile service from 1947 to 1965.

HISTORY

19.01.43	Ordered as *Guildford Castle* K 378.
23.05.43	Laid down as *HMCS Hespeler* K 489. **Builder**: Hull - Robb (Leith); Engine - Walker (Wigan).
13.11.43	Launched.
11.03.44	Completed.

WARTIME VOYAGES

Date	ESG	Senior Officer	Convoy	No of Ships	Arrive/ Sail	Location	Notes
15.03.44					Sail	Leith	Noi/c Leith 101100/3. Anticipate *H* will be ready to sail 15/16 March to Tobermory for Methil & Tobermory
17.03.44					Sail	Methil	
04.04.44					Arv	Londonderry	
21.04.44	EG C5	*Dunver*	ONS 233	111	Sail	Londonderry	CinC N.A. *H* to join Mid-Ocean ES. Force with Group C5 - D/W.A. 18004. April *H* has joined C5 Group today: This probably ON 233
01.05.44	EG C5	*Dunver*	ONS 233	111		4817N 4518W	
03.05.44	EG C5	*Dunver*	ONS 233	111	Arv	St John's	
08.05.44	EG C5					At Sea	
09.05.44	EG C5		(HX 290)	93	Sail	St John's	
10.05.44	EG C5	*Dunver*	(HX 290)	93	Sail	St John's	
19.05.44	EG C5	*Dunver*	(HX 290)	93	Arv	Londonderry	
27.05.44	EG C5	*Dunver*	ONF 238	67	Sail	Londonderry	
30.05.44	EG C5	*Dunver*	ONF 238	67		5558N 2330W	
05.06.44	EG C5	*Dunver*	ONF 238		Arv	St John's	Defective (SMO)
14.06.44	EG C5	*Dunver*	HXM 295	81	Sail	St John's	
17.06.44	EG C5	*Dunver*	HXM 295	81		4730N 4608W	
25.06.44	EG C5	*Dunver*	HXM 295	81	Arv	Londonderry	
04.07.44	EG C5	*Dunver*			Sail	Londonderry	
04.07.44	EG C5	*Dunver*	ONM 243	89		Oversay	
04.07.44	EG C5	*Dunver*	ONM 243	89	Sail	Londonderry	
14.07.44	EG C5	*Dunver*	ONM 243	89	Arv	Halifax	
20.07.44	EG C5	*Dunver*			Sail	Halifax	
22.07.44	EG C5	*Dunver*			Arv	St John's	
23.07.44	EG C5	*Dunver*	(HX 300)	166	Sail	St John's	
23.07.44	EG C5	*Dunver*			Arv	St John's	
30.07.44		*Hespeler*		6		5248N 2155W	Convoy of Escort Oilers
03.08.44	EG C5	*Dunver*	(HX 300)	166	Arv	Londonderry	
11.08.44	EG C5	*Dunver*	ONS 248S	104	Sail	Londonderry	
12.08.44	EG C5	*Dunver*	ONS 248S	104		5558N 0915W	
14.08.44	EG C5	*Dunver*			Arv	Londonderry	
16.08.44	EG C5	*Dunver*			Sail	Londonderry	Defective to Newfoundland
22.08.44	EG C5	*Dunver*	ONS248S	104	Arv	St John's	
24.08.44	EG C3	*Prince Rupert*	HXM 304	90		4640N 4225W	
29.08.44	EG C5	*Dunver*	HXF 305	99	Sail	St John's	

Date	ESG	Senior Officer	Convoy	No of Ships	Arrive/ Sail	Location	Notes
01.09.44	EG C5	*Dunver*	HXF 305	99		4624N 4443W	
08.09.44	EG C5	*Dunver*	HXF 305	98	Arv	Londonderry	EG C5 on operation CW from 8-14 September. Canadian Naval Mission Overseas paper 21.10.44 (165-1-30)
15.09.44	EG C5	*Dunver*			Arv	Londonderry	On conclusion of operation CW
23.09.44	EG C5	*Runnymede*	ONF 255	85	Sail	Londonderry	
23.09.44	EG C5	*Runnymede*	ONF 255	85	Sail	Londonderry	
24.09.44	EG C5	*Runnymede*	ONF 255	85		5520N 1102W	
29.09.44	EG C5	*Runnymede*	ONF 255	85		4535N 2945W	
06.10.44	EG C5	*Runnymede*	ONF 255	85	Arv	St John's	
09.10.44	EG C5	*Runnymede*	HX 312	77	Sail	St John's	
11.10.44	EG C5	*Runnymede*	HX 312	77		4428N 4638W	
18.10.44	EG C5	*Runnymede*	HX 312	47		5120N 0850W	
19.10.44	EG C5	*Runnymede*	HXA 312	30	Arv	Londonderry	
23.10.44	EG C5	*Runnymede*				At Londonderry	
27.10.44	EG C5	*Runnymede*				At Londonderry	
30.10.44	EG C5	*Runnymede*	ON 263	69	Sail	Londonderry	
07.11.44	EG C5	*Runnymede*	ON 263	69		4440N 3935W	
11.11.44	EG C5	*Runnymede*	ON 263		Arv	Halifax	
18.11.44	EG C5	*Runnymede*			Sail	Halifax	
21.11.44	EG C5	*Runnymede*	SC 161	48		4452N 5315W	
28.11.44	EG C5	*Runnymede*	SC 161	51		5327N 3405W	
03.12.44	EG C5	*Runnymede*	SC 161	51	Arv	Londonderry	
05.12.44	EG C5	*Runnymede*			Sail	Londonderry	
15.12.44	EG C5	*Runnymede*	ONS 38	28	Sail	Londonderry	
19.12.44	EG C5	*Runnymede*	ONS 38	28		5030N 1840W	
21.12.44	EG C5	*Runnymede*	SC 161	48		4452N5315W	
26.12.44	EG C5	*Runnymede*	ONS 38	26		4305N 4203W	
31.12.44	EG C5	*Runnymede*			Arv	St John's	
05.01.45	EG C5	*Runnymede*	SC 164	43	Sail	St John's	
08.01.45	EG C5	*Runnymede*	SC 164	43		4515N 3940W	
15.01.45	EG C5	*Runnymede*	SC 164	43		5540N 1420W	
18.01.45	EG C5	*Runnymede*	SC 164	43	Arv	Londonderry	
27.01.45	EG C5	*Runnymede*	ON 281	27	Sail	Londonderry	
29.01.45	EG C5	*Runnymede*	ON 281	27		5050N 0543W	
08.02.45	EG C5	*Runnymede*	ON 281	27	Arv	St John's	
17.02.45	EG C5	*Runnymede*	(HX 338)	70	Sail	St John's	
28.02.45	EG C5	*Runnymede*	(HX 338)	70	Arv	Londonderry	
08.03.45	EG C5	(*Runnymede*)	(ON 288)	108	Sail	Londonderry	
21.03.45	EG C5	(*Runnymede*)	(ON 288)	108	Arv	St John's	
25.03.45	EG C5				Sail	St John's	
27.03.45	EG C5				Arv	Halifax	Refit

Date	ESG	Senior Officer	Convoy	No of Ships	Arrive/ Sail	Location	Notes
09.04.45	EG C5					Halifax	Refit
31.07.45					Sail	Balboa	
08.08.45					Arv	San Diego	
15.08.45					Arv	Esquimalt	For disposal P4

A summary of her voyages with C5 Escort Group is given later under the heading of that Group.

1947   She was purchased by the Union Steamship Company and converted and re-named *Chilcotin* (Official Number 178070) specifically the for the Company's Alaskan summer cruises, with additional features for tourist entertainment. She was awarded a passenger licence for 200; first class berths 106; deck none; and cargo capacity of 250 tons.

Feb 1958   Sold to Sun Line, Monrovia and re-named *Capri* and registered for service in the Great Lakes and Gulf of St Lawrence. In the 1958-59 Lloyds Register she is listed as *Stella Maris* ex *Capri*-58 ex *Chilcotin* -58.

1960-61   Registered as *Stella Maris* ,Sun Line, Greek Flag for Mediterranean and Red Sea cruises. Similar entries follow for the period 1961 - 65.

1965-66   Entered as owned by Alaska Cruise Lines, British Flag for Mediterranean and Red Sea Service.

28.01.66   Destroyed by fire and broken up at La Spezia, Italy.

HMCS HUMBERSTONE

Battle Honours
Atlantic 1944-45

HMCS Humberstone.   *(Ken MacPherson via Vanwell Publications)*

Ordered as *Totnes Castle* but laid down as *Norham Castle* she was transferred to the Royal Canadian Navy and commissioned at Glasgow on 6 September 1944 as *HMCS Humberstone*. After working up at Tobermory she joined the C8 Escort Group and continued with that group escorting mid ocean convoys until the end of the war in Europe. She was paid off at Esquimalt on 17 November 1946, sold to Chinese owners in 1946 and converted for mercantile service as *Taiwei*. She underwent five more name changes before becoming the Korean *South Ocean* in 1954. She was broken up at Hong Kong in 1959.

During the war she escorted 11 convoys comprising 538 ships without loss due to enemy action.

HISTORY

19.12.42	Ordered as *Totnes Castle*.
30.08.43	Laid down as *Norham Castle*. **Builder**: Hull - Inglis (Pointhouse);
	Engine - Harland & Wolff (Govan) & Fawcett (Preston).
12.04.44	Launched.
06.09.44	Completed and commissioned.

WARTIME VOYAGES

Date	ESG	Senior Officer	Convoy	No of Ships	Arrive/ Sail	Location	Notes
27.09.44							NSHQ 081828/9 On completion working up *H* is allocated CinC C CAN
10.10.44	EG C8					At Tobermory	
16.10.44					Sail	Tobermory	
16.10.44	EG C8				Sail	Tobermory	
17.10.44					Arv	Londonderry	
20.10.44	EG C8	(*Leaside*)			Sail	Londonderry	
21.10.44	EG C8	(*Leaside*)	ON 261	39	Arv	Larne	
21.10.44	EG C8	(*Leaside*)	ON 261	39	Sail	Belfast	
23.10.44	-	*Leaside*	ON 261	39		5000N 1000W	
30.10.44	EG C8	*Leaside*	ON 261	38		4440N 4135W	
10.11.44	EG C8				Sail	St John's	
14.11.44	EG C8	*Stone Town*	HX 318	37		4745N 3258W	
20.11.44	EG C8	*Stone Town*			Arv	Londonderry	
27.11.44	EG C8	*Stone Town*	ONS 37	31	Sail	Londonderry	
28.11.44		*Stone Town*			Arv	Belfast	
29.11.44	EG C8	*Stone Town*	ONS 37	31	Sail	Belfast	
10.12.44	EG C8	*Stone Town*	ONS 37	31	Arv	St John's	
20.12.44	EG C8	*Stone Town*	SC 163	49	Sail	St John's	
26.12.44	EG C8	*Stone Town*	SC 163	49		5212N 2930W	
31.12.44	EG C8	*Stone Town*	SC 163	49	Arv	Londonderry	
13.01.45	EG C8	*Stone Town*	ONS 40	32	Sail	Londonderry	
15.01.45	EG C8	*Stone Town*	ONS 40	32		5502N 1348W	
22.01.45	EG C8	*Stone Town*	ONS 40	33		4247N 4040W	
26.01.45	EG C8	*Stone Town*	ONS 40	33	Arv	St John's	
01.02.45	EG C8	*Stone Town*	(HX 335)	53	Sail	St John's	
11.02.45	EG C8	*Stone Town*	(HX 335)	53	Arv	Londonderry	
21.02.45	EG C8	*Stone Town*	ON 286	55	Sail	Londonderry	
06.03.45	EG C8	*Stone Town*	ON 286	55	Arv	Halifax	
12.03.45	EG C8	(*Stone Town*)	(HX 343)	66	Sail	Halifax	
24.03.45	EG C8	(*Stone Town*)	(HX 343)	66	Arv	Londonderry	
01.04.45	EG C8	(*Stone Town*)	(ON 294)	85	Sail	Londonderry	
17.04.45	EG C8	(*Stone Town*)	(ON 294)	85	Arv	St John's	
22.04.45	EG C8	(*Stone Town*)	(HX 345)	74	Sail	St John's	
04.05.45	EG C8	(*Stone Town*)	(HX 345)	74	Arv	Londonderry	
12.05.45	EG C8	(*Stone Town*)	ONS 50	15	Sail	Liverpool	
26.05.45	EG C8	(*Stone Town*)	ONS 50	17	Arv	St John's	
04.06.45					Sail	St John's	
12.06.45					Arv	St John's	
17.06.45					Sail	St John's	
01.07.45					Arv	Cristobal	

Date	ESG	Senior Officer	Convoy	No of Ships	Arrive/ Sail	Location	Notes
03.07.45					Sail	Balboa	
18.07.45					Arv	Esquimault	19.07.45 For disposal

1946	Sold to Chinese owners, converted for mercantile service and renamed *Taiwei*.
1947	Renamed *Chang Chen*.
1949	Renamed *King Kang*.
1950	Renamed *Tai Shan*.
1951	Renamed *Flying Dragon*.
1951	Renamed *San Blas*.
1954	Renamed *South Ocean*; Korean owners.
09.59	Scrapped at Hong Kong.

Only one report of the proceedings of the C8 Escort Group has been traced. This was for the convoy ON 286 during the period 21 February 1945 to 4 March 1945.

To start with convoys ON 286 and OS112/KMS 86 steamed together in company. Because of thick fog the Milford Haven section of the convoy did not sail. During the afternoon of 22 February *SS Tintern Abbey* of OS 112/KMS 86 collided in thick fog off K4 Buoy with *SS Barbara Freiche* of ON 286. *Tintern Abbey*, damaged along her starboard side, was able to proceed independently to Cardiff. *SS Barbara Freiche* continued with the convoy

The fog cleared the next day and the two convoys and their escorts were able to sort themselves out and proceed on their separate ways.

Three MAC ships accompanied ON 286. Routine dawn, midday and dusk patrols were flown each day, the three ships sharing out the duties.

Humberstone oiled at sea on 26 February. She took in 130 tons in one hour 52 minutes. No steadying line was used. The usual series of exercise were carried out by the group whilst at sea.

HMCS HUNTSVILLE

Battle Honours
Atlantic 1944-45

HMCS Huntsville.

(*Ken MacPherson via Vanwell Publications*)

Laid down as **HMS Wolvesey Castle** she was transferred to the RCN and commissioned on 6 June 1944, on the Clyde. She worked up at Stornoway and joined the C5 Escort Group late in July and remained with that group until the end of the war in Europe. She escorted 12 mid ocean convoys across the Atlantic comprising 852 ships of which two were lost due to enemy action. In 1945 she completed a refit at Halifax from May to September when she was placed in reserve. She was paid off for disposal on 15 February 1946 and sold that year and converted for mercantile service.

HISTORY

20.01.43	Ordered as **HMS Wolvesey Castle** K 461.
01.06.43	Laid down: **Builder**: Hull & Engine Ailsa (Troon).
24.02.44	Launched.
06.06.44	Commissioned as **HMCS Huntsville** K 499.
15.06.44	Completed.

WARTIME VOYAGES

Date	ESG	Senior Officer	Convoy	No of Ships	Arrive/ Sail	Location	Notes
25.06.44					Sail	Greenock	AM 031747b/5 When ready for sea *H* should be sailed to Tobermory to work up, on conclusion CinC W is requested to sail her as requested by CinC MA
26.06.44					Arv	Stornoway	
16.07.44					Sail	Stornoway	
17.07.44	EG C5	*Dunver*			Arv	Larne	
17.07.44					Arv	Londonderry	
24.07.44	EG C5	*Dunver*				At Londonderry	Boiler clean
28.07.44	EG C5	*Dunver*				At Londonderry	
06.08.44	EG C5	*Dunver*				At Londonderry	
11.08.44	EG C5	*Dunver*	ONS 248S	104	Sail	Londonderry	
12.08.44	EG C5	*Dunver*	ONS 248S	104		5558N 0915W	
21.08.44	EG C5	*Dunver*	ONS248	104	Arv	St John's	
22.08.44	EG C5	*Dunver*			Sail	St John's	
24.08.44	EG C5	*Dunver*			Arv	Halifax	
27.08.44	EG C5	*Dunver*			Sail	Halifax	
29.08.44	EG C5	*Dunver*			Arv	St John's	
29.08.44	EG C5	*Dunver*	HXF 305	99	Sail	St John's	
01.09.44	EG C5	*Dunver*	HXF 305	99		4624N 4443W	
09.09.44	EG C5	*Dunver*	HXF 305	99	Arv	Londonderry	
15.09.44	EG C5	*Dunver*				At Londonderry	On conclusion of operation CW
22.09.44	EG C5				Sail	Londonderry	
23.09.44	EG C5	*Runnymede*	ONF 255	85	Sail	Londonderry	
24.09.44	EG C5	*Runnymede*	ONF 255	85		5520N 1102W	
29.09.44	EG C5	*Runnymede*	ONF 255	85		4535N 2945W	
06.10.44	EG C5	*Runnymede*	ONF 255	85	Arv	St John's	
09.10.44	EG C5	*Runnymede*	HX 312	77	Sail	St John's	
11.10.44	EG C5	*Runnymede*	HX 312	77		4428N 4638W	
18.10.44	EG C5	*Runnymede*	HXA 312	30		5012N 0925W	
19.10.44	EG C5	*Runnymede-*	HXA 312	30	Arv	Londonderry	
27.10.44	EG C5	*Runnymede*				At Londonderry	
30.10.44	EG C5	*Runnymede*	ON 263	69	Sail	Londonderry	
07.11.44	EG C5	*Runnymede*	ON 263	69		4440N 3935W	
11.11.44	EG C5	*Runnymede*	ON 263	69	Arv	Halifax	
20.11.44	EG C5	*Runnymede*				Halifax	Repairs Complete 25 Nov
24.11.44	EG C5					At Halifax	

Date	ESG	Senior Officer	Convoy	No of Ships	Arrive/ Sail	Location	Notes
26.11.44	EG C5				Sail	Halifax	
03.12.44	EG C5	*Runnymede*			Sail	St John's	
31.12.44	EG C5	*Runnymede*	ONS 38	28	Arv	St John's	
04.01.45	EG C5	*Runnymede*	SC 164	43	Sail	St John's	
08.01.45	EG C5	*Runnymede*	SC 164	43		4515N 3940W	
15.01.45	EG C5	*Runnymede*	SC 164	43		5540N 1420W	
16.01.45	EG C5	*Runnymede*	SC 164	43	Arv	Londonderry	
27.01.45	EG C5	*Runnymede*	ON 281	27	Sail	Londonderry	
28.01.45	EG C5	*Runnymede*	ON 281	27	Sail	Milford Haven	
29.01.45	EG C5	*Runnymede*	ON 281	27		5050N 0543W	
08.02.45	EG C5	*Runnymede*	ON 281	27	Arv	St John's	
16.02.45	EG C5	*Runnymede*	(HX 338)	70	Sail	St John's	
28.02.45	EG C5	*Runnymede*	(HX 338)	70	Arv	Londonderry	
08.03.45	EG C5	(*Runnymede*)	(0N 288)	108	Sail	Londonderry	
09.03.45	EG C5		(ON 288)	108	Sail	Milford Haven	
21.03.45	EG C5	(*Runnymede*)	(ON 288)	108	Arv	St John's	
28.03.45	EG C5	(*Runnymede*)	(HX 346)	61	Sail	St John's	
08.04.45	EG C5	(*Runnymede*)	(HX 346)	61	Arv	Londonderry	
13.04.45	EG C5					Londonderry	Repairs complete 16 Apr
18.04.45	EG C5	*Runnymede*	ON 297	81	Sail	Londonderry	
29.04.45	EG C5	*Runnymede*	ON 297	81	Arv	St John's	
08.05.45	EG C5				Sail	St John's	
16.05.45					Arv	Philadelphia	C.S. Halifax 012025/6 *H* completes 31.7 For disposal

1946   Acquired by Wellington Kent Ltd, St John's NF and re-named ***Wellington Kent***. Lloyds Register records that the ship's power unit was replaced by Oil Engine 4SA 8 Cl made and fitted in 1947 by Enterprise Eng. & Frdy. Co.

1951   Re-named ***Belle Isle***.

1963   Registered under Allister Towing, Halifax (Lloyds Register).

1965   No longer recorded in Lloyds Register. Believed to have been sunk in a collision off Trois-Rivières.

The ship's voyages with the C5 Escort Group are summarised under the heading for that group.

HMCS KINCARDINE

Battle Honours
Atlantic 1944-45

HMCS Kincardine. (*Ken MacPherson via Vanwell Publications*)

Laid down as **HMS Tamworth Castle**, she was transferred to the RCN and commissioned at Middlesborough on 19 June 1944. She worked up at Tobermory and Stornoway. Before joining the C2 Escort Group she had to return to her builders for repairs. On completion of these she moved to Londonderry in mid September and was employed on local duties until 2 October when, with her Group, she voyaged with her first convoy. For the remainder of the war in Europe she stayed with C2 Escort Group on trans-Atlantic mid-ocean convoy duties. During that

time she escorted 11 convoys comprising 550 ships. Two of these were lost due to enemy action.

During July 1945 she was briefly allocated to **HMCS Cornwallis** for training duties followed by a minor refit at Liverpool N.S. She was placed in reserve at Halifax in October where she paid off into reserve 27 February 1946. Later in that year she was sold to the French Government and resold in 1947 to Moroccan interests and renamed **Saada**. She was broken up in 1953/54.

HISTORY

19.01.43	Ordered as **HMS Tamworth Castle** K 393.
22.08.43	Laid down. **Builder**: Hull & Engine - Smiths Dock (Middlesborough).
26.01.44	Launched.
19.06.44	Commissioned as **HMCS Kincardine** K 490.
03.07.44	Completed.

WARTIME VOYAGES

Date	ESG	Senior Officer	Convoy	No of Ships	Arrive/ Sail	Location	Notes
09.07.44					Arv	Rosyth	
09.07.44					Sail	Rosyth	
09.07.44					Sail	Tees	
13.07.44					Arv	Tobermory	
01.08.44					Arv	Londonderry	
01.08.44					Sail	Tobermory	
06.08.44	Unall					At Londonderry	
11.08.44	EG C2					At Londonderry	
13.08.44	EG C2				Arv	Londonderry	
21.08.44					Sail	Londonderry	
23.08.44					Arv	Tyne	For Tees: NO I/c Tees 061756/9. Estimate *K* will be ready for sea 9/9.
23.08.44	EG C2				Arv	Tees	
12.09.44					Sail	Londonderry	
12.09.44	EG C2				Sail	Londonderry	
21.09.44	EG C2				Arv	Londonderry	
02.10.44	EG C2				Sail	Londonderry	
03.10.44	EG C2				Sail	Milford Haven	
04.10.44	EG C2	*Longueuil*	ON 257	40	Sail	Londonderry	
07.10.44	EG C2	*Longueuil*	ON 257	40		4931N 3615W	
11.10.44	EG C2	*Longueuil*	ON 257	40		4620N 4424W	
14.10.44	EG C2	*Longueuil*			Arv	Halifax	
19.10.44	EG C2	*Longueuil*	SC 159	64	Sail	Halifax	
30.10.44	EG C2	*Longueuil*	SC 159	64		5435N 1535W	
02.11.44	EG C2	*Longueuil*	SC 159	64	Arv	Londonderry	
13.11.44	EG C2	*Longueuil*	ONS 36	45	Sail	Londonderry	
14.11.44	EG C2	*Longueuil*	ONS 36	45	Sail	Campbeltown	
14.11.44	EG C2	*Longueuil*	ONS 36	45		N Channel	
21.11.44	EG C2	*Longueuil*	ONS 36	55		4430N 2635W	
28.11.44	EG C2	*Longueuil*	ONS 36	56		4350N 4355W	
29.11.44	EG C2	*Longueuil*			Arv	St John's	
04.12.44	EG C2	*Longueuil*	HX 323	19	Sail	St John's	
12.12.44	EG C2	*Kindardine*	HX 323	19		5119N 0912W	
13.12.44	EG C2	*Kindardine*	HX 323	19	Arv	Londonderry	
22.12.44	EG C2				Arv	Larne	
24.12.44	EG C2	*Kindardine*	ON 274	63	Sail	Belfast	
26.12.44	EG C2	*Kindardine*	ON 274	63		5050N 0920W	
04.01.45	EG C2				Sail	St John's	
12.01.45	EG C2	*Longueuil*	HX 331	63	Sail	St John's	
15.01.45	EG C2	*Longueuil*	HX 331	63		4535N 4302W	
23.01.45	EG C2	*Longueuil*	HX 331	63	Arv	Londonderry	
02.02.45	EG C2	*Longueuil*	ON 282	55	Sail	Milford Haven	

Date	ESG	Senior Officer	Convoy	No of Ships	Arrive/ Sail	Location	Notes
14.02.45	EG C2	*Longueuil*	ON 282	55	Arv	St John's	Attacked suspected U-boat 03.02.45
19.02.45	EG C2	*Longueuil*	SC 167	38	Sail	St John's	
02.03.45	EG C2	*Longueuil*	SC 167	36	Arv	Londonderry	Two ships sunk
12.03.45	EG C2	*Longueuil*			Arv	Cardiff	
12.03.45	EG C2	*Longueuil*	ON 290	71	Sail	Londonderry	
13.03.45	EG C2	*Longueuil*	ON 290	71	Sail	Cardiff	
25.03.45	EG C2	*Longueuil*	ON 290	71	Arv	St John's	
30.03.45	EG C2	*Longueuil*	SC 171	22	Sail	St John's	
12.04.45	EG C2	*Longueuil*	SC 171	22	Arv	Londonderry	
21.04.45	EG C2	*Longueuil*	ON 298	70	Sail	Londonderry	
03.05.45	EG C2	*Longueuil*	ON 298	70	Arv	St John's	
09.05.45	EG C2	*Longueuil*	ON 298	70	Sail	St John's	
21.05.45					Arv	Londonderry	
21.05.45					Arv	Londonderry	
30.05.45					Sail	Londonderry	
05.06.45					Arv	St John's	
06.06.45					Sail	St John's	
07.06.45					Arv	Halifax	For disposal

1946	Sold to the French Government.
1947	Sold to Les Cargoes Fruitiers Cherifiens Soc: Anon; and renamed *Saada* Registered by Lloyds for services in the Mediterranean; decks for light cargo only.
1953-54	Lloyds Register Stamped 'Broken up.'

KINCARDINE ATTACKS SUSPECTED U-BOAT

Reporting on the attack on 3 February 1945 on the suspected submarine contact, The Commanding Officer, Act Lt Cmdr R.P. Brown RNCVR, wrote:-

"The original contact was obtained by **HMCS Longueuil** *on the port bow of the convoy ON 282 at about 1310 on 3 February 1945.* **Kincardine** *then in position 'Baker' was ordered to join. Contact was obtained on a bottomed object at 1415. Seven Squid attacks were made. The object appeared to be lying in a North - South direction, giving typical submarine beam echoes on Easterly and Westerly runs. The heavy weather caused a great deal of 'quenching' and at slow speeds 'masking' was marked. 'Q' contact was excellent in most attacks. Firing time was obtained from the Q trace. Good 147B traces were obtained in the first, fourth and seventh attacks. Oil was observed in the area throughout the attacks. It dispersed too rapidly for samples to be obtained. After the seventh attack* **Kincardine** *was ordered to return to the convoy."*

HMCS LEASIDE

Battle Honours
Atlantic 1944-45

HMCS Leaside. *(Ken MacPherson via Vanwell Publications)*

Laid down as **HMS Walmer Castle** and transferred to the RCN on 21 August 1944. She was allocated to the C8 Escort Group and remained with that group on mid ocean escort duties.

Leaside joined the C8 Escort Group in October 1944. Her first convoy escort voyage was with convoy ON 261. One report indicates that **Leaside** was the Senior Officer on this occasion. For all subsequent voyages the Senior Officer was **Stonetown**. Between 20 October 1944 and 12 May 1945 **Leaside** escorted at least eleven ocean convoys. Unfortunately the record for the C8 Escort Group is not complete and only one Report of Proceedings was found. This related to an uneventful voyage. Details of the convoys thought to have been escorted by **Leaside** appear at the end of this history.

HISTORY

19.01.43	Ordered.
23.09.43	Laid down as **HMS Walmer Castle**. **Builder**: Hull & Engine - Smiths Dock, (Middlesborough).
10.03.44	Launched.
21.08.44	Commissioned and transferred to RCN as **HMCS Leaside**.
05.09.44	Completed.

WARTIME VOYAGES

Date	ESG	Senior Officer	Convoy	No of Ships	Arrive/ Sail	Location	Notes
11.02.44					Arv	Londonderry	
09.09.44					Sail	Tees	N.S.H.Q. 221945/8 On completion of working up *L* is allocated to CinC N.A.
09.09.44					Arv	Rosyth	
12.09.44					Sail	Rosyth	
13.09.44	Unall				Arv	Tobermory	
29.09.44	Unall					At Tobermory	
03.10.44	EG C8				Arv	Londonderry	
10.10.44	EG C8					At Londonderry	
17.10.44	EG C8					At Tobermory	
20.10.44	EG C8	(*Leaside*)			Sail	Londonderry	
21.10.44	EG C8	(*Leaside*)	ON 261	39	Sail	Belfast	
01.11.44	EG C8	(*Leaside*)			Arv	St John's	
10.11.44	EG C8				Sail	St John's	
14.11.44	EG C8	*Stonetown*	HX 318	37		4745N 3258W	
20.11.44	EG C8	*Stonetown*			Arv	Londonderry	
27.11.44	EG C8	*Stonetown*	ONS 37	31	Sail	Londonderry	
30.11.44	EG C8	*Stonetown*	ONS 37	31	Sail	Milford Haven	
10.12.44	EG C8	*Stonetown*	ONS 37	31	Arv	St John's	
20.12.44	EG C8	*Stonetown*	SC 163	49	Sail	St John's	
31.12.44	EG C8	*Stonetown*	SC 163	49	Arv	Londonderry	
13.01.45	EG C8	*Stonetown*	ONS 40	32	Sail	Londonderry	
15.01.45	EG C8	*Stonetown*	ONS 40	32		5502N 1348W	
22.01.45	EG C8	*Stonetown*	ONS 40	33		4247N 4040W	
26.01.45	EG C8	*Stonetown*	ONS 40	33	Arv	St John's	
01.02.45	EG C8	*Stonetown*	(HX 335)	53	Sail	St John's	
11.02.45	EG C8	*Stonetown*	(HX 335)	53	Arv	Londonderry	
11.02.45					Arv	Londonderry	
21.02.45	EG C8	*Stonetown*	ON 286	55	Sail	Londonderry	
06.03.45	EG C8	*Stonetown*	ON 286	55	Arv	Halifax	
12.03.45	EG C8	(*Stonetown*)	(HX 343)	66	Sail	Halifax	
24.03.45	EG C8	(*Stonetown*)	(HX 343)	66	Arv	Londonderry	
01.04.45	EG C8	(*Stonetown*)	(ON 294)	85	Sail	Londonderry	
17.04.45	EG C8	(*Stonetown*)	(ON 294)	85	Arv	St John's	
22.04.45	EG C8	(*Stonetown*)	(HX 345)	74	Sail	St John's	
04.05.45	EG C8	(*Stonetown*)	(HX 345)	74	Arv	Londonderry	
11.05.45	EG C8	(*Stonetown*)	ONS 50	17	Sail	Londonderry	
26.05.45	EG C8	(*Stonetown*)	ONS 50	17	Arv	St John's	
04.06.45					Sail	St John's	
12.06.45					Arv	St John's	
17.06.45					Sail	St John's	

Date	ESG	Senior Officer	Convoy	No of Ships	Arrive/ Sail	Location	Notes
01.07.45					Arv	Cristobal	
03.07.45					Arv	Balbao	
18.07.45					Arv	Esquimalt	For disposal

16.11.45	Paid off for disposal.
1946	Sold to Union Steamship Co. and converted to a coastal passenger vessel and renamed *Coquitlam*
1952-53	Lloyds Register records No 07109 *Coquitlam* Alaska Cruise Lines Ltd.
1957-58	Lloyds Register: No 57372 *Coquitlam* United Steamships Ltd: Vancouver. British Flag, Class BC. Class withdrawn 12/53.
1958-67	Lloyds Register: *Glacier Queen* ex *Coquitlam* (1958) Alaska Cruise Lines.
1967-68	As above but now Canadian Flag.
1968-74	As above.
1974-75	*Glacier Queen* ex *Coquitlam*; M.J. Stanley U.S.A.
1976-80	As above. Last entry in Lloyds Register.

In 1970 the ship was towed to Seattle and stripped in anticipation of becoming a floating restaurant at Valdez, the proposed southern terminus of the Alaska oil pipe line. It was reported that the hulk sank in Cook Inlet, Alaska on 8 November 1978, but was raised, towed to sea and scuttled in January 1979. This, however, does not correspond with the record in Lloyds Register as given above.

CONVOYS THOUGHT TO HAVE BEEN ESCORTED BY LEASIDE.

Convoy	No of Ships	Period	Route	Senior Officer
ON261	39	21.10 - 01.11.44	UK - St John's	*Leaside*
HX 318	37	10 - 20.11.44	St John's -UK	*Stonetown*
(ONS 37)	31	27.11 - 10.12.44	UK - St John's	*Stonetown*
SC 163	49	20 - 31.12.44	St John's - UK	*Stonetown*
ONS 40	32	13 - 26.01.45	UK - St John's	*Stonetown*
(HX 335)	53	01 - 11.02.45	St John's - UK	*Stonetown*
ON 286	55	21.02 - 06.03.45	UK - Halifax	*Stonetown*
(HX 343)	66	12 - 24.03.45	Halifax - UK	*Stonetown*
(ON 294)	85	01 - 17.04.45	UK - St John's	
(HX 345)	74	22.04 - 04.05.45	St John's - UK	
(ONS 50)	17	12 - 26.05.45	UK - St John's	

Convoy codes in parenthesis indicate those convoys whose sailing and arrival dates closely match those of *Leaside* .

HMCS ORANGEVILLE

Battle Honours
Atlantic 1944-45

HMCS Orangeville.   (*Ken MacPherson via Vanwell Publications*)

Orangeville was laid down as *HMS Hedingham Castle*. She was transferred to the RCN and commissioned on 24th April 1944. After working up at Tobermory she was allocated to the C1 Escort Group and spent the remainder of the war in Europe on mid ocean escort duty in the North Atlantic. *Orangeville* escorted 15 convoys comprising 1,022 ships.

HISTORY

19.01.43	Ordered as *Hedingham Castle*.
23.07.43	Laid down: **Builder**: Hull - Robb (Leith); Engine - G Plenty (Newbury).
26.01.43	Launched.
24.04.44	Commissioned as *HMCS Orangeville*.
10.05.44	Completed.

WARTIME VOYAGES

Date	ESG	Senior Officer	Convoy	No of Ships	Arrive/ Sail	Location	Notes
01.05.44					Sail	Leith	N.S.H.Q. 261707z/4 '*O*' Commissioned 24/4
11.05.44					Arv	Methil	
11.05.44					Sail	Methil	
13.05.44					Arv	Tobermory	
29.05.44					Arv	Londonderry	
29.05.44					Sail	Tobermory	
04.06.44	EG C1		ONS 239	98	Sail	Londonderry	
06.06.44	EG C1		ON 239	98		5518N 1150W	
16.06.44	EG C1		ONS 239	98	Arv	St John's	
23.06.44	EG C1		HXF 296	93	Sail	St John's	
26.06.44	EG C1		HXF 296	93		4710N 4245W	
02.07.44	EG C1		HXF 298	115	Arv	Londonderry	
10.07.44	EG C1		ONF 244	58	Sail	Londonderry	
11.07.44	EG C1		ONF 244	58	Sail	Londonderry	
16.07.44	EG C1		ONF 244	58		5327N 3814W	
19.07.44	EG C1		ONF 244	58	Arv	St John's	
31.07.44	EG C1		HXM 301	131	Sail	St John's	ADM 217/518 *Orangeville* left St John's on 30th July
03.08.44	EG C3		HXM 301	131		4958N 3348W	
04.08.44	EG C1		HXM 301	131		5048N 2831W	But see under 3rd Aug '44 - different Escort Group code No
08.08.44	EG C1		HXM 301	131	Arv	Londonderry	
15.08.44	EG C1				Arv	Larne	
21.08.44	EG C1					At Londonderry	ADM 217/520 *Orangeville* left Londonderry on 19th August 1944
27.08.44	EG C 1		ONM 249	154	Arv	St John's	
01.09.44	EG C1				Sail	Londonderry	
13.09.44	EG C1				Sail	Stornoway	
21.09.44	EG C1				Arv	Londonderry	
27.09.44	EG C1				Arv	Larne	
29.09.44	EG C1		ONS 33	51	Sail	Loch Ewe	
01.10.44	EG C1		0NS 33	53		5515N 1040W	
10.10.44	EG C1				Arv	St John's	
17.10.44	EG C1		ON 33	52		4733N 3637W	Date may be 7th October
19.10.44	EG C1		HX 314	63	Sail	St John's	
23.10.44	EG C1		HX 314	64		4720N 3458W	
29.10.44	EG C1				Sail	Londonderry	
30.10.44	EG C1				Arv	Londonderry	

Date	ESG	Senior Officer	Convoy	No of Ships	Arrive/ Sail	Location	Notes
09.11.44	EG C1		ON 265	55	Sail	Londonderry	
19.11.44	EG C1		ON 265	55	Arv	St John's	
28.11.44	EG C1		HX 322	38	Sail	St John's	
05.12.44	EG C1		HX 322	39		5045N 2208W	
09.12.44	EG C1		HX 322	39	Arv	Londonderry	
19.12.44	EG C1				Sail	Belfast	
26.12.44	EG C1		ON 273	62		4420N 3415W	Hague gives 45 ships
29.12.44	EG C1		ON 273	62	Arv	St John's	Hague gives 45 ships
07.01.45	EG C1		HX 330	46	Sail	St John's	
08.01.45			WHX 330	2		4225N 4930W	
15.01.45	EG C1		HX 330	46		5020N 1210W	
17.01.45	EG C1		HX 330	46	Arv	Londonderry	
30.01.45	EG C1		ONS 41	35	Sail	Londonderry	
17.02.45	EG C1		ONS 41	35	Arv	St John's	
22.02.45	EG C1		HX 339	79	Sail	St John's	
04.03.45	EG C1		HX 339	79	Arv	Londonderry	
09.03.45	EG C1					At Londonderry	Repairs complete 11 March
11.03.45	EG C1		ON 289	78	Sail	Londonderry	
12.03.45	EG C1		ON 289	78	Sail	Londonderry	
28.03.45	EG C1		ON 289	78	Arv	St John's	
03.04.45	EG C1		HX 347	62	Sail	St John's	
15.04.45	EG C1		HX 347	62	Arv	Londonderry	
21.04.45	EG C1		ON 298	70	Sail	Liverpool	
05.05.45	EG C1		ON 298	70	Arv	Halifax	
06.05.45	EG C1				Sail	Sydney	For disposal

05-08.45	Refit at Liverpool N.S. and placed in maintenance reserve at Halifax.
12.04.46	Paid Off.
1946	Sold for conversion to mercantile use under the Chinese flag and re-named *Ta Tung*.
1951	Taken over by the Nationalist Chinese Government and renamed *Te-An*.

CONVOYS ESCORTED BY HMC SHIPS ARNPRIOR & ORANGEVILLE

Convoy	No of Ships	Period	Route	Senior Officer	Castle Class
ON(S) 239	98	04.06 - 15.06.44	UK - St John's	*New Glasgow*	*Orangeville*

12 June *Fredericton* & *Orangeville* attacked suspected U-boat. This was later classified as Non-sub by Commodore 'D' Londonderry.

HX(F) 296	93	23.06 - 02.07.44	St John's - UK	*New Glasgow-*	*Orangeville*

With difficulty the convoy met at Westomp in fog. Full count of ships not possible until 26 June.

ON(F) 244	58	11.07 - 19.07.44	UK - St John's	*New Glasgow*	*Orangeville*

Uneventful passage. Resulting from all escorts successfully oiling from MAC emergency tanker *Alexia*. Resulting in arrangements made for 6 more tanker MAC ships to be fitted with emergency oiling at sea equipment

HXM 301	131	31.07 - 08.08.44	St John's - UK	*Chebougue*	*Orangeville*

Uneventful passage. *Orangeville* standing by MAC ship.

ON(M) 249	154	19.08 - 29.08.44	UK - St John's	*New Glasgow*	*Arnprior*

Orangeville remained at Londonderry with engine defects. Swordfish from *Alexia* crashed into Commodore's bow. Crew rescued by *New Glasgow*. Persistent fog throughout most of the passage.

HXS 306	121	05.09 - 17.09.44	St John's - UK	*New Glasgow*	*Arnprior*

Four MAC ships sailed with the convoy. Full air cover provided 9th to 12th inclusive. Low visibility or heavy weather prevented flying on the other days

ONS 33	33	29.09 - 10.10.44	UK - St John's	*Chebougue*	*Orangeville* *Arnprior*

Chebougue torpedoed and *Arnprior* assumed SO.

HX 314	63	19.10 - 29.10.44	St John's - UK	*Arnprior*	*Orangeville* *Arnprior*

Convoy routed on a southerly course.

ON 265	55	09.11 - 19.11.44	UK - St John's	*Arnprior*	*Orangeville* *Arnprior*

Poor station keeping in the convoy.

Convoy	No of Ships	Period	Route	Senior Officer	Castle Class
HX 322	38	28.11 - 09.12.44	St John's - UK	*Hallowell*	*Orangeville* *Arnprior*
ON 273	65	19.12 - 29.12.44	UK - St John's	*Hallowell*	*Orangeville* *Arnprior*
HX 330	46	07.01 - 17.01.44	St John's - UK	*Hallowell*	*Orangeville* *Arnprior*
ONS 41	35	31.01 - 17.02 45	UK - St John's	*Arnprior*	*Orangeville* *Arnprior*

Claimed to have been the slowest convoy across the Atlantic due to very severe weather.

Convoy	No of Ships	Period	Route	Senior Officer	Castle Class
HX 339	79	22.02 - 04.03.45	St John's - UK	*Arnprior*	*Orangeville* *Arnprior*
ON 289	78	11.03 - 28.03.45	UK - St John's	*Arnprior*	*Orangeville* *Arnprior*
HX 347	62	3.04 - 15.04.45	St John's - UK	*Arnprior*	*Orangeville* *Arnprior*
ON 298	70	21.04 - 05.05.45	UK - Halifax	*Arnprior*	*Orangeville* *Arnprior*

HIGHLIGHTS OF THESE VOYAGES

Convoy ON(S) 239

At 1845 12 June in position 'B' ahead of the tenth column, *Fredericton* gained a contact classified as 'submarine'. A ten charge depth charge pattern was dropped. The contact was maintained, sporadically, whilst the convoy passed by. Once the convoy had passed, the contact was attacked with Hedgehog and *Orangeville* made several attacks with Squid. Depth charge attacks were made by *Halifax* and New *Glasgow*. *Orangeville* carried out the last attack at 2139Z with Squid. At this point the hunt was abandoned chiefly because *Orangeville* and *Fredericton* were now thirty miles astern of the convoy.

At the time, Commanding Officers were fairly confident that they were attacking a submarine. Later, reflection caused the S.O. to believe that the contacts resulted from different density layers and temperature gradients in the sea. A notable feature of this action was the ability of *Fredericton* to maintain contact whilst the columns of ships passed either side of the hunting Frigate.

Convoy ONS 33 (29.09 - 12.10.44)

HF/DF bearings of a U-boat's transmission were obtained by *Arnprior* and *Orangeville* on 30 September 1944. These placed the U-boat close to the convoy. *Chebougue* (S.O.) with *Chambly* and

*A starboard quarter view of **HMCS Orangeville**.*   (Ben Warlow Collection)

Orangeville proceeded at best speed to find the U-boat. **Orangeville** cut through the convoy to do so. The U-boat dived and a box search was started whilst **Chebougue** returned to the convoy. At 2100 **Chebougue** illuminated a surfaced U-boat and shortly afterwards was torpedoed in the stern. **Orangeville** and **Arnprior** went to her assistance, **Arnprior** arriving first. She went alongside and took off the Senior Officer and most of the Officers and crew. The CO, Lt. Cdr Oliver and a skeleton crew remained on board whilst **Chambly** took her in tow.

Describing the action Lt Cdr M.V. Oliver RCNR wrote in a letter to Comdr. R. Pike:-

"To answer your question about the U-boat, I certainly saw it in the morning, about 0830. We saw a puff of smoke ahead of us, - I climbed up to the Crowsnest, and she was clearly visible. This was after running down a HF/DF bearing. We did not see her at night before we were torpedoed, but she was very clear on the radar."

"The torpedoing caused a hell of a lot of interest in the RN. The C.A.T. was working efficiently, (almost drowning out the noise of the Asdic transmission). We complied with the correct Step Aside procedure, (even erring if anything, on the side of caution in that we altered course 22° to Starboard when the range was 5,700 - instead of altering at 4,000 yards.)."

"He dived at 5,700 yards, hence the alteration. Admiral Max Horton, V.C, (CinC WA) was particularly interested, and sent a plane down to Swansea for me to go to Derby House. . . . .".

"You see, the RN did not believe in the efficiency of the C.A.T., they would have nothing to do with it - believing , it had not been sufficiently tested or proven. They continued to use Foxer which towed noisemakers, one from each quarter, (we thought them cumbersome). . . . ."

ONS 41 (31.01 - 17.10.45)

ONS 41 set a record for being the slowest convoy taking 21 days to cover the two thousand miles from Ireland to the rendezvous off Newfoundland some days bucking the westerly gales, the convoy didn't move at all.

On 7 February it blew so hard, the convoy finally had to 'heave-to'...we were astern of the carrier behind the convoy. The O.O.W of the carrier had a good wind indicator and 'flashed' us the wind velocity. At 1400 it was 60 knots, by 1500 it was 80. After that we had trouble seeing him because our eyes were cut with the flying spray but the signalman managed to get the last message . "Its gone over the gauge. Must be over 100 knots".

We were in a real hurricane. The big black waves were mountainous, the bow would dig in and tons of water would come crashing on to the bow, drench us on the bridge and pick up and shake the ship as it went by. At times we wondered if the bow would shake off the weight of water and come up again, but it always did, and our salvation was we would float over the top like a cork.

To keep our bow heading into the sea we had to keep enough revs on to maintain steerage way but were overtaking the convoy and had to turn around. We had heard that the castle the ***Hesperus*** (sic) had rolled 60° and water had gone down the ventilators into the boiler room. The 'seventh wave' is reputed to be the smaller and holding my breath I gave the order to put the helm over. We did roll our rails under but the ship righted herself and rode the following seas without broaching to. After that we knew our "Fruit Jar" could weather anything the Atlantic could come up with.

(Source: *Comdr. R. Pike RCNVR (Retd) 'History of **Orangeville**').*

Orangeville's Deck Log for the 7th February 1945 records the wind strength at 0400 as being Force 4 with Sea and Swell 3/4 . Four hours later the wind had risen to Force 7 with a sea and swell of 5/3. The Log records 'Numerous rain squalls reducing visibility to 3 cables. Wind force 8 with gusts to 9. The

HMCS Orangeville *in April 1944.*   *(MoD/Crown Copyright)*

peak of the storm occurred between the hours of 1300 and 1800. Winds recorded at Force 11 with the sea and swell increasing to 7/7. These seas continued until well into the night even though the wind slowly dropped to Force 9 by 0400 on 8 February. The convoy had hove to at 1715/7th on a course of 255°. *Orangeville* zigzagging across the stern of the convoy which was becoming increasingly scattered. By midnight with the ship on a course of 250° at 110 revs the convoy was on her port side. The decision to regain contact with the convoy was made at 0300 and the course altered to 070° and steamed at 140 revs. Contact was gained by radar with six merchant ships and course altered back to 250° steaming at 100 revs. at 0500. By 0700 *Orangeville* was in radar contact with 9 merchant ships. Rounding up the convoy continued until 1420 when, with the wind easing back to Force 7 and the sea and swell moderated to 4/7, the convoy proceeded on course at 6 knots. By 1140 the next day (9th) 28 ships had reformed and there were only 5 stragglers. By this time the wind was still at Force 7-8 with sea and swell 6/7. Normal routine seems to have resumed by 0400 on 10 February.

HMCS PETROLIA

Battle Honours
Atlantic 1944-45

HMCS Petrolia.   (*MoD/Crown Copyright*)

Petrolia was laid down as **HMS Sherbourne Castle**. She was transferred to the RCN and commissioned on 29 June 1944. After working up at Tobermory she was allocated to the C4 Escort Group engaged in escorting mid ocean convoys across the Atlantic. She remained with that Group until the end of the war in Europe.

HISTORY

24.01.43	Ordered as **HMS Sherbourne Castle**.
21.06.43	Laid dow. **Builder**: Hull & Engine - Harland & Wolff (Belfast).
24.02.44	Launched.
29.06.44	Handed over to the RCN and Commissioned.
14.07.44	Completed.

WARTIME VOYAGES

Date	ESG	Senior Officer	Convoy	No of Ships	Arrive/ Sail	Location	Notes
22.07.44					Sail	Belfast	0215526/6 *P* is allocated to CinC NA on comple tion of working up
23.07.44					Arv	Tobermory	
06.08.44	Unall				Sail	Tobermory	
08.08.44					Arv	Aultbia	
09.08.44					Sail	Aultbia	
09.08.44					Arv	Stornoway	
11.08.44	EG C4	*Wentworth*				At Sea	
14.08.44	EG C4	*Wentworth*			Arv	Tobermory	
22.08.44	EG C4	*Wentworth*			Arv	Londonderry	
22.08.44	EG C4	*Wentworth*			Sail	Tobermory	
01.09.44	EG C4	*Wentworth*	ONS 251	141	Sail	Belfast	
02.09.44	EG C4	*Wentworth*	ONS 251	141	Sail	Londonderry	
04.09.44	EG C4	*Wentworth*	ONS 251	141		5317N1245W	
13.09.44	EG C4	*Glace Bay*	ONS 251-	141	Arv	St John's	
21.09.44	EG C4	*Wentworth*	HXS 309	74	Sail	St John's	Canadian sources give 77 ships. 1 turned back, auxilairy machinery defects
27.09.44	EG C4	*Wentworth*	HXS 309	74		4822N 2754W	
01.10.44	EG C4	*Wentworth*	HXS 309	36		5135N 0805W	74 ships according to Hague.possibly some of the ships had already been diverted to destina tion ports.
02.10.44	EG C4	*Wentworth*	HX 309	36	Arv	Londonderry	
06.10.44	EG C4	*Wentworth*	HXS 309	74		At Londonderry	
10.10.44	EG C4	*Wentworth*				At Londonderry	
14.10.44	EG C4	*Wentworth*	ONS 34	37	Sail	Londonderry	
15.10.44	EG C4	*Wentworth*	ONS 34	37	Sail	Londonderry	
23.10.44	EG C4	*Wentworth*	ONS 34	37		4555N 2515W	
04.11.44	EG C4	*Wentworth*	HX 317	45	Sail	St John's	
07.11.44	EG C4	*Wentworth*	HX 317	45		4751N 3225W	
13.11.44	EG C4	*Wentworth*	HX 317	45	Arv	Londonderry	
24.11.44	EG C4	*Wentworth*	ON 268	60		At Larne	
24.11.44	EG C4	*Wentworth*	ON 268	60	Sail	Belfast	
24.11.44	EG C4	*Wentworth*	ON 268	60	Sail	Belfast	
28.11.44	EG C4	*Wentworth*	ON 268	60		4728N1620W	
05.12.44	EG C4	*Wentworth*	ON 268	60	Arv	St John's	
13.12.44	EG C4	*Wentworth*	HK 325	57	Sail	St John's	
24.12.44	EG C4	*Wentworth*	HX 325	57	Arv	Londonderry	
03.01.45	EG C4	*Wentworth*	ON 276	69	Sail	Belfast	

Date	ESG	Senior Officer	Convoy	No of Ships	Arrive/ Sail	Location	Notes
14.01.45	EG C4	*Wentworth*	ON 276	69	Arv	Halifax	
21.01.45	EG C4	*Wentworth*	HX 333	53	Sail	Halifax	
29.01.45	EG C4	*Wentworth*	HX 333	53		4959N 2222W	
03.02.45	EG C4	*Wentworth*	HX 333	53	Arv	Londonderry	
11.02.45	EG C4	*Wentworth*	ON 284	66	Sail	Londonderry	
24.02.45	EG C4	*Wentworth*	ON 284	66	Arv	St John's	
04.03.45	EG C4	*Glace Bay*	HX 341	71	Sail	St John's	
16.03.45	EG C4	*Glace Bay*	HX 341	72	Arv	Londonderry	
22.03.45	EG C4	*Glace Bay*	ONS 45	27	Sail	Londonderry	
23.03.45	EG C4	*Glace Bay*	ONS 45	27	Sail	Londonderry	
23.03.45	EG C4	*Glace Bay*	ONS 45	27	Sail	Belfast	
08.04.45	EG C4	*Glace Bay*	ONS 45	27	Arv	St John's	It is assumed that *Bowmanville* arrived at St John's the same day
12.04.45	EG C4	*Glace Bay*	HX 349	56	Sail	St John's	Canadian source gives 55 ships. 2 turned back: 1 poor bunkers, 1 engine defects
24.04.45	EG C4	*Glace Bay*	HX 349	56	Arv	Moville	Convoy split 5125N 0843W at 0200Z/ 22.04.45
03.05.45	EG C4	*Glace Bay*	ONS 49	56	Sail	Londonderry	
03.05.45	EG C4	*Glace Bay*	ONS 49	56	Sail	Moville	
16.05.45	EG C4	*Glace Bay*	ONS 49	56	Arv	St John's	
23.05.45	EG C4	*Glace Bay*	HX 357	83	Sail	St John's	Canadian source gives 82 ships. 2 turned back with defects
02.06.45	EG C4	*Glace Bay*	HX 357	83	Arv	Londonderry	
10.06.45	EG C4				Sail	Clyde	

August 1945	Refit at Charlottetown.
October 1945	Placed in maintenance reserve at Halifax.
08.03.46	Paid off at Liverpool N.S and soon afterwards sold to New York buyer and re-named *Maid of Athens*.
1947	Transferred to the Indian Registry and re-named *Bharat Laxmi*. Continued in service until 1965.
1965	Broken up at Bombay.

During her Naval Service she escorted 14 convoys including ONS 251 of 141 ships. In total she escorted 895 merchant ships of which only one was lost due to enemy action.

HMCS ST. THOMAS

Battle Honours
Atlantic 1944-45

HMCS St Thomas in May 1944.　　　　　　　　　　　　　　　*(MoD/Crown Copyright)*

The corvette **HMCS St Thomas** was laid down as **HMS Sandgate Castle**. She was transferred to the RCN and commissioned at Middlesborough on 4 May 1944. After working up at Tobermory she was temporarily allocated to anti submarine patrol work in the Western Approaches. At the end of July 1944 she was allocated to the C3 Escort Group and worked with that group until the end of the war in Europe on Mid-ocean convoy duty in the North Atlantic. She was the only Castle Class Corvette in the group. Whilst escorting convoy HX 327 **St Thomas** sank **U-877** and rescued all of her crew.

HISTORY

19.01.43	Ordered as **HMS Sandgate Castle**.
23.06.43	Laid down. **Builder**: Hull & engine - Swan Hunter & Wigham Richardson (Wallsend).
28.12.43	Launched.
04.05.44	Commissioned and handed over to RCN.
18.05.44	Completed.

WARTIME VOYAGES

Date	ESG	Senior Officer	Convoy	No of Ships	Arrive/ Sail	Location	Notes
30.05.44					Arv	Rosyth	
30.05.44					Sail	Tees	N.S.H.Q. 082306z.05:- On completion of working up *St T* is allocated to CinC N.A.
31.05.44					Sail	Rosyth	
02.06.44					Arv	Tobermory	
14.06.44	Unall				Arv	Londonderry	
20.06.44	Unall				Sail	Londonderry	For boiler cleaning operation C.W.
01.07.44	Unall				Sail	Londonderry	Operation CW
05.07.44						5828N 0910W	A/S Search: Operation CW
15.07.44	Unall				Arv	Londonderry	
24.07.44	Unall				Arv	Tobermory	Depart Londonderry same day
29.07.44	Unall				Sail	Tobermory	
30.07.44					Arv	Larne	
30.07.44					Sail	Tobermory	
03.08.44	EG C3				Sail	Londonderry	
04.08.44	EG C3	*Ettrick*	ONF 247	95		5612N 1315W	*Prince Rupert* takes over as SO on 10th Aug
13.08.44	EG C3	*Prince Rupert*	ONF 247	95	Arv	St John's	
22.08.44	EG C5				Sail	St John's	
23.08.44					Sail	Balboa	
24.08.44	EG C3	*Prince Rupert*	HXM 304	90		4640N 4225W	
07.09.44	EG C3	*Prince Rupert*	HXM 304	90	Arv	Londonderry	
14.09.44	EG C3	*Prince Rupert*	ONF 253	64	Sail	Londonderry	
14.09.44	EG C3	*Prince Rupert-*	ONF 253	64		Oversay	
25.09.44	EG C3	*Prince Rupert*	ONF 253	64	Arv	Halifax	
01.10.44	EG C3	*Prince Rupert*	HX 311	48	Sail	Halifax	
11.10.44	EG C3	*Prince Rupert*	HX 311	48		5138N 0733W	
12.10.44	EG C3	*Prince Rupert*	HX 311	48	Arv	Londonderry	
16.10.44	EG C3					At Londonderry	
20.10.44	EG C3					At Londonderry	
25.10.44	EG C3				Sail	Londonderry	
25.10.44	EG C3				Arv	Londonderry	
31.10.44	EG C3	*Kokanee*	ON 262	50		4520N 2040W	
06.11.44	EG C3	*Kokanee*	ON 262	50	Arv	St John's	
13.11.44	EG C2	*Kokanee*	HX 319	46	Sail	St John's	
21.11.44	EG C3	*Kokanee*	HX 319	46		5030N 2532W	
25.11.44	EG C3	*Kokanee*	HX 319	46	Arv	Londonderry	
03.12.44	EG C3	*Kokanee*			Sail	Larne	

Date	ESG	Senior Officer	Convoy	No of Ships	Arrive/ Sail	Location	Notes
04.12.44	EG C3	*Kokanee*	ON 270	48	Sail	Belfast	
09.12.44	EG C3	*Kokanee*	ON 270	48		4504N 2502W	
12.12.44	EG C3	*Kokanee*	ON 270	48		4408N 3159W	
16.12.44	EG C3	*Kokanee*	ON 270	48	Arv	St John's	
23.12.44	EG C3-	*Kokanee*	HX 327	45	Sail	St John's	
26.12.44	EG C3	*Kokanee*	HX 327	45		4410N 4140W	Sinks *U-877* 27.12.44. All crew rescued
01.01.45	EG C3	*Kokanee*	HX 327	17		5118N 0915W	Hague gives 44 ships
04.01.45	EG C3	*Kokanee*	HX 327	45	Arv	Londonderry	
13.01.45	EG C3	*Kokanee*	ON 278	47	Sail	Belfast	
15.01.45	EG C3	*Kokanee*	ON 278	31		5018N 0932W	47 ships according to Hague
22.01.45	EG C3	*Kokanee*	ON 278	48		4433N 4235W	
25.01.45	EG C3	*Kokanee*	ON 278	48	Arv	St John's	
03.02.45	EG C3	*Kokanee*	(HX 336)	47	Sail	St John's	
15.02.45	EG C3	*Kokanee*	(HX 336)	47	Arv	Londonderry	
27.02.45	EG C3	*Kokanee*	(ONS 43)	23	Sail	Liverpool	
13.03.45	EG C3	*Kokanee*	(ONS 43)	23	Arv	St John's	
19.03.45	EG C3	*Kokanee*	(HX 345)	74	Sail	St John's	
01.04.45	EG C3	*Kokanee*	(HX 345)	74	Arv	Londonderry	
06.04.45	EG C3	*Kokanee*				Londonderry	Repairs complete 10 April
12.04.45	EG C3	*Kokanee*			Arv	Cardiff	
13.04.45	EG C3	*Kokanee*	(ON 296)	65	Sail	Milford Haven	
30.04.45	EG C3	*Kokanee*	(ON 296)	65	Arv	Halifax	
23.08.45					Sail	Balboa	
09.09.45					Arv	Esquimalt	For disposal

1946	Sold to Union Steamship Co: converted for passenger service and re-named *Camosun*.
1958	Re-named *Chilcotin*.
1958	Re-named *Yukon Star*.
1974	After several years laid up, scrapped at Tacoma.

On the 26th June 1944 whilst working on A/S patrols in operation CW *St Thomas* made an HF/DF report that resulted in the sinking of *U-719* by a Hedgehog attack from *HMS Bulldog*. *St Thomas* did not attack the target because of the direct hit achieved by *Bulldog*. She was also criticised for not following the correct procedure when reporting the initial HF/DF contact.

Subsequently on 29th June *St Thomas*'s Squid failed to fire when attacking a doubtful contact. The failure of the Squid was attributed to human error by an in-experienced LTO deputising for the senior man who was sick at the time. However, excellent results had been obtained with the Asdic Type 147B depth predictor.

St Thomas was involved in the close escort of 13 trans-Atlantic convoys comprising 838 ships.

Only two Reports of proceedings were found for the C3 Escort Group. The first of these concerned the passage of convoy ON(F) 253 14 - 25 September 1944. This was a routine uneventful passage except perhaps for the unusual Asdic conditions that were reported occurring on the morning of 22nd September in position 44°59'N 43°05'W when numerous non-sub echoes were detected by all the ships of the escort. These never held over a range of 1,000 Yards. The echoes were of a 'sub' quality and the extent of the target was usually 10° at 1,000 yards.

It was thought that this was due to a marked negative temperature gradient which prevailed from the time that they crossed 20° W till the end of the voyage. It was observed that the temperature of the sea water increased from 60°F to 67°F during a two hour period.

*A close up shot of the bow and bridge structure of **HMCS St Thomas**.*

(*Ken MacPherson via Vanwell Publications*)

THE SINKING OF U-877

The passage of HX 327 of 45 ships (23/12/44 - 02/01/45) was routine and uneventful until the 26th December when a third class and distant transmission from a U-boat was detected. Later in the day *St Thomas* sighted an apparent rocket low down and far on the horizon. Because of the distance and the few escorts present none were despatched to investigate.

The next morning at 0755 in position 46°25'N, 36°36'W *Edmunston* in position 'N' obtained a doubtful Asdic contact which she investigated and subsequently lost. At 0815, *St Thomas*, in position 'G' attacked a contact . A second pattern with Squid was fired 0917. *Sea Cliff* was detached to assist. *St Thomas* lost contact. At 1030, after an unsuccessful search, course was about to be set to rejoin the convoy, when the U-boat surfaced, two and a half miles away and sank shortly afterwards. Fifty two survivors were picked up. The Commanding Officer, three other officers and thirty men by *St Thomas*, one officer and nineteen men by *Sea Cliff*.

The account of the action by the survivors is of interest. *U-877* had been allocated weather reporting duties, but because of a faulty transmitter she was unable to signal her reports. Control, in the absence of reports, conclude correctly that her transmitter was faulty and ordered *U-877* to act independently. Uncertain what action to take, course was set in a westerly to south westerly direction. On 27th December the U-boat was proceeding on the surface for the third time since leaving Kristiansand twenty days earlier. A contact was received on the *Fliege* and the boat dived. Screw noises were reported to be in the vicinity. These were disregarded by the C.O who considered that the G.S.R warning must have been an aircraft and that the hydrophone noises were from the boat itself. The first contact was about 0700 and about two hours later the first depth charges were dropped. These were estimated to have been at a depth of 60m (197 feet) and fairly far astern of the U-boat, which was at 20m (66 feet). No damage was done, except to the lamps in the P.O's mess. One prisoner stated that the hatch over the Diesel room had not been properly secured during the dive, and water had entered the Diesel room.

The U-boat had reached a depth of 80m (262 feet) when a second pattern of charges fell, causing a leak aft, which began to flood the stern compartment and the boat sank (stern first) at an angle of 40° to 50° to a depth of 340 to 350m (1,115 to 1,148 feet).

St Thomas had obtained a contact at about 0615, and after some hesitation because of fish noises classified it as submarine. At 0630 she fires Squid set to 100 feet. Asdic gave the U-boat's depth as 520 feet. At 0700 contact was regained and an attack made with Squid at 6 knots, the U-boat's depth being established as 400 feet. Contact was lost after the attack and never regained.

After this attack a great excess of pressure developed in the boat and the pumps were out of action, but tanks were blown and both motors put at full ahead. The boat rose to about 160m (524 feet) and the CO ordered the Engineer Officer to reduce to dead slow and to keep her at that depth. However, this was not possible and she started to slide back down again. The blowing of all tanks and the maintenance of three quarters speed brought the boat violently to the surface. The Captain was thrown out on the deck through the conning tower hatch, severely injuring his head and the CPO Navigation was also injured. The CO at first ordered the crew to man the 37mm guns, but apparently his order was never carried out and the next order was to abandon ship. The last to leave was the Engineer Officer, who scuttled the boat by opening the vents.

(Source: NSS 1487-49 Report on the Interrogation of Survivors from U-877, a 740 ton U-Boat sunk 27th December, 1944. National Defence Headquarters, Ottawa).

HMCS TILLSONBURG

Battle Honours
Atlantic 1944-45

HMCS Tillsonburg.   (*Ken MacPherson via Vanwell Publications*)

Originally laid down as **HMS Pembroke Castle**, she was transferred to the RCN and commissioned on 29 June 1944. After working up at Tobermory she was sailed independently to St John's NF to join the Escort Group C6. Thus, unusually, her first convoy being an east bound one. **Tillsonburg** remained as the only Castle Class Corvette within the C6 Escort Group, for the remainder of the war in Europe, engaged in mid Ocean escort of trans Atlantic convoys. She escorted 12 convoys comprising 646 ships.

HISTORY

19.12.42	Ordered as **HMS Pembroke Castle** K 450.
03.06.43	Laid down: **Builder**: Hull & Engine - Ferguson (Port Glasgow).
12.02.44	Launched.
29.06.44	Completed, Commissioned and handed over to the RCN.

WARTIME VOYAGES

Date	ESG	Senior Officer	Convoy	No of Ships	Arrive/ Sail	Location	Notes
26.08.44	EG C6	*Eastview*			Sail	Londonderry	
07.09.44	EG C6	*Eastview*			Sail	St John's	
18.09.44	EG C6	*Eastview*	HXF 308	60	Sail	St John's	
21.09.44	EG C6	*Eastview*	HXF 308	60		4635N 3930W	
24.09.44	EG C6	*Eastview*	HX 308 (ME)	59		4915N 2220W	
27.09.44	EG C6	*Eastview*	HXF 308	58		Tuscar Rock	
28.09.44	EG C6	*Eastview*	HXF 308	58	Arv	Londonderry	
06.10.44	EG C6					At Londonderry	
10.10.44	EG C6	*Eastview*				At Londonderry	
12.10.44	EG C6	*Eastview-*	ON 259	40	Sail	Londonderry	37 ships according to Hague
18.10.44	EG C6	*Eastview*	ON 259	40		4955N 2227W	Convoy badly scattered. 37 ships according to Hague
23.10.44	EG C6	*Eastview*	ON 259	37		4812N 4207W	
25.10.44	EG C6	*Eastview*	ON 259	37	Arv	St John's	
25.10.44	EG C6	*Eastview*				At St John's	
07.11.44	EG C6	*Eastview*	HX 316	40		51112N 1155W	
10.11.44	EG C6	*Eastview*	HX 316	39	Arv	Londonderry	
19.11.44	EG C6	*Eastview*	ON 267	40	Sail	Belfast	
19.11.44	EG C6	*Eastview*	ON 267	40	Sail	Belfast	
21.11.44	EG C6	*Eastview*	ON 267	40		5113N 0932W	
28.11.44	EG C6	*Eastview*	ON 267	42		4435N 3758W	
02.12.44	EG C6	*Eastview*	ON 267	43	Arv	St John's	
10.12.44	EG C6	*Eastview*	HX 324	55	Sail	St John's	
12.12.44	EG C6	*Eastview*	HX 324	56		4601N 4103W	
19.12.44	EG C6	*Eastview*	HX 324	55	Arv	Londonderry	
29.12.44	EG C6	*Eastview*	ON 275	39	Sail	Belfast	
08.01.45	EG C6	*Eastview*	ON 275	39		4452N 5230W	
09.01.45	EG C6	*Eastview*	ON 275	39	Arv	St John's	
19.01.45	EG C6	*Eastview*	SC 165	35	Sail	St John's	32 ships according to Hague
22.01.45	EG C6	*Eastview*	SC 165	35		4948N 4210W	
29.01.45	EG C6	*Eastview*	SC 165	33		5518N 1343W	
02.02.45	EG C6	*Eastview*	SC 165	32	Arv	Londonderry	
13.02.45	EG C6	*Eastview*	ONS 42	33	Sail	Liverpool	
03.03.45	EG C6	*Eastview*	ONS 42	33	Arv	St John's	
08.03.45	EG C6	*Eastview*	HX 342	72	Sail	St John's	
20.03.45	EG C6	*Eastview*	HX 342	72	Arv	Londonderry	
27.03.45	EG C6	*Eastview*	ON 293	82	Sail	Londonderry	
10.04.45	EG C6	*Eastview*	ON 293	82	Arv	St John's	
10.04.45	EG C6	*Eastview*	HX 350	87	Arv	St John's-	

Date	ESG	Senior Officer	Convoy	No of Ships	Arrive/ Sail	Location	Notes
28.04.45	EG C6	*Eastview*	HX 350	87	Arv	Londonderry	
06.05.45	EG C6	*Eastview*	ON 301	61	Sail	Londonderry	Claimed by the S.O. to be the last west bound convoy to sail across the Atlantic during the 2nd Great European War.
18.05.45	EG C6	*Eastview*	ON 301	61	Arv	St John's	
27.05.45	EG C6	*Eastview*			Sail	St John's	
06.06.45	EG C6	*Eastview*			Arv	Londonderry	
14.06.45	EG C6				Sail	Clyde	

June 1945 Arrived St. John's N.F and briefly based there and at Sydney and Halifax.
15.02.46   Paid off at Halifax.
1946   Sold to Chinese owners for mercantile service and re-named *Ta Ching*.
1947   Re-named *Chiu Chen*.
1951   Taken over by the Nationalist Chinese Government and re-named *Kao-An*.

HX 308 (60 SHIPS) 18-28 SEPTEMBER 1944

A successful and uneventful passage. The convoy comprising 60 ships which included two M.A.C. ships. The latter were very co-operative, flying three patrols daily whenever weather permitted. Shore based aircraft from Newfoundland were supplied for 14 hours on September 19th and 5 hours on September 20th.

The TBY on *Tillsonburg* caused problems because the ship's staff were unaware that crystals could be used with this set. *Eastview* (S.O.) was supplied with a TBY for tuning purposes.

At the request of CinC WA the MAC tanker *Empire MacKay* was exercised in fuelling escorts as operational requirements permitted.

Towards the end of the voyage the Commodore received changes of destinations of ships in convoy, reorganisation began. It turned out that the new organisation put the south-bound section on the north side of the convoy and the northbound section to the south. The Commodore insisted that the southbound portion should cross his bows on breaking off. To the astonishment of all, this manoeuvre was executed without accident.

There is no ROP for convoys ON 259 and HX 316.

ON 267 (40 SHIPS) 17.11 - 01.12.44
C6 HMCS EASTVIEW (COMMANDER BROCK)
ADM 217/602

Group consisted of *HMC Ships Eastview*, *Tillsonburg*, *St Lambert*, *Peterborough* and *Cobourg*.

The Group proceeded from Moville to Larne on 17 November for exercises. *Eastview*'s asdics broke down and she proceeded to Belfast for repairs rejoining the Group the following day. On completion of

HMCS Tillsonburg in September 1944.   (*MoD/Crown Copyright*)

exercises the Group proceeded to Bangor Bay to fuel from Scottish Musician. The Group weighed and proceeded to sea on Sunday 19 November.

After oiling problems in unsuitable weather and waiting for better conditions destroyer escorts detached from convoy leaving four escorts for the convoy.

Wednesday 29 Nov; *Tillsonburg* ordered to take charge of homing of W4 Escort Group. Group detached from Convoy and headed for St John's on Thursday 30th Nov, arriving alongside St John's 11.30 Friday 1st December.

HMCS EASTVIEW C6 GROUP ON 275
29TH DEC 1944 - 19TH JAN 1945
(ADM 217/603)

(Commander J.V. Brock RCNVR)

A successful and uneventful passage. Good weather was experienced.

Tillsonburg's sailing was delayed because she was awaiting the train arriving from Larne with ratings returning from long leave. On 3 January *Tillsonburg* spent over an hour "sitting" hooked up to the tanker, unable to fuel because of some defect with the tanker. Fuelling was abandoned with the approach of darkness.

On 30th December at 2100 a radar contact turned out to be a small Irish coastal fishing vessel which refused to obey sound or light signals ordering him to stop. A burst of machine gun fire over the mast of this fishing vessel proved a most effective means of impressing upon him that international signals made by both sound and light were to be obeyed. After closing him eventually we exchanged remarks and opin-

ions which would hardly bear repetition but which it is hoped made abundantly clear that Britannia rules the waves.

ANTICIPATED CONTACT WITH U-BOAT(S)

Thursday 4th January; 2300 Submarine situation reports indicated only one U-Boat within range of MAC ship aircraft. Suggested possibility of picking up a weather reporting U-Boat. Consequently at 0600, **Empire Mac Dermott**, with great credit to herself and Fleet Air Arm personnel, flew off three aircraft by moon-light to search most likely bearing.

0940. Aircraft returning, nothing sighted. First aircraft crashed on landing due to collapse of port oleo as a result of pitching flight deck. Port main plane damaged when aircraft came to rest. Plane had to be jettisoned to clear Flight Deck. No injuries sustained by crew.

Later in the day U-Boat situation reports and intercepted German messages indicated in fact that a U-Boat was in the immediate path of the convoy. so at 1301 the escorts were formed as a fleet screen in line abreast ahead of the convoy which at that time was well formed up and steaming in good weather at over ten knots. One ship was left in position 'S'.

From January 3rd **Tillsonburg**'s radar 251M was out of action. It was necessary to use the MAC Ship's set for shore based aircraft, **Tillsonburg** being the only escort of the Group, fitted with this type of radar beacon.

Tillsonburg celebrated the New Year with a successful gunnery exercise on a derelict raft which she sank by gunfire.

There was no ROP for the next convoy ESC 165 from 19 January to 2 February 1945. This was followed by a routine uneventful west bound voyage with ONS 42. That is until the 14 February when bad weather reduced the convoy speed to 2½ knots.

HMCS EASTVIEW C6 ONS 42 11th FEB - 1st MAR 1945 (ADM 217/605)

A fairly routine and uneventful passage with a convoy of 35 ships. The various sections of the convoy joined up over a period of two days. At one time three sections of the convoy were spread over an area of fifteen miles.

Tillsonburg carried out gunnery practice in the Londonderry Exercise area prior to collecting the Liverpool Section.

On the 14th the convoy was supported by Force 33 (EG 21) and by EG 31, the latter screening ships joining from astern.

On Friday 16th the weather began to deteriorate and some ships started to straggle. At times during this period of bad weather the convoy speed was reduced to 2? knots. Much smoke and many stragglers. By Tuesday 20th Feb the convoy was back in form so that by Friday 23rd the convoy speed had increased to 8 knots.

On Thursday 22nd Feb convoy ON 285 escorted by B2 crossed the track of the convoy 15 miles astern. HF/DF bearings were taken of transmissions on 2410 Kc/s and proved very satisfactory.

The next convoy, HX 342 from the 8th to 20th March 1945 was uneventful. Near Westomp a U-boat was reported by an aircraft to be ten miles ahead and the convoy did a credible emergency turn in 1? minutes from the time the Senior Officer had informed the Commodore. Whilst this was in progress **Tillsonburg** picked up an A/S contact and attacked. Other ships from the Group joined in the hunt.. In

his comments Cdr Brock wrote, "The enemy was not contacted by surface forces and although I am unable to assess the reliability of the aircraft sighting report, I feel it is unlikely that a U-boat was present."

The voyage with Convoy ON 293 (82 ships) was conspicuous for the hair raising situation that developed in thick fog when the convoy was clearing the St George's Channel south of Tuscar Rock. Visibility was poor (4-5 cables) and due to accumulated error of both convoys the two met on opposite courses. The convoy was still in an unformed state when RADAR contacts showed the approach of MKF 41 on a collision course with a combined closing speed of approximately 23 knots. Disaster was narrowly averted by prompt action as both convoys executed without incident emergency turns to port. This reflected great credit on all the Merchant Ships of both convoys in that turns were executed in both case in approximately 90 seconds after the receipt of the order from Escort Commanders.

By 4th April the weather was described as 'foul' with the convoy stretched out and steaming at 4 knots. The following day the Commodore's ship broke down. All the ships were rolling heavily in a beam sea; course was altered northwards and the speed of advance 3 knots. Six straggling ships coming up from astern. In consultation with the Commodore it was decided in view of the probability of encountering ice ahead, that the convoy should be reformed making R/T fitted ships leaders of columns. However, no ice was encountered.

With convoy HX 350 (88 ships), 17-28 April 1945, a routine passage was executed in exceptionally good weather. *Empire Reynolds* however, suffered a 'Man Overboard' on 19th April. The Rescue ship and *Tillsonburg* proceeded to the scene and the man was recovered by the Rescue ship's boat "hale and hearty" after his cold bath (water temperature 54°F)

This was followed by Convoy ON 301 (61 ships) 6-18 May 1945, claimed by Cdr. Brock to be the last westbound convoy to be escorted across the Atlantic during the Second Great European War. The enemy was not encountered.

The 9th May 1945, VE Day, did not pass unheralded with Convoy ON 301. To express our grateful appreciation and respect for the Allied Merchant Navies, all naval escorts present fired an eleven gun salute, followed by a Fue de Joie consisting of five depth charges. The firing of the Gun Salute and the dropping of depth charges were controlled by R/T and provided a spectacular and much appreciated gesture of good will. The Commodore then ordered all Merchant Ships to fire four rockets as a salute to the Navy. This mutual demonstration of thankfulness and pride while a small thing compared to Moscow's 4,480 guns or the noise in Trafalgar Square, gave vent to our noisy exuberance in a most fitting manner."

Questioned on his next visit to Londonderry by the HQ Staff on this unusual expenditure of ammunition, Cdr Brock claimed that it was covered by KR& AI. which allows such a demonstration on the occasion of an overwhelming victory for His Majesty's Arms. The SGO minuted "See KR & AI art 87. It would seem that S.O. C6 temporarily promoted himself to the rank of "Governor" in order to authorise the salute; propose NA."

On the 15th May in anticipation of encountering ice, *St Lambert* was stationed seven miles ahead of the convoy on 'Ice Patrol'. At 0740 on the 17th she reported an iceberg ahead and visibility down to about two cables. The convoy made evasive alterations of course to port by sound signals. Not all the ships heard these and the convoy began to split into two sections. Pendant 123 *Aalsum* struck a berg, damaging her forepeak. She reported that she could continue with the convoy. There were several bergs in the vicinity of the badly scattered convoy. The plot indicated that the bergs would easily pass down through the split in the convoy. A very nervous quarter of an hour was spent by all concerned until the escort astern reported that the bergs were clear

HNoMS TUNSBERG CASTLE

Battle Honours
Atlantic 1944   Arctic 1944

HNoMS Tunsberg Castle.   *(Royal Norwegian Naval Museum)*

The **Tunsberg Castle** was loaned to the Royal Norwegian Navy to replace the corvette **Potetilla**. She was owned by the Royal Navy but manned by a Norwegian crew. The Royal Navy paid all expenses.

After working up at Tobermory she was allocated to the B2 Escort Group and was employed on convoy escort duty to and from Gibraltar with that group from late May 1944 to the end of August that year. Subsequently she was variously employed with the B6, B2 and B3 Escort Groups with **Highlander** or **Cotton** as Senior Officer.

Arising from the liberation of the eastern part of Finmark it was decided to deploy Norwegian naval vessels to that area. As part of this movement **Tunsberg Castle** was sailed with Convoy JW 62. After the successful conclusion of this operation **Tunsberg Castle** was sailed for Batsfjord on the 11th December 1944 where on the 12th she struck a mine and sank.

HISTORY

06.03.43	Ordered as **Shrewsbury Castle**.
05.05.43	Laid down: **Builder**: Hull & Engine - Swan Hunter & Wigham Richardson (Wallsend).
16.08.43	Launched.
17.04.44	Given Norwegian Flag and renamed **Tunsberg Castle**.
29.04.44	Completed.

WARTIME VOYAGES

Date	ESG	Senior Officer	Convoy	No of Ships	Arrive/ Sail	Location	Notes
03.05.44	EG B2	*Hesperus*			Sail	Tyne	
21.05.44	EG B2	*Hesperus*			Sail	Tobermory	
30.05.44	EG B2	*Hesperus*			Arv	Larne	
03.06.44	EG B2	*Hesperus*			Sail	Londonderry	
05.06.44	EG B2	*Hesperus*	OS 79/ KMS 53	27		?420N 1245W	
14.06.44	EG B2	*Hesperus*	OS 79/ KMS 53	27	Arv	Gibraltar	
20.06.44	EG B2	*Hesperus*	MKS 52	19	Sail	Gibraltar	Hague records 17 ships
21.06.44	EG B2	*Hesperus*	MKS 52	19		3525N 0830W	
23.06.44	EG B2	*Hesperus*	SL 161/ MKS 52	45		3620N 1535W	Hague records 41 ships
30.06.44	EG B2	*Hesperus*	SL 161/ MKS 52	44		5430N 1101W	
02.07.44	EG B2	*Hesperus*	SL 161/ MKS 52	44	Arv	Londonderry	
13.07.44	EG B2	*Hesperus*	OS 83/ KMS 57	29	Sail	Londonderry	
14.07.44	EG B2	*Hesperus*	OS 83/ KMS 57	32		5557N 0945W	Hague gives 29 ships
22.07.44	EG B2	*Hesperus*	OS 83/ KMS 57	31		3810N 1750W	
25.07.44	EG B2	*Hesperus*	OS 83/ KMS 57	31	Arv	Gibraltar	
29.07.44	EG B2	*Hesperus*	MKS 56	18	Sail	Algiers	
30.07.44	EG B2	*Hesperus*	SL 165/ MKS 56	35	Sail	Gibraltar	Hague gives 35 ships
05.08.44	EG B2	*Hesperus*	SL 165/ MKS 56	39		4615N 1824W	
07.08.44	EG B2	*Hesperus*	SL 165/ MKS 56	32		5152N 1540W	
10.08.44	EG B2	*Hesperus*			Arv	Liverpool	
29.08.44	EG B6					Campbeltown	
01.09.44	EG B6				Sail	Liverpool	
04.09.44	EG B2	*Cotton*			Arv	Larne	
08.09.44	Force 33	*Highlander*	ONF 252	90		Nr Oversay	
09.09.44	EG B2	*Cotton*			Sail	Londonderry	
09.09.44	Force 33	*Highlander*	ONF 252	98		5610N 1128W	In support of B2
10.09.44	Force 33	*Highlander*	ONF 252	98		5317N 1549W	
18.10.44	EG B3	*Highlander*	ON 260	27		5045N 0905W	
28.11.44	7th EG	*Cygnet*			Arv	Aultbea	
29.11.44	7th EG	*Cygnet*	JW 62	31	Sail	Aultbea	
05.12.44	7th EG	*Cygnet*	JW 62	31		7240N 3120E	

Date	ESG	Senior Officer	Convoy	No of Ships	Arrive/ Sail	Location	Notes
10.12.44					Sail	Kola Inlet	Sailed independently on 11.12.44 destined for Batsfjord
12.12.44							*Tunsberg Castle* mined & sunk at entrance to Batsfjord.

The force transferred to operate in Finmark waters consisted of the corvettes *Tunsberg Castle* and *Eglantine*, auxiliary minesweepers (Isles Class) *Jelöy*, *Karmöy*, *Oksöy* and *Tromöy*. Admiral Danielsen was in command of the force, which operated independently, but under the Russian high command. *Tunsberg Castle* was ordered to sail to Norway on 26 November 1944 and sailed the next day for Loch Ewe to join Convoy JW 62. She was attached to the 7th Escort Group (SO *Cygnet*). A small specially trained group of Norwegian soldiers travelled with the convoy. These were to be landed in the gap between the retreating Germans and the allied forces.

A task force consisting of *Tunsberg Castle* (with 1 officer and 10 soldiers of the Norwegian army embarked) *Eglantine*, *Karmoy* and *Tromoy* sailed on 11 December from Polyarnye bound for Batsfjord with supplies for the population there. The town had been abandoned and destroyed by the Germans. Some of the inhabitants had managed to avoid being forcible evacuated and were in a desperate situation without food and shelter in the arctic winter.

The task force was commanded by Commander senior grade E. Hostveldt, the Commanding Officer of the Norwegian Navy in Kirness. The two corvettes were to support the minesweepers and provide anti U-boat cover. Arriving off the entrance to the fjord outside Batsfjord the two minesweepers escorted the corvettes with oropesa sweeping gear. At about 1000 the force observed some lights blinking near the Makkaur lighthouse and *Tunsberg Castle* was ordered to investigate. The minesweepers hauled their gear, and *Eglantine* returned out to sea in the cleared channel. At 1004, with Makkaur lighthouse bearing 010° 1,500 metres, the *Tunsberg Castle* was hit beneath the stern, and a second explosion about 15 metres to starboard of the vessel. Some 20-25 metres of the stern were ripped off , and five of the crew (located at the stern) were killed in the explosion. Two others were wounded, and both the engine and boilers put out of action. The *Tunsberg Castle* had sailed out of the swept channel. The sinking wreck drifted into the channel again and the *Eglantine* was able to come alongside. The remaining crew and the soldiers were safely transferred at 1045 when Lt. Cdr Th. Jacobsen was the last man to leave the vessel. *Tunsberg Castle* sank at 1145 in position 70°44.5'N 30°09'E. Some of the crew had abandoned the ship in rafts or jumped overboard. These were picked up by the *Eglantine* and *Tromöy*. The force returned to Polyarnye.

It is almost certain *Tunsberg Castle* struck a German EMC mine laid on 31 October 1944 by the German destroyer *Z-33* as part of a flanking minefield in the exact spot as *Tunsberg Castle* was later lost. The second explosion was probably another mine exploding in reaction to the first, or a depth charge from the *Tunsberg Castle*. She had armed depth charges with a 50ft setting, and they probably exploded. However this cannot be positively confirmed as the wreck is still not located and surveyed (05.09.01)

*(Source: The account of the sinking of **Tunsberg Castle** is derived from personal communications from Commander 1st Grade Ingvar Fosheim Commanding Officer Royal Norwegian Naval Museum and Rear Admiral Ole F. Berg Rt. who was serving as a Midshipman on the **Tunsberg Castle** at that time. The Editor is most grateful for these sources)*

Section Four
ESCORT GROUPS

Previous page: **HMS Allington Castle** (*Lt D. Harris*)

ESCORT GROUP REPORTS

Most of the Castle Class Corvettes operated in Escort Groups containing two or more of these ships. To avoid tedious repetition, summaries of the Reports of Proceedings of the relevant Escort Groups are provided, thus affording the reader an overview of the convoy work undertaken by these ships. Actions, primarily the concern of any one ship, are described in Section 3 under the individual ship.

LIVERPOOL ESCORT POOL

By December 1944 the threat to the Gibraltar convoys when on ocean passage from the air and from U-boats was considered to be comparatively low. Consequently the escort strength whilst on ocean passage was reduced and the relevant escort groups re-organized. This resulted in a number of Castle Class Corvettes being allocated to the Liverpool Escort Pool (LEP). The ships involved were:-

Amberley Castle; Knaresborough Castle; Leeds Castle; Oakham Castle; Oxford Castle and *Rushen Castle.*

The identification of these ships' voyages whilst in the LEP has been primarily through the 'Pink List' and from references from the Ship Movement Order files. There is little information available from the Reports of Proceedings, because, with the exception of *Knaresborough Castle* and *Rushen Castle*, the senior Officer of the escort was not identified. Accounts of the voyages of these two ships whilst operating from the Liverpool Escort Pool are given in Section 3 under the individual ships' histories.

B-1 ESCORT GROUP

CONVOY SC 158; 7th - 18th OCTOBER 1944 (72 SHIPS)
B-1 ESCORT GROUP HMS CHELMER (SO) Cmdr J.H. Elder DCS RN.
(The report of Proceedings for the outward bound voyage was not found).

This was an uneventful passage. There had been some dispute at the start of the voyage between W-5 and B-1 as who was in command of the escorts, W-5 maintaining that B-1 was merely in support.

When approaching the UK *Empire Mallory* developed a leak caused by the heavy rolling of the ship. She reported that sediment from the cargo of zinc concentrate had blocked the pump intakes. On the 17th the Master reported that the position was serious. The wind had reached gale force, but the convoy was riding comfortably with a stern sea. *Empire Mallory* reported that she was listing dangerously to starboard but could maintain 10 knots for 12 hours. Eventually she passed ahead of the convoy and arrived safely at Moville.
(ADM 217/326)

CONVOY ONS 35 UK - HALIFAX 30th OCTOBER - 11th NOVEMBER 1944.
B-1 ESCORT GROUP: HMS CHELMER (SO) Cmdr J.H. Eaden DSC RN.

Escorts included *Tintagel Castle* and two MAC ships, *SS Macoma* and *SS Adula*.

In the afternoon of the 30th October *SS Lombardy* had to stop to investigate engine defects. *Tintagel Castle*

was ordered to stand by her. Repairs were completed on the 31st and they rejoined the convoy.

No 55 **Egton** had problems with her crankshaft. A steel dowel pin was required to effect repairs. **SS Macona** produced a pin in record time from her workshop. This was transferred to **Egton** by **Tintagel Castle**, who also transferred a second pin on the 11th (Editor's recollection).
(ADM 217/328)

CONVOY HX 320 NF TO UK 17th - 30th NOVEMBER 1944 (32 SHIPS)
B-1 ESCORT GROUP: HMS CHELMER (SO) CMDR J.H. Eaden DSC RN.

HM Ships Inman, *Tintagel Castle* and others; Report does not give a list of the escorts. *HM Ships Vimy*, *Narcissus* and *HMCS Calgary* joined on 28th as additional escorts.

The *Abrial Gibbon* (No 83) created a diversion by reporting sighting a periscope. Three officers including the Master and the watch on deck had seen the periscope. Although B-1 seemed to doubt the authenticity of this report an emergency ship-shore was broadcast. In due course *Tintagel Castle* recovered an old weighted wooden spar. This was done from the whaler in difficult seas. The full story of this incident is related in the *Tintagel Castle* history.

Air cover was provided by the MAC ship *SS Empire MacAlpine* carrying four Swordfish. Bad weather, force 7 wind and confused swells, prevented routine patrols. The only operational flight carried out - which was to investigate the wherabouts of the straggler *SS Drupa*, was succesful, but the aircraft sustained damage to her landing gear when flying on. The aircrew suffered no casualties.
(ADM217/327)

CONVOY ON 271 9th - 22nd DECEMBER 1944 (70 SHIPS)
B-1 ESCORT GROUP: (SO) CMDR J.H. EADEN DSC RN IN HMS TINTAGEL CASTLE

HM Ships Inman, *Lotus*, *Poppy* & *Dianella* in company.

Rendezvous effected with the Clyde and Belfast sections on 9th December. The Milford Haven section joined on the 10th and the English Channel section on the 11th. Heavy weather encountered. On the 17th the convoy was spread out over a frontage of 25 miles and a depth of 35 miles. On the 20th, with a southerly gale wind force 8 veering slowly and increasing in strength one vessel with only 2.5 days fuel remaining was detached to St John's NF escorted by *HMS Poppy*.
(ADM 199/581 and ADM217/565).

CONVOY HX 328 HALIFAX TO UK; 28TH DECEMBER 1944 - 8th JANUARY 1945 (56 SHIPS)
B-1 ESCORT GROUP: (SO) CMDR J.H. EADEN DSC RN IN HMS TINTAGEL CASTLE

HM Ships Inman, *Lotus*, *Poppy*, *Dianella*, *HMCS Cap de la Madaleine* in company. The latter temporarily attached.

Four hours after leaving St John's the weather was reported as south-westerly gale wind force 8-9 and heavy snow. Homing procedures were used to effect the meet of escorts and convoy. This worked very well.

On the 30th December, 52 ships were found. One of these returned to Halifax as being unable to keep up with the convoy. One of the other stragglers reported as having a tank adrift in her hold.

Problems were encountered when oiling at sea in heavy weather because of the shortness of the oiling hose. Arising from this experience General Orders were amended to the effect that Masters of Oilers should be asked

by the relevant escorts to stream the additional 210 feet of hose carried for oiling during rough weather. *(ADM 217/566)*

CONVOY ON 279 UK - HALIFAX; 18th - 29th JANUARY 1945 (47 SHIPS)
B-1 ESCORT GROUP: (SO) CMDR J.H. EADEN DSC RN IN HMS TINTAGEL CASTLE

HM Ships Dianella, *Poppy*, *Lotus*, and *Starwort* in company (*Inman* undergoing engine overhaul at Londonderry. She joined the convoy later).

Junctions of the various sections of the convoy were carried out in heavy weather and in one case hazardous conditions. The Mersey Section joined in severe weather on opposite course. So as to disembark pilots the convoy sheltered in Cardigan Bay in conditions of high wind. Eight pilots were transferred in a force 8 wind by the whaler of *Tintagel Castle*, *Cape Mario*'s skiff and *Kemthorn*'s motorboat. "*The boats crews exhibited good seaman ship under difficult conditions.*"

Early in the morning of the 20th *HMS Starwort* attacked a suspected submarine. She was supported by *Inman*. Several attacks were carried out in the ensuing 2? hours. It was concluded that the target(s) were wrecks known to be in the vicinity. However, it was possible that the first contact was that of a submarine. The SO in his report raised the problems created by contacts in depths of less than 100 fathoms and of the tactical importance of not allowing close escorts to be diverted by 'doubtful' contacts.

On the 23rd *Tintagel Castle*, Engineer Officer was transferred to *Poppy* to assist in engine defect repairs. It was concluded that these could not be carried out at sea. *Poppy* 's speed was reduced to 10 knots.

CONVOY HX 336 6th - 16th FEBRUARY 1945 (48 SHIPS)
B-1 ESCORT GROUP: (SO) CMDR J.H. EADEN DSC RN IN HMS TINTAGEL CASTLE

HM Ships Inman, Dianella, *Poppy*, *Lotus*, and *Starwort* in company.

An uneventful passage. The weather was moderate and convoy discipline good.

The Rescue Ship dealt successfully with several cases of illness. In one case of peritonitis the patient's life was saved by the use of penicillin. The patient was transferred from No 42 *R.J. Reynolds* to the Rescue Ship *Accrington*. Following an urgent request for penicillin a supply was made available from No 92 *William A Carter* and transferred by *Dianella*.

The escorts suffered numerous defects that effected their efficiency. *Dianella* and *Tintagel Castle* had problems with Radar. Their sets were out of action during the last five days of the passage because the necessary spares were not carried by the Group. The MAC ship *Empire MaCCabe* was able to repair *Lotus*'s vapour valve spindle; *Dianella* was reduced to a maximum speed of 12 knots for 1? hours because of a defective feed pump and *Starwort* had to be steered from aft by her steering engine for 5 hours whilst the telemotor system was repaired.
(ADM 217/567)

CONVOY ON 287; 25th FEBRUARY - 8th MARCH 1945 (93 SHIPS)
B-1 ESCORT GROUP: HMS CHELMER (SO) CMDR J.H. EADEN DSC RN.

HM Ships *Tintagel Castle*, *Poppy*, *Dianella*, *Starwort* and *HMCS Lindsay* in company. *HM Ships Inman* and *Lotus* were detached for special duty.

Assembling of the convoy was considerably hampered by persistent fog and the considerable congestion of traf-

fic in the St George's Channel and South Irish Sea because of the combination of ON, OS and KMS convoys, their relevant sections and escorts meeting at junction points. Superimposed on this was the presence of the varied changing support groups. At one time there were 17 escorts present. This was accompanied by heavy signals traffic. *Chelmer* recorded handling 645 signals over the first three days of the voyage.

Tintagel Castle was engaged on several occasions in being in close support of individual ships that had either broken down or strayed from their convoy.
(ADM 217/330)

CONVOY HX 344 HALIFAX - UK; 15th - 28th MARCH 1945 (71 SHIPS)
B-1 ESCORT GROUP: HMS CHELMER (SO) CMDR J.H. EADEN DSC RN

HM Ships Tintagel Castle, *Poppy*, *Dianella*, & *Starwort* in company. The MAC ship *Empire MacDermott* provided air cover.

The presence of pack ice and growlers had threatened to close St John's harbour so the group sailed on March 15th and took refuge at Argentia. The US Authorities placed the facilities of the base at the Group's disposal. On passage *Tintagel Castle* experienced some difficulty with fragments of ice entering the condenser intake whilst on passage through thin ice (Editor's recollection).
Fog once again interfered with making contact with the convoy. *Tintagel Castle* was detached to escort the *Johnan Printz* who had been intercepted and to shepherd the stray back to the convoy. The vessel had become lost in the fog and was on her way to St John's. The remainder of the passage was without event.
(ADM 217/329)

CONVOY ON 295 7th - 20th APRIL 1945 (96 SHIPS)
B-1 ESCORT GROUP: HMS CHELMER (SO) COMMANDER R. THOMPSON DSC RD RN

HM Ships Inman, *Tintagel Castle*, *Dianella*, *Poppy*, and *Starwort* in company. *HM Ships Vanquisher*, *Alisma* and *Sunflower* joined with the English Channel section.

The Group had sailed from Moville on 7th April 1945. *Tintagel Castle* and *Poppy* sailing separately to act as escort for *HM Submarine Sidon* and to escort the joiners from Milford Haven. These joined the convoy early on the 9th.

On the 10th April *Poppy* gained an Asdic contact and was joined by *Chelmer*. The convoy was turned to port to make room for the hunt. After the initial attack an 'Observant' was carried out until the convoy was clear when it was decided that the contact was a non-sub and the ships rejoined the convoy. That night at 2035B in position 47°50'N, 09°49'W *Tintagel Castle* gained a contact and carried out two attacks on an object at a depth of 40 feet. There being no movement it was thought that the target was a wreck and at 2148 *Tintagel Castle* left the doubtful contact to rejoin the convoy.

At 2350B *Vanquisher* in position L sighted an U-boat on her port side and opened fire. At 2355 *Chelmer* illuminated the area ahead of *Vanquisher* and while doing so the U-Boat was reported to have dived. At 0009 *Vanquisher* was ordered to establish a datum and control an 'Observant' with *Alisma* who had been ordered to support him. Shortly afterwards they gained contact and *Tintagel Castle* who was returning from her previous contact, reported as being within two miles. She was ordered to join in and a deliberate hunt was started.

When *Tintagel Castle* arrived on the scene *Vanquisher* who was in firm contact with the U-boat acted as directing ship enabling *Tintagel Castle* to obtain a firm contact on a bearing of 050° 1,350 yards. Speed was reduced to 6 knots and at 1,000 yards a slow and deliberate attack was started with the U-boat moving slowly to the right. All instruments were checked and lined up. With the range down to about 800 yards and contact obtained with 147B, the depth of the U-boat was estimated as 700 feet. At 600 yards a firm contact was made

with Q and the depth accurately observed to be stable at 600 feet. Nine and a half minutes after contact had been made the centre bearing was 080° at 400 yards and the U-boat's course and speed plotted as 100° - 3 knots. The Squid was fired at 2327Z, exactly 10 minutes after contact had been made. The bombs exploded 28 seconds later and a minute later a muffled explosion was heard followed 20 seconds later by an even louder muffled explosion. This was felt by **HMS Inman** who was five miles away. **Vanquisher** was questioned and confirmed that she had not fired depth charges.

Five minutes after the first attack, contact was regained at a range of 500 yards on a bearing of 290°. The range was opened in preparation for a second attack. During the run out rattle and whistle effects were heard and the target appeared to have stopped. The second attack was made 11 minutes after the first at a depth of 300 feet. Three minutes later the target was reported 'stopped'. Two small underwater explosions were heard between eight and ten minutes after the second attack. The contact slowly faded.

At about an hour after the first attack another small under water explosion was heard and a Squid attack started. This was abandoned a minute later because the contact was not good enough. At this point **Tintagel Castle** was ordered not to remain on the scene beyond 0200Z. After a long stern case **Tintagel Castle** resumed her station on the convoy at 1255Z on the 11th April. This was some 13? hours after the start of the attack and 18? since **Tintagel Castle** had left her screening position to investigate what was eventually classifies as a non-sub contact. This serves to emphasise the tactical dilemma of the Escort Group Commander in balancing the need to conserve a secure A/S screen around the convoy and the eagerness of his COs to press home and bring all attacks to a successful conclusion. **Tintagel Castle** and **Vanquisher** were credited with the sinking of **U-878**.

Commodore D, Western Approaches, Londonderry, referring to this attack commented "This action illustrates several points of good drill - notably the admirable co-operation and thoroughness and a sound appreciation of the value of modern anti U-boat equipment. It is pleasing to note that a very keen ship of a keen, hard working Group has had at last a chance to display her worth."

(*ADM 217/331; ADM 199/895* the last report in the volume)

CONVOY HX 352 26th APRIL - 8th MAY 1945
B1 GROUP HMS CHELMER (SO) COMMANDER R. THOMSON DSC RD RN

HM Ships Tintagel Castle, *Inman*, *Dianella*, *Starwort*, *Poppy* in company.

The group sailed from St John's at 0945 local Time 27th April to join HX 352 at Westomp (43°59' N 49°50' W). The convoy was about 2 hours ahead of schedule. Dense fog was encountered shortly after leaving harbour. Icebergs and growlers were known to be in the area. The Group was formed in divisions in line-ahead disposed 2 miles abeam apart, the distance apart of ships in column being one mile. The meet took place in a comparatively clear patch.

This passage was (*FNG's recollection*) undertaken almost entirely in fog or low cloud making sun or star sights almost impossible.

The report states that **Tintagel Castle** with the Bristol Channel Section was detached in dense fog on 6th May. (*ADM 217/332*)

CONVOY ON 303, 16th MAY - 30th MAY 1945 (74 SHIPS)
B1 ESCORT GROUP HMS CHELMER COMMANDER R THOMPSON, DSC RD, RN.

HM Ships Tintagel Castle, *Lotus*, *Poppy*, and *Inman* in company

The Escort Group sailed from Londonderry at various times on May 16th and 17th 1945; **Lotus** to Milford Haven whilst **Poppy** and **Tintagel Castle** proceeded to the Clyde; **Inman** to Belfast. **Chelmer** was delayed in sailing by a defect but sailed to the Clyde early on May 17th. The OS 129/KMS 103 and its escorts joined the

convoy from Liverpool and was detached on the 19th in position 51°30'N 07°47'W. Although the passage through the Irish Sea passed off without incident the Milford Haven Section of the Convoy was joined successfully in dense fog. Dense fog and low visibility was the weather theme for the remainder of the passage. The Channel Section of ON 303 joined in position 49°58'N 10°04'W at midday on the 19th. The convoy was supported by the Escort Group 19 (*Loch Shin* (SO), *Cotton* and *Antigua* from early on the 19th to the evening of the 20th.

On the 20th *Vesper*, who had been escorting the Channel Section reported having sighted a possible schnorkel, dropped astern and dropped a pattern of depth charges by eye. The convoy was turned away to starboard and observant carried out by *Chelmer* and *Clematis* (escort with *Vesper* of the Channel Section). Smoke only had been seen, and as the MAC Ship's aircraft was known to have earlier dropped a marker in the vicinity, *Vesper*'s sighting was considered doubtful from the outset. An hour after the initial sighting the convoy resumed its original course.

Vesper and consorts were detached at noon on the 21st May to join HX 355. On the 23rd and 24th May two ships were detached to proceed independently to their respective destinations. This left some 72 ships in the convoy. On the 26th May the *Hadley F Brown* reported that she had 10ft of water in the No 1 hold. The Master was concerned lest the bulkhead should not stand up due to the movement of the ship and asked to be allowed to proceed to St John's. In view of the ice reports it was decided that he should remain with the convoy and detach with the ships bound for Newfoundland ports. In the meantime *Chelmer* transferred two 20 ton hand worked pumps, there being no suitable 110 Volt pumps available.

ENCOUNTER WITH ICEBERGS IN FOG.

The convoy had been in thick fog, visibility zero almost continuously for four days since 23rd May when on the 27th May at 1602 in position 43° 08'N 49°18'W course 233° 9.5 knots *Chelmer* ahead of the convoy (position AL) obtained a radar contact at 3 miles ahead eight degree on the starboard bow. A number of confused echoes were reported. While investigating and with visibility down to about 50 yards the SO found himself in close proximity to a very large iceberg. The full length of which could not be seen but it was thought to have been up to ? miles. There was also another berg to the northward as well as growlers.

It was inevitable that collisions would occur. Either the convoy would hit the ice at 9.5 knots or turn 90° together, in which case a number of ships would collide with each other. The SO chose the second alternative and asked the Commodore to do a 'Double Item' turn (90° to Port together). This turn was executed 20 minutes after the first radar report. Almost immediately the Commodore's ship *Villanger* was reported in collision. The convoy was ordered to stop. For some time the R/T and W/T channels were flooded with reports of collisions and damage. A signal was despatched for tugs to be sent out.

Both the Commodore's and Vice Commodore's ships had been in collision and the *Empire Stewart* was ordered to take over the duties of Commodore and the main body of the convoy was handed over to *Inman*. By this time the convoy ships were considered to have lost way and *Chelmer*, *Poppy*, *Tintagel Castle* and *Lotus* were closing ships with a view to rendering assistance where necessary and to find the Commodore. He was transferred to *Tintagel Castle* and embarked on *Chelmer* the next morning.

In the meantime the SO had devised a plan to withdraw the convoy from the danger of the ice. All ships were ordered to proceed on a course of 090°. Then to stop again and turn together to 180° and proceed on this course until well clear of the area before resuming a westerly course. This was successfully accomplished and at 1930 the turn to the south was carried out without further collisions.

By the time darkness fell (not that it made any difference to the visibility) *Inman* with the main body of the convoy was well clear whilst *Poppy* and *Lotus* were shepherding stragglers. *Chelmer* and *Tintagel Castle* remained in the vicinity of the icebergs looking for seriously damaged ships.

By 2230 it was apparent that 20 ships had been damaged and only one had actually hit the ice. In only three cases did the damage sound dangerous. There had been reports of ships being holed and compartments filling

up but no SOS had been made nor was there any reason to expect one. All ships appeared to be able to proceed. **Chelmer** and **Tintagel Castle** moved on with the rear ships.

A signal from C in C N.A indicated clear weather to the south. **Inman** went on ahead and found the Meteorological report to be very good. The **Empire Stewart** led the main body of the convoy out into the clear and by 1527/28th had formed up the convoy and set a course 300° at 7.5 knots. **Poppy** and **Lotus** acted as goal keepers at the turning point. **Chelmer** and **Tintagel Castle** brought up the extreme rear on an intercepting course at 10 knots. An hour and a half later **Inman** reported 68 ships present in the main body and that one ship (**Ovbula**) had been detached in accordance with previous orders. This return to normal was emphasised at 1830 when Commodore White had disembarked from **Chelmer** and was again in charge of the convoy on board the **Samthar**. Later that night a US Ship, with call sign P4EJ, reported that he had three ships from ON 303 in company still in fog. He was asked to help them to rendezvous with the convoy in the afternoon of the next day in a new rendezvous position which had been broadcast on BAMS.

The tugs **Tenacity**, **Chippawa** and **Commanche** had been sailed from Newfoundland with orders to proceed to the scene of the collisions. It did not seem that they would be required but it was arranged for them to meet the convoy on its new route in case any ship should be found to want a tug to stand by.

The relief Escort Group joined the convoy at 2130/28th and **Inman**, **Poppy** and **Lotus** were detached to proceed to St John's. The relief Escort Group (EG W8) took over the convoy at 0730/29th. The convoy now consisted of 72 ships. The whereabouts of all but two of those not in company was known and there was reason to believe that these two were proceeding ahead independently. **Chelmer** and **Tintagel Castle** proceeded to St John's Newfoundland arriving there at 1000/30th.

In his concluding remarks in his report the SO B1 wrote, *"I think one of the outstanding features of this episode was the splendid way in which the Master of the* **Empire Stewart** *immediately took charge of the convoy when the Commodore and Vice Commodore's ships had been too badly damaged to enable them to carry on. The manner in which he controlled the scattered ships, led them out of the danger area and formed up the convoy was a fine example of skill and leadership".*

When forwarding the Escort Group Commander's report to C in C Western Approaches, the Commodore (D) Western Approaches , included the following comments in his covering minute; *".......At 1602 on the 27th May, with visibility about 50 yards,* **Chelmer** *obtained Radar contact ahead at 6,000 yards and whilst investigating this, found it to be a particularly large ice-berg, estimated by Senior Officer B1 Group, to be more than a mile in breadth. it was directly in the path of the convoy. Commander Thompson immediately decided that the convoy must be diverted rather than stopped and ordered the convoy to turn 90° to port together. This resulted in a total of ten collisions affecting twenty ships and causing damage of varying degree, though in no instance was there any loss of life nor any ship lost. This difficult situation and subsequent happenings is fully described in the Narrative. I consider that Commander Thomson acted with commendable promptness and took the only possible course".*

*"The Commodore's ship (***SS Valange***[sic]) was damaged; also the Vice Commodore's, but the Master of the* **Empire Stewart** *took over the duties of Commodore in a particularly commendable manner (see paragraph 41 of the Narrative). A brief summary of the damage done was assessed by 2230 that night - twenty ships damaged in varying degree but only seriously damaged in three cases, whilst all were able to proceed unassisted. Only one ship hit the ice".*

The Director of Anti-U-Boat Division (C.D. Howard-Johnston) commented; *"I do not think it is being wise after the event to state that the implication of A.C.I 412, paragraph 3, was relevant, (Extract - "One or more escorts detached ahead have proved successful in locating icebergs which may be indicated to the Convoy...").*

....I think it is important to find out:-

    (a)   How is it that **Chelmer** *did not get a longer range contact from such a large object;*

(b)   Why **Poppy**, also stationed in a van position, did not locate the ice at long range;

(c)   What objections there were to complying with the sense of A.C.I. 412, paragraph 3.

"........it is suggested that it be made clear to Western Approaches at this stage that the Admiralty takes a serious view of the matter, which it is expected will have been fully enquired into in the usual Service manner".

The Director of Trade Division (W.A. Stephens) on 24th June 1945 submitted the chart showing how the convoy had already been diverted to the southward to pass through a position about 120 miles south of a known area of ice on the Eastern edge of the Grand Banks north of 44°30'N. At the day of the encounter the convoy was some 80 miles south of the southernmost reported ice position. He continues to explain that;-

"Owing to escort considerations it was necessary for the ON/HX traffic to be routed reasonably near to Halifax and St Johns for ships joining and leaving. In the ice season C. in C. C.N.A. had always therefore to keep these convoys as far to the northward as appeared safe. The situation shown on the chartlet does not suggest any failure on his part to route the convoy reasonably clear of known dangers.

As regards the actual encounter with the ice, it will be seen from the copy of the Commodore's report enclosed that the circumstances were very difficult indeed with fog and rain making the visibility practically nil at a time when immediate and wide avoiding action was imperative.

*On the whole I think the Commodore and the merchant ships did pretty well to avoid any more serious consequences. All the ships got in under their own power and no lives were lost. **Empire Stuart**'s performance was particularly meritorious and the sense of the Commodore's and SO Escort's remarks on this has been conveyed to her owners".*

Sir Robert Atkinson (then Lieut. Atkinson RNR) the Commanding Officer of **Tintagel Castle** during her first commission, commenting on the above account, also expressed surprise that **Chelmer** did not detect the ice at a longer range. He continued "On one occasion TC did precisely that - illuminated the huge iceberg by starshell since we couldn't contact the Commodore. The convoy turned immediately, there were no collisions" (personal communication).

Lieutenant R Dykes RNVR recalled this episode in a contribution to the News Letter of the Castle Class Corvette (Frigate) Association. He wrote:-

"I had just completed an afternoon watch of very heavy rain and nil visibility. Enjoying a cup of tea when "Away Seaboat's Crew" was piped. I went onto the bridge to find that ships had either hit an iceberg or in their attempt to avoid the iceberg had altered course in thick fog and collided with each other.

*The convoy commodore's ship **Villanger** had been damaged and it was necessary to go and collect the commodore and his staff from the **Villanger** and bring him aboard **Tintagel Castle**. So away we went with no difficulty in pulling towards the damaged ship. Going alongside the **Villanger** we found that the ship had been damaged before and aft of the midship superstructure down to the waterline. The duration of this transfer was some 2 to 2? hours - first taking the personal luggage of the Commodore's staff - then two journeys to collect staff and the Commodore.*

With the Commodore and his staff safely onboard evening was drawing in and our next task was to round up all stragglers ands instruct them to proceed South to clear the fog. When starting the middle watch I found that we were still searching for ships in the fog. As soon as one had been found by radar we would proceed at speed to close it and pass instructions for it to steer South. About 0200 in the middle watch, radar picked up a target some twenty miles distance - Captain was informed and eventually came to the bridge. In the meantime we altered course and increased to full speed to close the target.

In due course we closed the target to about two miles and I reduced speed, however the Captain required to maintain full speed.

Distance continued to reduce and the Captain continued at full speed. Visibility was very poor and speed was eventually reduced, when suddenly the lookout in the bows ran aft and at the same time a starboard light appeared out of the fog right ahead, then a white light to port and one to starboard indicating that we were close to hitting someone amidships. The telegraph was put at 'Full Astern' and we continued to move towards the merchant ship - the sudden change in engine movement to full astern whilst the ship had considerable forward speed created violent vibrations throughout the ship and as we were continuing to close the merchant ship (the alarm bells were sounded which promptly cleared lower deck of the ships company). Whilst all this was going on, a lone voice from midships of the merchant ship called us to go astern - we slowed to a halt some feet from the merchant ship - never did know its name.

*All quietness prevailed and the middle watch ended. Most returned below decks including the Commodore, although No 1 decided he was not going off the bridge. Next morning the Commodore was transferred to the SO Escort in **HMS Chelmer** and eventually the convoy was handed over to a local escort force.*

*Shortly after the Group's arrival at St John's the Group was disbanded and **Tintagel Castle** ordered to return to the UK independently. This was a remarkably peaceful voyage. Good weather the whole time but the sudden change from wartime to peacetime conditions took some getting used to. It was most gratifying, when some four days out from the UK that a surrendering U-boat flying the black flag was encountered. She was ordered to maintain station on our port bow kept in vigilant view by the closed up 4-inch Gun's crew until she was detached near Londonderry."*

B-2 ESCORT GROUP

The first reference to the B2 Escort Group including a Castle Class Corvette is on the 17th February 1944. At that time the Group's Senior Officer (S.O.) was carried by **HMS Mourne**, escorting convoy HX 278 of 60 ships. With **Berkeley Castle** in company. By the end of February 1944 both **Rushen Castle** and **Oxford Castle** had been allocated to the Group, but were still working up at Tobermory.

At the end of March 1944 the Group had been taken over by **HMS Hesperus** as S.O. **Rushen Castle** and **Oxford Castle** had already joined the Group. **Flint Castle** joined in early April 1944.

The lack of precise data on the B2 Escort Group illustrates the fact that the records in the Public Records Office for the Western Approaches Command are not complete.

The evidence of the Pink List and Convoy and Escort Dispositions suggests that for much of late March and early April 1944 the Group was involved in exercises and local duties.

Between the 23rd of April and the 12th September 1944 the Group was engaged in escorting convoys between the UK and Gibraltar. Eight Convoys totalling 290 ships were escorted without loss.

HMS Cotton became Senior Officer at the start of the voyage of OS88/KMS 62; Apparently for that voyage only. The records suggest that the convoy split into its two main parts on the 10th or 11th September 1944 and **Cotton** and **Morpeth Castle** escorted the KMS portion to Gibraltar **Berkeley Castle**, **Carisbrooke Castle** and **Oxford Castle** returning to the UK independently.

Between the 12th September 1944 and the 10th December 1944 there is no mention of the B2 Escort Group. It reappears on that date with **Morpeth Castle** arriving at Gibraltar and leaving on the 16th. After

that the Group was employed on the Atlantic convoys. There is no indication of which ship was Senior Officer until 10th May 1945 when **Morpeth Castle** is designated as S.O. With the lack of Reports of Proceedings it is not possible to state what other escorts formed the Group.

Reports of proceedings that are available are reproduced below.

B2 ESCORT GROUP
CONVOY KMS 53
SAILED FROM CLYDE 02/06/44

HMS Hesperus
Ocean Escort comprised **Hesperus** (S.O. B-2 Group) **Flint Castle**, **Gardiner**, **Cotton**, **Rushen Castle**, **Tunsberg Castle**, **Cape Argona** (Rescue Trawler) **Campania** (Escort Carrier)
(Source ADM 199/686)

Note: No ROP's for the B-2 Group have been found for the Group on the Gibraltar run earlier than that for Convoy OS83/KMS57

CONVOY KMS57/OS83
13/07 - 25/07/44
SAILED FROM LIVERPOOL 12/07/44

HMS Hesperus
Ocean escort was **Hesperus** (S.O.B-2) **Gardiner**, **Cotton**, **Rushen Castle**, **Oxford Castle**, **Flint Castle**, **Tunsberg Castle**, **Fencer**, **Evenlode**, **Delphinium**, **Usk**, **Southern Sea**, **Bergamot**, **G.S. King George II**, **Colombo** & **Awe**. The Group sailed from Moville on the afternoon of 13th July to act as escort for Convoy OS83/KMS57. Ships named after **Tunsberg Castle** were not part of the B2 Escort Group. They probably formed the escort after Gibraltar.

In the evening of the 13th **Hesperus** searched for No 73 **SS Tweedbank** reported to have collided with No 61 **SS Empire Fal**. She was reported stopped at 1838 in position 250° Oversay 12 miles. It was ascertained that when the Aultbea portion turned to the Liverpool portion's course of 280° at the RV **SS Empire Fal** hit **SS Tweedbank** forward of the bridge on the port side. **Tweedbank** reported making considerable water and was instructed to return to the Clyde. **SS Empire Fal** was closed by **Tunsberg Castle** and, reporting damage forward and flooding, and was also instructed to return to the Clyde.

About an hour later in position 55°38'N 07°18'W **Hesperus** intercepted a signal from an aircraft to his base. **Gardiner** was immediately ordered to detach and search for a dinghy with survivors from a crashed aircraft in position Inistrahull 150° 2 miles - this being only 14 miles from the convoy. On approaching Inistrahull **Gardiner** observed rockets and flares from the lighthouse. Nothing was seen to NW of Tor Rocks, but when passing close to the Eastern end of Tor Beg, a red dinghy was seen between Tor Rocks and Inistrahull.

The ship was taken through the passage and men observed to be in the dinghy. This was practically on top of Tormore rocks and drifting to the west with the tide. It was not possible to get very close to the dinghy because of the rocks. At 2300B the whaler was lowered and the four airmen recovered in a choppy sea., wind being against tide.

Shortly afterwards a launch was seen approaching and ordered to close. The airman were taken aboard half an hour after the launch of the whaler and given medical attention and dry clothes. One was suffering from injuries and severe shock; the others from shock. *Gardiner* proceeded to smoother waters to facilitate the transfer of the men to the launch and at 0015 14th July the airmen were transferred to the rescue launch. The airman from 21st Squadron reported that the remaining five of the crew had been lost.

The convoy was without anti U-Boat incident. *HMS Fencer* provided air cover. The three Swordfish were, in view of the U-Boat situation and weather, used only for dawn/dusk patrols when conditions allowed. The many 'Bogeys' kept *Fencer*'s Wildcats busy and a section was usually in the air before an IFF response was received.

One merchant ship broke down several times because of the fracturing of coupling bolts to the centre coupling of her propeller shaft. Both *Tunsberg Castle* and *Oxford Castle* kept guard over her on separate occasions whilst she was stopped and effecting repairs.

On the 21st July all escorts (except *Gardiner*; diesel) oiled from *SS Benedick*. The weather was moderate wind force 4 sea and swell 33, improving during the day. The buoyant hose method without steadying line was used successfully by all ships. Because of the shortage of oil the Castles were restricted to approximately 50 tons each. At full pumping pressure about 100 tons were transferred to both *Hesperus* and *Cotton* in 80 minutes each. The Castles also took about the same time to oil but this was because the pumping rate was halved owing to the presence of a blister in the hose.

All the ships in the group were fitted with the new type displacer paravanes during the recent lay over period. Foxers were successfully streamed and recovered by all ships in turn as an evolution.

The Group also exercise laying a smoke screen round the convoy.

Various material problems were encountered. New TBS aerials had been fitted to *Flint Castle* and to *Oxford Castle*. Excessive vibration in the masts of the Castles caused the dipoles to come out of their sockets. *Flint Castle*'s were particularly troublesome. As a result *Flint Castle* had to be kept in close V/S touch with *Hesperus*.

Flint Castle's MK V Sperry Gyro was out of action for the latter part of the voyage due to ball bearings in the south rotor race breaking.

Oxford Castle had problems with the Bowden cable operating the radar Type 272 aerial. Considerable slack developed.

(Source ADM 199/686 and 199/315)

CONVOY KMS61/0S87
SAILED FROM MILFORD HAVEN 26/08/44

HMS Hesperus

Ocean escort comprised *Hesperus* (SO) *Allington Castle*, *Flint Castle*, *Rushen Castle*, *Leeds Castle*, *Knaresborough Castle*. *Oxford Castle*, *Cotton*, *Fowey* & *Gardiner*, sailed from Belfast 0900 25th August 1944. *Cotton*, *Gardiner* & *Oxford Castle* detached 175° K.1 Buoy in accordance with previous orders. *Fowey* was detached on the evening of 26th August to proceed to Moville.

SS Benedick escorted by *Knaresborough Castle* & *Leeds Castle* joined during the morning of 27th August in position 50°26'N 06°02'W the escorts taking station on the convoy. *Allington Castle* joined at 1300.

Asdic contact attacked by *Rushen Castle* and *Hesperus*

In the late afternoon of 26th August in position 49°25'N 10°22'W *Rushen Castle* in station 'E' counter attacked an Asdic contact with depth charges. *Hesperus* proceeded to investigate and obtained a firm con-

tact at 1,200 yards. The plot confirmed this as **Rushen Castle**'s target. **Rushen Castle** had reported a slight movement, but **Hesperus** found the target stationary with no Doppler. The target fading at 400 yards indicated that the target was on the bottom. The position was on the Great Sole Bank, depth of water by echo sounder, 63 fathoms.

Hesperus then made a Hedgehog attack. The pattern exploded 17 seconds after entering the water. Herrings were the only result. **Rushen Castle** was sent in to make a Squid attack. This appeared to be accurate. Only fish and Squid scum resulted. The echo was now decidedly 'woolly' and as the situation report indicated the possible presence of fifteen U-Boats in the vicinity, it was decided not to carry out any more attacks. **Hesperus** returned to the convoy and **Rushen Castle** was ordered to remain in the area for half an hour before rejoining.

It was considered that the contact was a non-sub. No result was obtained from the echo sounder. The contact was definitely on the bottom. The Hedgehog and squid attacks should have provided definite prove of the presence of a U-Boat.

In accordance with CinCWA's instructions **Knaresborough Castle**, **Leeds Castle** and **Allington Castle** were detached at 1610 on 30 August in position 44°13'N 11°46'W.

Oiling at Sea

The weather prevented oiling at sea until 30th August. It was decided that the three escorts to be detached that evening should attempt to oil whilst the screen was definitely adequate. **Hesperus**, **Knaresborough Castle** and **Leeds Castle** oiled successfully from **SS Benedick**, but **Allington Castle** was delayed two hours due to loss of buoys and before she had taken any oil, instructions were received for the three additional Castles to proceed forthwith to Greenock. As **Rushen Castle** and **Oxford Castle** had more than ample endurance and in view of the number of escorts present, it was not considered advisable that they should oil. Details of oiling follow.

SHIP	AMOUNT	RATE	TIME
Hesperus	90 tons	140 ton/hr	1 hour 16 mins
Knaresborough Castle	72 tons	103 tons/hr	1 hour 20 mins
Leeds Castle	80 tons	107 ton/hr	1 hour 21 mins.
	242 tons		

Times taken are from picking up the hose to letting go. Buoyant hose method without steadying line was used.

Signed

G.V. Legassick Commander R.N.R.

Castle Class Corvettes escorted eight convoys of the UK-Gibraltar series comprising 292 ships and nine convoys of the HX/ON series with a total of 556 ships. 848 ships were escorted without loss. Summarised details follow

B2 ESCORT GROUP CONVOYS ESCORTED WITH CASTLE CLASS CORVETTES

PERIOD	CONVOY	NO OF SHIPS	CASTLES	NOTES
05/02-0/02/44	HX 278	60	*Berkeley Castle*	
24/04-06/05/44	OS75/KMS49	23	*Rushen Castle, Flint Castle Oxford Castle, Tunsburg Castle*	
10/05-21/05/44	SL157/MKS48	49	*Rushen Castle, Flint Castle Oxford Castle, Tunsburg Castle*	
03/06-16/06/44	OS79/KMS53	27	*Rushen Castle, Flint Castle Oxford Castle, Tunsburg Castle*	
20/06-02/07/44	SL161/MKS52	44	*Rushen Castle, Flint Castle Oxford Castle, Tunsburg Castle*	
13/07-20/07/44	OS83/KMS57	29	*Rushen Castle, Flint Castle Oxford Castle, Tunsburg Castle*	
29/07-09/08/44	SL165/MKS56	39	*Rushen Castle, Flint Castle Oxford Castle, Tunsburg Castle*	
24/08-12/09/44	OS88/KMS62	28	*Rushen Castle, Morpeth Castle Oxford Castle*	There is uncertainty with regard to the corresponding North bound voyage
10/12/1944	OS97/KMS71	29	*Morpeth Castle*	Reported arriving Gibraltar
16/12-24/12/44	MKS71G	24	*Morpeth Castle*	
08/01-18/01/45	(ON271)	69	*Morpeth Castle*	
27/01-06/02/45	(HX334)	74	*Morpeth Castle*	
14/02-28/02/45	(ON285)	70	*Morpeth Castle*	
11/03-22/03/45	(HX342)	71	*Morpeth Castle*	
02/04-18/04/45	(ONS46)	24	*Morpeth Castle*	

PERIOD	CONVOY	NO OF SHIPS	CASTLES	NOTES
21/04-05/05/45	(HX351)	57	*Morpeth Castle*	
10/05-24/05/45	(ON302)	75	*Morpeth Castle*	
29/05-07/06/45	HX358	56	*Morpeth Castle*	The last HX convoy

Convoy codes in brackets indicate the matching of convoy sailing date with the recorded sailing date of the escort(s).

B3 ESCORT GROUP

The following notes are derived from records of the Public Records Office (PRO). And unless stated otherwise all source references are those of the PRO.

Within the ADM 217 series of Western Approaches Station Reports the earliest report of the B3 Escort Group is that for the voyage Gibraltar - UK with convoy SL 159/MKS 50, May - June 1944. The report for the preceding outward bound voyage was not found.

The B3 Escort Group with a Castle Class Corvette forming part of the Group escorted 16 convoys comprising 674 ships without loss from April 1944 to May 1945. These convoys are summarised below

CONVOYS ESCORTED BY THE B3 ESCORT GROUP WITH A CASTLE CLASS CORVETTE IN COMPANY

PERIOD	CONVOY	NO OF SHIPS	CASTLES
04/04/44 - 17/04/44	OS 73/ KMS 47	45	*Leeds Castle*
23/04/44 - 03/05/44	SL 155/MKS 46	49	*Leeds Castle*
14/05/44 - 23/05/44	OS 77/KMS 51	31	*Tintagel Castle, Knaresborough Castle, Leeds Castle*
30/05/44 - 10/06/44	SL 159/MKS 50	36	*Tintagel Castle, Knaresborough Castle, Leeds Castle*
23/06 - 04/07/44	OS 81/KMS 55	26	*Tintagel Castle, Knaresborough Castle, Leeds Castle*
10/07/-/21/07/44	SL 163/MKS 54	42	*Tintagel Castle, Knaresborough Castle, Leeds Castle*
02/08 - 13/08/44	OS 85/KMS 59	34	*Allington Castle, Leeds Castle, Hurst Castle Knaresborough Castle, Tintagel Castle*
18/08 - 31/08/44	SL 167/MKS 58	29	*Allington Castle, Leeds Castle, Hurst Castle Knaresborough Castle, Tintagel Castle*
28/09 - 07/10/44	ON 256	73	*Flint Castle*
14/10 - 25/10/44	HX 313	43	*Flint Castle*
06/11 - 17/11/44	ON 264	67	*Flint Castle*
25/11 - 06/12/44	HX 321	37	*Flint Castle*
14/12 - 26/12/44	ON 272	45	*Flint Castle*
02/01 - 12/01/45	HX 329	36	*Flint Castle*

PERIOD	CONVOY	NO OF SHIPS	CASTLES
11/04/ - 28/04/45	ONS 47	17	*Flint Castle*
03/05/ - 15/05/45	HX 353	64	*Flint Castle*
Total Ships Escorted		674 without loss	

CONVOY SL159/MKS50 (36 SHIPS)
30th MAY - 10th JUNE'44

HMS Towy (SO); HM Ships Antigua, Knaresborough Castle, Leeds Castle, Anguilla & Tintagel Castle.

Sailed from Gibraltar at 0600 on 30th May 1944 with 5 ships in convoy. Contact to be made with SL 159 5 miles south of Europa Point and subsequently with MKS 50, 40 miles east of the Straits.

It became apparent that some ships in the convoy(s) were not aware of the intention to meet the MKS east of the Straits and return during darkness hours. Two ships went into Gibraltar to bunker and many despairing signals were received from other ships that their destination was the UK.

At 1320 R/V was made with MKS 50 two hours ahead of its expected position. Various 90° turns enabled the convoy to mark time - although this was not easy with a newly joined convoy, which had to form a narrow front before passing through the Straits. *HMS Dart* took all the Gibraltar merchant ships and escorts astern, breaking them off on passing Europa Point.

At 0257 on 3rd June OS 78 was contacted by radar at 19 miles and *HMS Activity* joined from that convoy to provide air cover until the 10th June. Various escorts oiled from *Activity*.

Early on the 7th June in position 49°20'N 18°24'W *HMS Cotton* and another escort made contact with the convoy and the oiler *San Tirso* was detached with them to join convoy OS 79.

At 1200 on 9th June, in position 54°30'N 10°42'W the convoy split, the Loch Ewe section proceeding under escort of *Leeds Castle*. *Towy* and the remainder of B3 Group, *HMS Activity* and *HM Trawler Vizalma* proceeded independently to Greenock and reaching position A at 0630 on 10th June
Source ADM 217/228

CONVOY OS 81/ KMS 55 (26 SHIPS)
23rd JUNE - 4th JULY '44:

HMS Towy (SO); HM Ships Antigua, Knaresborough Castle, Leeds Castle, Anguilla, & Tintagel Castle. together with *HMSMS Salamis.*

The Group sailed from Moville at 1100Z 23rd June. Contact made with the convoy at the Oversay R/V where the Loch Ewe section was joining up. *HMS Inman* and her Support Group swept ahead of the convoy until 0430 24th June leaving at position 56°02'N 10°14'W to sweep ahead of convoy HXM 295.

The convoy was re-organised on the 23rd June leaving three short columns in the centre to give *Activity* room to operate aircraft without leaving the convoy - this was particularly desirable as there were few escorts available to screen her outside the convoy. Whales caused numerous false alarms.

On the 23rd June *Knaresborough Castle* and *Tintagel Castle* were detached to R/V with SL 161 in order to escort the oiler *Scottish American* to join OS 81/KMS 55, the three rejoining on the 27th June in position 47°16'N 19°27'W

Considerable swell on the 28th prevented escorts from oiling. Four escorts oiled on the 29th and the remaining three on the 30th June.

Air cover was provided during the 30th June by two Fortresses from the Azores and a Catalina from Gibraltar KMS 55 was handed over to the Med Escort at 0630 on 4th July off Europa Point and B3 Group proceeded to Gibraltar.
(Source ADM 217/229)

CONVOY SL 163/MKS 54 (42 SHIPS)
10th - 21st JULY 1944

HMS Towy (SO) (Cmdr Hugh King); *HM Ships Antigua*, *Knaresborough Castle*, *Leeds Castle*, *Anguilla* & *Tintagel Castle*

An uneventful passage. There was some discrepancy between the sailing orders and convoy papers (20 miles) for the R/V and it was necessary to make a diversion so as to avoid a UGF convoy under escort by the 41st Group. *HMS Athene* took station within the convoy.

"Air cover was provided by *Campania* which also provided useful AA exercises for the escorts with drogue towing Wildcats during the 14th-16th July inclusive. *Campania* carried out excellent air searches; operating aircraft in the dark with a skill and speed that made it appear very easy."
(ADM 217/230)

CONVOY OS 85/KMS 59 (34 SHIPS)
2nd - 13th AUGUST 1944
UK TO GIBRALTAR

Tintagel Castle (Carrying the SO) *Knaresborough Castle*, *Leeds Castle*, *Allington Castle*, *Hurst Castle* & *HMS Anchusa*. Also joined by *HMNZS Arbutus* and *HM Ships Antigua*, & *Campania* (latter joined 3rd August 1330 in position 54°51'N 11°48'W having been delayed by defects). *HMS Bullen* joined on 5th August (51°29'N 16°00'W) to replace *Anguilla* who was unable to sail from the Clyde owing to hull defects.

At 2003 on 6th August *Leeds Castle*'s HF/DF sense aerial fell down the funnel, but was safely retrieved from its hiding place amongst the tubes of No 1 boiler and replaced.

HMNZS Arbutus detached on 8th August to proceed to Bermuda.
(ADM/217/564; see also ADM/199/315: Reports of Convoys UK - Mediterranean and Sierra Leone SL 143-166, MKS 35 -67, OS 81 - 86 & KMS 55 - 60)

CONVOY SL 167/MKS 58 (29 SHIPS)
18th - 30th AUGUST '44
GIBRALTAR TO UK

HM Ships Tintagel Castle (Carrying the SO) *Antigua*, *Knaresborough Castle*, *Leeds Castle*, *Allington Castle*, *Hurst Castle* & *HMS Bullen*.

This was the occasion when it was necessary to join 5 ships from Gibraltar to a west bound convoy MKS 58 when east of the Straits. The convoy was an hour late at the rendezvous and low visibility compounded the difficulty. Eventually it was decided to postpone the join until after the passage through the Straits.

At daylight the following morning it was found that three of the Gibraltar ships had strayed during the night, two of these were found 17 miles astern.

At 0730 on 20th August in position 35°29'N 10°14'W R/V was made with SL 176. The convoy was formed with the exception of three stragglers, but one of them, No 34 *Empire Planet*, continued to drop back. The convoy speed was reduced for her, but she failed to rejoin. On the 23rd she was sentenced to the Stragglers' Route. This had the desired effect and the *Empire Planet* soon began to overtake the convoy.
(Source: ADM 217/563)

HMS EXE B3 ON.256 (73 SHIPS)
28th SEPT - 7th OCT 1944 ADM 217/130

The Group comprising *HM Ships Exe* (SO), *Lavender*, *Vervain*, & *Flint Castle* sailed from Bangor Bay at 055/28th Sept to rendezvous with the various sections of the convoy. All 75 ships were assembled early on the 30th in 50°00'N 10°00'W.

The passage was uneventful and the Group were relieved by W2 EG at Westomp 47°45'N 48°51'W.

NOTE: Air cover was provided by MAC ship *SS Empire MacColl* with three serviceable aircraft. When weather allowed two Swordfish were flown on A/S sector searches at dawn and in the afternoon so as to land at last light. Other searches were also flown as requested by SO. "The efficient and tireless air cover thus provided was accomplished by only two aircrews and *Empire MacColl* is to be congratulated on their performance. The Master's Air Staff Officer was on the Sick List for the greater part of the voyage."

HMS EXE B3 HX.313 (43 SHIPS)
14 - 25th OCT '44

Group consisted of *Exe* (SO), *Gardiner*, *Vervain*, *Flint Castle*, *Borage*, & *Lavender*. Group sailed from St. John's at 1350 14th October 1944 and arrived in UK base on 25th October. Convoy met at 44°12'N 48°00'W. W4 Group then filled the Outer Screen Stations and B3 took up close escort. W4 left on the 16th to join ON 258.

Fresh westerly gale blew throughout 16th and 17th and by the evening of the 17th it was necessary to inform shore authorities that the convoy would be unable to alter course to port for position CG (50°28'N 27°05'W) on 18th Oct owing to risk of damage to deck cargoes from swell and intend to proceed direct to position 51°01'N 19°02'W.

On the 18th the wind backed and decreased so it was possible to fuel the Flower Class Corvettes

Vervain, *Lavender*, *Borage*, who are to be congratulated on their success under very difficult conditions.

By the evening a rapidly falling barometer and freshening SE wind heralded a gale which was unique in the experience of everyone on *Exe*.

The Gale reached its full strength (wind force 10) in the early hours of 19th October and the convoy scattered widely in low visibility, some ships heaving to, others running before mountainous seas, being forced to alter course to starboard by the veering wind.

Escorts spent the 20th searching for scattered ships; 42 out 44 made the noon rendezvous on 21st with *SS W.S. Baer* and *SS Michael de Kovasts* the only stragglers. MAC *SS Empire MacAndrew* deserves credit for collecting 10 merchantmen and leading them to the convoy.

It is regretted that a badly injured man from *SS George Hawley* died under shock of operation on board Rescue Ship *Eddystone* on 21st Oct.

The MAC ship was unable to fly any routine patrols because of the bad weather conditions throughout the passage.

CO of *Exe* was delighted with his new radar Type 277:

> *"Performance was unaffected by gale weather, save for the increase in 'Sea Returns.' The continuous rotation of the aerial presented a clear picture in the P.P.I display and it was possible to manoeuvre the Group as a unit in thick fog off Newfoundland and to make the approach to St John's with confidence."*

HMS EXE B3 ON.264 (67 SHIPS)
6-17th NOV'44 ADM 217/132

The Group comprising *Exe*(SO), *Gardiner*, *Flint Castle*,*Borage*, *Lavender*, and *Geranium*. The Group sailed from Liverpool on 4th Nov. The convoy was fully formed up on the 5th.

Lavender made ASDIC contact in the evening of the 5th and was assisted by *Flint Castle* who was unable to confirm the contact. While rejoining, *Lavender* obtained a second contact and attacked with Hedgehog. Explosions heard but it was thought that these were bottom contacts. *Flint Castle* was unable to confirm the contact.

Gales on the night 6th/7th caused the convoy to be scattered. 67 ships eventually rounded up. One lost; thought to have romped ahead.

On the evening of the 8th the visibility cleared sufficiently for the whole convoy to be seen from the SO's ship. The first time since sailing on the 4th.

On 13th *Exe* stopped port engine because of excessive vibration in the 'A' bracket. She took up station in position 'S' for the remainder of the passage having a maximum speed of only 12 knots.

The Group were relieved at Westomp 42°00'N 47°37'W on the 15th . *Exe* proceeded to Bay Bulls for docking and *HM Ships Gardiner* (SO), *Borage*, *Flint Castle* and *Geranium* proceeded on an A/S sweep as instructed by F.O. Newfoundland. The Group arrived at St John's at 1700/18th Nov.

HMS EXE B-3 HX.321 (37 SHIPS)
25th NOV - 6th DEC 1944 ADM 217/131

The Group; *Exe* (SO), *Gardiner*, *Flint Castle*, *Borage* and *Geranium* sailed from St John's 1200/25th Nov 1944 to meet Convoy HX.321 at 44°41'N 50°37'W effected 0900/26th.

The Atlantic passage was characterised by a succession of Northerly and North Westerly gales generating heavy swells. These forced the convoy to alter away to starboard from the route to nurse the Liberty

Ships which rolled excessively.

At 2230/4th in position 51°09'N 09°25'W the 30th Escort Group took station six miles astern of the convoy to support the convoy in case of U-Boat attack; the lee of Ireland giving sea conditions suitable for Schnorkel. They detached at 0800 in position 51°50'N 07°02'W.

Flint Castle and *Geranium* were ordered on the 6th when in position 54°01'N 04°56'W by CinC WA to detach from the Irish Sea Portion and return to Liverpool.

Notes

Exe detected MAC aircraft (*Adula*) while flying at 1,000ft at 70,000 yards (277 set). The *Adula*, a MAC emergency escort oiler was carrying US special navy fuel Specific Gravity 9424, flash point 175°. Escorts were asked by CinC N.A. to exercise the oiler in fuelling at sea for at least three occasions or until Master is satisfied. (The report does not state if this was done - possible not, in view of the state of the sea and weather).

HMS EXE, B3 ON 272 (45 SHIPS)
14 - 26th DEC '44 ADM 217/133

1. The Senior Officer, B3 Escort Group in *Exe*, with *HM Ships Geranium* and *Borage* in company, sailed from Bangor Bay at 0900/14th December 1944, to rendezvous with the Clyde and Belfast portions of ON 272 in position 090° New Island 4° miles at 1030.

2. *HMS Flint Castle* overtook at 1300, having, abandoned an HF/DF calibration in Belfast Lough, due to bad. weather.

3. All portions of the Convoy were delayed by a southerly gale, and rendezvous was not effected with the Liverpool section, *HNMS Acanthus* and *HMS Vascama*, until daylight, 15th in position 51°02'N 05° 38'W. *HNMS Acanthus* joined B3 Group and *HMS Vascama* returned to base.

4. The Milford Haven portion with Commodore F. H. Taylor in *Empire Balfour* was met at the Tusker Rock rendezvous (185° Tusker Rock 20 miles) at 1200/15th.

5. At 0800/15th *Flint Castle* reported Condenser trouble and was detached to proceed into Milford Haven. She rejoined by 2200/17th in position 48°49'N 12°40'W.

6. As the convoy was delayed by south westerly winds, the Channel Section (STATICE, Senior Officer Escort) turned back, and homed onto the main body on an opposite course. Visibility was under one mile, and, in spite of radar contacts, this section came in from ahead until it was necessary to inform them they were standing into danger unless they altered course. At 1430 convoys in position 51°50'N 06°03'W passed starboard to starboard on opposite courses, and the Channel Section became lost in the haze to the northward. *Borage* was sent to relieve STATICE Group and very ably rounded up the Channel Section and brought them in astern for the night.

7. *Port Darwin* embarks Commodore and Staff.

The Commodore's ship *Empire Balfour* was having difficulty in maintaining convoy speed. At 1530/18th the Commodore transferred together with his staff and equipment to *Port Darwin*. The transfer was very efficiently affected by the boats from the Rescue ship, *SS Melrose Abbey*.

8. It was not until the 19th December that the Convoy of 45 ships all reached assigned stations and speed could be increased to 9 knots.

9. ***HNMS Acanthus*** detached to Join B.2

At 1830/21st in position 44°38'N 27°47'W ***HNMS Acanthus*** was detached to proceed to rejoin B2 Escort Group. Before leaving she was re-fuelled from ***SS Egero***. Both oiler and escort are to be congratulated for the speed in which 85 tons of fuel were transferred in a heavy swell and failing light.

10. ***Empire Bombadier*** and ***Strix*** detached.

At 1100/24th in position 43°55'N 40°45'W the tankers ***SS Empire Bombadier*** and ***Strix*** were detached to proceed independently for Galveston, Texas.

11. Rendezvous with Western Escort

At 1600/26th in position 43°18'N 52°02'W rendezvous was affected with W2 Escort Group. B3 Group then detached and proceeded to St. John's Newfoundland.

Section 3 - Remarks on Air Escort.

(a) Suitable flying weather for ***MacAlpine***'s aircraft was not experienced until the 19th. Thereafter, when wind and weather allowed, Dawn and Dusk searches by two aircraft on the bows of the Convoy were flown off to a depth of 75 miles, while one aircraft was used to patrol around the Convoy (at visibility distance). On the 25th and 26th an appreciation of the movement of U-boats in the Newfoundland area indicated the sectors from 250° to 310° being most dangerous to the Convoy. Accordingly on these days searches in this sector to a depth of 80 miles were flown.

2. Air Cover provided by Shore Based Aircraft.

   On the 15th December, Liberator aircraft, JPN 10, provided air cover from 1430 until 1730. The aircraft was never seen in the thick fog then prevailing. On 25th December Liberator Aircraft, JPN 6 and JPN 8, provided air cover from 1000 until 2000. Homing procedure and V/S and R/T communication with these aircraft were satisfactory. They were employed in searches to a depth of 50 miles in sectors 240° to 300° and 300° to 360°. Two U-boats being estimated to be to the eastward of Newfoundland bound Northeast and Southwest respectively.

Section 6 - Communications

(f) Lost Aircraft Homed

On the morning of the 19th December, the MAC Ship reported one of her dawn patrol aircraft as lost. The aircraft was successfully homed by lost aircraft procedure in accordance with A.C.I. Article 116, para. 15. A signal from the ***SS MacAlpine*** stated that the 'remarkable accuracy' and speed in passing of the bearings had acted as a great fillip to the morale of the air crews.

The incident speaks well for the HF/DF calibration given to ***Exe*** in the Clyde, just prior to sailing with the Convoy.

Section 8 - Exercises

1. On the 20th, Smoke Floats were dropped by *Exe*, *Flint Castle* and *Geranium*, as targets for Low Angle gunnery exercise for Convoy ships. Later *Exe* used her mobile rocket projector to fire rocket flares for H.A. barrage practice for her main armament.

2. On the same day C.C.M, L.O.X.O. and Recognition exercises were carried out by the Group's Communications Staffs.

3. On the 21st and 22nd, MAC Ship aircraft returning from patrols exercised Radar ratings in the Group in IFF Stud changing routine. A sequence of changes previously agreed upon by the Senior Officer and the MAC Ship was compared with the results signalled in from the escorts. A good standard of accuracy was attained.

4. On the 23rd a Homing exercise for a lost aircraft was carried out, *Flint Castle* and *Exe* both taking part. Very accurate bearings were reported by the MAC Ship, bringing the aircraft in over the centre of the convoy.

5. On the 24th, *Exe* streamed her splash target and towed for L.A.shoots by each of the other escorts. *Flint Castle*, provided the best shoot.

HMS EXE B3 HX 329 (36 SHIPS)
2nd - 12th JAN '45

The Group, *HM Ships Exe* (SO), *Geranium*, *Borage*, *Flint Castle*, and *HMCS Stellarton*, sailed from St John's at 1700/2nd January 1945. Rendezvous with HX 329 was made in position 44°04'N 51°54'W.

On the 5th *SS Spinanger* reported a case of acute appendicitis. The Group Medical Officer transferred the patient to *Exe* by seaboat and a successful operation was performed that night. The patient's recovery was hastened by the intravenous injection of glucose saline solution. Whilst *Exe* carries a small quantity of this drug additional supplies were obtained from *SS Conrad Weiser*.

Empire MacKay's Swordfish developed engine trouble on the 6th whilst on A/S patrol. The aircraft had lost contact with the convoy. The lost aircraft was homed to safety by *Exe*.

The passage was without incident until within home waters. At 1915 on the 12 January the Liverpool portion of OS 104 was encountered on the starboard bow, steering a collision course, and it was necessary to switch on navigation lights and alter course 90° to starboard to clear. This resulted in the Convoy becoming somewhat scattered and *William Hall* was not seen again until passing Port Patrick.

The SO, Paterson, in his ROP complained that it was difficult to find out what is going on in home waters after being away for a month and suggested that SO's should receive a special SITREP when arriving at 15°W. Staff response was "...(He should be) aware that all coastal waters are dangerous areas and make his dispositions accordingly. That is all that is required. The fact that a ship is torpedoed off Holyhead or a U/B sunk off Tusker is irrelevant. He must be prepared for attacks at all times."

On arrival at the UK *Leeds Castle* underwent a refit which lasted until the end of March. The ship then spent a period in the Plymouth area, rejoining *Exe* and the B3 Escort Group on 9th April 1945. During this period of absence *Leeds Castle* does not appear to have been replaced by another Castle Class Corvette. The account of the B3 Escort Group resumes on 11th April 1945 with their voyage with ONS 47.
(ADM 217/134)

HMS EXE B3 GROUP, CONVOY ONS 47 (17 SHIPS)
11th - 28th APR '45

The B3 Escort Group consisting of *Exe* (SO), *Gardiner*, *Geranium* and *Flint Castle* with *Seychelles* additional, sailed from Liverpool on 11th April. *Flint Castle* had sailed a day earlier in order to calibrate HF/DF equipment at Belfast. She rendezvoused with the Belfast section on the 11th.

Whilst the Clyde section was closing up on the 12th *Gardiner*'s Unifoxer was destroyed by an explosion, presumed to be a Gnat. *Flint Castle* and *Seychelles* dropped scaring depth charges and an enemy report was transmitted. Because *Gardiner* had been zig-zagging and had just steadied when the explosion occurred it was considered that this had been caused by a mine and the enemy report cancelled. However, *Flint Castle* reported a serious problem with her condenser as a result of dropping two depth charges at 16 knots set to explode at 150 and 100 feet. She was sent to Londonderry for repairs; rejoining the convoy on 15th. Subsequently similar condenser problems occurred on the same day after she had fired a full pattern of Squid set to explode at 500 feet. However, the problem sorted itself out.

On the 18th April the *SS Nurtureon* developed boiler trouble and straggled. She told *Gardiner* that she had a very ill man aboard. The doctor was sent and found the man dying from a perforated ulcer. The Master had been treating him for the past three days for cramp. The man was buried at sea later that day.

The 23rd April was provisioning day. *SS Cap Fagnet* was supplied with 60lbs of beef and 200lbs of potatoes by *Gardiner*. Fresh provisions were also transferred from *Seychelles* to *Geranium*.

On 27th April W4 EG took over the convoy and the B3 Group proceeded to St John's arriving there on 28th April.

Section III Remarks on Air escort

(a) MAC Ship

1. Weather conditions allowed aircraft to fly off on ten days of the trip. On the afternoon of the 14th and the morning of the 15th, aircraft provided good cover. For the remainder of the trip dawn and dusk patrols were flown off when the weather was suitable.
2. On 15th April, aircraft were of assistance in homing *Flint Castle*.
3. Throughout the trip aircraft took part in exercises.
4. Aircraft crash landing on at 2000/25th April.

(b) Shore based aircraft

Call Sign	Time with Convoy	Comment
JXW1	121200 - 121850	This aircraft was used to search for a suspected sub which later proved to be a mine. Sighted a mine at 1337. At 1537 attacked an oil slick & homed *Exe* to the position. Communications good.
JEW1	100500 - 13 1702	This aircraft arrived with R/T receiver broken down. At 131015, a Sunderland contacted B3, said he was escort and disappeared. This aircraft had not been advised and call sign was not known. JZW1 had no knowledge of him either.

Section IV - Remarks on Convoy

SS Llandaff

The master, the Vice Commodore, was a perfect nuisance throughout the voyage. When leading a column he was always romping and when put at the end of a column he persisted in straggling. He was relieved of his post as Vice Commodore and then paid no attention to the Commodore's signals.

SS Nurtureon

It is felt that there is very little excuse for the Master of this ship for delaying reporting a man seriously ill for three days - until he became a straggler. The man was transferred to **HMS Gardiner** and died of a perforated Gastric Ulcer on board **Gardiner**.

SS Pendeen

She has faulty boilers and dropped back twice to stop leaks in tubes. Should not be allowed to join a convoy until the boilers have been repaired.

HMS EXE B3 HX 353 (64 SHIPS)
3rd -15th MAY '45 ADM 217/139

The Group comprising *Exe* (SO), *Seychelles*, *Flint Castle*, *Gardiner*, and *Geranium* sailed from St John's on 3rd May; *Seychelles* and *Flint Castle* escorting WHX 355 to Westomp. The Group met W1 EG and HX 353(64 ships) on 4th May in position 45°49'N 51°45'W. Several Spanish fishing vessels were encountered. W1 detached on 6th May.

On that day heavy swell was encountered causing the merchant ships to roll excessively. Course was altered to ease this, especially to ease the Liberty ships carrying deck cargoes. Heavy rolling continued to be experienced as the weather got worse; several course alterations were made to ease the movement of the ships; finally on the 8th the convoy hove to on a course 030°. On the following day with no improvement in the weather *Geranium*, who was running short of fuel, banked one boiler. However, the weather moderated in late evening and the convoy altered course to 070°. *Geranium* was able to fuel on the 10th.

On the 14th and 15th escorts detached with various sections.

B4 and 30th ESCORT GROUP

The Castle Class Corvettes that operated with the B4 Escort Group were reformed as the 30th Escort Group. Like the ships of the 31st Escort Group, they too continued to operate together in the immediate post European phase of WWII on Air Sea Rescue duties. It is therefore convenient to consider the two Groups together.

B4 ESCORT GROUP

The original core of the Group comprised *Helmsdale* (Senior Officer; Commander C.W. McMullen, DSC RN), *Highlander* and *Bayntun*. These were joined by *Kenilworth Castle* and *Portchester Castle* on 3rd May 1944. *Pevensey Castle* and *Launceston Castle* joined later once they had completed their early training. A summary of the convoys escorted between 03.05.44 and 19.08.44 is given below.

CONVOYS ESCORTED BY THE B4 ESCORT GROUP BETWEEN 03.05 - AND 19.08.44

PERIOD	CONVOY	NO OF SHIPS	ROUTE	REMARKS
03.05 - 13.05.44	OS 76/KMS 50	35	UK - Gibraltar	Gale force winds encountered
20.05 - 03.06.44	SL 158/MKS 49	47	Gibraltar - UK	
12.06 - 24.06.44	OS 80/KMS 54	29	UK - Gibraltar	
29.06 - 11.07.44	SL 162/MKS 53	36	Gibraltar - UK	Convoy unsuccessfully attacked by glider bombs
22.07 - 02.08.44	OS 84/KMS 58	27	UK - Gibraltar	
08.08 - 19.08.44	SL 166/MKS 57	31	Gibraltar - UK	
	6 Convoys	205 ships without loss		

Kenilworth Castle and *Portchester Castle* escorted all the above convoys, *Pevensey Castle* and *Launceston Castle* escorted the last two. Summaries of the Reports of Proceedings for those convoys follow.

CONVOY OS 76/KMS 50 (35 SHIPS)
3rd - 15th MAY 1944
UK-GIBRALTAR

The Group comprised *Helmsdale* (SO), *Highlander*, *Foley*, *Kenilworth Castle* and *Portchester Castle*.

Gale force winds caused slow progress in the first few days. On the 8th May, in thick fog, radar contacts and TBS communications narrowly averted a collision with an American convoy that was 70 miles ahead of its reported position. Emergency turns by the convoy were smartly executed - even so the convoys missed each other by only a mile and a half. Extensive air cover was provided by B-17 Fortress aircraft from the Azores.
(*ADM217/364*)

CONVOY SL153/MKS49; 46 SHIPS, 3 LSTS 2 SUBMARINES
20th MAY - 3rd JUNE 1944
GIBRALTAR TO UK

The Group comprised *Helmsdale* (SO), *Highlander*, *Foley*, *Kenilworth Castle* and *Portchester Castle*

Because there were only five escorts the position 'S' was not occupied. Air cover was provided from Gibraltar and the Azores. On the 25th May a Ju-290 shadower was sighted, but it evaded the two fighters scrambled from *Nairana*. Shadowers were again reported on the 26th. One Ju-290 was shot down by Hurricanes from *Nairana* 12 miles from the convoy. Unfortunately one Hurricane failed to pull out of a dive during this attack and the pilot was lost. *Inglis* was sent to pick up five Germans - reported as being 'good swimmers'. The convoy was wheeled 70° to port on orders from CinC WA. The convoy was now supported by two carriers. Escorts and carriers being stationed so as to provide the carriers with the maximum A/S protection whilst providing the carriers sufficient room for manoeuvre. See 'A.A. protection' in Section 2 for a more detailed discussion on carrier support for the Gibraltar convoys.

On 29th May *HMS Emperor* arrived in support. Now, with additional support of the 15th and 9th Escort Groups, the convoy had 15 escorts and three carriers to protect it. Unfortunately, the weather prevented the enemy from attacking the convoy and falling into the trap prepared for him. At dusk on that day the two support Groups detached. The carrier *Activity* and the oiler *Scottish American* were also escorted back to their OS convoy by *Hadleigh Castle* and *Carisbrooke Castle*.

Nairana laid on extensive Swordfish patrols around the convoy during the night of 29th/30th May and at dawn sent out deep patrols to search for the U-Boat known to be to the south west of the convoy.

Strong beacon W/T signals were detected by several ships. It was thought that an aircraft had dropped a homing beacon, but it became apparent that the beacon was situated in Portugal or Spain.

On 30th June *Emperor* flew off 4 Hellcats to carry out dummy attacks on the convoy and exercise the escorts in air defence.

At this stage it also became necessary to transfer provisions to the Dutch Submarine *Dolfijn*. The opportunity was taken to exercise the submarine boarding party. The sight of eight men rowing a whaler full of provisions in mid Atlantic prompted *HM Submarine Trespasser* to enquire "Is Captain Bligh in the boat?"
(*ADM 217/365*)

OS 80/KMS 54; 29 SHIPS, 2 SUBMARINES
12th - 23rd JUNE 1944

Initially the escort was supplemented by **Bulldog** (SO), **Duncan**, **Oxford Castle**, **Bullen** and **Goodall**. At night they were stationed 20 miles ahead of the convoy to avoid mutual radar interference. This Group detached at 1800 on 13th June. Air cover was provided by three Catalinas.

On 19th June **Searcher** had an accident on her flight deck whilst landing on fighters and lost a man overboard. **Highland** and **Portchester Castle** who were astern at the time carried out a thorough but fruitless search. The convoy was handed over to **HMS Fleetwood** off Europa Point on the 28th June. At the outset Commander McMullen (SO) was concerned over the make up of the convoy. The two submarines had been placed in the lead of the carrier lane. He considered that the submarines could become a serious embarrassment to the carrier if she wished to operate aircraft ahead of the convoy. Secondly the Commodore's ship was given pendant 81, which was not central. This was due to the ship being in the Freetown section. With the agreement of the Commodore, the Commodore's ship was given pendant 61 and the submarines stationed between columns 5 and 6. In reporting these matters Commander MacMullen suggested that arrangements along those lines should be followed in future. Staff Officer to CinC WA concurred with this view.
(ADM 217/366)

SL162/MKS 53; 37 SHIPS
29th JUNE - 10th JULY 1944

During the lay-over period a Group regatta was held, won by **Portchester Castle** , followed by a day of exercises. The Group comprising **Helmsdale** (SO), **Highlander**, **Bayntun**, **Foley**, **Kenilworth Castle**, and **Portchester Castle** sailed on 29th June. On 1st July at dusk a smoke laying exercise was carried out with the merchant ships participating. This paid dividends when an attack developed two days later. **HMS Activity** (carrier) joined the next day. Fighters from the carrier carried out close range dummy attacks on the escorts for gunnery training.

On the 3rd July, one hour after sunset three shadowers were detected by radar. Escorts were immediately disposed in AA defensive positions. At the time there was a very light breeze fine on the starboard bow of the convoy and ? full bright moon fine on the starboard quarter elevation 30°. Escorts and the convoy were ordered to make smoke and quite good cover had been maintained by the time the first attack developed. Even so, because of the very large area covered by the convoy, there were some significant gaps.

Two attacks were made on the convoy - both came in from ahead of the convoy and towards the moon. In response to radar reports Oerlikon, rocket flares and star shell were fired in the direction of the enemy by escorts ahead as a blind barrage. The enemy, having flown 800 miles to the attack dropped only three bombs. No ships were hit. The enemy was in the vicinity of the convoy for an hour. Smoke laying over this prolonged period brought its own problems. Ships with C.S.M. gear getting short of supply and **Kenilworth Castle** developed a small fire in her boiler room.

The firing of star shell and rocket flares was considered to be effective as they were between the enemy and the convoy. If the scene had not already been floodlit by a bright moon, this action might have been dangerous. Incidentally, although the aircraft closed to within 3,000 yards of the escorts ahead of the convoy, none of them were seen.

During the attack a number of unexplained radar echoes were obtained by both **Helmsdale** and **Highlander**. These were recognised by the operators as some form of radar decoy, although not reported as such. It was assumed that this was their first encounter with 'window'.

The escorts were able to replenish smoke floats from ships in the convoy on the 4th July. In the meantime the wind had gone round to the port beam of the convoy. It was decided to bring the wind onto the quarter if another attack developed so as to make the smoke hang. Accordingly the convoy was wheeled 20° to starboard at dusk with the intention of wheeling another 20° if an attack occurred. No attack developed and the convoy course was resumed at 0100Z.

The remainder of the voyage was comparatively uneventful. One of *Activity*'s Swordfish obtained a good ASV contact 18 miles on the convoy's port beam. Two escorts were detached to investigate and arrived at the marker in 40 minutes - but a 90 minute search proved fruitless.

The rising wind veered to the North West and one merchant ship who was very light in ballast quickly dropped astern. Contact was lost with her when she was 12 miles astern of the convoy. However, she managed to rejoin the convoy two days later. The Master of another ship died from heart failure on the 6th July. On the 9th July the hard westerly wind developed to gale force. The convoy arrived safely at its various destinations on the 10th July.

(ADM 217/367)

OS 84/KMS 58; 24 MERCHANT SHIPS, CABLE SHIP BULLFROG, HM SUBMARINE SUBTLE, TWO LCTS IN TOW BY SS EMPIRE CATRO 22nd JULY - 3rd AUGUST 1944

The Group comprised *Helmsdale* (SO), *Highlander*, *Bayntun*, *Foley*, *Portchester Castle*, *Kenilworth Castle*, *Pevensey Castle* and *Launceston Castle*. *HMS Stormcloud* (Fleet Sweeper) and *Lord Nuffield* (Trawler) sailed as additional escorts. After spending 36 hours on Group exercises with *Philante* the Group sailed from Moville on 22nd July 1944. The convoy was met in the afternoon and *HMS Biter* joined as convoy Escort Carrier.

The voyage was uneventful under very favourable weather conditions. *Biter* was asked to carry out dawn and dusk defensive patrols round the convoy and to carry out long ranger offensive sweeps. A considerable amount of night flying was carried out, but without making any contact with the enemy.

Shortly after dawn on 26th July one Swordfish reported that she was about to ditch. *Helmsdale*, *Bayntun* and *Highlander* carried out a high speed sweep to the aircraft's reported position five miles from the convoy. The crew were picked up unharmed by *Helmsdale*.

On the 27th July *Kenilworth Castle* was called upon to destroy some heavy flotsam which was a danger to shipping. This was successfully achieved with the Squid.

On 31st July *Helmsdale* and *Highlander* were detached off Cape Spartel and carried out a special operation "Return Trigger". The nature of this operation was not reported. The two ships arriving at Gibraltar on the 3rd August.

(ADM 217/308)

SL 166/KMS 57; 31 SHIPS HM SUBMARINES UNRULY AND UNSPARING WERE ESCORTED BY KENILWORTH CASTLE 8th - 18th AUGUST 1944

This was a calm and peaceful voyage. The most interesting part being when two incoming convoys were successfully passed in the Straits; "though it is considered that passing convoys in the Straits would not be a safe or desirable operation in thick weather or during a full gale by night."

On arrival in the UK on 19th August all the Castle Class corvettes of the Group underwent boiler cleaning and then re-assembled for Group training prior to resuming operations.

(ADM 217/369)

TRANSITION FROM B4 GROUP TO 30th ESCORT GROUP

The Group comprising *Helmsdale* (SO), *Pevensey Castle*, *Morpeth Castle*, *Kenilworth Castle*, *Launceston Castle*, *Portchester Castle*, and *Hurst Castle* sailed at various times on the 29th and 30th August 1944 to join forces with Force 33 patrolling the North West Approaches. It is possible that the Group also included *Highlander* and the Norwegian Castle Class Corvette *Tunsberg Castle*. These two ships were also reported to be in support of convoy ONF 252 together with the other ships of the B4 Group.

On the 31st August *Pevensey Castle* was detached from the SO, accompanied by *Ambuscade*, *Launceston Castle* and *Hurst Castle*, with orders to patrol between 55°20'N and 56°N with the object of preventing a U-Boat from escaping to the west. The ships were disposed in line abreast distance 4 miles on a course of 000° and 180° 12 knots between the limits of the patrol area. At 0615 on 1st September courses were altered to proceed to a reported sighting of a U-Boat. At 0810 course was altered in response to a more recent reported position and speed reduced to 12 knots with the intention of forming the ships up in station and starting a sweep from the westward. It was thought that the U-Boat had probably bottomed on being detected.

Launceston Castle was well astern of station having been on the outside of all the turns. *Hurst Castle* and *Ambuscade* were ahead. *Hurst Castle* turned back to loose bearing and had just turned again into station when she was torpedoed and sank in about six minutes with the loss of 17 lives. Survivors being picked up by *Ambuscade*. A more detailed account of this loss is given in Section 3 under the heading *Hurst Castle*.

On the 9th September *Portchester Castle* (Lieut: A.G. Scott RNR) was with the Group screening ahead of an ONF[1] Convoy. The escorts were disposed line abreast some 4 miles ahead of the convoy. *Portchester Castle* was the port wing ship. She obtained a contact at a range of 2,100 yards and ran over the target to confirm its classification. She ran out to open the range to 700 yards and then attacked with Squid. Five seconds after the explosion of the bombs the stern of the U-Boat broke surface dead in the centre of the disturbed water from the explosions. Fire was opened with the 4-inch and Oerlikons and course altered to ram. The submarine passed close down the starboard side and depth charges set at 50 feet were released from the starboard thrower and stern rails. The submarine appeared to roll over to starboard and sank. *Portchester Castle* lost contact but this was regained by *Helmsdale* who directed *Portchester Castle* onto the target, who attacked again. This was a well directed and accurate attack. It was quickly followed by a slight underwater explosion, followed five minutes later by a heavy underwater explosion. This and subsequent wreckage observed on the surface provided sufficient evidence for the U-Boat Assessment Committee to asses the attack as "U-Boat known to be sunk". This was the *U-484* and the first U-Boat to be sunk by a ship fitted with a single Squid. A suitable congratulatory signal was sent by the Admiralty. A more detailed account of this attack is given in Section 3 under the heading *Portchester Castle*.

From the 10th to the evening of the 13th September the Group was engaged in patrolling in the vicinity of 57°N 12°W and on the 13th the search area was moved towards 56°40'N 11°30'W in response to a reported ASV contact. These various movement being controlled by the SO Force 33. Subsequently on the 13th the Group were detached to join the 3rd Escort group to provide support to HX 306, (120 ships), the second largest HX convoy to sail across the Atlantic. The two groups covered the van of the convoy 8 miles ahead. It was when the B4 Group joined in support to this convoy that it was re-designated the 30th Escort Group.

---

[1]This may have been ONF 252, but the Report mentions ONF 305, but this is probably a misprint. That convoy did not sail until May 1945.

30th ESCORT GROUP

The 30th Escort Group operated in the Western Approaches, in the Western area of the English Channel and also between Scapa Flow and the Faeroes. The work was mainly concerned with carrying out Anti Submarine patrols and supporting convoys as they passed through their patrol area. The area of operations of the Group is shown below:-

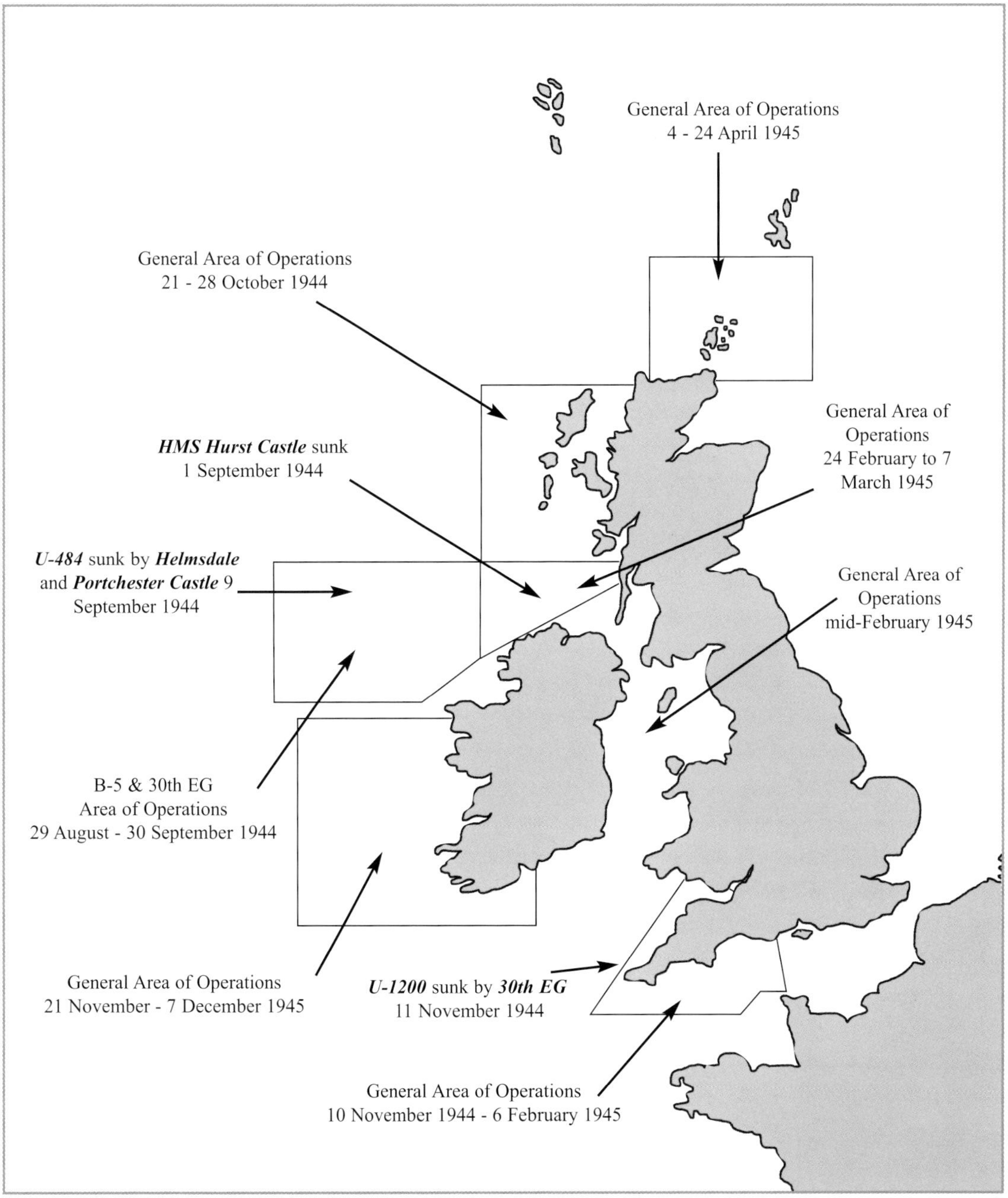

General Area of Operations
4 - 24 April 1945

General Area of Operations
21 - 28 October 1944

HMS Hurst Castle sunk
1 September 1944

General Area of
Operations
24 February to 7
March 1945

U-484 sunk by **Helmsdale**
and **Portchester Castle** 9
September 1944

General Area of
Operations
mid-February 1945

B-5 & 30th EG
Area of Operations
29 August - 30 September 1944

General Area of Operations
21 November - 7 December 1945

U-1200 sunk by **30th EG**
11 November 1944

General Area of Operations
10 November 1944 - 6 February 1945

13th - 30th SEPTEMBER 1944

On the 15th September 1944 the 30th EG and 3rd EG detached from convoy HX 306 and together carried out a dog-leg sweep to 15°W thence to the North East. In the meantime it seems that **Portchester Castle** had returned to Londonderry as she is reported to have joined the 5th Escort Group PM on the 15th September from Moville.

On the 16th the 30th EG is reported as sweeping East/West through areas B1 and B2[2] until the 20th when the Group investigated an aircraft contact in position 54°52'N 09°29'W. Meanwhile **Portchester Castle** and **Kenilworth Castle** were detached to investigate the curious behaviour of a Liberator which carried out an attack with depth charges; only one of which was said to have exploded, and then flew away without making any contact.

The initial contact point was reached at 1945A and good R/T communication established with the aircraft, which carried out searches to a depth of 10 miles. The Group swept through the area with an expanding box to a depth of 12 miles. A Gamma search was instituted during the night across a possible escape route of the U-Boat, but with no results. This type of work soon became 'normal' routine for the Group for the next eight months.

Following on from this the Group swept areas C1, C3 and B3 without incident during the following 48 hours, leaving the areas on 23rd September and returned to Moville.

The Staff Officer's comments on the Report of Proceedings is not without interest. "... It seems that there were two different aircraft involved, one of which did home 30th EG and established good R/T communications. On the way to it, which was still 20 miles away, two corvettes closed to investigate the Liberator's splashes of markers - now called depth charges - clearly an entirely different occurrence."

"The SO had been ordered to leave area B at 1300/23 to lay over. In point of fact he warmed the bell and left that area at 10.15, in order (as he explained later) to sweep through B4, which was not his area at all, and was in fact the direct route home. At 1541, when he should have been at sea, CinC ordered him to investigate an ASV contact, possible U-Boat - but as stated in his report - he arrived in harbour at 1530, and by the time he got the signal, he was up river at Londonderry, so the ASV contact was not examined. CinC has already verbally ordered NFA[3] on this affair."
(ADM 199/500)

5th - 18th OCTOBER 1944

After two days exercising at Larne where bad weather hampered the programme, the Group re-fuelled at Moville on 5th October and sailed for patrol in area D.2 at 2100 that day.

At 11.20 on the 6th a Swordfish reported by V/S sighting an oil slick 10 miles west of Oversay. The Group proceeded there with all despatch even though it was expected that the oil slick would turn out to be the strong tidal eddies frequently experienced in that location. However, oil was found to be rising to the surface and a firm contact was obtained by **Pevensey Castle**. This was attacked by **Portchester Castle** with Squid and a large amount of high octane petrol was brought to the surface. A few minutes later the petrol burst into flames just as **Pevensey Castle** was coming in to deliver her attack. **Pevensey Castle** was enveloped in the flames, but passed through without harm except for extensive damage to her paint work. (A more detailed account of this incident is given in Section 3 under **Pevensey Castle**).

The Group resumed patrol and during the next three days experienced the usual non-subs and contacts with wrecks all of which had to be investigated. **Kenilworth Castle**'s Asdics broke down and she was sent to Moville

---

[2] It has not been possible to accurately determine the co-ordinates of this and other designated patrol areas mentioned in these reports.

[3] No further action.

for repairs rejoining 24 hours later. **Launceston Castle** developed problems with her steering gear and she was detached to Londonderry for repair, rejoining on the 10th. In the meantime **Foley** was detached from EG 10 to fill the gap.

On the 12th **Launceston Castle** was again in trouble. This time with defective radar. She was sent back to Londonderry but managed to effect repairs en route and returned to the Group, which in the meantime had moved to patrol areas B2 and B4. Subsequently, on the 13th and 14th in areas A4 and A2. In anticipation of joining convoy ONS 34 (45 ships) the Group patrolled through the north west corners of areas D1 and C. The convoy was met shortly before midnight on the 14th. The next day the Group was augmented by three ships from the C4 Escort Group. **HMC Ships North Bay**, **Petrolia** (Castle Class Corvette) and **Atholl**. The protec-

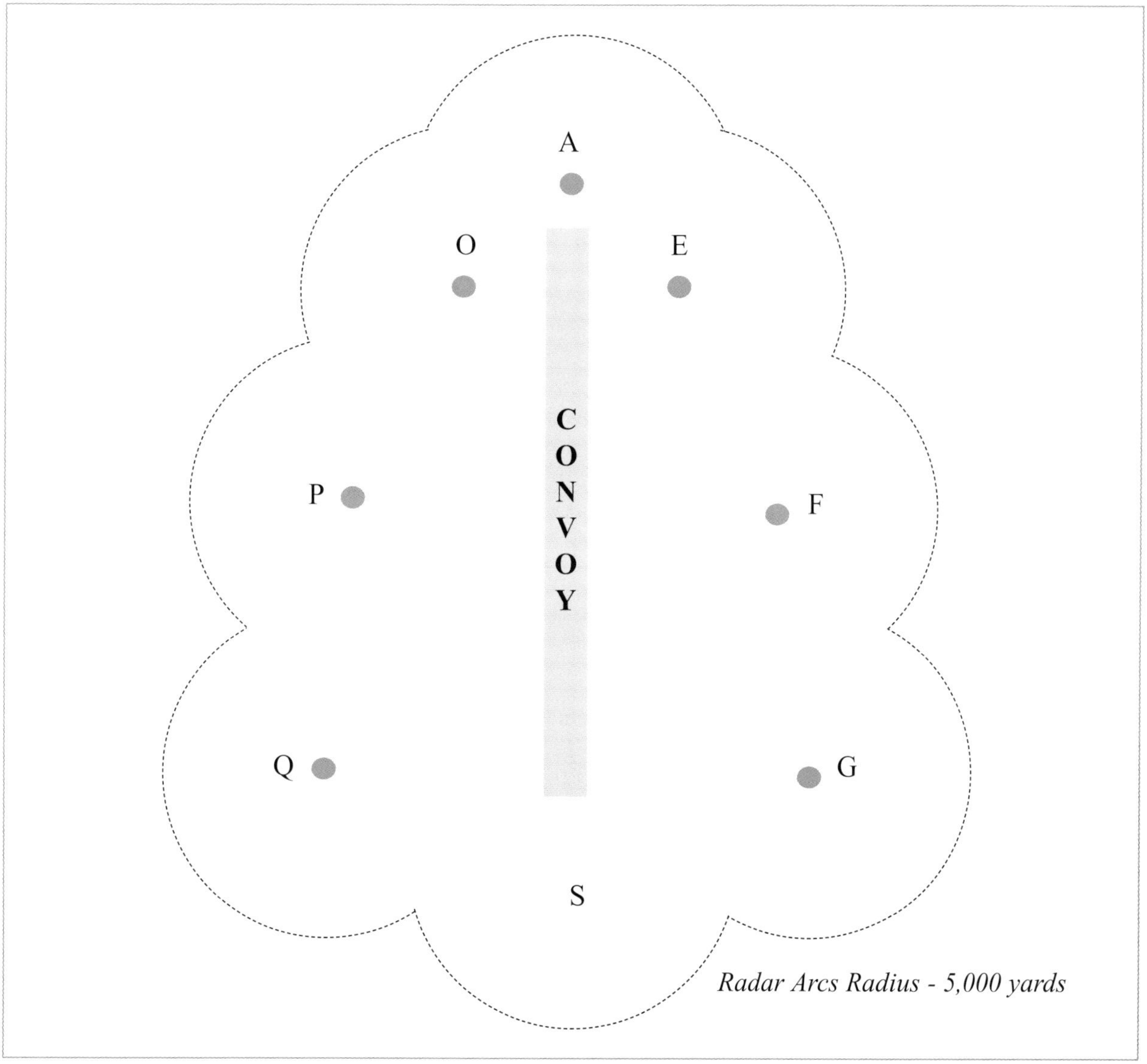

A

O   E

C
O
N
P   V   F
O
Y

Q   G

S

Radar Arcs Radius - 5,000 yards

CONVOY SCREENING DIAGRAM
Long Convoy of two Columns

tion of a convoy of 35 ships disposed in two columns stretching to a length of 6 miles gave cause for considerable thought. The escort stations solution is given in the preceding figure. The flanking escorts being stationed from 4,000 yards to 6,000 yards from the convoy's columns and 2,000 yards ahead and astern of the convoy. *(ADM 199/500)*

21st - 28th OCTOBER 1944

After a short layover, the Group comprising *Pevensey Castle* (SO Commander D.A. Rayner DSC VD RNVR), *Kenilworth Castle* and *Portchester Castle* sailed from Londonderry on the 21st October 1944. The Group patrolled to the west of the Outer Hebrides. The main emphasis was concerned with detecting a U-Boat believed to be within the area and to prevent it from entering the Minches. No contact was made and the patrol was remarkably free of contacts with non-subs.

Because both *Kenilworth Castle* and *Portchester Castle* had been a year out of dock the maximum operating speed of the Group was restricted to 12.5 knots, although 13 knots could be obtained for a short period.

In his report Commander Rayner expressed his frustration over an occasion when an aircraft delayed transmitting a sighting report for 50 minutes. During that time he was sailing away from the sighting position. It was found that this was due to the 15 RAF Group broadcasting the "Control Zone Scheme in force" at the time and preventing the aircraft from transmitting. It was noted that "Subsequent to this event 15 Group have taken steps to obviate the recurrence of such delays in receiving an aircraft's report." *(ADM 217/727)*

8th - 14th NOVEMBER 1944

The Group comprising *Pevensey Castle* (SO), *Launceston Castle*, *Kenilworth Castle* and *Portchester Castle* attempted to carry out various exercises at sea but were once again frustrated by the weather. On the 10th November the Group proceeded southwards through the Irish Sea. This was uneventful until at 0058 on the 11th with the ships in line abreast 3,000 yards apart, *Portchester Castle* obtained a radar contact bearing 183° 23,000 yards. This was originally classified as a ship, but when it faded, as possibly an aircraft. *Pevensey Castle* investigated the bearing and obtained a definite echo at 25,000 yards, which gave course of 250° on the plot. The contact was held continuously for 5 minutes before it faded. Course was altered to 187° on the assumption that if it was a U-boat it would maintain its course of 250° at 4 knots. At 0235 *Launceston Castle* obtained a firm Asdic contact whose course was 250° 2? knots. She attacked with Squid at 0240.

This was the start of an action lasting 70 hours resulting on the destruction of *U-1200* in position 50°24'N, 05°42'W. Over the three days contact was maintained continuously - very largely by *Launceston Castle*, whose radar was defective. Attacks were made as follows:-

Launceston Castle	Squid 10, Depth Charges 1
Portchester Castle	Squid 4, Depth Charges 1
Pevensey Castle	Squid 2
Kenilworth Castle	Squid 1
Drury	Hedgehog 1
4th Escort Group	Massed Depth Charge attack 1

The echo sounder trace produced by *Portchester Castle* showed a contour markedly resembling that of a bottomed submarine and was considered to be a notable piece of evidence. The estimated length of the target was 243 feet. 147B traces indicated a depth of 400 to 430 feet.

Oil was observed after *Launceston Castle*'s third attack. This was accompanied by a strong smell of 'tar' and a considerable area was thinly covered (by oil) by mid-day the next day. Air bubbles appeared at various times,

particularly after **Pevensey Castle**'s first attack and after the massed depth charge attack by the 4th Escort Group. A gallon oil tin was recovered. This showed pressure damage.

Included in Commodore 'D' Londonderry's comments on this action was the observation that, "The paucity of A/S defects and breakdowns during this prolonged action indicates careful maintenance by the Group". Relevant track charts are shown overleaf; A copy of a possible explanation for the abnormal range at which RADAR echoes was obtained is also include.

(ADM 217/735)

14th - 19th NOVEMBER 1944

The Group left port on the 14th November 1944 during a North West gale to proceed on patrol to the south west of Ireland. A radar contact was made at 2249 at a range of 17,000 yards. This was held for four minutes when it faded. The plot indicated a course of 160° 15 knots. The Group altered course dead into an old swell with a fresh North East sea running across. As a result very heavy quenching was experienced by all ships. Simultaneously an electrical storm was experienced. This produced St. Elmo's fire on bridge fittings and HF/DF aerials as well as interfering with R/T reception. A search was carried out but no Asdic contact was made until six hours later. This was lost almost immediately but regained an hour later at 0611/15th November.

Ten Squid attacks were carried out on the 15th (**Portchester Castle** 4; **Launceston Castle** 5 and **Pevensey Castle** 1). On the 16th the Group was joined by the 4th Escort Group and a single ship barrage attack with depth charges was carried out by **Bentick**. The increasing severity of the weather made maintaining contact no longer possible. At 1430/16th B4 Group broke off to patrol to the South and the 30th Escort Group to the North Westward.

During the night the wind moderated and contact was regained at 0830/17th, within 500 yards of the Group's Dan Buoy.

During this operation the Group had suffered several defects which had been reported to CinC WA. These together with a rising Westerly wind made it unlikely that the contact could be held for very long. Consequently CinC WA ordered the 4th Escort Group to take over the contact and for the 30th Escort Group to return to base. The Group left the area 65 hours after the initial radar contact had faded. Commenting on this action Commodore 'D' Londonderry wrote:-

"Though there is no undeniable evidence of the presence of a U-Boat, the combined evidence of -

    a) The disappearing radar contact,
    b) The subsequent Asdic contact,
    c) Air bubbles
    d) The presence of oil,
    e) **Pevensey Castle**'s 147B recorder trace
    f) **Portchester Castle**'s echo sounder trace

point to the presence of a U-Boat which indeed may have been 'killed'."

However, CinC WA was more sceptical. In forwarding the report to the Admiralty he concluded his covering letter with the remarks;

". . .Having regard to the depth of water and the adverse weather conditions, some doubt exists as to whether the Asdic contact was a U-Boat or a wreck."

(ADM 217/733)

N

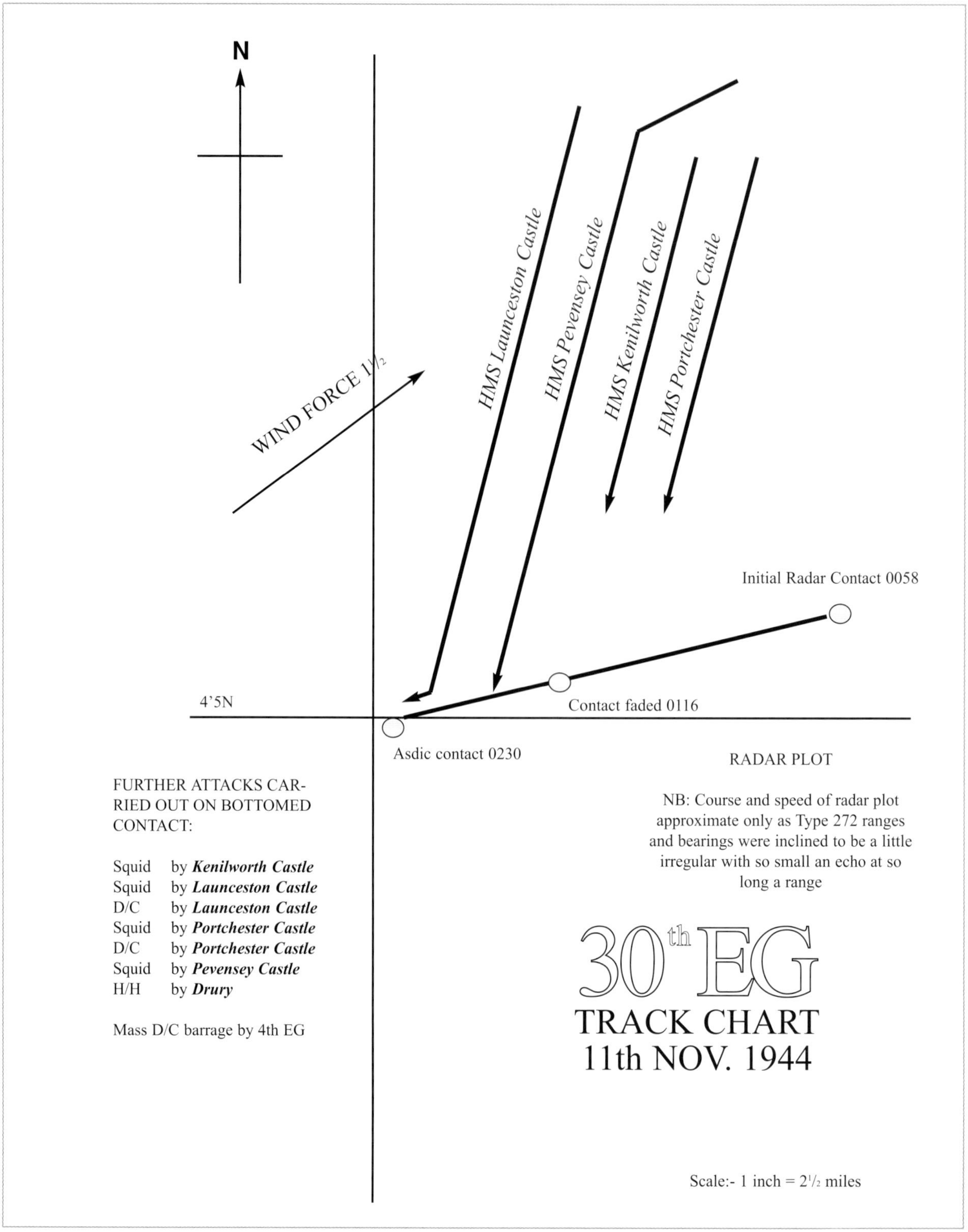

HMS Launceston Castle

HMS Pevensey Castle

HMS Kenilworth Castle

HMS Portchester Castle

WIND FORCE 1½

Initial Radar Contact 0058

4'5N

Contact faded 0116

Asdic contact 0230

FURTHER ATTACKS CAR-
RIED OUT ON BOTTOMED
CONTACT:

Squid   by *Kenilworth Castle*
Squid   by *Launceston Castle*
D/C   by *Launceston Castle*
Squid   by *Portchester Castle*
D/C   by *Portchester Castle*
Squid   by *Pevensey Castle*
H/H   by *Drury*

Mass D/C barrage by 4th EG

RADAR PLOT

NB: Course and speed of radar plot
approximate only as Type 272 ranges
and bearings were inclined to be a little
irregular with so small an echo at so
long a range

30th EG
TRACK CHART
11th NOV. 1944

Scale:- 1 inch = 2½ miles

ABNORMAL RADAR CONTACT
A possible explanation

With reference to the radar contact obtained at 23,000 yds on 11th November 1944. Radar contact on a U-Boat at 23,000 yds is not impossible with radar Type 272P. Conditions were perfect at the time and the echo was probably caused by a "freak" effect.
The following is a brief description of one theory which is supposed to cause "freak" effect.

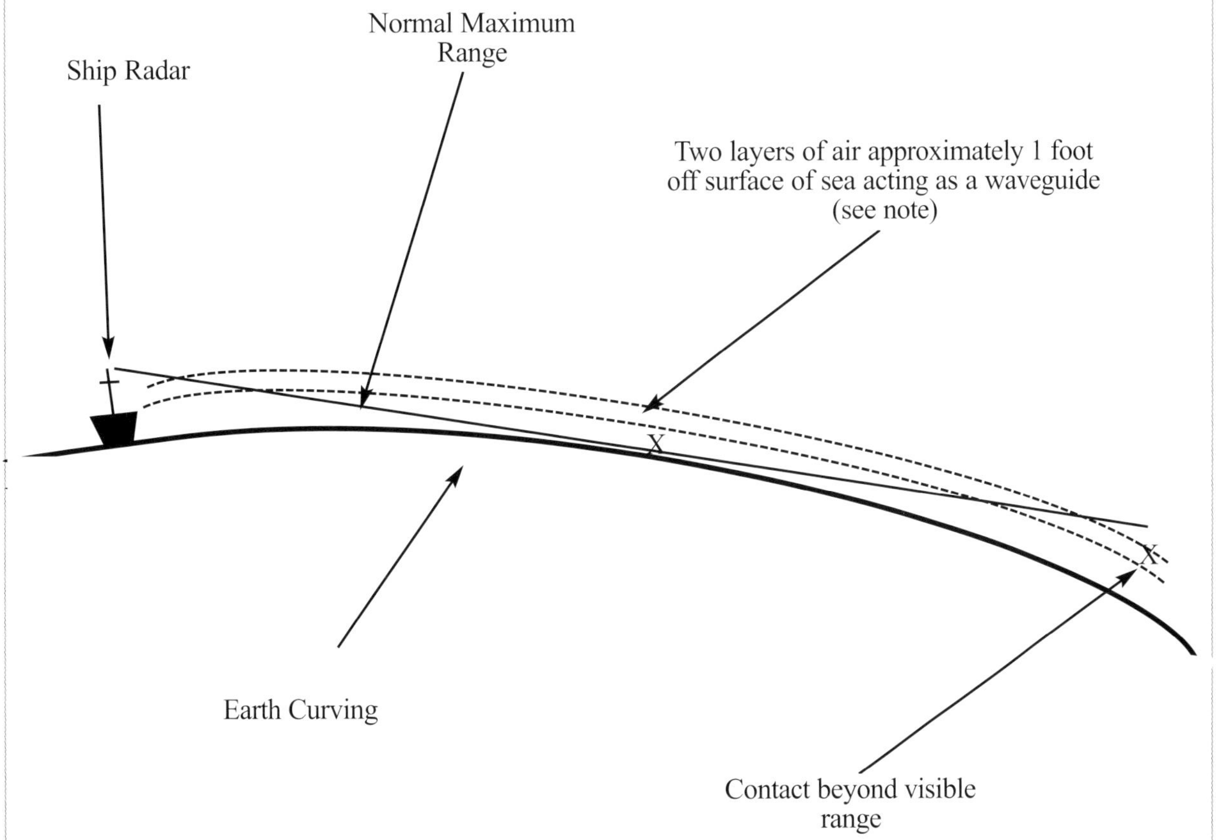

Ship Radar

Normal Maximum Range

Two layers of air approximately 1 foot off surface of sea acting as a waveguide (see note)

Earth Curving

Contact beyond visible range

Note: (or one layer of air and the sea acting as a waveguide)

It is believed that the Americans have been investigating this interesting phenomena which is the rule rather than the exception in the tropic waters of the Pacific.

Information of this theory was obtained from Lt.Cdr Milas RCNVR, Group Radar Officer, EG 26

21st NOVEMBER TO 7th DECEMBER 1944.

The Group, now comprising **Pevensey Castle** (SO), **Portchester Castle**, **Kenilworth Castle**, **Launceston Castle** and **Caistor Castle** sailed on the 21st November 1944 to patrol in the vicinity of 52°N 11°W, arriving at a slightly revised patrol line to the south east at 0830, 23rd November.

Because three ships had important bearings to run in and only 126 revolutions being available; equivalent to 10 knots, the speed made good with zig-zagging was only 9 knots. A strong head wind held back the ships so that only 8 knots was being made good. Commander Rayner was frequently frustrated by the windage and comparative slowness of the Castle Class Corvettes.

The patrol area lay in the western approaches to the Celtic Sea.

On the 23rd November the Group investigated two non-sub contacts. In each case the effects of a strong tide and wind were responsible for giving an impression that the target was moving. In one case the investigating ships were not convinced of this until a Dan Buoy had been laid.

Various non-sub contacts were made during the following two days. Careful record being held of their locations for future reference and for the information of other Groups that may encounter them.

From the morning of the 26th until 0900 on the 29th, the Group was convinced that they were attacking a probable U-Boat bottomed on the sea bed. The contact was excellent and air bubbles followed Squid explosions. Two underwater explosions were also noted following Squid attacks. Had the radar contact been held for longer, then there would have been more reason to claim that the contact had been with a U-Boat. The underwater explosions and bubbles at least indicated that the target was man made.

Commodore 'D' Londonderry commenting on the episode wrote:

> *"It is considered that there is no definite evidence of the presence of a U-Boat - - it is noted that there is a wreck - - which is close to the position given by SO EG 30 and which coincides exactly with the position given by **Launceston Castle**."*

CinCWA addressing the Admiralty observed that "It (the wreck) has since been re-located by the 10th Escort Group on 23rd December 1944 when it was marked by a 'winner'[4]

"It is considered that the 30th Escort Group Commander D.A. Rayner D.S.C. V.D. R.N.V.R displayed ability in attacks on this contact."

The Group remained on patrol until the 1st December when it was ordered to take over a contact being held by the 14th Escort Group following an attack by two ships of C8 Escort Group. The 30th Escort Group took over the contact in a force 8 south west gale. SO 14th EG who had known the contact in better weather conditions considered that it was a wreck. The 30th EG investigations confirmed this opinion. CinC WA was advised and the Group was ordered to resume patrol after recovering Dan Buoys.

During the night of 4th/5th December the Group supported the passage of HX 321 (36 ships) through their area. On relief on the 5th December the Group returned to base arriving there on 7th December.

Pevensey Castle endured an exciting but worrying time when her steering gear broke down some 4 miles from the Lough Foyle buoy and had to revert to hand steering. Temporary repairs were effected during the night and she was able to make the passage up river without assistance.
(ADM 217/745)

15th - 29th DECEMBER 1944

The Group, now under the command of Commander E. Hewitt RD RNR. Sailed from Moville (less **Kenilworth Castle**) on 15th December for exercises in the Campbeltown area. Again bad weather interrupted the proceedings to the extent that all gunnery exercises had to be cancelled. On the 25th **Portchester Castle**

---

[4] An electronic device identifying the object to an investigating ship as a known wreck

stood by a merchant ship in difficulties off Sanda Island.

The Group proceeded to Belfast Lough for fuel and sailed for their patrol area on the 18th. *Caistor Castle* was detached to Milford Haven for repairs to her radar. She rejoined on 22nd December.

On reaching their patrol area in the western approaches to the English Channel, the Group came under the operational orders of CinC Portsmouth. During the night, which was very dark, the Group trailed its coat within 5 miles of Alderney, but were ignored by the enemy.

On the 21st and 22nd December the Group patrolled at the western end of their area of operations and responded to various calls to investigate reported contacts. *Portchester Castle*, considered within the Group to be the expert, was frequently called upon to lead the investigations, none of which were classified as submarine and which usually turned out to be wrecks.

On the next day the Group proceeded to the position where a ship had been either mined or torpedoed. In the course of a box search, followed by a north and south sweep, a firm contact was attacked by *Portchester Castle* and *Caistor Castle*. Lumps of granulated cork, as from a refrigerator ship, surfaced, suggesting that the target was a wreck. The action was aborted and course set for Durlston Head in case the submarine was making good her escape by creeping along close to the shore line. The area was swept eastward when 2 miles off the coast towards the Isle of White. This was broken off at midnight to provide support to convoy HX 325 (59 ships[5]).

Patrolling continued during the 24th to 27th December. The occasion being enlivened by investigating a contact being held by a group of MTBs. These had held the contact for two hours. However, because of the poor weather conditions, they were unable to attack. The contact was attacked by *Pevensey Castle*. One of the Squid barrels failed to fire. The contact was classified as non-sub and patrolling was resumed. *Caistor Castle*, however, had to be detached to Portsmouth with a defective oscillator.

A similar situation with MTBs occurred on the 25th. A group of three MTBs were holding a contact which the Group classified as non-sub. The MTBs were not satisfied with this, insisting that *Pevensey Castle* was not in contact with the same target as they were. *Portchester Castle* confirmed the contact as non-sub. The MTBs plastered the area with depth charges and for the sake of good relations with another arm of the service, *Portchester Castle* attacked three times with Squid. The hunt was called off at 2200 and the ships resumed patrol. *Portchester Castle* was detached to Cardiff for refit on 26th December.

The *SS Empire Javelin* with 1,500 troops on board was mined or torpedoed on December 28th. The Group came in sight of the ship at 1700 when she was already well down by the stern. *Spragge* was carrying out 'Observant' around the casualty whilst *L'Escarmouche*, *Hargood* and 2 LSTs were picking up survivors. At 1713 a second explosion occurred right aft of the ship which quickly sank. 'Observant was immediately ordered. Once this was completed 'Scabbard was carried out by the Group with ships in line abreast. *L'Escarmouche* had been lying alongside an LST with about 700 survivors on board and reported damage. She and both LSTs were detached to Le Havre when they had completed their work. It was reported that all hands had been picked up. *Hargood* and *Cavalier* joined in the sweep until 2158 when *Hargood* reported having 59 survivors on board including some injured. She was detached to Le Havre.

Several non-sub contacts were made and the Group was relieved by the 10th Escort Group on the 30th December. By then an area 6 miles deep and 23 miles long had been double swept across tide. The datum point being the point where the wreck sank. The Group returned to Portsmouth for a short layover.

During the patrol it was found that the anti-Gnat 'Step Aside' procedure proved much simpler in practice than had appeared from the signal initiating it. It was concluded that the simplest method of achieving a gradual reduction in speed was to call 92 revolutions (8 knots) the anti-Gnat speed. The engine room now knew that if speed is reduced to those revs they must reduce revs according to the scale laid down. This proved simple and effective. It relieved the Officer of the Watch of the necessity of keeping a careful time check, when his attention is, rightly, on other things.
(ADM 217/570)

---

[5] This was the full size of the convoy. At this stage of its voyage there were probably not so many ships.

31st DECEMBER 1944 - 13th JANUARY 1945

The Group left Portsmouth to proceed on patrol on the 31st December. **Pevensey Castle** had to return to Portsmouth with an engine room defect rejoining the Group on the 7th January. **Caistor Castle** acting as SO during the absence of **Pevensey Castle**.

Patrolling was carried out in response to instructions received from time to time from CinC Portsmouth. There were the usual distractions and investigations of non-sub contacts. Various convoys and sections of convoys were supported as they passed through the patrol area. On the 6th January when in the vicinity of Alderney, the Group came under fire from the enemy shore batteries. Three salvoes fell within 200 yards astern of **Kenilworth Castle** as the Group retired northwards at high speed, meanwhile making white smoke and zig-zagging.

The Group were relieved by the 17th Escort Group on January 10th and proceeded to Portland, refuelled and stayed alongside pending the arrival of the 26th Escort Group. This Group arrived on January 11th and the 30th Escort Group sailed for Londonderry. A fresh northerly gale hindered progress. The weather moderated on the 13th, but at 0735 **Kenilworth Castle** stopped with an engine defect. **Pevensey Castle** and **Launceston Castle** carried out 'Observant' around her until daylight, when **Pevensey Castle** took her in tow. Ten knots was made during the tow which was slipped at 1325 **Kenilworth Castle** having made good the defect. The ships arrived at Moville at 1830 on the 13th January.
(ADM 217/571)

21st JANUARY - 5th FEBRUARY 1945

During this period the Group operated at the western end of the English Channel under the orders of CinC Plymouth. The Group had an erratic start. **Kenilworth Castle** being sailed to Belfast for a quick dry dock on 20th January. **Pevensey Castle** and **Caistor Castle** slipped from Londonderry, but before **Caistor Castle** could clear the port she had to re-secure because of dense fog.

On arrival at Moville **Pevensey Castle** and **Launceston Castle** carried out a 4-inch radar range exercise and a full calibre shoot. **Caistor Castle** was also able to join in latter.

Pevensey Castle and **Caistor Castle** sailed on the 22nd January having been further delayed by minor engine defects. They reached the patrol area on 24th January being joined by **Launceston Castle** later in the day and **Kenilworth Castle** on the 25th.

There followed the usual routine of investigating suspected contacts and providing support to convoys as they passed through the area. On 28th January whilst in support of TBC[6] 50 the **MV Cromarty** caught fire in the midship accommodation quarter. **Pevensey Castle** laid alongside and extinguished the fire. Commenting on the incident, Commodore 'D' Londonderry wrote:

> *"It is considered that the handling of **Pevensey Castle** on the windward side of **MV Cromarty** showed good seamanship on the part of Commander Hewitt. The fire parties, under the able leadership of Lieutenant Campbell RNVR Executive Officer, **Pevensey Castle** worked with courage and determination and their action is highly commended."*

This incident is described fully under the heading **Pevensey Castle** in Section 3.
(ADM 217/573)

The movements of the Group between the 5th and 19th February are uncertain. There is no Report of Pro-

---

[6] Code for Thames - Bristol Channel convoy.

ceedings covering this period. The 'Pink List' records **Pevensey Castle**, **Caistor Castle** and **Kenilworth Castle** leaving Plymouth on the 6th February and at sea on the 12th. However on the 19th all the Group, except **Portchester Castle** re-fitting at Cardiff, are reported as being in Londonderry boiler cleaning.

24th FEBRUARY TO 7th MARCH 1945

The Group left Lough Foyle on 24th February 1945 to relieve the 19th Escort Group off Altacarry and arrived in position in moderate visibility and a freshening gale. The weather continued to worsen and **Pevensey Castle** shipped a sea over her quarterdeck which poured down a ventilator and flooded the 60Kw generator. The remaining generators provided sufficient power to fight the ship. However, the tank storage of diesel oil for the 15Kw diesel generator would only suffice for 48 hours. The spare drum of diesel carried on deck had burst during the heavy weather. The situation finally resolved itself by the diesel generator developing a fault that could not be repaired at sea. **Pevensey Castle** returned to Londonderry leaving **Caistor Castle** in command. **Pevensey Castle** rejoining on 28th February and assuming the duties of SO Force 33.

The patrol was without any incident of significance, except that on 5th March **Pevensey Castle** and **Launceston Castle** detached from the convoy being supported by the Group to investigate a reported aircraft sighting. On arrival one Sunderland and one Liberator were circling a flare marker. An expanding square search was started. A deep Asdic contact was obtained and attacked. The target was stationery and considered to be bottomed even though the depth was 152 fathoms. **Launceston Castle** attacked with a depth setting of 875 feet resulting in a gush of oil. By this time **Caistor Castle** and **Kenilworth Castle** had arrived on the scene. It was decided to hold and surround the target all night. At daylight the target was still stationery and considered to be dead. The group returned to Moville.
(ADM 217/767)

The Group are reported as being at Lochalsh from the 27th March to 30th March, and arriving at Scapa Flow on the 3rd April 1945.

4th - 24th APRIL 1945

During this period the Group operated from Scapa Flow under the operational command of CinC Rosyth. The area of operations extended from the vicinity of Cape Wrath in the West to 1° West to the east and from the northern shores of the Scottish mainland to 60° North. That is as far north as the southern tip of the Shetland Islands. An exception to this was when the Group screened **Brittany** whilst she was 'laying an obstruction' in a position west of the Faeroes.

Throughout the period numerous contacts were examined all of which were finally classified as non-subs. Some of these being either wrecks or rocks. Convoys were supported in response to orders from CinC Rosyth.

A fairly typical days work describes the routine - April 16th 1945: On arrival off May Island the 1st Division detached to patrol towards the Farn Islands. When proceeding to investigate a radar contact to the northward, which subsequently proved to be a trawler, two non-sub contacts were investigated, one of which was attacked by **Portchester Castle**. The Division then returned to the vicinity of the swept channel where **Launceston Castle** had a good contact. This was attacked four times. A quantity of wreckage came to the surface, but found to be unmistakably of merchant ship origin and too large to have been jettisoned by a submarine as bluff. Contact was abandoned and course set for Farn Island. A signal was intercepted from the escorts of FS 84 indicating that a ship had been torpedoed. The Division proceeded at full speed to close them in anticipation of orders from CinC Rosyth.

On arrival at the scene an hour later **Viceroy** was found to be holding one contact and **Woolston** another. The Division immediately initiated a search across the tide. The convoy escorts left to rejoin their convoy after an hour. The 1st Division attacked several bottom contacts. There were so many of them that it was not possible

to investigate them thoroughly.

Viceroy obtained the best contact in position 55°37'N 01°28'W. This was attacked four times by *Viceroy* and twice by the Division.

The search was shifted northward at 0425/17th. Only one contact was investigated and attacked. A run over with echo sounder showed it to be a wreck. The search was abandoned at 1212 and course set for May Island where convoy EN 87 was met and supported northward.

To better cover the area *Caistor Castle* (SO) with *Kenilworth Castle* formed the 2nd Division and operated independently from the 1st Division. (*Pevensey Castle*, *Portchester Castle*, and *Launceston Castle*).

On separate occasions both *Portchester Castle* and *Kenilworth Castle* suffered from brickwork failure in a boiler. Repairs were effected at sea, but speed was reduced to 10 knots when steaming on one boiler.

False alarms were caused when the 1st Division encountered a small contact on April 22nd at a range of 10,000 yards. The first attempt to illuminate with rockets was foiled by the strength of the wind and low cloud, but a second spread illuminated a small Faeroes trawler which thereafter kept a white light burning. At about the same time, *Portchester Castle* at the eastern end of the patrol line closed and illuminated a second craft. This was the last day of the current northern patrol. The Group was relieved by the 23rd Escort Group and proceeded to Londonderry, arriving there on 24th April 1945.

(ADM 217/575)

4th - 17th MAY 1945

The Group less *Pevensey Castle* (SO in *Portchester Castle*) with *Launceston Castle*, *Caistor Castle* and *Kenilworth Castle* in company sailed early on 4th May to patrol and provide support to convoys in the Irish Sea.

Between the 4th May and 6th May the Group supported six local convoys, mainly proceeding between Milford Haven and Holyhead and between the Clyde and Bristol Channel. *Pevensey Castle* re-joined the Group on May 6th having overcome a main engine defect. Later on the same day the Group were ordered to return to Moville immediately. The Group arrived there at 2330.

On May 7th 1945 High Tea barrier stores[7] were loaded and the Group sailed at 0930 to lay a barrier to the westward. At 1415 the operation was postponed. The Group became Force 33 and proceeded northward to support Convoy RA 66 (27 ships). Support was withdrawn early on 8th May and the Group patrolled between Rathlin Island and Barra Head.

From 9th May to 14th May the Group was employed in intercepting and directing U-Boats coming in to surrender along the 'Blue Route'. The patrol area was extended to 58°N, 11°W. Three U-Boats were encountered; *U-956*, *U-825* and *U-255*.

During the patrol four British mines were sunk by gunfire at various locations. Doubtful Asdic contacts investigated and attacked. All turned out to be non-sub; either wrecks or shoals of fish. The Group returned to Moville at 1100 on 17th May.

(ADM 217/798)

19th MAY TO 2nd JUNE 1945

The Group less *Portchester Castle* sailed from Lough Foyle on 19th May and proceeded to Loch Erribol arriving there the next day. The Group came under the command of Senior Officer, Loch Erribol in *HMS Philante*.

Armed guards were provided in the U-Boats that had already arrived there. On 21st May *Caistor Castle* joined 21st EG in escorting ten U-Boats to Loch Alsh returning to Loch Erribol at 2300 the next day.

---

[7] Code name for Sona buoys.

On 24th May the Group were ordered to proceed to Bergen calling in at Scapa Flow enroute to fuel and pick up the necessary charts; *Portchester Castle* joining the Group at Scapa Flow. The early part of the 25th May was occupied in covering up as much red lead as possible and making the ships presentable for a triumphant entry into Norway. The Group sailed at 1700 covered with wet paint.

The ships arrive off Korsfjord at 2100, 26th May, and pilots were embarked on two ships. In close order and at full speed the Group proceeded up the inner lead to Bergen. In spite of the late hour, and the lack of telephone communications on the small islands, the ships received a tumultuous welcome all the way up, several enthusiasts courting death as they passed through the line in their dorys. The ships berthed at Bergen at 2300.

On the orders of 10th Cruiser Squadron in *HMS Birmingham*, the ships were opened to the public on the following day and large quantities of simple food were consumed by appreciative Bergenese. *Pevensey Castle* alone feeding 300 children and the other ships a like number.

On Monday 28th May the official ceremony of returning the base to its original owners took place. On the representation of SO 30th Escort Group a squad of men from the Group were included to represent Western Approaches Command.

Operation 'Cut out', the segregation of three Type XXI submarines, was carried out the same day and the Group provided guards to see their crews on their way to a prison camp about 10 miles down the Fjord, to which they were taken in two small trawlers. The Germans appeared very cheerful, making song and music en route. The guards thinking that they were singing party songs, countered by singing *"Don't Fence Me In"*. None of the German officers in the party would admit any knowledge of English until the trawlers arrived at the pier where they had to disembark. When, finding no transport awaiting them, they became good linguists, until the Norwegian pilot said to the officer in charge, *"The Roosians had to walk."* Thereupon the Germans fell silent and commenced the three mile trek up the hill to Fejide, which had previously been a concentration camp.

A conference was held in the German Naval Headquarters the following day, attended by 13 U-Boat commanders who were to form the group convoy on May 30th. They were compliant, especially the commanding officer of *U-1206* named Jager, who said he knew the ropes having surrendered his submarine in Harwich in 1918. This officer was made responsible for passing signals to the remainder on passage.

The Group less *Caistor Castle*, who was left behind to escort the three Type XXI U-Boats, slipped at 0800 30th May, the U-Boats slipping at the same time. All proceeded down the fjord without incident, escorts being spaced at intervals down the line until clear of the fjord where submarines formed up into three columns.

The passage to Scapa was without incident apart from the sinking of a mine by *Launceston Castle*. On arrival at Switha the local escorts took over; the Group securing to buoys in Gutter Sound.

The Group sailed from Scapa at 0615, 1st June, and arrived off Lough Foyle Buoy the following day at 1100. *(ADM 217/578)*

B5 and 31st ESCORT GROUPS

With one or two exceptions the Castle Class Corvettes forming part of the B5 Escort Group became the ships of the 31st Escort Group. Even after the Groups had been disbanded on the conclusion of the European phase of WWII the same ships continued to operate together on Air Sea Rescue duties. It is therefore convenient to consider the two Groups together.

B5 ESCORT GROUP

The first record of the B5 Escort Group in the 'Ship Dispositions' list occurs on the 3rd February 1944, with the Group (SO *Havelock*) escorting convoy HX 277 (69 ships). *Hadleigh Castle* being named as one of the escorts. *Hadleigh Castle* having arrived at Argentia on the 30th January 1944 on the conclusion of her visit to the United States and Canada.

After working up *Hadleigh Castle*, the first of the class, had gone to the USA in December 1943 with the Canadian C4 Escort Group (SO *Hotspur*) escorting ON 215 (58 ships). *Hadleigh Castle* had then demonstrated the capabilities of the Squid to the Canadian and USA Naval Authorities.

On the 23rd February 1944 the B5 Group consisting of *Hadleigh Castle* (SO), *Volunteer*, *Lavender*, *Buttercup* and two other escorts who's names were not readable in the file, sailed to provide the escort for ON 225 (59 ships). The convoy's route was altered to almost follow a Great Circle. Poor visibility was encountered for most of the voyage which passed almost without incident.

When in the vicinity of the Great Banks *HMS Lavender* on the port bow of a very scattered convoy, was steaming at 10 knots without Foxers being streamed; because the equipment had broken down. She sighted a periscope on the port bow distant 400 yards. The ship was immediately turned to ram and at the same time obtained an A/S contact on the same bearing and range as the sighting. At a range of 250 yards the Commanding Officer realised that the 'periscope' was a grey painted six inch spar projecting vertically from a partially submerged structure. This was definitely not a submarine. *Lavender* altered course to starboard and the spar passed down the port side 100 yards away.

When the spar was abeam a small explosion occurred and almost immediately a substance like cotton waste was thrown up, some of which struck the ship's side and rebounded. It was considered that the explosion occurred under the ship, and that it was mild and close to the surface. The spar was not disturbed by the explosion.

The A/S contact, classified as 'Submarine stopped' was held in the direction of the spar. The ship continued past the spar at 12 knots. The spar was lost to view in the fog.

Two minutes later a heavy prolonged explosion occurred in the direction of the spar. The explosion showed on the A/S trace and was heard by *Hadleigh Castle* 20 miles away. Sixteen minutes later another heavy and prolonged explosion occurred dead astern of the ship now on a course of 240°.

At Base the reception of the report of this incident produced a flurry of 'minutes' and speculation. Finally, CinC WA, advising the Admiralty of the incident wrote:

"From the information available the presence of a U-Boat cannot be definitely established at the time when the explosion took place in the vicinity of HMS. Lavender, and the nature of the explosions cannot be determined with any certainty'
It appears that the object sighted by HMS Lavender, might have been one of the following:-

(i)   A decoy in the form of a dummy periscope by a U-Boat with the object of attracting the atten-

tion of an escort, which would then provide a good torpedo target. - in this event the explosions might be attributed to torpedoes.
(ii) A Radar Reflecting Buoy (Thetis)
(iii) A Meteorological Buoy.

Having regard to the visibility (400 yards) and the intervals between explosions the explanation in (i) above appears unlikely.
It is not easy to reconcile the explosions in conjunction with a Meteorological Buoy.
It is noted that the position in which the occurrence took place was on the edge of the Newfoundland Bank. The probable explanation, therefore, appears to be that the object was a Radar Reflecting Buoy (Thetis) and that the explosions were mines."

The Admiralty's last word on the subject was :-

*"With reference to your submission....concerning the Report of Proceedings of **HMS Hadleigh Castle** whilst escorting Convoy ON.225, I am to inform you that it is considered that the object sighted by **HMS Lavender** was probably a Radar Decoy Spar Buoy (R.D.S.) and that the explosions were caused by torpedoes fired in the vicinity."*

BY COMMAND OF THEIR LORDSHIPS

During April 1944 the Group was re-organised with **HMS Exe** becoming the Senior Officer. The other ships forming the Group were, **Dumbarton Castle**, **Carisbrooke Castle**, **Berkeley Castle**, **Hadleigh Castle**, and **Moyola**. The four Castle Class Corvettes formed the core of the Group.

After exercising the Group at Larne and elsewhere the Group escorted Convoy SL 156/MKS 47 (50 ships plus 14 LSTs) to Gibraltar. The Group continued to escort convoys between the UK and Gibraltar until the end of August 1944 when the 31st Escort Group was formed. **Berkeley Castle** (Commander N.W. Duck RNR)became the Senior Officer's ship. The other ships forming the Group were:-

> **Hadleigh Castle**
> **Carisbrooke Castle**
> **Dumbarton Castle**
> **Lancaster Castle** .

CONVOYS ESCORTED BY THE B5 ESCORT GROUP FROM 13th APRIL 1944 - 23rd AUGUST 1944

DATE	CONVOY	No of Ships	N or S Bound	REMARKS
13/04 to 24/04	OS74/KMS48	29	S	
01/05 to 11/05	SL156/MKS47	64	N	Convoy included 14 LSTs

DATE	CONVOY	No of Ships	N or S Bound	REMARKS
23/05 to 05/06	OS78/KMS52	23	S	*HM Ships Ascension, Evenlode & Coldstream* additional escorts. Anti Glider bomb exercises carried out.
09/06 to 20/06	SL160/MKS51	44	N	*HM Ships Ascension & Evenlode* included in the escort. Passage without incident
02/07 to 13/07	OS82/KMS56	26	S	*HMS Bellwort* replaces *HMS Ascension*. Passage without incident
19/07 to 31/07	SL164/MKS55	33	N	Convoy supported by Escort Carrier *HMS Fencer*. On 26th & 27th U-Boat detected by radio transmission as being within 100 to 60 miles of the convoy. Air patrols failed to make contact. 12 ships capable of 11 knots detached on 29th escorted by *Exe, Hadleigh Castle, Carisbrooke Castle & Berkeley Castle* 30th *Dumbarton Castle* detached with Loch Ewe portion of 27 ships
10/08 to 21/08	OS86/KMS60	23	S	*Hadleigh Castle* now SO. *Bamborough Castle* joins the Group. *Carisbrooke Castle* returns temporarily to Moville because of a hot engine bearing. *HMS Activity* (Escort Carrier) supported convoy until 21st. 17th U-Boat detected 65 miles south of the convoy. Convoy altered course 40° to starboard for 4 hours. 19th *HM Ships Ascension & Goodall* detached to hunt U-Boat sighted by aircraft. 20th *Berkeley Castle & Bamborough Castle* detached to assist in U-Boat hunt
30/08 to 10/09	SL168/MKS59	33	N	No Report of Proceedings found for this voyage. Reports in the 'Ship Disposition List' suggest that the Group was re-designated as the 31st Escort Group whilst on this voyage.

Hadleigh Castle carried 20 boxes of bullion on the last voyage from Gibraltar to UK. This was said to be Polish gold evacuated from the country just before or at the beginning of the war.

31st ESCORT GROUP

Cdr N.W. Duck RNR (SO)

The Group comprising **HM Ships Berkeley Castle** (SO), **Hadleigh Castle** and **Dumbarton Castle** ex the B5 Escort Group arrived in Clyde on the 10th September 1944 having completed the escort of Convoy SL186/MKS59 from Gibraltar. For the remainder of the month the Group were either at Larne or Londonderry. Prior to assembling at Larne for exercises in their new role on the 22nd/23rd September, the Group remained at the Clyde, probably boiler cleaning. On the 27th September the Group were reported as forming part of Force 33 patrolling the Western Approaches. They provided support to ONS 33 (C1 Escort Group being the ocean escort).

Force 33 comprised several patrol groups of frigates and corvettes patrolling the Western Approaches and providing support for convoys as the tactical situation required. Initially this and similar 'Forces' were controlled directly from Western Approaches Command. As their commander's gained experience the detailed control came more and more under the direct control of the Senior Officer of the Force.

Between the 20th October 1944 and the 14th May 1945 the Group carried out seven operational patrol periods from the Western Approaches to the English Channel to north of the Shetland Islands. The locations and period of these operations are shown overleaf. A major characteristic of these operations was the large number of contacts that had to be investigated and attacked and, as far as this group was concerned, invariably turning out to be non-subs; usually wrecks. This placed considerable strain on the Asdic teams and one cannot but admire the manner in which they obviously maintained a consistent high standard of operation. The Reports of Proceedings do not provide a complete record of the number of Squid attacks that were carried out. But there can be no doubt that the ships of the Group became highly expert at scoring direct hits on bottomed targets.

Captain 'D', Greenock in a minute agreed with Commander Duck's assessment of the efficiency of the Group. Commander Duck had written:-

> "I consider that the A/S efficiency of the Group high, and the ships are now thoroughly expert at hitting bottomed targets, the only target which has presented themselves for months. I find the A/S ratings are disappointed if we are unable to identify the actual spot we have hit from the number of hatch covers brought to the surface. I am continually surprised at the unfailing keenness of the A/S ratings in spite on the months of coastal work and the hundreds of disappointing attacks on ordinary wrecks."

Perhaps it was this apparent difficulty in being unable to clearly distinguish between an echo generated by a submarine and that produced by a wreck that induced the authorities to arrange for the ships of the Group to run over **HM Submarine Sealion** whilst she lay on the bottom. The general opinion arising from this exercise was that the Asdic characteristics were exactly the same as the average wreck on the bottom.

Brief descriptions of the various operations follow.

20th OCTOBER - 4th NOVEMBER 1944

The Group comprising **Berkeley Castle** (SO), **Hadleigh Castle** and **Dumbarton Castle** sailed from Greenock on the 20th October 1944. A series of exercise had been planned for the next three days. These were to include full calibre gunnery shoot, A/S exercise, submarine boarding and towing exercises followed by day and night tactical exercises. The gunnery shoot had to be cancelled because of insufficient

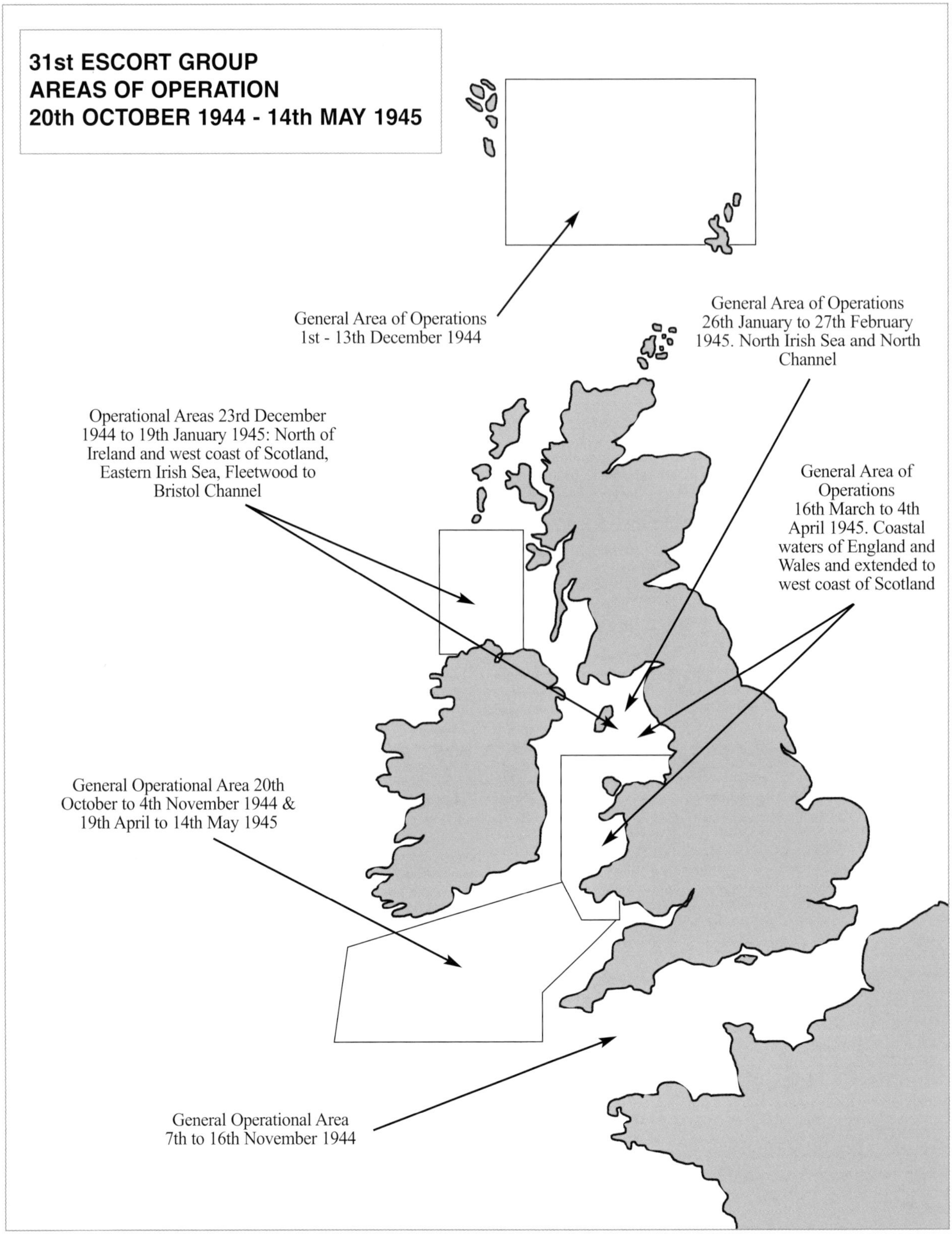

**31st ESCORT GROUP
AREAS OF OPERATION
20th OCTOBER 1944 - 14th MAY 1945**

General Area of Operations
1st - 13th December 1944

General Area of Operations
26th January to 27th February
1945. North Irish Sea and North
Channel

Operational Areas 23rd December
1944 to 19th January 1945: North of
Ireland and west coast of Scotland,
Eastern Irish Sea, Fleetwood to
Bristol Channel

General Area of
Operations
16th March to 4th
April 1945. Coastal
waters of England and
Wales and extended to
west coast of Scotland

General Operational Area 20th
October to 4th November 1944 &
19th April to 14th May 1945

General Operational Area
7th to 16th November 1944

visibility. But all the others were carried out and the weather conditions improved. It was noted that the radar Type 272P performed poorly when exercising in the detection of schnoerkels. Whereas these were visible by eye up to a range of 5,000 yards, the radar failed to detect them beyond 2,400 yards.

The first patrol area was in the north western approaches to the North Channel. Two unexplained underwater explosions were observed with an interval of about three minutes between them. The ships swept along the probable direction from which an attack might have come. No contact was obtained and after four hours the Group altered course to the south west in accordance to CinC WA's instructions. The SO considered that the explosions were probably due to mines. He discounted the probability of a U-Boat having initiated a periscope torpedo attack under the prevailing weather conditions. (Wind NW force 6/7; rough seas and swell). The signal reporting the event did not reach base until over ten hours later. All this did not go down too well at Liverpool. The Staff Officers remarked that:-

1.   The observed effect is consistent with a deep explosion.
2.   The probabilities appear to be either mines or torpedoes exploding on the bottom at the end of their run.

"There was evidently some doubt in their minds (as there is in ours) as to whether it was mine or torpedo. Any suggestion of a torpedo should have provoked a vigorous and prolonged search, which does not appear to have been carried out.
It was unfortunate that the signal was delayed in transit until 2100, over 10 ten hours too late for us. EG 30 was not on the spot until 2100, over ten hours too late."
"I agree also with SOO that the incident should have inspired an immediate signal and an exhaustive search. **Berkeley C** *carried the SO. There may be others like him who will ignore this coattrailing by the enemy so close to our doorstep. We have not yet got used to the fact that the "unmarked and unrestricted" submarines in the Londonderry Sanctuary are now U-Boats."*

The new patrol area was to the south west of the Celtic Sea with the group operating under the command of the SO of the 10th Escort Group. During the next nine days numerous targets were attacked all of which turned out to be non-subs. This in spite of two reports from aircraft of disappearing contacts. It was during this period that the Group was reinforced by the appearance of **Bamborough Castle**. **Dumbarton Castle** had also rejoined the Group, having been delayed by radio defects. On the 3rd November **Lancaster Castle** joined and relieved **Bamborough Castle** who was detached in accordance with CinC Plymouth's instructions.

On the 4th November the Group was relieved by the Sixth Escort Group and proceeded to Devonport for a lay-over.

7th - 16th NOVEMBER 1944

The Group comprising **Berkeley Castle** (SO), **Lancaster Castle**, **Hadleigh Castle**, and **Dumbarton Castle** slipped berths from Devonport and proceeded to their patrol area in the Western Approaches to the English Channel.

During the next eight days the Group attacked six non-sub targets and supported 5 convoys. One of these was UC 44B, one of the 14 knot westbound group of convoys heading for the United States. These convoys (CU/UC) were originally tanker convoys, but because of their fast speed were often joined by freighters and liners whose speed was greater than that of the standard HX convoys. The 31st EG were often detailed to provide support for these convoys but found it difficult to do so because of their speed. On this occasion the convoy was a little ahead of schedule with the result that the Group were unable to

catch them up and had to be content to support them from the stern.

On the 14th November the Group was relieved by the 10th Escort Group and proceeded to Greenock, arriving there on the 16th.

29th NOVEMBER - 13th DECEMBER 1944.

The Group comprising **Berkeley Castle** (SO), **Hadleigh Castle**, **Bamborough Castle**, and **Lancaster Castle** sailed from Greenock on 29th November 1944 and initially supported convoy ONS 37 (31 ships) until the 1st December when they detached from the convoy and proceeded to Scapa Flow arriving there on the 2nd December. After refuelling the Group immediately proceeded to their new patrol area between the Shetland and Faeroe Islands. Virtually the whole period was occupied in systematically patrolling the area with the occasional interruption from aircraft sighting reports. Commenting on the operation Commander Duck wrote:

> *"The patrol was noticeable for its quietness and remarkably fine weather. The few daylight hours available were spent either in Group or individual exercises."*

At that time of year there would have been only five hours of daylight per day in those latitudes. The Group returned to Greenock on the 13th December 1944.

23rd DECEMBER - 19th JANUARY 1945

During this period the Group consisting of **Berkeley Castle** (SO), **Hadleigh Castle** and **Dumbarton Castle** operated in the North Western Approaches and in the Irish Sea. **Lancaster Castle** was delayed at Greenock with boiler defects. On arrival in their patrol area the Group became part of Force 33 (**HMS Louis** SO).

In the evening of the 26th December **Dumbarton Castle** obtained a contact. Although this was classified as 'doubtful' contact was held from 1611 on the 26th to 1125 on the 27th in spite of adverse weather and Asdic conditions. 18 attacks were made, including one depth charge attack. Eventually, with insufficient evidence of the presence of a U-Boat, the contact was classified as 'non-sub' and abandoned.

The support groups operating in the coastal waters of the UK had to carry out a diverse range of tasks. They had to carry out protective patrols aimed at intercepting any lurking U-Boats. They were required to provide additional escort cover to convoys as they passed through and sometimes beyond their patrol area; and whilst carrying out these jobs be ready to react immediately to reports of U-Boat attacks or sightings by aircraft. The following diary of events of the remainder of the Group's work during this period provides an insight in to what was required.

28th Dec	Group supported the very badly straggling JW 63 convoy - 32 stragglers over 26 miles increasing to 40 miles. When the van of the convoy reached the Loch Ewe Buoy, the Group patrolled westwards whilst the convoy entered the Loch. 1300 Group supports a section of Convoy ONS 39.
29th Dec	1230 The section of the convoy joins the main convoy and **Berkeley Castle** assumes command of all the escorts. The Group sweeps ahead of the convoy.
30th Dec	0500 The Group detaches from ONS 39 and joins SC 163 (46 ships **HMCS Stonehouse** SO) 31st Group disposed astern.
31st Dec	0345 Group detaches from SC163 and proceeds to patrol off Barra Head.
1st - 2nd Jan	Group proceeds to Lisahally for fuel and layover.

3rd Jan	Group less **Dumbarton Castle** (delayed by steering defect-joins 1745) and proceeds to patrol area 55°N 56°30'N - 06°W 08°30'W

3rd Jan Group less **Dumbarton Castle** (delayed by steering defect-joins 1745) and proceeds to patrol area 55°N 56°30'N - 06°W 08°30'W

4th Jan Group patrolling western edge of patrol area and heaves to in face of full North-Westerly gale. At 0945 **Carisbrooke Castle** rejoins the Group after refit.

6th Jan Group patrolling north of Ireland. Three ships in line ahead formation astern of one ship 4 miles ahead towing single P.N.M. unit. Heavy gales continue.

8th Jan Continuing patrol along meridian 8°W; Gale abated.

10th Jan Left patrol area to meet convoy ENG 68 off Barra Head.

11th Jan Meet convoy ENG 68. 1732 Group detached to proceed with all despatch to position 53°19'N 04°48'W where two ships have been torpedoed.

12th Jan Group diverted to a second area but before getting there diverted to a third where aircraft had reported a U-Boat.

13th Jan En route to reported position of U-Boat **Berkeley Castle** and **Carisbrooke Castle** attacked a bottomed contact but could not agree on its classification. SO 3rd Escort Group ordered a square search sides 5 miles around the datum position. During the day four wrecks attacked and **Lancaster Castle** ordered to Liverpool with defective boiler brickwork.

14th Jan Group joined 3rd Escort Group in an A/S sweep towards the Irish coast. The 3rd EG detached at 1220. Group continued to sweep between 54°40'N; 53°18'N and 05°20'W and 05°45'W.

15th Jan Group searched the area between Arkhas Bank and Bardsey Island. 1300 Group directed towards 53°40'N; 05°14'W where ship reported to be mined. En route Group diverted to location where a suspected U-Boat was sighted by aircraft. **Carisbrooke Castle** detached to stand by the wreck of mined ship; subsequently joined by **Berkeley Castle** and **Dumbarton Castle** when search initiated around wreck position.

16th Jan Group detailed to support various convoys including one consisting of three fast fuel tankers from Liverpool steaming at 14 knots. The Group were just able to keep up by not zig-zagging.

17th Jan Group patrolling area between Isle of Man and Anglesey and then detached to support convoys.

18th Jan 6th Escort Group relieved the 31st E.G at 1006 which then proceeded to Greenock, arriving there for layover at 0300 on the 19th Jan.

During the period described above, the Group attacked nine non-subs classified as wrecks and supported six convoys.

26th JANUARY - 27th FEBRUARY 1945

The Group operated in the North Irish Sea and the North Channel. During this period Asdic conditions were exceptionally good except between the Mull of Kintyre and Rathlin Island and the bays of the North East Irish coast. Typically fish echoes which broke up often after a few transmissions were encountered hourly. These echoes were loud and gave a good trace and doppler effect.

It was found that small irregularities in the sea bottom provided a large proportion of contacts. These, had of course, to be investigated.

These all too frequent non-subs place a great strain on the Asdic team, who in spite of this remained keen and efficient. However, towards the end of the operational period, there developed a tendency to delay reports to the Officer of the Watch and to classify the contact before reporting.

During this period the Group provided additional A/S support to 40 convoys. Twenty seven of these

were coastal convoys, 11 were Ocean convoys and 2 were fast tanker convoys. Sometimes these convoys comprised only a hand full of ships - occasionally only one ship.

10th MARCH - 4th APRIL 1945

The Group were operating in the coastal waters off the west coast of Scotland, England and Wales. Numerous non-sub contacts were encountered and attacked. Weather conditions often contributed to the difficulties of classifying contacts. This may be illustrated by the occasion when **Dumbarton Castle** obtained a good Asdic contact on 31st March. Between 1049 and 1545 **Berkeley Castle** and **Dumbarton Castle** made 8 squid attacks. The adverse weather conditions were such that they were unable to obtain a good echo sounder trace of the object of attack until after the last attack, when it then became obvious that the ships were attacking a wreck.

Two days earlier it was fog that caused problems. The Group had been sweeping in the North Channel towards the Clyde Light Vessel with a view to meeting convoy ON 293. Fog descended on the area. It coincided with the untimely convergence of several convoys. These were ONS 293 (82 ships), HX 344 (71 ships) and BB 65. HX 244 was about 12 hours ahead of schedule. Thus within a fog bound confined area there was anything up to about 170 ships including escorts, each attempting to feel their way past each other. "This made the North Channel like a main line railway station with escorts madly rushing from departure to arrival platforms." (*SO 31st EG Report of Proceedings*).

The safe passage of these ships would have been impossible without the combination of radar and disciplined signalling procedures. On this matter Commander Duck referring to his Group wrote:-

> "*V/S and flag signalling is good throughout the Group but TBS is still unsatisfactory. This is almost entirely due to material defects. Speed and brevity being marred by repetitions occasioned by lack of sensitivity in aerials. Frequent W/T and R/T exercises have drilled the Group to a high standard. I think it worthy of mention that the W/T staff of* **HMS Berkeley Castle** *have transmitted some three hundred messages and coded nearly 12,000 groups since January 8th this year without any serious error. I consider this reflects great credit on the W/T staff.*"

During this period (10th March to 4th April) the Group supported 31 convoys of which:-

> 12 were ocean convoys
> 15 were coastal convoys
> 4 code unidentified.

19th APRIL - 14th MAY 1945

During this period the Group was operating mainly in the South Western Approaches. The support of convoys passing through the area was once again an important feature of their work. The Group now comprised **Berkeley Castle** (SO), **Hadleigh Castle**, **Lancaster Castle**, **Dumbarton Castle**, and **Carisbrooke Castle** . **HMS Allington Castle** joined the Group for a short while towards the end of the period.

On 22nd April **Berkeley Castle** whilst on passage between two convoys attacked a contact and brought up a lot of wreckage. After the three Squid explosions there was a fourth, indicating that a magazine must have been hit. This resulted in a patch of the sea surface being set on fire. Shortly after this **Hadleigh Castle** was detached to Holyhead to attend to a hot bearing. She rejoined on the 24th. That evening **Berkeley Castle** attacked a good A/S contact which was held and investigated for just over 12 hours before being abandoned as a non-sub.

On 29th April **Hadleigh Castle** and **Lancaster Castle** were detached to investigate an aircraft sighting of a U-boat. The situation became confused because several reports were received each giving a different position but all apparently referring to the same U-boat. Eventually Senior Officer 10th Escort Group signalled that he was investigating and the two Castles were recalled.

The Group went to Milford Haven for a short layover on 30th April. **Berkeley Castle** taking advantage of the rest period to repair condensers that had been causing problems.

The group left Milford Haven on 2nd May with **Allington Castle** in company to support HX 351 (57 ships) off Cork. En route **Hadleigh Castle** reported torpedo HE when the Group was steaming in line abreast at 13 knot, ships one mile apart. The Group turned north to investigate and in those wreck infested waters non-subs were soon contacted. The first division of the Group, **Berkeley Castle**, **Dumbarton Castle** and **Carisbrooke Castle** left the search area at 1757 to provide support to HX 351 when the convoy was 5 miles clear of the search area. The second division **Hadleigh Castle** (SO) **Allington Castle** and **Lancaster Castle** continued with the search until the outward bound combined convoy ON 300/KMS 100 had passed the area. They then joined that convoy and, early the next day were joined by the rest of the Group. The Group remained with the convoy. The KMS 100 convoy split from the main convoy at 0001 on 4th May. The 31st EG remained with the KMS section until its junction with the Channel section. V.E. Day was officially declared at 1500B by the Prime Minister and no ships requested repetition of the Admiralty's signal timed 1500B "*Splice the Main Brace*". Our moderate celebrations consisted of steaming through the convoy...with "*Well done the Merchant Navy*" flying and the "*Post Horn Gallop*" blaring out its cheerful message through the upper deck loudspeaker. At 2200 on the 5th May the Group detached to join the northbound MKS 98. The Group remained with that convoy until the evening of the 7th May. Earlier in the day one of the close escorts, **HMS Lavender**, observed an underwater explosion and thought that it may have been a Gnat. **Rushen Castle** the SO of the close escort considered that it might have been a mine detonated by **Lavender**'s P.N.M unit. **Berkeley Castle**, **Allington Castle** and **Dumbarton Castle** joined **Lavender** in investigating the incident. The Group detached from the convoy at 1700 to support convoy MH 106.

The Group continued to support various convoys until 12th May when ordered to proceed to Loch Alsh with all despatch but **Carisbrooke Castle** had to be detached to Greenock with engine defects. The remainder of Group reached Loch Alsh at 0700 on the 13th May. In the afternoon the Group under the command of SO EG 14 (**HMS Hesperus**) escorted eight surrendered U-Boats to Lough Foyle arriving there at 0100. Commander Duck wrote:

> "*This privilege was very much appreciated by the Group; at last the dogs of war were allowed to see the rabbits that they had been searching for so ardently.*"

The Group detached to proceed to Greenock, arriving there at 2335B. So ended the European War for the 31st Escort Group.

7th ESCORT GROUP

Castle Class Corvettes escorted 12 'Russian Convoys' comprising a total of 364 merchant ships of which six were sunk by enemy action. One Castle Class Corvette, the **Denbigh Castle** was torpedoed outside Kola Inlet. She was subsequently beached and capsized. Earlier **Denbigh Castle** had succeeded in shooting down one Ju-88. An excellent piece of work considering that this was the first time that she had been in action against enemy aircraft. The Norwegian Castle Class Corvette **HNorMS Tunsberg Castle** was mined and sunk in Arctic waters, but not whilst on Russian Convoy escort duty. On the other hand **Bamborough Castle** sank **U-387** on 9th December 1944 and **Alnwick Castle** sank **U-425** on 17th February 1945. A summary of the Russian convoys escorted by Castle Class Corvettes follows:-

7th ESCORT GROUP
RUSSIAN CONVOYS ESCORTED BY CASTLE CLASS CORVETTES

PERIOD	CONVOY	NO OF SHIPS	ROUTE	REMARKS
15/09 - 24/09/44	JW 60	31	UK - Kola Inlet	
28/09 - 04/10/44	RA 60	32	Kola Inlet - UK	2 merchant ships sunk
28/11 - 05/12/44	JW 62	38	UK - Kola Inlet	
10/12 - 20/12/44	RA 62	30	Kola Inlet - UK	
28/12 - 08/01/45	JW 63	38	UK - Kola Inlet	
11/01/ - 27/01/44	RA 63	30	Kola Inlet - UK	
02/02 - 13/02/45	JW 64	29	UK - Kola Inlet	**Denbigh Castle** shot down a Ju 88 & later was torpedoed and beached in Kola Inlet
17/02 - 01/03/45	RA 64	31	Kola Inlet - UK	**Alnwick Castle** sinks **U-425**; **Bluebell** blown up; **Lark** sunk; 2 merchant ships sunk; hurricane force winds encountered.
11/03 - 20/03/45	JW 65	26	UK - Kola Inlet	**Lapwing** sunk; 2 merchant ships sunk
23/03/- 01/04/45	RA 65	26	Kola Inlet - UK	
16/04/ - 27/04/45	JW 66	27	UK - Kola Inlet	
29/04 - 15/05/45	RA 66	26	Kola Inlet to UK	**Goodall** sunk; **U-307** & **U-286** sunk by other escorts

A summary of the narratives describing these voyages follow. They are generally extracts from the reports of the Admiral in command of the convoy operations.

CONVOYS JA & RA 60
15th SEPTEMBER - 5th OCTOBER 1944

The introduction of the Castle Class Corvettes to Russian Convoy work was quiet in that their first voyage to Russia and back was almost without incident. *Allington Castle* and *Bamborough Castle* joined the 7th Escort Group on the 13th September at Loch Ewe for the first time in preparation for forming part of the close escort of the two convoys. The outward bound JW 60 arrived at Kola intact without incident. The Grimm Group of six U-boats deployed to intercept the convoy failed to do so. On the return journey convoy RA 60 sailed from Kola Inlet on 28th September. On the 29th the convoy overran a U-boat which succeeded in sinking two merchant ships. Gnat torpedoes were also fired at the escorts but without success. The surviving 28 merchant ships arrived at Loch Ewe on 5th October 1944.

CONVOYS JA & RA 62
26th NOVEMBER - 20th DECEMBER
SOURCE ADM 199/602 PAGES 137 -140 & 164/5

HMS CYGNET

GENERAL REMARKS

I. <u>Time of departure of J.W. Convoys from Loch Ewe in winter.</u>

It would be a considerable advantage if J.W. convoys could be sailed in winter at daylight instead of 1430, so that they could get formed up before dark. On this occasion conditions were nearly perfect with a full moon and good visibility, but even so stragglers were not properly closed up until daylight the following morning.
Under conditions of poor visibility, and sailing so late in the day it would be inevitable that W/T silence would be broken on V.H.F. and very possibly on 2410 K/cs as well.

II. <u>Speed of entry into ports</u>

Now that submarines have taken to operating close in off our ports and off Kola Inlet it appears to be very necessary to speed up the entry of ships into ports. The rate of intake of the Clyde portion of JW 62 into Loch Eve was in the region of 5 per hour, and the hold-up appears to be due to the limited number of boats available to lead merchant ships to their berths.
It would be much better if they were instructed to pass the boom and wait inside rather than outside the harbour; if necessary they could anchor in a temporary berth until boats were available. At Kola the delay is due to the time taken to get pilots onboard; if they embarked further up the inlet a larger number of ships could be got into safety more quickly. On this occasion the *Fort Highfield* was found cruising out towards Kildin Island to waste time before entering.

III.   <u>Air Attack.</u>

Very little entertainment was provided by the Ju-88's, two were heard above the clouds, but none seen.

There was a certain amount of congestion of escorts in Van Sector. as some of the 9th EG had not had time to get back to join the close screen and remained, in the vicinity of the first group.

IV.   <u>Radar and Station keeping.</u>

For ships fitted with old type Radar sets, stations are not easy to maintain in Baker Peter Two, and there is no doubt that the Radar has to be employed on station keeping for considerably longer periods than is desirable. This is particularly the case when the convoy is at all scattered or there is much straggling.

2. In convoy JW 60, *Rodney* stood out well in the middle of the convoy and hence it was comparatively easy to obtain a reasonably accurate ZZ position. It is possible that the use of Type 253 P on button Baker by the cruiser has possibilities in easing this situation though it would of course mean an increase in the use of Type 242.

HMS CYGNET
19th DECEMBER 1944

<u>SECTION 1 - NARRATIVE OF EVENTS</u>

<u>CONVOY JW 62</u>

<u>26th November</u>

0912	*Cygnet* and *Westcott* sailed from Clyde.
1500	Met convoy LXK3 (feeder convoy of 18 ships for JW.62) off Altacarry Head. Took up screening positions - *Cygnet* Able, *Westcott* Sugar.
1645	2nd Escort Group (Senior Officer - *Wild Goose*) joined to give A/S support as far as Barra Head.

<u>27th November</u>

0920	Convoy arrived Loch Ewe Buoy and commenced entering harbour.
1245	*Kent* (Rear Admiral Commanding First Cruiser Squadron) arrived Loch Ewe.
1337	*Cygnet* and *Westcott* entered harbour, fuelled and anchored.

<u>29th November</u>

1030	Conference for convoy JW.62 and escorts at NCSO's Office.
1400	*Cygnet* (Senior Officer) passed boom with *Tunsberg Castle*, *Eglantine*, *Lapwing*, *Allington Castle*, *Bamborough Castle*, *Tortola*, *Somaliland*, *Bahamas* and *Tavy* (EG 20) in company.
1435	Convoy sailed, formed up and proceeded via route 'RED'.

| 1555 | Escorts took up positions as in Composite Screening Diagram, Admiralty Convoy Instructions as Follows: |

Ship	Day	Night
Cygnet	Able	Able
Lapwing	Charlie	Dog
Tunsberg Castle	Love	Nike
Eglantine	Baker	Charlie
Allington Castle	Dog	Fox
Bamborough Castle	Mike	Nan
Tavy	Sugar	Sugar
Somaliland	Peter	Roger
Bahamas	Fox	How
Tortola	Nan	Peter

| 1630 | *Onslow* (Captain (D) 17), *Keppel* and *Westcott* passed en route for Faeroe Islands. *Lapwing* with Asdic defects, detached to Join Captain (D) 17. |
| 2000 | Streamed displacer units. |

30th November

0200	9th Escort Group *St. John* (SO), *Port Colborne*, *Itene*, *Stormont*, *Monnow* and *Lark* joined from Scapa and formed advanced VS screen 8 miles ahead of convoy.
0915	Air Escort (Catalina) joined for 8 hours - ordered to VIPER.
1025	*Lark* ordered to take up position on close screen in place of *Lapwing*.

1st December

| 0830 | *Campania* (Rear Admiral Commanding First Cruiser Squadron), *Bellona*, *Nairana*, *Caesar* (Capt D6), *Cassandra*, *Cambrian*, *Caprice* joined company in position 63°56N 03°14W. |
| 1130 | *Onslow* (Capt D17) *Onslaught*, *Oribi*, *Offa*, *Orwell*, *Obedient*, *Keppel*, *Westcott*, *Bulldog*, *Beagle*, and three Norwegian trawlers joined company. Escorts formed Screening Diagram No.1. in accordance with Appendix II of C.S.1's No.980/9/8 of 22/11/44. |

2nd December

0750	Unidentified aircraft reported in vicinity of convoy.
0830	Aircraft passed overhead - not observed due to cloud.
2330	*Somaliland* (20th E.G.) reported boiler trouble and ordered to join close screen.

3rd December

| 1115 | Escorts took up day screening positions. |
| | Escorts took up night screening positions. |

4th December

0905	*Tunsberg Castle* joined Cygnet in Group One vice *Lapwing* detached to join Support Group No.G.
1206	9th and 20th Escort Groups ordered to carry out A/S Hunt up track of convoy.
1710	First HF/DF bearings of U-oboats reported by *Keppel*.

5th December

0700	*Cygnet* streamed PNM units. Numerous HF/DF bearings of U-boats in vicinity throughout day.

6th December

1100	9th and 20th Escort Groups rejoined convoy.
1430	Russian escorts joined.
1630	White Sea portion of JW 62 detached escorted by Russian escorts with 9th Escort Group sweeping ahead.
1805	Swordfish TBR attacked surfaced U-boat in position 2120 ZZ 29.
2045	*Caesar* (D6), *Cambrian* and *Keppel* investigating radar contact.
2059	*Keppel* reported unexplained explosion - presumed Gnat.
2150	Convoy formed two columns - *Cygnet* and *Tunsberg Castle* screened port side, 20th Escort Group starboard side.

7th December

0215	All ships of convoy entered Kola Inlet - *Cygnet, Bulldog* and *Beagle* proceeded to carry out A/S hunt in general area of aircraft attack. *Keppel, Lark* and *Westcott* hunting in Western half of area. No contacts obtained.
1200	Recovered Foxers.
1230	*Cygnet, Bulldog* and *Beagle* entered Kola Inlet.

CONVOY RA 62

9th December

1356	*Cygnet* (SO) *Lapwing, Allington Castle, Bamborough Castle* sailed from Vaenga to carry out A/S search of area South of 69°59'N between Longitudes 33° and 35° East. Aircraft from *Nairana* operating in approaches to Kola Inlet co-operating. *Cygnet* obtained small disappearing radar contact at 2800 yards range. No Asdic obtained.
1732	*Bamborough Castle* obtained radar contact at 4000 yards range which disappeared after 6 minutes.
1740 - 2200	*Cygnet, Lapwing, Allington Castle* and *Bamborough Castle* carried A/S hunt during which *Bamborough Castle* carried out two Squid attacks and oil patch was observed
2310	*Lark* joined company.

10th December

0602	***Allington Castle*** and ***Bamborough Castle*** detached to join close screen of convoy.
1800	***Cygnet, Lark*** and ***Lapwing*** took up appointed stations on convoy Screening Diagram No.2. HF/DF bearings during day indicated U-boats in contact with convoy.

11th December

0615	***Cassandra*** reported torpedoed in approximate position 72°72'N 32°50'E.
0656	20th Escort Group detached to escort ***Cassandra*** to Kola Inlet
0920	Screening disposition adjusted to cover windward bow of convoy.
1900	Escorts resumed Screening Diagram No.2. Numerous HF/DF bearings of U-boats still in contact.

12th December

0108	Two unidentified aircraft reported in vicinity of convoy.
1045	Observed enemy aircraft on fire crash into sea (shot down by fighter from ***Nairana***)
1400 - 1500	8 Ju-88 Torpedo Bombers made two attacks on convoy - emergency turns executed - no losses reported. (1500 position 71°55'N 01°54'E).
1600	***Monnow*** rescued 4 German airmen from raft. U-boats still in contact with convoy during day.

13th December

0849	Unidentified aircraft reported in vicinity of convoy.
1534	Aircraft from CVE's reported sighting U-boats on surface. HF/DF bearings indicated U-boats still in vicinity of convoy.

14th December

0134	Unidentified aircraft reported in vicinity.
1215	***Cygnet*** recovered PNM Units .
1709	9th Escort Group (negative ***Monnow***) detached and proceeded Greenock.
PM	U-boats withdrew out of range.

17th December

0900	***Campania*** (CS 1), ***Nairana***, ***Bellona***, 6th Destroyer Flotilla and ***Onslaught*** left convoy in approximate position 62°22'N 04°19'W and proceeded to Scapa.
1300 - 2100	South Easterly Gale - Convoy straggling and hove to. Subsequent muster showed No.11 only ship not present when convoy reformed.

HMS CYGNET
ENCLOSURE 1

ANTI-SUBMARINE HUNT CARRIED OUT BY HM SHIPS CYGNET, LAPWING, ALLINGTON CASTLE AND BAMBOROUGH CASTLE

(All times are Zone -3)

1. On 9th December, at 1800 in position: 69°39'N 33°26'E *Bamborough Castle*, *Cygnet*, *Allington Castle* and *Lapwing* were carrying out an A/S search disposed in line abreast in the above order, 3000 yards apart, course 345°, speed 11 Knots, when *Cygnet* obtained a small disappearing Radar contact bearing Green 010° range 2800 yards. Shortly after, hydrophone effect was heard ahead by Asdics, but it quickly ceased. No echo contact was obtained, but Asdic conditions were poor as is usually the case in these waters; ships were, however, transmitting on "Q" as well as main oscillator to enhance the chances of detection. The contact was considered doubtful.

2. At 1831 ships were turned 180 degrees together and swept back for 30 miles, when the original course was resumed. No further contact was obtained until 1932 when *Bamborough Castle* reported a radar contact bearing Red 050°, range 5,700 yards which was held for six minutes when it faded at 3,500 yards. *Bamborough Castle* dropped one depth charge as a "shake-off" measure for a possible "gnat". The Group's Course was altered to the bearing by Blue turn and speed reduced to 8 knots.

3. At 1940 *Bamborough Castle* reported she was in Asdic contact and a few minutes later attacked with Squid. *Cygnet* closed the position of the attack, marked by a calcium flare and ordered *Lapwing* and *Allington Castle* to carry out operation Observant.

4. At 1959 *Cygnet* obtained Asdic contact bearing 195° range 1,400 yards, no doppler, bearing moving very slowly left. Plot indicated that this was the same contact which *Bamborough Castle* was now closing, to carry out her second Squid attack, so *Cygnet* took over duties of Directing ship.

5. *Bamborough Castle* fired at 2005 and reported depth of target as 400 feet, whereas *Cygnet* had obtained a weak trace on 147B indicating a depth of 120 feet when the range was approximately 700 yards. The Range Recorder trace faded at 650 yards but no contact was gained by "Q".

6. *Cygnet* regained contact shortly afterwards but this was classified as "doubtful" and the trace was not convincing. No depth could be obtained by 147B and nothing was heard on "Q" attachment. After passing down the port side contact was lost at 600 yards, and not regained.

7. *Bamborough Castle* carried out a third Squid attack at 2057, having regained contact after losing it for nearly half an hour, and soon after reported that this attack had produced an oil patch. *Cygnet* closed and confirmed this; the smell of diesel oil was most marked, but the darkness made it impossible to find the position of the source so that it could be plastered with depth charges. *Bamborough Castle* was unable to regain contact.

8. The hunt was continued until 2335, but there was no tangible evidence of destruction except that *Bamborough Castle* reported some pieces of wood floating in the oil patch.

9. Since the object of the search was the sweeping of the approaches to Kola Inlet and the position of this attack was far removed from the convoy's route, it was unfortunate that the Group could not remain on the scene of the action longer. Ships were therefore reformed in line abreast and course set to the Eastward to search this area and to investigate two positions where contacts had been reported by aircraft operating from *Nairana*.

A brief visit to the scene of the action at daylight was made by *Cygnet*, *Lark* and *Lapwing*, but the oil slick was no longer visible.

I consider that without doubt a U-boat was present, and damaged, in this action, but in the absence of other information coming to light, it is not possible to state that the damage was sufficient to ensure the U-boat's destruction.

(Source ADM 199/602 pages 137-140, 164)

Note: **Bamborough Castle** was subsequently credited with the sinking of *U-387* by this action. (*Source: Axel Niestle 1998; German U-boat Losses During World War II. Details of destruction.*)

HMS BAMBOROUGH CASTLE   9/12/44
FORM S. 1203, SECTION H
NARRATIVE

1. **HM Ships Cygnet**, (S.O.E.G.7) *Lapwing*, *Allington Castle* and **Bamborough Castle** were sailed from Vaenga Bay, Kola Inlet, at 1200Z on 9.12.44. The object being to detect and destroy U-boats which here reported to be waiting in the approaches to Kola Inlet, for Convoy RA 62 which was due to sail on the following day.

2. At 1621 ships were disposed abeam to starboard in the order **Bamborough Castle**, **Cygnet**, **Lapwing**, **Allington Castle** course 345° speed 11 knots when radar contact was obtained on the port bow bearing 292°, range 5700 yards, amplitude 2x,

3. On gaining contact ship was turned towards to investigate and at 1628 the radar echo faded, range 3500 yards bearing 285°. This was reported to EG 7 in **Cygnet**.

4. On the echo fading, speed was reduced to 6 knots and one depth charge, set to 100 feet, was dropped. This precaution was taken because one of the PNM units had not been functioning correctly and was, at that time, being recovered, (safe anti-gnat revolutions with Foxers streamed gives approximately 6 Knots),

5. Ship proceeded on the last known bearing of the U-boat and at 1638, ten minutes after losing contact by radar, A/S contact was gained, bearing 233°, range 1400 yards. This was quickly classified as 'Submarine' and a Squid attack commenced. At 700 yards range depth was found by 147B to be 360 feet and with this knowledge revolutions were increased in an attempt to get the ship's speed somewhat nearer seven knots. It is not considered that this had any effect in the short time before firing.

6. Squid was fired at 1628, range 310 yards, depth 380 ft.

7. The submarine took no evasive action up to the time that Squid was fired, but remained stern on doing about 3 Knots. Immediately the bombs exploded loud whistle effect was heard on the bearing. It would appear that the U-boat captain was not expecting an attack and had not previously heard of Squid.

8. On opening the range contact was lost at 1200 yards owing to Foxer interference from ships in company. Two minutes later at 1700, contact was regained, range 1100 yards, and the second attack commenced. **HMS Cygnet** confirmed the contact at 1700 and took over directing ship.

9. Squid was fired at 1705, range 320 yards, depth 420 ft.

10. Between the first and second attacks speed was reduced to 6 knots owing to the possibility of the U-boat coming shallow and firing a gnat. Contact was not obtained by 147B. until the range was down to 500 yards consequently this attack was carried out at 6 knots. Finding that the U-boat intended to stay deep, speed was increased after this attack and was thereafter maintained at 7 knots.

11. On closing the range for the next attack contact was lost at 650 yards range. This is considered to have been due to the range recorder operator, who was listening out on 'Q' failing to get contact. This may have been due to the 'First Operator' getting his 'cut ons' very fine and the 'Q' not gaining contact, the ship not being fitted with A/S box relay A 3000.

12. Contact was now lost for 23 minutes, but by sweeping the arc suggested by plot, was eventually regained at 1729, at a range of 2100 yards. Foxer interference was very slight at this time.

13. Not being quite certain in my own mind that this was the U-boat with which we had regained contact I decided to run over without firing and get depth by 147B and also try the echo sounder. The contact was confirmed by 147B and by plot but not by echo sounder.

14. Contact was held while opening the range and in the third attack, at 2057, Squid was fired at 360 yards, depth 460 ft. Contact was lost after this attack and no further contact classified as 'Submarine' was obtained.

15. Returning to the position of the third at attack a large patch of oil was discovered, it was at least 1000 yards in diameter. Near the centre of this patch several pieces of wood were sighted. One piece about four to six feet long and four to six inches across appeared to be painted white. Three or four other pieces, from two to four feet long and from one to half an inch across, and several smaller pieces were light in colour and appeared freshly broken. Owing to the fact that Foxer displacers were streamed the ship could not be manoeuvred to pick up any of these pieces.

16. The oil patch ended, in a long streak to windward and on steaming along this the source of the oil streak was found. At 1930 this source was approximately 2000 yards from the centre of the large oil patch. On returning to the source of the oil slick at 2020 it was, by plot, half a mile further to windward. Land fixes were taken at 1930 and at 2520 and the charted position on both occasions was the same.

17. No A/S contact could be obtained to windward of the oil slick and the echo sounder was also tried without success,

18. The distinctive smell of diesel oil was most marked at the source of the oil slick but all attempts to obtain a sample were fruitless. A towel, which was towed astern, did not even smell of oil when recovered.

FORM S 1203 SECTION H

1. A/S conditions were good with occasional wake echoes.

2. Went deep, turned stern on to every attack, and, after the first attack, altered course 90 degrees when the ship was at about 700 yards range,

3. Tried without success.

4. Lost A/S contact and U-boat probably destroyed.

5. See narrative paragraphs 15 to 18.

6. The area to windward of the oil slick should have been plastered with depth charges to have got more conclusive evidence of destruction. Why I did not do this, I shall never understand.

8. That there is a definite danger of losing contact with a deep U-boat owing to the narrowness of the 'Q' beam if the ship is not fitted with A/S box A 3000.

9. That a clock should be fitted in the A/S but where all operators can see it, to enable them to note times on the edge of the A/S recorder paper. This clock must have a clearly marked dial with a second hand, if possible.

Sgd ? / Work(?)
Lieut. Commander RNR, Commanding Officer.

(Source ADM 199/602 page 164/5)

JW 63 AND RA 63: 7th - 20th JANUARY 1945

SECRET
OPERATION GREYSTROKE REPORT OF PROCEEDINGS

(Vice-Admiral Commanding Tenth Cruiser Squadron)
ADM 199/602 pages 285-7, 289-292
(No4/734/10 of 24th January, 1945)

SECRET

II

No.143/H.F. 01325/14/234.. ADMIRALTY.
Copies to:-   Commander-in-Chief, Western Approaches.
                   Flag Officer Carrier Training,
                   Vice Admiral Commanding, Tenth Cruiser Squadron.
                   Rear Admiral Commanding, First Cruiser Squadron.
                   Commodore (D), Home Fleet.)

Concur generally with Vice-Admiral Commanding, Tenth Cruiser Squadron.

1.   As regards Vice-Admiral Commanding, Tenth Cruiser Squadron's paragraphs 2 and 3 the undesirability of employing these old ships in JW and RA convoys in winter weather is fully appreciated, but with the existing shortage of arcticised escorts it may be necessary to use them in order to provide the number required.

2.   Commander-in-Chief, Western Approaches, has been asked not to include any 'B' class destroyers in the Western Approaches escorts for these convoys during the next two or three months as their endurance is so limited. He has been able to comply with this request when detailing the escorts for JW and RA 64.

3.   Remarks on any other special. points raised will be forwarded separately.

Home -Fleet
27th January 1945   A D M I R A L

SECRET

Subject	**OPERATION GREYSTROKE**
From	**VICE ADMIRAL COMMANDING TENTH CRUISER SQUADRON**
Date	**24th January, 1945 No. 4/734/10**
T o	**THE COMMANDER-IN-CHIEF HOME FLEET**
Copies to:-	**Commander-in-Chief, Western Approaches**
	Flag Officer, Carrier Training
	Rear Admiral Commanding 1st Cruiser Squadron
	Commodore (D), Home Fleet Destroyers)

1.   The passage of JW 63 was remarkable for the fact that for the first time I believe in the history of these convoys no contact was made with the enemy. As far as the air was concerned this was probably due to bad flying conditions keeping the enemy air forces grounded at the critical period of the passage. It is not so easy to understand why no U-boats were encountered or to decide whether this was due to a change in policy or to the fact that the enemy was quite unaware of the passage of the convoy.

2.   The return journey mainly resolved itself into a fight against adverse weather conditions. These were severe and caused much straggling amongst the ships in convoy. The night of 16th January, when it became necessary for *Vindex* and half the escorts to heave to, was particularly unpleasant and I was in some anxiety regarding the safety of the older destroyers. After this gale they all reported various defects including leaky oil tanks. Had they been forced to stop on account of these their position would have been very serious. Although it does not do to be too pessimistic on account of what was undoubtedly an exceptionally bad week's weather I am of the opinion that the 'V' and 'W' destroyers and possibly *Keppel* are not really fit for the winter voyage to Kola. *Keppel* is twenty and the 'V' and 'W' destroyers are nearly thirty years old and they suffer accordingly.

3.   It was not possible to refuel any destroyers on the return Journey. An attempt was made on the morning of the 16th but had to be abandoned. This raises the question of the desirability of sending the short-leg 'B' class destroyers on this voyage in winter.

4.   The only means of communication with the Commodore of the Convoy was by light. It is suggested that the commodores of these convoys should always be provided with a portable T.B.Y. set. This would be particularly valuable in the case of impending air attack.

5.   Despite all that was said at the Convoy Conference regarding the necessity for keeping close station and the dousing of lights there was much apparently unnecessary straggling as well as signalling with bright lights. The outstanding case of the former was the oiler *Lachlan* who on previous voyages has always kept good station. On this occasion she dropped six miles astern of the convoy on the first day of the return voyage. The Master in reply to a signal reported there was nothing wrong. Presumably the drop in her speed was caused by inexperienced Engine Room personnel and it is suggested their efficiency should be enquired into before this valuable ship is sent on another voyage to Russia.

As regards lights one example of extreme stupidity was when the leading ship of column 3 or 4

signalled with a very bright light "Pass down the line Course is 359°." Unfortunately I was unable to discover for certain which ship had done this.

6.   Perhaps the outstanding feature of the return voyage was the excellent work done by the destroyers in rear of the convoy who were indefatigable in their efforts to round up stragglers and were continuously employed in so doing for the whole voyage under the direction of Commander C.W. McMullen, DSC, in **HMS Scorpion**. The action of Acting Lieutenant-Commander E.E.G. Boak, Royal Canadian Navy of **HMCS Sioux** in collecting three MVs. after the gale of the 16th/17th and bringing them safely to the Faeroes was noteworthy.
The attempt by **Scorpion** to tow the **MV Longwood** into Thorshavn and by **Allington Castle** (Acting Lieutenant Commander P.A. Read, (Royal Naval Reserve) to go alongside that ship to rescue the crew on the night of the 19th/20th January were both most praiseworthy and it was unfortunate that owing to the weather they were unsuccessful. I consider the Commanding Officers of both these ships to be entitled to much credit.

7.   Reports of Proceedings of ships comprising the escort will forwarded when received together with any remarks arising from them.

8.   General narrative of events is attached as Enclosure No 1

(Signed)   F. DALRYMPLE-HAMILTON.
                    VICE ADMIRAL

OPERATION - GREYSTOKE
NARRATIVE

ALL TIMES ZONE "A"

1. Vice Admiral Commanding Tenth Cruiser Squadron in **Vindex** with **Diadem** in company sailed from Scapa at 1250 on 31st December, 1944, screened by **Scorpion**, **Scourge**, **Sioux**, **Algonquin**, **Zebra** and **Zambesi**, and proceeded Eastabout off Orkneys and through the Fair Island Channel to Position 'Charlie', thence along the Red Route to overtake convoy JW 63. The convoy was met at Noon on 1st January 1945, in position 63°45'N 02°20'W and **Vindex** entered the Carrier Box at 1315. The Escort Oiler **Blue Ranger**, escorted by **Keppel**, **Walker** and **Westcott** left the Faeroes at 2000 on 31st December 1944, and joined JW 63 during the forenoon of 1st January 1945.

2. While at the Faeroes, **Keppel** reported that, due to a wire round her starboard propeller, she was unable to exceed 15 knots. In view of this she was ordered to exchange stations with **Serapis**, one of the close screen. This wire was eventually cleared by Russian divers provided by the Northern Fleet whilst **Keppel** was berthed alongside at Polyarnoe.

3. At 1143 on 3rd January when in position 70°22' N 60°17'E, an unidentified aircraft detected by radar bearing 275° ZZ 25 miles was reported by **Diadem**. **Vindex** flew off two fighters to intercept. The enemy aircraft crossed to the Eastwards astern of the convoy and the echo faded. At 115° ZZ 20 miles at 1155. **Diadem** reported that one lookout stated he sighted the aircraft which he took to be a large flying boat. However, due to much cloud the fighters failed to intercept and were landed on at 1207. It is doubtful if the aircraft did in effect, sight the convoy.

4. At 1615 on 6th January in position 72°14'N 34°53'E **Scorpion** in position 'Item' obtained an Asdic contact classified as submarine. A hunt was carried out by **Scorpion** and **Scourge** and a number of attacks were made. Contact was lost, however, and, after carrying out 'Observant', the destroyers broke off the hunt at 1830 and rejoined.

5. The Senior British Naval Officer, North Russia's signal timed 060934A January had been received at 1035 on 6th January. This gave the local escort's E.T.A. at position 'MX' as 0700 on 7th January, which meant they would meet the convoy during daylight on that day. This arrival could be made without breaking W/T silence to make an amended E.T.A. at 1925, however, Commander-in-Chief, Home Fleet's signal timed 061703A January to the Senior British Naval Officer, North Russia was received, stating that the convoy's estimated E.T.A. Kola was A.M. 8th January. It then became necessary to assume that in the absence of further information the local escort would be sailed to conform to this estimate and that unless the correct E.T.A. was signalled no local escort would meet the convoy, the White Sea portion would not be detached, and the convoy would arrive unexpectedly without navigational arrangements for its reception having being completed. Vice Admiral Commanding Tenth Cruiser Squadron's signal timed 062030A January was therefore passed on port wave at 2140, and the risk of detection accepted.

6. Five destroyers were fuelled, from escort oilers during the passage.

7. No other events of interest took place during the voyage. Red Route was adhered to throughout

8. At 1200 on 7th January the Russian Local escort was met in position 69°30'N 35°01'E and eight ships comprising Group One of the White Sea portion were detached. **Vindex** and **Diadem** streamed paravanes P.M. on 6th January. **Diadem** was detached at 1230 on 7th January to proceed ahead at 28 knots to Kola. The convoy formed two columns at 1300 when in position 0500 Kildin Island Light 11 miles and **Vindex** parted company at this time and proceeded to Kola at 16 knots screened by **Zebra**, **Zambesi**, **Scourge** and **Sioux**. Captain (D), Twenty-third Destroyer Flotilla, in **Myngs** took charge of remaining escorts and screened the convoy into harbour. **Vindex** anchored in Vaenga Bay at 1600 on 7th January.

9. Thick fog descended as the rear half of the convoy entered the Inlet. In consequence, part of the convoy was compelled to spend the night at anchor in the outer reaches of the Inlet. This portion was, however, able to proceed and berth at Murmansk the following day. The Twenty-third Destroyer Flotilla were able to reach Vaenga Bay before the fog set in but the Seventh Escort Group who were covering the rear of the convoy were unable to enter and had to spend the night at sea, arriving at Vaenga Bay at Noon on the following day.

10. **Vindex** had onboard twelve Norwegian officers and twenty-three ratings with a large quantity of 'Crofter' stores. The Russians were very dilatory in making arrangements for their disembarkation. This was not done until the evening before the sailing of Convoy RA 63, in spite of repeated reminders and hasteners made by Senior British Naval Officer, North Russia. This appears to be the normal fate of 'Crofter' personnel and stores on arrival in Russia and is a cause of great inconvenience to the ships carrying them.

11. The Convoy conference for Convoy RA 63 was held in **Vindex** the afternoon of 10th January. The Convoy sailed at 0800 on 11th January and got away in good time. The Seventh Escort Group sailed three hours in advance of the convoy and swept along the convoy route, thereafter meeting the convoy off Toros Island. **Vindex** screened by **Zambesi Zebra**, **Walker** and **Westcott** sailed from Vaenga Bay at 0900 and proceeded to overtake convoy at 1200. **Diadem** sailed independently and proceeding at high speed, overtook convoy at the same time. **Vindex** and **Diadem** had streamed paravanes.

12. A strong South Westerly gale veering to West South West was experienced during the night of 12th/13th January and in consequence many merchant ships straggled badly. Rear escorts under the direction of **Scorpion** did excellent work in rounding up stragglers in difficult conditions. The Escort Oiler **Lachlan** was a persistent straggler and on several occasions was unable to maintain convoy speed of eight knots even in comparatively good weather. At 1024 on 15th January **Allington Castle** reported that she had lost a man overboard.

13. At 1710 on 14th January **SS Amaso Delano** reported that her ballast had shifted owing to stress of weather and requested that course might be altered down wind for two hours to enable her to re-stow. Course was altered to comply with this request and **SS Amaso Delano** rejoined some time later.

14. At 2010 on 15th January when in position 69°07'N 06°37'E and again at 2110 HF/DF 'B bar' signals from a U-boat were intercepted on a bearing of 120°. The estimated range was over 30 miles but inside ground wave, A/S patrols were flown to a depth of 25 miles but no sighting resulted and no further signals were intercepted.

15. During the forenoon of 16th January , **SS John Gibraltarbon** was forced to stop for two hours with condenser defects, and **SS Longwood** reported that all generators were out of action and one furnace had collapsed. **Scourge** and **Sioux** were ordered to stand by these ships, who were later reported to be rejoining.

16. At about 1900 on 16th January, the wind rapidly increased in force from the Northwards and by 2100 had reached, Force 12 on the Beaufort scale. At 2027, **Westcott** reported that she had been forced to heave to on a course of 340°. At 2050, when in position 66°08'N 001° 40'E, Vice Admiral Commanding Tenth Cruiser Squadron requested the Commodore to heave to the convoy, but he decided to run before the gale. By this tame, **Vindex** was experiencing great difficulty in steering and hove to at 2113. Escorts were ordered to conform.

On receipt of the Commodore's decision to run before the gale, and having been informed by Captain (D), Twenty-third Destroyer Flotilla, that he was still able to continue on the convoy course, escorts were told that if they had not yet hove to and were able to continue with the convoy they should do so.

The following escorts hove to: **Vindex, Scorpion, Scourge, Sioux, Algonquin, Zebra, Zambesi, Keppel, Walker, Westcott, Lark, Cygnet, Alnwick Castle**. The remainder continued with the convoy.

By 2300, the wind had reached a speed of 80 knots and a very high sea was running with an estimated height of 45 feet.

Zambesi reported at 2344 that she had lost one man overboard.

The wind started to abate slowly at about 0200 on 17th January, and conditions gradually improved until at 0930 on 17th January escorts were informed by Vice Admiral Commanding Tenth Cruiser Squadron that **Vindex** would turn to a course of 205° and escorts were ordered to conform By 1000 on 17th January, reports indicated that, although escorts were badly scattered, they had turned safely and were running before the gale. **Scorpion** and **Scourge**, who were near **Vindex** were ordered to form a screen.

17. Captain (D), Twenty-third Destroyer Flotilla, who was with the Commodore, reported he had about twenty merchant ships in company and that he was proceeding to Thorshavn to reform the convoy. He

had detached **Serapis** to proceed ahead to the Faeroes to inform all authorities of the situation and to ask for the necessary B.A.M.S. message to be made directing all ships to Thorshavn.

18. **Sioux** reported at 1311 on 17th January that she had with her **SS Longwood** and **SS Amaso Delano** and was proceeding to the Faeroes.

19. At 0950 on 18th January, three Swordfish aircraft were flown off from **Vindex** to search astern to a depth of eighty miles for any stragglers. Only one, **SS Stephen Leacock**, was found and she was directed by the aircraft to alter course for the Faeroes.

At 1030, visibility was reduced to one cable by heavy snow, and **Vindex** turned back to the Eastward to find a clear patch to fly on aircraft which had been ordered to return. By 1230, all aircraft had been landed on safely.

20. By about 1300 on 18th January, all ships had been accounted for. Twenty-five were in company with the Commodore; three were with **Sioux**; **Lapwing** was escorting one; and the remaining one had been located by aircraft (vide paragraph 19 above) **Diadem** was sent on ahead independently to Thorshavn, and **Vindex**, with **Scorpion**, **Scourge** and **Westcott** entered harbour ahead of the Commodore at 1430 on 18th January.

On arrival, the flag of Vice Admiral Commanding Tenth Cruiser Squadron was transformed to **Diadem**.

21. At 1530 on 18th January, wind increased from the Northward with heavy snow. By 1630 the blizzard had reduced visibility to less than one cable. This came at a particularly unfortunate moment as the convoy was then in the process of entering harbour. The result of this was that only eighteen ships were able to anchor in Nolso Fjord. A muster the following day revealed the fact that four ships were at anchor in Hesto Fjord to the Northwest of the deep minefield, and three more were at anchor off Sando, close South-East of the minefield. Four more were anchored in the open sea to the Eastward of Sando, and **SS Fort Island** had apparently remained at sea for the night as she was observed approaching the harbour from the Eastward at 1400 on 19th January.

22. Continuous A/S patrols were maintained off the Northern and Southern entrances to Nolso Fjord by two ships at each entrance.

23. At 1831 on 18th January **SS Fort Highfield** made an 'SOS' and reported 'IN COLLISION. STRUCK AMIDSHIPS HOLED BADLY'. At 1915 on 18th January, **Allington Castle** reported that she was standing by **SS Fort Highfield** North of Hesto Island. The Master stated that his ship had been damaged in collision with an unknown merchant ship and was in danger of sinking. **Allington Castle** reported that she was guiding **SS Fort Highfield** to the anchorage, and at 2237, this ship anchored two miles to the Eastward of Thorshavn. A Salvage Officer from the Base was sent on board to investigate the damage, and **Allington Castle** went alongside to render all possible assistance.
The following day, no apparent damage could be seen from outboard, and the Master stated that "there was a hole in his bunker but the pumps had the leak under control." He could not identify the ship which he stated had collided with him and no other ship reported having been in collision or appeared to have a damaged bow. The possibility of **SS Fort Highfield** having grounded must not be overlooked. Repairs were expected to be completed by Monday 22nd January.

24. At 1933 on 18th January, **Walker** reported that **SS Longwood** was anchored in position 173° Burin

Light, 6.5 miles and was unable to start main engines.

The following day, at 1040 *Scorpion* reported that *SS Longwood* would be unable to move main engines for four days and that if the wind blew hard from the Eastward she would be in danger of grounding.

Naval Officer-in-Charge was asked if he could render assistance and Trawlers *Buchans* and *Exponent* were ordered to proceed to *SS Longwood* and endeavour to tow her to the anchorage; *Scorpion* standing by to assist. This attempt proved unavailing, and at 1523 *Scorpion* reported that she was attempting to tow *SS Longwood* with one trawler on each quarter to assist steering. After considerable difficulty due to the swell, the tow was passed but *SS Longwood* was unable to weigh or slip her cable, and this had to be sawn through by hand. Eventually this was accomplished and *Scorpion* commenced towing, but unfortunately the tow parted at 2138 and the weather prevented any further attempts. *SS Longwood* anchored again close to her original position. Owing to the weather conditions and the risk of U-boat attack, *Scorpion* was ordered to remove the crew to await the arrival of a rescue tug which had been requested. The trawlers tried to go alongside but could not manage it and *Exponent* had to return to harbour with damaged steering gear. During the night, *Allington Castle* made repeated attempts to go alongside but was prevented from doing so by the sea conditions.

At daylight on 20th January, *Scorpion* was relieved by Captain (D) Twenty-third Destroyer Flotilla in *Myngs*, with *Savage* and *Sioux*. At 1235 the entire crew of fifty nine having abandoned ship in their own boats were picked up by *Myngs* and *Savage* and landed at Thorshavn.

Allington Castle and *Alnwick Castle* were ordered to remain at the Faeroes to give A/S protection to *SS Longwood* under the orders of the Naval Officer-in-Charge, Faeroes, until the arrival of the rescue tug, and then to provide escort to the United Kingdom.

25. The Kirkwall portion of the convoy, consisting of *SS Empire Stalwart*, *Blue Ranger*, *Fort Massie*, *Barbara Freitchie* and *Edward N. Hurley* were sailed at 1500 on 19th January escorted by *Zebra*, *Zambesi* and *Scourge*. *SS U.S.O.* was not sailed with the Kirkwall portion owing to a misunderstanding of the Commander-in-Chief Western Approaches' signal timed 171135A January, which read "US Oiler *Barbara Freitchie*". This mistake was not realised until after the Kirkwall portion had sailed. *SS U.S.O.* was sailed with the Clyde portion for Loch Ewe as stated in my signal timed 192309A January.

26. After discussion with the Commodore, it was decided that the most practical method of passing sailing orders to the convoy in view of the frequent blizzards, lack of boats, and wide dispersal of ships, would be to request Admiralty to transmit the orders on B.A.M.S. This was accordingly done.

27. The Clyde portion sailed at 1030 on Saturday 20th January, escorted by the Senior Officer, Seventh Escort Group, in *Cygnet*, with the Seventh Escort Group (less *Allington Castle* and *Alnwick Castle*) and four Fleet destroyers, *Scorpion*, *Stord*, *Algonquin*, *Serapis*.

On weighing, *SS John Gibraltarbon* reported that her anchor was foul of telegraph cable and *SS Andrew Turnbull* reported she had nine turns in her cable and was unable to clear it. *SS John Gibraltarbon* was able to clear her anchor and proceeded with the convoy. *SS Andrew Turnbull* was unable to follow suit and, being by this time so far astern of the main body, she was ordered to remain at anchor to await the arrival of the tug. The Naval Officer-in-Charge Faeroes, was informed of this and it was suggested he might arrange for the rescue tug to swing *SS Andrew Turnbull* clear before proceeding to *SS Longwood* provided this did not prejudice the more important operation in any way.

SS Andrew Turnbull was at anchor in Hesta Fjord. The telegraph cable between Faeroes and the United Kingdom was reported by the Naval Officer-in-Charge to be broken in two places. This is much regretted but it is not surprising under the circumstances.

28. *RFA War Bharata*, the oiler stationed in Skaalefiord has no arrangements for heating oil fuel. This slows up the operation of fuelling to a great extent, and it is recommended that oilers stationed in the Faeroes during the winter months should be fitted with the necessary oil fuel heating arrangements.

29. Throughout the passages, air patrols were flown as required. No U-boat contacts or sighting were obtained by aircraft during the period. No aircraft were lost or casualties to personnel sustained in spite of unfavourable weather conditions at times.

30. Vice Admiral Commanding Tenth Cruiser Squadron in *Diadem*, with *Vindex* in company, screened by Captain (D) Twenty-third Destroyer Flotilla in *Myngs*, with *Savage* and *Sioux*, proceeded at 1700 on 20th January for Scapa arriving at Hoxa Gate 0915 on 21st January, 1945.

SHIPS OF CONVOY RA 63 WHICH WERE LEFT BEHIND AT THE FAEROES WERE:

SS Longwood   Anchored in position 173° Burin Light, 6.5 miles. Engines totally out. of action; crew landed at Thorshavn.

SS Fort Highfield   Anchored two miles East of Skaale village. Repairs to holed bunker expected to be completed Monday 22nd January

SS Andrew Turnbull   Anchored in Hesto Fiord with nine turns in her cable.

HM Ships Alnwick Castle and *Allington Castle* remaining to give A/S protection to *SS Longwood* under orders of Naval Officer-in-Charge, Faeroes.

(Source ADM 199/602)

PASSAGE OF JW & RA 64
3rd - 26th FEBRUARY 1945
OPERATION HOTBED.

Rear Admiral Commanding, First Cruiser Squadron's No 544/9/8

ADM 199/759 Pages 322-341, 346, 292-295, 314, 317

No, 372/HFO 1325/241.
Copies to: Vice Admiral Commanding, Tenth Cruiser Squadron
Rear Admiral Commanding, First Cruiser Squadron

Forwarded.

2. The outstanding features of the passage of JW and RA 64 were the persistent bad weather, attacks by torpedo carrying aircraft in spite of the bad weather and the close approach of the U-boats to the entrance of the Kola Inlet. The bolder tactics on the part of the U-boats resulted in the loss of ***Denbigh Castle*** during the arrival of JW 64 two merchant ships joining RA 64 from the White Sea, and ***Bluebell***, and one merchant ship and damage to ***Lark*** during the sailing of RA 64.

3. The safe departure of RA convoys from the Kola Inlet now that the U-boats are concentrating off the entrance is causing me concern. To reduce the straggling and time taken to form up the convoy and to shorten the departure route, I have requested that pilots should be dispensed with in the majority of ships and that a searching sweep should be carried out to the north eastward to enable a more direct route to be taken out of the local U-boat danger zone.

4. The breaking of wireless silence by Coastal Command aircraft on meeting the convoy has been discussed with representatives of 18 Group. It has been agreed that the responsibility will in future rest with the Senior Officer of the Convoy.

5. I consider that the small losses from JW and RA 64 under the most trying weather conditions and sustained enemy air attack reflects great credit on the Rear Admiral Commanding, First Cruiser Squadron and the officers and men of the convoy and escorts.

6. Remarks on any further special points raised and recommendations for Honours and Awards will be forwarded separately.

Home Fleet.   Henry Moore
13th March, 1945.   ADMIRAL

From   The Rear Admiral Commanding, First Cruiser Squadron

Date   28th February, 1945 No 544/9/8

To   The Commander-in-Chief, HOME FLEET
Copies to:-   The Commander in Chief, Western Approaches
                 The Flag Officer, Carrier Training
                 The Vice Admiral Commanding, Tenth Cruiser Squadron
                 The Commodore,(D), Home Fleet
                 Captain (D), 17th Destroyer Flotilla
                 Captain (D), 2nd Destroyer Flotilla
                 The Senior Officer, 7th Escort Group

PASSAGE OF JW 64

1. Convoy J.W.64 sailed from Clyde p.m. 3rd February, 1945. I left Scapa at 1200 5th February, 1945, with my flag in *Campania*, with *Nairana*, *Bellona* and 6 destroyers in company, and carried out flying training during the afternoon. The convoy was detected 18 miles ahead at 0600 on 6th February, 1945, and was joined at 1045. *Zebra* had to be detached to Faeroes with engine trouble and did not rejoin.

2. C.A.P. was flown from 0940 until 1440 in the hope of intercepting the Zenit aircraft which could be heard in the vicinity. It was not detected, but it seems probable that it reported the convoy as at 1628 an enemy reconnaissance aircraft was detected at 28 miles which proceeded to shadow. 2 Wildcats were immediately scrambled by *Campania* and one hour later succeeded in shooting down what proved to be a Ju-88. Unfortunately one of our own fighters, Sub-Lieutenant Smyth, was lost in this fight, and although a Swordfish and 2 destroyers were sent to search the area, no trace of him was found.

3. From now on we were shadowed by enemy aircraft at intervals, day and night until the day before reaching Kola. The next bogey appeared at 0434 on 7th February, 1945, and shadowed until 0650. At 0730 in anticipation of a dawn torpedo attack I instructed the screen to remain in the night cruising disposition which had previously proved very suitable with its two concentric circles of escorts.

4. At 0745 a number of Ju-88 torpedo aircraft were detected and one of these was quickly shot down by *Denbigh Castle* on the outer screen, who was on her first operation since commissioning. I altered the course of the convoy 90° to Starboard towards the dawn by emergency turns, so as to bring the enemy's most favourable attacking sector astern. About a dozen enemy aircraft seemed from the radar to be trying to attack in two groups from the North West and South West during the next one and a quarter hours, but they did not press home their attacks or penetrate the inner screen, and only four escorts found targets to shoot at before they retired about 0900.

5. Meanwhile *Nairana* had scrambled 2 Wildcats but in the bad light and low cloud were unable to intercept, although one Ju-88 was sighted at 0855. The presence of fighters may have been one of the reasons for the lack of spirit shown by the enemy. At 1100 however, the fighters succeeded in intercepting a shadowing Ju-88 which was last seen at 1000 feet diving steeply in to thick cloud and rain with his starboard engine on fire and the port engine smoking heavily, a probable kill.

6. During the afternoon *Campania* flew our one antique night fighting Fulmar which she was still trying

to make serviceable after many hours of hard and unfruitful labour. The second Fulmar had not even been fit to leave Hatston.

7. During the middle and morning watches of 8th February, 1945, the convoy was shadowed at intervals and again for a short time at 0840 when our fighters failed to intercept. Air searches and patrols were flown during the day to try to locate U-boats which it was thought might by now be in position to waylay the convoy. **Opportune** and **Rhodedendron** were fuelled. The Fulmar was given another air test.

8. Between 1615 and 1750 three enemy shadowers appeared and started making homing signals, apparently for U-boats. These were jammed on 434 kc/s and later on 466 kc/s and 448 kc/s, when the enemy shifted frequency. Although the value of jamming was questionable it was felt that it was to our advantage to make the enemy shift frequency. The shadowers remained in company, homing and reporting well into the first watch.

9. This seemed a suitable time to use the Fulmar. It took the air at 1736 and for a short while prospects seemed promising and it actually arrived within 10 miles of one of the shadowers, but without locating by A.I or seeing it, the night being very dark with no moon. However, R/T communication got worse and worse and eventually, after other fruitless attempts, it was landed on at 1900, crashed into the barrier, and is now no more.

10. A/S searches and patrols were flown during the night to try to find the U-boats which were thought to be in the vicinity, but nothing was found. I had proceeded slightly to the Northward of the route given me before turning East, and it appeared from HF/DF bearings intercepted that the convoy passed some distance round the Northern flank of a U-boat patrol line.

11. Enemy shadowing aircraft re-appeared at 1000 on 9th February, 1945. They were attacked unsuccessfully by Wildcats and retired after a short while. D/F bearings of the enemy aircraft's M/F was used with some success to help the A.D.R to track the bogeys after they had faded.

12. Swordfish patrols were continued during the day, but searches were not flown owing both to the weather and enemy air activity. In the evening all flying was stopped by the weather.

13. A few HF/DF bearings were received in the dog watches apparently from U-boats some distance to the Southward and South Eastward.

14. On the 10th February, 1945, the first shadower arrived at 0340 and remained until 0630. At 0951 an aircraft was reported closing from the Southward. At first it was thought that this was a Russian aircraft, on the strength of a corrupt message received from the Senior British Naval Officer, North Russia. However, 10 minutes later **Sioux** turned it away with one engine on fire and reported that it was a Ju-88 and had dropped a torpedo. Fighters failed to intercept.

15. This was the only warning received of the torpedo attack which was on its way. It was fortunate for us as it gave the screens time to start moving into their anti-aircraft positions and brought everyone to the alert. The weather and light were poor with low 10/10ths cloud, rain squalls, and between whiles visibility of about 5 miles.

16. At 1019 the main attack started to appear on the radar approaching from the starboard bow. **Whitehall**, the right hand ship of the extended screen ahead, saw two groups of about 8 Ju-88's each, closing at sea

level; one of which groups was coming straight for her. She and **Lark** broke up this formation with their gunfire, causing it to take violent evasive action, and then when three aircraft detached themselves to attack **Whitehall** with torpedoes, she sent one away damaged, shot down the second, shared the third with **Lark**, and successfully avoided all torpedoes. Fine work by a veteran with a close range armament of only 2 Oerlikons each side. **Nairana**'s fighters and **Orwell** on the starboard inner screen also shot down aircraft at this stage and **Cygnet**, **Sioux**, **Onslow** and the fighters each got probables or damaged their aircraft.

17. Meanwhile I had turned the convoy 90° away from these attacks by emergency turns to bring them on the quarter, and more fighters had been flown off.

18. Further attacks then developed from various directions, the biggest threat coming from the starboard bow. These torpedoes were combed in due course by other emergency turns, some exploding in the wakes inside the convoy. Reports received from the screen of torpedoes approaching were most useful.

19. Meanwhile **Campania**'s fighters had got one probable and damaged another. More kills were obtained by **Onslaught** and by the port wing column of the convoy, which with the help of **Campania** and escorts dropped their Ju-88 neatly among the rear ships, and a number of aircraft were damaged by other escorts. Unfortunately our fighters returning to the carriers damaged were also fired at indiscriminately by escorts and merchant ships, in spite of a warning by convoy R/T that they were returning. This showed a quite inexcusable lack of fire discipline even taking into the account the bad visibility, low cloud and the pace of events. There is little resemblance between a Ju-88 and a Wildcat, and none with a Swordfish. One of **Campania**'s damaged fighters ditched astern of the carriers and the pilot was quickly recovered by **Opportune**. It was our only loss.

20. After 1110 there was a lull but at 1130 more Ju-88's came in. One was probably shot down by **Nairana**'s fighters, escorts and convoy and. that finished the attack.

21. Total score for the attack is assessed at 7 Ju-88's shot down, 4 probables, 8 damaged, out of 20-25 which took part, some of which may not have carried torpedoes. We lost one wildcat, the pilot of which was saved, and suffered no damage in spite of the sweeping claims of Lord Haw-Haw.

22. The rest of the day was quiet. Icing stopped flying in the afternoon with heavy snow showers later.

23. At 0600 on the 11th February, 1945 an enemy aircraft located the convoy and then left. During the forenoon the convoy was re-organised with the White Sea Section to port. Close A/S patrols were flown, but later had to be stopped on account of icing.

24. On 12th February, 1945, **Bamborough Castle** and **Oksöy** had both dropped astern with defect. They were ordered to proceed in company to Kola.

25. At 1330 the Russian escort was met and the White Sea Section of the convoy detached with **Lark**, **Lapwing**, and **Alnwick Castle** as extended screen as far as the entrance to the White Sea and thence to Kola. Considerable difficulty was experienced in getting the Commodore of the White Sea Section to take charge and alter course to port, and it was not until 1530 that he parted company. All this time the Russians had been flashing with very bright lights in the increasing darkness with U-boats almost certainly not far away.

26. Meanwhile A/S patrols had been flown and the approaches to Kola searched without result. At 1820

these had to be discontinued owing to bad visibility, after one of *Campania*'s Swordfish had crashed over the side while landing. The crew were safely picked up by *Onslaught*.

27. At 2100, to the Eastward of Kildin Island, I sent *Bellona* into Kola at high speed and proceeded ahead with *Campania* and *Nairana* screened by *Zambesi* and *Zealous*. It was pitch dark, snow, and poor visibility. Pilots were embarked off Toros Island at midnight and the ships proceeded to Vaenga arriving over 24 hours late owing to the strong head winds during our easterly run.

28. Meanwhile the convoy formed into two columns and proceeded up harbour during the middle watch. No signs were seen of U-boats but at 0015 *Denbigh Castle* reported that she had been mined just outside the entrance, the last merchant ship being then well on its way in. Visibility was very poor but I now consider this was a U-boat working close inshore, as subsequent minesweeping by the Russians found no trace of mines. An A/S sweep by escorts in the vicinity was unsuccessful.

29. *Denbigh Castle* was hit right forward and was soon in a precarious condition much down by the bow. It was greatly to the credit of her Officers and Ships company that she was kept afloat. *Bluebell* did excellent work in towing her in. Eventually the situation became so serious that it was decided to beach her in Bolshaya Volokovaya Bay, which was done by the Russian tug which had by then arrived with a salvage pump. Unfortunately *Denbigh Castle* later turned over on her side.

30. Attempts were made for two days to recover the C.B.'s and S.P.'s stowed below and secret material by *Bellona*'s divers, working from *Bamborough Castle* under the direction of the Commanding Officer, *Denbigh Castle*. In spite of gallant work in icy water and temperatures a long way below freezing this proved impracticable with the standard British equipment. The Type 277 Office was, however, wrecked by an explosive charge.

31. *Lark*, *Lapwing* and *Alnwick Castle* arrived Kola p.m. on 13th February, 1945, after an uneventful passage.

32. On 14th February, 1945, two merchant ships arriving from the White Sea under Russian escort were torpedoed just outside the entrance to the Kola inlet in almost the same position as *Denbigh Castle*.

OPERATION OPENDOOR.

33. At 2026 on 14th February, 1945, Captain (D), 2nd destroyer Flotilla, in *Zambesi*, with *Zealous*, *Zest*, and *Sioux*, was sailed on receipt of your signal to evacuate refugees from Soroy. I sailed *Sioux* in addition so that Captain (D), 2nd Destroyer Flotilla should have a destroyer in support in case of enemy interference during the evacuation, the situation he would find being far from clear in view of the conflicting messages received via Admiralty and via Senior British Naval Officer, North Russia.

34. All went well. 500 men, women and children were successfully evacuated without incident and transferred to merchant ships of RA 64 on return to Kola on the 16th February, 1945

PASSAGE OF RA 64

35. It was clear that on sailing RA 64 would have to force its way through a strong concentration of U-boats in the approaches to Kola. One U-boat was working right in the entrance where it had torpedoed 3 ships in the last few days. While H/F D/F fixes and Russian reports showed that others were clustered

along the first 40 miles of the convoy route and could not be avoided. Russian counter measures were confined to day flying and a few small craft patrolling the entrance and were quite ineffective. There was no night flying, no hunting groups, and no thought on their part of taking the offensive against the U-boats so handily placed

36. I decided to send all suitable escort vessels to hunt the approaches as far as 35°E during the night before sailing, and I arranged for Russian aircraft to flood the area on the day of sailing so as to keep U-boats down, for Russian escorts to follow the convoy until dark to take charge of any damaged ships, and for Russian tugs to stand by. I decided against sending a carrier out to operate during the night before sailing, both on account of the doubtful conditions for flying, intense cold, and dark, patches of fog and 'Arctic smoke', and so on, and also because of the concentration of U-boats, extending even into the waters where *Nairana* bad operated before RA 62 sailed.

37. **HM Ships Cygnet** (Senior Officer, 7th Escort Group), **Lark**, **Lapwing**, **Alnwick Castle** and **Bamborough Castle** accordingly sailed at dusk on 16th February, 1945, to sweep the approaches as far as longitude 35°E. At midnight **Lark** made Asdic contact with a U-boat which was attacked by **Alnwick Castle** with Squid at 0059. It surfaced at 0107, was picked up by radar, illuminated and hit by gunfire and finished off with squid. It sank vertically stern first at 0136 in position 69°32'N 35°50'E, leaving many corpses. One survivor was picked up. The U-boat was **U-425** of 540 tons, 10 days out from Narvik.

38. At 0708 17th February the Senior 0fficer, 7th Escort Group reported a disappearing radar contact in position 100° Tsyp Navolok point 9 miles, but failed to regain contact.

39. At 0745 the leading ships of the convoy passed Toros Island and the convoy started forming, screened by all remaining destroyers and escorts except the four detailed for the carriers. A number of Russian escorts also sailed later and did a certain amount of indiscriminate depth charging.

40. The convoy was very slow in getting out, in spite of all exhortation at the convoy conference, and at 1000 it was reported that 8 were still inside the Inlet. **Lucerna**, the escort tanker, had broken down for a few hours with engine defects and in view of her importance I left **Zealous** to bring her on if ready by noon. However, she then showed no signs of completion so had to be left behind and **Zealous** rejoined.

41. At 1024 **Lark** who was part of the screen sweeping ahead the convoy was torpedoed in position 052° Kildin 12 miles and had her stern blown off. **Lapwing** and **Bamborough Castle** swept round **Lark** in addition to 6 Russian motor boats, but could get no firm contacts. At this time I was just about to leave harbour with the carriers and cruiser astern of the last merchant ship, and asked Senior British Naval Officer North Russia to send the Russia escorts to look after **Lark** and to try tow her back to harbour.

42. At 1158 No. 34. **Thomas Scott** was torpedoed in approximate position 69° 23'N 34°28'E, within sight of **Lark**. **HM Ships Onslaught**, **Bluebell**, **Alnwick Castle**, **Cygnet** and **Whitehall** searched the area without success, but did enable the rear ships of the convoy who were still covering many miles astern, to pass and catch up without further incident.

43. The crew of **Thomas Scott** immediately abandoned ship although the ship was floating on an even keel with little sign of damage, in a calm sea surrounded by escorts. When this was reported to me I ordered **Onslaught** to keep the Norwegian refugee passengers but to send the crew to the Russians who had then arrived to take over. I consider that the subsequent loss of this ship before reaching harbour under tow might well have been prevented had her Officers and men stuck to their posts and done their duty. I con-

sider the premature abandonment of this ship should be the subject of enquiry. I see no justification for it.

44. At 1410 the carriers had joined the convoy and an hour later ***Bluebell***, ***Whitehall*** and ***Onslaught*** had also rejoined. ***HM Ships Cygnet***, ***Lapwing***, ***Alnwick Castle*** and ***Bamborough Castle*** were still with ***Lark*** as all attempts to make the Russian escorts take her over had proved unavailing, though they had taken over the merchant ship.

45. At 1525, half an hour after altering course to the Northward, ***Bluebell*** on the inner screen on the port beam of the convoy was torpedoed. She appeared to be turning towards a contact and to be hit on the port quarter. She blew up and disappeared, leaving one survivor, some corpses and wreckage. The Captain (D), 17th Destroyer Flotilla, ordered 'Artichoke', but no contact with the U-boat was made. The loss of this gallant little ship is much regretted. She had done fine work a few days previously in towing the damaged ***Denbigh Castle*** into harbour.

46. At 1740 Russian escorts at last took over ***Lark***, and our 4 escorts started to rejoin, after taking onboard all surplus Officers and men. ***Lark*** was subsequently reported to have been towed safely into harbour.

47. At 1850 ***Serapis*** on the inner screen on the port bow obtained a contact and counter attacked with depth charges. The convoy altered course to clear by emergency turns. Five minutes later ***Whitehall*** on the port bow also obtained this contact and fired a pattern and after marking the position carried out an 'Observant' round it. ***Serapis*** and ***Whitehall*** continued to hunt for an hour and then turned over to ***Zealous*** and ***Sioux*** and rejoined the screen. These continued the hunt until 20 miles astern without success and then rejoined. Subsequent teasing tactics by Swordfish were unsuccessful.

48. Meanwhile the air had been flooded throughout the day with numbers of Russian aircraft, which appeared to be mostly fighters, without result. On getting clear of the 'Smoke' outside the approaches to Kola Inlet, the carriers had also flown aircraft to patrol round the convoy where U-boats were known to be waiting and to search ahead on the convoy route. Positions of torpedoings were also investigated and 'teasing tactics' afterwards carried out in these areas, but all without result. After dark aircraft were sent to search along D/F bearings obtained, but had no contacts. One aircraft ditched on taking off but the crew were promptly recovered by ***Onslaught***.

49. By 0500 18th February, 1945, the Senior Officer, 7th Escort Group had rejoined with his four escort vessels. The day was uneventful there were no indications of U-boats. Air searches were unfruitful, and at 1530 flying had to be stopped owing to weather.

50. The first gale now arrived, with a big swell and sea and a wind of 60 knots between gusts from ahead with sleet. Before the peak was reached the convey was located by enemy aircraft at 0330 19th February, 1945. By morning the convoy was scattered.

51. By 2300 19th February, 1945, the weather was improving and in the morning at first light reforming of the convoy was started. By 0900 20th February, 1945, 29 ships were in station leaving four stragglers of which 2 were approaching from astern.

52. Reforming of the convoy had been a matter of urgency as at 0420 20th February, 1945, enemy aircraft had started shadowing and it was more than likely that a torpedo attack would follow. Escorts did well to round them up so quickly.

53. At 1000, groups of aircraft were detected approaching from the port bow and crossing ahead of the convoy, whose course was 270°. The sea was still very rough with a strong wind but *Nairana* flew off fighters to intercept. The convoy and stragglers were warned of what was coming on 500kc/s.

54. As the threat was now from the starboard bow, an emergency turn of 45° to port was ordered, followed by another 45° to port when the situation clarified. This put the majority of attacking aircraft on the quarter and it was from this direction that the majority of the attacks developed, although one or two small groups of aircraft also came in from the Southward (ahead).

55. A feature of these attacks was the large number of torpedoes which exploded prematurely, apparently on breaking surface in the trough of the rough seas, as well as on crossing wakes of ships. There were no casualties in the convoy or among the stragglers, one of whom was attacked but not hit.

56. **HM Ships Onslow**, **Zealous**, and **Nairana**'s fighters each shot down an aircraft confirmed. **Nairana**'s fighters and **Bamborough Castle** both got a probable, and 2 were damaged by **Rhodedendron** and one each by **Sioux** and **Lapwing**. Total 3 + 2 + 4. **Campania** only had one fighter serviceable, which was not flown off. It seems that over 25 aircraft took part in the attack. By 1140 all enemy aircraft had withdrawn, the last being driven away by Wildcats.

57. I consider the highest credit is due to **Nairana** and her Wildcats.They operated with great success and landed on safely in a really rough sea with a wind over the deck on landing of over 50 knots.

58. It was again unfortunate that some merchant ships fired at the returning wildcats. Luckily without fatal results in spite of warning by R/T and all that was said at the convoy conference. There was no excuse for it whatsoever.

59. At 1230 **HM Ships Savage**, **Scourge**, and **Zebra** joined from Scapa. By 1800 31 out of 33 ships of the convoy had been accounted for.

60. At 0435 21st, February, 1945 the usual enemy shadowers arrived. One was fired at by the screen at 0630 and then retired. Another appeared for a short time at 0950. Some of these bogeys transmitted a number of 'A', presumably to enable shore stations to fix or U-boats to home. The weather was still bad with strong head winds.

61. At 1400 flying just became possible for two hours and a sweep round the convoy was made for the two missing stragglers. One was found and gathered in. The other, **Crosby Noyes**, was not located and was not heard of again until she reported her position on the afternoon of the 27th February, 1945, some 300 miles astern of the convoy which was then in the latitude of the Shetlands.

62. At 1700 **Whitehall** who had been suffering continual feed water trouble was detached to the Faeroes.

63. At 0045, 22nd February, 1945, an enemy shadower located and reported the convoy, and shortly afterwards a few HF/DF bearings of U-boats were obtained, mostly in an easterly direction. A heavy swell across the wind prevented flying. Other bogeys were detected at 0200 and 0330 but may not have found the convoy.

64. A strong gale reaching 70 - 80 knots' blew up during the day, from ahead. These constant gales and strong winds from ahead which persisted throughout the voyage caused much difficulty in keeping strag-

glers with the convoy. Engine trouble, defective steering, ice chipped propellers, shifting cargoes, and splitting decks were among the very genuine reasons for dropping astern, and at times stopping.

65. By the evening, conditions were much worse, the barograph producing an almost vertical fall and a similar rise later. The convoy got much scattered. Some followed the Commodore on a course of 160°. Others were hove to. *Campania* had to heave to after rolling, over 45° each way.

66. At 0515 23rd February, 1945, though still blowing a full gale, an enemy aircraft appeared and must have reported a badly scattered convoy. The weather started to improve slightly and *Campania* was able to lead round gradually to port and at 1045 rejoined the convoy some 40 miles to the Eastward, which then had 20 ships in company and a good proportion of the escorts.

67. By dragging the convoy to the Westward across the line of advance we eventually managed by 1700 to collect all but one of the missing ships and the proper course was resumed.

68. I had been expecting air attack all day as a result of the night's sighting, but fortunately for the convoy in its unformed state no enemy aircraft found it. Unfortunately, however, they did find our one unlocated straggler and at 1420 No.43. *Henry Bacon* reported on 500 kc/s that she was being attacked by aircraft and then that she had been torpedoed and was sinking. A D/F bearing was obtained and a section of Wildcats sent out, who found the ship, climbed and enabled its position to be fixed by radar, but were too late to intercept the enemy. She was 100° 47 miles from the convoy and it seems probable that she got ahead of the Commodore during the night gale and missed the signal altering course to the Westward although this was passed on Convoy R/T.

69. The Captain (D), 2nd Destroyer Flotilla, in *Zambesi* with *Zest* and *Opportune* was sent to rescue survivors. They picked up 65 survivors including Norwegian men, women and children, refugees from Soroy, and rejoined by midnight. Survivors reported that the ship had been attacked by 15 aircraft and claimed possibly to have shot down two.

70. The gale continued strong from ahead, gusting up to 70 knots. There was much trouble with stragglers and their defects.

71. At 0720, 24th February, 1945, a Liberator arrived and we were escorted throughout the day. Unfortunately, each Liberator in turn chose to orbit, calling loudly on Convoy R/T and presumably acting as a useful beacon for the enemy and it took some time to stop them talking. It is clear that they were not aware that W/T silence was in force.

72. Two stragglers, one with engine and one with steering defects, were some 15 miles astern with two destroyers as escort. The strong gale continued from ahead with no sign of improvement, and the fuel situation in *Bellona*, destroyers and *Rhodedendron* was becoming serious. The convoy was advancing at a 'nominal' speed of 3 knots. At 1100 I detached *H.M. Ships Zealous*, *Zebra* and *Opportune* to the Faeroes to fuel and rejoin as soon as possible.

73. At 1900, the Captain (D), 23rd Destroyer Flotilla arrived from Scapa in *Myngs* followed shortly by *Scorpion* and *Cavalier*. On their arrival I detached *Savage* and *Orwell* to the Faeroes to fuel and rejoin as soon as possible, placed *Cavalier* in the close screen, and told the Captain (D), 23rd Destroyer Flotilla, to take over the two defective stragglers astern with *Myngs* and *Scorpion* and escort them direct to the Faeroes. One was steering by hand tackle, the other had constant engine trouble.

74. On 25th February, 1945, the wind was still force 8 but had moved to the Westward which allowed a slight increase of speed above the former 3 knots. At 1700 **Rhodedendron** was detached to the Faeroes to fuel and rejoin the convoy, and at 1830 **Onslaught** was detached to the Clyde with her cargo of Norwegian refugees.

75. During the night the wind though still very strong moved further to the Northwest-ward which allowed the convoy to make about 7 knots for a few hours, the fastest speed for very many days.

76. At 0930 on 26th February, 1945, **Serapis** and **Scourge** were detached to the Faeroes to fuel and rejoin the convoy, and at noon **HM Ships Zealous**, **Zebra** and **Opportune** rejoined after fuelling. The wind again increased to gale force and reduced the convoy speed, but in the lull when the wind, was down to 40 knots **Zambesi** had succeeded in taking 50 tons of fuel from **Black Ranger** and so avoided having to be sent to the Faeroes.

77. At 1830 **Savage** and **Orwell** were in touch rejoining, so I left the convoy in charge of **Zealous**, proceeding ahead with **Bellona**, **Nairana**, **Onslow** (The Captain (D), 17th Destroyer Flotilla), **Zambesi** (The Captain (D), 2nd Destroyer Flotilla), **Zest** and **Sioux** to Scapa. We arrived at 0915 on the 27th February, 1945, 10 days out from Kola.

REMARKS

78. The outstanding features of JW 64 and RA 64 were the continuous heavy seas and adverse gales which persisted during the Easterly run of JW 64 and for practically the whole passage of RA 64 the increased part now being played by enemy aircraft, the concentration of U-boats outside Kola when RA 64 sailed, and absence of U-boats during the remainder of the passage.

WEATHER

79. The effect of the weather was to reduce the speed of RA 64 to between 3 and 6 knots for most of the passage, to disperse it twice, and to prevent any thought of fuelling escorts. All but four of the destroyers had to be detached to the Faeroes to fuel and it was fortunate that none of the usual short legged escorts like **Beagle** and **Bulldog** were present.

SHADOWING AIRCRAFT.

80. Both convoys were shadowed at intervals day and night from just North of the Faeroes to one day out from Kola. It was noticeable that enemy shadowing aircraft flew in the most adverse weather. The usual procedure was a search by 3 or 4. BV-158 or Ju-88 flying about 25 miles apart in the middle or morning watch, when the convoy would be shadowed and reported. for 2 or 3 hours, and homing signals made if in the U-boat waters North of Latitude 70°N. Shadowers were, however, liable to appear at any time, though by day they usually left very quickly, presumably owing to a healthy respect for our fighters. They were obviously using ASV picking up the convoy at about 20 - 25 miles.

NIGHT FIGHTERS

81. I have already in my report on JW 62 and RA 62 drawn attention to the need for night fighters in the winter convoys, to the great chances they would have in suitable weather, and to the healthy effect it would have on the enemy if some of his night shadowing aircraft were shot down. The one night fighting Fulmar

provided was too obsolete and too full of defects to be of use. It is galling when shadowed night after night with no chance of retaliation, to read in A/A.W.D. 626/44 of 11th November 1944, in a lecture on experience in the Pacific Theatre of war that some Admirals and Commanding Officers are still unwilling to undertake the arduous task of providing a standing night patrol.

TYPE 277

82. I must draw attention to the extreme importance of having Type 277 and good communications in the flagship in these convoys. In this respect we were fortunate in *Campania* although the blind arc astern was always an anxiety. Enemy torpedo attacks approach at sea level, visibility has usually been poor, and it is on the information provided from Type 277 that the convoy has to be manoeuvred, the screening ships kept informed of the directions from which attacks are developing and fighters vectored to intercept. Besides this, Type 277 almost always gives the first warning of the coming attack.

83. I am quite sure that without the good Type 277 detection and good communications provided by *Campania*, heavy losses would have occurred in the air attacks, and will occur in future air attacks if the flagship is not suitably equipped.

ENEMY Ju-88 TORPEDO ATTACKS

84. Having fixed the position of the convoy by shadowing aircraft a few hours previously, enemy tactics appear to be to send out a main group of perhaps 16 torpedo aircraft, accompanied by one or two smaller groups, all flying out to intercept at sea level. On finding the convoy these split up to attack in pairs from different bearings, then retiring and attacking again later with the second torpedo carried.

85. In practice co-ordination of attacks has been poor. Groups have been broken up by the fighters and by gunfire from the outer screen in BP 2, and a proportion of the aircraft have broken away to attack ships on the outer or inner screen who have proved quite capable of looking after themselves. Of the remainder many have fired their torpedoes against the convoy at too long a range as a result of coming under fire from the inner screen. A number of torpedoes do, however, enter the convoy.

86. Against these I have found it quite practicable to manoeuvre the convoy by emergency turns of 45° although it is advisable to do a second turn of 45° before too long on account of station keeping. It takes time to get signals through, in practice at least 2 or 3 minutes depending on visibility, and even then it is advisable on turning to pass the course by Convoy R/T as some ships always miss the signal. With a large convoy it is obviously impossible for every ship to be combing torpedoes, but much can be done to reduce the targets presented.

87. An initial turn to bring the dawn or dusk ahead of the main attack astern undoubtedly upsets the enemy, who either fires his torpedoes from an unfavourable position if committed to the attack or circles round at 15 miles range trying to reach a more favourable bearing, which is easily prevented by another emergency turn at the right moment. For the smaller subsidiary attacks however, reliance has to be placed on the screen and, in the last resort, on the convoy for driving them off. The danger to stragglers is, however, great. Had the attack on the 20th February, 1945, taken place an hour or two earlier, before the convoy had reformed, after being dispersed by weather, or had the attack on the 23rd February, 1945, found the convoy while it was still dispersed, instead of one unfortunate straggler, heavy casualties might have been incurred.

89. It was noticeable that the Ju-88 attacks on 20th February, took place in surprisingly bad weather conditions, winds of 45 knots, low clouds, poor visibility, squalls of sleet and very rough sea which, however, proved too much for many of their torpedoes.

90. The cruiser is badly placed in the middle of the convoy to deal with torpedo attacks. As a result of experience she was given discretion to move to a position astern of the lee column adjoining the pocket when torpedo attack developed, where she is well placed for protecting the carriers and the rear of the convoy, while keeping out of the carriers' way.

FIGHTERS

91. Carrier fighters did extremely well, operating in very bad weather, shooting down a number of Ju-88 breaking up attacks before they developed and finally landing on successfully in most adverse conditions. The outstanding problem is to stop the merchant ships firing at them as they must be free to return to their carrier at any time if they are damaged. Fire discipline in merchant ships leaves much to be desired and escorts were also to blame in JW 64, though above reproach in RA 64. As a partial remedy fighters were routed back via the rear of the "box" but this cannot be relied on in all cases, as a damaged fighter may return by the most direct route.

92. More fighters will have to be carried. We started with 10 between the two carriers but after the attack on the 20th February, 1945, these were reduced at one time to 4 serviceable in *Nairana* and 1 in *Campania*. Each carrier needs its full complement of 8, especially with the longer daylight hours of the summer.

KOLA

93. The problem of entering and leaving Kola without losses, or even of safety while at Kola is now in a very unsatisfactory state. The approach is confined to a 40 mile passage eastward along the shore before turning North, a fact of which the enemy is well aware.

94. Suspicion of minefields in the entrance to Kola as a result of damage to *Denbigh Castle* and to two merchant ships next day in the same area revealed the inadequacy of Russian mine sweeping arrangements, all the better sweepers having moved to the Petsamo-Kirkness area. Searching sweeps were carried out at my request by two small sweepers, as far as could be ascertained and fortunately showed no minefield present. Little if anything appears to be done to ensure a swept channel and the initial Russian reaction to being asked to sweep the entrance was to ask for British minesweepers.

95. Failure to find mines made it clear that one or more U-boats were operating in the actual entrance to the Inlet, presumably with 'snorts', as well as those patrolling every few miles along the coast waiting for the convoy. How to get an unformed convoy through those U-boats unscathed is major problem to which the only answer would seem to be, so to hunt and harry the U-boats as to force them to withdraw further from the coast. This the Russians should do but don't.

96. I consider it most important that each convoy should be so strong in long endurance escort vessels that a continual offensive can be undertaken in the approaches during the whole period the convoy is at Kola, so as to drive the U-boats further away, in addition to such commitments as helping the Russians with the White Sea section. Fleet destroyers are not suitable for this purpose. Modern escort vessels are needed, and in no other way can I see how losses are to be prevented. The question of alternative approach routes to Kola also needs consideration.

97. Apart from the U-boat menace in the approaches, I consider it most probable that when there is no longer loose ice in the Inlet, a U-boat with 'snort' will proceed up to Vaenga and attack ships anchored there. There is nothing to stop it and a suitable U-boat could at any time torpedo the carriers, cruiser and oilers lying at Vaenga with little risk to itself. Russian counter measures consist of a few small boats at the entrance dropping occasional charges. They are useless, there are no obstructions and the risk in a month or two's time will be a very real one. It is important that it should be realised now, and the Russians encouraged both to keep the approaches clear and to take more adequate measures to ensure the safety of ships anchored at Vaenga.

ESCORTS FOR JW/RA CONVOYS.

98. The requirements for escorts are good endurance, good A/S, and good A/A, and a few destroyers are also needed for their speed and surface armament. The numbers needed for A/S and A/A protection are 8 on the inner screen and 10 on the outer screen and one or two extra if possible to replace casualties, (e.g. **Zebra** - engine trouble, **Whitehall** - feed water trouble, in JW 64/RA 64 in addition to casualties from enemy action). In view of the offensive which must be carried out at Kola against U-boats it is most desirable that as many long endurance sloops, frigates and modern corvettes as possible should be included. Old destroyers and corvettes cannot pull their weight.

A/S

99. The destruction of a U-boat off Kildin Island by **Lark** and **Alnwick Castle** was very creditable. On the other hand that **Lark**, a merchant ship and **Bluebell** should be torpedoed next day without any retaliation on the U-boats concerned is a most unsatisfactory state of affairs. Day and night air searches for U-boats known to be present were this time disappointing and yielded no results. No U-boats were met on passage except in the approaches to Kola.

100. We lost badly in the U-boat war. One U-boat was sunk, against 2 escorts and one merchant ship sunk and one escort damaged.

GENERAL

101. All escorts had a most gruelling and uncomfortable time with the constant bad weather. Their effectiveness as A/A screens was very encouraging. Aircraft shot down during JW 64 and RA 64 totalled:-

Fighters	4 confirmed		5 probables.		2 damaged.
Gunfire	8	"	2	"	13
TOTAL	12	"	7	"	15

Against this we lost one merchant ship straggler sunk by torpedo aircraft and 2 fighters, the pilot of one of which was saved. The main convoy suffered no damage.

COMMUNICATIONS RADAR AND AIRCRAFT DIRECTION

T.B.S.

102.   There were a slightly higher number of technical failures than is usual in these operations which

emphasizes the necessity for first class maintenance and the need for the second T.B.S. to be fitted. The value of using MCW, giving as it does a slightly increased range, was often apparent in this operation especially for the passing of long messages.

AIR ATTACK

103. R/T radar reporting was carried out on the air plot control wave, for the benefit of carriers and **Bellona** only. **Campania** who acted as the controlling ship employed the new sitrep system on this frequency. It was not found necessary to open up the air plot relief wave, primarily owing to the comparatively small number of fighters available.

104. In view of the distance of ships on the close and outer screen from **Campania**, it was necessary to carry out a broadcast of the air situation in addition to the R/T radar reporting. This commenced on T.B.S. and when it was appreciated that an attack (as opposed to shadowing) was imminent, was carried out on 2410 kc/s with the object of:

(a) combining the broadcast to escorts with that to merchant ships.

(b) reducing delays by avoiding the necessity of controlling a ship to read back for the benefit of ships near the limit of T.B.S. range.

(c) freeing T.B.S. for the passing of visual reports by the outer screen and for inter communication generally

105. In view of the comparatively large number of aircraft including hostile and friendly's within about 20 miles of the Convoy, many of them at zero feet, coupled with the number of visual reports received, the problem of keeping the air plot up to date was far from easy.

106. **Campania**'s A.D.R. team did this excellently and this enabled her:

(a) to direct her own fighters.

(b) supply **Nairana** with sufficient information to enable her to direct her own fighters.

(c) keep the command accurately informed as to the air situation and to any especial threat that was developing.

(d) keep all escorts and merchant ships in touch with the air situation.

(e) keep an eye as necessary on the A/S patrol and endeavour to vector him out of harms way.

I consider great credit is due to **Campania** for the manner in which she carried out these duties.

107. A factor which stood out was the high noise level in the A.D.R. due mainly to the various internal broadcasts being so frequently in use. It is important that these conditions should be simulated in all practices.

2410 Kc/s - WATCH BY MERCHANT SHIPS

108. It is considered important that all merchant ships in these convoys should be capable of keeping loud-speaker watch on 2410 kc/s. Enemy aircraft invariably approached low and the range of detection, even with Type 277, did not allow for adequate warning to be passed by V/S to the convoy. Furthermore, during air attacks, it is necessary that merchant ships should be informed of the movement of our own fighters.

109. In the rare event of it being required to manoeuvre the convoy by radio alone as was necessary on two occasions with RA 64, in bad weather, the use of 2410 kc/s is considered preferable to that of 500 kc/s. The use of 2410 kc/s is also considered to be valuable in supplementing visual signals for emergency turns during air attack when it is imperative that there should be no delay in executing these.

110. Up to the present time the normal and alarm organisation for these convoys have been respectively A and B. During this operation the convoy was instructed to set watch on convoy R/T when air attack was considered probable but I was never certain whether all ships had the necessary equipment to comply with these orders.

111. I would therefore recommend that the radio organisation for these convoys should be:

    (a)   Continuous loudspeaker watch on 2410 Kc/s by all ships (or all ships fitted)
    (b)   Maximum watch on BAMS.
    (c)   Stragglers - Maximum watch on BAMS shifting to 500 kc/s

112. It is possible that all merchant ships may not have the necessary equipment to comply with this proposed organisation; it is however considered that it should be adopted by ships suitably fitted and under these conditions consideration should be borne in mind when the convoy form Al is prepared, such ship being stationed as leading ship of columns and the remainder being spaced equally round the convoy.

113. Observing that the great majority of merchant ships in these convoys are American it is suggested that the lack of a receiver could probably be rectified at an early date if it was sufficiently realised by the American authorities that the provision of this equipment would materially assist in the defence of the convoy.

TYPE 277

114. The supreme value of this set and, conversely, the comparatively little use of Type 281 in this particular operation was clearly demonstrated and to such an extent that it is considered that it would be courting trouble to sail one of these convoys without one of the larger ships of the escort being fitted with this equipment.

115. Owing to the present siting of the aerial outfit, the Type 277 in *Campania* has a blind arc some twenty five degrees either side of the stern. When it was apparent that the enemy air force were taking a serious interest in the convoy, the *Denbigh Castle* was instructed to pay particular attention to stern bearings with her Type 277 and she was included in the air reporting organisation and placed on the inner screen.

116. After the loss of *Denbigh Castle*, *Alnwick Castle* was used for this purpose with RA 64, and to enable her to carry out these duties more efficiently, the Second Fighter Direction Officer in *Bellona* was lent to

her for the passage.

117. It is recommended that this procedure be followed in future operations unless there are two large ships in the escort fitted with Type 277. It is considered essential that the frigate or corvette selected should be loaned a FDO and preferably at least two RP 3's if possible from a carrier.

ENEMY ASV

118. On a large number of occasions during this operation enemy aircraft were shadowing at night, and time after time it was quite apparent from their movements as seen on the air plot, that they were using A.S.V. for this purpose. Watch was being kept in *Bellona* but enemy radar transmissions were only intercepted on one occasion, the frequency being used being 596 mc/s.

119. It therefore seems probable that the operating frequency of A.S.V. equipment at present more generally fitted lies outside the band of the P.29 receiver. If, from an intelligence aspect, it is of sufficient importance it is suggested that special search receivers should be embarked in future operations.

HF/DF REPORTING

120. The standard of HF/DF reporting was somewhat lower than usual. Formerly the experts in this respect have been the Western Approach Destroyer's. It appears that the more recently commissioned Home Fleet Destroyers require exercises and it is for consideration that some should be arranged.

121. In this connection a very realistic exercise used to be carried out at Larne, ML's being employed to transmit messages on a few H/F frequencies, escort vessels in the area taking bearings and reporting them. It might be possible to arrange for similar exercises to be carried out in the Orkney exercise area.

18 GROUP

122. Aircraft from 18 group escorting RA 64 broke silence on 2410 kc/s on the following occasions on February 24th.

Call sign	Time
BNP 5	0814, 0820,& 0855
BNP 9	0925
BNP 1	1240 & 1255
BNP 3	1245

On all these occasions aircraft asked for strength of signal and were instructed to keep silence. During this period it was particularly desired to keep H/F silence as the enemy appeared to be unaware of our position.

123. With reference to C3 04234 (44), Article 244, paragraph 6, it is noted that the instructions contained in the previous Edition of A.C.I (e.g. CB 04234(3), paragraph 49), left no margin for doubt on this point whereas the existing article requires the aircraft to be aware of the radio policy in force in the convoy.

124. Since the interval between the time of briefing and their E.T.A with a convoy is necessarily a long one, it is recommended that when escorting JW/RA convoys the onus of breaking silence other than to report the enemy should continue to rest with the Senior Officer present.

WEATHER MESSAGES

125. The situation as regards weather messages as reported in Appendix I of my No. 398/9/8 of 19th December, 1944, continues to be unsatisfactory. I think it would be very helpful if the Fleet Meteorological Officer could take passage in one of these operations to witness conditions and make detailed recommendations.

7TH ESCORT GROUP

126. I would like to pay tribute to the standard of efficiency of communications in the 7th Escort Group generally and in *Cygnet* the ship of the Senior Officer in particular. I have done 3 of these operations with the 7th Escort Group and their efficiency in communication has been consistently high.

Reports from Escorting ships together with my remarks will be forwarded shortly.

Sgd R (?) McGrigor
REAR-ADMIRAL

Accompanying this Report:-

Plan One: Passage of JW.64 3rd to 13th February, 1945
Plan Two: Passage of RA.64, 17th to 27th February, 1945

Plan Three: Approaches to Kola Inlet, showing RA 64 departing, 17th February, 1945

REPORT OF PROCEEDINGS - 7TH ESCORT GROUP
COVERING ESCORT OF CONVOYS JW 64 3rd FEBRUARY - 1st MARCH 1945

(Senior Officer, 7th Escort Group, HMS CYGNET's letter No.025 of 4th March 1945)

No.3995/191

DIRECTOR OF ANTI-U-BOAT DIVISION, ADMIRALTY, LONDON.

1. Forwarded.

2. The successful attack by *HMS Lark* and *HMS Alnwick Castle* on the night of l6h/l7th February 1945 resulted in one prisoner being taken.

3. Recorder traces and plot from *HMS Alnwick Castle* are forwarded herewith. Recorder traces and plot from *HMS Lark* were destroyed when she was torpedoed on the following day.

4. An interesting feature of this A/S action was the course of action by the Senior Officer, 8th Escort Group in *HMS Lark* when he gained contact.

5. *HMS Lark* was not fitted either with ahead throwing weapon or 147B and the Commanding Officer was anxious not to drive the submarine deeper, where it would, in these waters, in the normal course of events probably be lost owing to temperature layers.

6. He accordingly waited for the aid of a Castle Class corvette fitted with 147B and Squid, and although running over the contact two or three times made no attempt to attack it himself. No difficulty was experienced in holding contact astern, with Unifoxer.

7. The Squid-fitted ship gained contact immediately on arrival and discovered by 147B that the depth of the U-boat was only forty feet.

8. A deliberate attack was carried out with the result that before a second pattern could be fired the U-boat surfaced and surrendered.

9. Throughout the entire action the U-boat appears to have acted in a completely casual manner, no noticeable avoiding action being taken, and the sole survivor stated that at the time of the attack he was in his hammock. He said that the submarine was the *U-425*, ten days out from Narvik. Norwegian money was found on him.

10. He also added that they had sunk a small British warship a few days previously and had fired five torpedoes. That had been their only success on this patrol.

11. This information was obtained from him during the voyage back to the United Kingdom, but as no one in the ship claimed to have any substantial knowledge of German it is possible that errors may have crept in to the translation.

12. The crew of the U-boat were seen to abandon the vessel which was observed to sink stern first. There

is no doubt that the submarine was destroyed.

13. As a matter of interest the submarine, on surfacing to surrender fired red and green flares which, it is understood, were the Russian aircraft recognition signal for the day.

H. Jauncey
CAPTAIN (D).
GREEENOCK.
6th March 1945.

GENERAL REMARKS
HMS CYGNET
4th March 1945

I.   REPORT OF PROCEEDINGS OF HMS WHITEHALL

Much credit is due to the Commanding Officer of **HMS Whitehall** for getting his ship back safely under extremely trying conditions, and there is no doubt that in the winter months ships of that class are a liability and not an asset on the North Russian Run, as not only are they liable to suffer considerable weather damage, but the fuel problem is ever present when fuelling at sea cannot be carried out.

II.   SQUID AMMUNITION.

Now that more squid fitted ships are being employed as escorts for the JW and RA convoys it seems desirable that a small stock of Squid Ammunition should be maintained in North Russia to enable ships to top up when required.

III.   ENTRY INTO AND DEPARTURE FROM KOLA INLET.

(a) Now that U-Boats are operating in the close approaches to the port it has become very necessary to see what additional steps can be taken to safeguard the convoys entering and leaving.

(b) There is no doubt that the speed of both entering end leaving could be improved if the pilots were embarked and disembarked in the vicinity of Salni Island. As regards entering it would then be possible for the convoys to maintain its speed until past Toros Island; if the entry takes place at night two ships fitted with good Radar should be stationed ahead of the two columns to lead in at full convoy speed; there is really plenty of room to enter or leave in two columns, as there is no outward bound traffic when a convoy is entering and vice versa. This procedure would obviate the present very slow entry of the convoy in what must now be regarded as a very definite danger area. When leaving, the convoy could be formed in two columns before the leader is allowed to pass Toros Island and thus a better speed would be possible and forming up would take less time.

(c) Owing to the large prohibited area off Kola the convoys route is so stereotyped that it is easy for the U-Boats to get into the tracks of the convoys and when Asdic conditions are bad there is practically nothing that the escorts can do to help. It therefore, seems that it is high time that the Russians undertook some

sweeping so that the route can be changed and some degree of surprise thereby achieved. From Russian D/F reports, which seemed to be very reasonably accurate and sinkings, it would appear that there were at least 4 and possibly five U-Boats in the close approaches extending as far as Tsyp Navalok in the West and MX in the East, with the majority stationed on the route to (?).

(d) Escorts sweeping the approaches before the convoy sails undoubtedly achieve a certain amount but if Asdic conditions are poor, they really only give warning that a convoy is leaving without any commensurate gain to counter balance the loss of surprise.

(e) Possibly as the days get longer more value will be obtained from the Russian aircraft in keeping the U-boats down, though this may well be nullified by the use of more SCHNORKEL fitted U-Boats. There is, however, no doubt that it is no longer a suitable area in which to operate a carrier prior to the convoy sailing and the only other possibility would be to land some of their aircraft at Vaenga. It is realised that this raises a considerable maintenance problem, but there does not seem to be any other way of ensuring good air support.

IV.   AIR ATTACKS

The results achieved against the Ju-88's were most satisfactory and excellent H.A. practise was obtained, but there is no doubt that they were a very untrained squadron and delivered very poor attacks. With the improvements in Radar and hence better warning being obtained, the day of the torpedo aircraft attacks seem to have passed unless it is mixed with some other form of bombing to distract attention. The single armed reconnaissance aircraft is really more likely to do damage than a massed attack which everybody knows is coming in.

HMS CYGNET
3rd MARCH, 1945

SECTION II   ENCOUNTER WITH THE ENEMY (All time Zone-2)

HMS Denbigh Castle mined or torpedoed

On 13 th February at 0016, whilst JA 64 was entering Kola Inlet *Denbigh Castle* reported that she had been mined in position 140° Nevilaski Light 4 miles. *Serapis* and *Bluebell* closed to render assistance, whilst *Cygnet*, *Whitehall* and *Zest* carried out an A/S patrol to the seaward and to the westward. At 0159 *Bluebell* reported that she had *Denbigh Castle* in tow, but that the latter's bows were blown off and although the forward bulkhead was holding there was no safety margin. *Denbigh Castle* used her own pump to hold the inrush of water, and a Russian tug arrived alongside her later to assist.

From 0155 to 0550 *Cygnet* was employed in investigating and attacking a bottomed contact in position 082 degrees Tsyp Navolok light 0.75 miles, but this was eventually considered to have been 'non-sub', and course was set for Kola. At 0630 *Cygnet* passed *Denbigh Castle* in tow of *Bluebell* with *Serapis* standing by, Russian tugs took over from *Bluebell*, and beached *Denbigh Castle* in Volokavaya Bay.

Sinking of German U-Boat by *HMS Lark* and *Alnwick Castle*

On the night of 16th/17th February, ships of the 7th and 8th Escort Groups were employed in carrying out

on A/S search in the approaches to Kola Inlet prior to the sailing of RA 64.

Ships were disposed in line abreast in the order **Lapwing**, **Bamborough Castle**, **Cygnet** (SO), **Alnwick Castle**, and **Lark** from left to right, 2,000 yards apart, course 280° speed 10 knots, carrying out zigzag No.45. Visibility was good, wind WSW force 3 no swell. Escorts had Unifoxers streamed, and apart from their slight interference, Asdic conditions were good.

At 0016 **Lark** reported on T.B.S. that she was investigating an Asdic contact on her starboard side, and since it was classified 'firm' at 1200 yards **Alnwick Castle** was ordered to join her. And the remainder of the Group turned 180°. **Lark** passed ranges and bearings to **Alnwick Castle** until the latter reported firm contact at 0043. **Lark** not being fitted with A.T.W or Type 147B, wisely ordered her consort to attack with Squid and a pattern was fired at 0059.

Meanwhile **Cygnet**, **Lapwing** and **Bamborough Castle** were forming up to carry out operation 'OBSERVANT', sides North and South but using 3 mile legs so as to minimize interference by Unifoxers to the attacking ships.

At 0101 **Lark** reported her Asdic set out of action, so **Bamborough Castle** was ordered to join **Alnwick Castle**. This was cancelled at 0109 when **Lark** reported her Asdics fit for action again. Three minutes later **Alnwick Castle** reported lost contact and commenced 'OBSERVANT' on a datum course of 240 degrees, round the calcium flare dropped on her Squid pattern. **Lark** reported she had regained contact at a range of 800 yards at 0117, followed almost immediately by the report "Submarine in sight bearing 110 degrees". Starshell were first sighted and then a lively encounter witnessed when both **Lark** and **Alnwick Castle** engaged the U-boat with 4-inch, close range weapons, a pattern of Squid, set shallow, and the Port D/C thrower. During this action the U-boat was observed to fire a red and green coloured cartridge

At 0123 **Alnwick Castle** requested permission to board, but cancelled this a minute later when the U-boat had been observed to sink stern first and **Lark** ordered her to pick up survivors. The position of the sinking was 040° Tsyp Navolok 10° miles (69°31'10N 33°49'30E). **Alnwick Castle** lowered a boat and succeeded in picking up one live German.

At 0234 the Group reformed and the A/S search continued to the Westward. **Alnwick Castle** reported a fading radar contact at 0520 bearing 355 degrees 4.5 miles, and although **Lark** could not confirm the contact, it was considered worthwhile detaching the two ships to search the area. Unfortunately, no opportunity presented itself for a repeat performance of their earlier success, and at 0700 both ships were ordered to rejoin.

Whilst sweeping back to the Eastward, course was shaped so as to pass through the area in which the U-boat had been sunk, and at 0835 **Cygnet** sighted a yellow inflatable dinghy containing a corpse in position 325 degrees Kildin Lighthouse 10 miles (69°31'10N 33°53'00E) also a considerable quantity of oil covering a large area.

Lark Torpedoed

At 1024 ships were steering 090°, speed 10 knots, carrying out zigzag No. 45, Unifoxers streamed, visibility was extreme and Convoy RA 64, was in sight to the Southward range 8 miles, also 6 Russian T-Boats steaming at high speed towards the group, when an explosion was observed aft in **Lark**. The Group was immediately ordered to carry out 'OBSERVANT' round **Lark**, who reported her stern blown off and unable to steam. Depth charges were dropped intermittently, and **Lapwing** ordered to prepare to take **Lark**

in tow. The Russian T-Boats were by now steaming round *Lark* at high speed, dropping occasional depth charges - this did improve the chances of detecting the U-boat. The position of the torpedoing was 0520 Kildin Lighthouse 12 miles (69°30'28N 34°35'30E).

At 1155, No.34 in the convoy was reported as having been torpedoed, her position then being about 5 miles to the South West of *Lark*. A few minutes later a report was received of a periscope sighting just off the Port quarter of the convoy as it was forming up, so at 1220 *Alnwick Castle* was ordered to join *Cygnet* and a search was carried out in the approximate area of the sighting. A boat with survivors from No.34, was passed at 1240 (they were informed that a destroyer was about to pick them up; *Onslaught* was seen closing to do so). No contacts having been obtained by 1300, and the convoy well clear of the area *Cygnet* and *Alnwick Castle* swept back to *Lark* and continued with OBSERVANT.

Several Asdic contacts were obtained within the next two hours, both *Alnwick Castle* and *Bamborough Castle* fired Squid Patterns, but all were of a doubtful nature. One Russian Destroyer arrived at 1415 and made on unsuccessful attempt to take *Lark* in tow, eventually getting the towing wire round its own propellers. All efforts to persuade the other Russian escorts, which were standing by the abandoned merchantman, to join *Lark* so that the Group could rejoin the convoy were abortive.

Bluebell was reported torpedoed at 1523, the flash of the explosion was observed to the Eastward, so it was decided to remove all non-essential personnel from *Lark*. *Alnwick Castle* and *Bamborough Castle* were detailed for this operation which was completed by 1640. The Russian tug and escorts eventually arrived at 1656, when *Lark* was handed over to them and *Cygnet* and *Bamborough Castle* set course to rejoin the convoy.

HMS BAMBOROUGH CASTLE'S REPORT
HMS BAMBOROUGH CASTLE
27th FEBRUARY 1945

Sir,
I have the honour to submit the following report on action between His Majesty's Ship *Bamborough Castle*, escorting convoy RA 64, and enemy torpedo bombers which attacked at 1006A on the 20th February, 1945 in position 72°58'N 17°46'E.

2. HM Ship was distant 10 miles, on bearing 250° from the centre of the convoy, stationed 360° distant 4,000 yards from *HMS Allington Castle*, (Senior Officer of Group IV of the extended screen), carrying out an independent zigzag on convoy course of 270°.

3. The weather at the time was; wind S.W. force 4, sea and swell 34, visibility variable from 2 to 3 miles with drizzle.

4. At 1000A when on course 300°, enemy aircraft were sighted, bearing 180° distant three miles on course of approximately 360°. These aircraft were identified as nine Ju-88 torpedo bombers, in a 'V' formation of three groups of three. Oerlikon fire was opened on the leader when he came within range. Two planes promptly released their torpedoes and all turned away. The leader was seen to be hit several times with Oerlikon fire and was on fire when last seen. This plane disappeared in the mist on a bearing of 150°, steering about 180°. This plane was not considered sufficiently damaged to justify claiming a probable.

5. With the torpedoes dropped course was altered to comb tracks. Two underwater explosions were heard about ten minutes later it was thought that these were torpedoes exploding at the end of their run. No W/T report of these torpedoes being fired was made as they were seen to be running clear of all ships and W/T traffic was already heavy.

6. Several more enemy aircraft were sighted between 1010A and 1045A but none came within gun range or attempted to attack. They all appeared to be trying to thread their way between the groups of the outer screen and sheered off as soon as they sighted an escort.

7. All the planes which were sighted were Ju-88 torpedo bombers.

Sgd
Lieutenant Commander, R.N.R.
Commanding Officer.

HMS ALNWICK CASTLE'S REPORT

FROM: **THE COMMANDING OFFICER, HMS ALNWICK CASTLE**
DATE: **19th FEBRAURY,1945   REF. A.C. 145**
TO: **THE SENIOR OFFICER, 7TH ESCORT GROUP**

REPORT OF PROCEEDINGS

All times GMT

On the night of the 16th February, 1945, whilst on anti submarine sweep off Kola Inlet, ships in company, **HMS Cygnet** EG 7 (SO), **HMS Lark, HMS Lapwing, HMS Bamborough Castle**. Course of sweep 280° **HMS Alnwick Castle** being one mile on **HMS Lark**'s Port beam, Unifoxers streamed. At 2315, **HMS Lark** gained contact and **HMS Alnwick Castle** was ordered by Senior Officer to join her. **HMS Alnwick Castle** turned towards, and reduced to 8 knots and contact at 2340, ran over, confirmed contact was submarine and at 2359 attacked with Squid; depth of submarine by Type 147 was 40 feet. Contact was lost in run out, **HMS Alnwick Castle** turned and steered course as advised by plot, no contact gained, and about to commence Observant round last known position of submarine, when at 0017 on the 17th February, 1945, radar reported small echo bearing 001° at 1100 yards. HM Ship increased to full speed to close, illuminated the target with rocket projectiles, and the U-boat was sighted, and engaged with close range weapons and 4-inch gun. Hits on the conning tower were obtained by bridge oerlikon but no hits by 4-inch observed. A pattern of Squid set to 20 feet was fired by eye, but it fell short by about 50 yards. **HMS Lark** crossed ahead firing at submarine; cease fire was ordered. When within 100 yards of submarine, searchlight was switched on and depth charge from Port thrower fired which fell about 10 to 15 yards short, but in line. Conning tower was observed to be very badly damaged and crew abandoning, and many were in the water shouting. Submarine was observed to sink stern first at 0036, bows coming out of the water.

    HMS Alnwick Castle closed position to pick up survivors, boat being lowered, but only one survivor

was found, it is considered that extreme cold overcame the reminder before they could be reached. HM Ship then rejoined group to continue sweep. On passing over area at daylight, the Senior Officer reported seeing oil and one corpse in rubber dinghy.

Sgd H.A. Stonehouse
Lieutenant Commander, RNR

EXTRACT FROM CAMPANIA'S REPORT

JW 64/RA 64 continued. Another hurricane, lasting 24 hours, scattered the convoy for a second time. The furious seas were exhausting for us in a 16,000- tons ship, but in the destroyers and smaller escorts it must have been a thousand times worse. In the **Campania**, it was almost impossible to stand without support. Men walking along the alleyways looked like drunks staggering from side to side. I tried going from the bridge to the wardroom aft: one moment I felt like a fairy with my feet hardly touching the ground, and the next I was like an elephant with feet of lead - I could hardly get my feet off the ground. To get to the wardroom required almost as much effort as walking three miles. I just got there when the ship gave a terrific roll from side to side. She went through 81 degrees. Tables screwed to the deck were wrenched from their fixings; chairs, crockery, books, settees everything was slung in a heap of debris in one corner, and on top of the mound of struggling officers. It was amazing no one was hurt. Yet even more amazing, everyone was laughing. The Germans would have cursed; Italians probably have wept; but these British men were laughing. In the alleys and messdecks it was the same. The sailors were laughing, and in the operations room a few minutes later I found Captain Short. He was standing with a mug of cocoa in one hand and a huge sandwich in the other. He was talking to the Admiral and they were both grinning as though they had paid a bob to ride on a non-stop switchback.

After twenty-four hours the wind began easing and we started reforming the convoy for a second time. We began to take stock of the situation. It was not very encouraging. One merchant ship reported a split deck, as a result of the bad weather, another was steering with block and tackle because her steering gear had been smashed. Others could move no quicker than walking pace. Destroyers reported smashed boats and wrecked gear. Then once again the Ju-88s arrived. But instead of the convoy they chose a single straggler - the **Henry Bacon** - nineteen of them attacked her. She didn't have a chance, but she fought for a quarter-of-an-hour and damaged two aircraft before she went down. I'm glad to say our destroyers picked up most of her gallant crew. For the rest of the dreary voyage we rolled and rocked along at three or four knots; an occasional hour or two at six knots was a luxury. Then, when we were almost in sight of Britain the sun came out, a pale watery sun that showed up the salt-caked funnels of the merchant ships and escorts against the wintry sky, but to us, this sun was a symbol of home. Bone weary and exhausted though we all were. Admiral McGregor had got us home.

ARCTIC CONVOYS JW 65 & RA 65
EXTRACTS FROM "THE WAR AT SEA" VOL.III
S.W. ROSKELL

On the 11th March (1945) JW 65 of 24 ships, left the Clyde for Murmansk, under the charge of Admiral Dalrymple-Hamillton, who was flying his flag in the **Campania**. This time the enemy's intelligence gave him better warning of the movement, and two days after the convoy's departure six Schnorkel U-boats sailed from Narvik to patrol west of Bear island, while others concentrated off Kola Inlet. On the 14th the Germans started to fly daily air searches; but they failed to find the convoy, and it passed safely through

the U-boat patrol line. The fact that this convoy enjoyed unusually good weather until just before reaching its destination makes the failure of the German reconnaissance all the more inexplicable. On the 20th March, when the convoy was approaching Kola Inlet a snowstorm put a stop to all flying from the escort carriers at a critical juncture, and the six U-boats lying in wait were able to seize their opportunity. They sank the sloop *Lapwing* and two merchantmen right outside the entrance.

The Russian Navy had meanwhile carried out a request that a channel should be swept through the German minefield north of Kola, to enable the convoys to approach or leave Murmansk by a shorter and more direst route. We made the first use of this route when RA 65 of twenty five ships, sailed on the 23rd March. The frigates of the escort once again went ahead of the convoy to harass the U-boats, nine of which were now lying in wait, with time four destroyers put up a pyrotechnic display on the old route to draw the enemy in that direction. This ruse, combined with the strong anti-submarine measures, was wholly successful; for no U-boat even reported the sailing of the convoy until it was well on its way to the west. Although the enemy then sent several U-boats in pursuit, and also flew air searches, they did not succeed in locating the convoy, all of whose ships reached British ports safely."

7th ESCORT GROUP HMS CYGNET
CONVOYS JW 66 AND RA 66
15 APRIL - 8 MAY 1945

Group comprised *Cygnet* (SO) *Oxlip*, *Lotus*, *Honeysuckle*, *Rhododendron*, *Allington Castle*, *Alnwick Castle*,*Bamborough Castle*, *Farnham Castle*.

April 16th at 2300 Group passed boom with the Castles taking up positions as close escort for the convoy. The next afternoon *Allington Castle* reported defective steering gear and she returned to harbour for repairs. Passage northward was without serious incident. Some of the escorts reporting minor faults that were put right after a short time. At 0600 April 25th *Cygnet* assumed SO and advanced screen from *Zealous*.

Advanced Screen *Farnham Castle*, *Alnwick Castle*, *Stord*, *Cygnet*, *Offa*, *Bamborough Castle*. The close screen was mainly Flower Class plus some Russian s/m chasers. During the morning scaring depth charges were dropped frequently. 1231 *Alnwick Castle* attacked a possible submarine with Squid; *Farnham Castle* sent in support. At 1300 both ships reported the contact as 'non-sub'. Shortly afterwards Foxers were recovered on the orders of D2 and speed reduced to 8 knots. Two of the close escort were ordered to place a smoke screen around the convoy. After some alarms due to contacts subsequently classified as non-sub, the first ships entered Kola Inlet at 1433. The Group turned and proceeded seaward to form a patrol and proceeded to patrol the entrance to Kola Inlet. EG 19 also formed a patrol in line abreast to seaward. The escorts entered Kola Inlet shortly after 2100 after a successful passage of the convoy without loss.

RA 66 Homeward Passage

April 29th 1230. Orders for a preliminary sweep off Kola Inlet passed to EG7 and EG9. The Group weighed at 1645 and proceeded to patrol their designated area. *Rhododendron* had a temporary hick-up with her steering gear. Patrolling started at 1830 course 030° speed 8 knots in line abreast 3,000 yards apart.

The Group was formed into two divisions for this purpose. The first division consisting of *Cygnet*, *Honeysuckle*, *Lotus* and *Farnham Castle* was ordered to sweep to the western half of the areas allocat-

ed. The second division under *Alnwick Castle* and consisting of *Alnwick Castle*, *Rhododendron*, *Oxlip*, and *Bamborough Castle*, was ordered to sweep the eastern half. The sweep was carried out about 2 miles astern of the 19th Escort Group who proceeded the 7th Escort Group out of harbour to carry out a sweep to the northward.

At 1902 *Loch Inch* (19th EG) was observed to fire a pattern of Squid and shortly afterwards opened fire astern with close range weapons. A surfaced U-boat was sighted about 4,000 yards ahead of *Cygnet*. It appeared to be fully surfaced and was stern on when first sighted. The U-boat turned slowly to starboard until she was beam on to *Cygnet*. The U-boat was engaged with *Cygnet's* forward group of 4-inch guns and she sank at 1910 vertically, stern first. *Cygnet* fired 28 rounds from twin 4-inch guns and 10 were considered to be hits on or near the conning tower. The whole action lasted 8 minutes.

Cygnet and *Lotus* covered *Loch Inch* who after the U-boat sank, lowered a whaler, until she continued with her sweep at 1928 (*Loch Inch* recovered survivors from the U-boat).

HMS Goodall was torpedoed at 1938 about 3 miles ahead, while engaged in the sweep to the northward with EG19. *Honeysuckle* and *Farnham Castle* were sent to pick up survivors and rescued 17 and 24 respectively. *Honeysuckle* went alongside the wreck and in doing so the ship's side was severely scorched (from oil burning on the sea surface) and holed above the waterline.

At 2045 and 2145 *Cygnet* obtained contact in positions 259° KK 11 and 281° KX 9.2 miles. These contacts were heavily depth charged and were later believed to be non subs.

At 2111 *Rhododendron* reported to *Alnwick Castle* that a torpedo had been fired at *Alnwick Castle* who later searched a definite submarine contact which was attacked with two patterns of Squid which produced no evidence of destruction. The subsequent decision of the U-boat Assessment Committee was:- Taking into consideration information obtained from German records, the attack is assessed "Probably Slightly Damaged" (*Ref A.U.D. 949/45 26th September 1945 & ADM 199/1786*)

Alnwick Castle was then ordered to remain in the vicinity and search the area with *Rhododendron*, until the convoy came out.

The 7th Escort Group meanwhile reached the limit of their sweep and turned and joined the convoy with out further incident at the entrance to Kola Inlet at 2334.

The greatest credit is due to the commanding officer of *HMS Rhododendron* in the way he placed his ship alongside the burning wreck and rescued survivors from *Goodall*.

It is remarkable after five and a half years of war yet another ship has been sunk and members of the crew were not wearing life belts or life lines thereby causing greater loss of life than may have otherwise been the case.

SECRET

OPERATION ROUNDEL - PASSAGE OF CONVOYS JW 66 AND RA 66

Page 2 of Rear Admiral Commanding Tenth Cruiser Squadron's Report
No D1/734/12 dated 9th May 1945

All the escorts and the sixteen sub-chasers; the latter's unpredictable movements (as he put it) might help to bewilder the enemy. The carriers, screened by three destroyers and **Bellona** stood off to the North-East, and their aircraft did some extensive searching and depth-charging of the water ahead of the convoy. Lines of sono-buoys were also dropped by Swordfish to help detection but they unfortunately gave no contacts. The carriers put in some really intensive flying and are to be congratulated on their work.Just as I had decided on the QZ channel for entry, the Senior Officer Nineteenth Escort Group reported mines detected by Asdic to the Northward of the entrance to it; a very smart piece of Asdic work, but somewhat embarrassing. As this point could be avoided and the water in the vicinity had been passed over by the Nineteenth Escort Group and the Russian White Sea escort, I decided that the risk was less than that of taking the longer passage through dangerous water via MX. The safe entry of the whole convoy reflects great credit on Captain (D) Second Destroyer Flotilla and on the Commodore, Sir Roy Gill KBE, RD, RNR, who kept his ships in a compact order and at good speed until well inside.

Captain (D) Second Destroyer Flotilla and five destroyers then returned to bring the carriers and **Bellona** into harbour, the passage being made during the darker hours. Smoke was tried but a following wind spoilt it and destroyers were not available to act as smoke layers steaming on a reverse course. As it was, each destroyer steamed along in its own small white smoke cloud looking rather like a poached egg.

Polyarnoe

6. While at Vaenga I went to Polyarnoe to see the Senior British Naval Officer to make arrangements with him for the sailing of RA 66. Admiral Golovko gave a 'prasnik' for the Senior British Naval Officer, myself and the Captains. The toast-drinking I was glad to find not nearly as formidable as formerly. The Admiral was extremely friendly and there was much veiled talk of meeting us all at Vladivostok before long, which seemed a good omen. He was also most cooperative and fell in with everything I asked for. This included the provision of hunter craft to drop depth charges and the switching on of all lights and radio beacons two evenings before we sailed, to simulate the departure of the convoy in the hopes of misleading the U-boats. Our part was to increase the Port wave traffic and carry out a T.B.S. exercise. He also agreed to search for the mines reported by the Senior Officer, Nineteenth Escort Group and to provide destroyers and hunter craft to follow the convoy out five miles astern for rescue work. Both on entry and leaving, the Russian Catalinas did some very useful and successful work, searching for, and attacking, U-boats. This novel helpful attitude on the part of the Russians is, I am sure, the direct result of the friendly relations established by Rear Admiral H.J. Egerton who I am also sure turned the scale to allow operation 'Trammell'.

Departure of RA 66.

7. I decided to sail RA 66 on Sunday 29th April during the darker hours, to give an extra day's rest to escorts and put an extra strain on the waiting U-boats. The rest was rather interfered with by the strenuous exchange of hospitality between the Russians and the destroyers at Polyarnoe. Further, **Rhododendron** had a dynamo defect which might not have been ready before 29th.

8. The Seventh and Nineteenth Escort Groups went out at 1800 to search out and attack any U-boats near the track of the convoy. The convoy formed in four columns while still in the Fjord and Captain (D) Second Destroyer Flotilla took them out again without losing a ship. The carriers and **Bellona** sailed as soon as the destroyer screen could be taken from the convoy.

Loss of **HMS Goodall**

9. I deeply regret the loss of this fine Frigate with her Captain and so many of her officers and men. She was torpedoed just after her Group had successfully sunk a U-boat during the searching operations before the convoy sailed. (This has been reported on separately in my No.734/12 of 6th May. 1945)

The conduct of the Commanding Officer, **HMS Honeysuckle** laying his ship alongside under hazardous conditions to rescue survivors was most praiseworthy. On Thursday I attended a memorial service on board **Vindex** for those who were lost.

Estimate of U-Boat threat on Sailing.

10. The following is an estimate of the U-boats present in the area :-

One U-boat found and sunk by the Nineteenth Escort Group. Another which torpedoed **Goodall**, and was attacked by **Cotton** and **Anguilla** and was probably destroyed. One whose torpedo was seen to miss **Alnwick Castle**, sighted and attacked by Russian aircraft. A fourth sighted and attacked by **Zodiac**. Numerous other contacts by screening destroyers, none of which were confirmed.

I can only repeat what has appeared frequently in similar reports, that the passage of a large convoy out through the approaches to Kola with a pack of U-boats concentrated on their route in water notoriously bad for Asdics is most hazardous.

That this took place without loss to the merchant ships is a singular achievement on the part of the Senior Officers, Nineteenth and Seventh Escort Groups, who, with their Escort Groups, cleared the way, not, unfortunately, without loss to themselves; and on the part of Captain (D) Second Destroyer Flotilla, who, in command of his vigilant escorts, carried the responsibility for this part of the passage. The discipline of the merchant ships under their Commodore contributed greatly to their own safety.

Return Passage of RA 66

10. The weather was again favourable and the conduct and speed of the convoy exemplary

11. As was to be expected the Convoy was not so lucky in remaining undetected. Ju-88 reconnaissance air-craft obtained contact at 1722 on 1st May and thereafter groups of 3, 4 and on one occasion 5 came in at about 8 hourly intervals to verify our Position, Course and Speed. Wildcats were used to drive them off as soon as they appeared on the Radar screen. A paucity of Radar reports and the very high speed of these reconnaissance Ju-88s made interceptions difficult. **Vindex** fought off two; in one the German obviously saw the fighters first and in the second the Ju-88 was attacked and damaged.

12. It looked as though the Germans would try and synchronise an air and U-boat attack in the vicinity of Bear Island. I therefore passed within 20 miles of this Island and kept the Nineteenth Escort Group until clear of this area. The convoy then proceeded along the 74th parallel to near the meridian of Greenwich

before turning south to keep at a good range from Bardufoss. The last reconnaissance was at 1830 on 3rd May after which we were left in peace as I imagine the Vice Admiral Commanding First Cruiser Squadron's most successful operation was occupying their full attention. I fully expected an attack by Torpedo planes but for some reason they were deterred from making the attempt.

Ice

13. A Swordfish was flown to Bear Island and could see no sign of ice near the Island. There was no sign of ice in our North-Westerly position 74° North 2° East but the sea temperature in that region was 29° Fahrenheit.

Signals

14. Much internal signalling would be saved if all signals from shore authorities which concern the escorts were addressed 'All Escorts of Convoy'. A number were addressed individually to CS 10, D 2, EG 7, EG 19.

Russian Aircraft

15. Although the Russian Catalinas were very effective in the area round Kola they are less so in the longer flights in the Barents Sea. HF/DF bearings indicated a U-boat track from the Rybachi Peninsula to the Bear Island Strait. If this could be watched by the Catalinas they would be of much more use on this than on their present flights to inspect the convoy. As their IFF seldom works they cause confusion and risk fire from our ships or attack by our fighters.

Minefields

16. From evidence of the prisoners taken from the U-boat sunk by Nineteenth Escort Group, it was not damaged by the mines laid by *Apollo*, but it is hoped that others were. The mines resisted depth-charging but became rather expensive in Foxers which had to be slipped whenever escorts neared the fields. With regard to the mines reported by Senior Officer, Nineteen-Escort Group, Russian minesweepers were observed to be searching the area when we sailed, and, Senior British Naval Officer, North Russia, will no doubt report the result.

Route

17. Red Route was followed by both convoys except that between positions G and D, RA 66 passed through 74° North 2° East, 74° N 20°E 74°N 02°E and then to position ZA 71°N 01°E (to meet *Blue Ranger*)

Carriers

18. The work of the carriers was most impressive. I met many of the young pilots and observers in both ships and I cannot speak too highly of the way they responded to all calls for patrols and interceptions, often under conditions of thick weather and probable icing, and their disappointment at the lack of opportunities for more offensive action. The general efficiency with which *Vindex* and *Premier* operated their aircraft was most marked.

19. As JW and RA 66 were the last convoys of the series PQ, QP JW and RA subjected to lawful enemy attack, I should like to pay a tribute to our predecessors whose experience and ingenuity have evolved all the methods we used to safeguard the convoy.

REAR ADMIRAL

(Source ADM 199/1339 180-182)

B21 ESCORT GROUP

Early in September 1944 the B21 Escort Group was formed with **Hesperus** as Senior Officer and **Rushen Castle**, **Flint Castle Bluebell** and **Pimpernel**. After one voyage to Gibraltar and back **Hesperus** left the Group and **Rushen Castle** (Lieut Cmndr C. Warwick DCS**, RNR) took over as Senior Officer, with two Flowers **Pimpernel** and **Clover** forming the Group which continued to escort convoys to and from Gibraltar. However, it should be noted that in his ROP for Convoy OS90/KMS 64 the Senior Officer stated that "...this was the first voyage of the newly formed B21 Group."

This arrangement continued until mid-December 1944 when **Rushen Castle** was allocated to the Liverpool Escort Pool (LEP). She continued to work the Gibraltar route as Senior Officer; but not infrequently becoming the only escort.

Between 4th September 1944 and 12th December 1944 the B21 Escort Group escorted seven convoys totalling 245 ships. These were:-

SL 169/MKS 50	23 Ships	09/09 - 17/09/44	
OS 90/KMS 64	30 "	24/09 - 01/10/44	
SL 172/MKS 63	23 "	09/10 - 16/10/44	
OS 93/KMS 67	30 "	25/10 - 01/11/44	
SL 175/MKS 66	38 "	07/11 - 14/11/44	
OS 96/KMS 70	40 "	23/11 - 27/11/44	Convoy dispersed
SL 178/MKS 69	61 "	05/12 - 12/12/44	

7 Convoys   245 Ships.

These voyages were undisturbed by the enemy and generally without incident. On the first voyage as Senior Officer, Rushen Castle experienced condenser problems during the first 24 hours and had to put in to Milford Haven for repairs - rejoining the convoy a day later. The trouble persisted so that both boilers were given a three minute blow down every four hours so as to control salinity in the boiler water.

At the Commodore's request an L.A gunnery practice was organised for the convoy. Smoke floats as targets were dropped for each of the seven columns. All ships fired an average of four rounds, and after making 14 emergency turns the convoy was almost in perfect station. Fourteen hits were scored by ten ships. Gunlaying was either good or very poor. No ships were damaged.

On the return voyage (SL172/MKS63) there was an interesting occurrence when a ship echo was reported by radar 7 miles ahead and steering straight towards the centre of the convoy. **Rushen Castle** increased to full speed to intercept, but was unable to raise the other ship by light even at a range of less than 1,000 yards. A red shaded Aldis lamp being used. When the stranger was on the port quarter identities were exchanged and **HMS Redpole** was given the course and distance to take her clear of the convoy. She was a considerable distance from her expected position given in the Situation Report. The SO commented "that had we been in other waters, we should have opened fire when she was abeam of us , as we were ready to do so." At Headquarters the SO commented "**Rushen Castle** does not state whether she endeavoured to "Challenge" **Redpole**. It would appear that he did not, but exchanged identities since he considered that the other ship to be friendly. This was correct. Should he have challenged, there is no objection to using a red Aldis. The criteria when challenging by flashing is to use a light which is sufficiently bright :-

      a)   To attract attention and
      b)   To be read by the other ship, with a minimum of flashing.
(The brightness of the light used can only correctly be gauged by the 'man of the spot'.)

If **Rushen Castle** had been in 'other waters' and there had been possibility of meeting a friendly ship, he would assuredly have lit up the other ship before pressing the trigger." (*ADM 217/586 539/IRP*)

Whilst on passage **Rushen Castle** carried out an endurance test on anti Gnat equipment. Type B Displacer P/Vs and towing gear were streamed for 6 days 15 hours. The distance run was 1,900 miles with the ship carrying out a 40/50 degree zigzag across the front of a nine column convoy making good 7 to 7.5 knots. It was concluded that the test demonstrated that escort corvettes of a slow convoy (7 - 10 knots) can steam with Type B displacers streamed for at least 7-8 days in moderate to bad weather and heavy swell. Fifteen degrees of helm can be used with safety for carrying out a broad zigzag of 40 to 50 degrees at speeds of 10 to 12 knots.

On another occasion whilst passing westbound through the Straits of Gibraltar an aircraft on patrol dropped parachute flares close to and over the convoy. The type 253 of all the escorts was switched on and IFF was obtained from the aircraft. Nevertheless the captain of the aircraft, who was presumably searching for the U-boat reported to be in the area, placed the convoy under a 'Blackpool Illumination' making the ships visible for ten miles, and disclosing his own position to any U-boat within forty miles. **Rushen Castle** suggested that if aircraft wish to practice illumination they should choose a Support Group, rather than a convoy.

Whilst escorting convoy SL 178/MKS 69 in which some of the ships had originated from the Eastern Mediterranean **Rushen Castle** received a signal from the Commodore to the effect that an army deserter on a ship from Haifa had been found in the hold. Assistance from the crew was suspected but there was no proof. The Commodore required advice on the appropriate procedure. **Rushen Castle**'s reply which was reproduced in the Western Approaches Bulletin for the information of others, read:-

"Reference Army Deserter.

1. Master should make a thorough investigation with a view to establishing identity and a note taken in writing of the proceedings. Deserter to be asked formally if he has any statement to make, and such statement if any to be signed and witnessed.
2. Deserter should be kept under lock and key and under armed guard, if considered necessary. D.E.M.S. ratings may be used for this purpose.
3. Military Authorities at port of destination should be informed on arrival. The latter should send escort for deserter. Report of investigation and statement should be handed over to N.C.O. in charge of escort, and receipt obtained for deserter.
4. Suggest Master takes no action regarding suspected assistance from crew until he has taken advice on the matter from shore authorities. K.R.&.A.I. does not cover this problem. We do not hold copy of Merchant Shipping Act"

It would of course have been comparatively easy for Army men employed on the docks to stow away, and with the help of the crew, could remain undiscovered until the ship docked, when the stowaway could literally don a bowler hat and walk ashore.

The maintenance of sensitive equipment at sea was a re-occurring problem. In addition to frequent condenseritis problems **Rushen Castle** also suffered from frequent defects to the 272 Radar set. These defects were attributed by the C.O to excessive vibration of the mast and he referred to tests that he understood to have been carried out on **Hadleigh Castle** .

The Base Radar Officer minuted as follows:-

Rushen Castle *has suffered more than most ships with 272 from faults in the aerial system. The effect of vibration on type 272 is well-known and has been reported to Admiralty on several occa-*

sions. However, I do not think that there is a case for asking for the lattice mast to be heavily rein-
forced to reduce vibration, (supposing that this were possible), as the mast was designed to take the
277 aerial, (a much more robust structure than the 272 aerial system), and from experience so far
gained with 277, the mast appears to be quite adequate for this purpose.

The majority of the faults could sometimes and now normally are, prevented by regular inspec-
tion and tightening up of components concerned. I have asked Capt. (D) Liverpool's TR.O to pay
particular attention to ensure that regular inspection is carried out at sea of components such as the
pedestal gearing system, which can only be stripped in harbour, are taken down and examined as
opportunities occur.

The difficulty of broken leads has been overcome by fitting a junction box in the lantern so that
only this portion has to be replaced, a job which can be carried out in HM Ships in about a quar-
ter of an hour".

Another problem common to all the Castle Class Corvettes was the shipping of seas onto the quartedeck.
After **Rushen Castle**'s main dynamo was put out of action when a heavy sea shipped in the port waist
flooded down the dynamo ventilator intake. It was suggested that the dynamo ventilators might be raised
to the level of the engine room casing, as in the event of the ship being pooped, both ventilators would be
flooded as the water would not clear fast enough through the scuppers, and freeing ports in the bulwarks.

Capt. (D) Liverpool commented:

"The dynamo ventilators are now situated between six and seven feet above the main deck level and
should be quite satisfactory except in the case of a direct green sea when siting at the level of the
engine room casing would be little if any better."

B22 ESCORT GROUP

The first record of a Castle Class Corvette within the Group is on the 14th March 1944 with **Oxford**
Castle allocated to the Group when she arrived at Tobermory for working up. At that time the Senior
Officer of the Group was borne by **Hesperus**. **HMS Cotton** took over on 4th September 1944. **Leeds**
Castle apparently assumed command of the Group for one voyage in January 1945, but by the end of that
month the Senior Officer was **Oxford Castle**. Apart from the one report of **Leeds Castle** joining the Group,
Oxford Castle was the only Castle Class Corvette included in the Group which was solely concerned with
escorting the Gibraltar convoys. Accounts of the Group's voyages are therefore included in the those of
Oxford Castle.

B23 ESCORT GROUP

This Group, engaged on escorting convoys to and from Gibraltar were involved in providing an escort to 330 ships in 11 convoys from 12th September 1944 to 30th April 1945. Reports of Proceedings were not found for all those convoys. Those that were are summarised below.

HMS KNARESBOROUGH CASTLE B23 OS 89/KMS; 33 SHIPS
12-23 SEPT '44
(COMMODORE H.J. ANCHOR OBE RD RNR)
ADM 217/578 & ADM 199/317
10th EG IN SUPPORT 16th-17th

Close escort comprised *Knaresborough Castle* (SO) (Commander D. M. MacLean RNR), *Oxlip*, and initially *Bluebell*,who was replaced by *Leeds Castle* on 15th September.

The Group left Clyde on 12th Sept in poor visibility but were diverted to Belfast because their convoy was 24 hours late. Meanwhile *Oxlip* had signalled that two ships of the convoy, *Empire Archer* and *Fjordass* had grounded on N.W. Rathlin. Tugs were sent for and *Oxlip* and *Bluebell* stood by them. In due course the ships were refloated *Fjordass* proceeded to the Clyde and *Empire Archer* to Belfast, holed and down by the head.

On the 17th September the 10th EG who had been in support for eight hours parted company. Now, with only three escorts for the convoy a spare radar set was put aboard *SS Devis* placed in the rear of the convoy so that she could keep radar guard astern of the convoy during the dark hours. *Leeds Castle* thought it was in contact by radar with a U-boat on the 16th and attacked with squid by plot. Apart from this, it was an uneventful passage. The Group arrived Gibraltar on 23rd, KC having sunk a mine by 4-inch gunfire on the 22nd.

HMS KNARESBOROUGH CASTLE B23 SL 171/MLS 62; 23 SHIPS.
29 SEPT- 9 OCT'44
ADM 217/579

Composition of the group; *Knaresborough Castle* (SO), *Leeds Castle*, *Sharpshooter*, and *Oxlip*.

The Group slipped from the South Mole on 29th Sept to meet MKS.62 of 22 merchant ships plus *HM Submarine Truant* and *HMS Vienna*.

When passing through the swept channel met an east bound convoy. There was little room to pass and the MKS convoy had to make two ten degree emergency turns to starboard to avoid a foul-up and at the same time to reduce the distance between columns. *Leeds Castle* developed main engine problems and returned to Gibraltar. She rejoined the Group on the afternoon of the 30th. On that day the SL convoy was successfully merged; number of ships not stated. Later in the day the weather started to deteriorate with wind and sea increasing from the NNE. On the 2nd the convoy was making 7 knots. On the 3rd and

4th wind force reported as 7. this caused the convoy to fall behind schedule with Admiralty SITREPS consistently putting the convoy tens of miles ahead of her position.

During the night of 3rd /4th **Barin Renfrew** reported a smouldering fire deep in one of her bunkers and later she asked for assistance at her first port of call in moving the coal in that bunker.

At the suggestion of the Commodore the SO detached the Liverpool section early so that the ships could take advantage of the tide. This upset the HQ Staff because the early arrival of the ships caused administration difficulties at the port, and it was against orders. Signal sent to Capt. D Liverpool to that effect. **Leeds Castle** continued to have condenser problems - these were fixed by base staff during lay-over.

The Group passed the Clyde Boom on the 9th.

In his report SO B23 (Commander D. M. Maclean RNR) sought the provision of additional staff as well as a separate Commanding Officer. This was discussed on the minute sheets in some length. Firstly there are not enough specialist officers around for appointment to small 3 ship Groups, and if they were they would be considered as under training for transfer to the Far East Fleet. It was also noted that "...the SO should be borne additional (to the Commanding Officer) is contrary to the policy adopted in all the RN EGs where the Senior Officer is invariably the Commanding Officer as well, except in those cases where a temporary transfer to another ship is made. (This happened with **Tintagel Castle** when the Group SO and staff were transferred for a few voyages - this caused a certain amount of accommodation difficulties).

HMS FOWEY (SO) B23 ESCORT GROUP OS 92/KMS 66; 34 SHIPS
HMS ALLINGTON CASTLE & HMS KNARESBOROUGH CASTLE IN COMPANY
14th - 26th OCTOBER 1944
ADM 217/48 & 199/317

The main features of this voyage was that there were five merchant ships each towing two LCTs and the severe and prolonged gale that occurred from the 17th to 22nd of October 1944. The weather began to deteriorate very rapidly on Tuesday the 17th. During the morning **LCT 488** being towed by **SS Sanfoyle** along with **LCT 489** reported having suffered heavy damage and that the crew would have to abandon ship. At this point it was agreed with the Commodore that all the towing ships should heave to and they were ordered to do so.

Shortly after this **SS Nairnbank** reported that he had lost touch with one of his tows, **LCT 494**. **Allington Castle** was ordered to assist in rescue operations. The Senior Officer then signalled CinC WA reporting the situation and requesting that additional escorts should be sent out to assist. By this time weather conditions had developed to full gale proportions.

The situation of the LCTs continued to worsen. At 1215 **LCT 7022** was reported holed, making water and about to abandon ship. An hour later **LCT 480** was reported by her towing ship to be sinking and being abandoned by her crew. At the same time **LCT 494** in tow by **SS Nairnbank** was requesting assistance.

Allington Castle and **Knaresborough Castle** were ordered to detail any ships in the convoy as required to assist in the rescue operations.

At 1442 **Allington Castle** lost one man overboard whilst preparing the quarter-deck for rescue operations. At that time it seemed that **LCT 488** was able to proceed under her own power towards Milford Haven. **Knaresborough Castle** and **Allington Castle** were ordered at 1503 to return to the convoy. However thirty minutes later **LCT 488** was in serious trouble, her pump had broken down and she was rapidly making water. **Knaresborough Castle** was ordered to stand by her. At 1559 **LCT 480** in tow of **SS City of Lyons** was in distress and about to abandon ship. **Allington Castle** was informed, but it was unknown if she would be able to assist, as she was looking for **LCT 494**.

Half an hour later *SS Nairnbank* reported that *LCT 7014* was in distress ands wished to abandon ship. Her other tow, *LCT 494*, had also sought help four hours earlier. *SS Nairnbank* reported that so as to save one of the LCTs he would have to slip the other.

At 1715 *SS City of Lyons* reported that one of his tows (number not given) as being full of water and sinking. At 1730 *SS Sanfoyle* reported that *LCT 489* had broken adrift.

In the meantime *HM Ships Tobago* and *Kingcup* were approaching the scene and *Allington Castle* was carrying out homing procedures with *Kingcup*. At the same time the Senior Officer of B2 Escort Group reported that he was in touch with *LCT 7014*.

By 2000 *Allington Castle* had rescued the crew of *LCT 480* and sunk the wreck by gunfire. He was ordered to search for *LCT 489*.

Shortly before 0100 on the 19th *Kingcup* reported *LCTs 7022* and *7023* as still being in tow of *SS Ocean Vanity*, and, although damaged, they were expected to last out until daylight. Shortly after this *SS Badjeston* (not a towing ship) sought urgent assistance. He was unable to manoeuvre alongside an LCT (number not given).

At 0300 19th *Kingcup* was in contact with *Ocean Vanity* and her two LCTs. By this time *LCT 491* was in serious trouble. At 0445 *Allington Castle* reported having all survivors from *LCT 491* on board and about to sink it with gunfire.

By noon on the 19th the situation was that all the convoy was badly scattered. Only 12 ships were in sight of the Senior Officer, and as far as was known *LCTs 489*, *494*, and possibly *7022* were adrift and unaccounted for. *LCTs 4023* and *7015* were possibly still under tow. At 0845 *Knaresborough Castle* reported that *LCT 488* had sunk at 0540 and that he had picked up some survivors, loosing his seaboat in the process. *Kingcup* reported that *LCTs 7022* and *7023* were still in tow of *Ocean Vanity* and that he was taking them to Falmouth. *Kingcup* took the two LCTs in tow with the crews still on board, but later on took the crews off. During the afternoon the weather gradually moderated, but deteriorated again a few hours later.

During the morning of the 20th October it became apparent that several merchant ships had suffered weather damage. *Allington Castle* was ordered to stand by them. By noon it was learnt that two of the ships were in no immediate danger. They had hove to and did not require assistance.

At 1554 on the 20th *SS Lagarto* called for immediate assistance. His bridge, boats and compasses having been washed away by heavy seas. *Allington Castle* was instructed to stand by him. The weather at this time was gale force 9 with high seas. The Commodore ordered the convoy to heave-to on a course of 280°. *Allington Castle* had great difficulty under these conditions in finding *Lagarto*, but received valuable help from *SS Bosphorus* who assisted in homing procedures. She found *Lagarto* at 2000. She was running before the wind, badly damaged and making water, but in no way in danger of sinking. One crew member had been washed overboard.

By Saturday morning (21st October) the weather was improving. *Allington Castle* with *Lagarto* were hove to and the latter was securing her deck cargo. The weather continued to improve. *HMS Drury* who had been despatched by CinC WA to take over the care of *Lagarto*, was in sight of *Allington Castle* at 1726 and *Drury* took over *Lagarto* at 1747. *Allington Castle* proceeded to rejoin the convoy. At 1100 on Sunday he reported being in company with 12 stragglers. Homing procedures were carried out with both *Allington Castle* and *Knaresborough Castle*.

Knaresborough Castle rejoined the convoy at 1620 followed by *Allington Castle*, with 12 merchant ships, at 1735.

The whole incident occurred over a period of 5 days of almost continuous very severe weather conditions. The Senior Officer's report of proceedings does not give any indication of the number of lives lost; he would not have been in a position to have done so. There can be no doubt that without the superb handling of the two corvettes and the high standard of seamanship under extreme conditions of their crews, the casualties would have been very much greater.

The remainder of the voyage was without incident. At the conclusion of his report the Senior Officer commented :-

General Remarks

Escort Group B23 consisting of only three ships **HMS Fowey, HMS Allington Castle**, and **HMS Knaresborough Castle** was recently formed, and operating together for the first time. Events during the voyage very definitely proved that three ships are inadequate when escorting a convoy of the dimensions of KMS 66/OS 92, which consisted of no less than 35 merchant ships, 3 HM Submarines and 9 Tank Landing Craft in tow. Although the likelihood of submarine attack is much smaller than formerly, risk of such attacks must still be deemed to exist, and it was impossible to afford anything remotely resembling an anti-submarine screen with this small number of escorts. Furthermore the fact of other emergencies arising such as heavy weather, scattered convoy, casualties and heavy weather damage, ships requiring urgent assistance and medical assistance, must not be overlooked. All the above occurred during the voyage and it was most obvious that the group was all too pitifully small to cope with the situation. Had there been more escorts present, much needless loss of life from the T.L.C' s could have been prevented. It is therefore strongly urged that in future no escort group consists of less than five ships, and that more than one ship in the should carry a Medical Officer.

(Sgd.) G.E. NEWEY   Lieutenant Commander RNR
Senior Officer B 23 Escort Group

HMS FOWEY S.O. B23 EG 0S95/KMS 69; 31 SHIPS.
12th - 24th NOV 1944
(ADM 199/317)

Composition of the Group *Fowey* (SO), *Leeds Castle* & *Bluebell*, sailed 12th Nov 1944 from Clyde to rendezvous with Belfast section. The complete convoy was assembled on the 14th.

On the 15th two Spanish Trawlers were sighted and intercepted by *Leeds Castle* . *Bluebell* boarded one and both trawlers were escorted towards Falmouth by *Bluebell*. The following day, on Admiralty instructions, *Bluebell* returned towards the convoy having ordered the trawlers out of the 'prohibited area'. *Bluebell* rejoined the convoy at 2305 16th.

Apart from a short spell of poor weather resulting in some scattering of the convoy, it was an uneventful voyage. Medical assistance was given to one ship where an acute case of cerebral meningitis was diagnosed. On approaching the Straits, a Greek ship *Nicolas*, which had developed defective steering gear three days earlier, was ordered to reduce speed so as not to arrive at Gibraltar before daylight there being numerous trawlers about with extensive nets. Bluebell was detailed to remain with the ship.

In the afternoon of the 23rd the convoy was dispersed. *Fowey* and *Leeds Castle* moored alongside the oiler hulk and the next morning slipped and berthed within Gibraltar harbour.

HMS KNARESBOROUGH CASTLE (SO) B-23 OS 117/KMS 91; 25 SHIPS
17-26 MARCH'45

Composition of the Group not clearly stated it appears to have been **Knaresborough Castle**, **Amberley Castle**, **Ayrshire**, **Northern Gift**, **Madeline** and **MFV1075**.
The convoy was lying at anchor off bar light vessel on 17th and sailed on 18th. On the 20th the ON Section detached with C7 Group (**Rhododendron**, **Lanark**, **Coppercliff**, **Amherst**, & **Hawkesbury**).

Knaresborough Castle closed some Spanish trawlers in position 47°57'N 08° 33'W, *Alisma* was ordered to detach and take the trawlers to Milford Haven.

On the 26th *HMS Woodruff* was ordered to take over the Group from *Knaresborough Castle*. who proceeded into Gibraltar; the convoy was dispersed off Europa Point.

HMS KNARESBOROUGH CASTLE MKS 92; 41 SHIPS
31st MAR - 5th APRIL '45

The Gibraltar section of the convoy sailed on 31st March 1944 escorted by *Knaresborough Castle*, *Hyderabad*, *Willowherb* & *Spirea* (SO).

Knaresborough Castle 's sailing was delayed but joined the convoy in the Straits of Gibraltar and assumed SO duty. The Casablanca section merged on 1st bringing the convoy up to 41 ships and *HM submarine Storm*.

Three escorts were detached on the 3rd to join convoy O3.119/KMS.93. On the 4th *Knaresborough Castle* destroyed a large raft with a depth charge. On 5th *HMS Fowey* and others joined the convoy. *Fowey* assumed command. Throughout this passage *Knaresborough Castle* had a lot of trouble with malfunctions with Asdics, radar, and HF/DF.

HMS FOWEY OS 120/KMS 94; 21 SHIPS
2nd TO 8th APRIL 1945

Escorts included *Rushen Castle*, *Flint Castle* and *Knaresborough Castle*.

The voyage was without incident. Numerous non-sub contacts were attacked when in coastal waters. The assembly of the convoy was hampered by dense fog.On leaving Liverpool Fighter Direction Exercises were carried out. This was followed by dummy attacks by three Hurricane aircraft for exercising fire distribution. *Fowey* provided a smoke screen using both funnel and C.S.A smoke.
(Source: ADM 199/317)

HMS KNARESBOROUGH CASTLE B-23(?) OS 125/KMS 99; 23 SHIPS.
27th - 30th APR '45

The escorts comprised *Knaresborough Castle* (SO), *Amberley Castle* & *Oxford Castle*

The convoy was joined by EG C7 SO *HMCS Lanark* who assumed command of the operation. The convoy was further reinforced by EG 8 *HMS Loch Achray* (SO).

In the evening of 28th the convoy divided, ON 299 proceeded 4 miles ahead of the OS/KMS convoy with EG C7. *Knaresborough Castle* assumed command of the OS/KMS convoy with escorts *Amberley Castle* & *Oxford Castle*.

On 30th April *Knaresborough Castle* with *Amberley Castle*, *HMCS Lunenburgh* & *HMS Narcissus*, *SS Dewbury* (rescue ship) and EG 8 detached to join convoy MKS 97. *Oxford Castle* continued with OS 125/KMS 99 as sole escort .

Towards the end of the convoy period there arose a difference of opinion between KC and SO 8 regarding disposition of the escorts CinC WA ordering SO 8 to assume command.

APPENDICES

Previous page: **HMS Pevensey Castle**.

Appendix One
CASTLE CLASS PRODUCTION

Ordered 12 December 1942

Name	Pt No	Laid Down	Launched	Completed	Remarks
Allington Castle	K689	22.07.43	29.02.44	19.06.44	

Ordered 19 December 1942

Name	Pt No	Laid Down	Launched	Completed	Remarks
Bamborough Castle	K412	01.07.43	11.01.44	30.05.44	
Caistor Castle	K379	26.08.43	22.05.44	29.09.44	
Denbigh Castle	K696	30.09.43	05.08.44	30.12.44	
Farnham Castle	K413	25.06.43	25.04.44	31.01.45	
Gorey Castle	K529	02.11.43	30.10.44	12.05.45	*Hedingham Castle* (1943)
Hadleigh Castle	K355	04.04.43	21.06.43	18.09.43	
Kenilworth Castle	K420	07.05.43	17.08.43	22.11.43	
Lancaster Castle	K691	10.09.43	14.04.44	15.09.44	
Maiden Castle	K443	00.00.43	08.06.44	00.11.44	Completed as mercantile convoy rescue ship *Empire Lifeguard* (1944)
Oakham Castle	K530	30.11.43	20.07.44	10.12.44	
Pembroke Castle	K450	03.06.43	12.02.44	29.06.44	RCN *Tillsonburg* (1943)
Rayleigh Castle	K695	00.00.43	19.06.44	00.10.44	Completed as mercantile convoy rescue ship *Empire Rest* (1944)
Totnes Castle	K447	30.08.43	12.04.44	06.09.44	*Norham Castle* (1943) then RCN *Humberstone* (1943)

Ordered 19 January 1943

Name	Pt No	Laid Down	Launched	Completed	Remarks
Alnwick Castle	K405	12.06.43	23.05.44	11.11.44	

Name	Pt No	Laid Down	Launched	Completed	Remarks
Barnard Castle	K694	00.00.43	05.10.44	00.00.45	Completed as mercantile convoy rescue ship *Empire Shelter* (1945)
Caldecot Castle	K...				Cancelled December 1943
Dover Castle	K...				Cancelled December 1943
Dudley Castle	K...				Cancelled December 1943
Flint Castle	K383	22.07.43	29.02.44	19.06.44	
Guildford Castle	K378	25.05.43	13.11.43	11.03.43	RCN *Hespeler* (1943)
Hedingham Castle	K396	23.07.43	26.01.44	10.05.44	RCN *Orangeville* (1943)
Knaresborough Castle	K389	22.04.43	28.09.43	05.04.44	
Launceston Castle	K397	27.05.43	27.11.43	20.06.44	
Sandgate Castle	K373	23.06.43	28.12.43	18.05.44	RCN *St Thomas* (1943)
Tamworth Castle	K393	25.08.43	26.01.44	03.07.44	RCN *Kincardine* (1943)
Walmer Castle	K460	23.09.43	10.03.44	05.09.44	RCN *Leaside* (1943)
York Castle	K537	00.00.44	20.09.44	00.02.45	Completed as mercantile convoy rescue ship *Empire Comfort* (1945)

Ordered 23 January 1943

Name	Pt No	Laid Down	Launched	Completed	Remarks
Bere Castle	K...				Cancelled December 1943
Calshot Castle	K...				Cancelled December 1943
Hever Castle	K521	29.06.43	24.02.44	15.08.44	RCN *Copper Cliff* (1943)
Leeds Castle	K384	22.04.43	12.10.43	15.02.44	
Morpeth Castle	K693	23.06.43	26.11.43	13.07.44	
Nunnery Castle	K446	12.08.43	26.01.44	08.10.44	RCN *Bowmanville* (1943)
Oxford Castle	K692	21.06.34	11.12.43	10.03.44	
Peel Castle	K...				*Monmouth Castle* (1943) Cancelled December 1943
Pevensey Castle	K449	21.06.43	11.01.44	10.06.44	
Rhuddlan Castle	K...				Cancelled December 1943
Rising Castle	K398	21.06.43	08.02.44	26.06.44	RCN *Arnprior* (1943)

Name	Pt No	Laid Down	Launched	Completed	Remarks
Scarborough Castle	K536	00.00.44	08.09.44	00.01.45	Completed as mercantile convoy rescue ship *Empire Peacemaker* (1945)
Sherborne Castle	K453	21.06.43	24.02.44	14.07.44	RCN *Petrolia* (1943)
Thornbury Castle	K...				Cancelled December 1943
Tintagel Castle	K399	29.04.43	13.12.43	07.04.44	
Wolvesey Castle	K461	01.06.43	24.02.44	15.06.44	RCN *Huntsville* (1943)

Ordered 2 February 1942

Name	Pt No	Laid Down	Launched	Completed	Remarks
Amberley Castle	K386	31.05.43	27.11.43	24.11.44	
Berkeley Castle	K387	23.04.43	19.08.43	18.11.43	
Carisbrooke Castle	K379	12.03.43	31.07.43	17.11.43	
Dumbarton Castle	K388	06.05.43	28.09.43	25.02.44	
Hurst Castle	K416	06.08.43	23.02.44	09.06.44	

Ordered 6 February 1942

Name	Pt No	Laid Down	Launched	Completed	Remarks
Portchester Castle	K362	17.03.43	21.06.43	08.11.43	
Rushen Castle	K372	08.04.43	16.07.43	24.02.44	
Shrewsbury Castle	K374	05.05.43	16.08.43	29.04.44	RNoN *Tunsberg Castle* (1944)

Ordered 3 March 1943

Name	Pt No	Laid Down	Launched	Completed	Remarks
Appleby Castle	K...				Cancelled December 1943
Tonbridge Castle	K...				Cancelled December 1943

Ordered 4 May 1943

Name	Pt No	Laid Down	Launched	Completed	Remarks
Norwich Castle	K...				Cancelled December 1943
Oswestry Castle	K...				Cancelled December 1943
Pendennis Castle	K...				Cancelled December 1943

Ordered 10 July 1943

Name	Pt No	Laid Down	Launched	Completed	Remarks
Alton Castle	K...				Cancelled December 1943
Warkworth Castle	K...				Cancelled December 1943

It was planned to close Modified Flower class corvette production in Canada and put the shipyards to building Castle class corvettes. In the end, with the Battle of the Atlantic swinging in favour of the Allies, the plan did not come to fruition and all of those Castle class ships ordered from Canadian yards were cancelled before construction began.

Ordered 15 March 1943

Name	Pt No	Shipbuilder	Cancelled
Aydon Castle	K...	Kingston Shipbuilding	Cancelled December 1943
Barnwell Castle	K...	Kingston Shipbuilding	Cancelled December 1943
Beeston Castle	K...	Kingston Shipbuilding	Cancelled December 1943
Bodiam Castle	K...	Collingwood Shipyards	Cancelled December 1943
Bolton Castle	K...	Collingwood Shipyards	Cancelled December 1943
Bowes Castle	K...	Kingston Shipbuilding	Cancelled December 1943
Bramber Castle	K...	Collingwood Shipyards	Cancelled December 1943
Bridgnorth Castle	K...	Collingwood Shipyards	Cancelled December 1943
Brough Castle	K...	Collingwood Shipyards	Cancelled December 1943
Canterbury Castle	K...	Midland Shipbuilding	Cancelled December 1943
Carew Castle	K...	Midland Shipbuilding	Cancelled December 1943
Chepstow Castle	K...	Collingwood Shipyards	Cancelled December 1943
Chester Castle	K...	Collingwood Shipyards	Cancelled December 1943
Christchurch Castle	K...	Midland Shipbuilding	Cancelled December 1943
Clare Castle	K...	Collingwood Shipyards	Cancelled December 1943

Clavering Castle	K...	Collingwood Shipyards	Cancelled December 1943
Clitheroe Castle	K...	Collingwood Shipyards	Cancelled December 1943
Clun Castle	K...	Midland Shipbuilding	Cancelled December 1943
Name	**Pt No**	**Shipbuilder**	**Cancelled**
Colchester Castle	K...	Midland Shipbuilding	Cancelled December 1943
Corfe Castle	K527	Collingwood Shipyards	Cancelled December 1943
Cornet Castle	K528	Collingwood Shipyards	Cancelled December 1943
Cowes Castle	K...	Collingwood Shipyards	Cancelled December 1943
Cowling Castle	K...	Midland Shipbuilding	Cancelled December 1943
Criccieth Castle	K...	Morton (Quebec)	Cancelled December 1943
Cromer Castle	K...	Midland Shipbuilding	Cancelled December 1943
Devizes Castle	K...	Kingston Shipbuilding	Cancelled December 1943
Dhyfe Castle	K...	Collingwood Shipyards	Cancelled December 1943
Dunster Castle	K...	Midland Shipbuilding	Cancelled December 1943
Egremont Castle	K...	Kingston Shipbuilding	Cancelled December 1943
Fotheringay Castle	K...	Morton (Quebec)	Cancelled December 1943
Helmsley Castle	K...	Morton (Quebec)	Cancelled December 1943
Malling Castle	K...	Morton (Quebec)	Cancelled December 1943
Malmesbury Castle	K...	Morton (Quebec)	Cancelled December 1943
Raby Castle	K...	Morton (Quebec)	Cancelled December 1943
Trematon Castle	K...	Morton (Quebec)	Cancelled December 1943
Tutbury Castle	K...	Morton (Quebec)	Cancelled December 1943
Wigmore Castle	K...	Midland Shipbuilding	Cancelled December 1943

Canadian Castle Class

Name	Pt No	Laid Down	Launched	Completed	Remarks
Arnprior	K494	21.06.43	08.02.44	26.06.44	Ex-*Rising Castle* (1943)
Bowmanville	K493	12.08.43	26.01.44	08.10.44	Ex-*Nunnery Castle* (1943)
Copper Cliff	K495	29.06.43	24.02.44	15.08.44	Ex-*Hever Castle* (1943)
Hespeler	K489	25.05.43	13.11.43	11.03.43	Ex-*Guildford Castle* (1943)
Humberstone	K497	30.08.43	12.04.44	06.09.44	Ex-*Norham Castle* (1943) then Ex-*Totnes Castle* (1943)
Huntsville	K499	01.06.43	24.02.44	15.06.44	Ex-*Wolvesey Castle* (1943)
Kincardine	K490	25.08.43	26.01.44	03.07.44	Ex-*Tamworth Castle* (1943)
Leaside	K492	23.09.43	10.03.44	05.09.44	Ex-*Walmer Castle* (1943)
Orangeville	K491	23.07.43	26.01.44	10.05.44	Ex-*Hedingham Castle* (1943)

Name	Pt No	Laid Down	Launched	Completed	Remarks
Petrolia	K498	21.06.43	24.02.44	14.07.44	Ex-*Sherborne Castle* (1943)
St Thomas	K488	23.06.43	28.12.43	18.05.44	Ex-*Sandgate Castle* (1943)
Tillsonburg	K496	03.06.43	12.02.44	29.06.44	Ex-*Pembroke Castle* (1943)

Norwegian Castle Class

Name	Pt No	Laid Down	Launched	Completed	Remarks
Tunsberg Castle	K374	05.05.43	16.08.43	29.04.44	Ex-*Shrewsbury Castle* (1944)

Empire Class Convoy Rescue Ships

Name	Pt No	Laid Down	Launched	Completed	Remarks
Empire Comfort		00.00.44	20.09.44	00.02.45	Ex-*York Castle* (1945)
Empire Lifeguard		00.00.43	08.06.44	00.11.44	Ex-*Maiden Castle* (1944)
Empire Peacemaker		00.00.44	08.09.44	00.01.45	Ex-*Scarborough Castle* (1945)
Empire Rest		00.00.43	19.06.44	00.10.44	Ex-*Rayleigh Castle* (1944)
Empire Shelter		00.00.43	05.10.44	00.00.45	Ex-*Barnard Castle* (1945)

Appendix Two
COMMANDING OFFICERS[1]

Ship	Commanding Officer	Appointment	Rank	Seniority
Allington Castle	W.G. Ogden DSC BA	25.04.1944	Temp Lt Cdr RNVR	18.09.1939
Allington Castle	P.A. Read	10.09.1944	Lt Cdr RNR	31.05.1937
Allington Castle	P. Aylwin	15.12.1945	Lt RN	16.08.1940
Alnwick Castle	H.A. Stonehouse DSC	20.07.1944	Act Lt Cdr RNR	11.01.1940
Amberley Castle	E.F. Hall DSC	10.08.1944	Temp Lt RNVR	18.12.1942
Amberley Castle	R. Edwards	04.09.1944	Act Lt Cdr RNVR	19.06.1940
Amberley Castle	R.S. Mortimer	03.09.1945	Temp Lt RNR	05.06.1940
Anrprior	S.D. Thom	08.06.1944	Act Lt Cdr RCNR	05.09.1939
Anrprior	T. B. Edwards	28.08.1945	Act Lt Cdr RCNR	18.07.1940
Bamborough Castle	M .S. Work DSC	28.03.1944	Temp Lt RNR	10.04.1940
Bamborough Castle	H. Vernon	11.04.1945	Temp Lt Cdr RNR	31.03.1944
Bamborough Castle	R.W. Anstice OBE	03.12.1945	Cdr RN	30.06.1943
Berkeley Castle	N.W. DUCK DSC RD	11.09.1944	Cdr RNR	31.12.1943
Berkeley Castle	A.C. Palmer DSC	08.03.1945	Temp Lt Cdr RNVR	25.12.1940
Bowmanville	M.S. Duffus	15.09.1944	Act Lt Cdr RCNVR	21.05.1940
Bowmanville	A.D. Ritchie	04.04.1945	Lt RCNVR	07.09.1943
Bowmanville	M.S. Duffus	21.04.1945	Lt Cdr RCNVR	21.05.1940
Bowmanville	W.J. Ransom	25.10.1945	Lt RCNVR	07.07.1945
Caistor Castle	H. Hutchinson	14.06.1944	Act Lt Cdr RN	01.11.1944
Caistor Castle	W.T. Huntriss MBE	04.07.1944	Lt RNR	06.02.1942
Caistor Castle	J.J. Bowick	24.03.1945	Act Lt Cdr RNVR	10.06.1939
Carisbrooke Castle	W.H. Forster	11.10.1943	Temp Lt RNR	19.06.1941
Copper Cliff	F.G. Hutchings	24.07.1944	Lt Cdr RCNVR	24.04.1944
Copper Cliff	F.W. Bogardus	04.12.1944	Act Lt Cdr RCNVR	29.08.1938
Copper Cliff	F.G. Hutchings	12.01.1945	Lt Cdr RCNR	01.01.1945
Copper Cliff	W.M. Combe	20.08.1945	Lt RCNR	
Denbigh Castle	G. Butcher DSC	18.08.1944	Lt Cdr RNVR	09.10.1939
Dumbarton Castle	P. F. Broadhead	05.11.1943	Lt Cdr RNR	01.01.1940
Dumbarton Castle	R.C. Heron	23.11.1944	Temp Lt Cdr RNVR	05.04.1940
Dumbarton Castle	H.D. Hayes	01.10.1945	Lt RNR	09.08.1940
Farnham Castle	W.E. Warwick	14.10.1944	Temp Act Lt Cdr RNR	30.05.1940
Flint Castle	W.R. Sitwell[2]	01.01.1943	Lt RN	19.03.1943

[1] Wartime or immediate post-war.
[2] Anecdotal evidence gives Stitwell as being in command from the date of first commissioning. The Navy List does not record anyone as being in command of Flint Castle until March 31st 1945.

Ship	Commanding Officer	Appointment	Rank	Seniority
Flint Castle	L. Polke	15.11.1945	Temp Lt RNVR	15.11.1945
Hadleigh Castle	H.V. Gordon DSC	02.11.1943	Act Lt Cdr RNVR	15.03.1940
Hadleigh Castle	C. Sandeman	01.12.1943	Lt RN	01.08.1942
Hadleigh Castle	A.C.D. Leach	26.12.1943	Lt RN	01.11.1938
Hadleigh Castle	R.C. Boyle DSC	12.02.1944	Cdr RN	30.06.1938
Hadleigh Castle	C.C. Kuper	22.11.1944	Temp Lt RNVR	15.01.1943
Hadleigh Castle	B.T. Wortley	19.05.1945	Lt Cdr RNR	11.10.1939
Hedingham Castle	W.N. Bishop Leggett	01.03.1945	Temp Lt Cdr RNR	29.05.1940
Hedingham Castle	E.E. Roberts	22.11.1945	Temp Lt Cdr RNR	28.10.1940
Hespeller	N.S.C. Dickinson	28.02.1944	Lt Cdr RCNVR	01.01.1944
Hespeller	G.P. Manning	14.11.1944	Lt RCNVR	31.10.1939
Humberstone	H.A. Boucher	27.06.1944	Act Lt Cdr RCNVR	05.09.1939
Humberstone	J.W. Golby DSC	19.08.1945	Act Lt Cdr RCNVR	11.12.1939
Humberstone	G.C. MacDonald	06.09.1944	Lt RCNVR	19.07.1941
Humberstone	C.L. Campbell	16.10.1944	Lt RCNVR	04.09.1939
Humberstone	H.A. Boucher	27.11.1944	Lt Cdr RCNVR	27.11.1944
Huntsville	C.B. Hermann	10.04.1944	Act Lt Cdr RCNVR	01.05.1941
Huntsville	C.F. Usher	21.07.1945	Lt RCNVR	20.08.1938
Hurst Castle	H.G. Chesterman DCS*	01.02.1944	Lt. RNR	21.07.1938
Kenilworth Castle	J. D. Love	03.09.1943	Temp Lt RNR	07.12.1939
Kenilworth Castle	J.J. Allon	11.10.1943	Temp Lt RNR	19.03.1941
Kenilworth Castle	J.O. Williams	20.03.1945	Act Lt Cdr RNR	30.06.1940
Kenilworth Castle	J.B. Newland	29.11.1945	Lt Cdr RNR	30.10.1942
Kincardine	R.P. Brown	09.03.1944	Act Lt Cdr RCNVR	19.02.1941
Kincardine	A.E. Gough	28.08.1945	Act Lt Cdr RCNVR	
Kincardine	A.H. Campbell	04.10.1945	Skpr Lt RCNR	14.11.1941
Knaresborough Castle	J.R. Freeman	05.11.1943	Lt Cdr RNR	14.11.1937
Knaresborough Castle	J.F. Marchant	09.10.1944	Act Temp Lt Cdr RNR	15.07.1940
Lancaster Castle	W.S. Jolliffe	05.05.1944	Temp Lt Cdr RNR	29.04.1940
Lancaster Castle	M Sokolov	01.09.1945	Act Temp Lt RNR	01.03.1944
Lancaster Castle	J.B. Simpson	08.11.1945	Temp Lt RNR	
Launceston Castle	W.E. Coggin	02.10.1943	Temp Lt Cdr RNR	
Launceston Castle	R.M. Roberts	15.04.1944	Lt RNR	11.01.1941
Launceston Castle	G.H. Riches	21.06.1945	Act Lt Cdr RNVR	24.09.1940
Leaside	G.G.K. Holder	03.07.1944	Lt RCNVR	26.11.1939
Leaside	H. Brynjolfson	16.06.1945	Lt RCNVR	01.05.1941
Leaside	C.P. Balfry	01.09.1945	Lt Cdr RCNR	01.01.1945
Leeds Castle	J. Mackay	01.12.1943	Lt Cdr RNR	11.01.1940
Leeds Castle	W.T. Hodson DSC	05.05.1944	Act Lt Cdr RNVR	07.11.1939
Leeds Castle	E.M. Quarrie	15.10.1945	Lt Cdr RNR	01.11.1941

Ship	Commanding Officer	Appointment	Rank	Seniority
Leeds Castle	J. Ashforth DSC	10.01.1946	Lt RN	16.11.1940
Morpeth Castle	E.R. Pate DSC	15.03.1944	Act Lt Cmdr RNR	05.04.1940
Morpeth Castle	L.F.L. Hill	01.06.1945	Lt Cdr RNR	08.11.1944
Oakham Castle	A.H. Lyons	16.08.1944	Act Lt Cdr RNVR	20.12.1940
Oakham Castle	D.H. Cope DCS	30.12.1945	Lt RNR	14.06.1944
Oakham Castle	H.A. Stonehouse DSC	09.07.1945	Act Lt Cdr RNR	11.01.1940
Orangeville	F.R. Pike	24.04.1944	Act Lt Cdr RCNVR	25.08.1938
Orangeville	G.A. Powell	17.07.1945	Act Lt Cdr RCNVR	01.07.1940
Oxford Castle	H.E. Holden DSC	10.11.1943	Lt Cdr RNR	04.03.1942
Petrolia	P.W. Spragge	29.06.1944	Lt RCNVR	11.11.1940
Petrolia	N.M. Simpson	26.06.1945	Lt RCNVR	01.05.1942
Petrolia	R.H. Ellis	08.08.1945	Lt RCNVR	
Petrolia	J.J. Hodgkinson	12.09.1945	Lt Cdr RCNR	
Pevensey Castle	C.W. Leadbetter	16.04.1944	Act Lt Cdr RNR	24.03.1940
Pevensey Castle	D.A. Rayner DSC VD (SO 30th EG)	01.09.1944	Cdr RNVR	30.06.1943
Pevensey Castle	E. Hewitt RD (SO 30th EG))	12.12.1944	Cdr RNR	31.12.1941
Pevensey Castle	W.L. Turner DSC	20.05.1945	Lt Cdr RNR	14.11.1940
Pevensey Castle	W.E. Warwick (SO 30th EG))	01.11.1945	Lt Cdr RNR	30.05.1940
Portchester Castle	A.G. Scott	04.08.1943	Lt RNR	04.03.1940
Rushen Castle	R.C. Warwick DSC*	01.12.1943	Temp Lt Cdr RNR	31.01.1941
St Thomas	J.B.K. Stewart	21.06.1945	Lt RCNVR	
Rushen Castle	J.K. Craig	25.06.1945	Temp Lt Cdr RNR	22.11.1939
Rushen Castle	E.W. Clubb	07.12.1945	Lt RNR	11.07.1942
St Thomas	L.P. Denny	04.05.1944	Act Lt Cdr RCNR	21.01.1940
St Thomas	B. Hynes	27.01.1945	Act Lt Cdr RCNVR	21.09.1939
St Thomas	A.D. Ritche	19.03.1945	Lt RCNVR	07.09.1943
St Thomas	B. Hynes	04.04.1945	Act Lt Cdr RCNVR	21.09.1939
Tillsonburg	W. Evans	10.04.1944	Lt Cdr RCNVR	01.01.1944
Tillsonburg	A.D. Ritche	17.01.1945	Lt RCNVR	07.09.1943
Tillsonburg	W. Evans	03.03.1945	Lt Cdr RCNVR	01.01.1944
Tillsonburg	G.E. Gilbride	10.07.1945	Lt RCNVR	13.01.1943
Tillsonburg	F. Angus	05.09.1945	Lt RCNVR	27.04.1942
Tintagel Castle	R. Atkinson DSC**	01.02.1944	Lt RNR	23.10.1940
Tintagel Castle	C.A. Hoodless	09.06.1945	Lt Cdr RNR	01.05.1940
Tunsberg Castle (RNN)	Mc C Homan	01.03.1944	Temp Lt RNR	23.10.1940
Tunsberg Castle (RNN)	Th. Jacobsen	17.04.1944	Lt Cdr RNN	

Appendix Three
ROLL OF HONOUR

HMS Allington Castle

Chatham Naval Memorial - Kent

BARNES, Ordinary Seaman, DOUGLAS, C/JX 549647. *HMS Allington Castle*. Royal Navy. 18th October 1944. Age 19. Son of John Alfred and Edith Barnes, of Whittlesea, Cambridgeshire. 76, 2

LAWRENCE, Petty Officer, CHARLES MURGATROYD MIDGLEY, C/SSX 23690. *HMS Allington Castle*. Royal Navy. 15th January 1945. 80, 2.

HMS Amberley Castle

Portsmouth Naval Memorial - Hampshire

BALMER, Stoker 2nd Class, JAMES, P/KX 526780. *HMS Amberley Castle*. Royal Navy. 18th November 1944. Son of William and Isabella Balmer, of Jarrow, Co. Durham. Panel 86, Column 2

HMS Bamborough Castle

VATCHER, Stoker 1st Class, ERNEST EDWARD, P/KX 129942. *HMS Bamborough Castle*. Royal Navy. 18th February 1945. Age 32. Son of Charles William and Thurza Vatcher; husband of Marjorie E. L. Vatcher, of Enfield, Middlesex. Panel 89, Column 3.

HMS Berkeley Castle

BRYAN, Able Seaman, FRANK, C/JX567341. *HMS Berkeley Castle*. Royal Navy. Died ashore 29th June 1945. Age 37. Son of William and Mary Bryan; husband of Muriel Gwendoline Bryan, of Bowes Park, Middlesex. Panel 85.

HMS Denbigh Castle

Plymouth Naval Memorial - Devon

ATKINSON, Ordinary Telegraphist, JOHN, D/JX 575021. *HMS Denbigh Castle*. Royal Navy. 13th February 1945. Age 21. Son of Joseph and Edith Atkinson, of Ulverston, Lancashire. Panel 94, Column 2.

BETTANY, Ordinary Seaman, JOHN, D/JX 541380. *HMS Denbigh Castle*. Royal Navy. 13th February 1945. Age 18. Son of Horace and Evelyn Bettany, of Coventry. Panel 94, Column 2.

CHARLES, Telegraphist, LEIGHTON HENRY, D/JX 327365. *HMS Denbigh Castle*. Royal Navy. 13th February 1945. Age 20. Son of Thomas Wade Charles and Brenda Charles, of Uplands, Swansea. Panel 94, Column 2.

EALEY, Ordinary Seaman, LAWRENCE CHARLES GORDON, D/JX 541388. *HMS Denbigh Castle*. Royal Navy. 13th February 1945. Age 19. Son of Frederick and Rose Ellen Ealey, of Newport, Monmouthshire. Panel 94, Column 2.

JAMES, Leading Seaman, ROWLAND KEITH, D/JX 342214. *HMS Denbigh Castle*. Royal Navy. 13th February 1945. Age 35. Son of Ernest Percival and Jane James; husband of Adeline James, of Burley-in-Wharfedale, Yorkshire. Panel 93, Column 3.

MacSWEEN, Petty Officer, NEIL, D/X 9811B. *HMS Denbigh Castle*. Royal Naval Reserve. 13th February 1945. Son of Donald and Isabella MacSween, of Lochboisdale, Isle of South Uist. Panel 95, Column 2.

PATTERSON, Coder, AUBREY, D/JX 293539. *HMS Denbigh Castle*. Royal Navy. 13th February 1945. Age 21. Son of Thomas and Jane Patterson, of Lisburn, Co. Down, Northern Ireland. Panel 94, Column 2.

SMART, Able Seaman, WALTER WALLACE, D/JX 302599. *HMS Denbigh Castle*. Royal Navy. 13th February 1945. Age 20. Son of George Smart and of Ellen Smart (nee Williams). Panel 94, Column 1.

SMITH, Ordinary Seaman, THOMAS FREDERICK JAMES, D/JX 537736. *HMS Denbigh Castle*. Royal Navy. 13th February 1945. Age 18. Son of Thomas William and Martha Susan Smith, of Barkingside, Essex. Panel 94, Column 2.

TAYLOR, Able Seaman, JOHN ARTHUR CLINTON, D/JX 566787. *HMS Denbigh Castle*. Royal Navy. 13th February 1945. Age 23. Son of George and M. A. Taylor, of Jarrow, Co. Durham. Panel 94, Column 1.

WILLIAMS, Able Seaman, STANLEY, D/JX 220791. *HMS Denbigh Castle*. Royal Navy. 13th February 1945. Age 28. Son of Albert Gregg Williams, and of Florence Williams, of Liverpool. Panel 94, Column 2.

HMS Tintagel Castle

LOWNDES, Stoker 1st Class, ALFRED GEORGE, D/KX 137990. *HMS Tintagel Castle*. Royal Navy. 25th May 1945. Age 22. Son of James and Eva Muriel Lowndes, of St. Helens, Lancashire. Panel 94, Column 3.

HMS Flint Castle

Edinburgh (Seafield) Cemetery - Edinburgh

MURT, Able Seaman, EDWARD, D/JX 356121. *HMS Flint Castle*. Royal Navy. 22nd December 1943. Age 19. Son of Edward and Mary Ann Noall Murt, of St. Ives, Cornwall. Sec. P. Coll. grave 804.

HMS Hadleigh Castle

St. Johns (Mount Pleasant) Cemetery - Newfoundland

DOUTHWAIT, Ordinary Telegraphist, CRADOC, P/JX 403928. *HMS Hadleigh Castle*. Royal Navy. 2nd January 1944. Age 19. Son of Sidney and Edna Douthwaite, of West Auckland, Co. Durham, England. Sec. A. Plot 6. Grave G.

HMCS Humberstone

Halifax Memorial, Nova Scotia

MURRAY, Able Seaman, James Burton V/69565. *HMCS Humberstone*, Royal Canadian Nayy Volunteer Reserve 4th March 1945. Panel 13.

HMS Hurst Castle

Chatham Memorial - Kent

ARBUCKLE, Leading Seaman, GEORGE, C/SSX 26900. *HMS Hurst Castle*. Royal Navy. 1st September 1944. Age 23. Son of George and Esther Arbuckle, of Eythorne, Kent. 74, 3.

ASH, Able Seaman, WILLIAM ERNEST, C/JX 379298. *HMS Hurst Castle*. Royal Navy. 1st September 1944. Age 19. Son of Ernest Victor and Martha Ash, of East Dulwich, London. 75, 1.

BENNETT, Ordinary Seaman, DONALD LIONEL, C/JX 672323. *HMS Hurst Castle*. Royal Navy. 1st September 1944. Age 16. Son of William and Olive Ruth Bennett, of Salisbury, Wiltshire. 76, 2.

BYNER, Stoker 1st Class, ALBERT LEONARD, C/KX 145387. *HMS Hurst Castle*. Royal Navy. 1st September 1944. Age 35. Son of William and Rachael Byner; husband of Mrs. Byner, of Shepherd's Bush, London. 77, 3.

DARBY, Stoker 2nd Class, ALFRED, C/KX 665318. *HMS Hurst Castle*. Royal Navy. 1st September 1944. Son of Joseph and Carrie Darby, of Denaby, Yorkshire. 78, 1.

DUFFY, Engine Room Artificer 4th Class, MICHAEL, C/MX 58231. *HMS Hurst Castle*. Royal Navy. 1st September 1944. Age 21. Son of Michael and Mary Duffy, of Edinburgh. 77, 2.

EARL, Stoker 1st Class, SIDNEY ALBERT, C/KX 154377. *HMS Hurst Castle*. Royal Navy. 1st September 1944. Age 20. Son of Thomas and Hester Earl, of Islington, London. 77, 3.

ELLIS, Able Seaman, SAMUEL JOSEPH, C/JX 317390. *HMS Hurst Castle*. Royal Navy. 1st September 1944. Age 21. Son of Samuel Joseph and Hannah Ellis, of Woolwich, London. 75, 2.

KELLY, Leading Cook (S), JAMES HANN, C/MX 72943. *HMS Hurst Castle*. Royal Navy. 1st September 1944. Age 28. Son of Arthur R. and Sarah H. Kelly; husband of Mrs. J. P. Kelly, of Roker, Sunderland, Co. Durham. 78, 3.

NAYLOR, Chief Stoker, ROBERT MADDOCKS, Mentioned in Despatches, C/KX 79092. *HMS Hurst Castle*. Royal Navy. 1st September 1944. Age 34. Son of George and Mabel Anne Naylor. 77, 2.

ROFF, Ordinary Seaman, LEONARD, C/JX 654037. *HMS Hurst Castle*. Royal Navy. 1st September 1944. Age 19. Son of Alfred E. and Sarah Ann Roff, of Ruislip, Middlesex. 76, 3.

SAVIDGE, Ordinary Seaman, STANLEY ERNEST, C/JX 641914. *HMS Hurst Castle*. Royal Navy. 1st September 1944. Age 18. Son of Albert Stanley and Lily Savidge, of Tonbridge, Kent. 76, 3.

TURNER, Leading Stoker, SIDNEY GEORGE, C/KX 583048. *HMS Hurst Castle*. Royal Navy. 1st September 1944. Age 30. Son of James Clark Turner and Alice Mabel Turner; husband of Elizabeth Turner, of Glasgow. 77, 3.

WARES, Ordinary Seaman, JOHN HENRY, C/JX 652642. *HMS Hurst Castle*. Royal Navy. 1st September 1944. Age 19. Son of Mr. and Mrs. G. Wares, of Brighton. 76, 3.

WRIGHT, Ordinary Seaman, WILLIAM, C/JX 639841. *HMS Hurst Castle*. Royal Navy. 1st September 1944. Age 19. Son of Benjamin G. and Eliaabeth Wright, of Whitley Bay, Northumberland. 76, 3.

HMS Kenilworth Castle

Londonderry City Cemetery - County Londonderry

COLEMAN, Sub-Lieutenant (E), ALBERT WILLIAM, *HMS Kenilworth Castle*. Royal Naval Volunteer Reserve. 4th January 1944. Age 30. Son of Henry W. Coleman and Clara A. Coleman, of Twickenham, Middlesex. C. of E. Plot. Sec. F. Grave 42.

HMS Launceston Castle

FERNIE, Midshipman, ALEXANDER LINN, *HMS Launceston Castle*. Royal Naval Volunteer Reserve. 16th January 1945. Age 19. Son of William Linn Fernie and Agnes Doris Fernie; grandson of Mrs. E. M. Loch, of Ealing, Middlesex. R.C. Plot. Sec. M. Grave 12.

HMCS Leaside

PATERSON , Sick Berth Attendant, John Archibald. *HMCS Leaside*. Royal Canadian Navy Volunteer Reserve. 8th May 1945, Age 19, C of E plot F. Grave 49

HMS Oakham Castle

Wembley (Alperton) Burial Ground - Middlesex

COPE, Lieutenant, DESMOND HENRY, D S C, ***HMS Oakham Castle***. Royal Naval Reserve. 31st May 1946. Age 24. Son of Frank William Enoch and Elsie Cope, of Wembley. Plot D.D. Grave 112.

HMS Oxford Castle

Lossiemouth Burial Ground - Moray

SIM, Telegraphist, DOUGLAS HAIG, D/JX 186464. ***HMS Oxford Castle***. Royal Navy. 8th June 1947. Age 27. Son of Robert John and Margrat Sim, of Lossiemouth; husband of Elizabeth Doreen Sim, of Old Swan, Liverpool. Grave 1167.

HMS Pevensey Castle

Freetown (King Tom) Cemetery

LONGMAN, Chief Stoker, SIDNEY ALFRED, P/K 67280. ***HMS Pevensey Castle***. Royal Navy. 2nd October 1945. 9. D. 1.

Blackpool Cemetery - Lancashire

McFARLANE, Able Seaman, JAMES, P/JX251063. ***HMS Pevensey Castle***. Royal Navy. 29th May 1944. Age 31. (served as MOORE, Peter). Son of Capt. John Currie McFarlane and of Ida May McFarlane (nee Causebrook), of Pretoria, Transvaal, South Africa. Sec. P.P. Grave 10.

HNorMS Tunsberg Castle

KARLSEN, Odvar, Midshipman
NESSE, Arthur, Able Seaman
ROLFSEN, Jens Kristian, Midshipman
SCHREUDER, Arnold, Able Seaman
THORESEN, Oluf Edvard, Able Seaman

Appendix Four
ESCORT GROUPS REPORTED TO INCLUDE
CASTLE CLASS CORVETTES

Escort Group	Corvettes	Senior Officer's Ship
B1	*Flint Castle, Portchester Castle, Tintagel Castle*	*Chelmer, Tintagel Castle, Inman, Poppy, Lotus*
B2	*Bamborough Castle. Berkeley Castle, Carisbrooke Castle, Dumbarton Castle, Flint Castle, Morpeth Castle, Oxford Castle, Rushen Castle, Tunsberg Castle*	*Highlander, Hesperus, Mourne Cotton, Morpeth Castle*
B3	*Allington Castle, Flint Castle, Hurst Castle, Kenilworth Castle, Knaresborough Castle, Leeds Castle, Tintagel Castle, Tunsberg Castle*	*Inman, Tintagel Castle, Burza Towy, Exe, Highlander*
B4	*Carisbrooke Castle, Hadleigh Castle, Kenilworth Castle, Launceston Castle, Morpeth Castle, Pevensey Castle, Portchester Castle*	*Helmsdale*
B5	*Bamborough Castle, Berkeley Castle, Carisbrooke Castle, Dumbarton Castle, Hadleigh Castle*	*Havelock, Hadleigh Castle, Exe*
B6	*Tunsberg Castle*	
B7	*Carisbrooke Castle, Berkeley Castle, Kenilworth Castle, Portchester Castle*	*Chelmer, Vidette*
B21	*Flint Castle, Rushen Castle*	*Hesperus, Rushen Castle*
B22	*Morpeth Castle, Oxford Castle*	*Cotton*
B23	*Allington Castle, Knaresborough Castle, Leeds Castle*	*Knaresborough Castle, Fowey*
C1	*Arnprior, Orangeville*	*New Glasgow, Chambly Cheboque, Arnprior, Hallowell*
C2	*Kincardine, St Thomas*	*Lonquell, Kincardine*

Escort Group	Corvettes	Senior Officer's Ship
C3	Hespeller, Orangeville, St Thomas	Kokane, Saskatchewan, Ettrick, Prince Rupert
C4	Bowmanville, Petrolia	Wentworth, Hotspur
C5	Hespeller, Huntsville, St Thomas, Tillsonburg	Runnymede
C6	Coppercliff, Tillsonburg	Eastview, Coppercliff
C7	Coppercliff	Lanark, Coppercliff
C8	Leeside, Humberstone	Stonetown, Leeside
7th	Allington Castle, Alnwick Castle, Bamborough Castle, Denbigh Castle, Farnham Castle, Lancaster Castle	Cygnet
8th	Alnwick Castle, Farnham Castle	Lapwing
15th	Carisbrooke Castle, Berkeley Castle, Portchester Castle	Saladin
30th	Caistor Castle, Kenilworth Castle, Launceston Castle, Pevensey Castle, Portchester Castle	Pevensey Castle
31st	Carisbrooke Castle, Berkeley Castle, Dumbarton Castle, Hadleigh Castle, Lancaster Castle	Berkeley Castle
39th	Kenilworth Castle, Leeds Castle, Flint Castle	Rochester
40th	Berkeley Castle, Carisbrooke Castle, Dumbarton Castle	Exe
LEP	Amberley Castle, Knaresborough Castle, Leeds Castle, Oakham Castle, Oxford Castle, Rushen Castle.	

Appendix Five
AN EXAMPLE OF
COMMANDING OFFICER'S STANDING ORDERS

1.a. Officers are to make and keep themselves acquainted with those parts of the following orders which affect them.
K.R. & A.I's, C.A.F.O's and A.F.O's, Local orders issued by the Senior Officer under whom the group is operating.

b. Officers concerned are to draw my attention to any new orders which require action by the ship.

c. The particular attention of officers is drawn to the following articles of K.R. & A.I's

All Officers:	1, 9, 10, 153, 154, 156, 177, 178 ,514, 514A, 619, 620, 635, 635A, 925A, 1072, 1076, 1129, 11 38,
Executive Officers:	149, 536, Chapter 16, Chapter 11, 1160, 1245.
Navigator:	Chapter XXXII, XXXV
GCO:	Chapter XXXIV, Section III
A/S C/O:	Chapter XXXIVA.
Gunner:	1067 - 1069, Chapter XXXIV Section 3 and 4, Chapter XLII Sections 1 and 2.
Engineer Officer:	Chapter XXXVIII
Medical Officer:	Chapter XXXVIA and XXXVIII

2.Duties of Officers

1st Lieutenant	(I)	Executive Officer.
	(II)	President Ward Room mess,
	(III)	President and Treasurer Canteen Committee,
	(IV)	Security Officer.
	(V)	Anti Gas Officer.
	(VI)	Waste Products Officer
Staff Officer	(I)	Group Navigator
	(II)	Staff Duties.
.	(III)	Action Plot.
Sub Lt. RNVR	(I)	Ship's signal Officer
	(II)	C.B. S.P. and Cypher Officer charge documents

	(III)	Aircraft recognition Officer
	(IV)	Ward Room Mess Secretary
	(V)	Communication and Miscellaneous Division
	(VI)	OOQ Aft

Sub Lt. RNVR	(I)	A/S C.O.
	(II)	Accountant Officer
	(III)	Sports Officer.
	(IV)	Education Officer.
	(V)	Quarterdeck Division.
	(VI)	Censor and Mail Officer.

Sub Lt. RNVR	(I)	G.C.O.
	(II)	Squid Officer
	(III)	Cable Officer.
	(IV)	Correspondence Officer,
	(V)	Focsle. Division.
	(VI)	Magazine.

Lt. RNVR	(I)	Torpedo Officer
	(II)	Boats officer
	(III)	Training officer
	(IV)	Boarding officer

Engineering Officer	(I)	Central Stores
	(II)	Q.U's and B.R's
	(III)	E.R. Division
	(IV)	Damage Control Officer

Engineer Officer	(I)	Central Stores
	(II)	Q.Y's and B.R's
	(III)	E.R. Dvision
	(IV)	Damage Control Officer

| Group Officers will attend to | | HF/DF |
| | | Radar |

3. Officer of the Day in Harbour

The officer of the day as detailed by the First Lieutenant is responsible for the safety and proper conduct of the ship and ship's company.

He is to see that a favourable and immediate response is made to every request for assistance, and that every communication to the ship is promptly dealt with.

He is to pay particular attention to the welfare of the ship's company and is immediately and thoroughly (to) investigate any requests, complaints, losses or defaults.

Evidence in serious cases (these that might involve court martial proceedings) is always be taken in writing, after giving a clear warning In the words of K.R. & A.I. 537 Para 6. In cases of drunkenness the Medical officer should always see the men concerned for the man's own protection.

In bad weather O.O.D. has authority to order steam to be raised; to let go another anchor and to set anchor watch. He is also to take the normal seaman like precautions such as taking transits and bearings, or using the lead line to detect dragging, and to hoist boats and ladder., recall libertymen, start the gyro, to ensure the safety of the ship and crew.

He is to see that the routine ordered is carried out and is to go around the deck at regular intervals during the night, particularly during the middle and morning watches.

All boats are to be hoisted at night, unless my permission to leave a boat down has been obtained.

He is to report 2100 rounds to me.

He is to pay particular attention to the piping and answering of pipes from other ships.

4. Punishment

The First Lieutenant is hereby authorised to award the punishment as laid down in K.R.& A.I. 536B.

The O.O.W. or O.O.D. if a Lieutenant, is hereby authorised to award punishment as laid down In K.R. &. A.I. 536D.

All leave breaking and damage and loss cases must be brought before me for ultimate decision.

5. Leave

Officers not required for duty on board may have leave when the service and First Lieutenant permit.

The Captain should be informed if leave is required in the forenoon, over night. or when the ship is at least 2 hours notice or less

6. Steam

When steam is ordered on main engines, both boilers are to be connected; engines are to have been tried., and telegraph and communications tested by the time ordered,

NOTE.

Sirens may not be tested in harbour in wartime. A responsible rating is to make certain that steam to the siren is opened up in case they may be required in emergency.

Steam for Capstan may be ordered either by the Executive Officer or O.O.W. as required.

7. Telegraphs

SLOW	40 revs or 4 knots
HALF	Revs as ordered on the revolution telegraphs
FULL	Full speed with the steam available. Only to be used in conditions of emergency

Shortly before the engines are required the order 'Stand By' will be passed to the engine room.

Should the telegraph be moved before this order has been passed. the engine room is to query the order before obeying the telegraph.

The order 'finished with engines' be passed when the engines are no longer required.

8. Officers of Watch at Sea

(a) Unless otherwise ordered there are to be two O.O.W's during the dark hours. One of them is to have a W.K.C.

(b) The O.O.W. is entirely responsible for the safety of the ship under all conditions unless and until I have for-

mally assumed charge.

(c) I am entirely available at all times of the day & and night and the O.O.W is never to hesitate to call me for any unusual occurrence, sighting, change of weather or visibility or if he is in the least difficulty or doubt. I would rather be called unnecessarily many times, than not be called once when I should have been.

(d) The Officer of the Watch is to act immediately if I am not on the bridge in any emergency. His power to carry out a counter attack without sounding the general alarm signal is clearly stated in Admiralty M.A.S.W. 1246/43

(e) On sighting a periscope or torpedo track anti-gnat precautions must immediately be taken unless the position of the U-boot in respect of the convoy justifies the risk of being torpedoed.

(f) In the event of sighting a hostile or unidentified aircraft sound aircraft action alarm, pass bearing and estimate range to guns. Call me and increase speed. and open fire with short range weapons when aircraft comes near. Make sure that what you have to do is quite clear in your mind as you may not have many seconds in which to ponder if the emergency arises. Once everybody is closed up to action stations your responsibility is less, but unless we are quick in the beginning we may never reach that stage.

(g) Remember that YOU and not the signalman. are responsible that the correct reply is made if we are challenged at any time, so always know the challenge and reply when you are on watch. NEVER challenge another ship unless I am on the bridge and the ship's company is closed up at action stations, with guns loaded and trained on the other vessel. This does not necessarily apply to challenging suspicious aircraft, of course, for in such case you should have already sounded the alarm and can then proceed to identify it.

(h) Always note the bearing and time when you sight any suspicious or extraordinary object, ship, light or aircraft.

9. Confidential and Secret Books and Documents

All C.B.'s and S.P.'s are to be mustered quarterly by the officers detailed.
Signal books in use are to be mustered at noon at sea by the O.O.W. and at 0800 each day in harbour by O.O.D, and this fact noted in deck-log. If the ship sinks the confidential and secret books sinks with her in their safes. Books in use are to be placed in a weighted bag and thrown overboard.

10. Emergency Steering Arrangement (Secondary Steering Position)

In the event of a break down of the telemeter system in the steering engine, the engine room is to be ordered to shift to hand steering and the helmsman ordered to place the wheel amidships and to keep it there. A steering party of at least 4 hands under the petty officer of the watch or the Coxswain is then to be sent aft to steer by hand when the E.R.A. has connected up. The steering party is to report by the telephone to the bridge when ready and this telephone is to be continually manned by the Petty Officer in charge of the party. The ship may be conned either by telephone from the bridge or by voice pipe from secondary steering position aft.

11. Requestmen etc

Requestmen will be held on Thursdays if practicable.

12. Smoking

Attention is called to K.R. & A.I. Article 1081
At sea , No SMOKING is to take place on the weather decks whilst the ship is darkened.

In harbour smoking may take place on the weather decks while the ship is darkened until the receipt, and during the period, of an air raid warning

13. Spirits

An executive Officer is always to be present whenever the spirit room is opened, and is to wait and see it closed.
In harbour this officer will be the Officer of the Day; at sea he will be detailed by the Executive Officer. He is to check that the correct quantity of spirit in drawn, and is to supervise its subsequent issue to each mess, and is to sign the daily account book accordingly.
No raw spirit is to be issued other than to Chief & Petty Officers,

14 Ammunition (Private)

With reference to K.R & A.I. Art. 1073 para. 232 (a) all such ammunition approved by me to be kept on board is to be stowed in a locked cupboard

15. Secret Correspondence

All most secret correspondence is to be handed to the captain personally, or in his absence to the Senior Executive Officer on board for opening and action. Such letters are to be registered in the secret document book immediately, and the receipt acknowledged as indicated and then the letter locked in a steel chest.

16. Cameras

No one is to have a camera on board without my permission in writing. (In the case of ratings this will only be granted as a request to me, with a record of my decision in the Captain's request book)
No one is to take photographs in or from the ship without my permission or in my absence the permission of the Executive Officer.
The First Lieutenant is detailed as Ship's photographic officer. He is to keep a record of all cameras on board and is to make himself acquainted with the latest orders on the subject.

17. Subsidiary Non-Public Funds

The following non-public funds are authorised to be kept on board as follows:-

FUND	Name of Secretary and/or Treasurer
Ward Room Mess Fund	Sub. Lieut France
Ward Room Wine Fund	Sub. Lieut France
Ship's fund including, Tombola Fund	Sub. Lieut Hughes

(2) Audits are to be carried out In accordance with K.R & A.I. Art. 635A, for the Monthly period ending 30th Jun, 30th October, and 28th February. Audited statements on Form S, 256, are to be submitted to me by the 15th July, November and March. Accounts are also to be audited in accordance with K.R.& A.I. Art 620, on charge of secretaries. Auditing Officer will be detailed by me.
The attention of all officers keeping accounts is directed to K.R. & A.I. Arts. 619, 921, 623, and 635A.

18. Keys

(1). No ship's keys are to be taken out of the ship. Keys of any locked places are to be handed over to the Q.M. for safe custody

(2) The Q.M. is to be in charge of the key board which is to be kept locked and its key is to be kept on the person of' the Q.M.

(3) The Q.M. is responsible for the keeping of the key book. When any keys are issued they are to be signed for by the recipient in the key book and the date and time are to be entered therein. When keys are returned the Q.M is to note the time and sign the key book. It is the responsibility of the person returning the keys to see that this is done.

The Q.M. is to report to the officer doing the rounds any keys that have not been returned by 1630.

The following places are to be kept locked except when work is actually going on in them.

Captain's Office	Ward Room store	Clothing Store
Central Store	Paint Shop	Gunners Store
Canteen Store	Provision Store	Canteen
Electrical Store	Spirit Room.(see 13)	

The keys of Officers cabins when an officer is on leave are not to be issued without personal authority of the officer of the day.

The keys of the spirit room are to be kept on the magazine key board.

(8) The key of the dangerous drug cupboard is to be in the possession of and on the person of the Medical Officer or the Commanding Officer.

When both Medical Officer and Sick Berth Attendant are ashore the Sick Bay is to be locked and the key returned to the key board.

19. Magazine Keys

One key of the magazine key board is to be kept in my custody and the other issued to O.O.D. The O.O.D. is to keep this key on his person.

20. The following books are to be presented each Saturday for Signature

Magazine Log Books	Gangway Check Book
Engine Room Log	Rounds Book
Deck Log	Registered Mail and Parcel Books
Wine Books	A. & A. Book.
All Departmental Defect Books	Record of Punishment,
Short Leave Book.	

21. Rounds

The First Lieutenant is to do the round at sea and the Officer of the Day in port, at 2100. Particular attention is to be paid to the secure fastening of all spaces which should be locked.

22. Alarm Bells

Alarm Bells are to be tested daily at sea. Before this is done a warning is to be piped around the ship and on completion of the test the fact is also to be piped.

23. Gangway Wine and Spirits

All transactions in dutiable goods, whether from merchants or other ships are to be entered in the gangway book. This includes short period loans or exchanges with other ships even if there is no monetary transaction.

24. Canteen Bills

All canteen bills are to be paid up promptly and any defaulting in this matter is to be brought to my notice.

K.R & A.I's	=	Kings Regulations and Admiralty Instructions.
C.A.F.O.	=	Confidential Admiralty Fleet Orders
A.F.O.	=	Admiralty Fleet Orders

Appendix Six
HMS TINTAGEL CASTLE
Boarding Party Standing Orders

The boarding party consists of the following men:

S.P.O.	Vinnicome
Sto.	Williams
LTO	Sluggett
A.B.	Smith
A.B.	Thomas
Sig.	Belben
Tel.	Jenkins
Coder	Weir

Seaboat to consist of L.Sea Carr (Coxswain) and at least two others of the seaboats crew.

At the order "Away seaboat's crew and Boarding Party" the above hands will leave their place of action and muster at the double alongside the whaler with gasmasks, rubber lifebelts already worn. A.B's Thomas and Smith on hearing the pipe will collect all boarding gear from the support and stow into the boat.

One bag containing 6 torches and spare Lanchester magazines.
Three Lanchester machine guns with bayonets attached.
Four revolvers with ammunition pouches.
One box of revolver ammunition.
One ensign stowed in bag.

The tool bag of the stoker's (to include 4 wheel spanners) should also be stowed with this boarding gear where it can be obtained without delay.

A.B. Smith is detailed to muster the above gear in the gun support on proceeding to sea; reporting to me when it is correct. He is to place in my cabin the box containing all grenades, where it is to be placed under lock and key. On returning to harbour he is to request permission from me to return all boarding gear to their correct stores and this is to be carried out just prior to passing the boom.

The 20 ft. length of chain and grapnel is to be stowed in the seaboat at all times, whilst at sea also two small fenders and two heaving lines. A.B. Smith is to see that this gear is placed in the boat when mustering the above boarding gear and report it stowed into the boat at the same time as the boarding gear. When returning to harbour the chain and grapnel are to be stowed in the starboard gun support fenders and heaving lines in the Wash Deck lockers.

A.B's Thomas and Smith having obtained the boarding gear and placed it in the seaboat are then to see that it is distributed as follows:-

1 revolver to the Boarding Officer
1 revolver to S.P.O. Vinnicome.

1 revolver to L.T.O. Sluggett.
1 revolver to Tel. Jenkins.

1 Lanchester with magazine ready to each of themselves and one to the seaboat's crew.

Torches: 1 to the Boarding Officer

1 to A.B. Smith.
1 to A.B. Thomas.
1 to Coder Weir.
1 to Tel. Jenkins.
1 for spare.

The S.P.O, Stoker, & L.T.O. will provide their own, also the TEL if possible.

Lifebelts are to be worn partially blown up, Gasmasks to be slung on the chest.

A.B. Smith.

His duty will be armed guard. On entering the seaboat he is to place himself right forward with the grapnel and boarding chain. He is to have his Lanchester ready for use from the time the seaboat is slipped. When coming alongside the submarine and at the order "BOWS" he is to have the grapnel ready for throwing, and throw same as soon as possible. The bowman will help him in any way that is necessary. Immediately the grapnel is secured he is to board with the boarding chain (20 ft. chain) and make his way to the conning tower (by this time the remainder of the boarding party should be aboard). When he has reached the conning tower he is to secure the chain by the hook provided and throw the remainder down the hatch taking care at the same time not to show any part of himself above the hatch. He is to remain on the conning tower taking charge of any bundles the sub crew may bring up with them, until A.B. Thomas has taken over. He is to return to the seaboat, if it is still alongside for his Lanchester and then return to A.B. Thomas to search any prisoners on the upper deck.

A.B. Thomas.

His duty will be of armed guard. He is to remain aft in the whaler with his Lanchester loaded and ready. When the seaboat is alongside he is to board the submarine following A.B. Smith to the conning tower where he is to take charge allowing no one to interfere with the work of A.B. Smith. He is to clear the conning tower of all except the boarding party. He is to see that no one is near the guns of the submarine. Whilst in charge of the conning tower he is also to keep order on the upper deck, keeping prisoners aft of the conning tower and clear of any gun or hatch and if necessary use force to see that his orders are carried out. His orders are to be obeyed first time and he is to see that they are obeyed immediately. He is to cover A.B. Smith in his work of searching the prisoners. Prisoners are to be kept apart from the boarding party and not allowed to interfere with the seaboat should it still be alongside. He is to have a whistle and should he hear the whistle of the officer below he is to repeat the signal to those on the upper deck.

S.P.O. Vinnicome & Sto. Williams.

Their duties are to attend to the trim and buoyancy of the submarine immediately they get below. They are to provide themselves with the necessary tools.for this job which are to be placed in a small bag in a position known to both men where it can be readily obtained. Torches are also to be provided by them and maintained in a workable order at all times. A lanyard to be attached. They are both to board the submarine as quickly as possible making their way to the conning tower where they will enter the submarine immediately after the boarding officer and carry out their duties of trimming the ship.

L.T.O. Sluggett.

His duty is to restore as soon as possible the lighting of the control room. He is to provide himself with the tools, in a bag, required for this or any other electrical job, and is to carry a torch to which is attached a lanyard.

Sig. Belben

He is to provide himself with a set of hand flags, flashing lamp and one signal pad. He is to board the submarine and when aboard is to place himself on the conning tower, and to establish communication with the ship as soon as possible informing the Boarding officer as soon as this is done. He is also to report on the tanks, whether they are blowing or not and whether the fore or after tanks whichever the case may be. Before leaving the bridge at the pipe "Away boarding party" he is to collect 1 Very light and a number of red cartridges.

Tel. Jenkins

His duty is to enter the submarine and collect all papers and documents that he can lay his hands on and for this purpose he is to provide himself with a waterproof bag. He will be armed with a revolver and carry a torch. He will be the last down the conning tower hatch and as soon as he has collected all papers he will return to the conning tower.

Coder Weir

His duties being chiefly that of interpreter and messenger between the Boarding Officer and the Boarding Party. He will be provided with a torch.

   The seaboat is to be manned by L.Sea Carr and any two of the seaboats crew who may be mustered by the pipe "Away boarding party and seaboats crew." His duty is to remain in the boat when the boarding party has entered the submarine. To stand off, within hailing distance, and should he remain alongside to prevent any member of the sub's crew from getting aboard. He will be provided with a Lanchester for defence purposes only.

   A whistle will be carried by the Boarding Officer for the following use:- When the boarding party are in the control room and it is required to abandon the room by the entire party, series of short blasts will be given. On hearing this each man will get to the upper deck immediately.

   A.B. Thomas will have another whistle and he is to repeat the above signal for those on the upper deck to abandon the submarine. The whaler should it be lying off at the time is to close the submarine on hearing the whistle and take off those of the boarding party who are on the upper deck. None of the submarine's crew is to enter the whaler until the whole of the boarding party is picked up.

Signed

R F Dykes, Boarding Officer

Appendix Seven
INSTRUCTIONS FOR FORMING AN 'OBSERVANT' SEARCH

When an Observant Search is to be carried out ships will comply with the following instructions:-

(1) Regardless of the direction of the approach course, the sides of the square will lie North - South, East and West.

(2) The Datum Point will be indicated by a ship of the group, a sea marker or a bearing and distance from the Senior Officer.

(3) The search will normally be carried out in a clockwise direction; side of the square will be divided into sections of one mile in length.

(4) Starting from the North West corner of the square these sections will be numbered from No 1 onwards consecutively in a clockwise direction. (Thus in an Observant with 3 mile legs there will be 12 Sections; 4 mile legs 16 Sections, etc.)

(5) As each ship reaches the perimeter of the search, she will report to the Senior Officer the section she is entering (e. g, ASSIZE entering 13). Later arrivals will be guided by these reports in deciding; what section to steer for, so that ships may be evenly spread round the perimeter. The length of the perimeter divided by the number of ships carrying out Observant gives the correct distance apart of ships.

(6) Unless otherwise signalled, ships will make good 12 Knots zig-zagging independently.

(7) If an Inner Observant is formed it will normally be carried out in a clockwise direction with 2 mile legs.

(8) Ships will not cross the Observant Square except to reach a position on the Inner Observant.

(9) The Signal for forming an Observant Search will be made as follows :- Codeword 'Observant' followed by the Datum Point (indicated as in Para 2) and a numeral indicating the length of each leg
  e.g.   1 - Observant Flare - 4
  e.g.   2 - Observant 130 NANSON 1 - 5

(10) If, while carrying out Observant, ships are told to indicate their position, they will report in order of fleet numbers the number of the section which they are then in; or, if passing, from one section to the next, they will give the numbers of the two sections separated by a tackline.

  e. g,   WINSLEY 15
     KEYSTONE - 4 - tackline 5
     Positions on the Inner Observant will be preceded by the word. 'Inner'
  e.g,   SHADOW - Inner 6

(11)   Figure illustrating Inner Observant and Outer Observant of 4 mile legs:-.

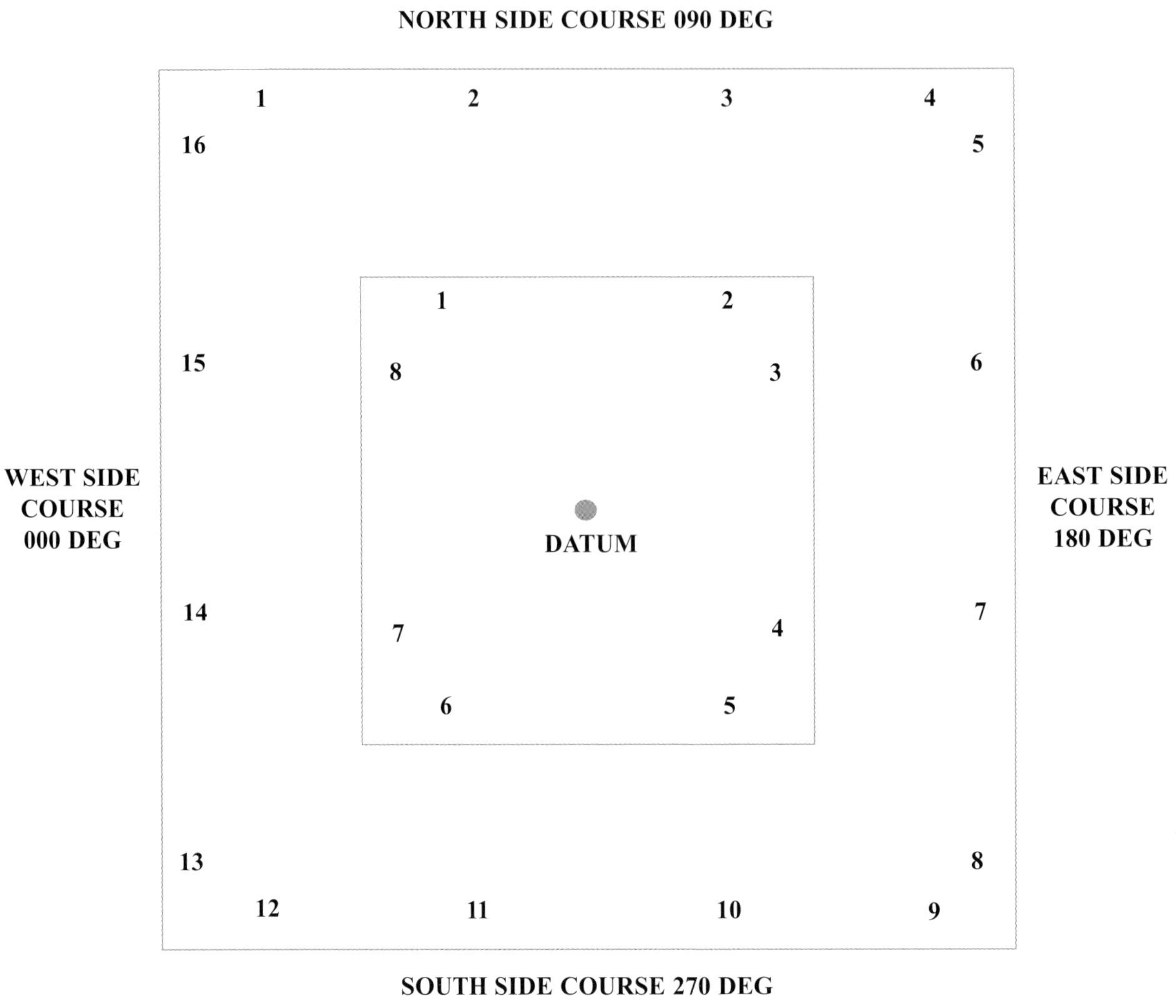

NORTH SIDE COURSE 090 DEG

| 1 | 2 | 3 | 4 |

16   5

WEST SIDE   **EAST SIDE**
COURSE   **COURSE**
000 DEG   **180 DEG**

15   6

       1   2

8   3

DATUM

7   4

14   7

      6   5

13   8

| 12 | 11 | 10 | 9 |

SOUTH SIDE COURSE 270 DEG

Note:

No specific instructions for forming an 'Observant' were found in the RoPs pertaining to Escort Groups with Castle Class Corvettes. This, from the 6th Escort Group, is presented as a typical example of the procedures used.

Appendix Eight
OPERATION BANANA

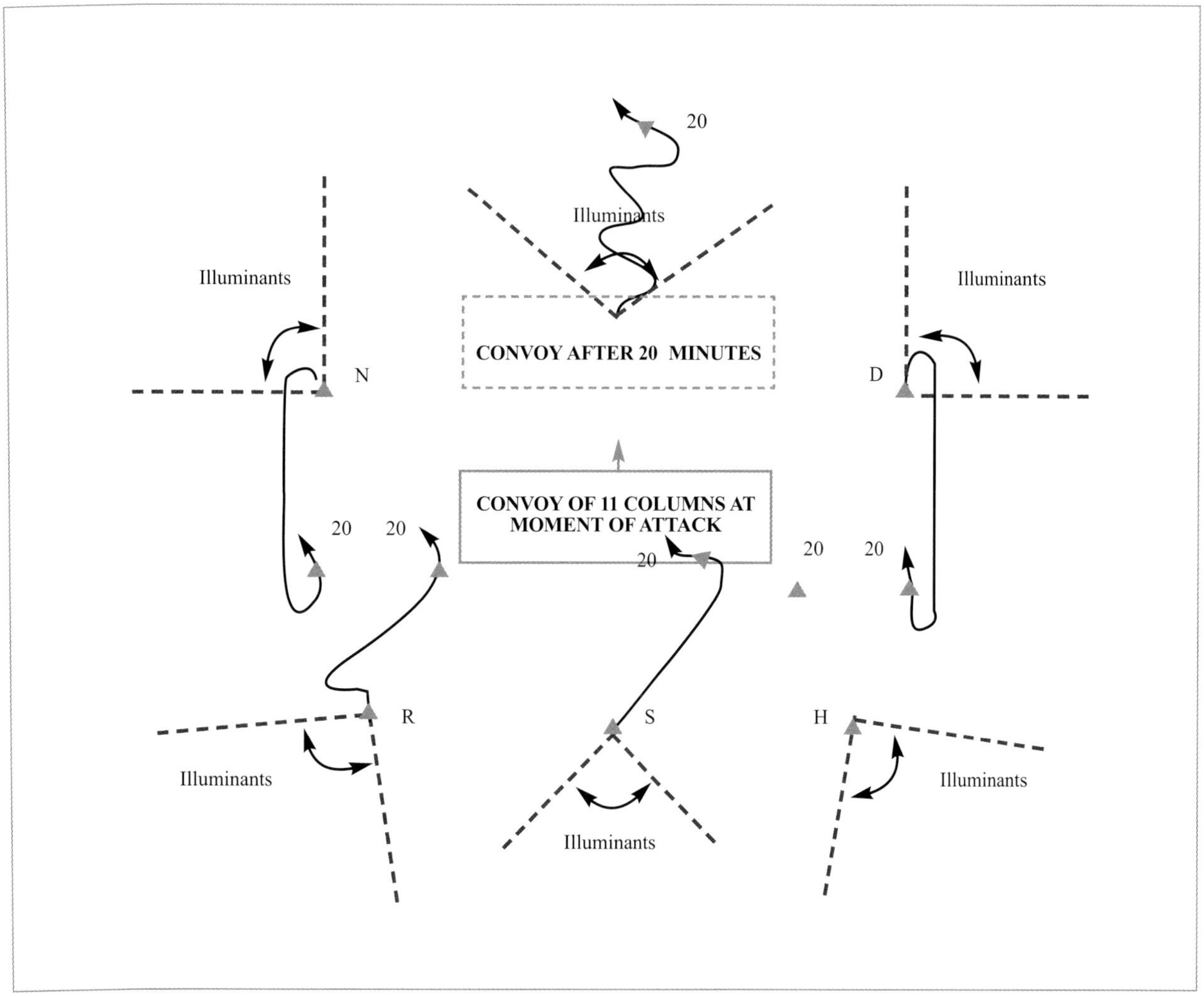

20

Illuminants

Illuminants

Illuminants

CONVOY AFTER 20 MINUTES

N

D

20   20

CONVOY OF 11 COLUMNS AT MOMENT OF ATTACK

20   20

20

R

S

H

Illuminants

Illuminants

Illuminants

Position of convoy and escorts after 20 minutes is shown. Escorts D, H, R and N then sweep zigzagging on convoy course making good convoy speed.

Appendix Nine
OPERATION SCABBARD

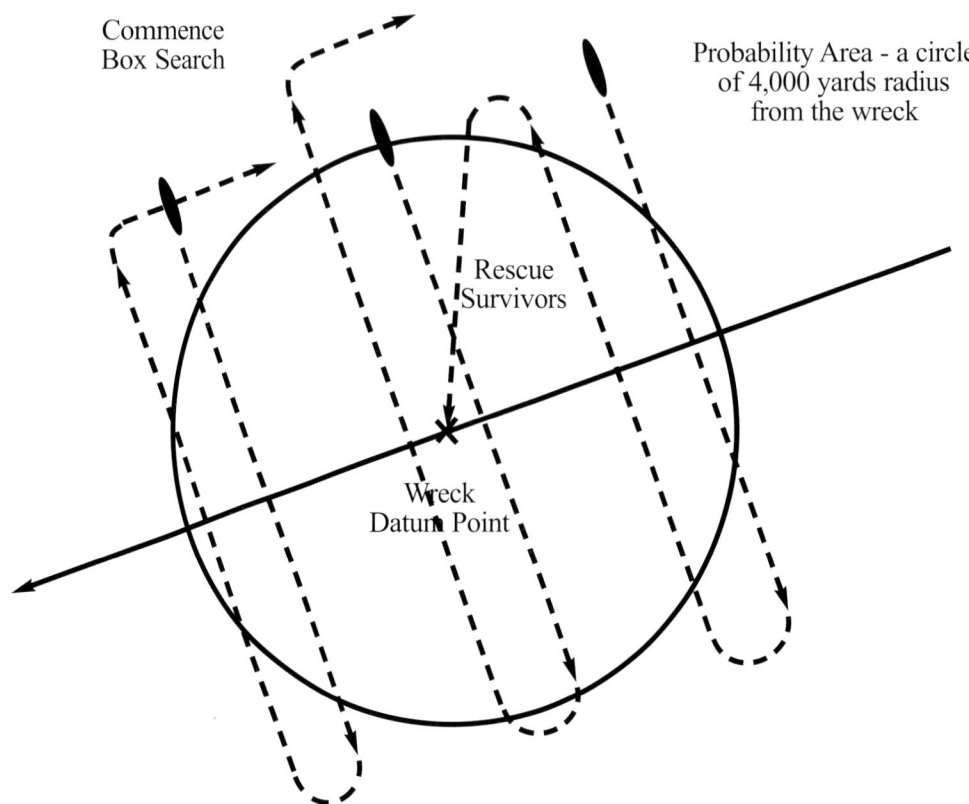

Commence
Box Search

Probability Area - a circle
of 4,000 yards radius
from the wreck

Rescue
Survivors

Wreck
Datum Point

Appendix Ten
OPERATION ARTICHOKE

The operation was designed to cover the probable actions of a U-boat commander when operating in an area where his evasive measures may include bottoming.

It was assumed that the U-boat would bottom anywhere inside the 100 fathom line (183 metres), rising to carry out attacks by periscope by day and to depths of not more than 80 feet (24.5 metres) by night to fire torpedoes into the brown of the convoy HE. After the attack the U-boat may again bottom but will first get clear of the datum point calculated by escorts.

On a ship being torpedoed the escort(s) seeing the torpedoing will fire two white rockets, if a Merchant Ship has not already done so.

The ship in position 'S' will proceed to the vicinity of the wreck and if possible ascertain on which side the ship was torpedoed. She will than proceed to carry out 'Observant' using the wreck as datum.

The escorts in position 'P', 'L', 'A', 'B' and 'F' to turn onto the reciprocal of the convoys course and when 4,000 yards astern of the ship which was torpedoed to commence a sweep along the line of advance of the convoy. The general actions are illustrated by the accompanying diagram.

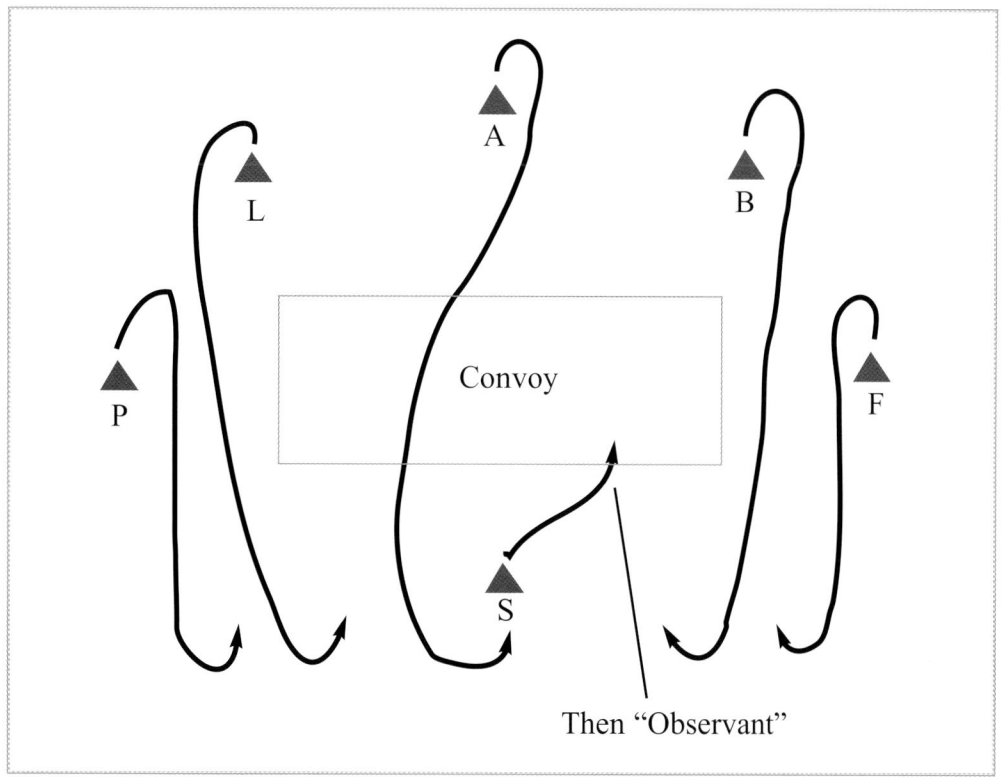

Appendix Eleven
ANTI-GNAT PROCEDURES

SECRET.   <u>REPORT OF PROCEEDINGS</u>   **Ref: 08**

<u>Thirty First Escort Group</u>

<u>Appendix 5. - Anti-Gnat Policy</u>

(1)   Whilst operating as a Support Force in coastal waters, all ships are to keep Unifoxers streamed from dawn to dusk, (i.e. between the times when periscope visibility is considered to be above 2,000 yards. Note: a minimum speed of 10 knots through the water is required to avoid our own minefields in coastal waters and for minimum efficiency of noise level etc.)

(2)   This is :-

(a)   To allow ships to close a U-boat without the delay necessitated by "Step-aside" tactics and

(b)   to accustom Asdics Operators to the detection of echoes through the noise of Unifoxers.

(3)   In fog and at night (except on bright moon light nights) the Group will sweep at anti-gnat speed.

(4)   Immediately a U-boat discloses its presence by sighting, HE, torpedo track or an unexplained explosion etc, all ships, are to drop one depth charge set to 100 feet (unless Unifoxers are streamed) and alter course at least 20 degrees.

(5)   When supporting Convoys and augmenting the close Escort, ships in position on the screen abeam and ahead of the Convoy are to stream Unifoxers. Ships in astern positions are NOT to stream them.

(6)   In daylight when acting independently of Convoys, a continuous weave zig-zag of not loss than 30 degrees either side of the mean course will normally be carried out at a sweeping speed of 12 knots,

(7)   On every occasion of recovering Unifoxers, the bars are to be inspected for wear and changed if necessary.

(8)   Ships detached independently are to take full anti-gnat precautions (i.e. stream Unifoxers and zig-zag continuously).

(9)   On leaving the area of a doubtful contact, speed should not be increased above anti-gnat speed until the range of the contact is at least 5,000 yards.

(10) When clear of coastal waters (i.e. out side the 100 fathom line) the "step aside" procedure as laid down in paragraphs 17 to 21 of W.A.G.O. 706, is to be followed by ships which have no Unifoxer streamed.
All Officers of the watch are to be instructed in the procedure for "step aside" and are to carry stop watches.

(Source: ROP 31st Escort Group 19/04 - 14/05/45 ADM 217/219)

On the other hand the S.O. 30th Escort Group took a more pragmatic view.

EXTRACT FROM 30TH ESCORT GROUP

REPORT OF PROCEEDINGS 15TH TO 29TH DECEMBER 1944

GENERAL

The Group has been too busy operationally during the latter part of the period for exercises to be carried out, as alarms due to bottomed targets have been very frequent. In addition the Group has been working in conjunction with other units on patrol, and not as a group.

As regards the new step aside procedure, this has proved much more simple in operation in practice than appeared from the signal, and after the first two days exercise it worked very well.

Remarks were called for as to the best way to effect the gradual decrease in speed in ships with reciprocating engines. Various methods were tried but the simplest had been found to call 92 revolutions (8 knots) an anti gnat speed, and the engine room now know that if speed is reduced to these revs, from anything higher they must do so according to the scale laid down.

This has proved simple and effective both in practice and when suspicious contacts have been reported. It relieves the Officer of the watch of the necessity of keeping a careful time check when his attention is on other things.

(Source ADM 217/570)

The recommended rate of reduction in engine revolutions given in amplification of W.A.G.M. 102 (N) was:-

Reduce to 70 Revs as follows:

Speed in Revolutions	Time in Minutes and Seconds	Reduction per 15 secs
185	0 to 30	20 Revolutions
	30 to 1-45	10 Revolutions
	1-45 to 3-00	5 Revolutions
175	0 to 15	20 Revolutions
	15 to 1-45	10 Revolutions
	1-45 to 3-00	5 Revolutions
165	0 to 15	20 Revolutions
	15 to 1-30	10 Revolutions
	1-30 to 2-45	5 Revolutions
155	0 to 1-30	10 Revolutions
	1-30 to 2-45	5 Revolutions

Speed in Revolutions	Time in Minutes and Seconds	Reduction per 15 secs
145	0 to 1-15 1-15 to 2-30	10 Revolutions 5 Revolutions
135	0 to 1-00 1-00 to 2-15	10 Revolutions 5 Revolutions
125	0 to 45 45 to 2-00	10 Revolutions 5 Revolutions
115	0 to 30 30 to 1-45	10 Revolutions 5 Revolutions
105	0 to 15 15 to 1-30	10 Revolutions 5 Revolutions
100	0 to 1-30	5 Revolutions
95	0 to 1-15	5 Revolutions
90	0 to 1-00	5 Revolutions
85	0 to 45	5 Revolutions
80	0 to 30	5 Revolutions
75	0 to 15	5 Revolutions

(4) When it is required to revert to the normal method of obeying the Revolution Telegraph, the order "Ship Clear of Danger Area, obey Revolution Telegraph in Normal Manner" will be passed to the Engine Room by telegraph.

(5) It is noted that this procedure for reducing speed is only to be used when speed is reduced to 70 Revolutions. For all other reductions of speed when in the "Danger Area" the normal method is to be used.

Source PRO ADM 217/231

Appendix Twelve
EXERCISES AT SEA

The following are examples of the wide ranging exercises carried out at sea when the conditions were suitable.

B1 ESCORT GROUP CONVOY ONS 35
30th OCTOBER - 11th NOVEMBER 1944: EXERCISE BONE

OBJECT

(1)   To exercise MAC aircraft in reporting the position of a U-boat located during air patrol
(2)   To exercise MAC aircraft in striking, locating and attacking a U-boat and in initiating homing procedure for escorts
(3)   To exercise escorts in striking and in homing procedure on U-boat reported by aircraft.

METHOD OF EXECUTION

On the order "Carry out exercise BONE" being made by B1 to aircraft on patrol, this aircraft is to drop a marker ahead of the convoy at a distance of between 12 and 15 miles, and within the limit of 10° of the convoy's Mean Line of Advance. Marker to be renewed as necessary to identify datum.
This marker is assumed to be a U-boat on the surface and will be reported as such by the aircraft releasing it. Senior Officer Escort will order air strike and detail escorts to support.
Aircraft and HF/DF fitted escorts are to be prepared to carry out Homing Procedure CHARLIE on 2410 Kcs.

ORDERS FOR ESCORTS

Surface escorts, on arrival at datum carry out OBSERVANT, returning to station on completion. Ant Gnat precautions in accordance with ON5N are to be observed. All escorts are to keep a plot.

IFF POLICY

In accordance with W.A.G.O. 349 Striking aircraft are to use code 2.

COMMUNICATIONS

All enemy reports are to be prefixed "FOR EXERCISE".

TERMINATION OF EXERCISE

Exercise may be cancelled at any time by the order "NEGATIVE BONE".

REPORTS

On completion a brief report is to be signalled to Senior Officer escort.

TACTICAL EXERCISES
6th NOVEMBER

Operations PINEAPPLE and BANANA were exercised, ships carrying out Starshell sweeps controlled by B1.
Rocket illuminants were fired.
(Source ADM 217/328)

SECTION 8

(1) The following Group Exercises were carried out during the passage of HX 344

DATE		EXERCISE	REMARKS
Mar 18th		Equal Speed Manoeuvres	Well executed
Mar 20th		Group pass in bearings obtained of Coastal Command Aircraft DUN 4 on 385 Kc/s	Bearings satisfactory
Mar 21st	BEX- 41	Fire a bouquet of Rocket Illuminants on reciprocal to diagram line of bearing from the convoy.	Satisfactory
	BEX-69	Forward lighting has failed. Rig emergency lighting.	Satisfactory
	BEX- 71	Rig suction hose to 4" Magazine assuming it has been flooded in an emergency.	Satisfactory
	BEX-73	Shore up the collision bulkhead.	Satisfactory
	BEX-34	Engage smoke burst with close range. weapons on a safe bearing.	Satisfactory
	BEX-25	Carry out Flag Hoisting Exercise	Satisfactory
	BONE 51	IFF Exercise.	Results satisfactory Equipment gave normal performance in all ships with the exception of Type 253P in *Tintagel Castle*, which gave weak response

DATE	EXERCISE		REMARKS
Mar 22nd	BEX-66	Barometer problem	Answers satisfactory
	BEX-82	A/S Problem	Answers satisfactory
	-	Plotting Exercise	Satisfactory
Mar 23rd	BEX-86		
	BEX-87	T.B.S. Wave Changing Exercise	Very good
	BEX-84		
Mar 24th	BEX-88	Cyphering and decyphering exercise	Satisfactory
	BEX-16	Report D.R. Position using lettered co-ordinates	Satisfactory

BEX SERIES 4.

BEX-83 HF/DF fitted ships code and pass the following on the appropriate channel:- PREFIXED FOR EXERCISE. Enemy submarine transmitting Naval Enigma on Series local bearing 320 Second Class Distant at 1325Z

BEX-84 T.B.S. shift to Frequency A

BEX-85 T.B.S. shift to Frequency B.

BEX-86 T.B.S. shift to Frequency C.

BEX-87 T.B.S. shift to Frequency D.

BEX-88 The following message is to be encyphered. by an officer and. Checked by decyphering by another officer. Times and number of groups are to be reported.
EMERGENCY.
To: C in C WA. (R) Admiralty. COM (D) W.A. From: H.M.S. ....

Possible schnorkel sighted by Officer of Watch. My position, course and speed 54°10'N 05°15'W, 180°, 9?. Suitable. T.O.O. 161924Z.

BEX-89 The following message is to be encyphered by an officer and checked by decyphering by another officer. Times and. number of groups are to be reported.

To: C in C W.A. (R) Admiralty. COM CD) W.A. From: H.M.S. . . .
My 161924.Z. Have attacked. A/S contact classified submarine with Hedgehog. Two explosions 11 seconds after firing. Oil and debris on surface. No charted wreck in vicinity. Investigating. Suitable.

T.O.O. 162030Z.

BEX-90   The following message is to be encyphered by an officer and checked by decyphering by another officer. Times and number of groups are to be reported.

IMMEDIATE.
To: C in C W.A. (R) Admiralty. COM (D) W.A.   From: H.M.S ......,.
My 162030Z. Three bodies recovered, together with debris. Diesel oil on surface. No further A/S contact. Consider U-Boat destroyed. Intend rejoining convoy. Suitable.
T.O.O. 162115Z.

BEX-91   The following message is to be encyphered by an officer and checked by decyphering by another officer. Times and number of groups are to be reported.

IMMEDIATE.
To: C in C W.A. (R) Admiralty. CoM (D) W,A. From: H.M.S. . .
ON 214. Empire Viking rejoined. My position, course and speed at 2000Z
48°17'N 26°42'W 280° 10.   T.O.O. 272325Z.

BEX-92   Prepare to tow aft.

BEX-93   Cruising Watch Depth Charge Party to drill.

BEX-94   Action Depth Charge Party to drill.

BEX-95   Fire a green Very light.

BEX-96   Fire a white Very light.

BEX-97   Fire a red Very light.

BEX-98   Rig gear to embark depth charges aft from oiler.

BEX-99   Place Oil Navigation Lights.

BEX-100   Landing Party to muster with equipment.

BEX-101   Report proof and breaking strains of:-

(A) 4" White Hemp
(B) 6" Grass.
(C) 3?" F.S.W.R.
(D) 1?" Chain Cable

(Source ADM 217/329)

From SO B3 Escort Group R.O.P. 14th December to 26th December 1944 (*ADM 217/133*)

<u>Section 8 - Exercises</u>

1. On the 20th, Smoke Floats were dropped by *Exe*, *Flint Castle* and *Geranium*, as targets for Low Angle gunnery exercise for Convoy ships. Later *Exe* used her mobile rocket projector to fire rocket flares for H.A. barrage practice for her main armament.

2. On the same day C.C.M, L.O.X.O. and Recognition exercises were carried out by the Group's Communications Staffs.

3. On the 21st and 22nd, MAC Ship aircraft returning from patrols exercised Radar ratings in the Group in IFF Stud changing routine. A sequence of changes previously agreed upon by the Senior Officer and the MAC Ship was compared with the results signalled in from the escorts. A good standard of accuracy was attained.

4. On the 23rd a Homing exercise for a lost aircraft was carried out, *Flint Castle* and *Exe* both taking part. Very accurate bearings were reported by the MAC Ship, bringing the aircraft in over the centre of the convoy.

5. On the 24th, *Exe* streamed her splash target and towed for L.A. Shoots by each of the other escorts. *Flint Castle* , provided the best shoot.

From R.O.P. B4 Escort Group Convoy M.K.S. 53 (*ADM 217/367*)

<u>30th June</u>

The convoy formed 4 columns at dawn and escorts were disposed in line abreast as in A.C.I. Article 130 A. Next day the 1st July, the S.L. portion was met and taken over from *Enchantress* and the total convoy of 37 ships was then formed. During the afternoon *Anthony* was ordered to investigate a Portuguese Merchant Ship the *Africa Occidendant*; she boarded this ship - relations were amicable and she found Navicerts in order.

During dusk twilight a smoke laying exercise was carried out with the concurrence of the Commodore, merchant ships taking part. It is thought this exercise paid a good dividend as escorts gained experience which proved valuable when attack actually developed two nights later.

<u>OILING AT SEA</u>

Under normal operating conditions Castle Class Corvettes carried sufficient fuel to make oiling at sea unnecessary. However, WAGOs laid down that ships should be exercised in this manoeuvre whenever possible. An example of the result of such an exercise follows:-

<u>Oiling at Sea</u>

The weather prevented oiling at sea until 30th August. It was decided that the three escorts to be detached that evening should attempt to oil whilst the screen was definitely adequate. *Hesperus*, *Knaresborough Castle* and *Leeds Castle* oiled successfully from *SS Benedick*, but *Allington Castle* was delayed two hours due to loss of

buoys and before she had taken any oil instructions were received for the three additional Castles to proceed forthwith to Greenock. As **Rushen Castle** and **Oxford Castle** had more than ample endurance and in view of the number of escorts present, it was not considered advisable that they should oil. Details of oiling follow.

Ship	Amount	Rate	Time
Hesperus	90 tons	140 ton/hr	1 hour 16 mins
Knaresborough Castle	72 tons	103 tons/hr	1 hour 20 mins
Leeds Castle	80 tons	107 ton/hr	1 hour 21 mins.
	242 tons		

Times taken are from picking up the hose to letting go. Buoyant hose method without steadying line was used.

Appendix Thirteen
DOUGLAS SEA AND SWELL SCALE

SWELL

SEA	0 No Swell	Low 1 Short or Average	Low 2 Long	Moderate 3 Short	Moderate 4 Average	Moderate 5 Long	6 Short	Heavy 7 Heavy	8 Long	9 Confused
0 Calm	00	01	02	03	04	05	06	07	08	09
1 Smooth	10	11	12	13	14	15	16	17	18	19
2 Slight	20	21	22	23	24	25	26	27	28	29
3 Moderate	30	31	32	33	34	35	36	37	38	39
4 Rough	40	41	42	43	44	45	46	47	48	49
5 V Rough	50	51	52	53	54	55	56	57	58	59
*6 High	60	61	62	63	64	65	66	67	68	69
*V High	70	71	72	73	74	75	76	77	78	79
* Precipitous	80	81	82	83	84	85	86	87	88	89
¥9 Confused	90	91	92	93	94	95	96	97	98	99

Note: In this scale a new departure has been introduced in that length of swell and height of swell are, from the point of view of observations, considered separately and then combined together for coding.

A Short Swell means a swell where the length or distance between each successive top of swell is small.

A Long Swell means a swell where the length or distance is large.

A Low Swell means a swell where the height between the lowest and highest part of the swell is small.

A Heavy Swell means a swell where the height is great.

* These are considered to represent seas which occur with a swell or in the open ocean, for instance, the highest sea recorded in sheltered waters would be 5, or under exceptional circumstances (eg a hurricane) 6 or 7 might be used. The idea of the roughness would be conveyed by the force of the wind.

¥ Occasioned by current, tide, sudden shift of wind, and not necessarily strong wind.

N.B: This scale is provisional pending acceptance by International Meteorological Committee

Appendix Fourteen
TABLE SHOWING THE FORCE OF THE WIND AS REGISTERED BY BEAUFORT'S NOTATION

Nautical Miles per Hour	Force	Description
0-1	0	Calm
2-6	1-2	Light Airs
7-10	3	Light Breeze
11-16	4	Moderate Breeze
17-21	5	Moderate Breeze
22-27	6	Strong Wind
28-33	7	Strong Wind
34-40	8	Gale
41-47	9	Gale
48-55	10	Storm
56-65	11	Storm
Above 65	12	Hurricane

Appendix Fifteen
PROBLEMS ARISING WHEN ESCORTING LARGE CONVOYS

These notes arise from the passage of Convoy ONS 233 escorted by C5 Escort Group; 21 April 1944 to 3 May 1944. It appears that this was the first time that such a large slow convoy (111 ship) had been sent across the Atlantic. See ADM 217/525 for the full ROIP narrative.

25. SECTION 1 APPENDIX 1

Remarks in amplification of my 261705B on escorting large convoys with small escorts.

TO: ONS 233 PASS TO COMMODORE   **FROM :CinCWA**
(R) A.I.G. #303

ONS 233. In view of large number of ships, report whether convoy experiencing difficulty in complying with my 232151.
(2) Have you any useful proposals for future large convoys 251607b.

Paragraph 1 refers to am alteration of course associated by a re-route.

TO: AIG #303   **FROM: S.O. C5**

(1) PARAGRAPH 1 YR 251607. NO BECAUSE VISIBLITY WAS GOOD.
(2) PARAGRAPH 2
(A) TO REDUCE TRAFFIC ON 2410 MOST DESIRABLE TBS BE FITTED ALL ESCORTS. DESPITE WHIPPING IN DEPTH OF CONVOY FOUR TO SIX MILES DEPENDING ON WEATHER HENCE DISTANCE TOO GREAT FOR MUCH V/S EXCEPT IN HIGH VISIBILTY. IF STATE 'Y' WERE IMPOSED DIFFICULTIES OF INTER ESCORT COMMUNICATION WOULD BE ACUTE.
(B) RESCUE SHIP OR INTELLIGENT REAR COMMODORE AT REAR OF CONVOY WITH SIGNAL STAFF AND TEN INCH LAMP. COMMODORE ALSO NEEDS TEN INCH LAMPS.
(C) ESCORT TO BE LARGE ENOUGH TO PERMIT OF ONE BEING DETACHED FOR EMERGENCIES. E.G. SHIPS TEMPORARILY DISABLED.
(D) MAIN REQUIREMENT NO SHIP LESS THAN 9 KNOTS, CONVOY AT PRESENT SLOW IN BAD WEATHER THAT MANY SHIPS CANNOT STEER. RESULT CHAOS.
(3) COMMODORE CONCURS IN 2(A), (B), (C) AND (D) ARE COMMODORE's VIEWS WITH WHICH I AGREE. REFERNCE 2(C) ONE ADDITIONAL ESCORT WOULD BE AN ADVANTAGE.

261705B

1. ONS 233 numbered 111 ships disposed in 14 columns with 2 MAC ships in 74 and 82.

2. Station keeping was only moderate, particularly in the outer columns and at no time was the convoy

less than four miles in depth and in bad weather this increased to six and even seven miles. This was despite a considerable amount of whipping in and I much agree with the Commodore's suggestion that a Rear Commodore with full signal staff should be stationed at the back of the convoy. The convoy front did not exceed eight miles and could normally be kept at six and a half miles.

3.   Number of Escorts required.

Six escorts does not leave much to spare to allow for breakdowns in radar and A/S or for detaching ships either to investigate reports of U-boats or to stand by merchant ships suffering from temporary breakdowns. One additional escort would be a considerable help, even if no breakdowns occurred, there is work enough for two in the rear to chivvy laggards. For the last five days *Dunver*'s A/S had a maximum range of 700 yards and *Hespeler* had neither A/S or radar working, thus the effective escort was only four corvettes, with both A/S and radar in action. It is also very necessary that this number of escorts be maintained in waters where , though submarine risk is low, ordinary marine risks due to icebergs and fog is appreciable.

4.   Use of MAC ship Aircraft.

With the reduction in escort numbers these aircraft take on an enhanced value. They are of the greatest use for reporting the positions of ships which have fallen astern, when escorts cannot be spared and such tasks as reporting icebergs on the track.
If a patrol round the convoy is not necessary, then, in the absence of definite U-boat information, sweeps ahead of the convoy appear to be the best employment as it is the only direction in which it would be at all possible to send slow escorts for any distance to investigate sightings.
In view of the great importance of having aircraft available, it may well be desirable to conserve aircraft in the early stages of the voyage, even though flying weather is good, to a greater extent than would be necessary with small convoys and a large number of escorts. It is realised that this is normally an undesirable practice but in the case of large convoys it would seem justified.

5.   Fuelling of Escorts

As it is most undesirable for escorts to be away from their positions in the disposition longer than is necessary, it may well not be possible to carry out as much exercise fuelling and topping up of escorts that do not actually require fuel, as would normally be the case.

6.   Communications

With the much greater distances apart of escorts that are entailed, V/S is not satisfactory for inter escort communication except in the highest visibility. Consequently there is a great increase in R/T traffic and to obviate excessive use of 2410 K/cs it is most strongly recommended that all escorts in Groups used for escorting these large convoys be fitted with T.B.S.
The value of T.B.Y. communication with the Commodore is very great as it materially helps to reduce the burden on his very overloaded communication staff. In fog and low visibility it is invaluable. It is only a pity that it is so temperamental about screening and care must be taken to get the set and the ship in the best possible position if good results are to be obtained.

7. <u>Conclusion</u>

As no experience was gained with regard to enemy action these remarks deal only with normal convoy business entailed by the large number of ships present. The sum total of increases asked for are not great, amounting only to the fitting of T.B.S. in escorts and if possible the provision of a seventh escort.

Appendix Sixteen
A COMMODORE'S COMPLAINT

11. My most depressing and worrying trip and that in spite of very favourable weather no ships lost and one submarine sunk.

Maybe the trip feeling started in New York where I read of French-Canadian sabotage and resistance to war effort. Then at Halifax I heard of their sabotage of HMC ships so that when ship after ship broke down and one caught fire, I again thought of sabotage

My own course and speed as well as navigation and W/T D/F gave me continual anxiety. Also I missed the support, which one nearly always gets, of the Vice-Commodore and others.

As NCSO Halifax was so keen on it, I accepted an A1 form with the 9 LSTs filling the rear positions in each of nine columns. After 36 hours, I changed the LSTs over into 2 columns of their own (numbers. 11 and 12) on starboard wing of convoy, and I am confident that the latter is the preferable arrangement.

12. No suggestions for improvement, except perhaps the impossible request that only perfect people or angels should be drafted to the merchant navy. Having now worked with the latter for almost four years, and fully realizing their many excellent qualities I may, I hope, be allowed to laugh at them (and at myself) for some of our less creditable moments,, and I will try so to do (however imperfectly) in the Damon Amyon manner:

(a)   One little ship, fussy like an old doll with the itch, she just can't keep on going straight on and firing her little peashooters. "No" she says, "let me go astern of the convoy please where I find room to use my rods `cos I'm a twelve gun doll indeed." Now this doll is mighty gabby, and slow, but it all seems soso to me, so I says to her sure she can drop back and fire. But soon my eye is popping out of my head, like when you see a lone doll on Broadway, cos as soon as this doll drops astern, she turns and steams merrily away firing happily with every peashooter on the bucket. When all the equilisers is fired, she turns back and tumbles at last that she is 5 miles astern and it takes her 12 hours to get back into the convoy.

(b)   One morning, I thinks the gang will soon be getting near the Great Banks, and into the fogs so it's time we do a last bit of practice. There's one lunkie (a square-head, see) with the moniker of Scandinavia Sam. He's been going along amiable and making no fuss howsoever. Well, I makes a signal to them all, all friendly, saying "You guys, will you please read up your Mersigs and all about fog-manoeuvering and we'll soon have a grand parade and don't forget 3 and 11 is repeating columns." So at 1000 off goes my whistle and off go lots of other whistles and some are quick and some are slow and some don't go at all. And the lunkie, he's 113, makes no noise howsoever. Well, I says, it's silly waiting like this; `allo make a signal to Sam saying "Why don't you whistle?" "Why as to my whistle," replies Scandinavia Sam. "Why, that's been on the blink for days".

(c)   One night the wind is howling like a pitchman and the ship is knocking about not a little, and it is indeed what sailors call a great storm. I am thinking it is a good if I am at home, when I hear that the **Southern Belle** is blinking out a signal saying, "Help, there's some men just floating past in the water." Help indeed, I thinks, this is a more than somewhat tough break for any guys in the water. Is it possible that the corvette ahead is capsizing or is it a lifeboat? Anyway, I decide break R/T silence and I tell the S.O. Escort there are guys in the sea. "Whisst" he says and "whisst" I thinks. But I knows the rescue ship is a hop kid and next Morning he signals me that he looks and finds a raft with red lights nicely burning but no men. So I tell little **Belle** about this

and she says "Sure, that is our raft that is washing overboard just before I sees the red lights in the water." So I thinks **Southern Belle** is perhaps not one with much zing in her furthermore.

(d)   One rusty old bucket can't get the R.V. through her noggin. So she winks over as nice as you please for me to check the coding of same. So I checks the R.V. and it's O.K. and I says so to her and I also says "What is the trouble?" Then Rusty replies "I'm steering 223° but you signals 228°."

(sgd) (Charles Turle ?)
Commodore RNR
MV Bonaire
15.3.44.

Source ADM 199/1337

Appendix Seventeen
CANTEEN MESSING

H. Cooper-Bland of **Denbigh Castle** wrote:-

As I remember, Canteen Messing was a system that was favoured in small ships as it required only one cook in the galley plus of course the officer's cook.

The crew would already be divided into messes. Each mess would have it's own Mess Caterer, who would be responsible for drawing what was available from the ship's canteen. In these transactions money was not involved. Goods, or the value thereof would be debited to the particular mess account.

The Caterer would also make a roster of "Cooks of the day"; it would be two ratings who that day would have responsibility of preparing the meals for that day. They would in effect do everything except cook it. When ready it would be taken to the galley where it would be cooked. The duty cooks of the day would then collect and serve the food under the direction of the Mess Caterer. They would also be responsible for clearing away.

As I have already mentioned it was the Mess Caterer's task to draw the rations and buy from what was available. At the end of each month a list was published showing the amounts spent, which would be balanced against a catering allowance, of so much a head.

The signal mess, to which I belonged was the only mess that I ever heard of that ended up in the black; not having overspent their allowance.

Our mess caterer, who was the Yeoman, seemed to be very proud of his budgeting skills. I don't think many members of the mess felt quite the same about it, as it meant that if there was any kind of luxury going we didn't have it; it would be too dear.

An example of this I recall was when there was some tinned fruit to be had, needless to say we didn't have any; far too expensive.

The reputation that our mess gained was a constant embarrassment to us all. We suffered the derision of all and sundry. Gash in many forms was often dumped on mess deck table with remarks like, "There you are you poor hungry Sods."

While I think that this type of catering was very popular you always had to remember that however well you had prepared a meal you were always at the mercy of the cook. On our ship we were fortunate in having a good one.

Stoker Reg (Rattle) Ravencroft of **Kenilworth Castle** time as Mess Cook did not last very long.

He had not had much experience in the cooking line, so when he was told to provide a dinner for the mess, he filled a tray with rice and bunged it into the galley oven

It was not long before an irate ship's cook dragged him into the galley to witness rice pudding oozing out of his oven. Ordered to shovel it out, he eventually got down to the bottom of the tray. There seemed to be enough rice to feed the entire ship's company. The surplus was thrown overboard where it weighed down the swooping gulls.

He had better success with his 'creamy coffee'. The secret ingredient being the addition of custard powder This was greatly appreciated by the lads . That is until one day they discovered lumps of yellow gobs at the bottom of the pot. Thereafter he not allowed to be messman again.

They got their own back by volunteering his services to sweep the funnel during 'Cleaning Ship'. He had to wear a muslin mask and his underwear which he slung overboard when he emerged looking like Old King Cole.

Appendix Eighteen
CARRIAGE OF BULLION

Flint Castle (SL 165/MKS 56 - 30/07/44)
Hadleigh Castle (SL 170/MKS 61 - 01/09/44)
Morpeth Castle (Sl 170/MKS 61 - 20/09/44)
Rushen Castle (MKS52, 21/06/44, SL 165/MKS 56 - 30/07/44)
Oxford Castle (SL170/MKS61 - 20/09/44)

All are reported to have carried small quantities of gold bullion (between 15 and 40 tons) to the U.K. whilst escorting the convoys and dates indicated above,

To: Norman Goodwin. Archivist (April 4th 2002)

From: R.C.Warwick. Regarding "*Other Queries*" Spring 2002

I served in **Rushen Castle** from her commissioning in 1943 to the end of the German War when I became C.O of an Assault Ship building in Canada for the Pacific.

1. BULLION.

This came from the Bank of Poland and was shipped down to Gibraltar for safekeeping when war was declared. It was packed in individual wood covered "bricks". We stowed it in the magazine. The Bank of England representative who met us with a truck in Gladstone Dock was provided with a working party of five sailors. He kindly gave each of his helpers £1 for their assistance.

2. RAF SPANISH COAST DEFENCES PHOTOGRAPHS

On the same voyage back from Gibraltar we were approached by the RAF who had a number of large parcels wrapped in canvas and weighted with lead. A little over one ton. These packages they wished us to stow handily on our bridge so that in the event of being threatened with capture they could be thrown overside.

The commanding officer informed the RAF personnel that the ship was "tender" enough as it was and did not need a ton or more added. "What was the treasure in these packages anyway?"

The CO was told that this represented four years work by the RAF in photographing the coastal defences of Spain and would create a diplomatic incident if this work was discovered. The CO ordered the packages to be put into the magazine with the Polish gold. The RAF personnel came aboard in Liverpool to collect their "treasure" but did not reward the sailors helping them. Pity.

****

From Harry James (Coder & writer on **Morpeth Castle**)

"My memory of the trip we made carrying gold are mainly of the great difference between the way it was handled on loading and unloading. The consignment arrived heavily escorted and I remember flashing lights and motor cycle outriders. When it was off loaded at Liverpool, there

was only a solitary policemen visible on the jetty though I have no idea who was within the warehouse behind him. The boxes were small but heavy as much as one man could reasonably carry. I was not part of the proceedings at either end. I only witnessed it from the deck. I was later told that it was French gold which had been sent abroad at the outbreak of hostilities."

Appendix Nineteen
MANOEUVRING AT SEA:
EFFECTS ON ENGINE AND BOILER ROOMS

When considering the Castles, the Engine Room itself, was faced with a very large cumbersome engine which was slow to respond to extreme changes but with low order increases or decreases there would be no problem. So that, from a control point of view and all other things being equal oiling at sea was less of a worry than, say a creep attack. However if the pressure of the steam supplied from the boiler room to the engine varies, then the engine revs change and must be adjusted. The objective of the Boiler room is to supply steam at constant quality and pressure to the engine room. To achieve this the Boiler Room must control certain variables eg:-

> fuel oil temperature and pressure
> number of burners in use
> quantity of air to furnace (via pressurised boiler room)
> water level in the boiler.

To name but a few.

> A sudden reduction in demand for steam results in:-

>> High boiler water levels and steam pressure
>> *(in the extreme, both dangerous)*

> A sudden increase in steam demand, results in:-

>> Low boiler water levels and steam pressure
>> *(also in the extreme, dangerous)*

and with a higher probability of making black smoke, a war time no no.

The problem was that they had no way to store steam so that a change in demand had to be met by an instant increase or decrease in the generation of heat (more readily achieved with oil than with coal).

Therefore, although the Engine Room itself, whilst under way, had many variables other than steam pressure to which it must adjust, it was the Boiler Room, when the ship was manoeuvring , that would encounter most problems.

Appendix Twenty
OILING AT SEA

THE OILERS

The Athel Line ships were pre-eminent as Naval oilers. They had been designed to carry molasses and were provided with heavy scantlings and the sheer strake had a thickness of 1.8 inches. They were therefore ideally suited as oilers.

The Athel Line ships were stationed at Londonderry, St John's N.F. as well as at Reykjavik and Scapa Flow. They were also used as escort oilers, travelling with the convoys and oiling the escorts at sea as required.

Prominent amongst these was the **Scottish Heather** (Captain L. Blanch) She survived a torpedo attack by **U-225** (Leimkukler) on 27 December 1942, after refuelling escorts of the convoy ONS 154. The damage was such that the order was given to 'abandon ship'. However thirteen crew members remained on board. The following morning the skeleton crew managed to get the ship under way and pick up her boats. Captain Blanch then took the ship back to Rothesay arriving there on 2 January 1943. The ship was given an extensive refit at Smiths Shipyard.

Considerable improvements were made to the 'oiling at sea' equipment. The ship was also fitted out to carry reserve depth charges for the convoy escorts. Under the command of Captain T. Maxwell the **Scottish Heather** made sixteen Atlantic crossings between April 1943 and May 1944. Altogether the ship completed over 100 refuelling operations.

Six owned and three vessels managed by the Athel Line were fitted for bunkering escorts. In recognition of these ships, My Lords Commissioners of the Admiralty wrote:

> *"One hundred and fifty-four vessels were equipped for fuelling Warships at sea; and in the course of its two and a half years existence the Escort Oiling Service carried out more than 4,000 separate oiling operations, which involved the transfer of 35,000 tons of fuel in every condition of weather. It thus took a prominent share in winning the Battle of the Atlantic.*
>
> *Nine ships of your Company were employed on this novel and often arduous work, which was undertaken in addition to their normal duties by officers and men with a zeal and competence which deserved and achieved success. To this success the Direction and Management of your Company have contributed materially by their active co-operation and help.*
>
> *My lords would be glad if an expression of their appreciation could be conveyed to the Masters, Officers and Crews of the ships named in the accompanying schedule for their contribution to a service of vital operational importance."*

To this the Company added:-

> *"By their steadfast courage and devotion to duty Masters, Officers and Crews made an unsurpassed Contribution to Victory, of which everyone associated with the United Molasses Company Limited has reason to be proud."*

20th April 1946

Appendix Twenty-One
SHIPS' NEWS SERVICES

Most ships operated a News Service of one kind or another. Very little of this output has survived. This piece from *HMS Morpeth Castle* is of some historical interest.

The 'Morpeth Castle' News Service

Owners: Osborne & Duncan

Operated by: Link and Co.

Message from Admiral Dönitz to all German Forces

My Comrades. Our Fuhrer has fallen; faithful to his great ideas of preserving the peoples of Europe from Bolshevism, he has laid down his life and won the death of a hero. With him has gone one of the greatest heroes of German history. In proud reverence before him we lower the flag.

The Fuhrer has appointed me to be his successor as Head of the State and Supreme Commander of the German Armed Forces. I have assumed command over all services of the German Armed Forces with the intention of continuing the struggle against Bolshevism until our Fighting Forces and hundreds of thousands of our families in the East are rescued from slavery and annihilation.

Against the English and Americans I must continue the struggle as long as they oppose me in the struggle against Bolshevism.

The situation depends on you who have already accomplished such historical deeds and who now refuse to see the end of the war as unconditional surrender. I expect discipline and obedience. Only by unreserved execution of my orders will chaos and defeat be avoided.

He is a coward and a traitor who at this juncture shrinks from his duty, and thereby brings death and slavery to German women and children. The trust carried out for the Führer is now without further orders owed by each and every one of you to me as the successor appointed by the Führer.

German Soldiers do your duty. The life of our people is at stake.

Signed.

Dönitz

Grossadmiral and Supreme Commander of Armed Forces.

*The message was broadcast in plain language to all German fleet. Picked up by **Morpeth Castle** and translated into English by Lieut. Duncan (Ex-schoolmaster)*

Appendix Twenty-Two
U-BOAT SURRENDER ORDERS

8th May 1945: 30th Escort Group ordered to proceed to the Blue Surrender Route for U-Boats

This Blue Surrender Route was on a line between New York and Loch Eriboll, in the extreme north of Scotland. A continuous signal was being sent out by the German Admiralty instructing all U-Boats to proceed under water and surface on this line and proceed to Loch Eriboll. They would eventually meet an Escort Group who would hand them comprehensive instructions. A copy of these instructions and the English translation follows.
The 30th Escort Group left the Blue Surrender Route on 12th May 1945, being relieved by **HMS Zanzibar** in order that the Group could return to Londonderry for 48 hours VE Day rest.

**COPY OF ORIGINAL INSTRUCTIONS HANDED TO U-BOAT COMMANDERS
SURRENDERING THEIR SUBMARINES AND CREWS ON THE BLUE SURRENDER ROUTE
TO 30th ESCORT GROUP.**

8th MAY to 12th MAY, 1945

(a)   Zu die oberflacse kommen und an die oberflaose bleiben.

(c)   Ein schwarz oder blau ermatten fliegen mahrend der tag und mahrend die night die bositions Pampe brennen..

(d)   Alle munition wegwerfen, allen torpedo sichen sicser wiedergeben durch bistolem wegschaffen, und sicher minen wiedergeden.

(e)   Alles sicnal in die sprache schlicht machen.

(f)   Sich enthalton versenten oder in irgendwie machen der schladen fur ihr unterseerot.

(g)   Die stellung, der kurs und die sputen Jeder acht uhr zu die Funksprunkstation GKR an 500 kc/s und auch GZZ 10 an einem diesen frequenz 16845, 12685., 5970, kc/s Berickton.

(h)   Durch der wogfest zu loch Eriboll fur die revision. schreiten.

(i)   Ihr weg ist durch 58°Nord 11°West 59°Nord 05°30'West zu Loch Eriboll in 58°33 Nord 04°37'West.

An langen an Loch Eriboll dazwischen des uhr auf Sonnenaufgang und drei uhr Vorn der sonneuntergang.

English Translation:-

(a)   on coming to the surface, on the surface stay.

(c)   Fly a Black or Blue flag by day and burn a position lamp by night.

(d)   Throw away all ammunition. All torpedoes make safe. Remove detonators and defuse.

(e)   Make all signals in simple language.

(f)   Contain oneself, abstain from damaging your submarine in any way to hazard the voyage.

(g)   Report your course and speed every night at 8 o'clock to the radio station GKR on 500 kc/s and also GZZ 10 on one of these frequencies 16845, 12685, 5970, kc/s (Berickten)

(h)   Proceed to Loch Eriboll for the gathering (Reunion).

(i)   Your course is from 58°N 11°W by 59°N 05°30'W to Loch Eriboll in 58°33'N by 04°34'W.

Arrive at Loch Eriboll between sunrise and three hours before sunset.

Appendix Twenty-Three
HIGH TEA BARRIER

High Tea was the codeword for sonobuoys. These enabled aircraft with a means of listening to underwater sounds. The buoy had an operational life of 4 to 8 hours, after which it sank. Aircraft were able to track a moving submerged U-boat. The involvement of the 30th Escort Group with a 'High Tea Barrier' is explained by the following extract from the War Diary.

Monday, 7 May 1945, War Diary (Naval), 1-15 May 1945, Naval Historical Branch p.148.

<u>Operations</u>

<u>Western Approaches.</u>

HT ["High Tea"] barrier 200 miles west of Aran Is.
Commodore (D) WA is requested to sail 30th EG [EG30] to arrive 55°N,13°W at 0730B/8 and 21st EG [EG21] to arrive 55°N, 14°W at 0800B/8.

1.   On arrival at above positions, groups addressed are to lay HT barriers in a direction of 270°.

2.   Continuity of line is essential and to ensure this aircraft will drop a line of smoke markers using for datum the first marker laid by 30th EG.

3.   On completion of lays groups are to patrol parallel to and 10 miles to the northward of their respective barriers and co-operate with aircraft.

4.   Codewords   21st EG - "Loiter A"
                       30th EG - "Loiter B"
(C-in-C WA, 070011B to Commodore (D) WA, SO EGs 21, 30)

My 070011 not to all. Operation postponed owing to weather.

(2) 21st EG form Force 32 forthwith and proceed via Minches to operate in area between parallels 58° and 59° and meridians 04°30' and 06°30'[W]

1.   30 EG form Force 33 and operate in area between line joining Barra Head, Malin Head and line Altacarry, Mull of Kintyre.

2.   All convoys to be supported within these areas.

3.   (C-in-C,WA 071242B to SO EGs 21,30.)

Appendix Twenty-Four
BRITTANY BARRIER

The "barrier" laid by **HMS Brittany** was an anti-schnorkel obstruction, which appeared to have consisted of a series of buoys linked by wire cable designed to snag or damage a U-boat's schnorkel, thus forcing her to make use of the surface (and thus become vulnerable to attack, particularly by aircraft). Some quotations follow from the Naval War Diary which provide some detail of the role of the 30th Escort Group in the laying of anti-schnorkel barriers;

Monday, 9 April 1945, War Diary (Naval), 1-15 April 1945 - Naval Historical Branch. P144.

Operations

Northern Waters

Anti-Schorkel Obstructors.

AM 032223B request **Brittany** be sailed as convenient to commence laying of type OP obstruction at daylight 11 April evenly spaced over a length of 50 miles from position 60°40'N, 05°20'W on a line 160°

1. On completion **Brittany** to return to Greenock to re-load.

2. An early report as to mileage of obstruction laid and date and time of completion is required.

3. (D of BD, Adty., 091 706B to C-in-C, Rosyth, C-in-C HF)

Tuesday, 10 April 1945, War Diary (Naval), 1-15 April 1945 - Naval Historical Branch. Pp. 162-163.

Operations

Northern Waters

Brittany - Anti-Schnorkel Obstruction Lay

At about 1700B today Tuesday when Home Fleet units have returned to harbour R/V with Brittany departing Scapa at 1700B/10.

1. Escorting **Brittany** to 60°40'N, 05°20'W or as required by **Brittany**, where **Brittany** will commence to lay obstruction.

2. Support **Brittany** to north-eastward during laying operation.

3. Trawler **Narvik** will join later
(C-n-C, Rosyth, 101110B to SO EG 30)

Pass Switha Gate at 1700B today Tuesday and proceed to comply with AM 091706B which is being passed to 30th EG, routed by AM QZS.15 and through 59°53'N 04°45'W.

1.   You will be met off Stanger Head by SO EG 30 in *Pevensey Castle* with *Launceston Castle* and *Portchester Castle* who will escort until lay is completed. *HNMT Narvik* is being sailed to R/V on line of laying and will escort you to Greenock on completion. *Narvik* will keep constant W/T watch on 1570 Kc/s and hold naval code XA Cofox and Loxo.

2.   Attention is called to AM QZX.816

3.   Report is required in accordance with para 3 of AM 091706.

4.   Gate arranged. Acknowledge.
      (*C-in-C HF, (Ashore), 101142B to* **Brittany**.)

Brittany with SO EG 30 in *Pevensey Castle* with *Launceston Castle* and *Portchester Castle*.
(*C-in-C HF, Ashore 1017098.*)

Appendix Twenty-Five
PUBLICATION SPONSORS

The following have contributed to the publication of this book.

Ship	Name
Allington Castle	Beckett D.L. ; Hopkins J. ; Jeffery M.G. ; Meredith W.E. ; Montier J.C. ; Morgan E.G. ; Pond P.J. ; Rourke P. ; Sweeney J. ; Tucker W.J.
Alnwick Castle	Harland A.E. ; Thompson B.R.E.
Bamborough Castle	Burden D.W. ; Davis W.E. ; Groutage S.H.
Bamborough Castle/ Berkeley Castle	Wikeley J.D.
Berkeley Castle	Butler F.W.D. ; Stanley A.E. ; Tribe T.J.C.
Caistor Castle	Beer B.R. ; Bell P.G. ; Bowman B.R. ; Clough L. ; Hughes R.A. ; Pearson MBE K.J. ; Worsencroft F.L.
Carisbrooke Castle	Biffen M.C. ; Boulden L.J. ; Hickmott J.S. ; Howard H.G. ; Hudson L.A. ; Laidler W.J. ; Legget B.J. ; Long L.F. ; Rogers K.G. ; Saunders J. Wainwright OBE B.H.
Carisbrooke Castle/ Berkeley Castle	Richards R.J.
Denbigh Castle	Andrews L.G.S ; Bettridge R.A. ; Cooper-Bland H. ; Green R.A. ; Johnson J.L. Wright W.A.
Denbigh Castle/ Hedingham Castle/ Oxford Castle	Looker W.
Dumbarton Castle	Charlton G. ; Hart P De B.C. ; Phillips R. ; Shelley S.
Farnham Castle	Myson P.J.
Flint Castle	Beck J.W. ; Burrows P.C. ; Evans L. ; James K.E.M. ; Mitchell M. ; Simmons J.
Hadleigh Castle	Barrow B.M. ; Benham B.R. ; Joss J.J.B. ; Rodman P. ; Zeitz H.B.
Hadleigh Castle/ Humberstone	Crothers R.J.
Hedingham Castle	Maule G.A. ; Nugent J.A. ; Pickett S.C. ; Rendall R.F.

Hedingham Castle/ Launceston Castle	Carroll P.J.
Hurst Castle	Haynes R.A. ; Kemp F.L.R.
Kenilworth Castle	Crutch W.A. ; Daniel C.S. ; Welch J.
Kincardine	Pyke D.R.
Knaresborough Castle	Angel R.C. ; Childs J. ; Clarke V.F. ; Dando I.D.
Lancaster Castle	Baynon A.C. ; Green L. ; Rynn F.P.J. ; Swain H.T. ; Wright D.
Launceston Castle	Burrows E. ; Gould B.F.J ; Griffiths J.A. ; Hewitt R. ; Hicks C. ; I'Anson D.G. ; Jones E. ; Young J.S.
Launceston Castle/ Hedingham Castle	Seamer J.C.
Leeds Castle	Davis A.H. ; Myers D.F. ; Patrick T.M. ; Roberts P.E.
Morpeth Castle	Jameson H.B. ; Jeremiah N.C.
Oakham Castle	Hallet R.J. ; Karling B.J. ; Richmond F.G. ; Roberts M. ; Schlegel R. ; Shaw V.E.
Oakham Castle/ Flint Castle	Stanton E.W. ; Webb L.W.C. ; Davies J.H.
Oxford Castle	Barbour I.G.
Pevensey Castle	Gunner R.H. ; Ould D.J. ; Rees F. ; Roberts K.A.
Pevensey Castle/ Portchester Castle	Marsh S.R.
Portchester Castle	Bennett F. ; Castle R. ; Jones F.H. ; Sansom K.G. ; Selby I. ; Slocombe P. ; Wells-Brown D.A.
Rushen Castle	Adams H.J.H. ; Goodall R.S. ; Palmer G.R. ; Shipp A.B.F. ; Stubbs P. Warwick R.C.
Tintagel Castle	Booth R.F. ; Corlett J. ; Cornwall A.W. ; Green S. ; James H. ; Kimberley N.S. ; Mitchell M. ; Morrell Rev D. ; Taylor S. ; Weir A.D.
Tintagel Castle/ Allington Castle	Goodwin F.N.
Associate	Butler R.S. ; Cunliffe Mrs M.J. ; Dunlevy J. ; McLeod R. ; Sillence Mrs J. ; Townsend K.
Others	Huntley P.W. ; Jarzebek H. ; Skelton M.L.

Epilogue

"As darkness fell, those of us not fortunate enough to have been ashore for
VE day celebrations when the lights went on again, saw the lights go on again
at sea and were able to count our blessings by night as well as by day.
The sight of sixty odd ships, well formed in convoy and fully illuminated was
a truly remarkable one, and after five and a half years of complete darkness, a
little frightening to behold. However, we lighted up our pipes on the bridge
and having "cast away the works of darkness and put upon us the armour of
light', we were soon readjusted to persuing our lawful occasions for all the
world to see."

Commander J.V. Brock RCNVR

Senior Officer C6 Escort Group
(Passage of Convoy ON 301 - 6th to 18th May 1945)